THE LIMITS OF PUBLIC CHOICE

Public choice, 'the economic theory of politics', has been one of the most important developments in the social sciences in the last twenty years. This book argues that the claims made by many economists and their followers about the scope and richness of this approach are greatly exaggerated.

The book addresses a wide range of the approaches which come under the heading of 'public choice', paying particular attention to the work of Buchanan, Tullock, Downs and Olson. According to James Buchanan, public choice is based on the following key assumptions of economics:

- *self-interest* which is shown to be too far removed from observed political behaviour to be useful, even as a simplifying assumption

- *market exchange* – the metaphor of a political market is misleading because it privileges one factor amongst many

- *individualism* reveals an ideological as well as a methodological bias in public choice

Despite these problems, the author acknowledges that the recent popularity of economic thinking in the other social sciences – often referred to as 'economic imperialism' – has had a revitalizing effect. However it becomes counterproductive when it begins to crowd out other approaches, and in particular it argues for the richness of the sociological approach to politics, as a complement to the economic one.

Lars Udehn is a researcher and lecturer in Sociology at the University of Uppsala.

THE LIMITS OF PUBLIC CHOICE

A sociological critique of the economic
theory of politics

Lars Udehn

London and New York

First published 1996
by Routledge
11 New Fetter Lane, London EC4P 4EE

Simultaneously published in the USA and Canada
by Routledge
29 West 35th Street, New York, NY 10001

Typeset in Garamond by
Datix International Limited, Bungay, Suffolk
Printed and bound in Great Britain by
Clays Ltd, St Ives plc

British Library Cataloguing in Publication Data
A catalogue record for this book is available from the British Library

Library of Congress Cataloging in Publication Data
A catalogue record for this book has been requested

ISBN 0–415–08273–0 (hbk)
ISBN 0–415–12512–X (pbk)

To my parents, Elsa and Lennart

CONTENTS

FIGURES

ACKNOWLEDGEMENTS

A number of persons have read parts of the manuscript to this book and made valuable comments. They include, first of all, my friends and collegues Göran Ahrne, Thomas Coniavitis, Ulf Himmelstrand and Christine Roman, all of whom also gave much needed encouragement along the way. A special thanks goes to Ulf Himmelstrand who read the whole manuscript at an advanced stage and made detailed comments that certainly improved the end product.

I am also grateful to a larger circle of people who commented on various parts of the manuscript at seminars. Some of them I am afraid I might have forgotten, even though I did benefit from their remarks. What follows is a list of commentators I distinctly remember: Tom R. Burns, Jörgen Hermansson, Keith Jakee, Leif Lewin, Mats Lundström, Olof Pettersson, Bo Rothstein, Pablo Suarez and Stephen Turner.

Two anonymous reviewers have been a great help in making this book more readable than it would otherwise have been. One of them, in particular, made me change the arrangement of different parts radically and for the better I am sure.

Michael Hechter saved me from an embarrassing omission, by bringing my attention to a recent book of obvious relevance for my own work: Donald P. Green and Ian Shapiro, *Pathologies of Rational Choice Theory. A Critique of Applications in political Science* (Yale University Press, 1994). Unfortunately I became aware of this book only at the stage of proof reading and did not have the opportunity to let it influence my own argument. Green and Shapiro's main message is that the theoretical sophistication of rational choice is not at all matched by its empirical achievements; that, in fact, much of rational choice theory, as applied to politics, is either falsified or trivial. They also make the important point that rational choice gives rise to excessive *post hoc* theorizing. I largely agree with the verdict of Green and Shapiro and make a similar point myself in this book and, more specifically, in an earlier article (Udehn, 1992). My main concern, however, is different from that of Green and Shapiro. I wish to exhibit the principal limitations to an economic theory of politics and to suggest that sociology is a necessary complement.

x

ACKNOWLEDGEMENTS

I, finally, owe a debt of gratitude to the Swedish Council for Research in the Humanities and Social Sciences (Humanistisk-Samhällsvetenskapliga Forskningsrådet, or HSFR) for necessary financial support while writing this book. Having learnt from public choice theory that social life is exchange, I hope that the publication of this book may be conceived of as repayment of that debt, or at least part of it.

INTRODUCTION

We have seen, over the last three decades, an immense spread of economic thinking in all branches of social science (see, e.g. Hartley, 1992); a phenomenon commonly referred to as 'economic imperialism' (Tullock, 1972; Brenner, 1980; Stigler, 1984; Radnitzky and Bernholz, 1987; Udehn, 1992), or 'universal economics' (Radnitzky, 1992). Outside its traditional domain, the economic approach has proved most useful in the analysis of politics. Since the 1950s, there has been an invasion of economists into political territory. Many political scientists, too, have become impressed by the apparent power of this perspective and adopted its tools. Being a discipline with a topic, but no particular approach, political science is easily subjected to the influence of neighbouring disciplines (cf. Truman, 1955; Greer, 1969: 55; Riker, 1982a: 4).[1]

Another reason for economic imperialism is the failure of economics in its own domain. With the expanding role of the state in economic life and the consequent interdependence of economy and polity, traditional economic theory became increasingly inadequate for the explanation of macroeconomic phenomena. To retrieve themselves from this embarrassing situation, economists called for the inclusion, or endogenization, of politicians in economic analysis. The economist's way of doing this was by theoretical imperialism. Not only were political actors included in their analyses, but the economic approach was also applied to the domain of politics.[2]

FROM POLITICAL SOCIOLOGY TO POLITICAL ECONOMY[3]

Before economics became the exemplary model, political science received a strong impetus from sociology and social psychology (Dahl, 1961a: 764ff.; Lipset, 1969a: ix–xvi; Almond, 1991: 36–38; Petracca, 1991: 172).[4] There were three sources: behaviouralism, group theory and structural-functionalism. Of these, 'behaviouralism' was the most important and, in a wide sense of the term, included the other two.[5] In a narrow sense, 'behaviouralism' signified an empiricist approach to political behaviour.

The movement known as 'behaviouralism' in political science – not to be

1

confused with 'behaviourism' in psychology – was part of a larger movement in all social sciences. Its overriding aim was to turn the social sciences into hard sciences (Truman, 1955: 203ff.; Eulau, 1963: 31-35; Easton, 1967: 18ff.). This was to be achieved by systematic empirical study of human behaviour. Despite the transdisciplinary character of the movement, behaviouralism was to a considerable extent an importation from sociology, or its empiricist branch. The main instrument of research; the survey, came from sociology, as did some of the classic investigations (Eulau, 1967: 42).[6]

A second sociological and social psychological input, closely akin to behaviouralism (Truman, 1951b), was the group approach of Arthur F. Bentley, David B. Truman and Robert A. Dahl (see Weinstein, 1962; Greenstone, 1975). Bentley, for instance, was a sociologist by training, and he was no exception. In the formative years of the social sciences, there was no clear separation between sociology and political science. The single most important work in political group theory is David Truman's *The Governmental Process* (1951a). In this work, the basis of political group theory is entirely in social psychological and sociological theories of groups and of group behaviour (Truman, 1951a; ch. 2).

The third source of sociological influence was Talcott Parson's structural-functional theory of the social system (MacKenzie, 1967: 96ff.; Mitchell, 1967; Flanigan and Fogelman, 1967; Holt, 1967; Landau, 1968). This influence branched off in several directions: there was, first, an interest in comparative research, including developing areas, presumably involved in a process of modernization (Almond, 1956; Almond and Coleman, 1960; Almond and Powell, 1966). Second, there was a widespread interest in political culture and an emphasis upon the importance of social values for democracy, as exemplified by Gabriel A. Almond's and Sidney Verba's *The Civic Culture* (1963) and Seymour Martin Lipset's *The First New Nation* (1963). Third, there was a short upheaval for systems theory, which had, at least, something to do with Parsons' adoption of this approach in the 1950s. Among political scientists it was above all David Easton (1953/1971, 1957, 1965) and Karl Deutsch (1963, 1970), who worked with a systems theory of politics. Fourth, there was the analysis of mass democracy as 'symbolic politics' (Edelman, 1964, 1971).

It has been suggested that the traditional approach to politics, before the rise of behaviouralism and of political sociology, was a sort of institutionalism (Easton, 1953/1971: ch. 6; 1967: 15; Truman, 1955: 214–217, 230f.; Almond, 1960: 3f.; Almond and Powell, 1966: 3, 16f.; Dahl, 1961a: 766). Is institutionalism, perhaps, the particular approach of political science? I think not. Institutionalism is not specific to any social science. It is one of several approaches in all social sciences, and especially in sociology (cf. Riker, 1982–4).[7] If behaviouralism replaced institutionalism – and in a way it did – it did so in all social sciences, not just political science (cf. Truman, 1955: 210). On the other hand, 'one can scarcely imagine a political science in which institutions, as persistent patterns of political action, would not be a proper and central focus of concern' (Truman, 1965: 866). What distinguishes political science from economics and sociology, once more, is not the approach, but the topic (cf. Almond, 1966: 878). Political science is, or was, concerned with a delimited set of institutions; those institutions we call 'political institutions' and, in particular, with those institutions that, together, make up the state (cf. MacKenzie, 1970: 169ff., 185ff.). Traditional political science, before behaviouralism, was often comparative, descriptive and formal/legal (Truman, 1955: 215–217; 1965: 866–868; Almond, 1956: 393f.; 1966). The contribution of political sociology to political theory was (1) to treat political processes as special cases of more general social processes and (2) to situate political institutions in an environment of other institutions, or in short, in society (Lipset, 1959/1965: 83; 1967: 438; 1969a: xi). In order to distinguish between them, it would be possible to refer to the first as the 'sociology of politics' and only to the second as 'political sociology'.

At the end of the 1960s, however, political science went into a state of crisis, not as severe as that in sociology, but serious enough (cf. Gunnell, 1983: 28-38). Behaviouralism dissolved and was replaced by a post-behavioural theoretical pluralism (Easton, 1969; Almond, 1990: ch. 1). The strongest 'paradigm' eventually to emerge out of this plurality of voices was the economic approach to politics (cf. Easton, 1991: 286f.; Ordeshook, 1992: 196).[8] Economics replaced sociology as the main external source of inspiration for political scientists (see, e.g. Mitchell, 1968, 1969).[9] Great hopes were placed upon the new political economy – as twenty years earlier upon behaviouralism – as a means of making political theory more scientific or, at least, more explanatory (Petracca, 1991: 172f.). Behind these hopes lay an important development of the economic approach itself. In the 1940s and 1950s, it had become enriched by game theory, dealing with strategic behaviour – a phenomenon of some importance in political life (cf. Ordeshook, 1992: 188).

In his influential *Sociologists, Economists and Democracy* (1970/1978), Brian Barry set out to compare the sociological and the economic approaches to politics, and to democracy in particular. He came to the conclusion that the economic approach is superior to the sociological (Parsonian) approach in rigour and fertility (Barry, 1970, 1978: 84, 165–183; cf Mitchell, 1969: 121, 129–132). Unlike many other proponents of the economic approach, however, Barry is keenly aware of its limitations and raises some objections, which later became the standard critique of this school. If the economic approach is superior, this is not because it is terribly good, but because the sociological approach is even worse. This may very well be the case.

The shift in orientation 'from political sociology to political economy' is probably the most significant change in political science over the last decades (cf. Hedström, 1986; Ordeshook, 1990), but it is not the only one. Another important movement, in all social sciences, is the new institutionalism. This movement has been most marked in economics, simply because mainstream economics has, for a long time, been the least institutionalistic of the social sciences, but least marked in sociology, because it was always institutionalistic. In political science, the rediscovery of institutions is focused on the organizations of political life and, especially, on their relative autonomy *vis-à-vis* the rest of society (March and Olsen, 1984, 1989; Lane and Ersson, 1991). It is, thus, related to the new statism in political analysis (cf. Krasner, 1984: 225, 234ff.).

But while March and Olsen oppose their institutionalism mainly to the economic approach, Lane and Ersson set their institutionalism against political sociology. One reason for this may be that they are engaged in comparative research, and when it comes to comparison, economics has been largely silent. When you look for differences between societies and polities, you look for differences in social institutions and culture (cf. Kaplan, 1968: 37f.), people's rationality and biological drives presumably being the same. Thus in comparative politics, it is quite possible that the recent development has been from political sociology to institutionalism. In political science, at large, it is more reasonable to see the new institutionalism as a rival of the economic approach to politics – a statement which is problematic, because the new political economy is, to a large degree, also a new institutionalism.

Lane and Ersson give us a highly stylized story of a development from political sociology to institutionalism, but their account of political sociology is problematic in several respects: they single out one particular brand of political sociology and call it 'the sociological approach' (Lane and Ersson, 1991: 33); they incorrectly suggest that it is reductionistic (ibid., pp. 11, 31, 40, 51) and they refrain from mentioning that political sociology, itself, has developed in the same direction as comparative politics. The particular version of political sociology they wish to correct is the Parsonian brand of the 1950s and early 1960s, but political sociology is more than that. The greatest political sociologist of all times, Max Weber, was not a reductionist. Lane and Ersson also misrepresent Parsonian political sociology as implying a structural determinism: politics being a function of social structure. This is hardly correct, considering Parsons' recognition of the polity as one distinct subsystem in the total social system.[10] It may, finally, be pointed out that sociologists, such as Charles Tilly and Theda Skocpol, are very much part of the institutionalist ambition to bring the state back in and that political sociology, as a whole, has returned to the state, taking it seriously indeed (Badie and Birnbaum, 1983; King, 1986; Birnbaum, 1988).

Lane and Ersson are correct, however, to suggest that political sociology has been most interested in the relation between polity *and* society and especially in the influence of the latter upon the former (Lipset, 1959/1965: 83; 1969a: viiff.). But this does not imply any assumption of causal priority.

Political Science can be defined as the study of the interrelationship between society and polity, between social structures and political institutions. It is important to note that this definition does not assign causal priority to society over polity; political sociology is not solely the study of the social factors that condition the political order. Indeed, political institutions are themselves social structures, and hence are often the independent (that is, causal) factors that affect the nonpolitical social structures.

(Lipset, 1967: 440)

If political sociology has largely been concerned with the influence of society upon polity, this is division of labour, not reductionism (cf Easton, 1953/1971: 144–145).[11] The internal working of the state and its various organs, especially government and parliament, has simply been considered the special province of political science. If political scientists now rediscover their traditional province, this is certainly a good thing, but it is not a development in opposition to political sociology. As argued by Lane and Ersson (1991: 11, 50f.), it is a necessary complement. The new institutionalism launched by Lane and Ersson and, above all, by March and Olsen may have another topic than traditional political sociology, but it is very much the same approach. It may, therefore, be held to exemplify political sociology in sense (1) above, or the 'sociology of politics'. An important part of this version of the new institutionalism is a defence of the ideas of normative and symbolic orders and of social identity against the economic theory of politics.

POLITICS, ECONOMICS AND SOCIOLOGY

I have used a number of terms to describe the interdisciplinary nexus between economics, sociology and political science. A first set of terms has been used to denote the relation between economics as a discipline and politics as a subject matter: (1a) 'the new political economy', (1b) 'the economic theory of politics' and (1c) 'the economic approach to politics'. I will soon add the term (1d) 'public choice' to this list. A second set of terms captures the relation of sociology to politics: (2a) 'political sociology', (2b) 'the sociology of politics' and (2c) 'the sociological approach to politics'. I have already suggested a possible distinction between (2a) and (2b), so that the former is concerned with the relation between society and polity, whereas the latter is the use of sociological theory to analyse politics. However, since the term 'political sociology' is usually used in the latter sense and since I do not have much use for the distinction, anyway, I will follow common usage, and refer to the sociological theory of politics as 'political sociology'.

There is no corresponding set for political science. There is no political theory of, or approach to, society or economy. It is arguable, though, that there is a political aspect of, or a political dimension to, all social, or group, activity. The various terms used to distinguish between types of political

5

analysis: 'political philosophy', 'political theory' and 'political science', are but styles of political analysis.[12]

Concerning the first set, I suggest that (1a), while often used as a synonym, is best understood as being different from (1b). On analogy with 'political sociology', I suggest that 'political economy' is best conceived of as the study of the interdependency of economy and politics. This is clearly not equivalent to 'the economic theory of politics'.[13] The latter is sometimes referred to as 'public choice'. This is correct, in a wide sense of this term, In a narrow sense, 'public choice' refers to the Virginia School in political economy (see p. 9).

By 'approach', finally, I understand something more limited and more basic than theory. By 'approach' I understand the *core assumptions* of a theory, or discipline.[14] I have already made the provocative claim that political science lacks an approach of its own and is, therefore, easily subjected to influence by other disciplines. There is, in this respect, an asymmetry between political science, on the one hand, and economics and sociology, on the other. Political scientists use the economic and sociological approaches for their own purposes, but possess, themselves, no basic approach which can be used by economists and sociologists. According to the political scientist Heinz Eulau:

> At least two major approaches have crystallized in the last few years. On the one hand, there are those who, pointing to the basic *social* nature of man, see interindividual relationships and interactions – summarized in the concept of role – as the relevant theoretical point of departure. On the other hand, there are those who, influenced by classical economics, treat the individual not only as the empirical but also – in the model of the rational, self-interested, calculating, and utility-maximizing man – as the theoretical unit of analysis. Implicit in these differing approaches are fundamentally different views of reality. The 'sociological' approach, if it is proper to name it so, sees politics as a set of ordered relations among people, whereas the so-called 'economic' approach sees politics as a set of rules or strategies by which individuals order their relationships.
>
> (Eulau, 1969a: 17)

Eulau goes on to suggest that the economic approach is methodologically individualist, whereas the sociological approach is not. I believe that Eulau's characterization of the sociological and economic approaches is, by and large, correct, but I have reservations about the insertion of the word 'rule' in the last sentence of the quotation. Economic man is essentially rational, but not rule-following. This becomes clear in Jon Elster's explication of the divide.

According to Elster (1989a: 97ff.; 1989c, 1991b), there has been an enduring opposition, in social science, between two conceptions of man, associated with Adam Smith and Emile Durkheim, respectively: instrumentally rational *homo economicus* and norm-guided *homo sociologicus*. I will return to

Elster in Chapter 5 and confine myself here to mentioning that instrumental rationality is oriented to outcome, whereas norms tell us what is right to do, or not to do, in a certain situation, irrespective of outcome.

One of the most well-known explications of the economic approach is that of Gary Becker: 'The combined assumptions of maximizing behavior, market equilibrium, and stable preferences, used relentlessly and unflinchingly, form the heart of the economic approach as I see it' (Becker, 1976: 5). Becker's economic approach is not identical with Elster's *homo economicus*. First of all, Becker makes the additional assumptions of market equilibrium and stable preferences. Second, Becker substitutes utility-maximization for rationality, suggesting that the two are identical. I find this suggestion doubtful. I think it is possible to pursue a number of discrete ends, in an instrumentally rational manner, without being engaged in utility-maximization. It is even logically conceivable to minimize utility in a consistent and rational manner. In short, the two are distinct, but both are part of the economic approach. It might be added that economists often make the additional assumption that individuals' utility-functions are self-interested. As we will see (pp. 34 f.), this is especially so in the economic theory of politics. The assumption of stable preferences should be interpreted not just as constancy over time, but as similarity between people (Stigler and Becker, 1977: 76). Economic man is one, and constant; human nature and humanity consequently a homogeneous population.[15]

An elaboration of the sociological approach, which has proved valuable, for my purposes, derives from Göran Therborn. He suggests that sociology typically explains human action in terms of *cultural belonging* and *structural location*, or an interaction between the two (Therborn, 1991: 182ff.). Under the rubric 'cultural belonging' is included (a) shared social values and norms, (b) shared symbols and beliefs and (c) common identities. Structural location is more of a problem, because sociologists mean so many different things by the term 'structure'. For Therborn, a social structure is a fairly permanent 'distribution of resources and constraints' upon a set of actors. By 'resources' should be understood not only wealth but also symbolic and social capital, and rights (cf. Bourdieu, 1979/1986: 114; Giddens, 1984: 258–262).

The implication of Therborn's version of the sociological approach is that a view of sociological man as a follower of norms is too narrow. First should be added a cognitive side and a social identity. Second it must be added that sociological man is never an island, but always a party to social relations, most of which involve power or authority.

As I see things, economics and sociology are the two main approaches in social science and both rely to some extent on psychology. The sociological approach might equally well be called 'anthropological', since I fail to see any important difference between these disciplines. I prefer the former name, however, because it is most common to do so and, perhaps, because I am a sociologist myself. There are other ways to make this distinction, which are

7

not in terms of disciplines. I believe, for instance, that it would be possible to talk, without much distortion, about the economic approach as 'rational choice' and the sociological approach as 'institutionalism'. If I still prefer the language of disciplines, this is because it serves my purposes better.

THE PURPOSE OF THIS BOOK

The aim of this book is to offer a critique of the economic approach to politics.[16] The emphasis is on *approach*. I am not going to discuss the relative merits, or demerits, of all and every particular economic theory of politics. My critique is directed at the foundation and what follows from the shape of this edifice, in the form of limits to analysis. Making simplifying assumptions is always a choice and no choice is without consequences. Something is gained and something is lost – 'opportunity costs', as it were. My focus in this book is on what is lost by making the particular assumptions that, together, make up the economic approach.[17] This does not mean, however, that I will only discuss assumptions. I agree with Milton Friedman (1953) that the proof of the pudding is in the eating. Part of my strategy, therefore, will be to systematically explore and assess some of the most well-known predictions derived from the basic assumptions of the economic approach.

My motive for writing this book has been twofold. (1) Over the last ten years, I have been overwhelmed by an impression that increasing numbers of social scientists now believe that we could do without sociology; that the contribution of sociology to our understanding of society has been small and that economics is all that we need. I do not share this belief. I am convinced that sociology is important and makes up a quite indispensable part of social science. This is my main reason for writing this book. I have chosen to concentrate on political theory because this is where economic imperialism made its first inroads, and this is where it has been most victorious. (2) Economic imperialism has been accompanied by an ideological change of course in large parts of the Western world. The New Right has replaced the New Left as the loudest and most powerful ideological force. Since I believe that there is a relation between the two, and deplore the latter development, I have an additional reason to criticize the first development. This book is not, however, an ideological critique of public choice. Only in Chapter 4, do I touch on normative and ideological matters. My critique of public choice is empirical and theoretical.

My procedure, simply stated, will be first to present the economic approach to politics, then to criticize it and, finally, to present the sociological approach as an alternative, or supplement. The expository parts are warranted by the addressee of this book. It is written for social scientists from several disciplines – especially economics, political science and sociology – most of whom cannot be expected to be familiar with both economics and sociology. A special effort has been made to show that sociology has something to

8

contribute to the analysis of politics – something which has been seriously disputed in the heavy attack from economists and their allies for the last thirty years.

A problem with mixing exposition and critique is that the reader might have difficulty distinguishing between the two modes of discourse. What is exposition and what is critique? Or worse: what kind of work is this? The problem is aggravated by the fact that I intend some of the expository parts on sociology as an indirect critique of economic imperialism: simply by presenting sociological ideas, I hope to be able to convince the reader that political theory would be impoverished by doing without them, as economic imperialists suggest we should.

I am not going to argue, however, that the sociological approach is superior to, or even as good as, the economic approach. I believe that a comparison is difficult, to the point of being entirely devoid of meaning. To a large extent, the economic and sociological approaches highlight different aspects of politics. To the extent that they do, they cannot be compared in a simple way.[18] James Buchanan is fond of quoting Nietzsche, to the effect that we approach a subject through 'different windows'. This metaphor reflects an attitude, with which I sympathize. My quarrel is with those who make exaggerated claims concerning the universality and explanatory power of economic theory. The argument of this book is not that public choice is bad, but that there are definite limits to the economic approach to politics; that there are certain phenomena it is not well equipped to deal with, and some phenomena it cannot handle at all. Political phenomena not amenable to economic analysis – and there are plenty of them – have to be treated, however imperfectly, by the alternative approaches of psychology and sociology.

The economic theory of politics is sometimes equated with 'public choice' (Mueller, 1976: 395; 1979; 1; 1989: 1; McLean, 1987: 1). In this wide sense of the term, 'public choice' comprises the Virginia (Buchanan, Tullock, Tollison, Wagner, Brennan), Rochester (Riker, Ordeshook, Ferejohn, Fiorina, Shepsle) and Bloomington (Elinor and Vincent Ostrom) Schools of public choice, the Chicago (Becker, Stigler, Peltzman) School of political economy, Anthony Downs' economic theory of democracy, Mancur Olson's logic of collective action, and all other applications of the economic approach to politics. In a narrow sense, 'public choice' refers only to the Virginia School. Members of the latter have a special right to the name, because they invented it back in the 1960s, when starting the Public Choice Society and the journal *Public Choice*.[19]

In my critique of the economic approach to politics I will steer a middle course. I address and discuss public choice in the wide sense, but pay special attention, in Part I, to the Virginia School, and James Buchanan in particular. I think this is justified by the extraordinary importance of his contributions to an economic theory of politics. James Buchanan is generally recognized as the head of the Virginia School and received the Nobel prize for his role as founder of public choice. He has also done more than anyone else to clarify the meaning and proper use of economic theory in the analysis of politics. Another economist singled out for special attention is Mancur Olson, who is the point of departure and main target of critique in Part II of this book. Mancur Olson made the single most important contribution to an economic theory of politics in his *Logic of Collective Action*. No other book of public choice – not even Anthony Downs' *An Economic Theory of Democracy* – has made such an impact on the subsequent development of social science. This is probably because of its provocative thesis, which challenges conventional wisdom about collective action and other forms of human cooperation. *The Logic of Collective Action* strikes at the very heart of social science, and of sociology in particular. It is, therefore, well suited for making a comparison of economics and sociology as two different approaches to the basic problems of human cooperation and of social order.

It is common to make a distinction between *positive* and *normative* public choice (Mueller,1976: 23f.; 1979: 2–4, 263–270). My main interest is in 'positive' public choice, as advanced by people like Anthony Downs, James Buchanan, Gordon Tullock, Mancur Olson and William Niskanen, and not with the more explicitly normative theories of welfare economics, or social choice, and the normative version of the theory of the social contract (Rawls, Nozick, Gauthier). This does not mean that I uncritically accept the distinction between positive and normative theory as made by public choice theorists, nor that I fail to see the strong, if largely implicit, normative element in most public choice writing and that of Buchanan in particular. It should be mentioned that Buchanan, himself, has become increasingly aware of the normative character of his own theory of constitution and has also turned it in a normative direction. My main concern in this book will be public choice as a 'positive' theory of politics (see, however, Chapter 4). I plan a separate treatise on normative public choice.

Being a sociologist myself, my critique of public choice will be directed from a sociological point of view. This is the particular contribution of this book, but it also implies further limitations. I am not, for instance, going to pay systematic attention to the most basic element in the economic approach: the assumption of *rationality*. One reason for this is that the most weighty critique of the economic concept of rationality would be expected from the psychological point of view. Another reason is that so much has been written about rationality that I despair of being able to say anything at all interesting about this subject.

These are not the only limitations of this book. Like public choice itself,[20] I attend almost exclusively to Western parliamentary democracies, to the exclusion of other parts of the world and other political systems. I am concerned exclusively with domestic politics, to the exclusion of international relations. I only touch upon central topics of political theory, such as political parties, committees and coalitions. Finally, I largely neglect some recent contributions to political theory, such as postmodernism. The most conspicuous lacuna is the absence of feminist theory. My only excuse is ignorance, but I know it will not do. More surprising, perhaps, for a malestream sociologist, is that I have little to say about the subject of ideology and that I pay no attention at all to the recent debate about communitarianism.

A friendly critic has pointed out that the perspective of this book makes political science, itself, disappear – as if it did not exist in its own right. This complaint is justified, but I don't see it as much of a problem. There are lots of political scientists, better equipped than I am, to do full justice to this discipline. Every perspective involves a choice, and every choice is a loss of something. This book is about the economic and sociological approaches to politics. It is argued that political science has been influenced by these approaches, but certainly not that it lacks a history and an identity of its own. It is, indeed, possible to argue that political science is the oldest and most venerable among the social sciences, that its roots can be traced to Plato's theory of the ideal state and to Aristotle's comparative approach to constitutions. It is certainly the case that in the history of social theory, political theory occupies the most prominent place. It is probably correct to suggest that economics and sociology are but offsprings of political theory.

PLAN OF THIS BOOK

This book is divided into two parts. The first part, Chapters 1–4, is a presentation and critique of 'public choice' (as defined by James Buchanan) from a sociological perspective. The second part, Chapters 5, 6 and 7, is a comparison of the economic and sociological approaches to collective action.

Chapter 1 is an introductory presentation of two alternative perspectives on politics: the economic and sociological theories of politics, respectively. The first part of this chapter ends with James Buchanan's explication of 'public choice' as defined by three constitutive elements: the assumptions of (1) self-interest, (2) exchange and (3) individualism. This explication sets the stage for the following three chapters.

Chapter 2 is a critique of the assumption that political man, no less than economic man, is motivated solely by self-interest; that political man is economic man. Scrutinizing a large body of empirical research on the behaviour of politicians, bureaucrats and voters, I conclude that this assumption is definitely falsified as a scientific hypothesis about political man. Evidence indicates clearly that political man pursues not only self-interest but also the public interest and various group-interests. The fact that people vote at all is difficult to explain without assuming disinterested behaviour: expressive and/or normative. The assumption of self-interest may still be retained as a heuristic device. As such it may be of considerable fertility, if used cautiously and with an open mind that leads to alternative models, rather than to *ad hoc* adjustments of an irrefutable economic theory of politics. Chapter 2 ends with a short presentation of political sociology.

Chapter 3 discusses the empirical relevance of the market metaphor, or of politics-as-exchange. It is argued that exchange, while important, is not the essence of politics. The main import of the market metaphor is normative, not positive. While it is important to study forms of exchange such as log-rolling, bribery and bargaining, it is also important to recognize that these phenomena are limited and that there is much else in politics. Much that goes on in politics is persuasion, not exchange in the economic sense. Exchange of ideas is something completely different from exchange of goods and services. People try to persuade one another by rational argument and by rhetoric. The important difference is that in persuasion people try to change, not to satisfy, the wants of other people. Most important, social relations within political institutions are authority relations, not relations of exchange. State bureaucracies are systems of command, not of exchange.

In Chapter 4 I take issue with the individualism of public choice. My first argument is that public choice has developed in an institutionalist direction, thus creating a problematic tension between institutionalism and methodological individualism, at least if we understand methodological individualism as a principle of explanation. A second argument is that the main use of individualism in public choice is normative, not methodological. This is particularly evident in James Buchanan's theory of constitutional economics, but is apparent also in the rejection of welfare economics and in the theories of government failure propounded by representatives of public choice. Leading representatives of public choice are libertarians and belong to the New Right. As such, they place ultimate value on the individual, who is free to choose only on the market. Hence, the secondary importance attached to democracy, or popular sovereignty. Hence, also, the failure to incorporate power in the analysis of politics.

Chapter 5 deals with the problem of collective action: that rational egoists will not contribute to the provision of public goods, as first stated by Mancur Olson in *The Logic of Collective Action* (1965/1971). It takes the form of a survey of the extant literature devoted to solving this problem. It is argued that Olson's size argument has been shown to be defective, but that little has been added to his informal institutional analysis. The analysis of the collective action problem as an iterated N-person prisoners' dilemma did much to clarify its nature and eventually made us realize that there are several collective action problems, not all of them equally severe. But there are limits also to game theory, an insight which led some analysts to introduce heterogeneity among actors and social relations between them. A fundamental issue remains, however: do social relations solve the collective action problem or do they transcend it; do they work on incentives or on motives? The first inclination of economists is to suggest incentives. Because of certain problems associated with this hypothesis, however, a growing number of rational

12

choice theorists now consider explanations in terms of mixed motivations. I argue that this is the only possible way out of the dilemma. I also show that empirical evidence supports the assumption of mixed motivations, but that one particular explanation has not received due attention: evidence suggests strongly that communication is of vital importance for collective action. What is achieved by communication? The most promising suggestion is that communication creates a collective identity, which makes people think in terms of 'we', rather than in terms of 'I'.

Chapter 6 is a presentation of sociological theories of collective action. It is shown that sociologists have always assumed that people have mixed motivations. Contrary to Mancur Olson's accusations, therefore, sociologists are not guilty of logical failure. They have never seen the problem of collective action the way economists do. Sociologists always assumed that people develop collective identities and group solidarities that make them act to achieve common ends. They also believe that ideas, values, myths, utopias and symbols play a part in the activity of social movements.

Chapter 7, finally, treats the more general problem of social order. Mainstream sociologists always rejected the economic view of the matter. Sociology emerged as a discipline very much in opposition to *homo economicus* and to rational choice theories of social order: Hobbes' theory of the social contract, utilitarianism and the economic theory of market exchange. Against these theories, sociologists insisted that cooperation and social order are not possible without morality. Indeed, according to one of the most prominent sociologists, Emile Durkheim, society is a moral order. This is no doubt an exaggeration (or a persuasive definition), but it contains an important element of truth: social order is not just a rational order; it is not even possible as such. In addition, it is a normative order and, I suggest, also a cognitive order.

Part I

PUBLIC CHOICE: A CRITIQUE

1

TWO APPROACHES TO POLITICS

As indicated by its subtitle, this work aims at a sociological critique of the economic theory of politics, or public choice. Before I start on this task, however, I believe it is appropriate to offer a short presentation of the economic and sociological theories of politics, respectively. In the *Introduction* I suggested that public choice had replaced political sociology as a major current in political theory. Chronology, therefore, suggests that I should start with political sociology and then turn to public choice. The 'logic' of my argument, however, makes it reasonable to treat public choice first and to present political sociology as an alternative way of looking at politics.

PUBLIC CHOICE[1]

Two works have a special place in the early development of the economic approach to politics: Joseph Schumpeter's *Capitalism, Socialism and Democracy* (1942/1954) and Kenneth Arrow's *Social Choice and Individual Values* (1951/1963). In the first work, Schumpeter attacked the classical doctrine of democracy for being naive and unrealistic (Schumpeter, 1942/1954: ch. 21). Politics is not the expression of a general will and politicians do not seek the common good. In its stead, Schumpeter advanced 'another theory of democracy' (ibid., ch. 22), based on the following definition: 'the democratic method is that institutional arrangement for arriving at political decisions in which individuals acquire the power to decide by means of a competitive struggle for the people's vote' (ibid., p. 269). As we shall see in Chapter 3, Schumpeter's theory of democracy was not altogether new and not entirely his own, but it was the most influential source of the neo-liberal theory of democracy.[2] A clear forerunner of public choice is the following motivational assumption: the 'foremost aim of each party is to prevail over the others in order to get into power or to stay there' (ibid., p. 279).

In the second work, Arrow reaches a conclusion even more devastating for the theory of popular sovereignty: there are logical barriers to aggregating individuals' preference orderings into a social preference ordering. Hence, there can be no such thing as a general will, or a general social choice function. The implications for the possibility of a social welfare function is a continuing matter at issue. Making a number of reasonable assumptions about individual preference orderings, Arrow produces a formal proof for the so called general possibility theorem:

> *If we exclude the possibility of interpersonal comparisons of utility, then the only methods of passing from individual tastes to social preferences which will be satisfactory and which will be defined for a wide range of sets of individual orderings are either imposed or dictatorial.*

(Arrow, 1951/1963: 59)

The classics

Schumpeter and Arrow prepared the ground, but the first major contribution to a positive economic theory of politics was Anthony Downs' *An Economic Theory of Democracy* (1957). Because of the imprint of Schumpeter on this work, it is common to talk about the 'Schumpeter–Downs' theory of democracy.

The main novelty in Downs' pioneering study was to populate our political institutions with *homo economicus;* a human who acts rationally (Downs, 1957: 4ff.) and for his own selfish ends (27ff., 282ff.). For members of political parties, this means that 'they act solely in order to attain the income, prestige, and power which come from being in office'. Politics is reduced to a means for the politicians' private ends. 'Upon this reasoning rests the fundamental hypothesis of our model: parties formulate policies in order to win elections, rather than win elections in order to formulate policies (ibid., p. 28). This hypothesis is operationalized as the assumption that politicians in democratic countries seek to maximize votes (ibid., pp. 11, 31). Voters act so as to maximize their own utility; the benefits they expect to receive from voting in one way rather than the other; their so-called 'party differential' (ibid., pp. 36ff., 274). Surprisingly, Downs suggests that his 'model leaves room for altruism in spite of its basic reliance upon the self-interest axiom' (ibid., p. 37).

A consequence of this view of political man is the denigration of the role and importance of political ideologies. They are reduced, by Downs, to mere instruments in the competitive struggle for votes. The function of ideologies is to reduce uncertainty and information costs. Ideologies serve parties mainly by decreasing the need to inform voters about policy and by saving voters the trouble of collecting more detailed information about party programmes (ibid., ch. 7).

Downs' most lasting contribution to an economic theory of politics is his spatial theory of voting (ibid., ch. 8). Borrowing an idea originally used by Harold Hotelling in another context, Downs derives a number of hypotheses concerning the distribution of political parties along an ideological spectrum from left to right. The most well-known hypothesis suggests that parties in a two-party system tend to converge ideologically upon the centre (ibid., pp. 115–117). The reason is that parties can always count on the votes of the extremists on their side of the middle. Their chance of gaining more support, therefore, is to address the voters in the middle of the ideological spectrum. This hypothesis holds if voters' preferences are evenly distributed, or concentrated at the centre, not if there is strong ideological polarization (ibid., pp. 118–119).

A second important contribution to a spatial theory of voting stems from another public choice classic: Duncan Black's *The Theory of Committees and Elections* (1958/1971). Black is, perhaps, most well known for calling our attention to the phenomenon of cyclical majorities, which is an illustration of Arrow's general possibility theorem, but he is also the origin of the median voter theorem. According to this theorem, if in a committee the number of members is odd and their preference curves are all single-peaked, the most preferred outcome of the median voter is the only alternative that can get a simple majority against all other alternatives. If the number of members is even, but there is a chairman with the right to a casting vote, the preferred outcome of that member who is closest to the median, but on the same side as the chairman, can get a simple majority against all other alternatives (ibid., p. 16). Black does not make any assumption of self-interest and, as I will argue below, the spatial theory of voting does not depend upon any particular motivational assumption.

The spatial theory of voting has developed into one of the most important and most lasting contributions of economics to a science of politics.[3] In a recent work (*The Spatial Theory of Voting. An Introduction*, 1984), two of its most influential representatives, James M. Enelow and Melvin J. Hinich, divide this field into two branches: one dealing with committee voting, the other with mass elections. The main difference between them is that in the first case voting is between policy alternatives, while in the second case it is between candidates and with limited information. I will not go into details about the further advances in the spatial theory of voting (see Enelow and Hinich, 1990). I observe that it has been generalized so as to apply to several dimensions and candidates.[4] Also, in mass elections, voters are assumed to reduce information costs not only with the help of ideology, but by relying on the personality of candidates. People vote for candidates they trust to be honest. A third advance is to introduce institutions into the analysis. Special attention is called to agenda control. But for all these changes, one element remains unchanged: the assumption of self-interest. 'Spatial theory describes two classes of actors: voters and candidates. Both are assumed to be motivated by self-interest' (Enelow and Hinich, 1984: 2).

A third public choice classic appeared in 1962: James Buchanan and Gordon Tullock's *The Calculus of Consent*. A first objective of this work was the development of an economic theory of constitutions. A second objective was the analysis of decision-making rules.

Constitutional economics eventually became somthing of James Buchanan's specialty, developed in *The Limits of Liberty* (1975a), *The Reason of Rules* (1985; together with Geoffrey Brennan), *Explorations into Constitutional Economics* (1989b) and numerous articles. I deem constitutional economics an essentially normative enterprise and leave it until Chapter 4. The analysis of decision-making rules, while mainly an exercise in logic, has more of real world import. The main argument is that a rule of simple majority may lead to inefficient outcomes, because of the exploitation of the minority by the majority. The play of sectional interests leads to social waste.

Buchanan and Tullock open some new ground in the economic analysis of politics. They draw our attention to the significance of vote trading, especially log-rolling,[5] in democratic politics and use game theory to discuss coalition formation. Another novelty is the introduction of decision-making costs (transaction costs) in the economic analysis of collective decision-making. A third feature to notice is the early insistence upon the importance of institutions in economic analysis, which turns Buchanan and Tullock into pioneers of the new institutional economics. Most important, for my present purpose, is Buchanan and Tullock's advocacy of the use of *homo economicus* in political analysis. I will return to Buchanan's views on this matter in Chapters 2 and 4, but it might be pointed out, at this stage, that his views on this subject are rather complex. Buchanan is no simple-minded defender of the assumption of self-interest for all social scientific purposes.

Buchanan and Tullock were not alone in analysing coalition formation with the aid of game theory. The classic in this field is William Riker's *The Theory of Political Coalitions* (1962). A first important contribution of this work to the emerging tradition of public choice was to replace Anthony Downs' assumption of vote-maximization by the weaker, but presumably more realistic, assumption that people enter the game of politics mainly for the sake of winning. 'What the rational political man wants, I believe, is to win' (Riker, 1962: 22). This assumption may be regarded as a parallel to Herbert Simon's suggestion that firms *satisfice*, rather than maximize their profits. Riker's most noteworthy contribution, however, was the so-called 'size principle': '*In n-person, zero-sum games, where side-payments are permitted, where players are rational, and where they have perfect information, only minimum winning coalitions occur*' (ibid., p. 32). This is intended as a purely formal statement in game theory. The descriptive counterpart reads as follows: 'In social situations similar to n-person, zero-sum games with side-payments, participants create coalitions just as large as they believe will ensure winning and no larger' (ibid., pp. 32f., 47).[6]

A fifth classic of public choice, broadly conceived, is Mancur Olson's *The Logic of Collective Action* (1965/1971). The main thesis of this work is that rational egoists will not engage in collective action, unless the collective is small, or some private good is added to the benefit from the collective good. Since this collective action problem is the point of departure for Part II of this book, I refer the reader to Chapter 5 for a more detailed presentation of Mancur Olson's classic statement of this problem.

Political business cycles

Albert Breton's *The Economic Theory of Representative Government* (1974)[7] combines elements from Downs and from Buchanan and Tullock.[8] While his purpose is more in line with that of Downs, Breton criticizes the latter for neglecting institutions and transaction costs, elements brought into the analysis by Buchanan and Tullock. Writing after Olson and Niskanen, Breton also incorporates pressure groups and bureaucrats into the analysis. His principal actors, however, are political parties and citizens (ibid., p. 12). The governing party is assumed to maximize the probability of being re-elected (ibid., pp. 18, 41, 74, 123). The individual politician is more immediately concerned about things, such as 'personal pecuniary gains, personal power, his own image in history, the pursuit of lofty personal ideas, his personal view of the common good, and others which are peculiar to each politician' (ibid., p. 124). The citizen, who is not identical with the voter, but with the participant in the political process, is supposed to be motivated by his own interest (ibid., p. 74) and to 'choose among candidates the one who offers the bundle of policies with the highest expected utility' (ibid., p. 50). Citizens' utility functions include both private goods supplied on the market and public policies, comprising both public and private goods (ibid., p. 123). The discrepancy between the number of public policies demanded by a citizen and the number provided is called 'coercion'. The extent of aggregate coercion determines citizens' participation in the political process.

Breton's economic theory of representative government is in terms of the demand and supply of public policies. Public policies are demanded by citizens in a number of different ways, including voting and joining pressure groups; they are supplied by politicians and bureaucrats. The main purpose of Breton's analysis is to explain government expenditure in traditional economic terms, that is, as a function of demand and supply. His actual procedure, however, is less traditional. His main explanatory variable is the *institutional framework* (see ibid., pp. 205–207).

One hypothesis, advanced by Breton, is that governments, in order to be re-elected, try harder to please voters immediately before, than after, election day (ibid., pp. 131–135). One way of doing this is to manipulate the economy so as to minimize unemployment and inflation in the period before election (ibid., pp. 26–31). Breton does not actually go this far, but he is on the verge of suggesting the existence of a political business cycle.[9]

In traditional economics, government is supposed to be concerned with counteracting the occurrence of political business cycles. In theories of political business cycles, it is the other way round: politicians deliberately create business cycles. They do so in order to win votes and to be re-elected. There is a variety of theories of political business cycles based on different models of the relation between the economy and the polity (see Frey, 1978a: ch. 10 and 1978b). The first theory of this type seems to have been Marxism, which conceives of the state as an instrument for the capitalist class (see Borooah, 1988: 66–72). The classic piece is Michal Kalecki's article 'Political Aspects of Full Employment' (1943; see also Feiwel, 1974), which is the first contribution to a theory of 'the political business cycle'. In Kalecki's version it is big business, the 'captains of industry', that creates business cycles by opposing governmental policy of full employment. It does so because it dislikes governmental interference, generally, and public enterprise in particular, but most of all because it wishes to see a 'reserve army' of unemployed to keep the working class in its place. (Kalecki, 1943: 324–326).

The first contribution to a public choice theory of political business cycles was by William D. Nordhaus (1975; first version 1972). The idea is that politicians in power manipulate certain macroeconomic variables (inflation and unemployment), in order to win elections, thereby creating business cycles. The theoretical basis of this manipulation is the so-called 'Phillips curve', suggesting a trade-off between inflation and unemployment. By an expansionist policy, aimed at reducing unemployment before election, the governing party hopes to be re-elected. The consequent rise in the rate of inflation culminates after the election and does not affect the result.

> The typical cycle will run as follows: immediately after an election the victor will raise unemployment to some relatively high level in order to combat inflation. As elections approach, the unemployment rate will be lowered until, on election eve, the unemployment rate will be lowered to the purely myopic point.
>
> (Nordhaus, 1975: 184)

Nordhaus' model is based on a number of assumptions. One concerns the electorate: 'We assume individuals have the aggregate unemployment and inflation rates in their preference functions and that individuals prefer stable prices and low unemployment rates to high inflation and unemployment rates' (ibid., p. 171). Since voters are assumed to know little about macroeconomic performance and to be myopic, what matters is their own experience of unemployment, rising prices and lower incomes (ibid., p. 172f.). 'Parties are assumed to be interested only in election outcomes. They want to win elections. It is assumed they know voters' preferences ... perfectly. *The government therefore chooses economic policies during its incumbency which maximize its plurality at the next election*' (ibid., p. 174).

A similar attempt to demonstrate 'a potential in a democratic society for a politically motivated business cycle' was made by Duncan MacRae (1977: 239).[10] The precondition, once again, is the existence of a trade-off between unemployment and inflation, which is such that it is possible to have both low unemployment and low inflation in the election year. MacRae is not very specific about the utility functions of governments and voters. But, among the objectives of parties in power, 'an important one is to remain in power and thus continue to determine government policy' (ibid., p. 240). More specifically, parties are supposed to engage in 'vote-loss-minimizing behavior' (ibid., p. 240). A presupposition of this assumption is that parties in power lose votes between elections, as is, indeed, normally the case. Voters are assumed to be myopic and to react negatively to high inflation and unemployment.

The most important figure in the literature on political business cycles is Bruno S. Frey. He is not an orthodox member of the public choice movement and his model departs significantly from some of its core assumptions. I will return to Frey in my critique of the theory of political business cycles, and limit myself here to a very short presentation. The main gist of Frey's contribution is to situate the theory of political business cycles within a more comprehensive and more realistic model of the politico-economic system. His ultimate aim is the development of an empirical model of the type used in econometrics. Since the principal part is played by the polity, Frey calls it 'politometrics'. Unlike Nordhaus and MacRae, Frey does not concentrate on inflation and unemployment, but attaches even more importance to governments' attempts to buy votes by raising voters' consumption level.[11]

A more orthodox public choice view of political business cycles stems from Richard E. Wagner (1977). While agreeing that politicians create business cycles, Wagner is critical of the typical Keynesian, or macroeconomic, approach to the problem. The economy is not the kind of thing that can be controlled by manipulating a few aggregate variables. Thus, it is not likely that governments could control inflation and unemployment, as suggested by the theories of political business cycles, even if they wished to do so. Instead, self-interested politicians try to buy votes with more selective measures directed at particular groups. Political business cycles occur as an unintended by-product of government interference with an otherwise self-regulating market.

It may be wise to make a distinction between parties and politicians. According to methodological individualism, a party has no preferences. The usual procedure has been to construct the utility functions of parties and governments as aggregates of their members' utility functions, but this will not do. Politicians have the most diverse arguments in their utility functions. Parties and governments are supposed to have only one consistent set of preferences. At least, they can only maximize one utility function with their policy. One way of conceiving the relation between parties and politicians would be to see the former as a means for the latter. Parties would then be reduced to mere instruments for ambitious politicians, seeking power, prestige and riches.

The assumption that voters maximize their own expected utility has turned out to be the Achilles' heel of the economic theory of politics (see pp. 86–93). Despite the fact that it gives rise to some seriously disturbing questions, however, this assumption has remained an integral part of orthodox public choice (see, e.g., Tullock, 1976: 5; Mueller, 1976: 40; 1979: 97; 1989; 2). 'Expected utility', however, is an empty phrase until you specify the arguments in voters' utility functions. The usual specification is that voters are most concerned about the money that floats into their pockets; so-called 'pocketbook voting'. One hypothesis derived from this assumption is that voters react favourably to governments that lower the rates of inflation and unemployment while raising their income, or consumption level.

Bureaucracy

Politicians and voters are not the only figures in political life. A personage steadily growing in number and importance is the much despised bureaucrat. Having exploded the myth of the benevolent politician seeking nothing but the common good, public choice theorists shifted their attention to the bureaucrat; this loyal and self-denying servant of politicians and citizens bent on nothing but doing his/her duty. Against this idealized picture of a political eunuch, commonly ascribed to Weber, it is argued that bureaucrats, no less than other people, look after their own interests first and only secondly the interests of others.

The first public choice contribution to a theory of bureacuracy was Gordon Tullock's *The Politics of Bureaucracy* (1965/1987). It is not at all clear that the analysis in this work is 'economic' in the ordinary sense of this term (see Chapter 3). The reason is that Tullock relies heavily upon a distinction between the economic relation of exchange and the political relation between superior and subordinate (ibid., pp. 11–14). Relations in a bureaucracy, are of course, of the latter type. In his foreword to this book, Buchanan, nevertheless, argues that 'Tullock's approach to a theory of administration is an "economic" one' (ibid., p. 4). The reason is that 'Tullock's "politician" is, to be sure, an "economic" man of sorts' (ibid., p. 4). This is true, although Tullock is not very specific about him. He is supposed to be more or less rational, like the rest of us, and he is supposed to be 'selfish', operationalized as 'with "career centred motivation". Within the context of an organizational hierarchy, the more normal meaning may be simply stated as the desire to get ahead, to move up, in the hierarchy' (ibid., p. 29).

Anthony Downs made the next contribution to an 'economic' theory of bureaucracy with his *Inside Bureaucracy* (1967). As with Tullock's analysis, the epithet 'economic' is misleading as a trademark for the product. 'Sociological' would serve equally well. Not only are most of the hypotheses, advanced by Downs, structural; his homunculus is not altogether selfish. In fact, Downs operates with five human types, only two of which are narrowly selfish, while the remaining three exhibit a mix of egoism and altruism (Downs, 1967: 81ff.). True, Downs assumes that egoism is a stronger motive force than is altruism, but altruism is an essential part of some of his hypotheses.

The most consistent use of an economic approach to bureaucracy is William A. Niskanen's *Bureaucracy and Representative Government* (1971). Like Tullock and Downs, Niskanen assumes that bureaucrats are selfish and maximize their personal utility (Niskanen, 1971: 36f.; 1973: 20f.), but while Tullock and Downs focused upon the internal working of bureaux, Niskanen is more interested in their output. Treating them as production units on a par with firms, he asks, what, instead of profit, do bureaux maximize? His answer is: their budgets.

> Among the several variables that may enter the bureaucrat's utility function are the following: salary, perquisites of the office, public reputation, power, patronage, output of the bureau, ease of making changes, and ease of managing. All of these variables except the last two, I contend, are a positive monotonic function of the total *budget* of the bureau during the bureaucrat's tenure of office.
>
> (Niskanen, 1971: 38; cf. 1973: 22)

But this is not the whole story. Unlike profits, budgets include costs, which must somehow be introduced as a constraint upon budget maximization. The relation between supply and cost may be opaque in the activity of a bureau, but it is not entirely absent. In the least, bureaus have to keep their promises and produce what is expected of them. A full statement of the motivational assumption for bureaucrats, therefore, reads like this: 'Bureaucrats maximize the total budget of their tenure, subject to the constraint that the budget must be equal to or greater than the minimum total costs of supplying the output expected by the bureau's sponsor' (Niskanen, 1971: 42; cf. 1973: 27; 1978: 164).

Niskanen's analysis remains, to this day, the most influential contribution to a public choice theory of bureaucracy. But he is not alone. Tullock returns to this subject in *The Vote Motive* (1976: ch. 4) and in *The New World of Economics* (Tullock and McKenzie, 1975/1985: ch. 11), but treats it, this time, in a rather different vein. The analysis has become much influenced by that of Niskanen, even if Tullock is more careful in his statement of the motivational assumption. Bureaucrats are not supposed to be entirely selfish. Like the rest of us, they are 'partly selfish partly public-interested' (Tullock, 1976: 27), but selfish most of the time. The assumption of a single maximand for bureaucrats is deemed problematic, but Tullock finally settles for *size* as a possible candidate. The size of staff is assumed to be positively related to most of the things, including leisure, that individual bureaucrats might wish to attain in their jobs.

Albert Breton and Ronald Wintrobe (1975, 1979, 1982) have attempted an 'economic' analysis of bureaucracy. The most characteristic feature of their economic theory, however, is an emphasis on the element of exchange in the working of bureaucracy. I will return to this side of their argument in Chapters 3 and 4. The assumption of self-interest plays a minor role in Breton and

Wintrobe's analysis and requires only brief mention here. Bureaucrats are assumed to 'maximize well-behaved ordinal utility functions defined over informal services, policy characteristics, and the other objects that are traded in bureaucracies' (Breton and Wintrobe, 1982: 27). The vacuity is intentional. Breton and Wintrobe reject every attempt – including that of Niskanen – to specify bureaucrats' utility functions in more detail. Bureaucrats have different objectives, which are but different expressions of their supposed self-interest.

Interest groups

I have mentioned politicians, voters and bureaucrats. But there is, in our Western democracies at least, a fourth important political force: interest groups.[12] Following William Mitchell and Michael Munger (1991), we can distinguish four economic theories of interest groups: (1) Mancur Olson's theory of collective action, (2) the Chicago theory of economic regulation, (3) the Virginia theory of rent-seeking and (4) Gary Becker's theory of pressure groups. In addition, we could mention the theory of directly unproductive profit-seeking, or DUP activities, which has most in common with Mancur Olson's theory of interest groups and with the theory of rent-seeking.

The most well-known economic theory of interest groups, at least among non-economists, is that of Mancur Olson in *The Logic of Collective Action* (1965/1971). I am going to discuss this work at length, in Chapter 5 and turn instead to the sequel, *The Rise and Decline of Nations* (1982), which has more in common with other economic theories of interest groups and is more relevant for my present purposes. Olson presents *The Rise and Decline of Nations* as 'an outgrowth of *The Logic of Collective Action* and in large part even an application of it' (Olson, 1982: 18). I do not see that much continuity. *The Logic of Collective Action* is about the problem of collective action. It presents an economic argument why interest groups will not emerge. *The Rise and Decline of Nations* does not treat the problem of collective action. It assumes that this problem has been solved in a number of cases, i.e. that there already exists a number of interest groups competing for differential advantage (cf. Mitchell and Munger 1991: 516). One argument of *The Logic of Collective Action* which plays an important role in the sequel is that collective action is much more likely in small groups. In *The Rise and Decline of Nations*, this leads to the conclusion that certain interests (e.g. producers) are advantaged at the expense of others (e.g. consumers). The most advantaged interests will form 'distributional coalitions', engaging in unproductive bargaining over their share of the social product. In the long run, these distributional coalitions will act as a serious impediment to economic growth: directly by engaging in unproductive activity; indirectly by creating social rigidities with a stultifying effect on economic life. On both counts, they contribute to the decline of nations.

The Chicago theory of regulation is about interest groups *and* politicians, but primarily about the former. The classical piece is George Stigler's article 'The Theory of Regulation' (1971), reprinted together with related papers in *The Citizen and the State* (1975). Stigler begins by challenging the widely held view that regulation is 'for the protection and benefit of the public at large' (1975: 114). The truth of the matter is that regulation is, primarily, for the benefit of industries and occupations and, secondarily, for the benefit of politicians: representatives and their parties. Politicians, of course, seek office and therefore votes and campaign contributions, even bribes. The resource of politicians is coercive power, which they can use to regulate economic life to the advantage and disadvantage of different interests. The goods sought by interest groups include taxes, price-fixing, subsidies, licences, tariffs, quotas and other restrictions on entry. The main message of Stigler is that regulation is a *redistribution* of wealth from some groups to other groups in society and that it involves *deadweight losses* for society as a whole. The second message is that redistribution is not neutral, but favours certain groups at the expense of others: 'the representative and his party must find a coalition of voter interests more durable than the anti-industry side of every polity proposal' (Stigler, 1975: 125). More generally, regulation favours small and concentrated interests at the expense of large and diffuse ones.[13]

A somewhat unorthodox analysis of pressure group competition – at least for an economist from Chicago – emanates from Gary Becker (1983, 1985). His model includes only special interest groups – not politicians, bureaucrats or voters – competing for political influence. While recognizing that such competition involves deadweight (social) costs, Becker is less pessimistic than the other Chicago economists about its consequences. Pressure groups are not caught in a prisoners' dilemma, but engage in a Cournot-Nash noncooperative game, in which equilibrium is reached by a process of mutual adjustment of group pressure to the pressure of other groups. Each group, of course, exerts pressure so as to maximize the utility of its members.

Becker goes on to challenge the conclusion, reached by Olson and Stigler, that regulation favours small but strong interests at the expense of large and weak ones. Producer interests in regulation give rise to the countervailing power of consumers and taxpayers. What is more: 'Since deadweight costs encourage pressure by taxpayers and discourage pressure by recipients, taxpayers have an "intrinsic" advantage in influencing political outcomes' (Becker, 1983: 381). The reason for this is the asymmetry that deadweight costs add to taxes but detract from subsidies, hence all have an interest in diminishing deadweight.

So far, Becker is a lone voice in the public choice choir. The dominating economic theory of interest groups is the Virginia theory of rent-seeking, which has much in common with Mancur Olson's theory of distributional coalitions and with the Chicago theory of regulation. The idea of 'rent-seeking' is usually traced to an article by Gordon Tullock from 1967c on the costs of monopoly.[14] The actual costs of monopoly, Tullock argues, are usually underestimated, due to a failure to include all resources spent, and wasted, on obtaining and maintaining a monopoly situation (Tullock, 1967c). The term 'rent-seeking' was first used by Anne Krueger in an article of 1974 to denote profits deriving from government restrictions on economic activity, but also from illegal action such as bribery, corruption, smuggling and black markets (Krueger, 1974/1980: 51).

More generally, the term 'rent-seeking' refers to profit-seeking that leads to social waste rather than to surplus (Buchanan, 1980b: 3f., 8). Another term for rent-seeking is *directly unproductive profit-seeking*, or 'DUP' activities' (Bhagwati, *et al.*, 1984). Rent-seeking is competition for differential advantage which does not depend upon the market, but on special privilege. On the market, rents tend to dissipate. Rent-seeking, therefore, presupposes another institutional setting, including an interventionist government and interest groups. In the public choice theory of rent-seeking, government is the ultimate source of the evil and interest groups the derivative phenomenon (Buchanan, 1980b: 8ff.). In the theory of DUP-activities, rent-seeking emerges on the market, even though government intervention is a primary source of the occurrence of rents (Colander, 1984: 1ff.).

What are the forms of rent-seeking? The most common form, or method, of rent-seeking is lobbying for special privilege. What, then, are the sources of privilege? They might be regulations granting monopoly to some supplier of a good or service, or legitimation to the members of some professional organization. They might be tariffs, or quotas, protecting some branch of industry, or agriculture. They might be government contracts for the private provision of public goods and services. All these types of government intervention give rise to indirect transfers of income. But there are also direct transfers in the form of subsidies, social benefits and redistribution of income by means of progressive income taxation. Transfers, as such, involve no waste. To the extent that they do not influence the size of the pie, they give rise to a zero-sum game. But the competition for differential advantage, in the form of lobbying and other activities, turns it into a negative-sum game of social waste (Tullock, 1980, 1990).

It goes without saying that rent-seeking is positively correlated with corruption. If that is so, we might wish to believe that it is a problem mainly in the Second and Third Worlds, but not in the West. According to public choice theorists, however, it is also an increasing problem in our part of the world, both in its legal and in its illegal forms. What can be done about it? A starter would be if economists could be persuaded to engage in debunking rent-seeking society. With admirable faithfulness to public choice principles, Tullock (1984b) assumes that this is possible only if it can be shown to be in their own interest to do so. Kenneth J. Koford and David J. Colander (1984) suggest a number of measures aimed at 'taming the rent-seeker'. They include information, moralizing, adjusting property rights and changing the institutional framework. Only the last suggestion would appeal to Buchanan, who thinks that the 'classic American syndromes, incrementalism and pragmatism, must be nonstarters' in the fight against rent-seeking (Buchanan, 1980b: 367). The public choice cure is simple, if not to effect, at least to spell out: if rent-seeking is the result of an institutional setting including an interventionist state and powerful interest groups, limit the power of the former and the role of the latter will decline too. What is needed is nothing short of a constitutional revolution.[15]

Public finance

No presentation of public choice is complete without a mention of its contribution to a theory of public finance (cf. Mitchell, 1968: 79; Peacock, 1992).[16] In part, public choice is a by-product of James Buchanan's attempt to instigate a scientific counter-revolution in this field. Therefore, 'public finance is, indeed, the parent discipline out of which the more generally applicable public-choice theory, now sometimes called the "economic theory of politics", emerged' (Buchanan, 1979a: 10). In one of his first published articles, 'The Pure Theory of Government Finance' (1949), Buchanan advocates the replacement of an 'organismic' by an 'individualistic' theory of the state, which views the relation between government and individuals as one of exchange. According to this view, taxes, or costs, ought not to exceed the benefits accruing to the citizens from government services. The remainder of Buchanan's writings on public finance is devoted to arguing that they do and to explaining why.

His first effort in this direction is in his first published book, *Public Principles of Public Debt* (1958). In this polemical tract Buchanan declares war against the 'new orthodoxy', or 'new economics', of public debt. According to this theory of public finance, public debt, at least if it is internal, does not impose any burden upon future generations. The commonsense belief that it does is supposed to be based upon a false analogy between public and private debt. Buchanan sides with common sense and declares the 'new orthodoxy' to be utterly wrong.

Buchanan's early work on public finance was still not in the public choice tradition – there was as yet no such tradition. His first application of public choice to public finance is in *Public Finance in Democratic Process* (1967). But this was before the term 'public choice' was coined. On page 171, we read: 'Public finance, as a branch of scholarship, as a science, on the borderline between economics proper and political science is the *economics of politics.*' This, you may recall, was later to become the definition of 'public choice' (see p. 9). The main purpose of Buchanan's novel approach to the subject is to close the gap between individual benefits and costs associated with the provision of public goods. The traditional theory of public finance tended to take both taxes and policy goals as exogenously given – analysing the effects of the former and leaving the latter for the economist to determine, according to his preferred ethical values. This approach may suit an elitist society, or one with a 'benevolent dictator', but not the individualistic democracies of today's West.

Buchanan's 1967 book on public finance is primarily a programmatic treatise. One year later, he took a first step from programme to systematic theory in *The Demand and Supply of Public Goods* (1968). I am not going to delve deeply into Buchanan's theory of public finance. Eventually it developed into constitutional economics, which I will discuss, if briefly, in Chapter 4.

But Buchanan did not leave the field of 'public finance', more narrowly conceived. One of his main concerns, to this day, has been to contribute to a theory of *public expenditure*, explaining why it has reached heights that threaten to ruin us all. The main statement of Buchanan's views on this matter can be found in *Democracy in Deficit* (1977), written together with Richard Wagner. The main thesis in this work is that today's excessive public expenditure is the result of the fatal coincidence of democratic politics and Keynesian economics. The former creates an urge to spend, the latter provides a licence to do so.[17]

> In a democracy, the pressures placed upon politicians to survive competition from aspirants to their office bear certain resemblances to the pressures placed upon private entrepreneurs. Private firms compete among themselves in numerous, complex ways to secure the patronage of customers. Politicians similarly compete among themselves for the support of the electorate, and they do this by offering and promising policies and programs which they hope will get them elected or re-elected. A politician in a democratic society, in other words, can be viewed as proposing and attempting to enact a combination of expenditure programs and financing schemes that will secure him the support of a majority of the electorate.
>
> (Buchanan and Wagner, 1977: 96)

This is standard public choice. Competition between self-interested politicians, by itself, leads to oversupply. But output is, in the last instance, determined by demand. So why should voters demand more than an optimum level of public expenditure? The answer is fiscal illusion (Buchanan and Wagner, 1977: 127ff.; see also Buchanan, 1967: ch. 10). People do not feel the burden of taxes, especially indirect taxes, as heavily as they perceive costs paid with money out of their own pockets. We might even delude ourselves into believing that public goods are free. The task of the economist is to teach us that 'there ain't no such thing as a free lunch'. Equally important is the fact that public goods are paid in other ways than by taxes. One important alternative is money creation. Instead of raising taxes, which is certain to be unpopular, politicians may use the printing press for banknotes.[18] Because of the money illusion involved, people are more ready to accept the costs of inflation than the costs of additional taxes (Buchanan and Wagner, 1977: ch. 8). In so far as people do react negatively upon inflation, they tend to misperceive its cause, blaming business and labour unions instead of politicians. But inflation turns out to have more far-reaching consequences. It is depicted, by Buchanan and Wagner, as nothing less than a threat to our civilization, leading to the erosion of our moral and social order (Buchanan and Wagner, 1977: 64f.). A third way of financing a growing public sector is by borrowing. This is the main theme of *Democracy in Deficit*. According to Buchanan and Wagner, the main implication of the Keynesian legacy has been the legitimation of borrowing and deficit financing as sound economic policy. Buchanan and Wagner, of course, are of another opinion. Keynesian economic policy leads to excessive public expenditure. Because of their natural shortsightedness people are more willing to accept the public spending of borrowed money than of taxes. But public borrowing drains the private sector of capital and gives rise to a misallocation of resources (Buchanan and Wagner, 1977: ch. 7).

The root of the evil, then, is Keynesianism, but only in conjunction with democratic politics. Indeed, a main argument in *Democracy in Deficit* is that 'institutions matter' (Buchanan and Wagner, 1977: 127, 135, 144). One might be led, by this, to believe that there is a shift in explanatory burden from individuals to institutions. And maybe there is, but, as we have seen, the assumption of self-interest is still of vital importance. This becomes even more obvious when reading Buchanan's contribution to Thomas Borcherding's *Budgets and Bureaucrats: The Sources of Government Growth* (1977c):

> Without doubt, some considerable part of the observed growth in the public sector, at all levels, is directly traceable to the demands of the citizenry, genuine demands for more services accompanied by an increasing willingness to shoulder the tax burdens required for financing. But, once this is acknowledged, there can also be little doubt but that a significant and remaining part of the observed growth in the public sector can be explained only by looking at the motivations of those who secure direct personal gains from government expansion, gains that are unrelated to the benefits filtered down to the ordinary citizens.
>
> (Buchanan, 1977c: 6)

The electoral process offers, at best, a crude disciplinary check on those who depart too much from constituency preferences. Elections are held only at periodic intervals. Information is poor, and citizens have relatively little private interest in securing more. As a result, almost any politician can, within rather wide limits, behave contrary to the interests of his constituents without suffering predictable harm. If he

31

departs far from these preferences, he may fail to be reelected. But if the stakes are high, if the potential gains to him in 'political income' are sufficiently large, reelection may be willingly sacrificed.

(ibid., p. 13)

Another group which contributes significantly to an expanding public sector is that of governmental bureaucrats. 'Clearly their interests lie in an expanding public sector, and especially in one that expands the number of its employees' (ibid., p. 14). Buchanan's argument concerning bureaucrats is almost identical to that of Niskanen and need not be repeated here. A novel observation is that bureaucrats tend to vote in larger numbers, and for parties supporting the public sector, than does the rest of the citizenry. Another observation, supporting the assumption of self-interest, is that private enterprises are more productive than public enterprises (ibid., p. 17).

Not only has the public sector become too big, at the expense of the private sector; it actually obstructs the working of the latter. By interfering with the market mechanism, governments create the opportunity for rent-seeking. State interventionism leads to rent-seeking, stagnation and decay.

What can we do to curb the seemingly insatiable appetite of the gluttonous Leviathan? The remedy, suggested by Buchanan and Wagner (1977: ch. 12), is a return to the fiscal principles of yesterday, or before Keynes. This means, above all, a balanced budget laid down in the constitution.[19] A second cure would be to deprive civil servants of the right to vote (Buchanan, 1977: 14f.). A third way to cut down public expenditure, without reducing benefits, would be a shift from public to private provision of public goods and services (ibid., pp. 16–18).

Conclusion

I have made a short presentation of the main contributions to an economic theory of politics, or public choice. I will conclude this chapter by offering one authoritative statement of its most essential elements, or hard core. This statement will be the basis for the arrangement of the remaining chapters of Part I of this book.

According to James Buchanan, the theory of public choice is the application and extension of economic theory and economic tools to politics, or governmental choice (Buchanan, 1978: 3; 1979a: 13; 1986: 13, 19; Brennan and Buchanan, 1984: 185). Alternative names are 'the economic theory of politics' or 'the new political economy' (Buchanan, 1979a: 11). Politics is the activity having to do with the collective provision of collective, or public, goods; with public choice. Collective, or public, choice in its turn, is occasionally equated with non-market choice, but is more often limited to government or state activity.

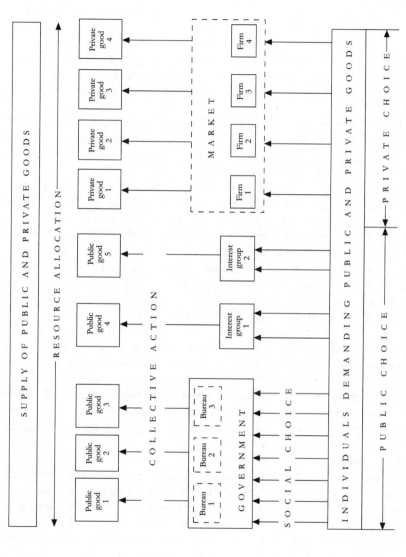

Figure 1.1 The context of public choice

In my vision of social order, individual persons are the basic component units, and 'government' is simply that complex of institutions
through which individuals make collective decisions, and through which
they carry out collective as opposed to private activities. 'Politics' is the
activity of persons in the context of such institutions.

(Buchanan, 1979b: 144)

A preliminary distinction, then, is between traditional economics as the
science of the private choice of private goods on the market and the new
political economy as the science of the public choice of public goods
through government (see Buchanan, 1972: 14–16; Brennan and Buchanan,
1985: 34–37).

Having followed Buchanan in his characterization of 'public choice' as 'the
economic theory of politics', my next query concerns his definition of economics. In his view of economics proper, Buchanan is very much of an Austrian
and a follower of his teacher Frank H. Knight. Economics is seen as a theory
of exchange; as *catallactics* (Buchanan, 1979b: 19ff.; 1986: 19ff.; 1989a: 14ff.).
Buchanan is opposed to seeing economics as a 'logic of choice', because logic
is empty and 'objective'. It says nothing about the choices and exchanges of
actual human beings. In particular, Buchanan is averse to Lord Robbins'
famous definition of economics as 'the science which studies human behaviour as a relationship between ends and scarce means which have alternative
uses' (Robbins, 1935/1972: 16). An undesirable effect of this definition, according to Buchanan, is that it opens the way for turning the economic
problem into a mathematical-technical problem to be solved by some objective utility function, but with no basis in the subjective evaluations and preferences of individual human beings. Buchanan's main target of attack is, of
course, welfare economics, which aims at maximizing an objective utility
function for the community as a whole. Lacking any connection with the
subjective utility of individuals, these social utility functions can only reflect
the preferences of economists themselves. The only way to 'solve' a social
utility function is by exchange on the market or, in politics, by the market
analogue of unanimous consent.

Buchanan, himself, does not maintain that there is a strict homology between economic (market) exchange and political exchange. Farthest in this
direction goes the Chicago School, who follow Gary Becker in treating the
assumption of market equilibrium as essential to the economic approach.
Members of the Rochester School of public choice, on the other hand, do
not at all embrace the model of politics-as-exchange (Riker, 1988; Ordeshook, 1992). This is probably because they are political scientists, not economists. As such, they tend to take institutions more seriously than economists
do. Their major tool is game theory, not traditional microeconomics.

When Buchanan turns to public choice, however, it is not exchange, but
self-interest, which appears to be the most important constitutive element in

the science of economics. The main task of public choice is to replace *homo politicus* by *homo economicus*. According to Buchanan (1972: 12ff.; 1986: 36–38; 1989b: 29, 64f.; Buchanan and Tullock, 1962/1965: 19ff.), it is an unacceptable inconsistency to work with different conceptions of man in the spheres of economics and politics; to assume that, on the market, man is moved solely by self-interest and in politics solely by the public interest.[20] This inconsistency is all the more serious when it appears, not between the two sciences of economics and politics, but within the discipline of economics itself. In welfare economics it is assumed, as a matter of course, that the rational egoist appearing on the market will suddenly turn into a benevolent despot when acquiring political power (see, e.g., Buchanan, 1973: 165, 169, 1975b: 177; Brennan and Buchanan, 1981: 386f.). In opposition to this unhappy state of affairs, Buchanan urges economists to 'close the behavioral system' (1972).[21] If traditional economics is the science of self-interested individuals trading private goods (and services) on the market, public choice is the science of self-interested individuals involved in complex exchange of public goods in the context of political institutions. This conclusion is reached by Buchanan himself. The public choice perspective, he says (Buchanan [1983] 1986: 19ff.; 1989a: ch. 2), is a combination of two elements: (1) the *homo economicus* postulate and (2) the politics-as-exchange paradigm.

The assumption of self-interest is the *differentia specifica* and defining characteristic of public choice. All adherents and commentators, except Iain McLean (1987: 3), seem to agree on this point, even though I notice a recent tendency to define self-interest in a vacuous sense, as compatible with altruism. Orthodox public choice, however, definitely operates with the definition of 'self-interest' as 'selfishness', even though most economists admit that real men and women, as distinct from simplified economic man, are not entirely selfish.

Homo economicus is what distinguishes public choice from rational choice, which assumes only rationality and is, therefore, compatible with altruism and with motives directed at the public interest (Margolis, 1981, 1982/1984). Public choice may be seen as one particular version of rational choice, characterized, above all, by consistent use of the assumption of self-interest. But there is one element that unites all versions of rational choice: methodological individualism.

There is, thus, a third element in the economic approach to politics: the principle of methodological individualism. As we have seen, Buchanan does not always mention methodological individualism explicitly among the core assumptions of public choice. Perhaps this is because it is the most self-evident element in any microeconomic approach to society. There is no doubt whatsoever that methodological individualism belongs in the hard core of public choice (see, e.g. Buchanan, 1949, 1966; 1975a: 1f.; Buchanan and Tullock, 1962/1965: vi–vii, 11–15, 265). Public choice, then, has three constitutive elements: the core assumptions of (1) *self-interest*, (2) *exchange* and (3) *individualism* (Buchanan, 1988: 104).

POLITICAL SOCIOLOGY

Political sociology emerged, as a special division of the amorphous discipline of sociology, along with a number of other subdivisions, such as the sociology of the family, of law, religion, education, science, art, medicine, etc., in the 1950s. This is not to say, of course, that sociology was silent about politics before this point in time. All classical sociologists wrote about politics, Marx and Weber in particular. I will have more to say about political sociology, and especially about the classical sociologists, in the remaining chapters of this book. What follows here is a very brief introduction to the subject.[22]

Orthodox political sociology

In contrast to public choice, political sociology rarely seeks explanations in terms of self-interest. There has been a tendency, at least in mainstream sociology, to assume that the state is an organ for the common good and that politicians and public officials serve the public interest (Parsons, [1959] 1967: 224).[23] There are notorious exceptions, of course, such as Marxism, which tends to assume that state power is in the hands of the ruling class and elite theories of power, which, in a similar manner, assume that political power serves the interest of an elite. The state and its servants was a major concern for the classical sociologists, but not so much for the political sociologists of the mid-century. Several factors conspired to turn their attention to voters, at least in Western democracies. In the studies of modernization and nation-building in other parts of the world, however, the state was still an important object of investigation. I suggest that political sociology in its mid-century heyday had five major concerns:[24]

1 the comparative study of political systems all over the world and, in particular, of the factors contributing to the legitimacy of political systems and regimes;
2 the analysis of the conditions for democracy and, in particular, of the political culture (social values and beliefs) necessary for democratic government;
3 the study of ideology, party alignment and voting behaviour in the democratic countries of the world, especially in the United States;
4 the study of mass movements and ideologies, and especially of the totalitarian ideologies of Nazism, Fascism and communism;
5 the study of state-building and nation-building, especially in the emerging nation-states in Africa and other non-Western parts of the world.

Common to all these concerns was an interest in the social basis of politics and, especially, in the various social cleavages – class, region, religion, ethnicity, sex, etc. – underlying politics. The dominating concern of traditional political sociology, however, was number 3: the explanation of individuals'

36

ideology, party alignment and, ultimately, their voting behaviour, in terms of social structure, socialization and party identification. It is common to recognize two (non-economic) 'paradigms' in the explanation of voting behaviour (Crewe and Denver, 1985: 2ff.; Denver, 1989: 24–28). The first is a 'social structural' paradigm suggesting that the individual vote is determined by location in social structure. This paradigm is associated with Paul Lazarsfeld and Bernard Berelson in *The People's Choice* (Lazarsfeld *et al.*, 1944/1948) and *Voting* (Berelson *et al.*, 1954/1956). The second paradigm explains voting in terms of 'party identification' and is associated with Angus Campbell *et al.* in *The Voter Decides* (1954) and *The American Voter* (1960). These two paradigms – the first more sociological, the second social psychological – are not at all conflicting and thrived for a while in peaceful coexistence. In fact, explanatory power is increased by their conjunction. Together they make up the long-term component that explains what Philip E. Converse (1966) has called the 'normal vote'. In addition, the actual vote is always subjected to the influence of a short-term component, consisting of the specific situation of the election: the state of the domestic economy, international relations, the record of the incumbent, the issues on the agenda, the personality of the candidates, media coverage, etc. Combining the main explanatory factors of traditional political sociology, we arrive at something like the synthesis shown in Figure 1.2.

Figure 1.2 is a good illustration of Göran Therborn's suggestion that sociologists explain human action in terms of structural location and cultural belonging (see p. 7 above). It might be added that cultural belonging is explained in terms of the experiences common to people in similar structural locations and in terms of socialization; and that the explanatory power of the model as a whole and of the different parts of it varies between countries.

One important difference between the economic and sociological approaches to politics is that the former starts with a given situation and given preferences and explains the vote in terms of these, while the latter is almost entirely concerned with explaining how it comes that people are in different situations and have different preferences.[25] To the extent that this is the case, the aims of the economic and sociological approaches to politics are complementary, not conflicting. The Michigan model falls, in this respect, somewhere in between the sociological and economic approaches. While typical sociological variables are included as 'determinants' of the vote, the focus is on the vote itself, and on the motives behind the decision to vote and to vote for a particular candidate (see Miller, 1994: 253, 255).

A second difference is that the economic approach explains the vote as a result of rational egoism, while sociologists tend to be more sceptical about rationality and to deny the ubiquity of self-interest. They do not deny, however, that individuals are to some extent rational and to a large extent self-interested. The Michigan group – the members of which are political scientists – is closer to public choice than is the Columbia group. The Michigan view of rationality, self-interest and ideology is, in fact, very close to that of

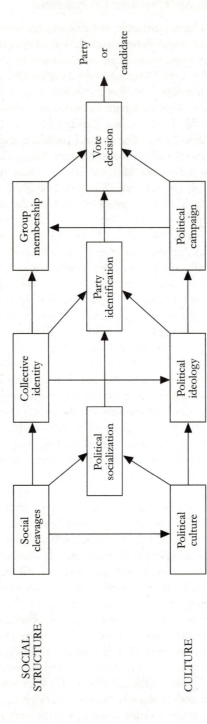

Figure 1.2 A sociological model of voting

Anthony Downs. While equally sceptical about voters' knowledge of issues and party programmes, the Michigan group differs somewhat on the issue of ideology. Downs saw ideology as a means of reducing uncertainty and of cutting information costs. The Michigan group see ideology as a rationalization of long-term self-interest (Campbell *et al.*, 1960: 201–215).

Traditional (political) sociology, it is true, neglected the element of calculation, or rational choice, in the individual's political activity. I say *neglected*, because sociology never denied the element of choice. It simply focused on the social determinants of choice; on the social constraints upon choice and on the social codes that make individual choice largely pre-programmed. But choice is always implicit in sociological analysis, and often explicit too. Even in a piece of Parsonian sociological theory of politics, there is a place for rational choice:

> This brings us to a crucial point in our discussion of the translation of cleavage structure into party systems: *the costs and the payoffs of mergers, alliances, and coalitions.* The height of the representation threshold and the rules of central decision-making may increase or decrease the net returns of joint action, but the intensity of inherited hostilities and the openness of communications across the cleavage lines will decide whether mergers or alliances are actually workable.
>
> (Lipset and Rokkan, 1967: 32)

The Parsonian branch of political sociology tended to emphasize values more than interests, but values are not antithetical to interests, and political sociology, as a whole, has not neglected the play of interest. The important difference between the new political economy and sociology is that the former recognizes only self-interest, while the latter focuses on *group-interest.* And, as we shall see in Chapter 6, sociology does not conceive of group-interest as reducible to self-interest. Group-identity and ideology make group-interest distinct from common self-interest.

Political sociology had its palmy days in the 1950s and the beginning of the 1960s. Since then it has been superseded by public choice as a major intellectual current in political theory, but it has not disappeared from the scene. Political sociology is still alive and kicking, but it has changed since the 1960s, both as an adaptation to external social change and as a result of the internal development of social science. It has been argued that political sociology has come closer to rational choice than it was thirty years ago. Subsequent empirical research indicates that the voter might be a bit more rational than he/she was supposed to be. In addition, the theoretical development of parts of political sociology has changed its focus from values to interests.

In their introduction to *Party Systems and Voter Alignments* (1967), Seymour M. Lipset and Stein Rokkan concluded (p. 50) that the European party systems of the 1960s reflect the cleavage structures of the 1920s. This conclusion was supported by Robert A. Alford's contribution to this volume (Alford,

1967), which shows that class voting was stable in the Anglo-American countries between 1940 and 1965. Lipset and Rokkan went on to argue, however (ibid., pp. 54ff.), that these party systems had become increasingly irrelevant and predicted drastic changes in future voter alignment. This prediction was borne out by the subsequent development. Five years later, Converse (1972: 301–322; 1976: ch. 4) reported the seeds of change in the United States and ten years later, change was evident; at least, if we are to believe Norman H. Nie, Sidney Verba and John R. Petrocik in *The Changing American Voter* (1976). They found a decline in class voting and party identification, but an increase in issue voting and ideological consistency in the United States.

Converse believed that change was the result of special circumstances and, therefore, temporary, but many social scientists saw it as a permanent change resulting from a transformation of Western society from industrial to postindustrial society. The most influential account of this transformation is Ronald Inglehart's idea of a 'silent revolution'. Political realignment was a result of the increasing importance of 'post-materialist' values held by the economically secure and highly educated new middle class in postindustrial society (Inglehart, 1971, 1977).

A consequence of the coming of postindustrial society would be that we now have voters who are less socially determined; more knowledgeable, because better educated and because of new media, more ideologically sophisticated, more interested and more individualistic in their rational choices of candidates and parties (see Dalton, 1988: chs 1–2; Denver, 1989: ch. 4; Lavau, 1990). The implication is not, however, that political sociology has come closer to adopting the assumption of self-interest. Quite the contrary: the new, individualistic, voter is usually supposed to be governed by post-materialistic values, rather than by self-interest (see, e.g., Dalton *et al.* 1984: 474).

A number of studies of Western electorates confirm this trend toward dealignment, party system fragmentation, electoral volatility and, perhaps, realignment along new political lines.[26] Extrapolating from this trend, parties have been predicted to decrease and social movements to increase in importance. Ideologies, which were supposed to be dead in the wake of World War II, have reappeared, but in new shapes and along different dimensions. What we see now, is a New Left and a New Right and, in addition, feminism and environmentalism. Economic voting seemed for a while to decline as a result of increased prosperity, and give way to a growing concern for 'non-economic' values. Today, economic growth has retarded and unemployment has made substantial portions of the population in the West anything but prosperous and economically secure. This 'post-materialist' culture looks more like a short parenthesis in the development of an ever-increasing, worldwide 'materialism'.[27]

Party fragmentation, dealignment and post-material values is a trend which probably has something to do with the rise of a new middle class in the coming postindustrial society. But this is just one trend that we can observe over the past thirty years. Party dealignment does not signify the end of class conflict and class politics. Classes are also represented by interest organizations and these have attained greater political significance as part of corporatist arrangements in many Western countries.

Orthodox, pluralist and functionalist, political sociology was shaped at a time when it seemed that nothing would hinder the continuing economic growth and prosperity of the West; the prospect was that all would be better off, without anyone being worse off and that conflict and ideology would come to an end (cf. Goldthorpe, 1984b). But very soon economic growth did come to an end, or retarded, and unemployment could no longer be combated by traditional means, not even at the cost of inflation. The traditional cures of Keynesian economic policy no longer worked and economists were at a loss to suggest anything better than the old medicine of *laissez-faire* – meanwhile the patient is dying. On top of it, the West has become subjected to increasing economic competition from the East and a continuing immigration from the South. This additional contribution to the work force was most welcome in times of economic growth and shortage of labour, but is less welcome now that there is competition for a shrinking number of vacant jobs and a surplus of labour. The result of this new economic situation has been an accentuation of class conflict and of new political forms to contain it. In addition, there has been an increase of ethnic conflict, both in Western Europe and, especially, in Eastern Europe after the fall of communism.

Theoretical developments

Turning to theory, we observe that new theoretical currents have appeared or, more correctly, *old theories have reappeared*, to challenge the ruling orthodoxy of the 1950s.[28] A simple way to describe this change is to say that it amounted to a renewed concern with *power*. By way of another well-known simplification, we might add that political sociology has replaced one of its core assumptions, *consensus*, by that of *conflict*. Since it is assumed that power largely resides outside parliament, there has been a concomitant shift of focus from elections, parties and government to classes, interest groups and the state. The main theoretical impetus behind this change has been Marxism, but it is much broader than that. Sociology was a centre of the political radicalism which swept the Western hemisphere, or its universities, in the 1960s and 1970s, and political sociology received its share of new and radical ideas. It might be added that there has been a geographic basis of theoretical change: while the ruling orthodoxy was centred in the United States, challenge to this orthodoxy has often been of European origin.

'Power' was a rare word in the vocabulary of orthodox political sociology. Part of the orthodoxy was the, usually unstated, assumption that the countries of the West are pluralist democracies and that the countries of the Third World were on their way to becoming such, unless led astray by the communist

East. Pluralist democracies are representative democracies; politicians are elected by the people and represent their values and interests. The sovereignty of elected politicians, therefore, is popular sovereignty. The existence of non-parliamentary power in the form of pressure groups was acknowledged, but their plurality guarantees that no group can dominate the rest. In pluralist democracies, the various interests counteract and balance one another as in a state of equilibrium. To continue the mechanical analogy, government policy is a vector sum of many forces of equal magnitude.

A first blow to the pluralist image of democratic society came with C. Wright Mills' revival of elite theory in *The Power Elite* (1956/1959).[29] The argument of Mills' book is that the United States since World War II has been governed by a political, economic and military elite, which takes all important decisions without hearing the rest of society. This power elite is not a hereditary aristocracy, but consists of people occupying strategic positions in the central political, economic and military institutions. The power elite is not a monolithic hierarchy, but a network of overlapping circles, exchanging members and sharing a common worldview.

The power elite is but one side of the coin. The other side of the United States of America is an emerging mass society – a society of atomized and apathetic individuals incapable of performing their duty as citizens of a state; of forming publics and of shaping public opinion. Stupefied by politicians and by the media, the mass is reduced to an object of manipulation.

Elite theories and theories of mass society – usually they go together – have been advocated both by conservative aristocrats and by radical democrats (cf. Kornhauser, 1960: 21ff.). They seem to agree that modern society is, or is on its way to becoming, a mass society governed by an elite. But they differ in their diagnosis. Conservative aristocrats, of course, believe that society must be governed by a select elite. They fear the mass and deprecate democracy, which gives it the right to vote. Radical democrats, on the other hand, see the existence of elite–mass society as a deficiency that must be remedied. The existence of a power elite is tantamount to the lack of popular sovereignty.

C. Wright Mills, of course, represents the democratic and radical view of the elite–mass society, but the origin of elite–mass *theory* of society is in the conservative-aristocratic view; it was a reaction to democracy and equality as constitutive features of modern society. I will linger a while on classical conservative elite–mass theory, because, as we will see, it is part of the background of public choice.

The main source of the conservative-aristocratic version of the elite–mass theory of society is Alexis de Tocqueville. In his *Democracy in America* (1835–40) you find the classic, and in its vividness still unsurpassed, description of the totalitarian elite–mass society.

I seek to trace the novel features under which despotism may appear in the world. The first thing that strikes the observation is an innumerable multitude of men all equal and alike, incessantly endeavouring to produce the petty paltry pleasures with which they glut their lives. Each of them, living apart, is as a stranger to the fate of all the rest ... Above this race of men stands an immense and tutelary power, which takes upon itself alone to secure their gratifications, and to watch over their fate. That power is absolute, minute, regular, provident and mild. It would be like the authority of a parent, if, like that authority, its object was to prepare men for manhood; but it seeks on the contrary to keep them in perpetual childhood: it is well content that the people should rejoice, provided they think of nothing but rejoicing ... Such a power does not destroy, but it prevents existence; it does not tyrannize, but it compresses, enervates, extinguishes, and stupefies a people, till each nation is reduced to be nothing better than a flock of timid and industrious animals, of which the government is the shepherd.

(Tocqueville, 1835–40/1961: 380f.)

According to Tocqueville, mass society is the result of the destruction of social groups and relations between the family and the state (Tocqueville, 1835–40/1961: 345ff.). Under the *ancien régime* a bulwark of secondary and intermediate powers, consisting of the nobility, the townships and the guilds, prevented central administration from becoming despotic. In modern society these social structures have vanished and what remains is a direct relation between individual (or family) and state. Like nature, society abhors a vacuum. Unless the old community structures are replaced by secondary groups, they will eventually be replaced by a totalitarian state. Some protection is afforded by the existence of local administration (Tocqueville, 1835–40/1961: 93–99), but the only guarantee against totalitarianism is a free press and freedom of association. One of the most striking features of American society, according to Tocqueville, was 'the immense assemblage of associations'; political and civil (Tocqueville, 1835–40/1961: 216–226; 1835–40/1961: 123–144). 'Americans of all ages, all conditions, and all disposition, constantly form associations ... Wherever, at the head of some new undertaking, you see the Government in France, or a man of rank in England, in the United States you will be sure to find an association' (ibid., pp. 128ff.).

The insistence on the political importance of associations, or secondary groups, has been a constantly recurring theme in the writings of sociologists and political theorists until this day (Wolfe, 1989b: 113 ff.). I will return to this theme in Chapters 6 and 7. It may be added that, unlike the elite theorists, Tocqueville did not see the coming of elite–mass society as inevitable, only as a frightening possibility. Nor did he take an altogether negative stance toward democracy and equality. His attitude was deeply ambivalent.

Classical elite theory is usually associated with two Italian sociologists, Gaetano Mosca and Vilfredo Pareto (who was also an economist and successor of Léon Walras in Lausanne) and the German sociologist Robert Michels.[30] Common to all classical elite theorists was a conviction that society, whatever the form of government, is in actual fact always governed by a small elite and necessarily so – the reason being a combination of the imperatives of organization and an unchanging human nature. An often quoted passage from Mosca states their position with sufficient clarity:

> Amongst the constant facts and tendencies that are to be found in all political organisms, one is so obvious that it is apparent to the most casual eye. In all societies – from societies that are very meagerly developed and have barely attained the dawnings of civilization, down to the most advanced and powerful societies – two classes of people appear – a class that rules and a class that is ruled. The first class, always the less numerous, performs all political functions, monopolizes power and enjoys the advantages that power brings, whereas the second, the more numerous class, is directed and controlled by the first, in a manner that is now more or less legal, now more or less arbitrary and violent, and supplies the first, in appearance at least, with the material means of subsistence and with the instrumentalities that are essential to the vitality of the political organism.
>
> (Mosca, 1896/1923/1939: 50)

Robert Michels, a follower of Mosca, emphasized the organizational causes of elite rule. In his classic *Political Parties* (1915/1962: 61),[31] he argued that 'Democracy is inconceivable without organization', and 'Organization implies the tendency to oligarchy' (ibid., p. 70):

> In every organization, whether it be a political party, a professional union, or any other association of the kind, the aristocratic tendency manifests itself very clearly. The mechanism of the organization, while conferring a solidity of structure, induces serious changes in the organized mass, completely inverting the respective position of the leaders and the led. As a result of organization, every party or professional union becomes divided into a minority of directors and a majority of directed.

This is not an empirical generalization summing up our accumulated experience of political organization, but a 'matter of technical and practical necessity. It is the inevitable product of the very principle of organization' (ibid., p. 72), Michels' famous iron law of oligarchy: 'It is organization which gives birth to the dominion of the elected over the electors, of the mandatories over the mandators, of the delegates over the delegators. Who says organization, says oligarchy' (ibid., p. 365). But the cause of oligarchy is not entirely technical; it is partly psychological. The power of leaders and their separation from the rank and file members of the organization causes a psychological transformation, which Michels depicts as 'corruption' (ibid., pp. 205ff.).

Pareto, finally, was more inclined towards psychological explanations.[32] His leaning towards systems theory made him aware that everything is dependent upon everything else, and psychological phenomena are therefore dependent on 'material' social phenomena. His own focus was on psychic phenomena. Pareto was also obsessed with rhythms, oscillations and cycles, and wished to explain the circulation of elites in terms of rhythmic movements in the sentiments of the population. In an early version of Pareto's theory of elite circulation, what he had in mind was simply what we would today call 'social mobility': the movement of individuals between the different strata in society. The elite is simply the upper level of the social pyramid, also called the 'aristocracy'. In Pareto's mature version of the elite theory, however, elite circulation is the replacement of old elites by new elites. The elite is now divided into two parts: a governing elite and a non-governing elite. The governing elite consists of that part of the elite which plays a significant part in government and political life. What Pareto originally called 'elite circulation' is now called 'class circulation'. There is a relation between elite circulation and class circulation, such that the latter counteracts the former. Elites co-opting the most able elements from the lower strata survive longer.

The psychological basis of Pareto's elite theory can be found in his concepts of *residues* and *derivations*. Residues are manifestations of sentiments and instincts, used by Pareto to explain human behaviour. I believe we can think of them as motives, or complexes of motives, found as character traits in individual human beings. Derivations are beliefs such as religions, myths, metaphysics and pseudo-science. Pareto's view of derivations make them equivalent to 'ideology', in the Marxist sense of that term. Two residues are important in Pareto's explanation of elite circulation: combination and group persistence. People dominated by the residue of combination are instrumental and calculating – think of them as economic man. People dominated by group persistence are loyal to their group and act on principle – think of them as sociological man. The first type is called, by Pareto, 'speculators', the second type *'rentiers'*. Following Machiavelli, he also calls them 'foxes' and 'lions'. In Pareto's view, new elites, seizing power, typically consist of lions, who are eventually replaced by the more cunning foxes, who meet their destiny in the form of new lions, and so on in the never-ending story of elite circulation. Even if it were true, this would not be much of an *explanation*, and Pareto tries to back it up by assuming as a law that all elites lose their vigour, becoming decadent and soft and finally unable to defend themselves against the attacks of new, confident elites.

Another part of the explanation is that elites use derivations to back up their claim to power. For old elites, derivations tend to lose credibility as it becomes obvious that ideals fail to materialize. New elites have the advantage of being as yet uncompromised. They can use the old battle cries of liberty, brotherhood, equality, justice, etc., and be believed by the masses, who, full of implicit faith, install them as their new masters.

Elite theories obviously have something in common with Marxism. Power is in the hands of a ruling elite, or class. One difference is that elite theories do not see political power as a derivative of ownership of the means of production. The elite is simply the elite. In the case of capitalist society, however, Pareto endorsed the Marxist view that it is a plutocracy. A second difference is that most elite theorists denied the possibility of ever getting rid of governing elites. Democracy and socialism are but the latest expressions of wishful thinking; effective in stirring people to action, but illusions. With the exception of the young Robert Michels and the old Mosca, classical elite theorists were opposed, not only to socialism, but also to democracy, perhaps because they feared that the latter would lead to the former.[33]

Around 1960 the revival of elite theory led to a reaction from pluralist quarters. Most well known is the rejoinder of the political scientist Robert A. Dahl.[34] In a short article (Dahl, 1958), he argued that elite theory, because of its conspiratorial component, is especially hard to test. He also maintained that the ruling elite model, while used in several studies, has not, as yet, been subjected to an appropriate test. Such a test must avoid the following mistakes: (1) it must not mistake a high potential for control with actual control. Actual control also presupposes a high potential for unity. (2) It must not confuse a leading stratum with a ruling elite. It is a commonplace that effective power is in the hands of a minority. But it is still possible that this minority consists of a plurality of powerful groups. The ruling elite model assumes that the ruling minority is also united. (3) It must not generalize from a single sphere of influence. The fact that one group is influential in one sphere does not imply that it is also influential in other policy spheres.

In his own classic investigation of *Who Governs?* (1961b), Dahl found that, in the city of New Haven at least, the power structure had changed from oligarchy to pluralist democracy, but it was far from 'democratic', if that means equality of power:

> Within a century a political system dominated by one cohesive set of leaders had given way to a system dominated by many different sets of leaders, each having access to a different combination of political resources. It was, in short, a pluralist system. If the pluralist system was very far from being an oligarchy, it was also a long way from achieving the goal of political equality advocated by the philosophers of democracy and incorporated into the creed of democracy and equality practically every American professes to uphold.
>
> (Dahl, 1961b: 86)

Dahl's critique hits elite theory only to the extent that it conceives of the elite as being one cohesive body acting in unison. This is how C. Wright Mills depicts the elite, but the classical elite theorists were less clear about its actual composition. Mosca seems at first to have assumed one single elite, but ended endorsing an elitist version of democracy not very different from Dahl's pluralist democracy, or as it has also been called, 'democratic elitism' (Parry, 1969: ch. 6).

More important, perhaps, is the critique directed at Dahl's concept of 'power' and its relation to methodical behaviouralism: '*I do not see how anyone can suppose that he has established the dominance of a specific group in a community or a nation without basing his analysis on the careful examination of a series of concrete decisions*' (Dahl, 1958: 466). This presumption was disputed by Peter Bachrach and Morton S. Baratz in their important article 'Two Faces of Power' (1962). Against Robert Dahl and behaviouralism, they argued that power is not a matter only of decision-making, but also of agenda setting. Power is also the ability to prevent certain issues from becoming subject to decision-making. It is exercised in *non*-decision-making as well as in decision-making (Bachrach and Baratz, 1963). Steven Lukes went further and argued that power has *three* faces or dimensions. Important as it is to recognize control of the political agenda as an additional 'dimension' of power, it is still not sufficient. 'The power to control the agenda of politics and exclude potential issues cannot be adequately analysed unless it is seen as a function of collective forces and social arrangements' (Lukes, 1974: 22). Bachrach and Baratz are 'still too committed to behaviourism' (ibid., p. 21), and too much concerned with 'actual, observable conflict' (ibid., p. 22). The third face of power is the ability to mould people's preferences by means of persuasion.[35] 'To put the matter sharply, *A* may exercise power over *B* by getting him to do what he does not want to do, but he also exercises power over him by influencing, shaping or determining his very wants' (ibid., p. 23). Power, then, is not limited to observable conflict and subjective interest. An adequate concept of 'power' must include potential conflict and real interests. Lukes' three-dimensional concept of 'power' may be interpreted as a nod of approval in the Marxist direction.[36]

Marxism has been the strongest current in post-behavioural and post-pluralist political sociology, at least in Europe. Because of the complexity and great variety of Marxist theories, it is quite impossible to survey this field in a few pages. I will limit myself, therefore, to a few observations and direct the reader to some other source for more enlightenment.[37]

Prima facie, Marxism may seem to be an unlikely basis for political theory. This is so for, at least, three reasons:

1. Marx never developed a systematic theory of politics himself. His most important, but unfinished, work, *Capital*, breaks off at the point where he intended to discuss the state. Engels tried to fill the gap, but did not get very far in developing a comprehensive Marxist theory of politics. In *The Origin of the Family, Private Property and the State* (1884), he points out that the state has not always existed and adds that it 'arose from the need to keep class antagonisms in check' (1884/1891/1972: 231). The state is typically the state of the dominant class, but in exceptional cases, when several classes compete for supremacy, the state may turn into a mediator between them. In *Anti-*

Dühring (1878/1969) and *Ludwig Feuerbach and the End of Classical German Philosophy* (1888/1976), Engels suggests that the state first arose as an organ for the common interest of members of tribes in irrigation and protection against external enemies and only later turned into a vehicle for class rule (1878/1969: 179; 1888/1976: 53). The modern state, however, is a capitalist machine, defending capitalism not only against the working class, but also against individual capitalists. The capitalist state is 'the ideal personification of the total national capital' (1878/1969: 330). As such, it has two primary tasks: to create the technical conditions necessary for capitalist production and to produce the ideology necessary for the acceptance of capitalist class domination.

2.   Marxism is, at least in some versions, the most 'reductionist' of all theories of politics. In the simplified scheme of historical materialism, political life belongs to the 'superstructure' and is conditioned, or determined, by the material base. Political forms cannot be comprehended by themselves, since they originate in the material conditions of life (Marx, 1859/1970: 20f.; Marx and Engels, 1846/1976: 61, 98f., 348). Engels tried to modify or, perhaps, clarify historical materialism, with respect to the relation between base and superstructure, in some letters written in the 1890s. Engels now suggests that the state is relatively independent of the base and of the interest of the ruling class. Within limits, it is capable of exerting an autonomous influence upon the course of events and even of reacting on the economic base (in Marx and Engels, 1975: 398f., 441f.).

3.   Marx, and especially Engels, did suggest that the state (as state) would disappear, or 'wither away' with the disappearance of classes in communist society. The 'government of persons' would be replaced by 'the administration of things' (Engels, 1878/1969: 333; cf., Marx and Engels [1872] in Marx 1974: 314) – an idea they had probably borrowed from Saint-Simon. This is not only a seriously mistaken belief, but a dangerous illusion, since it releases communists from the responsibility of seriously discussing their most important problem: the economic and political organization of communist society (cf. Udehn, 1981a: 53–55). Leaving rhetoric aside, however, Marx admitted the need for a state (or administration) in classless, communist, society (cf. Elster, 1985a: 453–458). 'While the merely repressive organs of the old governmental power were to be amputated, its legitimate functions were to be wrested from an authority usurping preeminence over society itself, and restored to the responsible agents of society' (*The Civil War in France* [1870], in Marx, 1974: 210). As this happens, the functions of the state cease to be political and become administrative. There now exists '1) no government function, 2) the distribution of the general functions has become a business matter, that gives no one domination, 3) election has nothing of its present political character' (ibid., p. 336). What functions will remain after this transformation of the state is not for Marx, but for future science, to say. An indication can be found in Marx's division of the social product in his *Critique of the*

Gotha Programme of 1875. A first part consists of investments necessary for production. More interesting is a second part which has three uses: (1) the diminishing '*general costs of all administration not directly appertaining to production*', (2) the increasing '*amount set aside for needs communally satisfied*, such as schools, health services, etc.' and (3) '*a fund for people unable to work*, etc., in short, for what today comes under so-called official poor relief' (Marx, 1974: 345). The remaining part is distributed as income for the working population. Marx dismisses bourgeois notions of 'justice' as ideology, but does not reject all moral principles. The famous principle of communist society is this: 'From each according to his abilities, to each according to his needs!' (Marx, 1974: 347).

Before proceeding, it might be noticed that Marxism and public choice have something in common: both theories express a deep mistrust of the notion of a 'public interest'. According to public choice, politicians and bureaucrats pursue their own interests; according to Marxism, they pursue the common interest of the bourgeoisie. If, however, we look at Marx's early political writings, before he and Engels created historical materialism, we find descriptions of political life that are indistinguishable from those made by public choice theorists. In his *Critique of Hegel's Doctrine of the State* (1843), for instance, we find Marx maintaining that 'for the individual bureaucrat, the purpose of the state becomes his private purpose, *a hunt for promotion, careerism*' (Marx, 1975: 108). Marx's critique of Hegel's idealist theory of the state is, on the whole, not dissimilar from Buchanan's individualist critique of the organicist theory of the state. In one of Marx's last works, *The Civil War in France* 1874, the state is again depicted in a way close to that of public choice: as a monster born of society, but emancipating itself from its true home and eventually turning against it. Instead of Leviathan, Marx uses less fictitious, but equally telling images: 'The centralized state machinery which, with its ubiquitous and complicated military, bureaucratic, clerical and judiciary organs, entoils (enmeshes) the living civil society like a boa constrictor' (Marx, 1974: 246). Marx's most commonly used metaphor, however, is of state employees as a band of corrupted parasites sucking the blood of civil society. Because of the ideological role of the state, Marx sometimes refers to state officials as 'priests'.

For Marx and Engels, the state is bound up with the existence of classes. At its most simple, 'the state is the form in which the individuals of a ruling class assert their common interests' (Marx and Engels, 1846/1976: 99), an 'instrument of class rule' (Marx, 1870 in 1974: 250). In capitalist society, it 'is but a committee for managing the common affairs of the whole bourgeoisie' (Marx and Engels, 1848/1967: 82).

The above is often called 'the instrumentalist theory of the state' (Jessop, 1982: 12–16; Elster, 1985a: 408). It looks simple enough, but much revolves around the specification of the 'common interest' of the bourgeoisie. The term 'common interest' excludes the fact that Marx and Engels had in mind the interest of particular members of the capitalist class. There is much to indicate that the task of the capitalist state is to solve the collective action problem of the capitalist class. But is it their short-term, or their long-term, collective interest in the extraction of surplus value? Or is it their long-term and enlightened interest in the survival of the capitalist system? If the state is an organ for the long-term interest of the bourgeoisie, it might in many cases act against the immediate interests of the capitalist class in order to protect it against itself. As we move progressively away from the immediate interests of the bourgeoisie, the instrumentalist theory of the state changes from a rational choice theory to a functionalist theory of social cohesion.

It is often pointed out that Marx's concrete political studies display an analysis of the state that is much more complex and subtle than in the simplified schema of historical materialism. In particular, they reveal that Marx was not a consistent reductionist. The state is treated as an autonomous actor in relation to social classes. In *The Class Struggles in France 1848–1850*, Marx argues that state power is indeed in the hands of the bourgeoisie and based on a compromise between its different fractions (Marx, 1973b: 41, 43). The working class had compelled the bourgeoisie to make some concessions in the February republic, but was soon defeated. According to Marx, the time was not yet ripe for the proletariat to emerge victorious. In his much celebrated *Eighteenth Brumaire of Louis Bonaparte*, Marx finds a regime that does not conform to expectations. Bonaparte is not the henchman of the bourgeoisie. 'As against the bourgeoisie, Bonaparte sees himself simultaneously as the representative of the peasants and of the people in general, as the man who wants to make the lower classes happy within the framework of bourgeois society' (Marx, 1973b: 246). By acting as a safeguard of bourgeois order, however, Bonaparte couldn't help but serve the long-term interest of its dominant class. By breaking the political power of the bourgeoisie, he protected and recreated their material power (ibid., p. 245). But this was possible only because, in the terminology of Jon Elster (1985a: 411), the bourgeoisie 'abdicated' power:

> the bourgeoisie confesses that its own interest requires its deliverance from the peril of its own self-government; that to establish peace and quiet in the country its bourgeois parliament must first of all be laid to rest; that its political power must be broken in order to preserve its social power intact; that the individual bourgeois can only continue to exploit the other classes and remain in undisturbed enjoyment of property, family, religion and order on condition that his class is condemned to political insignificance along with the other classes; and that in order to save its purse the crown must be struck off its head and the sword which is to protect it must hang over it like a sword of Damocles.
>
> (Marx, 1973b: 190)

On the basis of this analysis and some other pieces of evidence, Elster argues that Marx really maintained a general class-balance theory of the modern state.

It is a view of the state as an active, autonomous agent from the sixteenth century onwards, pursuing its own interests by harnessing those of others to its purpose. The basic explanation is to be found in the presence of several opposed classes, allowing the government to play an active rule by mediation and divide-and-conquer.

(Elster, 1985a: 426)

In modern (European) sociology, the most influential Marxist political theory has probably been that of Nicos Poulantzas, with roots in the ideas of Louis Althusser and Antonio Gramsci. The language of French structuralism, in which Poulantzas' theory is wrapped up, is an obstacle to the uninitiated reader, but I will try to avoid the most impenetrable profundities. According to Poulantzas, *'the state has the particular function of constituting the factor of cohesion between the levels of a social formation'* (1968/1978: 44). There are three 'modalities' of this general function: a technico-economic, a political and an ideological. The first consists in providing the legal framework for economic activity, the second of keeping political order by mediating in class conflict and the third in educating the citizens of the state.

By maintaining order in society, the state really promotes the interest of the dominant class, which gains most from the status quo. The official version of the state's duty, however, is, without exception, that it is the guardian of the public interest. By thus presenting itself, it seeks to hide its true class character (Poulantzas, 1968/1978: 123, 133). To the extent that the dominant class succeeds in launching its own interest as the public interest, it is 'hegemonic' (ibid., p. 137) – a term borrowed from Antonio Gramsci. The means whereby the state is made to appear as a vehicle for the public interest and, thereby, is enabled to maintain cohesion, is ideology (ibid., pp. 206ff.). Thus deceived, the dominated classes consent to being governed by the state, which is thereby rendered legitimate. If several classes, or class fractions, are dominant, they constitute a 'power bloc' (ibid., p. 234) – another term borrowed from Antonio Gramsci.

Poulantzas rejects the instrumentalist theory of state power. The state defends the long-term interest of the dominant class, but is not its servant. The state has a relative autonomy, within limits set by class struggle. Unlike Elster, Poulantzas does not wish to attribute to Marx a general class-balance theory of the state. State autonomy is possible also in the absence of an equilibrium (1968/1978: 166f., 259–262, 351–353). The reason for this is, probably, that Poulantzas wishes to make as clear as possible a distinction between Marxism and pluralist theories of equilibrium (ibid., pp. 264ff.). He is also critical of the corporatist and elite theories of state power (ibid., pp. 26ff., 325ff.). For Poulantzas, political power ultimately resides in social classes, and, especially, in the hegemonic social class.

Structuralist Marxism appeared and disappeared all of a sudden. Among the reasons for its disappearance was a widespread discontent with the radical denial of the human subject. In the end, few sociologists were willing to acquiesce in the reduction of the individual to a mere support of structures. More specifically, the extant use of functional explanations, not least by Poulantzas, has been severally criticized by rational choice Marxists (Elster, 1982; 1985a: 27–37; 1983: 59–69; Przeworski and Wallerstein, 1982: 235f.; Przeworski, 1985: 200–203).

Another, originally Marxist, tradition is the German critical theory of the Frankfurt School. The main descendant of this extinct school is Jürgen Habermas, who may very well be the most influential sociologist of our times, with intellectual roots both in Marxism and in orthodox sociology, especially the work of Max Weber. In his first systematic treatise of modern society, *Legitimation Crisis* (1973/1975), we find, in embryo, ideas that were to culminate in *The Theory of Communicative Action* (1981/1984; 1981/1987). In addition, there is in the earlier work an analysis of economy and state, which is only partly recapitulated in the latter work.

Habermas conceives of contemporary society as 'advanced capitalism', consisting of (1) an economic system, comprising a competitive, a monopoly and a public sector, (2) a political system and (3) a socio-cultural system. The economic system has an inherent tendency to economic crisis and also produces a number of 'negative' external effects. The state, which in early, liberal, capitalism was limited to being the guardian of law and order, is 'forced' by circumstances to intervene on an ever increasing scale in order to secure capital accumulation and to mitigate and remedy the consequences of market failure. By so doing, the state progressively replaces the market mechanism by a number of administrative techniques: monetary, financial and tax policy, regulations, etc., and by the production of public goods.

State intervention, however, produces problems of its own. The costs incurred by its new commitments lead to increased taxes, budget deficits, inflation and financial crisis. The conflict arising from the opposite demands that the state should, on the one hand, refrain from interfering with the allegedly self-regulating market mechanism and, on the other hand, correct market failures, is irresolvable. According to Habermas, there are definite limits to state intervention, which have to do with the principal impossibility of a rational administration of the economic system of advanced capitalism and of every complex social system.

Habermas' analysis of the problems of state intervention in advanced capitalism is much indebted to that of Claus Offe.[38] For him, the problems of advanced capitalism are generated by the fact that its subsystems are run by different and conflicting principles of operation. The economic system is based on exchange and commodification and the political-administrative system on authority and decommodification. Because the economic system is not self-sufficient and because it gives rise to negative externalities, the political-administrative system is forced to engage in 'crisis management' on an ever increasing scale. Since these subsystems operate on different principles, however, intervention does not result in the alleviation of problems, but leads to their multiplication. The political-administrative system has the impossible task both of creating optimal conditions for market exchange and of abating its undesired effects.

As Offe notices, himself, his diagnosis of our times is similar, in many respects, to that of 'government overload' and 'ungovernability', advanced by conservative and libertarian critics of the welfare state (Offe, 1984: ch. 2, 149ff., 164ff.). As such, it is similar also to the public choice analysis of public expenditure. A decisive difference is that Habermas and Offe, in a Marxist manner, see the root of the trouble in the capitalist economic system, not in the self-interest of politicians, or in the working of democratic political institutions. Another important difference is that Habermas and Offe recognize a third, socio-cultural, subsystem, which is the locus of members' normative integration in society. What happens in the economic and political systems decides the fate of nations, but it is not unaffected by developments in the socio-cultural system. For Habermas and Offe, therefore, the present crisis is, to an important degree, a legitimation crisis (Habermas, 1973/1975: 68–75; Offe [1975] 1984: 130–146).

Habermas and Offe are also among the first to observe certain tendencies in liberal democracies, which were to become comprehended as 'neocorporatism' (Habermas, 1962/1989: 196ff.; 1973/1975: 59ff.; Offe [1979, 1980] 1984: 73, 167).

Corporatism has been a major theme among political scientists and political sociologists for two decades, but seems now to be on the wane.[39] It all started in 1974 with three, independently written, articles by Gerhard Lehmbruch, R. Pahl and J. Winkler and Philippe C. Schmitter. Lehmbruch uses the term 'liberal corporatism' to denote 'a special type of participation by large organized social groups in public, especially economic, policy-making'. By 'participation' is understood '(c)onsultation and cooperation among administrations and organized interests' (Lehmbruch [1974] 1979a: 53). Pahl and Winkler conceive of corporatism as a type of economic system, the essence of which is '*private* ownership and *state* control' (Pahl and Winkler, 1974: 73). Winkler later suggested the following explicit definition: '*Corporatism is an economic system in which the state directs and controls predominantly privately-owned business according to four principles: unity, order, nationalism and success*' (Winkler, 1976: 103). Most influential has been the definition provided by Schmitter:

Corporatism can be defined as a system of interest representation in which the constituent units are organized into a limited number of singular, compulsory, noncompetitive, hierarchically ordered and functionally differentiated categories, recognized or licensed (if not created) by the state and granted a deliberate representational monopoly within their respective categories in exchange for observing certain controls on their selection of leaders and articulation of demands and supports.

(Schmitter [1974] 1979b: 13)

According to this definition, corporatism is a system of interest *representation*. Since corporatism is commonly regarded as a threat to representation, Schmitter later suggests that it is a form of interest *intermediation* (Schmitter, 1979a: 63). Lehmbruch, who maintains that corporatism has more to do with the output than with the input of the political system, argues that it is a form of *policy-formation*, characterized by the concerted actions of the state and the largest organized interests (Lehmbruch, 1979b: 149–152). I believe Lehmbruch has a point, since it is generally agreed that corporatism, as distinguished from pluralism, includes interest organizations as partners in the shaping and implementation of policy (cf. Cawson, 1978: 184). Schmitter (1981: 295f) acknowledges the existence of two types of corporatism; corporatism$_1$ and corporatism$_2$, but prefers to keep them conceptually apart. I agree with Cawson (1985: 8) that 'corporatism *is* corporatism$_1$ and corporatism$_2$ together.

Some writers go even further and see corporatism as a specific arrangement including exactly three partners: state, capital and labour. This view of corporatism, as *tripartism*, is common especially among Marxists using a class-theoretic approach (Jessop, 1979; Panitch, 1979, 1980). Corporatism is analysed as a state form fit for securing capital accumulation in advanced capitalism. It achieves this by pacifying the working class, thus containing the conflict between capital and labour. Corporatism is typically associated with social democratic regimes. Leo Panitch defines 'corporatism', minimally, as '*a political structure within advanced capitalism which integrates organized socioeconomic producer groups through a system of representation and cooperative mutual interaction at the leadership level and mobilization and social control at the mass level*' (Panitch, 1980: 173). Including this definition, Lehmbruch (1984: 61) recognizes three concepts of 'corporatism':[40]

(i) the development and strengthening of centralized interest organizations – or 'peak' associations – which possess a representational monopoly;

(ii) the granting to these associations of privileged access to government, and the growth of – more or less institutionalized – linkages between public administration and such interest organizations;

(iii) the 'social partnership' of organized labour' and business aimed at regulating conflicts between these groups, in coordination with government policy (usually in the form of 'tripartism').

There is merit in the view of corporatism as tripartism, because this may very well be the dominant form of corporatism in advanced capitalism. I nevertheless believe that it is better not to turn this fact into a part of its

54

definition (cf. Lehmbruch, 1979c: 299–302). I see little gain in wrapping up the concept of 'corporatism' in the strait-jacket of historical materialism, or the Marxist theory of capitalism; a place where it did not originally belong. I prefer to allow for the existence of other forms of corporatism at other times and in other places and even here and now. Following Max Weber (and Frank Parkin), Alan Cawson (1986: 14, 38) has argued that other interests than organized capital and organized labour may be party to corporatist cooperation. The important thing is the ability of organized interests to achieve monopoly status and this can also be accomplished by professional groups, excluding people not fulfilling the stipulated entrance requirements.[41]

> *Corporatism is a specific socio-political process in which organisations representing monopolistic functional interests engage in political exchange with state agencies over public policy outputs which involves those organisations in a role which combines interest representation and policy implementation through delegated self-enforcement.*
>
> (Cawson, 1986: 38)

Like neo-elitism and neo-Marxism, the theory of neo-corporatism grew out of a dissatisfaction with the prevailing pluralist image of liberal democracy. Most advocates of neo-corporatist theory are closer to elite theory and, especially, to Marxism than to pluralism. Even so, pluralists reject the claim that neo-corporatism is distinct from a pluralist political system. According to Gabriel A. Almond (1983: 251), 'corporatism is a variety of pluralism – to be distinguished from a more disaggregated competitive variety at one extreme, and a state controlled variety at the other'. Is corporatism, then, a limiting case of pluralism, bordering on monistic polity, as conceived by elite theory and the instrumentalist versions of Marxism? This is the view of Alan Cawson, who sees neo-corporatism as the oligopolistic result of competitive pluralism (Cawson, 1978: 185, 187ff.). Needless to say, it all depends upon how you define 'pluralism' and 'corporatism', but I prefer to conceive of them as distinct ideal types, representing certain features of political life that may be more, or less, pronounced and may even coexist in a particular political system. Cawson (1986: 27–40) maintains that they are *both* ideal types *and* extremes on a single continuum of concentration, but I find this view problematic. It is, of course, possible to construct a continuum as a compound variable, or index of several variables, but there is a limit to the fertility of this procedure. There is too much real discontinuity between pluralism and corporatism for a continuous scale between the two to be theoretically feasible. I do not deny, however, that, in some cases, there might be a 'continuous' development of pluralism into corporatism.

The decisive difference between pluralism and corporatism is not the number of interest organizations involved, even though 'pluralism' connotes many and 'corporatism' few. More important is the fact that corporatism is a much more closely knit nexus of state and interest organization than is pluralism. In corporatism, we don't see interest groups acting as pressure groups, but interest *organizations* disciplining their members in the interest of the state. Interest organizations are licensed by the state and attain a limited public status (Offe, 1981). They act as partners of the state, with one leg in civil society and the other in the state apparatus (cf. Grant, 1985a: 3).

I am more impressed by Cawson's suggestion that some Western political systems exhibit a dual structure, involving both pluralism and corporatism (Cawson and Saunders, 1983: 18–26; Cawson, 1986: ch. 7).[42] Pluralism and corporatism coexist, but in different parts of the political system. Corporatism dominates at the central level of the state and includes producer and professional interests, while pluralism is relegated to the local level of the state and includes primarily consumer interests. The coupling of dualism to different parts of the state apparatus is probably the most problematic part of the argument. The distinction between producer and consumer interest is of long standing and important both to public choice and to corporatism. Clearly producer interests are easier to organize and more powerful – therefore more likely to be assimilated by the corporate state.

The term 'corporatism' has been used to denote both a theory and a real world political structure. In its classical form, corporatism was a theory, or ideology, celebrating medieval, organic society, with its functional organization of society into occupational groups, or guilds. At the time of capitalist breakthrough a number of intellectuals feared that society would disintegrate, because of the destruction of traditional social communities and/or the emergence of antagonistic classes. The political organization of society in corporations would perform the double function of replacing old communities with new ones and of preventing the emergence of organizations based on class.[43] Eventually, corporatism was appropriated by the Fascists and thereby definitely discredited as an ideology, if not as a theoretical ideal type. Contemporary corporatism is called 'societal', 'liberal', or simply 'neo-corporatism', in order to distinguish it from earlier conceptions and political systems. In contradistinction to authoritarian 'state corporatism', imposed from above, neo-corporatism is anchored in civil society and coexists with liberal political institutions.

The recent upsurge in theorizing about corporatism is a response to certain developments in the economic and political systems of the West (see, e.g., Maier, 1984). I have already indicated that corporatism is associated with the prevalence of social democratic regimes. It is also associated with the existence of monopolistic and centralized organizations, representing the interests of capital and labour. A third observation is that corporatism seems to be most pronounced in small countries such as Austria, Norway and Sweden.

A precondition for corporatism in liberal democracies is that the parties to exchange define the situation as a positive-sum game (Grant, 1985a: 25; Schmitter, 1985: 44ff.).[44] There is no incentive to engage in tripartite exchange unless you stand to gain from cooperation. This definition of the situation is at odds with traditional Marxism, which emphasizes conflict between capital and labour and sees the state as necessarily partial in this conflict. Modern Marxists and social scientists of Marxist inspiration are more prone to see the existence also of common interests between capital and labour and of organized labour as powerful enough to exert a countervailing pressure on the state. I agree with those who recognize the relation between organized capital and labour as a mixed game of conflict and cooperation (Elster, 1982: 474–478; Przeworski and Wallerstein, 1982; Przeworski, 1985: ch. 5; Lange, 1984; Crouch, 1985: 64ff.) and with those who argue that organized labour may become strong enough significantly to influence politics to its own advantage (Korpi, 1983). I also agree that behind the common interests of capital and labour, and the countervailing power of the working class, there is a fundamental asymmetry of power emanating from the capitalist control over investment decisions (cf. Przeworski and Wallerstein, 1988).

But if capital and labour have both common and conflicting interests, we should expect corporatist cooperation to be unstable. We should also expect the strategies of actors to change as a function of changes in their relative power. Thus, it has been suggested that corporatism thrives in times of economic growth and a high level of employment, when there is more to divide and the working class has more bargaining power (Schott, 1985: 92ff.). It has also been argued that the leaders of labour have a stronger incentive to enter corporatist cooperation than have the rank and file members of workers' organizations. If this is so, we should expect corporatism eventually to lead to a split within organized labour (Panitch, 1979: 140ff.). Another feature of corporatism, making for instability, is the exclusion of many interests (e.g. consumer interests) and the eventual development of dualism also among producers. John Goldthorpe (1984a: 329–335), for instance, has pointed to the possible emergence of a divided labour market, with an increasing part of labour, mainly migrant labour, lacking effective organization. There is, finally, a problem of the legitimacy of corporatist arrangements which may be a bar to its institutionalization (Schmitter, 1985: 59–62; Cawson, 1986: 145–147). Democratic governments are supposed to represent voters, not organized interests.

For all these reasons, full-blown corporatism is a rare and precarious form of cooperation between the state and organized interests (cf. Maier, 1981: 49–56). It is an ideal type approximated, so far, only by a few countries in Western Europe and in some of these countries (e.g. Sweden), it is on the wane. There is no compelling reason to believe that corporatism will ever become a dominant feature of the political systems in the West and it cannot be expected to last, once it has been instigated. Interest in corporatism, therefore, has probably been exaggerated. But the verdict must not be unfair. The discussion of corporatism has been theoretically fertile and it did spawn a whole lot of valuable empirical investigations, which I have not mentioned in my short presentation.

A common critique of theories of corporatism has been that they focus on cooperation with the state, but lack a theory of the state. This is not correct with respect to the Marxists' theories of corporatism, which do have a theory of the state. But it may be argued that the Marxist theory of the state is inadequate as part of a theory of corporatism. Marxism is too reductionist and lack a theory of the state as an independent institution (Przeworski and Wallerstein, 1982: 235; Przeworski, 1985: 201). Corporatism, on the other hand, implies that the state is independent, both as an institution and as a strategic actor (Birnbaum, 1982; Williamson, 1989: ch. 6).

I will not enter this debate, but note that it ties in with another important current in recent political science and political sociology: the movement to 'bring the state back in' (Skocpol, 1982, 1985). What is requested is a return to the state as an actor and as an institution. The state, according to this movement, is more than an arena for contending social interests. It is a relatively independent and relatively autonomous actor, with powers of its own (Krasner, 1984). How much independence and autonomy differ between states is an important matter for comparative research. Methodologically stated, 'bringing the state back in' means turning the state from a dependent to an independent variable (Nordlinger, 1987: 359ff.; 1988: 881–885).

The new state-centred research strategy has been questioned by political scientists of the older generation. Gabriel Almond (1988) and Theodor Lowi (1988), for instance, argue that the state was *in* all the time. What was *out*, was the concept 'state'. The movement to bring the state back in, therefore, is not much of a revolution. If anything, it is a counter-revolution threatening to undo the achievements of three decades of analytical political science.

Another attack is mounted from Marxist quarters. Paul Cammack (1989), for instance, maintains that the attempt by advocates of statism – Theda Skocpol, in particular – to dissociate themselves from Marxism is possible only by making a mock of the latter. In actual fact, much state-centred research is continuous with Marxism and depends upon it, while celebrating Weber instead. This point is supported by Almond, who suggests that 'Skocpol's notion of the autonomy of the state has to be seen in the context of ... Marxist, neo-Marxist, and post-Marxist polemic' (Almond, 1988: 856).

I will not take a stand in these debates, but I register that Eric Nordlinger, in his reply to Almond, notices a similarity between the new state-centred research strategy and the new political economy (Nordlinger 1988: 880f.). They both wish to turn the state into an independent, or endogenous, variable. An important difference is that economists are methodologically more individualist and hesitate to treat the state as a corporate actor. They prefer individual actors such as politicians and bureaucrats.

A possible reason for this difference is that state-centred research in political science and sociology has been more macro-oriented. Among sociologists, at least, the attempt to 'bring the state back in' has largely been restricted to historical-comparative studies of long-run and large-scale developments (Badie and Birnbaum, 1979/1983; Birnbaum, 1988). One example is Charles

Tilly's research on the emergence of the modern territorial nation-state (Tilly, 1975a, 1990a). According to Tilly, the rise of the modern state is indissolubly linked to the waging of war. States made war and war made states. Another example is Theda Skocpol's *States and Social Revolutions* (1979), where she argues that the success of social revolutions is due to the weakness of states as much as, or more than, to the strength of the opposition. Her investigation is limited to the French, the Russian and the Chinese revolutions, but these cases support her argument. Of particular importance is the position of the state in the international system. A state in an especially exposed position – defeated in war, for instance – is an easy prey to revolutionaries.

In this short résumé of political sociology I have emphasized the influence of Karl Marx on recent political sociology, but I have not mentioned the influence of Max Weber. This imbalance must be corrected. The influence of Weber has been strong and it has increased in proportion as that of Marx has decreased. This is evident from the concern of Habermas and Offe with legitimacy, the emphasis in corporatist literature on organizational monopoly and from the attempt to bring the state back in (see, e.g. Badie and Birnbaum, 1979/1983 and King, 1986). Typical of the renewed interest, among sociologists, in the state, and therefore in the work of Max Weber, is Anthony Giddens' critique of historical materialism (Vol. 2) *The Nation-State and Violence* (1985) and Michael Mann's historical analysis of power in early societies in *The Sources of Social Power* (Vol. 1, 1986). In both works, explicit allegiance is paid to the work of Max Weber, but especially so in the work by Mann: 'My debt to [Weber] is enormous – not so much in terms of adopting his specific theories, but rather, in adhering to his general vision of the relationship between society, history, and social action' (Mann, 1986: 32). The debt to Weber is visible, above all, in the importance attached to the state and in the view of the state as based ultimately on coercion and violence. Hence, also, the importance of the military and of war – social phenomena long neglected by sociologists – in social development.

In my opinion, Marx and Weber are the greatest classical sociologists and they are also the greatest political sociologists. I think there is reason to make this confession, because much of this book will be about the existence and importance of social norms, something we associate with Emile Durkheim and Talcott Parsons, rather than with Marx and Weber. The reason for this launching of the orthodox sociology of Durkheim and Parsons is that they have more to contribute to a critique of public choice. Not because they are most right, but because they highlight those elements that are missing in public choice and, to some extent, also in Marx and Weber.

2

SELF-INTEREST IN POLITICS

The main ingredient in the theory of public choice, then, is the assumption of self-interest (see Chapter 1; see also, e.g., Mueller, 1976: 23; 1979: 1; 1989: 2 and van den Broeck, 1989: 11). Political man, no less than economic man, acts in his own selfish interest. As we have seen, Downs, Buchanan and Stigler find it inconsistent to operate with two different conceptions of man. If economics is correct to assume that man is first of all a selfish creature, then he/she must be so, not only on the market, but in politics too. The task of public choice, then, is, 'to close up the analysis of social interaction systems' (Buchanan, 1972: 11). The attempt to do so resulted in a set of new behavioural and, especially, motivational assumptions concerning people in their varying political roles.

In this chapter I will single out the most important behavioural assumptions used by public choice theorists to predict political phenomena. I will take a close look at the evidence for these assumptions, or, rather, for the predictions. In the light of the evidence, I reach the conclusion that the assumption of self-interest cannot be sustained. Political man is not the selfish creature suggested by public choice. I am not foolish enough to deny that he/she is much more selfish than we would like him/her to be.

The merit of positive public choice resides in its ability to explain and predict political phenomena (Buchanan and Tullock, 1962/1965: 28f.; Crain and Tollison, 1990). So what is the record of public choice? The answer is that it is rather bad. In a recent book by the Swedish political scientist Leif Lewin (1991), we find an effective refutation of positive public choice, at least to the extent that it relies on the assumption of self-interest (see also Barry, 1982; Kelman, 1988; Orren, 1988: 24–29; van Winden, 1991; Lindberg, 1991/1988). Invoking a massive body of empirical research, Lewin shows that the most common motivational assumptions used by public choice theorists cannot be sustained. Evidence suggests that political men and women are motivated by group interests and by the public interest, *as they conceive of it*, no less than by their own selfish goals (cf. Noll, 1985a: 19ff.).

Buchanan and Tullock (1962/1965: ch. 20) have pointed to the difficulty of directly testing the basic assumptions of public choice and asked us to suspend judgement until we are in a position to test some implications. Thirty years later, there are lots of implications to test and the risk of premature judgement seems to be small. According to the well-known canons of Milton Friedman (1953: 7ff.), there is no need to worry about the 'realism' of assumptions. Or as Anthony Downs (1957: 21) puts it: 'Theoretical models should be tested primarily by the accuracy of their predictions rather than by the reality of their assumptions.' What matters, then, is the predictive power of a scientific theory. Friedman has been interpreted as arguing that the realism of an assumption is 'quite irrelevant to its validity and worth' (Samuelson, 1963: 323). I will not recapitulate, or contribute to, the extensive discussion of Friedman's exact position: is he a Popperian, an instrumentalist or something else? Is he simply confused? I note that he defends the use of theoretical 'ideal types' (Friedman, 1953: 34) and also of 'useful approximations'. I have no quarrel with this interpretation of the assumption of self-interest, which is also that of Buchanan and Tullock. A possible difference between them is that the latter suggest that a test of implications is an indirect test of the 'realism' of assumptions. Being myself more inclined towards realism than towards instrumentalism, I side with Buchanan and Tullock, but for the purpose of this chapter, this is not important. The burden of my argument is that positive public choice fails to predict political phenomena. Whether this failure is due to a lack of 'realism', or a lack of fertility, on the part of the assumption of self-interest, is for my present purposes immaterial. 'To the extent that men behave as his model predicts, the economist can explain uniformities in social order. To the extent that men behave differently, his predictions are falsified. It is as simple as that' (Buchanan, 1972: 17).

My procedure in the remainder of this chapter will be to take a close look at the evidence pertaining to some of the most influential hypotheses supposedly derived from the assumption of self-interest. In some cases, I will focus on the alleged implications, in other cases on some operationalization of this assumption. In both cases, as I have already indicated, evidence is largely negative. Three problems, in particular, complicate the test of public choice theory (cf. Toye, 1976). (1) Some models lack the precision and consequent predictive content that is necessary for a test to be at all meaningful, or even possible. (2) Some specifications of the assumption of self-interest are equally compatible with the opposite assumption that people are benevolent. In these cases, an unambiguous test is impossible. (3) In some cases, we find no particular specification of the assumption of self-interest, but the results obtained do not rely upon this assumption for their validity.

A good illustration of the first problem would be Albert Breton's theory of representative government. When Breton presented his theory before The Institute of Economic Affairs, Lord Robbins (1978: 65) asked: 'Would you claim, Professor Breton, that your system of analysis has predictive value?' Breton's answer was affirmative. He pointed to the political business cycle as one prediction and the hypothesis that bureaucrats seek larger bureaux as another (Breton, 1978: 65). The first prediction, as I will show below, has failed to appear; the second, if it is true, has no necessary connection with self-interest. The main purpose of Breton's model, however, is to 'explain' government expenditure and taxation. But what about prediction and testability? This is more of a problem (see Toye, 1976: 440–442). Breton's model is quantitative, but includes variables that are not easily quantifiable: the coercion felt by citizens, the costs of political participation, the relative bargaining power of bureaucrats and politicians, etc. It is safe to say that the task is impossible. There will never be anything like a decisive test of Breton's model.

The second problem is exemplified by, for instance, Niskanen's hypothesis that bureaucrats try to maximize the budget of their own bureaux. As I will argue at some length below, such a motive does not necessarily reflect self-interest. Another example is the assumption that politicians, or parties, seek election, or re-election. This motive is part of the game of parliamentary democracy but neutral between self-interest and the pursuit of 'higher' goals. As Margolis (1982/1984: 97) puts it: 'Whether a politician is motivated by self-interest or group-interest or any compromise between, he must win votes to carry out his purpose.'[1]

The third problem may be illustrated by the spatial theory of politics. As a pure 'logic of choice', this theory does not depend upon the assumption of self-interest, at least not the theory of committee voting. All this theory requires is that people's preferences are single-peaked and spread over a continuous space.[2] This independence of any particular motivation was clearly recognized by Duncan Black (1958: 12): 'One may support a motion for the most altruistic of reasons while another supports it because he expects it to favour his own particular interests.' The same is true at the international level: 'The real root of the difficulty in international relations is not that nations are selfish, but that the solution is indeterminate' (Black, 1958: 145f.).[3] Black's spatial theory of voting is a mathematical or, more precisely, a geometrical theory. Because of this, 'predictions' – being inferences – cannot fail, but are independent of motive. Black's median voter theorem, for instance, is entirely *a priori* and analytically true. But like all theories of rational choice, the spatial theory of voting is also normative and, because of this, may turn into a number of synthetic truths. To the extent that people are rational and understand the mathematics of committee voting, they may utilize this knowledge to achieve the best outcome, given their preferences. In this case, if people are at all rational, we should expect some predictive success. A limitation of theories of rational choice is that predictive power is tied to common sense. For people to be able to vote as the theory 'predicts', they must already understand the theory and use it as a guide to their action.

The spatial theory of mass elections is a bit different. In Downs' version, it assumes that voters maximize their own utility, while politicians maximize votes. I fail to see that the first assumption is necessary for the results of the theory to obtain. It should suffice to assume that voters vote for the party which best represents their preferences, whether selfish or not. Things are somewhat different in the case of politicians, or parties. Here we have to assume a motive to maximize votes or, at least, to win the election, in order to produce the predictions made by Downs. But, as I have already suggested, this is not necessarily a manifestation of self-interest. Winning elections is part of the parliamentary game. As Robert Michels observed: '"Parliamentarism" signifies the aspiration for the greatest number of votes' (Michels, 1915/1962: 334). It may be the case, for instance, that the leaders of a party pursue the interest of their members, their supporters, or even all those whose interest they feel themselves called upon to represent. It may also be the case that they are convinced, right or wrong, that their policy is best for their country as a whole. They may even honestly believe that they have a special mission to lead their country to times of power and glory.

Interestingly, this point is borne out by the development of the spatial theory of coalitions. The essence of William H. Riker's theory of coalitions is the size principle and the theorem of a minimal winning coalition. A precondition for the efficacy of this principle is that politicians (candidates or parties) are intent upon winning at all costs. This in its turn presupposes that ideology, or policy, does not matter. This presupposition is usually false and has been replaced, in most theories of political coalition, by the assumption that policy, not office-seeking, is the important thing (Budge and Laver, 1986; 1992a). This change of assumption opened the door for spatial analysis. In coalition theory, then, the use of spatial analysis is incompatible with the assumption of self-interest, at least in the form of office-seeking.

Robert Axelrod's notion of a 'minimal *connected* winning coalition' represents a clear improvement upon Riker's 'minimal winning coalition' (Axelrod, 1970: ch. 8). The meaning of 'connected' is that coalitions are not only minimal in size but *close in policy space*, i.e., ideologically close. Axelrod hypothesized that minimal connected winning coalitions would form more often and last longer than other coalitions. He tested this hypothesis for the case of Italy and found it confirmed. Ideology does matter. The implication for the assumption of self-interest, however, is not clear. It could be that ideals set limits to self-interest. It could also be that ideology is a rationalization of self-interest. Minimizing ideological differences could then be a way of minimizing bargaining costs. Axelrod does not say. While devoting much space to defining '*conflict* of interest', he has little to say about 'interest'. He defines it in terms of 'utility', as revealed preference, but does not say that all preferences are selfish (ibid., pp. 16f.).

A second group of spatial coalition theories drops the size principle altogether – minority administrations are common – and becomes purely spatial. In these theories the median position in policy space acquires a special significance (Budge and Laver, 1993: 500ff.). The median politician has the strategic advantage of being able to turn both to the right and to the left for coalition partners. Ian Budge and Michael Laver have tested both groups of theories with data from eight European countries. They found most support for the purely spatial group of theories, indicating that the median position is more important than the size of coalitions (ibid., pp. 508f.). Policy does not explain all coalition formation, however. In addition, Budge and Laver mention the relative size of parties and long-standing ideological differences associated with social cleavages (1992b; 1993: 511, 519).

Similar considerations apply to Buchanan's and Tullock's *Calculus of Consent*. In sharp contrast to the impression created by Buchanan and Tullock, nothing in the positive content of this book relies on the assumption of self-interest. Their analysis of constitutions and of decision-making rules presupposes that people have *different* and conflicting interests, or goals, but not that these interests, or goals, are selfish. Self-interest is a sufficient, but not a necessary, condition for conflict of interest. There will be a conflict of interest also if people are motivated by some group-interest, or if they have different conceptions of the public interest; if they have different values. Buchanan and Tullock, of course, know this. In the introduction to *The Calculus of Consent* (1962/1965: 3f.), we find the following declaration:

> The analysis does not depend for its elementary logical validity upon any narrowly hedonistic or self-interest motivation of individuals in their behavior in social choice processes. The representative individual may be egoist or altruist or any combination thereof. Our theory is 'economic' only in that it assumes that separate individuals are separate individuals and, as such, are likely to have different aims and purposes for the results of collective action.

The same point recurs in the last chapter of the book: 'Accept,' they say, 'The fact that some men, some of the time, do act so as to promote partisan private or group interest through political means; accept that our model does help to explain many of the results' (ibid., p. 302). Also, 'Behavior in accordance with the precepts of the golden rule, literally interpreted, can lead to a conflict of individual interests that is equally intense as that which would arise under the operation of pure self-interest' (ibid., p. 303). But if this is the case, why Buchanan and Tullock's strong emphasis on the assumption of self-interest as the basis of their analysis in *The Calculus of Consent* (ibid., pp. 25ff., 266, 298) and as a defining characteristic of public choice?

In an article written shortly after (1966), Buchanan concedes this ambiguity in *The Calculus of Consent*. He now makes a distinction between 'logical theory' and 'positive theory'.[4] For logical theory, once again, no particular motivational assumption is needed. All that is required is that interests differ and that people act on their differing interests.

For a genuine predictive theory of politics, however, more is needed. If by 'Theory' we mean the development of hypotheses about behavior in the political process that can be conceptually refuted by observation of real-world events, some additional constraints must be placed on the manner in which separate interests differ. The most familiar of these constraints, again taken from economics, is the hypothesis that individuals act in politics as they are assumed to act in the predictive theory of markets, so as to maximize their expected utility, and that their behavior in doing so is measurable in terms of some objectively identifiable magnitude such as personal income or wealth. In politics, this 'positive' theory implies that individuals, and groups, act so as to further their economic position.

(Buchanan, 1966: 27f)

Having settled this matter, it is time to take a closer look at the particular motivational assumptions used by public choice theorists to derive testable hypotheses about political actors.

POLITICIANS

A theory presumably more dependent upon the assumption of self-interest is that according to which politicians create political business cycles. What is the evidence for this theory? Not at all impressive, as we shall see. Nordhaus made two predictions from his model: '(I) that the politically determined polity choice will have lower unemployment and higher inflation than is optimal and (II) that the optimal partisan policy will lead to a political business cycle' (Nordhaus, 1975: 185). As he admits, himself, the first is not easily tested, but it has been shown, by Brian Barry (1985b: 309–315), to be internally incoherent. There remains the second prediction. Nordhaus' own test (1975: 184–187), comprising nine countries, shows strong support in three countries (Germany, New Zealand and the United States) and weak support in two countries (France and Sweden). The remaining countries were Australia, Canada, Japan and the United Kingdom. Nordhaus' evidence has been criticized on several grounds, but even were it correct, it is not much. More is needed.

Duncan MacRae attempted to test, not whether there is a political business cycle, but whether the United States' government believes that the electorate is myopic, or strategic. A myopic electorate is a precondition for successful manipulation of the unemployment–inflation trade-off. MacRae (1977: 254–262) did find support for the myopic hypothesis in the case of Democratic administrations and for the strategic hypothesis in the case of Republican administrations. Whatever that is evidence for – probably that Democrats fight unemployment and Republicans fight inflation – it is not for the existence of a political business cycle.

Nordhaus' and MacRae's hypothesis about a political business cycle was tested by Benneth T. McCallum against an alternative hypothesis suggested by

Thomas Sargent and Neil Wallace, but based upon earlier work by Robert Lucas. The Lucas–Sargent proposition says that incumbent governments are unable to produce booms by the end of their terms, even if they wish to, because of the pre-emptive behaviour on the part of those concerned. The basis of this proposition is in the theory of rational expectations. If people expect governments to expand the economy before election, they will behave so as to undo the intended effects. McCallum's test (1977: 507–514) lends unequivocal support to the Lucas–Sargent proposition against the hypothesis of a political business cycle.

The most ambitious attempt to verify the theory of political business cycles can be found in Edward R. Tufte's *Political Control of the Economy* (1978). Tufte's point of departure, however, is that 'virtually no evidence confirming even the existence of an electoral-economic cycle is at hand' (Tufte, 1978: 5); a situation he wishes to remedy. In the first chapter of his book, Tufte reports a survey of 29 democratic countries aimed at answering the question whether there is an electoral business cycle, or not. For two countries relevant data were missing. Twenty-seven countries remained. In Tufte's opinion (1978: 11), 'The findings are clear. Evidence for an electoral-economic cycle was found in 19 of the 27 countries; in those 19, short-run accelerations in real disposable income per capita were more likely to occur in election years than in years without elections.' We may observe that Tufte's economic-electoral cycle is not identical with Nordhaus' business cycle. While the latter had to do with the trade-off between unemployment and inflation, the former concerns disposable income. But are the findings really that clear? I, for one, do not think so, and I am not alone (see, e.g. Barry, 1985b: 306f.; Lewis-Beck, 1988b: 141; Lewin, 1991: 65f.). Especially, if we look at the numbers presented and find that in 4 of the 19 countries counted as showing evidence of an electoral-economic cycle, the difference made by election is small indeed. Thus, clear evidence of an electoral-economic cycle can be found in little more than half of the countries and half is what we would expect by mere chance.

The main part of Tufte's book is devoted to a painstaking analysis of the United States. This part is more persuasive. I believe that Tufte succeeds in showing that incumbent presidents occasionally meddle with the economy in order to enhance their chances of re-election. They seem particularly eager to combat unemployment and/or inflation when election day is close and they sometimes use monetary policy to stimulate the economy. Most common, however, because most simple and most effective, is the strategy of pouring money into the pockets of voters immediately before election. Direct transfers in the form of social security benefits, veteran benefits, and the like, have a tendency to increase just in time to make large groups of people feel a bit more friendly towards the incumbent president and his party on election day (See Tufte, 1978: ch. 2).

Tufte's discussion of the United States, then, is, on the whole, convincing.

It does not, however, lend unambiguous support to a public choice theory of political business cycles. Among other things, Tufte demonstrates the influence of ideology upon economic policy (Tufte, 1978: ch. 4). This is not what we should expect from a theory of public choice and it is not part of the theory of political business cycles. As we have already seen, the assumption of self-interest implies that politicians' indifference curves stretch over the entire political spectrum.

Tufte's work is merely the beginning of something. A second serious effort at verifying the existence of a political business cycle was made by Martin Paldam (1979). His test was based on 49 stable governments in 17 countries between 1948 and 1975. The point of confining the investigation to stable governments was to exclude those without a real opportunity to manage a business cycle. Paldam's results are negative (Paldam, 1979: 338f.). While he does actually find some kind of election cycle, albeit a weak one, it does not fit the model at all and certainly not the model suggested by Nordhaus and MacRae. Data suggest that real growth is strongest in the second year and inflation in the third year after election. Paldam's own, tentative, interpretation of his findings is that parties make election promises which they have to fulfil if they win. The consequence is second-year expansion and third-year inflation (Paldam, 1981: 298–300).

Byung Hee-Soh tested the hypothesis of a political business cycle on a sample of 20 industrialized democracies between 1961 and 1980. Evidence was, once again, weak. 'All in all, twelve out of the twenty industrialized democratic countries show some indications of political business cycles' (Hee-Soh, 1986: 37). Hee-Soh did, however, find some variation between countries. Those using indexation against inflation and those with longer election terms *seem to be* less subject to political business cycles (ibid., pp. 39–44).

The search for political business cycles goes on. With ever more refined instruments, economists and political scientists, especially in the United States, continue their detective-like investigation of the case – for and against. So, for instance, has Grier (1987, 1989) detected a monetary election cycle, which, he suggests, supports Nordhaus' original model of a political business cycle. Beck (1987) detects the cycle too, but is confused by its timing: it peaks at election day, which means that the effects of money expansion would occur after election. His explanation is that the monetary cycle is a secondary phenomenon, reflecting the adaptation of monetary policy to fiscal policy. Williams (1990) also identifies the monetary cycle, but denies that it supports Nordhaus' model. Presidents facing declining popularity do manipulate the economy, but their main target is real income, not unemployment and/or inflation. Erikson (1990), finally, suggests that the cycle is confined to presidential elections, but is independent of mid-term Congressional vote.

The impression you get from reading the literature on political business cycles is of something like a mirage; an elusive phenomenon which appears only to disappear again; visible to some, but not to others, yet it must be there, out there, somewhere. The common opinion among competent judges, however, is that the evidence supporting the hypothesis of a political business cycle is weak, or non-existent (Lewis-Beck, 1988b: ch. 9; Lewin, 1991: ch. 3). In 1983, James Alt and Alec Chrystal characterized the situation thus:

No one could read the political business cycle literature without being struck by the lack of supporting evidence. There must be cases where politicians have undertaken electorally motivated interventions. It is difficult to imagine politicians not exploiting some extra information or other resources. But while this clearly happens, and happens particularly clearly in some cases, such cycles may be trivial in comparison with other economic fluctuations. Incumbents may be able to give themselves significant advantages relative to challengers. But the ability to intervene economically is only one of many possible incumbency advantages. The existence of such advantages may not make anything worse overall or in the long run.

(Alt and Chrystal, 1983: 125)

Douglas Hibbs reaches a similar conclusion in 1987:

The argument that business cycles frequently are driven by electoral politics is simple, important, and immensely appealing to laypeople and scholars alike. For these reasons the so-called political business cycle has received more attention, particularly outside of professional circles, than any other idea appearing in recent academic work on political economy. Yet the thesis that economic cycles often are influenced by the election calendar rests on rather fragile empirical foundation.

(Hibbs, 1987a: 255)

Directly observable fluctuations in macroeconomic outcomes, the qualitative and anecdotal record, and parameter estimates from theoretically constrained statistical models designed to take into account the impact of wartime fiscal thrusts, exogenous international shocks, structural and policy inertia, and contrasting partisan priorities all indicate that election cycles have not been a consistent feature of the postwar American political economy. Yet the qualitative and quantitative records reveal several likely instances of electorally focused economic expansion, although these appear idiosyncratically rather than systematically, with those of 1972 and 1984 being the principal illustrations. Of course, no incumbent president desires or plans to go into an election year with the economy in recession.

(ibid., p. 277)

The following conclusion seems possible: if there is a political business cycle of some kind, it is not a very widespread and not a very marked phenomenon, except, perhaps, in the case of a few presidential elections in the United States. The findings hardly support the public choice picture of politicians as selfish and unscrupulous people manipulating the economy to their own advantage and without a second thought about the negative consequences of their policy for the economy as a whole and in the long run. On the other hand, findings do not disprove this picture either. It may be that politicians would like to manipulate the economy in this way, but they can't, for a number of reasons: (1) lack of knowledge, (2) because, as Richard E. Wagner suggested, the economy is not amenable to cybernetic control, (3) because rational expectations pre-empt the effects, or (4) because voters punish politicians for irresponsible manipulation (cf. Chappell and Keech, 1985; Alesina and Rosenthal, 1989).

Even if there is no convincing evidence of a regular political business cycle, there can be little doubt that incumbent politicians occasionally do try to 'buy' votes in order to enhance their chances of re-election. They do so in a variety of ways: we are all familiar with pork barrel legislation, popular tax cuts, direct transfers and, above all, promises, immediately before elections. Maybe the 'new "political business cycles" theories' (see Alesina, 1988: 35–38) are more promising than the old ones? But even if they are, this does not prove that politicians are entirely irresponsible, or entirely selfish. They may honestly believe that everything they do is for the best of their country, or for those they represent. I admit that this suggestion is a bit farfetched, but it is not entirely impossible. Using economic policy as a means to be re-elected is indicative of self-interest. But, on the other hand, no one in his right mind denies that politicians, like other people, are to some degree selfish. The point I wish to make is that some use of economic policy to increase the probability of re-election does not prove that politicians are *all* selfish. It only proves that they are human, perhaps all too human.

An adequate explanation of economic policy must go beyond politicians and voters. More consistently than anyone else in the public choice camp, Bruno S. Frey has worked with developing a more adequate, because more realistic, model of the interaction of polity and economy. Like most of the others, Frey is out to prove the existence of a political business cycle, but he knows that it is difficult. Using time-series of aggregated data from the United States and the United Kingdom, Frey failed to find support for the existence of a political business cycle (Frey, 1978a: 132–141; 1978b: 97–104). But lack of evidence is not proof of non-existence. It might be possible to detect a political business cycle with a better model and a better method. This is what Frey attempts to do next. As one of the first, he uses multiple regression analysis, which makes possible a much more detailed look at the dynamic interaction of variables, with the possibility of controlling for disturbing influence. With this technique, Frey claims to find support for the existence of a political business cycle in the United States, the United Kingdom, Germany and Sweden (1978a: ch. 11; 1978b: 104–106; 1978c: 211–216;

1978d, 1979: 312–318). He also claims that his politico-economic model is superior to alternative models in terms of predictive power (Frey and Schneider, 1982).

It is important to point out, however, that Frey's model differs in important respects from earlier public choice models of the political business cycle. First of all, it is not a model of an *election* cycle. Frey's interest is not primarily in the impact of elections upon the economy, but in the interdependency of economic performance and *government popularity*, as measured by opinion polls. There is not even any presumption of a *cycle*. There may be – in fact, there is much more likely to be – interdependence without a cycle (cf. Alt and Chrystal, 1983: 113, note 6). Second, the model is not based on the Phillips curve. The typical response of governments to decreasing popularity is budget expansion. As with Tufte, growth of income appears as more important than both unemployment and inflation. Most important, Frey abandons the assumption that governments maximize votes, or even their probability of being re-elected. Governments are utility-maximizers. In Frey's model, this means that governments try to realize their ideology as reflected in their party programmes, subject to the constraint of re-election (1978a: 149; 1978c: 206, 211; 1979: 310f., 316–318). This is an unusual specification of utility-maximization. It becomes odd indeed, in the light of the following quotation: 'Government may be assumed to maximize its utility by pursuing economic policies in accordance with its ideological views concerning the desirable state of the economy, e.g., the relative weight to be accorded to efficiency compared to equity' (Frey, 1978c: 211). Considerations of equity would not normally be counted as part of utility-maximization and how does equity relate to governments' own utility? One way to resolve this puzzle is to assume that it is in the long-term interest of governments to pursue a policy consistent with party ideology, but in their short-term interest to seek re-election (see Frey, 1978c: 207). Both strategies contribute to keeping governments in power (see Frey, 1974: 232; 1978c: 209; 1978d: 245). A problem with this interpretation is that power, not utility-maximization, appears as the ultimate goal and this seems to be ruled out by Frey's explicit statement to the contrary: 'The party in power considers as its main goal putting its ideological views into reality. It must, however, ensure that it remains in office, because in opposition it has no possibility of realising its ideology' (Frey, 1978a: 149; see also Frey, 1978c: 203). Perhaps he simply cannot make up his mind: 'It is unclear why a party's own goal should at all times be the maximization of votes. It is easy to think of other goals such as staying in power for as long as possible, or the realization of its ideological preferences' (Frey, 1979: 310). It seems as if Frey is torn between the public choice assumption of self-interest and the insight that ideology matters to some extent, without being able to decide which is the more important. But if we assume that Frey settles for ideology, rather than power, which sometimes seems to be the case (ibid., p. 317), we are left with the problematic coincidence between a government's ideology and its own utility (cf. Van Winden, 1988: 29). His ultimate choice, however, seems to be in the other direction. While in his earlier writings ideology appears as the primary goal, subject to the constraint of re-election, things eventually turn out the other way around. 'The basic proposition of the politico-economic model that governments are interested in putting their selfish goals into practice in the political contest, i.e., to be re-elected, fares well compared to the competing proposition that governments are interested in the state of the economy (presumably to further the welfare of the population)' (Frey and Schneider, 1982: 252). Ideology now counts as a phenomenon of secondary importance. 'Government behaviour is not solely determined by the need to survive but also by *ideological considerations*' (ibid., p. 252).

Irrespective of Frey's indecisive wavering between ideology and self-interest, his model-building represents an advance compared to the original theory of the political business cycle. The attempt to develop a more realistic model of politico-economic interaction is laudable, if not without problems. The latest development of Frey's model goes in the direction of incorporating the central bank, bureaucracy and economic interest groups (1979: 318ff.; 1982: 242). This is a development in the right direction, except for the method. The play of economic interests takes the form of struggle and bargaining, phenomena not tractable to quantification, hence regression analysis (cf. Korpi, 1991: 327). Without metrics, no politometrics.

Economic policy is shaped in a field of forces including government, opposition, bureaucracy, interest groups, media and voters, and embedded in a larger field consisting of the international economy (cf. Van Winden, 1988 29ff.). There are important differences between countries, depending upon their different traditions, institutions and dominant ideologies. This, in its turn, depends much upon the relative strength of different interests, especially class interests.[5]

There are few safe findings about economic policy, and the theory of a political business cycle is not one of them. It seems safe to say, though, that economic policy is an important public issue in all parliamentary democracies and that it has increased in importance, relative to other issues, in the latest decades (Hibbs, 1987a: 127ff.; 1987b: 117–120). One implication of this is that voters attach much importance to macroeconomic performance. They tend to punish administrations with a bad record and reward governments when times are good, whether they deserve it or not.[6] This fact provides an incentive for politicians to create business cycles. If they don't, this is either because they can't, or because they are responsible, in addition to being selfish. I believe both are true, to some extent, but there is something politicians can do: they can expand the budget before elections, and they sometimes do. As Tufte pointed out (see p. 66 above), the easiest and most effective way of doing this is to increase the disposable income of voters shortly before elections. The feasibility of this method is limited by voters not being quite as myopic as is commonly assumed in models of political business

71

cycles and by the media helping them to remember and to see beyond election day. But it is still a possible method. Voters may be rational, but they are not as rational as suggested by the theory of rational expectations. We have to allow for an asymmetry of information between politicians and voters, leaving some scope for successful manipulation of the economy (see, e.g., Alesina, 1988: 16f., 35ff.; Alesina and Rosenthal, 1989: 374ff.).

Turning to unemployment and inflation, the most significant finding concerns its differential importance to voters and parties. Not surprisingly, unemployment is a matter of concern mainly to the lower classes. After all, they are the people most likely to be hit by it. Inflation is, for less obvious reasons, a source of worry mainly to the middle and upper classes (see Hibbs, 1987a: ch. 2, 138ff.; 1987b: 125–127, 158–163, 295ff.). A corollary of this fact is that left-wing parties take greater pains to combat unemployment, while right-wing parties concentrate on fighting inflation.[7] The extent to which governments pursue a partisan policy, and their success in doing so, is contingent upon the existence of a strong labour union, supporting or opposing them, as the case may be (Alvarez *et al.* 1991). But why is inflation so important? Isn't unemployment a much worse calamity? (see Schlozman and Verba, 1979: ch. 3; cf. Hibbs, 1987a: 55–62, 117–124; 1987b: 6). Maybe Kalecki was not that wide of the mark? (cf. Korpi, 1991: 325ff.). Is it even possible to reduce the 'Anti-inflationary hysteria', strongly supported by some public choice theorists, to 'reactionary twaddle' (Barry, 1982: 144; 1985b: 317)?

I have dealt, at some length, with the theory of political business cycles. I will strengthen my coming conclusion by a short note on George Stigler's so-called 'capture theory' of economic regulation. This theory fares no better than the theory of political business cycles when confronted with available evidence.

One of the first attempts to test the capture theory was made by James B. Kau and Paul H. Rubin (1979). Their conviction before the test was that Stigler's hypothesis is correct. Their conclusion after the test was that it is not. Kau and Rubin identified three explanations for the voting of Congressmen: (1) they might vote in the interest of their constituency, (2) they might vote in the interest of another Congressman, in exchange for a vote in their own interest (log-rolling) and (3) they might vote in accordance with their ideology. Kau and Rubin's attempt to explain away ideology failed. In the end, they had to admit that 'ideology is significant in explaining voting by congressmen on bills with primarily economic components. Thus, it seems difficult to continue to argue that ideology is not significant in explaining voting behavior' (Kau and Rubin, 1979: 384). An additional point made by Kau and Rubin is that economists, defending the assumption of self-interest, typically advocate pro-market policies that refute this assumption, presumably for ideological reasons (ibid., p. 367). The basis of the argument is the assumption that economists benefit from government intervention, because it creates a demand for their expertise.

Another attempt, by two economists, to test the self-interest hypothesis against the ideology hypothesis led to similar results: 'The evidence so far suggests the need for some broadening in the economic theory of politics.' This broadening includes 'rational altruistic-ideological promotion of self-defined notions of the public interest' (Kalt and Zupan, 1984: 298). The scope for ideology, however, seems to vary with the institutional setting of voting; e.g. how much discretion is possible on the part of representatives. Kalt and Zupan also conjecture that the capture theory might work better as a theory of elections than as a theory of issue-specific politics.[8]

The strongest case against the economic theory of regulation is probably that made by Martha Derthick and Paul J. Quirk in *The Politics of Deregulation* (1985). How come, they ask, politicians have succeeded in achieving substantial deregulation in industries such as airlines, telecommunications and trucking, despite the active opposition of strong productive interests and with the backing only of diffuse consumer interests? Their answer was that ideas matter (ibid., ch. 7; Quirk, 1988). Deregulation was possible because of an idea, promulgated by economists and adopted by politicians, that deregulation is in the public interest. 'Contrary to the economic theories . . . members of Congress do not act almost solely on the basis of electoral calculations. To a great extent they act on their judgement about the merits of issues and conceptions of the public interest' (Quirk, 1990: 191).

Thomas H. Hammond and Jack H. Knott (1988) try to salvage the economic theory of regulation, not by refuting Derthick and Quirk, but by suggesting that it may not be a general theory applicable to all cases of deregulation. Quirk agrees that this is indeed the case, but nevertheless insists that Stigler's capture theory or, for that matter, any economic theory, is likewise inadequate as a general theory of politics. Quirk makes an important point that the reader might bear in mind for the rest of this chapter. Hammond and Knott argue for the continuing relevance of economic factors and, therefore, of economic theories in the explanation of regulation. As Quirk makes clear, this point is not in dispute, but economic theory 'requires much more of such factors than mere relevance' (Quirk, 1988: 38). Denying that economic theory gives a complete explanation of politics is not tantamount to denying that it provides part of the explanation.

> Without doubt, the sources of behavior stressed in the economic theory of politics are often important, and economic theorists have enhanced our understanding of politics by working out some of their consequences. An economic analysis does not add up to a complete theory of policy-making, however, because other sources of behavior are also important.
>
> (Quirk, 1988: 39)

There is no denying that politicians seek income, prestige and power. They do, but not single-mindedly. As Christopher Hood has pointed out (1992: 210–212), politicians' salaries differ widely between countries, but are nowhere high, relative to salaries in the private sector, or even relative to bureaucrats. Steven Kelman (1990: 201f.) maintains that two motivations in particular are important for persons in elective office. The first is a desire for attention and adulation. 'Politicians seem to want, more than the average, to be liked. They crave media attention.' The second motive is 'the desire to participate in formulating good public policy, which work in the public sector can provide. People so motivated are "seeking power", but less power over individuals than power to do good.' Kelman's observations are a bit impressionistic, but he makes the important point that power-seeking, like office-seeking, does not imply self-interest. People may seek power in order to do good or, more generally, to promote some ideological vision of the good society.

There is also no denying that politicians seek office as the main means of achieving income, prestige and power. They do, but not all of them. If they did, how would you explain the existence, and persistence, of small parties, with no prospect of winning the election in the first place, but whose representatives and members nevertheless work year after year, sometimes a lifetime, for some distant goal they hope, most often in vain, will some day be realized? Of course, they may still be in it for some kind of gratification; for income and prestige, if not for power. This goes a long way to explain the activity of leaders, as in the public choice theory of political entrepreneurs. But most of them work without an income, and without prestige. In Max Weber's terminology (Weber, [1919] 1948: 84), they live *for* politics, not *off* politics. And this goes for the party activists in big parties too. This is the real puzzle, or 'paradox', as some would say.

Trying to explain the participation of party activists without income, prestige, or power, we confront the problem of collective action, which I will treat at length in Chapter 5. The economic solution to this problem is to invoke a host of 'selective incentives'. Party activists benefit personally from the activity itself, from altruism and feelings of solidarity, from a sense of duty and from following group norms. One could go on trying to fit party activists within a public choice framework, but it is not convincing. In the end, it seems much more reasonable to assume that members of small parties, as of social movements, work for some ideal they honestly believe in. Ideology matters, to some extent at least. This is true, not only of party activists, but of professional politicians. It is only more obvious in the case of party activists because of a lack of alternative explanations for their participation.[9]

BUREAUCRATS

The most discussed and most criticized public choice theory of bureaucracy is that of William A. Niskanen. According to him, bureaucrats are supposed to maximize the budgets of their bureaux. This is because the most important arguments in a bureaucrat's utility function – salary, perquisites of office, public reputation, power, patronage, output of the bureau – are all positive monotonic functions of the total budget of their bureaux.[10] This assumption is problematic in several respects.

First, Niskanen assumes not only that bureaucrats are motivated by budget-maximization, but also that they are successful in achieving this goal. But, then, we have two hypotheses, not one, and the second does not follow from the first (cf. Blais and Dion, 1990). The ultimate purpose of Niskanen's theory of bureaucracy, as of most public choice theories, is to explain the growth of the public sector and of public expenditure. For this purpose, the second hypothesis is more critical than the first. Budget-maximization is neither a necessary nor a sufficient condition for the growth of the public sector. Another necessary condition is that bureaucrats have the power to impose their budget-maximizing wills upon politicians and Niskanen assumes that they do. In this chapter my interest is only in budget-maximization as a motive on the part of bureaucrats. The power of bureaucrats to achieve their ends will be discussed in Chapter 3, and the effects of this on public expenditure in Chapter 4.

A second problem concerns the use of budget-maximization as a proxy for a variety of self-interested motives. As I have already suggested, budget-maximization is not a very convincing operationalization of self-interest. There are other conceivable manifestations of self-interest on the part of bureaucrats. Niskanen mentions 'ease of making changes' and 'ease of managing the bureau'. Presumably these are deemed unimportant, or else Niskanen would not settle for budget-maximization. But are they? 'On the job leisure' is mentioned as an important argument in the utility functions of many a bureaucrat (Peacock, 1978: 126; 1992: 76).

There is no necessary connection between budget-maximization and self-interest; hence no very good reason to assume that bureaucrats, even if they were self-interested, would generally try to maximize the budgets of their bureaux – not even those top bureaucrats who are in a position to do so (the vast majority of officials, of course, have no direct influence on the size of the budget). Sometimes, the way to make a career might be to reduce the budget or, at least, to save money.

A good critical discussion can be found in Dunleavy (1985). He argues convincingly that budget-maximization is not the maximand of a majority of bureaucrats. First of all it is wrong to conceive of a bureau as a monolith. Opening the black box reveals other possibilities, as well as important differences between bureaucrats. A strong motive of bureaucrats is to make a career, but this possibility exists without budget-maximization. Indeed, there may be a collective action problem involved in getting the whole staff to act in concert. One reason is differences between bureaucrats of different rank. Low-rank bureaucrats are most likely to support budget-maximization, but lack the means to do so. Top bureaucrats, on the other hand, do have the means, but often lack the motive, because they gain the least and must bear the cost of advocacy of budget-expansion. A second problem with budget-maximization is that only part of a bureau's budget goes to the staff and the relative size of that part varies greatly between bureaux, depending, above all, upon their respective tasks. Dunleavy (1985: 310) distinguishes between control, regulatory, transfer, contract and delivery agencies. As an alternative to budget-maximization, Dunleavy suggests 'bureau-shaping' as a proxy for utility-maximization on the part of top bureaucrats. A bureau-shaping strategy is typically designed to bring the bureau 'into a progressively closer approximation to "staff" (rather than "line") functions, a collegial atmosphere and a central location' (Dunleavy, 1985: 322).

The second problem with the budget-maximization hypothesis, then, is that there are many ways for a bureaucrat to act in his/her own interest. Budget-maximization is only one of them, sometimes consistent with self-interest, sometimes not, but perhaps more often so in the United States than in other countries (Hood et al. 1984: 164). Not necessarily because bureaucrats in this country are more selfish than in other countries, but because they have a better opportunity to pursue this objective. Given the plurality of possible selfish objectives, it is probably impossible to find a single maximand, at least one with empirical content (cf. Kogan, 1973; Breton and Wintrobe, 1975: 204–206, 1982: 26–29; Margolis, 1975; Peacock, 1978, 1992: 74–79; Jackson, 1982: 133f.).

A third problem with the budget-maximization hypothesis is that self-interest is not the only plausible motive for a bureaucrat wishing to increase the budget of his/her bureau. And a bureaucrat motivated entirely by a wish to serve the common good and convinced that the public goods supplied by his bureau contributes to this goal, would wish to increase the budget (cf. Goodin, 1982: 31f.). These complexities make it extremely difficult to test the budget-maximization hypothesis and extremely problematic to use it as an indication of self-interest. This may be the reason why evidence on the assumption of budget-maximization is scarce.

In his article 'Bureaucrats and Politicians' (1975), Niskanen cites some empirical studies that support his theory of bureaucracy and representative government. None of these studies, however, has a direct bearing upon the assumption of self-interest. Niskanen finds support for his hypotheses about overspending, inefficiency, oversupply and overcapitalization and the hypothesis that bureaucratic structure matters. But there is no need to invoke self-interest in order to explain these results. They are equally compatible with the assumption that bureaucrats are altruists, or that they are simply trying to do their duty, or any combination thereof.

John A.C. Conybeare (1984: 486) reports some negative evidence, suggesting that bureaux do not maximize their budgets. Christopher Hood, Meg Huby and Andrew Dunshire (1984) attempted to test the 'budget/utility theory' by asking how government expenditure translated into staff increases in Great Britain between 1971 and 1983. Their test had two parts. At an aggregate level, they found that government expenditure translates but imperfectly into pay and perks for bureaucrats. At the departmental level, they found a clear relationship between budget increase and bureau benefits in six out of ten departments. But even in these positive cases, top staff received less benefits than the lower ranks. Their conclusion was that the budget/utility theory is neither verified nor falsified by the results. There is also the attempt by Boyne (1987) to test the staff maximization hypothesis, advanced by Tullock among others. Evidence was negative. Boyne tested this hypothesis on the policies of English and Welsh local bureaucracies, but found nothing to support it. Despite the weak support for Niskanen's theory of bureaucracy, André Blais and Stéphane Dion (1990) conclude their review of the critique of Niskanen with the suggestions that (1) budget-maximization remains an eminently credible hypothesis and (2) that the hypothesis that bureaucrats stand to gain from increased budgets seems to be confirmed. I don't find this conclusion justified by the evidence, but even if it were, it would not matter much for my argument. As I have already suggested, budget-maximization is compatible with any motive on the part of bureaucrats. This becomes apparent if we look, instead, at Anthony Downs' theory of bureaucracy.

In his *Inside Bureaucracy* (1967), Downs gives a more complex and less 'economic' picture of the working of bureaucracy. Above all, he does not rely on the assumption of self-interest as the sole motive of the actions of bureaucrats. As I mentioned in Chapter 1, Downs recognizes five types of officials: climbers, conservers, zealots, advocates and statesmen (Downs, 1967: 88f.). Of these, only climbers and conservers act out of pure self-interest, while the remaining types mix egoism with altruism. Climbers, of course, come closest to the rational egoist. But climbing does not imply budget-maximization. As Dunleavy noticed, careers are possible without increasing budgets and are often easier to attain without working for this collective good. Also, as Julius Margolis (1975: 646ff.) has pointed out, the most common way to make a career, at least for top bureaucrats, is to move from bureau to bureau. If this is so, it is far from clear that budget-maximization is instrumental for climbers. Conservers, according to Downs, are *not* concerned with maximization. 'In contrast to climbers, conservers seek merely to retain the amount of power, income, and prestige they already have, rather than to maximize them' (Downs, 1967: 88). Zealots are those entirely devoted to the cause of their bureaux, and could therefore be expected to be the main budget-maximizers. Advocates are loyal to the broader organization, while statesmen are loyal to society as a whole and, therefore, resemble the 'ideal' public official most closely. According to Downs (1967: 5ff.), new bureaux are created by zealots and advocates. Now, bureaucracy grows, not only by the growth of bureaux, but by their multiplication. As Dunleavy pointed out, this is the way bureaucracy has grown recently. But, according to Downs, zealots and advocates are altruists. On Downs' analysis, therefore, altruism plays a significant role in the explanation of the growth of bureaucracy. The motive behind change in already existing bureaux may be a desire to do a good job, desire for aggrandizement, or self-defence against external pressures. The desire for aggrandizement, which most closely resembles Niskanen's budget-maximization, 'may be partly altruistic', while 'self-interest is a powerful cause of inertia' (Downs, 1967: 198–200).

The analysis of Downs, then, is very different from that of Niskanen. Altruism, rather than self-interest, leads to budget-maximization. My point is not that Downs is right and Niskanen wrong, even though I do believe that Downs is closer to the truth. My point is that evidence for budget-maximization is not evidence for self-interest.

VOTERS

In my assessment of the assumption of self-interest I have concentrated, so far, on politicians and bureaucrats, while discussing voters only occasionally. The public choice view of the matter is, of course, that voters, like all others, act in their own interest. According to Downs, voters seek to maximize their personal gain. Or, as Popkin *et al.* (1976: 805) believe American voters ask their president: 'What have you done for me lately?' A more narrow specification is that people vote so as to maximize their own wealth (see, e.g., Peltzman, 1980: 223). Using an old term, this is often described as 'pocketbook voting'. Before public choice, the term 'pocketbook voting' was used to designate *one* type, or aspect, of voting behaviour (see, e.g., Campbell *et al.*, 1954: 115; 1960: 381, 416). In public choice, however, the pocketbook (self-interest) is assumed to be the sole determinant of vote choice. But is it?

The assumption that voters maximize their own wealth or, more broadly, their utility, has turned out to be the most problematic of all. Already Downs had problems explaining why, on this assumption, people should bother to vote at all and, to this day, no satisfactory explanation of this fact has been produced and none seems possible within the frame of public choice. Before asking *why* people vote at all, however, I will examine *how* they vote, or why they vote as they do.

Early evidence pertaining to this matter was provided by Eva Mueller in an article on 'Public Attitudes toward Fiscal Programs' (1963). As the title indicates, her evidence is about attitudes, not about voting. It is well known that people do not always act in a way consonant with their expressed attitudes.

This is a limitation her results share with many other results presented in this section. While aware of the difficulties with attitudes, I do not believe that they are entirely unreliable as indicators of interest. Mueller wanted to find out whether attitudes toward public spending are in any way related to the expectation to benefit from this spending. If people are self-interested, we should expect them to support only such public spending as can be expected to result in a net benefit on their own balance-sheets. Mueller assumed that this is much more likely to be the case for people with low income than for people with high income. Support for this version of the self-interest hypothesis was very weak, and Mueller concluded that 'it is clear that other considerations are at work also and may even be more decisive (Mueller, 1963: 230).

Mueller's findings were confirmed by James Q. Wilson and Edward C. Banfield (1964), who hypothesized that some classes are more public-regarding than others. The evidence this time is stronger because it rests on data about voting, not about attitudes. Wilson and Banfield's data are from local politics, where 'it is sometimes possible to say that a vote in favor of a particular expenditure proposal is incompatible with a certain voter's self-interest narrowly conceived' (Wilson and Banfield, 1964: 876). If voters support such policies they can be assumed to be guided by the 'public interest'. Results suggested that some groups are. 'We have shown both that a considerable proportion of voters, especially in the upper income groups, vote against their self-interest narrowly conceived and that a marked ethnic influence appears in the vote' (Wilson and Banfield, 1964: 885). A comment: while it is correct to interpret a vote by rich people on programmes that benefit the poor as altruism, it is not necessarily correct to infer that the poor are less public-regarding if they vote in the same way. There is an asymmetry involved, which makes the comparison unfair.

The first serious blow to the hypothesis of pocketbook voting came from Kinder and Kiewiet (1979, 1981). Using data about individuals, they failed to detect anything but a faint relation between personal economic grievances and voting behaviour. Hence, little support for pocketbook voting. Instead, they found a weak, but significant, relation between people's vote and their collective economic judgement; their judgement of the state of the economy as a whole. Adopting a term from Paul R. Meehl, they dubbed this vote pattern *sociotropic* voting. Economic voting is a fact, but the people's choice does not reflect their own personal economic situation. Economic voting reflects their assessment of the national economic situation; inflation, unemployment and business climate; their estimation of the economic performance of the incumbent party and their belief about the competence of parties to run the national economy. Sociotropic voting seems to be more prevalent in presidential than in congressional voting (Kinder and Kiewiet, 1981: 145–148). By far the strongest relation was found to hold between voting and party identification, thus confirming one of the more important findings of political sociology (see Campbell *et al.*, 1960: ch. 6). Interestingly, the data presented by Kinder and Kiewiet (1981: 148–152) indicate that partisanship is affected by perception of party performance and party competence. It should be pointed out that Kinder and Kiewiet do not simply equate pocketbook voting with self-interest and sociotropic voting with altruism. The difference between them is not a matter of motivation, but of information. Nevertheless, they do admit that sociotropic voting is easier to reconcile with altruism, or benevolence, than is pocketbook voting (Kinder and Kiewiet, 1981: 132).

Kinder and Kiewiet's hypothesis about sociotropic voting was corroborated in Kiewiet's *Macroeconomics and Micropolitics* (1983: esp. ch. 6). National economic assessments were much more important than personal economic experiences as a determinant of voting. It should be pointed out, though, that Kiewiet did find evidence of some pocketbook voting in presidential elections (ibid., pp. 63–67); a finding which supports earlier observations by Fiorina and by Kinder and Kiewiet. In addition, the importance of retrospective economic voting was confirmed, as was the hypothesis, advanced by Hibbs in particular (see p. 72), that concern about unemployment increases support for the Democrats, while the Republican party is more trusted to fight inflation. Not surprisingly, those who support the public sector tend to vote for the Democrats, while those who wish to see less public spending vote Republican (ibid., p. 100).

The results obtained by Kinder and Kiewiet have been seriously questioned by Gerald Kramer (1983). He argues, first, that the seemingly discrepant results of micro- and macro-studies is a statistical artifact and, second, that evidence for sociotropic voting is equally compatible with the null hypothesis of pocketbook voting.[11] I believe, however, that the strength of Kramer's contention is seriously vitiated by some oddities in his argument. First, he persists in talking about a 'puzzle', an 'anomaly', or a 'discrepancy' between findings at the macro- and micro-level, respectively, even though he does recognize that correlations at the aggregate level are compatible with several alternative hypotheses about individual behaviour (Kramer, 1983: 92–94). He suggests that in many cases aggregate-level analysis is superior to individual-level analysis even when we are interested in individual behaviour. I find this surprising, since there are statistical barriers – the ecological fallacy – which prevent valid inferences from aggregate data on individual behaviour, in principle. To be sure, there are problems with individual-level analysis too, but at least they do not include the risk of committing the ecological fallacy. Finally, Kramer insists that a distinction between selfish and sociotropic voting must be based upon the incumbent government's real, rather than perceived, economic performance. Furthermore, only government-induced changes in personal income are relevant for an estimation of pocketbook voting (ibid., pp. 95, 102ff.). I agree that real economic performance is important, more important than perceived performance, but the immediate determinant of voting is perception rather than reality, no matter how erroneous perceptions might be. To the extent that we are interested in individual choice, therefore, 'appearance' may be more relevant than 'reality'. There is also the risk that government-induced changes 'disappear' in the myriad of possible sources of change in people's private economy, even that they compensate for other changes, however farfetched this suggestion might seem. Kramer is, of course, correct to conclude that evidence for sociotropic voting is not conclusive, but who would disagree? (Cf. Kiewiet and Rivers, 1984.)

Gregory B. Marcus (1988) tried to meet Kramer's criticism, by pooling the data used to test the hypothesis of sociotropic voting. Results, once again, confirmed the original analysis of Kinder and Kiewiet. While there was evidence for pocketbook voting, evidence for sociotropic voting was much stronger. Kinder, Adams and Gronke (1989), finally, responded to Kramer's critique in a rather casual manner. They tested the hypothesis of sociotropic voting once again, and in their own way, for the 1984 presidential election – this time against two other hypotheses: pocketbook voting *and* group voting. The latter hypothesis suggests that people vote out of concern for some group with which they identify. Support for sociotropic voting was even stronger than in earlier tests (Kinder *et al.*, 1989: 504f.). The public interest seems to be a stronger motive force behind voting than either self-interest or group-interest; at least, in the United States in 1984 (see, however, Conover, 1985). Or is it merely a matter of relevant information? It may be added that group-interest also seems to be stronger than self-interest if we consider its indirect effects upon voters' assessments of the national economy (ibid., p. 511f.). If Kinder, Adams and Gronke are correct, the question American voters ask their president is neither 'What have you done for *me* lately?', nor 'What have you done for my *group*?', but 'What have you done for our *country* lately?'

Evidence, so far, has been limited to the American voter. Is there anything to suggest that pocketbook voting might be more common in other countries? I find it hard to believe that American voters are less self-interested than voters in other countries. But there is another possibility: it is a widely held belief that American voters, because of their extreme economic individualism, tend to blame themselves, rather than the government, for their economic misfortunes (Sniderman and Brody, 1977; Schlozman and Verba, 1979: 103ff.).[12] If so, changes in American voters' private economy should not have a direct effect on their voting. Stanley Feldman (1982; 1984: 239–248) has argued that this is, indeed, the case. The reason self-interest has so little effect on vote choice is that a majority of American voters do not attribute responsibility for their economic hardships to their government. The 'American dream' of self-reliance and equal opportunity prevents people from locating the cause of their economic conditions outside themselves. But among those – a small minority – who do blame the government, self-interest does affect voting (Feldman, 1982: 449ff.; 1984: 240). If pocketbook voting is rare, this does not necessarily imply that self-interest is unimportant.

If Feldman's explanation is correct, we should expect to find more pocketbook voting in other, more collectivistic, countries, where the government is, to a larger degree, considered responsible for the welfare of its citizens. Michael Lewis-Beck has looked at economic voting in five European countries (Britain, France, West Germany, Italy, Spain). Evidence is clear. Economic voting is no less important in Europe than in the United States, but there is virtually no evidence, at all, for pocketbook voting, despite the fact that European voters are more prone to assign to their governments the responsibility for their own economic situation (Lewis-Beck, 1988b: 62). European voters, like American voters, show more concern about the collective economy than about their own pocketbooks (Lewis-Beck, 1986: 328; 1988b: 57, 62–65, 75–77, 90; Eulau and Lewis-Beck, 1985). But concern about collective economic conditions is only one determinant of voting. Equally important are class and religious cleavages, and ideological commitment (Lewis-Beck, 1986: 326–333; 1988b: ch. 4).

A novelty in Lewis-Beck's study is the distinction between a cognitive and an *affective* dimension of voters' reactions to policy. This distinction is justified by the results: affect appears as an important determinant of economic voting – in Europe as in the United States (Lewis-Beck, 1986: 318, 329; 1988b: 41f., 65). Among the first to introduce an affective dimension in research on economic voting were Pamela Johnston Conover and Stanley Feldman (1986). They argued first, that affect is distinct from cognition; second, that they interact and, third, that people's emotional reactions to economic matters are important for their evaluations of government performance – as important as their cognitive judgements. Their data corroborate earlier findings to the effect that the collective economy is more important than the private economy as a determinant of vote choice. Evidence is particularly clear in the case of cognition. When it comes to affect, people's personal economic situation is no less important for their evaluations of policy (Conover and Feldman, 1986: 65–71). The upshot of Conover and Feldman's analysis would be that voting is not as 'rational' as is often supposed (ibid., pp. 50f.). A rational choice approach that ignores emotions is to that extent inadequate. But what about self-interest? Conover and Feldman do not report any repercussions of their analysis on the assumption of self-interest, besides a support for the hypothesis of sociotropic voting. As far as I can understand, emotions may serve the interest of self, other, group or nation, but they may also be evoked by violations of impersonal principles of morality.

A further argument by Stanley Feldman (1983, 1988) is that public opinion and voting are, in part, structured by the distribution of certain core values and beliefs. A received truth, handed down by political sociology some thirty years ago, would have it that 'ideology', in a specific sense, plays no part in American politics. Feldman accepts this thesis, but suggests, in accordance with another received truth of political sociology, that individual values and beliefs may – even though they do not constitute ideologies – be important determinants of public opinion and of voting. He tests his hypothesis for three, commonly recognized, core values of American culture: economic individualism, equality of opportunity and free enterprise. Feldman finds that the first two, but not the third, are 'strongly related to policy positions, performance evaluations and candidate evaluation' (Feldman, 1988: 437; see also 1983: 18ff.). Not surprisingly, he also finds that 'differences in support for core beliefs are to some extent associated with long-standing cleavages in society' (Feldman, 1988: 427). Briefly: white, rich men believe in economic individualism; coloured, poor women believe in equality.

Social cleavages also make for differences in economic voting. M. Stephen Weatherford (1983) presents data indicating that people with more education seek information about economic policy in the media, while people with less education seek it in their own lives. A result of this difference in source of information would be that the upper and middle classes vote sociotropically, while the members of the working class vote with their pocketbooks. This tendency is reinforced by the fact that it is always members of the working class who suffer most when times are bad. I find Weatherford's argument, on the whole, convincing. I am not prepared, however, to accept his interpretation of the working-class pattern as self-interested (ibid., p. 159). If members of the working class base their economic voting on personal experience, this does not necessarily indicate self-interest. It may be a matter of information, rather than of interest (cf. Conover *et al.*, 1986: 584f.). And if interest does play a role, it may be a matter of class-interest, reflecting collective identity and fraternal solidarity, rather than self-interest (cf. Sears, *et al.*, 1980: 681; unsuspected support for this argument derives from Brennan and Lomasky, 1985: 209f.).

But other groups than the working class have a special stake in redistribution and social welfare: the elderly, who do not work, but are dependent upon insurance, social security and health care; state employees, who administer redistribution and social welfare; and women, who work in the public sector and who are relieved from responsibility when the state takes care of those who cannot take care of themselves. Thus, it is predicted by public choice theorists and others that the elderly, state employees and women will support the welfare state and its public sector more than other groups in society. It has also been predicted that, in highly developed welfare states, traditional social cleavages between classes will increasingly be replaced by new cleavages between the private and the public sector, between generations, and between the sexes.

The ideal case to test these hypotheses would be Sweden, the welfare state *par excellence*. One attempt to do so has been made by the Swedish sociologist Stefan Svallfors (1991). He did find some weak evidence for all three predictions, but he also found that class is still a much stronger 'determinant' of attitudes toward the welfare state than is either age, private/public sector, or sex. Similar results concerning the private and public sectors are reported by Holmberg and Gilljam (1987: 191–198) and, for the United States, by Sears and Funk (1990: 155). The latter also found that public employees are more averse to reductions in taxes and public spending than are other voters. The reason may be that they are afraid of losing their jobs (ibid., p. 160).

Svallfors' results are also reinforced by Erik Olin Wright and Donmoon Cho (1992), who confirm that Swedish state employees have somewhat more prostatist attitudes than do people working in the private sector. In the United States, the reverse is the case (see also Sears and Funk, 1990: 155). In the middle class, however, United States state employees are also more prostatist than their privately employed colleagues. A novel finding is that the public sector is not homogeneous. People working in *the state service sector* (public health, education, publicly owned utilities, public recreation) are more prostatist than people working in *the state political sector* (the police, the courts, the administrative organs of government, the military, the legislature). The difference between these two parts of the state is greater in Sweden than in the United States. In both countries, however, class cleavages are stronger than those beween the private and the public sector. Class cleavages are also much stronger in Sweden than in the United States.

Laurie A. Rhodebeck (1993) has tested the hypothesis that elderly people have stronger preferences for state-financed health insurance, social security and health care. She found that 'age is not particularly effective in structuring preferences on age-related issues; variation in opinion among the elderly often equals or exceeds variation in opinion across the generations' (Rhodebeck, 1993: 361). In fact, before the 1980s, sometimes called 'the decade of greed', elderly people were more satisfied with social security and health care than were younger people. They are more inclined, though, to vote for the candidate who is presumed to look after their interests.

The as yet small, but possibly widening, gender gap in politics has been interpreted by Pamela Johnston Conover (1988a) as a reflection of differences in fundamental values. She suggests that at least feminist women (not all women) share an *ethic of caring*, which explains their possibly greater concern for the disadvantaged in society.

More generally, Conover has criticized the common, but reductive, interpretation of group-interest as merely coinciding self-interests (1984, 1985). She argues that group-interest may reflect social identity and social solidarity, and be distinct from, even unrelated to, self-interest. Her argument is backed up by data, indicating, first, that group identifications influence the way people perceive and evaluate political issues (1984) and, second, that group-interest may be stronger than the public interest (1985). In the second study, people were asked (by telephone) which group they feel close to, then to make judgements about the economic conditions of themselves, their group and the nation; and, finally, to assess the effects of economic policy on themselves, their group and the nation. It seems, from the answers, that people show more concern for their group than for themselves and for their nation. One finding is of special significance for differentiating between self-interest and group-interest. People are very much concerned about unemployment in their group, even when they are not themselves affected by it. In a later article (1988b), Conover develops a theoretical model that reinstates the group at the centre of political theory. The main theoretical concept in her model is *group identity*. I will return several times in this book to the notion of 'group identity', which is often theoretically related to the idea of 'symbolic politics', as used by David O. Sears.

The assumption of self-interest has been tested in a broader context by David O. Sears and his various collaborators. Special attention has been given to racial issues, especially busing, but also to crime and war.[13] Sears *et al.* tested the hypothesis of self-interest against the alternative hypothesis of 'symbolic politics' (see Sears *et al.*, 1979, 1980). The result was no different than that arrived at by Kinder and Kiewiet, Lewis-Beck and Feldman. Evidence supporting the assumption of narrow, short-term self-interest is almost nil. In stark contrast to self-interest, which accounts for only a few per cent of policy attitudes and voting, symbolic attitudes 'explain' about 15 per cent, or eight times as much as self-interest (Sears *et al.*, 1980: 673; Sears and Funk, 1990: 169). But what is 'symbolic politics'? In Sears' usage, this somewhat nebulous term denotes a set of predominantly affective preferences, acquired at a relatively early stage in the individual's political socialization and comprising general and fairly stable dispositions, such as party identification, ideology and various prejudices (Sears, 1975; Sears *et al.*, 1980: 671; Sears and Funk, 1990: 149).

Sears and his collaborators are wise enough not to draw the conclusion that self-interest is ineffectual, even in politics. Instead they ask, first, why it is so relatively unimportant in politics and, second, in what circumstances it does play a role? A possible answer to the first question is that the relation between policy and self-interest is too obscure. Another possibility is that people are taught to pursue the common good in politics. The answer to the second question is that people do act in their self-interest when stakes are high and/or clearly visible, and when the government is considered responsible. They react negatively to taxes and to policies that threaten their homes and their jobs.

Sears *et al.* finally discuss the possibility that symbolic politics is an expression either of self-interest masquerading as group-interest or of long-term, enlightened, self-interest. These hypotheses are hard to refute, but to the extent that evidence can tell, it tells against both. Sears and his colleagues advance the alternative hypotheses that group-interest reflects group-solidarity and that symbolic politics reflects a learned concern for the common good. The strength of symbolic politics resides in its dependence on affective responses to certain symbols expressing people's political convictions and commitments (Sears, *et al.* 1980: 680–682; Sears and Funk, 1990: 166–170).

Thirty years' testing of the public choice assumption that people vote for their pocketbook has resulted in a great mass of disconfirming evidence, and little, if anything, in the way of confirmation. With hindsight, it is possible to say that, with respect to this particular assumption at least, we were closer to the truth before the advent of public choice.

> The relevance of governmental activity to individual goals may take many forms, varying from enduring and all-embracing relevance experienced by the ideologically persuaded individual to an occasional and probably casual feeling that 'Washington' could or should do something to alleviate or eliminate a personal grievance. The relevance may be perceived as strictly personal, as with the concern over taxes, or prices, which affect the individual's pocketbook. It may also be much broader, perceived as affecting not only the individual but his or her business or social associates as well. In the latter case, the issue involvement is possibly reinforced by a sense of group involvement in which the individual feels that his group, and not he alone, has a stake in some governmental action. Issue involvement may also be experienced in relation to governmental action which has no conceivable consequences for the individual's material well-being, or for that of family or friends, but which, rather, enhances or threatens values held by the individual.
>
> (Campbell *et al.* 1954: 115)[14]

I have discussed *how* people vote, and presented overwhelming evidence against the assumption that they vote with their pocketbook, or in some other entirely self-interested way. The real puzzle, for an economic theory of politics, however, is not *how* people vote, but *why* they vote. The expected benefit of voting for a particular party or candidate is often small and always surrounded by uncertainty. So why do people take the time and trouble to go to the polls? This 'paradox', as it is sometimes called, has haunted the minds of public choice since its very beginning. Downs had to resort to people's long-term interest in maintaining a democratic political system in order to explain the act of voting (Downs, 1957: 265–274). But as Barry (1970/1978: 23) points out, this doesn't help matters, since even this is irrational, given the infinitesimal effect of each vote. Barry concludes, correctly, that the economic approach cannot, except at the cost of emptiness, be modified so as to account for the fact that people do vote. Other factors, such as duty, self-expression, habit, perhaps even magic, must be invoked.

Gordon Tullock (1967b: 108–114) agreed that it is not rational for a self-interested individual to vote in a mass election. Simplifying somewhat, Tullock's payoff function may be written thus:

$$R = BP - C$$

Where R is the net benefit, or return, from voting, B is the benefit from casting your vote on your favoured party, as defined by Downs' party differential, P is the probability that your vote will make a difference to the outcome of the election, and C is the cost of voting. Because P is so diminishingly small in a mass election, costs will vastly exceed expected benefits. Altruism may affect the balance-sheet, but is unlikely to do so. For this to happen, 'The value put on the well being of others must be extremely great' (ibid., p. 114). The explanation offered by Tullock seems to be 'social pressures that make it wise for the individual to make the rather small investment necessary for voting' (ibid., p. 114). Social pressure may even make it costly *not* to vote.

William H. Riker and Peter C. Ordeshook were not at all satisfied with an analysis which makes it 'irrational' to vote. As a remedy for this unbearable situation, they constructed their own calculus of voting (Riker and Ordeshook, 1968; 1973: 62–69). A first argument against Downs and Tullock was that P does not equal my vote divided by the total number of votes, or even half of them. What matters in any decision whether to vote, or not, is subjective, not objective, probability. P, therefore, depends on voters' estimation of the relative strength of candidates, or parties. If a voter expects an even race, the probability of casting the decisive vote may approach imaginable size. Riker and Ordeshook are, of course, correct to insist that the relevant probability is subjective, but wrong to imply that people actually believe their own, single, vote will make a difference. Their decisive argument concerns the benefits of voting. Downs and Tullock counted only the benefits expected to come from the policy of the preferred candidate or party. But, according to Riker and Ordeshook (1968: 28; 1973: 63), there are many additional benefits from voting: There is (1) 'The satisfaction from compliance with the ethic of voting', (2) 'The satisfaction from affirming allegiance to the political system. . ., (3) the satisfaction from affirming a partisan preference. . ., (4) the satisfaction of deciding, going to the polls, etc. . ., and (5) the satisfaction of affirming one's efficacy in the political system'. Subsuming these satisfactions under D, we arrive at the following equation, representing Riker's and Ordeshook's calculus of voting:

$$R = PB - C + D$$

The rationality of voting now hinges upon D being large enough to outweigh the negative value of PB – C.

Riker and Ordeshook are, of course, correct to suggest that it is rational to vote for the reasons suggested by D, but this does not solve the problem (cf. Barry, 1970/1978: 13ff.). The question is whether it is rational to vote from an economic, self-interested, or some other utilitarian, outcome-oriented, point of view. Riker and Ordeshook beg that question by introducing ethical and expressive elements into their calculus. 'One essential element of our explanation is that the paradox of participation is solved by the construction of an ideology of obligation.' This ideology 'leads men to participate by reason of private incentives such as prestige, status, and duty' (Riker and Ordeshook, 1973: 60–61). This may very well be true, but duty, or obligation, has no place in an economic, or utilitarian, explanation. Things we do because of duty, or obligation, are things done irrespective of benefit or outcome. It may be that people derive satisfaction from doing their duty, but this does not save the economic approach, for such satisfaction can only exist as a by-product of duty. On this analysis, economics becomes parasitic upon sociology.

One of the most effective refutations of the economic interpretation of voting is that of Paul E. Meehl (1977). Demonstrating the ultimate 'irrationality' of voting from a utilitarian point of view, he argues, convincingly, that voting can only be explained – by using some quasi-Kantian, or sociological, perspective – in terms of duty, or obligation.[15]

A different attempt to rescue rational choice, as a viable approach to voting, came from John A. Ferejohn and Morris P. Fiorina (1974). Following Barry, they resolutely reject Riker and Ordeshook's addition of a D term as too much of an *ad hoc* solution. Their own strategy is to attack P in Downs and Tullock's original calculus of voting. In Downs and Tullock's analysis, voting takes place under *risk*, which implies that P is known. 'Rationality' is defined as 'maximization of expected utility'. The alternative, suggested by Ferejohn and Fiorina, is to conceive of voting as decision-making under *uncertainty*. This gives rise to a different conception of 'rationality' – and this seems to be the main point of their article: to open our eyes to the fact that there are several, alternative, concepts of 'rationality'. The particular alternative suggested by Ferejohn and Fiorina is that people behave as 'minimax regret decision makers', which means that they choose the act which minimizes their maximum regret (Ferejohn and Fiorina, 1974: 527f.). One presupposition of making this assumption is that people conceive of their vote deciding the election as a real possibility. Another presupposition is that people would very much regret being responsible for the defeat of their favoured party at the polls. The only way to make sure that there will be no reason for regret is, of course, to vote.

The attempt, by Ferejohn and Fiorina to save rational choice has been met by much scepticism.[16] I share that scepticism. The assumption that people act on a decision rule of minimax regret seems to me farfetched. I find it difficult to believe, for instance, that people do not at all consider the probabilities involved. I also doubt that the personal stakes in the outcome of mass elections are high enough to cause that much regret. In their response to criticism, Ferejohn and Fiorina (1975) make clear that they only intended to offer one possible solution to the problematic decision to vote, not to suggest that all voters act this way. Yes, but how many? A majority of citizens go to the polls.

For my purposes, it is also of some significance that Ferejohn and Fiorina do not discuss the motives for minimax regret decision-making. Why should people feel regret? For a loss of personal utility, or because they believe that the winning candidate, or party, is a national calamity? Ferejohn and Fiorina do not say, but the evidence of 'sociotropic voting' makes the latter alternative seem much more likely. This is also what Howard Margolis suggests as a solution to the 'paradox of voting' (Margolis, 1982/1984: 88–95). The personal stakes in an election may not be very high, but the consequences for society may be enormous. Therefore, if people vote with an eye to the public interest, they may find it worthwhile, even if the odds are microscopic.

The latest attempt I know of to avoid the scandal of a rational choice theory unable to explain the act of voting is by John A. Aldrich (1993). In his account, focus is shifted from individual voting to turnout over time. Aldrich rejects the minimax regret model and returns to expected utility. His argument, much simplified, is that voting is a low-cost, low-benefit, decision, offering politicians an opportunity to affect the decision by strategic manipulation of the rewards covered by the D term. But this is possible only if the D term is reinterpreted to include, not only a sense of duty and commitment to the value of democracy, but also the expression of party affiliation. With this new D term, it is possible to explain the decline, over the latest decades, in turnout, as due to a decline in party attachment. When individuals care less about who wins, they will be less motivated to vote. The fact that turnout is higher when candidates are close is explained, not by the increasing efficacy of voting, but by the higher intensity of campaigns.

Aldrich's article contains many interesting observations, but does not save the economic theory of voting. His explanation relies heavily on the D term, which he interprets as denoting an 'expressive' component, 'for the voter receives that value, per se, regardless of the outcome' (Aldrich, 1993: 251). Voting is an act of 'consumption', as well as an act of 'investment'. According to Aldrich, his is a rational choice theory because expressive voting is a source of utility for voters. Looking closer at the sources of this utility, however, we find some strange elements: a sense of duty, personal values (democracy) and party attachment. Like the other economic theories of voting, Aldrich's account is derivative of things non-economic. It is in fact close to the Michigan explanation of turnout.

In *The American Voter* (1960: ch. 5), Campbell *et al.* analysed voting turnout as a function of (1) partisan preference and (2) political involvement, the latter comprising four variables: (a) interest in the campaign, (b) concern over the election outcome, (c) sense of political efficacy (d) sense of citizen duty. All independent variables showed a clear positive correlation with the dependent variable of voting turnout. Correlation was strongest in the case of citizen duty. Aldrich's attention to party attachment is, of course, a return to the Michigan model, assigning primary importance to party identification and partisan preference. Aldrich's suggestion that voting is an act of consumption in addition to being an act of investment has a counterpart in the Michigan variable 'interest in the campaign'. One variable in the Michigan model, however, is lacking in Aldrich's and all economic explanations of voting: sense of efficacy. According to the theory of rational choice, a single vote has only infinitesimal efficacy in a mass election. How come people, nevertheless, develop a psychological sense of efficay of voting and how come that those who do are the most educated (Campbell *et al.*, 1954: 193), those who ought to know better?

The fact that people do vote – despite the often negligible and uncertain gains from doing so and despite the infinitesimal probability that their vote will have an effect upon the outcome of an election – is the first conspicuous anomaly confronting an economic theory of politics. We have still to see whether it is enough seriously to threaten the theory of public choice. According to Thomas Kuhn, the existence of an anomalous experience normally does not lead to the rejection of a paradigm. 'If any and every failure to fit were ground for theory rejection, all theories ought to be rejected at all times' (Kuhn, 1962/1970: 146). Imre Lakatos, likewise, observes that scientific theories emerge and survive in an ocean of – more or less serious – anomalies (Lakatos, 1970: 93ff., 133ff.). They both agree that paradigms, or research programmes, are not abandoned before there is an apparently superior alternative to replace them (Kuhn, 1962/1970: 77ff.; Lakatos, 1970: 119). Is there a better political theory than public choice? Unfortunately, in social science there is no simple answer to such questions. In the absence of any pragmatic criterion for scientific appraisal, much depends upon ideology and upon rhetoric (Hesse, 1980: ch. 8).

But even if the anomaly of voting does not lead to its overthrow, public choice is in trouble and there are indications of a crisis. One indication is a noteworthy article written by James Buchanan and Geoffrey Brennan (1984), in which they abandon most of positive public choice, and especially the theory of voting. As with Meehl, both the act of voting itself and the choice between alternatives is deemed 'irrational', from a utilitarian point of view. The reason is the absence of any clear connection between the act of voting and the outcome of an election when the electorate is large.

> Voters do, in fact, participate in electoral processes, and they care about political outcomes. But there is no logical connection between these two facts, and the absence of this logical connection is crucial. It arises from the fact that the relation between how any individual voter votes and the outcome of the election is virtually negligible. We cannot, therefore, explain voter behavior in terms of preferences over outcomes: Voter behavior must be explained on its own terms. People vote because they want to – period. And neither the act of voting nor the direction of the vote cast can be explained as a means to achieving a particular political outcome, any more than spectators attend a game as a means of securing the victory of their team.
>
> (Brennan and Buchanan, 1984: 187)

But if voting does not make sense in a utilitarian framework, how can it be explained? Brennan and Buchanan believe that much voting is 'habitual' (ibid., p. 191) and 'symbolic', or 'liturgical' (ibid., p. 196).

It may be pointed out that Brennan and Buchanan's rejection of public choice is not wholesale. It concerns only the positive, predictive, branch, but not their own normative, comparative, theory of constitutions. Brennan and Buchanan also wish to save part of the positive theory and especially that part which deals with lobbying (ibid., p. 197). This seems reasonable enough. Lobbying is often easy to understand in terms of narrow self-interest, especially in the case of business associations and corporations working upon the government in order to obtain competitive advantages. In this case, if the group is small, or 'privileged', lobbying may take the form of a straightforward economic transaction. Nevertheless, it has been argued by Mancur Olson that, when groups are large, the gains from lobbying are insufficient to motivate people to support a lobby. Thus we are led to consider the vexed issue of collective action, which is the subject of Chapter 5 of this book.

Geoffrey Brennan and Loren Lomasky went further and looked for something to replace the economic theory of voting. They found it in Adam Smith's *Theory of Moral Sentiments* (1759). Brennan and Lomasky are not the first to detect that there is another Adam Smith than the one economists usually infer from a reading of *The Wealth of Nations* (1776), but they are probably first to propose a 'Smithian theory of electoral behavior'. I will return to Adam Smith below and confine myself, here, to observing that Brennan and Lomasky infer from Smith a theory of voting as, in part, an expressive act revealing individuals' moral sentiments.

> After all, once it is recognized that the individual qua individual cannot rationally act in electoral settings on the belief that he is to be decisive, it is clear that participation in the voting process is rather like the participation of the spectator at a sporting event. The individual cheer for his team, and the combined effect of all such cheering may influence the course of the game – but such influence does not provide the *rationale* for the cheering. The cheering is an expression of support – nothing more. And the questions of which team persons will be led to support, and of which considerations weigh in the choice of the favored team – these questions demand a theory of spectator behavior. Where more natural to look for such a theory than in Adam Smith's *Theory of Moral Sentiments?*
>
> (Brennan and Lomasky, 1985: 206).

I do not know if Buchanan, Brennan and Lomasky are aware of this, but their theory has great similarities to the theory of 'symbolic politics'. Most of all, their resolution of the paradox of voting resembles the solution put forward by Talcott Parson (see pp. 142f.). The theory of voting as expressive behaviour may be seen as an alternative, excluding both self-interest (Saraydar, 1987) and civic duty (Hudelson, 1987) from an explanation of voting. Brennan and Lomasky (1987) have no such thing in their minds, and rightly so.

More important, for my present purposes, than the theory itself is what led Brennan and Lomasky to adopt it. Their point of departure is the collapse of the economic theory of voting.

> Any attempt to explain voting behavior – either *why* large numbers of individuals vote, or why they vote in the way they do – solely by appeal to narrow economic interests is, in our view, necessarily contrived and, in most of the common formulations, logically flawed.
>
> (Brennan and Lomasky, 1985: 191)

I attach great importance to the death sentences pronounced by Buchanan and Brennan on positive public choice. With their close affiliation to public choice as a school of thought, we should not expect them to give up a major part of its teaching without sufficient reason.[17] Equally important is the verdict of Morris C. Fiorina, according to Gary Becker (1990: 43f.), one of the most important advocates of economic thinking, or rational choice, in contemporary political science. Fiorina (1990: 336) admits that rational choice cannot account for the fact that people vote in mass elections, and even less, why some people acquire information in order to cast an *informed* vote. But the failure of rational choice does not imply that people do not have good reasons for voting. It is just that these reasons have little to do with personal gain.

Fiorina considers two alternative explanations, with which we are, by now, quite familiar. The first is civic duty, which he endorses but does not discuss. Instead, he fastens upon Brennan's and Buchanan suggestion that voting can be likened to a spectator sport (Fiorina, 1990: 337). Voters simply cheer on their favourite teams. Information is gathered in different ways and for different reasons. It may be gathered as a by-product of some other activity, as a collector's item, or as part of people's self-definition. The most important point, however, is that many people attach an intrinsic value to political information (ibid., p. 340). This is similar to Albert Hirschman's suggestion that political activity may carry its own reward (see p. 132). It is also similar to Aldrich's account above, but with this important difference: Fiorina does not try to force the expressive theory of voting into the strait-jacket of rational choice.

But if rational choice models are useless in explanations of mass voting, there is still the possibility that they can be used to explain other types of electoral behaviour. Fiorina suggests that rational choice might fare better in explanations of why various elites try to influence the elections in directions consonant with their goals. He mentions interest groups (cf. Brennan and Buchanan, above) and media elites 'concerned with selling information as a commodity rather than communicating the content of that information' (Fiorina, 1990: 341). In addition to disseminating information, elites also 'shape the information they communicate' (ibid., p. 134). Following Riker, Fiorina sees a new field opening up for rational choice analysis. I have my doubts about that (see p. 129), but I agree that 'electoral processes involve numerous actors other than the mass public', and also that 'Many of these actors have compelling personal motives to fabricate, accumulate and disseminate information' (Fiorina, 1990: 341).

POLITICAL MAN

It is time to reach a conclusion concerning the empirical standing of the assumption of self-interest in the economic theory of politics: evidence against it is overwhelming. There is no possibility left of retaining the hypothesis that political man is economic man, not even as a useful approximation, except perhaps in a few limited contexts where politics turns into business. There is still the possibility, of course, of using the model of economic man as a heuristic device. But the fertility of this device is bound to be limited, unless it is argued that the failures of a simplifying assumption are as enlightening as its success.

In social science, however, research programmes are rarely abandoned simply because they are refuted. The obvious reason for this is that all social scientific theories are refuted by experience. In this situation, the rational thing to do, it would seem, would be to choose the best among existing alternatives. This strategy, as I have already argued, usually fails, because of a lack of commonly accepted standards of evaluation. In addition, there is the problem that different social scientific approaches focus on different aspects of social reality. They are complementary, rather than conflicting. I venture the conjecture that competition in social science is much more between social scientists than between theories. I am aware that this conjecture is in the spirit of public choice.

Appeal to predictive success is not the only method of justification in social science. Also common is appeal to authority. Social scientific theories are often justified by the fact that they can be traced back to this or that authority in the history of a discipline. In the case of public choice the main authorities are Thomas Hobbes and Adam Smith, at least with regard to the assumption of self-interest. This is not the place to dig deeply into the history of ideas. I will confine myself to the most important source of the public choice insistence on self-interest: Adam Smith.[18] Attempts to justify the assumption of self-interest in the economic theory of politics almost always involve an appeal to the authority of Adam Smith.

In this section I am going to argue, first, that advocates of public choice do not have the support of Adam Smith when arguing that political man is really economic man. Second, I deny that there is any inconsistency in assuming that man acts differently in politics and on the market. Third, I will present one influential attempt to create a new model of rational choice, capable of dealing with this seeming inconsistency. Fourth, I will argue that sociological man is the offspring of Adam Smith's theory of human nature and superior to rational choice as a model of political man.

Smith on self-interest

Adam Smith is generally considered the main progenitor of economic man (see, e.g. Elster, 1989a: 97). But this is legend, not fact. Adam Smith was not an advocate of *homo economicus*. His account of human nature is, actually, much closer to *homo sociologicus* and Smith is also a main forebear of the latter homunculus.[19]

Among the worst falsifiers is George Stigler, who suggested that *The Wealth of Nations* is built on the 'granite of self-interest' ([1971] 1982: 136). Adam Smith's greatest success was

> in providing a theorem of almost unlimited power on the behavior of man. His construct of the self-interest-seeking individual in a competitive environment is Newtonian in its universality. That we are today busily extending this construct into areas of economic and social behavior to which Smith himself gave only unsystematic study is tribute to both the grandeur and the durability of his achievement.
>
> (Stigler [1976] 1982: 158)

This is Stigler's view, not Smith's, as I will show in this section. Adam Smith did not provide any theorem at all and he did not believe in the universality of self-interest.[20]

The claim that Adam Smith was a propagator of economic man is routinely backed up by the following quotation from *The Wealth of Nations*:

> It is not from the benevolence of the butcher, the brewer, or the baker, that we expect our dinner, but from their regard to their self-interest. We address ourselves, not to their humanity but to their self-love, and never talk to them of our own necessities but of their advantages.
>
> (Smith, 1776/1937: 14)

This is one of the most cited passages in the whole literature of social science, but it does not say that man is all, or even predominantly, selfish. It says that when I go out shopping I had better appeal to the self-interest than to the benevolence of shopkeepers. It is thus a statement about market transactions, but says nothing at all about other types of human actions (cf. Sen, 1987: 22–28 and Kristol, 1981: 206).[21] This becomes perfectly clear from the context in which the statement occurs. It occurs in a chapter on the division of labour as occasioned by the propensity of human nature to truck, barter and exchange one thing for another. Smith's argument is that in civilized society man 'stands at all times in need of the co-operation and assistance of great multitudes, while his whole life is scarce sufficient to gain the friendship of a few persons'. Therefore, while man is in constant need of help from his brethren, 'it is vain to expect it from their *benevolence only*' (Smith, ibid., p. 14, my italics).

The above is not the only passage in *The Wealth of Nations* where Smith mentions self-interest, and he does not say that it is limited to the market. The industry of the Catholic clergy, for instance, is also kept alive by 'the powerful motive of self-interest' (1776/1937: 742), in contradistinction to university teachers, who are led, by the same motive, to live as much at their ease as they can (ibid., p. 718). Self-interest, in the form of the 'uniform, constant, and uninterrupted effort of every man to better his conditition' (ibid., p. 326), is also the primary force behind that progress which leads to the wealth of nations.

> The natural effort of every individual to better his own condition when suffered to exert itself with freedom and security, is so powerful a principle, that it is alone, and without any assistance, not only capable of carrying on the society to wealth and prosperity, but of surmounting a hundred impertinent obstructions with which the folly of human laws too often incumbers its operations; though the effect of these obstructions is always more or less either to encroach upon its freedom, or to diminish its its security.
>
> (Smith, 1776/1937: 508).

It is the message of *The Wealth of Nations* that the market has the unique advantage of (1) setting free this powerful motive and of (2) channelling it – as if led by an invisible hand – in ways conducive to the common good.

The Wealth of Nations is Adam Smith's most famous book – at least *post mortem* – but it is not the only book he wrote. In his own day he was famous, above all, as the author of *The Theory of Moral Sentiments* (1759). This book begins:

> How selfish soever man may be supposed, there are evidently some principles in his nature, which interest him in the fortune of others, and render their happiness necessary to him, though he derives nothing from it, except the pleasure of seeing it. Of this kind is pity, or compassion, the emotion which we feel for the misery of others, when we see it, or are made to conceive it in a very lively manner.
>
> (Smith, 1759/1976: 47)

This statement – and the book as a whole – has been supposed to contradict the statements about self-interest in *The Wealth of Nations*. The problem of reconciling these seemingly opposite views about self-interest has been called '*Das Adam Smith Problem*'. I don't believe there is an Adam Smith problem. Smith never said, in *The Wealth of Nations*, that man is all selfish, and he never said in *The Theory of Moral Sentiments*, that man is not at all selfish. In both books he maintained that self-interest is a strong motive and in the former book he added that it dominates exchange on the market (cf. Coase, 1976: 540ff.). But suppose, for the sake of argument, that *The Wealth of*

Nations assumes universal self-interest, what becomes of *The Theory of Moral Sentiments?* The only way out, for someone seeking support for universal economic man in Adam Smith, would be to argue that he changed his mind between 1759 and 1776, and that his mature view of the matter is to be found in *The Wealth of Nations*.

This road is blocked. *The Theory of Moral Sentiments* went through six editions in Adam Smith's lifetime. The only substantial change is in the last of these editions, published in the year of his death (1790), but it is not a change that resolves the supposed Adam Smith problem. It is also reported that Adam Smith, himself, considered *The Theory of Moral Sentiments* superior to *The Wealth of Nations* (Campbell, 1971: 16; Lux, 1990: 106). We have to conclude, therefore, that *The Theory of Moral Sentiments* represents Smith's mature view of human nature. In the context of Smith's projected writings, *The Theory of Moral Sentiments* is clearly more fundamental and constitutes a necessary background to *The Wealth of Nations*, the latter being an application of the ideas of the former to commercial society (Macfie, 1967: ch. 4; Campbell, 1971: 16–19; West, 1976: 97f.; Werhane, 1991: ch. 3). Smith's nomination as 'father of economics' is the work of posterity. He did not conceive of himself as an economist and did not attach any particular importance to this subject: 'of all the sciences by far the most important, but hitherto, perhaps, the least cultivated [is] that of natural jurisprudence' (Smith, 1759/1976: 357). A reading of Smith as an 'economist' in the modern sense is bound to be misleading (Myers, 1983: 111). Looking at Smith's writings, as a whole, he appears, by modern standards, as more of a psychologist and sociologist than an economist (Macfie, 1967: chs 1–2; Campbell, 1971: 19; Wolfe, 1989b: 28; Eriksson, 1993: 257).[22] To this impression contributes his concern with institutions, which has only recently reappeared as a major concern of mainstream economists; his analysis of society as a whole, not just the market; his conception of society as divided into different orders or classes, with interests of their own; his analysis of the history of society, where commercial society is but one stage; his interest in rhetoric and education as means of persuasion, which shows that he did not treat preferences as stable and given to analysis; and last, but not least, his social psychological theory of morality in *The Theory of Moral Sentiments*.

Turning to this work, a first observation is that self-interest appears as a very strong motive here too and, above all, much stronger than benevolence.

Every man is, no doubt, by nature, first and principally recommended to his own care; and as he is fitter to take care of himself, than of any other person, it is fit and right that it should be so. Every man, therefore, is much more deeply interested in whatever immediately concerns himself, than in what concerns any other man.

(Smith, 1759/1976: 161; see also 167ff., 233)

People, then, care most for themselves, but, in addition, they do care strongly for their close kin and for their close friends. They also care, if less, for their colleagues in office, their business partners and their neighbours. Smith also recognizes such things as people's love of their country and their attachment to the social orders to which they belong – even a love for mankind, however weak and restricted to a few saints among men (Smith, 1759/1976: 359–386).

Smith's estimate of self-interest as much stronger than benevolence may have led some economists to believe that he would have accepted economic man as a good approximation to the truth and a fertile model of man in social science. As we shall see, there is no justification for this inference except, perhaps, in the case of economics (cf. Hollander, 1976: 139f.). First of all, it is perfectly clear that although benevolence is not as strong as self-interest, it is strong indeed in the case of family and friends. It is also quite obvious that Smith considered sentiments such as attachment to social orders and nations, if not equally strong, at least strong enough to make a difference in the world, hence needed for the explanation of many social phenomena, political phenomena included (cf. West, 1990:- 123f.).

Second, and more important, there is a countervailing power much stronger than benevolence. What prevents people from acting in their self-interest is their sense of justice, their conscience.

When we are always so much more deeply affected by whatever concerns ourselves than by whatever concerns other men; what is it which prompts the generous upon all occasions, and the mean upon many, to sacrifice their own interests to the greater interests of others? It is not the soft power of humanity, it is not that feeble spark of benevolence which Nature has lighted up in the human heart, that is thus capable of counter-acting the strongest impulses of self-love. It is a stronger power, a more forcible motive which exerts itself upon such occasions. It is reason, principle, conscience, the inhabitant of the breast, the man within, the great judge and arbiter of our conduct. It is he who, whenever we are about to act so as to affect the happiness of others, calls to us, with a voice capable of astonishing the most presumptuous of our passions... It is he who shews us the propriety of generosity and the deformity of injustice; the propriety of resigning the greatest interest of our own for the yet greater interests of others; and the deformity of doing the smallest injury to another in order to obtain the greatest benefit to ourselves. It is not the love of our neighbour, it is not the love of mankind, which upon many occasions prompts us to the practice of those divine virtues. It is a stronger love, a more powerful affection, which generally takes place upon such occasions; the love of what is honourable and noble, of the grandeur, and dignity, and superiority of our own characters.

(Smith, 1759/1976: 234f.)

This is Smith's main message, repeated again and again, in *The Theory of Moral Sentiments*. The major spring of moral behaviour is the man within the breast, our conscience, also called the 'impartial spectator', which makes us follow the moral rules of society even against our own self-interest (see, e.g., Smith, 1759/1976: 156f., 289, 422f.). But this view of human nature is really much closer to sociological man than to economic man. I suggest that *The Theory of Moral Sentiments* may be conceived of as a social psychological theory of the ontogenesis of sociological man.[23]

Human beings have the ability of 'sympathy'. In Smith's usage this does not mean an ability to feel pity, or compassion, nor is it an ability to enter into other people's minds. It is the ability of imagining that we are in the situation of other people. Because of this ability, we are also capable of sympathizing with the sentiments of others. Once again, we do not enter the feelings of other people, we imagine what our own feelings would be in their situation. On the basis of these sentiments, we either approve or disapprove of other people's behaviour. We are all spectators of other people's behaviour and the abstract representative of this multitude of actual and potential spectators is called, by Smith, the *impartial spectator*.

The next step in Smith's theory of morality is that we tend to act so as to please the impartial spectator. We do so because we love approval and praise. This part of the argument is compatible with a reductionist account of 'moral behaviour' as opportunistic and basically self-interested. Smith is aware that this is a possible interpretation, and emphatically denies its correctness:

> Man naturally desires, not only to be loved, but to be lovely; or to be that thing which is the natural and proper object of love. He naturally dreads, not only to be hated, but to be hateful; or to be that thing which is the natural and proper object of hatred. He desires not only praise, but praise-worthiness; or to be that thing which, though it should be praised by nobody, is, however, the natural and proper object of praise. He dreads, not only blame, but blame-worthiness; or to be that thing which, though it should be blamed by nobody, is, however, the natural and proper object of blame.

(Smith, 1759/1976: 208)

Smith goes even further in his rebuttal of reductionism: 'The love of praise-worthiness is by no means derived altogether from the love of praise' (ibid., p. 208); 'so far is the love of praise-worthiness from being derived altogether from that of praise, that the love of praise seems, at least in a great measure, to be derived from that of praise-worthiness' (ibid., p. 209).

Our desire to be praiseworthy can only be satisfied by acting in conformity with the dictates of a judge better informed than other people. This judge is the man within the breast, our own conscience.

> But though man has, in this manner, been rendered the immediate judge of mankind, he has been rendered so only in the first instance; and an appeal lies from his sentence to a much higher tribunal, to the tribunal of their own consciences, to that of the supposed impartial and well-informed spectator, to that of the man within the breast, the great judge and arbiter of their conduct. The jurisdictions of those two tribunals are founded upon principles which, though in some respects resembling and akin, are, however, in reality different and distinct. The jurisdiction of the man without is founded altogether in the desire of actual praise, and in the aversion to actual blame. The jurisdiction of the man within is founded altogether in the desire of praiseworthiness, and in the aversion to blameworthiness; in the desire of possessing those qualities, and performing those actions, which we love and admire in other people; and in the dread of possessing those qualities, and performing those actions, which we hate and despise in other people.
>
> (Smith, 1759/1976: 227)

The man within the breast is the impartial spectator internalized and made part of our own selves. 'We endeavour to examine our own conduct as we imagine any other fair and impartial spectator would examine it' (Smith, 1759/1976: 204). Smith's analysis of this internalization of the impartial spectator is with the help of a well-known metaphor: that of a mirror, or looking-glass:

> We suppose ourselves the spectators of our own behaviour, and endeavour to imagine what effect it would, in this light, produce upon us. This is the only looking-glass by which we can, in some measure, with the eyes of other people, scrutinize the propriety of our own conduct.
>
> (Smith, 1759/1976: 206)

The result of this internalization of the impartial spectator is a divided self. There is first the acting self under the sway of our passions, but there is also the man within the breast observing and judging the actions of the primary self (see Khalil, 1990).

> When I endeavour to examine my own conduct, when I endeavour to pass sentence upon it, and either to approve or condemn it, it is evident that, in all such cases, I divide myself, as it were, into two persons; and that I, the examiner, the judge, represent a different character from that other I, the person whose conduct is examined into and judged of. The first is the spectator, whose sentiments with regard to my own conduct I endeavour to enter into, by placing myself in his situation, and by considering how it would appear to me, when seen from that particular

point of view. The second is the agent, the person whom I properly call myself, and of whose conduct under the character of a spectator, I was endeavouring to form some opinion.

(Smith, 1759/1976: 206f.)

Smith's metaphor of the *other*, or of society, as a 'mirror' for the reflection of the *I* has been used by the sociologist Charles Horton Cooley in his well-known theory of the 'looking-glass self' (Cooley, 1902/1964: ch. 4). The idea of an impartial spectator was developed by the sociologist, or social psychologist, George Herbert Mead into a theory of the self as a social self (Mead, 1934/1962). The self consists of two parts: an 'I' and a 'me', the latter being Mead's counterpart to Smith's internalized impartial spectator. Mead's term for the impartial spectator is the 'generalized other'. Mead goes beyond Smith, however, in recognizing that some others are more important than other others, especially in the early development of the self. His term for these important others are 'significant others'. Cooley and Mead are the two pillars upon which rests the social psychological theory of symbolic interactionism, which together with Freud's theory of personality is the main micro-foundation of mainstream sociology and, perhaps, still the best theory of socialization there is.

The impartial spectator is also the source of the general rules of morality, which Smith explains as arising out of the self-disciplined attempt to act in ways that lead to approbation and to avoid actions that lead to disapprobation. Moral rules are arrived at by induction. Experience tells us what the impartial spectator commends. Morality tells us to do those things. Experience also tells us what the impartial spectator cannot go along with. Morality tells us not to do those things.

I hope that, by now, I have succeeded in convincing the reader that Adam Smith did not conceive of man as acting entirely, or primarily, from self-interest. It is still conceivable, if unlikely, that he would have supported the universal use of economic man for purposes of analysis. Several considerations tell against this possibility.

First, Smith was not a rationalist, or utilitarian. Like Hume, he was a critic of Hobbes' theory of the social contract, but unlike Hume he gave little weight to utility in the explanation of moral judgements (Campbell, 1971: 116–119; Holmes, 1990: 268; Eriksson, 1993). He did assign to utility a certain role both in the explanation and for the justification of morality, but it was a limited role. Morality owes its existence and normativity primarily to the passions, not to calculated interest. Of the three heads of contemporary schools in political economy – Hayek (Austrian), Stigler (Chicago) and Buchanan (Virginia) – claiming allegiance to Adam Smith, I believe Hayek is closest to Smith. Public choice is more Hobbesian than Smithian.

Second, Smith would not have endorsed Stigler's metaphor of self-interest

100

as 'granite' (see Werhane, 1991: ch. 3). Smith's own metaphor was in terms of more mouldable material:

> The coarse clay of which the bulk of mankind are formed, cannot be wrought to such perfection. There is scarce any man, however, who, by disicipline, education, and example may not be so impressed with a regard to general rules, as to act upon almost every occasion with tolerable decency, and through the whole of his life to avoid any considerable degree of blame.
>
> (Smith, 1759/1976: 270)

The difference between granite and clay is that the latter is easier to sculpt. In contradistinction to Stigler (Stigler and Becker, 1977), Smith did not believe that preferences are stable. Moral judgements, like judgements of taste, are disputable and change over time. Hence the need for moral education (Smith, 1759/1976: 363–365; 1776/1937: 736–740).

Most importantly, Smith was a consistent critic of economic reductionism. He argued with much energy against Epicurus, Hobbes and, especially, Mandeville for seeing self-interest behind every apparent manifestation of benevolence and morality (1759/1976: 54, 270, 473f., 485ff.).[24] His spirited attack on Mandeville is fully applicable to many economic reductionists of our own day.

> Though the notions of this author are in almost every respect erroneous, there are, however, some appearances in human nature, which, when viewed in a certain manner, seem at first sight to favour them. These, described and exaggerated by the lively and humorous, though coarse and rustic eloquence of Dr Mandeville, have thrown upon his doctrine an air of truth and probability which is very apt to impose upon the unskilful.
>
> (Smith, 1759/1976: 487)

The appearances in human nature that Smith refers to are the selfish passions, which Mandeville, like many contemporary advocates of the economic approach, believes are all there is in human nature:

> Dr Mandeville considers whatever is done from a sense of propriety, from a regard to what is commendable and praise-worthy, as being done from love of praise and commendation, or, as he calls it, from vanity. Man, he observes, is naturally much more interested in his own happiness than in that of others, and it is impossible that, in his heart, he can ever prefer their prosperity to his own. Whenever he appears to do so, we may be assured that he imposes upon us, and that he is then acting from the same selfish motives as at all other times.
>
> (ibid., pp. 487f.)

Smith, of course, agrees that there is more than a grain of truth in

Mandeville's depiction of human nature. The intensity of his attack, however, indicates a conviction that it is, nevertheless, fundamentally flawed. An important observation, made by Smith, is exactly how easy it is to turn a half-truth into the whole truth and how deceptive are theories that do.

> It is the great fallacy of Dr Mandeville's book to represent every passion as wholly vicious, which is so in any degree and in any direction. It is thus that he treats every thing as vanity which has any reference either to what are, or to what ought to be, the sentiments of others; and it is by means of this sophistry that he establishes his favourite conclusion, that private vices are public benefits.
>
> (ibid., pp. 493f.)

Not only was Smith critical of economic reductionism, he was critical of excessive theoretical simplicity in general.

> By running up all the different virtues, too, to this one species of propriety, Epicurus indulged in a propensity, which is natural to all men, but which philosophers in particular are apt to cultivate with a peculiar fondness, as the great means of displaying their ingenuity – the propensity to account for all appearances from as few principles as possible.
>
> (Smith, 1759/1976: 474; see also p. 508)

It may be argued that Smith indulged in this propensity, himself (Campbell, 1971: 40, 50, 55, ch. 3; Cohen, 1989: 53ff.; Eriksson, 1993: 258ff.), but he never accepted the reduction of man to one single dimension. Smith's conception of human nature was much more complex than economic man (Holmes, 1990). Therefore, when Stigler suggests that Smith's 'construct of the self-interest-seeking individual in a competitive environment is Newtonian in its universality', this does not reflect Smith's view. Indeed, self-interest, in the form in which it appears in *The Wealth of Nations*, is a dominant motive only in commercial society and it is explained in terms of 'sympathy'. It is because we want sympathy, and because we sympathize most with the rich, that we strive incessantly to better our own conditions (Smith 1759/1976: 112ff.; Campbell, 1971: 171–174; West, 1976: 107ff.; Cohen, 1989: 61).

The paradox resolved

Adam Smith, then, was not an advocate of economic man as universal man, but what about political man? Is political man reducible to economic man? I don't think so, and Smith did not think so either (see Whitehead, 1991). First of all, according to Smith, it is at least the task of politicians to pursue the public interest.

> The wise and virtuous man is at all times willing that his own private interest should be sacrificed to the public interest of his own particular

order or society. He is at all times willing, too, that the interest of this order or society should be sacrificed to the greater interest of the state or sovereignty of which it is only a subordinate part.

(Smith, 1759/1976: 384)

According to Stigler, however, Smith also assumed that politicians actually do act in the public interest, and this time his interpretation is correct. This is evident in Smith's repudiation of Mandeville:

All public spirit, therefore, all preference of public to private interest, is, according to him, a mere cheat and imposition upon mankind; and human virtue, which is so much boasted of, and which is the occasion of so much emulation among men, is the mere offspring of flattery begotten upon pride.

(Smith, 1759/1976: 488)

Is this an inconsistency, as Buchanan maintains, or a paradox as Stigler suggests? Not at all. Accepting Smith's model of mixed motivations, it is perfectly possible to assume, without inconsistency or paradox, that people act on different motives in different institutional settings. This is what Smith did, if less successfully in the case of politics than in the case of market exchange (Whitehead, 1991: 54ff.). Even so, there are good reasons for being more public-spirited in politics than on the market and some of them can be derived from the writings of Adam Smith.

Smith is, of course, under no illusion that all men and women are virtuous. He recognizes the existence of fraud and falsehood among politicians (Smith, 1759/1976: 130f.) and he anticipates public choice by suggesting that members of parliament seek election out of self-interest (ibid., p. 287). George Stigler ([1971] 1982: 137ff.) finds many examples of self-interested politicians in *The Wealth of Nations* and Edwin West (1990: chs 8 and 9) presents Smith as a precursor of James Buchanan's constitutional economics and of the public choice theory of rent-seeking. This is correct up to a point. Smith's main concern was the institutional design of a just society. Among the main threats to a just and decent society was the rent-seeking activity of business interests. 'People of the same trade seldom meet together, even for merriment and diversion, but the conversation ends in a conspiracy against the public, or in some contrivance to raise prices' (Smith, 1776/1937: 128).[25] Therefore: 'The government of an exclusive company of merchants is, perhaps, the worst of all governments for any country whatever' (ibid., p. 537). The reason for this is not, however, the inherent selfishness of merchants, but the nature of their trade, which makes their own interest opposite to that of their country. 'As sovereigns, their interest is exactly the same with that of the country they govern. As merchants, their interest is directly opposite to that interest' (ibid., pp. 602f.). 'No two characters seem more inconsistent than those of trader and sovereign. If the trading spirit of the English East India company

103

renders them very bad sovereigns, the spirit of sovereignty seems to have rendered them equally bad traders' (ibid., p. 771).

According to Smith, then, there is no inconsistency in assuming that merchants and sovereigns act differently; it is part of their respective trades, or roles, to do so. An important difference between Smith and public choice is that the former sees the threat to the public interest mainly in the competing interests of social orders, or classes, whereas the latter recognizes only individuals and their self-interests.

The explanation for this difference between politicians and merchants, I suggest, must be sought in Adam Smith's impartial spectator. The impartial spectator, both in the form of other people and in the form of our own consciences, tells us that it is right to be self-interested on the market, but public-spirited in politics. Nobody really expects the baker to give away his bread, but most people, advocates of public choice excluded, expect politicians to submit to the public interest. It is the task of individuals to take care of themselves and of those who work to take care of their families. But it is also the task of managers to maximize profit and of politicians to maximize the common good – and, by and large, they do. In the case of a sovereign, the public interest merges with prudent 'self-interest', or family interest, to create a union that is stronger than mere duty.

> Even a bad sovereign feels more compassion for his people than can ever be expected from the farmers of his revenue. He knows that the permanent grandeur of his family depends upon the prosperity of his people, and will never knowingly ruin the prosperity for the sake of any momentary interest of his own. It is otherwise with the farmers of his revenue, whose grandeur may frequently be the effect of the ruin, and not of the prosperity of his people.
>
> (Smith, 1776/1937: 854)

This is a Smithian and sociological resolution of the 'paradox'. Economists don't believe in the efficacy of obligation. They see the relation between citizens and politicians as that between principal and agent. I believe there is a normative element in most principal–agent relations and especially in the relation between citizens and politicians – politicians are not just hired, they are entrusted to represent citizens – but even for economists it should be possible to accept that politicians in power run their countries as managers run firms, and for similar reasons.

An economist, commenting on my manuscript, invoked the example of Italy in defence of public choice. No doubt, Italy presents a melancholy spectacle of corruption, and corrupt politicians can be found in all countries. It is possible, though, to draw another conclusion from this example than that public choice is correct. If the disgaceful behaviour of Italian politicians were normal behaviour, no one would react, since no one would expect politicians to behave differently. The word 'corruption' means, not only moral deterioration, but a deformity of the self. When Adam Smith wrote about fraud and falsehood among politicians (see above), it was in a chapter on the corruption of our moral sentiments. More important, the discovery of widespread corruption in Italian politics created a scandal that swept away the whole political establishment. Who did it? Smith's impartial spectator. In his own characteristic phrase, the behaviour of Italian politicians was more than 'the impartial spectator could go along with'. Smith is more useful than Hobbes and public choice even for the understanding of corruption.

It is of some importance to realize that Smith's concept of 'self-interest' is different from that of Hobbes (see also Chapter 7). According to the latter, self-interest leads to a war of each against all; according to the former, self-interest leads to peaceful market transactions. Hobbesian self-interest is *unbounded*, Smithian self-interest is *bounded*; it is the love and care of the self. Self-interest, for Smith, is a virtue. Like the other virtues, benevolence and justice, it presupposes the stoic virtue of self-command. As a virtue, self-interest takes the form of prudence; of long-term and enlightened self-interest. But more importantly, Smith's self-interest is bounded by justice and a sense of fair play (see Werhane, 1991: ch. 3 and Muller, 1993: Part II). Once this is recognized, the seeming inconsistency between political man and economic man becomes less dramatic.

James Buchanan is, at least from about 1983 onwards, aware that Smith was not a champion of economic man and also that he conceived of 'self-interest' as 'bounded' and different from that of *homo economicus* (Buchanan [1983] 1986: 238; [1983] 1989a: 33). He suggests, therefore, that the model of economic man is inadequate for positive theory both about the market and about politics. He seems to believe, though, that honesty is a more scarce resource in politics than in economics (Buchanan [1983] 1986: 89). I doubt it, but the important thing is that Buchanan no longer sees an inconsistency in assuming that elected politicians and public officials seek the public interest ([1983] 1989a: 29–32). The difference between politics and market is in the institutional setting.

So far, the argument has relied on the virtue of justice. If we add that individuals are to some small degree benevolent, and some individuals more than others, it might be argued that we find more benevolence in politics, simply because political institutions are more productive than the market of good deeds. Market and politics work according to different principles and breed different kinds of people and different kinds of conduct (cf. Lane, 1981). The market is unfit for doing good. It is good for resource allocation of private goods, but not for distribution according to need or for achieving distributive justice. The market is for private goods and political institutions for public goods (cf. Hahn, 1991). It's as simple as that.

I have discussed politicians (and bureaucrats) and turn now to voters. There are strong reasons to believe that voters have other motives than buyers on the market. I have already mentioned Brennan and Lomasky's

Smithian theory of voting as an expression of moral sentiments. Brennan and Lomasky suggest that institutional peculiarities make people predominantly self-regarding on the market and other-regarding in politics. Their explanation is that market transactions are consequential in a way that voting is not. The baker who gives away his bread will be forced out of business and lose his livelihood. The voter casting his/her vote on a party intent upon redistribution risks very little and shares the burden with other taxpayers.

Another peculiarity of the market contributes to making it inadequate for outlets of benevolence. As many economists (e.g. Hayek) have taught us, knowledge is local. People are, in most cases, the best judges of their own needs. In addition, as Adam Smith pointed out, we know only a few people and their needs. But we rarely know anything about the parties to our market transactions. It would be a totally gratuitous policy to be benevolent towards anonymous buyers and sellers on the market. It is simply impossible to act in the public interest on the market, except as an unintended consequence of our self-interest. The market signals private interests, but not the public interest. To the extent, therefore, that people, do entertain ideas about a 'public interest' that go beyond, or differ from, the results of market exchange, politics is the obvious way to realize those ideas. Indeed, according to many social scientists, this is the function and *raison d'être* of political institutions. Public choice theorists have been correct to question a naive belief in the benevolence of politicians, but wrong to reject the concepts of 'group-interest' and of 'public interest' altogether.

Some commentators have suggested that Adam Smith really does not operate with the assumption of self-interest at all, but with the idea of 'non-tuism', as later propounded by Philip H. Wicksteed (Werhane, 1991: 90). I agree that some of the things Smith says about self-interest, including the famous passage about the butcher, the brewer and the baker, is consistent with this idea, but I nevertheless doubt that this is what Smith had in mind. I turn to Wicksteed instead and the claim that not even the theory of market exchange relies for its validity on any assumption of self-interest.

According to Wicksteed (1910: ch. 5), economics does not rely on any motivational assumption at all, and least of all upon that of universal egoism.[26] A housewife buying food is, usually, more concerned about the needs and tastes of her children, than about her own satisfaction. Wicksteed, therefore, wishes to dispense with the idea of a particular economic motive altogether. What we need is the notion of a specific economic relation. The assumption of non-tuism says that individuals show no altruism towards the parties to their economic transactions. Buyers and sellers, typically, do not care for each other, but treat each other as means for their own ends, whether selfish or altruistic. According to Wicksteed, the economic nexus of market exchange is a particular sphere of social life characterized by economic means–ends relations free from the disturbing influence of altruism.[27]

Now, if not even the theory of market exchange depends upon the assumption of self-interest, then, of course, the paradox of George Stigler disappears. If there is an inconsistency at all, it is to be found in many economists, who typically assume that individuals are altruists towards their kin and, especially, towards their family (see, e.g., Becker, 1976: 282ff.; Margolis, 1982/1984: 24). The inconsistency involved is particularly obvious in the case of George Stigler (1982: 21, 25, 36f.), who interprets personal utility-maximization as including both self-interest and altruism towards family and close friends. The circle of family and friends, however small, is always 'larger' than the self.[28]

A new model of rational choice

In a recent introduction to *Public Choice*, Iain McLean drops the assumption of self-interest, arguing that economics assumes rationality, but not necessarily self-interest. Rationality is equally consistent with altruism (McLean, 1987: 3). This is correct. But McLean forgets that many economists consider the assumption of self-interest equally constitutive of economics as of rationality. More surprisingly, he forgets that this is the case with the founders and most adherents of public choice (see p. 35 above). Also, consistency is not enough. There is little reason to mess things up, by assuming altruism, unless it makes a significant contribution to the explanation of human action. McLean's argument is, of course, that it does. Most of his examples are cases of collective action (ibid., pp. 74ff.), but he also draws attention (ibid., pp. 12–14) to a work by the British sociologist Richard Titmuss on *The Gift Relationship* (1970): a study of blood donors in different countries, especially Great Britain and the United States. He is not the first to do so (see also Arrow, 1972; Hardin, 1982: 103, 216f.; Axelrod, 1984: 220; Hirschmann, 1985: 17f.; Taylor, 1987: 170–172). While in the United States blood is to a large extent a commodity, bought and sold on the market, in Great Britain (as in Sweden), it is provided by voluntary donors as a gift. Since the donors are not paid and can expect nothing in return, their gift is motivated by altruism. Actually, even though Titmuss uses the term 'altruism' (1970: 12f., 71), what he is talking about is morality and social norms (1970: 5, 12, 13).

McLean's revised version of 'public choice' is based upon Howard Margolis' influential 'new model of rational choice' (Margolis, 1981, 1982/1984, 1990, 1991). Margolis' objective is to provide the basis for 'an empirically tenable theory of public choice, a model of individual choice that does not fail catastrophically in the presence of public goods'. The presupposition is that 'the conventional model of choice does so fail, the most familiar illustration being its inability to account for the elementary fact that people vote' (Margolis, 1982/1984: 1). Margolis, 'new model of rational choice', then, is primarily a theory of social, or public, choice. The theory of private choice appears as a special case, applicable, especially, to behaviour on the market.

Margolis' main idea is to split up the individual in two (or three): one private man, motivated solely by self-interest (S-Smith), and one public man, motivated only by group-interest (G-Smith). Both are utility-maximizers, but their utility functions are separate and do not intermesh. Thus, there is no way of arriving at a single utility-function for both selves, as in Becker's economic approach to human behaviour. Instead, the choices of S-Smith and G-Smith are mediated by an arbiter, or referee (U-Smith), that allocates resources between them according to a rule of 'fair share':

> The larger the share of my resources I have spent unselfishly, the more weight I give to my selfish interests in allocating marginal resources. On the other hand, the larger benefit I can confer on the group compared with the benefit from spending marginal resources on myself, the more I will tend to act unselfishly.
>
> (Margolis, 1982/1984: 36)

Since Smith is, himself, a member of the group, resources allocated to G-Smith are, usually, also in the interest of S-Smith. G-utility includes some S-utility. As a consequence, group-interest and self-interest go a long way together, without clashing. Group-interest should not be conceived of as an objective entity, defying methodological individualism or, rather, ontological individualism. Nor is it group-interest as conceived by Margolis, or some other economist. Group-interest, in Margolis' model, is always group-interest as perceived by the members of the group. This means, of course, that, potentially at least, there are as many group-interests as there are members. In any case, Margolis' model of rational choice is not subject to the critique directed by public choice theorists and other methodological individualists at the organicist theory of the state and at welfare economics.

Margolis makes a distinction between two kinds of altruism: 'participation altruism' and 'goods altruism'. In the case of participation altruism, it is the act of giving, or participating, itself, which is valued, irrespective of the utility it confers upon other people. In the case of goods altruism it is the utility of others that matters, but not the act. In the language of Elster (1985b: 145ff.; 1989a: 37ff.), the first is 'process-oriented' and the second 'outcome-oriented'. Elster admits only outcome-oriented altruism. The motivation for participation, if it is rational, is selfish. It is not entirely clear to what extent Margolis and Elster are talking about the same thing. It would seem that Margolis thinks of 'participation' mainly as spending money on some cause, while for Elster 'participation' is spending time on some activity. I suspect that most participation that results from rational choice is, to some extent, also outcome-oriented and motivated by a mix of altruism and self-interest. I also suspect, though, that much participation is non-rational, non-selfish and insensitive to outcome: the result of social norms. Elster, as we shall see (pp. 260f.), gives plenty of scope for this possibility; Margolis none at all. I suggest that he should. The idea of 'participation altruism' is not intuitively clear. It has a tendency to dissolve into either egoism or duty.

Margolis' model has the great advantage, over the conventional model of rational choice, of being able to account for the simple fact that people do give and help. Not only as a means to more ultimate selfish ends and not only as an exception, but regularly and for 'higher' ends. Altruism is as much a part of human nature as is egoism. Margolis compares his tripartite model of man to that of Freud. S-Smith is, of course, the counterpart of Freud's Id, G-Smith is the Superego and U-Smith the Ego. It may be pointed out that Margolis' model is but one in a series of models of multiple selves currently invading the rational choice literature (see, e.g., Elster, 1986a). For my argument, the differences are more significant than the similarities. For Freud, the Superego is the forbidding father. It is society with all its norms. Not the altruistic G-Smith. Freud's model of man is much more congenial to sociological man than to any model of economic man. It is no accident that Freud has been used by prominent sociologists, such as Parsons and members of the Frankfurt School, to provide the psychological foundations of sociological man.

Of special significance, for my argument, is Margolis' rebuttal of the public choice argument for consistency. With Margolis' model, there is no inconsistency in assuming that man pursues his self-interest on the market and the public interest in politics. It is simply a matter of the most efficient – given his/her beliefs – allocation of resources. There is no rational outlet for group-interest on the market. The way it works would give rise to an entirely haphazard use of resources allocated to G-Smith. Also, on a perfectly competitive market, there is an irresoluble conflict between group-interest and self-interest. You cannot allow altruism to affect your choices without causing your own ruin. These are the rules of the game. However, if you wish to contribute to the common good, politics, in a broad sense, is the obvious way to do it (I suppose that this is an analytic truth).

Even though Margolis' model is an improvement upon the conventional model of rational choice, it is still a model of rational choice. G-Smith is a social man, of sorts, but he/she is not a sociological man. The social element in Smith is 'altruism'. Margolis uses this term in an inclusive sense, to denote morality, rather than a merely psychological inclination, as with Elster. Altruism, for Margolis, is primarily commitment to values affecting people's preferences. But no independent role is assigned to social norms as determinants of human action. Margolis' treatment of social rules and conventions is reductionist. We follow rules in order to reduce information costs (1982/1984: 49–51), or because of the rewards and punishments associated with compliance and non-compliance (Margolis, 1991: 358ff.). Although this may sometimes be true, it is far from the whole truth. Conformity to social norms is a matter of routine and/or duty, but rarely of rational choice. This is true even when conformity turns out to be rational according to some economist's calculation of benefits and costs. The decisive question is whether people themselves perform these calculations. If they don't, conformity replaces choice.

SOCIOLOGICAL MAN

There is much truth in Margolis' explanation. But it is not the whole truth. In a full explanation of the difference between economic and political man there must be some place also for sociological man. The difference between market behaviour and political behaviour is, partly, the result of differing social roles and attendant norms. If politicians pursue the public interest, this is not only because they are all altruists, or morally superior. It is because they are expected to do so; because it is their duty. It is part of 'Politics as a Vocation'.[29] Sociological man has a role to play even in economic life. The consumer is rarely narrowly selfish. Most consumers are parts of households and, as such, pursue the interest of the household as a group. In such a small group, often consisting of a family, altruism is a strong motive, but social roles are equally important. There are strong normative expectations of the heads of a household, and, especially, of parents, to share with the rest of the household and, in particular, with the children. Also, if managers maximize (or satisfice) profit, this is not only because they are selfish, but also because this is what they are expected to do; and I mean *normative*, not only *rational*, expectations. It is the duty of managers to maximize profit. It is definitely expected by the owners of the company; it is also expected by the remaining employees and even by people in general.

In the decades that have passed since Anthony Downs, James Buchanan and Gordon Tullock started erecting the edifice of public choice, they have all come to entertain second thoughts about the foundation. Downs and Buchanan, in particular, now deny that political man is economic man.[30]

In the 1980s, if I understand him correctly, Buchanan came to abandon economic man as a model suitable for the purposes of *positive* public choice.[31] Buchanan now occasionally admits that there is reason to believe that man behaves differently on the market and in politics. He goes even further and suggests that economic man is also an inappropriate model for market behaviour. 'I suggest that we cease and desist in any attempt to model man in his market *or* in his public choice behaviour as seeking exclusively or even predominantly to maximize the value of his net wealth' (Buchanan, 1989b: 31). Like most economists, Buchanan always knew that the assumption of self-interest is descriptively false (see, e.g. 1972: 16ff.; 1979b: 70ff., 166; 1981: 384–386). Before this idea gained wide currency, he argued that man has a *multiple self:* 'The elementary fact is, of course, that *homo economicus* does exist in the human psyche along with many other men and that behavior is a product of the continuing internal struggle between them' (Buchanan, 1979b: 207; see also pp. 224ff. and Buchanan and Tullock, 1962/1965: 20f.). What is new is the argument that economics, as a positive-predictive science, has to introduce arguments inconsistent with the assumption of narrow self-interest, or fail as a general theory of human behaviour. The loss in simplicity is a price that must be paid. Buchanan, nevertheless, suggests that we retain the assumption of self-interest for the purposes of a comparative analysis and evalution of alternative institutional arrangements (Buchanan, 1986: 32–38; 1989b: ch. 1 [with Brennan], 31f., 47, 63f.; Brennan and Buchanan, 1981: 382ff.; 1985: ch. 4). I will discuss these normative arguments in Chapter 4.

Anthony Downs began revising his economic theory of democracy shortly after the publication of *An Economic Theory of Democracy* (1957). In a clarifying article on 'The Public Interest: Its Meaning in a Democracy' (1962), his purpose was to rectify some omissions in his book. The biggest failing was not to have recognized that democracy cannot work, or even survive, without a minimal consensus on certain basic values (Downs, 1962: 25). More generally, Downs now argues that people act in the public interest, in addition to acting in their self-interest. His model of man has become more sociological: man is seen as the occupant of so many social roles, trading off the interests associated with each role against those of other roles. Of particular significance for political man is the role of citizen, in which individuals are assumed to act in the public interest (Downs, 1962: 18ff.). Downs does not believe, however, that including the public interest in his model will substantially alter the analysis and the predictions made in *An Economic Theory of Democracy*.

Downs' departure from economic theory is most explicit in his recent article on 'Social Values and Democracy' (1991), where he turns into a critic of orthodox public choice. Downs now argues that social values are vitally important for society and for democracy, and that a rational choice theory of society and of politics, therefore, is fundamentally flawed (Downs, 1991: 146ff.). I will not recapitulate Downs' new theory of democracy here. It is stated in the form of eight axioms of social life and a number of values making up the political culture of democratic society. A few points should be made, however.

First, there is irony in the fact that Downs should eventually come up with something very close to that sociological theory of democracy, which Brian Barry once wanted to replace by Downs' economic theory of democracy. Second, Downs' largely normative concern with consensus does not blind him to the fact that there are important cleavages in society. The fifth axiom reads: '*in most societies, individuals draw part of their personal identities from membership in relatively cohesive subgroups within the society. Examples are ethnic groups, tribes, religions*' (Downs, 1991: 150). Third, Downs still recognizes selfishness as stronger than benevolence. The fourth axiom reads: '*individuals in all societies tend – when they can – to give higher priority to serving their own interests, and the interests of those dearest to them, than the interests of others not so linked to themselves – even at the cost of sacrificing or exploiting others to benefit themselves*' (ibid., p. 149).

In my opinion, Downs' new theory of democracy could, with advantage, be read as an introduction to political sociology. Before turning to political sociology proper, however, I wish to say something about the sociological conception of human nature. Since sociological man is usually presented as an alternative to economic man, one might be led to believe that sociological man is the opposite of economic man: all benevolent, or entirely norm-guided. This is not the case, as I intend to show.

Sociological man is usually conceived of as the descendant of Aristotle's 'political animal' (*zoon politikon*), while economic man is the descendant of his 'rational animal'. I think this is correct. Aristotle made no distinction between the city state as (civil) society and as political community. But Aristotle's political animal is also a precursor of Adam Smith's man, which is further evidence that Smith's man is not economic man. According to Aristotle, man is a political animal because the individual human being is not self-sufficient. Man relies upon cooperation with others through exchange and division of labour (Aristotle, *The Politics*, 1962: 27ff.). Aristotle's point of departure is very much the same as Smith's in *The Wealth of Nations*. Aristotle goes on to maintain that 'humans alone have the perception of good and evil, right and wrong, just and unjust' (1962: 29). Smith agreed, but added a theory to explain this specifically human capacity, in terms of 'sympathy'. The state, according to Aristotle, is an organ for the common interest and good life of citizens and the good aimed at is justice (ibid., 127f.). Like Smith, Aristotle attaches primary importance to the legal rules of society and, especially, the constitution. Like Smith and a large majority of sociologists, Aristotle made a distinction between positive law and morality and insisted that the former must be grounded in the latter (ibid., p. 144). Finally, like Smith, Aristotle defended private property and bounded self-love in terms almost identical to those of Smith:

> every man bears a love towards himself and I am sure that nature meant this to be so. Selfishness is condemned and rightly so, but selfishness is not simply love of self but excessive love of self. So excessive greed to acquire property is condemned, though every man, we may be sure, likes to have his bit of property. And there is this further point; there is very great pleasure in giving, helping friends and associates, making things easy for strangers; and this can only be done by someone who has property of his own.
>
> (ibid., pp. 63ff.)

My next step will be to show that there is continuity between Adam Smith and Auguste Comte, the nominal father of 'sociology'. It is well known that Comte coined the term 'sociology' and made the term 'positivism' famous, but it is less well known that he also invented the term 'altruism'. In his second major work *Système de politique positive* (1851–54), Comte tried to instate the religion of humanity as the spiritual foundation of society. The term 'altruism' is simply a synonym for 'benevolence' and was used, by Comte, as a name for the message of this religion.

Comte, then, was a missionary of the religion of humanity, preaching altruism, but he had no illusion about its power. Like Smith, he considered altruism the highest virtue, but he also believed that 'the selfish instincts are naturally stronger than the unselfish' (Comte, [1851–1854] 1975 p. 382, see also p. 430). Comte was familiar with the work of Smith and may have been influenced by parts of it. He frequently used the term 'sympathy' and the following passage is at least indicative of the direct influence of Smith:

> If the altruistic instincts did not exist in us . . . the mutual services that this activity of industry calls out would certainly not be able to create them. Were this dismal hypothesis a true one, the reciprocal assistance of man to man would never become gratuitious, and the only moral influence that this aid would have, would be to develop a constant prudence of interest.
>
> (Comte [1851–1854] 1975: 407)

For Jon Elster (1989a: 97), and with good reason, 'sociological man' is associated with the name of Emile Durkheim. According to Durkheim, society is a moral order and man a follower of social norms. His sociology is in important respects a sociological version of the philosophy of Kant. But Durkheim was very far from denying the existence and omnipresence of egoism. The energy with which both Comte and Durkheim fought egoism shows that they saw it as a very powerful enemy. In Durkheim's view, for instance, it is strong enough to rule out the possibility of communism in modern society (Durkheim [1884] 1986: 86–96). Durkheim is critical of economic man, though. While agreeing that 'every science lives from abstractions', he maintains that this particular abstraction is of limited value (Durkheim [1890] 1973: 38). His own conception of human nature is dualistic: on one side there are sensations and appetites, on the other side are intellect and morality. The first part of this *homo duplex* is necessarily egoistic, the second part is universalistic, with morality in constant conflict with the egoistic passions. Durkheim concurs with Pascal: 'man is both "angel and beast" and not exclusively one or the other' (Durkheim [1914] 1973: 153). Durkheim is wrong to assume that passions are necessarily egoistic. There are social passions as well, but the point to be made here is that Durkheim did not deny the selfish part of man.

Perhaps the most important contributor to the shaping of sociological man is Talcott Parsons. In a famous article, Dennis Wrong argued that Parsons worked with an 'oversocialized conception of man' (Wrong, 1961). I agree with Wrong that a preoccupation with Hobbes' problem order and a critical attitude to economic man has led Parsons and other sociologists to overemphasize the social side of human nature. I agree that, as an ideal-typical abstraction, on a par with economic man, sociological man is as one-sided as the latter. For most social scientific purposes we must use a mixed breed. Wrong is wrong, however, to suggest that sociologists, like Durkheim

113

and Parsons, are blind to the other side of human nature. Parsons does not at all exclude self-interest, and sociological man is not unfamiliar with this motive. Parsons is critical of economic man as engaged in 'the rational pursuit of self-interest',[32] but so was Adam Smith. Social scientists familiar only with the stereotypes of these thinkers would expect them to be miles apart, but actually their views on motivation are essentially the same.

Parsons criticizes the economic model of man for being partly wrong and in part misleadingly simplistic. It is wrong because in addition to self-interest there is moral sentiment. It is overly simplistic, because self-interest is almost always harnessed and channelled by institutions into *specific patterns*, such as profit-maximization. Most institutionalized behaviour is part of social roles; behaviour expected of people in specific positions and situations. Now, according to Parsons, institutionalized role behaviour is typically a mix of self-intererst and moral sentiment. This is so because it is generally in the self-interest of people to do what is expected of them. The motive for complying with norms is, once again, mixed. One important ingredient is *self-respect*, which we get from acting in accordance with our moral beliefs. Another ingredient is *recognition*, which is for lots of people a self-interested motive stronger than net wealth maximization.

Of some relevance for political sociology is Parsons' classification of types of action by their mode of motivational orientation: intellectual activity (cognition), expressive action (cathexis) and moral action (evaluation). Instrumental action is a combination of cognition and cathexis. This tripartite typology is a theme with many variations in Parsons' theory of the social system. My point is that the normative type of action is only one of three. Sociological man is not a one-dimensional conformist, but a two-or three-dimensional creature.[33]

3

POLITICS AS EXCHANGE

The economic, or public choice, approach to politics consists, as we have seen, of three elements: the assumptions of self-interest, exchange and individualism. I have dealt with self-interest and turn now to exchange. Among public choice theorists, James Buchanan, in particular, sees economics as catallactics and an economic theory of politics as based on the market analogy. This is justified if exchange is, indeed, the essence of the market, and I believe that it is. But it is also possible to conceive of competition as the principal market mechanism. In that case, you may use the market analogy even when there is no exchange.

The relations between the principal political actors in our Western parliamentary democracies – politicians proper, bureaucrats, voters, interest groups, media – are not relations of exchange, or not predominantly so. To the extent that an element of exchange enters the interaction of political actors at all, this is beside, or within, more basic relations of power, authority and representation. Political exchange, therefore, when it takes place, is rarely between free and equal partners, as on a competitive market.

I do not, of course, deny the existence of exchange in politics, nor do I deny the value of subjecting it to scientific scrutiny, but this is not tantamount to adopting a conception of 'politics-as-exchange'. The prevalence of exchange in politics is a matter for empirical investigation – I suspect that such investigation would reveal interesting differences between political systems and cultures – and not of definition. Despite assurances to the contrary (Curry and Wade, 1968: xi), politics-as-exchange, or as market, is a metaphor of dubious standing and mainly normative import (cf. Davis, 1992: 45, 74). As a heuristic device, it may, of course, give rise to some new insights, but as a general approach, inviting us to see politics as exchange, it is misleading.

As Gabriel A. Almond (1991: 36) has pointed out, politics-as-exchange is only one of several metaphors that have been used in the study of politics. In addition there are politics as religion, warfare, game and dramatic performance. Another popular metaphor is politics as sports (Balbus, 1975). Jon Elster (1986c) mentions two important conceptions of politics: those implied by the analogies of the *market* and the *forum* (see also Beetham, 1993: 194).

115

His discussion of them is normative, but they are no less significant in positive political theory. The market analogy gives us a theory of politics starting from isolated individuals with fixed alternatives and given preferences, which they reveal by demanding certain policies. Politics is seen as a matter of aggregating private preferences into 'public' choice. The market analogy was not important to political theory until the advent of public choice. By contrast, the analogy of the forum goes back to Greek Antiquity, where politics was seen as a truly *public* matter, public choice being the result of open discussion among the citizens of the state. On this view of politics, individuals are not isolated, preferences are not given and public choice is not a matter of aggregation; it is a matter of discussion.

The analogies of market and forum give rise to two major conceptions of politics. But there is a third equally important conception: the view of politics as a matter of authority. In this chapter, I follow Charles E. Lindblom (1977: ch. 1) and recognize three principal mechanisms of social organization, or methods of social control: exchange, authority and persuasion. Exchange, then, is only one form of social interaction in politics and probably not the most important. Any theory of politics which concentrates on this relation, to the exclusion of other, equally important, relations, is severally limited in scope.

EXCHANGE

The term economics derives from the Greek word *oikos*, which means household. The work *Oeconomica*, attributed to Aristotle, but almost certainly written by someone else, is a treatise of both household and state, suggesting some sort of analogy between the two. One thing they have in common is that both are budgetary units (cf. Willer, 1992: 64).

Modern economists – especially the Austrians – have insisted that the market is a *catallaxy*, not an *oikos* and that economics is *catallactics*, the theory of exchange. This is a justified claim, even if there is an element of persuasion in the disqualification of centrally planned economies as objects of economic analysis. (They were obviously outdistanced and forced to abandon the economic race between nations.)

Now, Buchanan takes a further step and suggests that the state too is a *catallaxy* and political theory *catallactics*. This looks like a kind of category mistake. The state is not a *catallaxy*, it is an *oikos*, a budgetary unit, as we all know. James Buchanan knows it very well, because he is a specialist in public finance. But has anyone heard of a market developing a budget deficit? I don't want to exaggerate the importance of this argument – the state may be engaged in exchange with other states and with firms, and there may be many types of non-market exchange going on within the state apparatus – but I do believe that it casts serious doubt, *a priori*, upon the conception of 'politics-as-exchange'.

According to public choice, the principal actors on the political market are politicians, bureaucrats, voters and interest groups.

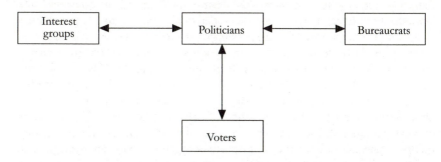

Figure 3.1 Actors on the political market

The political market has some peculiar characteristics which make it different from most economic markets. Since there is only one seller (government) the political market is monopolistic, except at elections, when there is competition between parties (cf. Buchanan and Tullock, 1962/1965: 104; Buchanan, 1979a: 19). Buyers are many, but very unlike buyers on the market because of the special significance attached to majorities in democratic politics. Other peculiarities arise from the fact that government trades in public goods (see Chapter 5) and even more because it deals in packages of public goods, to some extent meeting the demands of all citizens for diverse public goods. From this follows a further peculiarity: the package of public goods sold by government is financed in lump and indiscriminately by taxes. As James Buchanan (1954a) was among the first to point out, this makes political transactions radically different from economic transactions. Most important, there is no direct relation between what you pay and what you get. Many policies are intended to correct undesirable consequences of the working of the economic market. Because of this, it may be regarded as a metamarket, 'which deals not with the allocation of resources, but rather with the regulation and management of complex systems of markets and quasi-markets' (Crozier, 1991: 314). To this might be added, that many public goods are in the form of rules of the game, or constitutions; the legal framework within which both economic exchange and ordinary politics take place. In this case, uncertainty is almost absolute and exchange becomes consent. According to Buchanan, economic exchange is simple and political exchange complex (Buchanan, 1979a: 14).

Before I scrutinize possible examples of exchange relations in politics, I will voice two general complaints about the public choice analysis of the political market. First, relations between actors are often assumed to be asymmetric in terms of power and rationality, or, at least, information; hence the possibility for persuasion (Downs, 1957: 83ff.; Tullock, 1967b: ch. 8). In the theory of political business cycles, voters are manipulated by cunning politicians. In Niskanen's theory of bureaucracy and in the Chicago 'capture' theory of economic regulation, politicians are depicted as powerless and ignorant (cf. Riker, 1985: 198), mere playthings in the hands of interest groups and bureaucracy. A glaring example is Gary Becker, who argues that voters' preferences 'can be manipulated and created' through information and misinformation, that voters are 'easily persuaded' (Becker, 1983: 392f.), and who suggests that we drop 'the unrealistic assumption that the preferences of voters are fixed', six years after writing the already classic defence of economic assumption of stable preferences (Stigler and Becker, 1977). This lack of strategic rationality in one party to political relations makes rational choice theory applicable only to the other party and game theory not applicable at all. This is a pity for an economic theory of politics.

Second, there is a glaring inconsistency between different parts and advocates of public choice. Government, which is in some public choice theories depicted as omnipotent, is in other theories modelled as impotent. In the theory of government failure, it is both – it is possible, of course, that it is omnipotent in some respects and impotent in other respects, but this is only part of the answer. In the theory of political business cycles there is only one strategic actor, government, while the electorate is an object of manipulation. In the spatial theory of democracy both politicians and voters are strategic actors.

Alan Peacock (1992: 13f.) identifies three major political markets: (1) 'the "primary political market" in which politicians sell policies for votes', (2) 'the "policy supply" market in which bureaucrats will offer alternative administrative packages to promote the policy aims of elected governments' and (3) 'the "policy execution" market', involving a 'bargaining situation between regulators and regulatees'. I will treat these markets in reverse order. First, however, I suggest that there is a fourth market: parliament itself.

The most obvious examples of political exchange take place, not between politicians and other actors, but between politicians (or parties) themselves. The paradigm of exchange in politics is log-rolling, or vote-trading, between parties or politicians in parliamentary committees. This explains the prominent place occupied by vote-trading in the theory of public choice (see Mueller, 1979: 49–58; 1989: 86–95).[1] Not only is this phenomenon subjected to much attention, it is defended as an important part of an ideally working democracy. As Buchanan and Tullock (1962/1965: 267ff.) correctly observe, this is in diametrical opposition to public opinion, which brands log-rolling, not to mention vote-selling, as immoral. It is even against the law in some countries (Tullock, 1976: 41). This observation may be generalized. It seems as if all kinds of economic behaviour, or trade, are considered illicit in the political sphere. Bribery, for instance, is more illegitimate than is log-rolling. The proper way to influence matters political is by persuasion; by rational argument and exchange of ideas in a political forum.

But public choice is not public opinion. Buchanan and Tullock dismiss arguments against economic behaviour in politics as the expression of an ancient social morality which looked down upon economic trade and upon those engaged in this activity in general. Contrary to public opinion, they claim that vote-trading expresses the true spirit of democracy and, perhaps more important, that of individualism. The argument is that vote-trading also makes it possible for minorities to exert some influence and so to alleviate the tyranny of majorities. It also opens a possibility for the intensity of preferences to matter in political decision-making, something which is impossible with the voting rule 'one man, one vote'. Vote-trading provides a solution to the problem of cyclical majorities and brings us closer to the ideal of Pareto efficiency. This is the key to Buchanan's analysis of politics-as-exchange (see Buchanan and Tullock, 1962/1965: ch. 18; Reisman, 1990: 45–53). With this key to his theory of politics-as-exchange, we also realize that it is a predominantly normative theory, to be discussed in Chapter 4. The significance of vote-trading as a real world phenomenon is little known. We know that it takes place, but not how common it is.

A somewhat better known phenomenon, akin to vote-trading, is coalition formation. For parties to enter a governing coalition, they must arrive at a common platform and a cabinet. This inevitably involves exchange of particular policies and bargaining over the allocation of cabinet portfolios among the parties in the coalition (Laver and Shepsle, 1990). The analysis of coalition formation is one of the most important contributions of public choice to the science of politics, even though the full potential of game theory and spatial analysis emerges only when the dogma of self-interest is thrown overboard (see pp. 63f.).

Widening the circle to include other actors than politicians, we probably find most exchange in the relation between public officials and interest groups. This relation is often indirect, at least in pluralist democracies such as the United States, where it is typically mediated by lobbyists (There is, of course, also direct interaction between politicians and separate business corporations). There is probably an element of exchange in this interaction: politicians supply policies 'in exchange' for campaign contributions. More specifically, it is suggested that campaign contributions give access to politicians and representation to interest groups (Wright, 1989). The main role of lobbyists is to provide specialist information to politicians (Austen-Smith, 1993: 799f.) and possibly also to members of interest groups (Ainsworth and Sened, 1993). In addition to exchange, there is probably a lot of persuasion going on, lobbyists trying to convince politicians of the righteousness and popularity of certain policies. Another element is that of representation. Officials are supposed to be responsive to the needs and demands of citizens without getting anything in return. Lobbying is one way, however imperfect, in which officials get informed about the will of the people. We might say that politicians exchange policies for popular support, but this is a metaphor, not an indication of market exchange.

Whatever exchange is involved in the interaction between officials and interest groups is usually very imperfect in terms of *quid pro quo*. There are no market (price mechanism), no clearly defined goods and services and most uncertain terms of trade. Direct exchange is most common in the case of big business, simply because the most powerful producer interests have something specific, e.g. investments, to offer in exchange for certain regulations. There are, of course, also various forms of downright economic transactions between politicians, and interests, such as bribery and blackmail, the existence of which must unfortunately be acknowledged, but not exaggerated.

In some countries in Europe the relation between interest groups, or peak associations, and the state is said to take the form of corporatism (see pp. 53–58). This relation is characterized by cooperation, or exchange for mutual advantage, in a situation when a conflictual strategy appears damaging to all. Interest groups agree to show restraint in their demands, in exchange for public status and influence.

> The type of gains the actors stand to make from political exchange are twofold: direct and indirect. The *direct* gains are those which relate to the goods embodied in the political exchange relationship: for the interest groups, preferential access to the decision-making process with an increased ability to affect market outcomes and protect their monopoly status; for the state, increased effectiveness in the implementation of its policies and greater legitimacy accorded to its actions. The *indirect* gains relate to organizational needs. In the case of interest groups, the leaders have the opportunity of expanding their own patronage, power and prestige, and of expanding membership either by developing 'selective incentives' or through realizing the direct gains of the political exchange relationship. The state, on the other hand, may benefit from the creation of 'insider groups', giving them influence over decision-making for political purposes and excluding other groups; or, it may benefit from coopting groups into decision-making procedures and giving the leaders the illusion of having influence as a means to social control.
>
> (Bull, 1992: 269)

The relation between politicians and bureaucrats involves even less of exchange.[2] What, exactly, do they exchange? Politicians have the right to decide about the budget of bureaux, but what have bureaucrats to offer politicians? According to William Niskanen (1971: 25; 1973:14), 'A bureau offers a promised set of activities and the expected output(s) of these activities for a budget.' A problem with this suggestion is that these activities and these outputs are public goods for the benefit of the citizens of the state, not just its politicians. What the politician may possibly gain from an exchange with bureaucrats is re-election (cf. Niskanen, 1971: 137; 1973: 16; 1978: 164). The gain to politicians from the activities and outputs of bureaux is indirect.

An efficient bureaucracy is a good support for elected politicians at the polls. Niskanen has analysed the relation between politicians and bureaucrats as one of bilateral monopoly. There is a single buyer (the political sponsor) and a single seller (the bureau). Niskanen models the bureau as offering the sponsoring government a package of activities and outputs and the government as a passive recipient of these goods.

Niskanen presents his theory as an alternative to the dominating sociological theory of bureaucracy and, in particular, to the theory of Max Weber (1973: 3, 13f.). He also suggests that Weber was strongly influenced by the organic concept of the state (Niskanen, 1971: 5f.). This is, of course, pure nonsense. Weber was a methodological individualist and a consistent critic of the organic theory of society (see, e.g., Weber, 1922/1978: 13–18). Indeed, Weber's theory of bureaucracy is best understood as an attack on the idealized conception of it, implicit in the organic theory of the state (Beetham, 1974/1985: 63ff.). As has been noted by Mueller (1989: 248), Weber held a theory of bureaucracy not at all unlike that of Niskanen. Because of the dependence of politicians on the superior expert knowledge of bureaucrats and because of their ability to make this knowledge secret, the latter are most powerful and may dominate the former (cf. Smith, 1988). I will quote at length from Max Weber's *Economy and Society*, because of the widespread misunderstanding of Weber's ideal type of bureaucracy as a description of reality:

> The power position of a fully developed bureaucracy is always great, under normal conditions overtowering. The political 'master' always finds himself, *vis-à-vis* the trained official, in the position of a dilettante facing the expert. This holds whether the 'master,' whom the bureaucracy serves, is the 'people' equipped with the weapons of legislative initiative, referendum, and the right to remove officials; or a parliament elected on a more aristocratic or more democratic basis and equipped with the right or the *de facto* power to vote a lack of confidence; or an aristocratic collegiate body, legally or actually based on self-recruitment; or a popularly elected president or an 'absolute' or 'constitutional' monarch.
>
> (Weber, 1922/1978: 991f.)

> This superiority of the professional insider every bureaucracy seeks further to increase through the means of *keeping secret* its knowledge and intentions. Bureaucratic administration always tends to exclude the public, to hide its knowledge and action from criticism as well as it can.
>
> (ibid., p. 992)

> In facing a parliament, the bureaucracy fights, out of a sure power instinct, every one of that institution's attempts to gain through its own means (as, e.g., through the so-called 'right of parliamentary

investigation') expert knowledge from the interested parties. Bureaucracy naturally prefers a poorly informed, and hence powerless, parliament – at least insofar as this ignorance is compatible with the bureaucracy's own interest.

(ibid., pp. 992f.)

Unlike Niskanen, however, Weber believed that a parliament, functioning as a training ground for political leadership, might curb the power of bureaucracy. This belief is the basis of Weber's theory of democracy (see pp. 138f.). Much of the critique of Niskanen's theory of bureaucracy centres on the passivity of politicians and the failure to include voters in his model (see Chapter 4, pp. 199–201). In both these respects Weber's theory of bureaucracy is superior to that of Niskanen. Weber also knew something that seems to have escaped Niskanen's attention: governmental bureaux and legislatures are not actors on a market. If their relation is that of 'bilateral monopoly', this is only because they are both parts of the state apparatus and the state is one single hierarchy. According to Weber, politics is very much a struggle for power and so is the relation between bureaucracy and elected politicians, but this does not make it a relation of exchange. It is a problematic relation of political authority (Page, 1985: ch. 8), the problem being that of controlling bureaucracies (Gruber, 1987), but still a relation of authority. Whatever exchange takes place between politicians and bureaucrats is within a relation of authority and only possible because of this relation.

I summarize Weber's theory of how to control bureaucracy (see Figure 3.2). People elect members of parliament (1), which may exert some slight control of the bureaucracy through the right of parliamentary investigation (2). Much more important is the fact that parliament may function as a training ground for political leaders (3), with the capacity of gaining more control over bureaucracy (4). In addition, political leaders may turn directly to the people for popular support (5), which may further enhance their capacity to control the bureaucracy. In some democracies, e.g. the United States, political leaders are elected directly by the people, a system which favours strong leaders with demagogic skill and the capacity not just to control, but to direct bureaucracy in a desired direction. Superior to bureaucracy in terms of expert knowledge are only economic enterprises and interest groups (6), which act as countervailing powers setting limits to bureaucratic power. Another possible control, which I have not been able to detect in Weber, would be to make bureaucratic documents public (7).

I turn, finally, to the relation between politicians (parties) and voters. This, I submit, is not a relation of exchange at all, at least not in the ordinary economic sense. The classical theory of democracy says that the relation between elected politicians and voters is one of representation. Politicians represent voters. To accept this view of the matter, however, would be to beg the question, since this is exactly the view that public choice theory rejects.

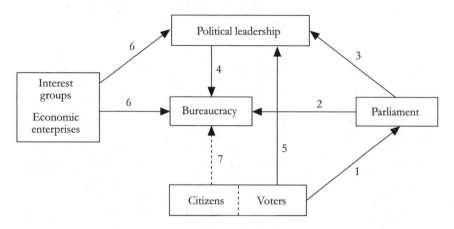

Figure 3.2 A Weberian model of the control of bureaucracy.

According to Alan Peacock (see p. 188), politicians sell policies for votes. But many votes go to parties and candidates that lose. What do you get in exchange for such a vote? Not policies anyway.[3] Also, voters do not 'buy' policies, they 'buy' programmes and promises. There is, thus, a very uncertain relation between the individual vote and eventual policies. As Brennan and Buchanan suggest (1984: 187), 'the relation between how any individual voter votes and the outcome of the election is virtually negligible'.

Suppose, however, that voters maximize their expected utility. In that case, what voters (and others) pay for policies is not just votes, but, above all, taxes. But, as public choice theorists never tire of complaining, there is no direct relation between what you pay in the form of taxes and what you get in the form of public goods and transfers. Therefore, as Anthony Downs (1960: 547–551) pointed out at an early stage, political transactions are not in the form of *quid pro quo*, as are private transactions on the market. The fact is, of course, that no transactions take place at all between voters and politicians. Taxes are extracted by means of coercive power, as public choice theorists like to point out when they wish to emphasize the difference between state and market (see, e.g., Brennan and Buchanan, 1980). Talk about 'transactions', or 'exchange', therefore, is merely metaphorical and, above all, normative. 'Ideally, the fiscal process represents a *quid pro quo* transaction between the government and all individuals collectively considered' (Buchanan, 1949: 499).

I will return to the coercive power of the state at the end of this chapter. Before that, I will continue dicussing the relation between voters and politicians, focusing attention on the most influential of all public choice theories: Anthony Downs' economic theory of democracy.

Spatial politics

The spatial theory of voting and party competition is not a theory of exchange. The important thing in this theory is exactly the spatial analogy, not any assumption of exchange. It is a rational choice theory, though, and a theory of competition. Because of this, it is an economic theory based on a certain analogy between party competition and market competition. But competition need not be 'economic' and it may be carried out by means which are not 'economic', in the sense of being within the reach of the economic approach. In the next section I will sketch a sociological theory of party competition, which has much in common with the spatial theory and which derives in part from the same source: Joseph Schumpeter's theory of democracy. In this section I will comment briefly on the limitations of the original spatial theory of mass elections and on its subsequent development.

The spatial theory of party competition, as first formulated by Anthony Downs, is probably the most significant and, therefore, probably also the most lasting contribution of public choice to political science.[4] Indeed, it is one of the most powerful theories there is in political science. Even so, this theory has some limitations which it shares with other economic theories of politics. As Downs now admits, himself: 'whole theories of political behavior have been built upon this rather narrowly focused "economic" approach. They include my own earlier *Economic Theory of Democracy*' (Downs, 1991: 144).

The main strength of the spatial theory of party competition is its wonderful simplicity and heuristic power. It stands out as one of the most illuminating ideal types in the history of the social sciences. This is due, in part, to the simplicity of the assumptions, but even more to the lucidity of the spatial image. This is not enough, however, to make it an important scientific achievement. The spatial metaphor has a long history in informal political discussion and the idea that, in a two-party system, parties tend to converge on the centre is also of commonsense origin (cf. Stokes, 1963/1966: 161; Austen-Smith, 1983). It is obvious to most observers that, in a two-party system, where each party can rely on the votes at their respective extreme, new votes are mainly to be found at the centre of the ideological continuum, if there is such a thing.[5] But to the extent that there is, we should expect a tendency to adjust party programmes to suit the median voter. Politicians in parliamentary democracies have always known this and sometimes acted accordingly. Political journalists and commentators, even a large part of the general public, have also known this to be the case long before Anthony Downs turned it into a scientific theory. The main contribution of Downs, then, was to turn a metaphor and a commonsense theory into a formalized social scientific theory, based on explicitly stated assumptions and yielding a number of testable hypotheses. An additional advantage of the spatial theory is that it has become increasingly formalized. Since, in a formalized theory, assumptions are usually made explicit, and when implicit are easy to detect, a formalized theory is usually easier to criticize.

The weakness of simple theories is, exactly, that they are simple. In the social sciences simplicity always means simplification and, consequently, lack of realism and limitation of scope. The spatial theory of mass elections, for instance, is largely limited in its application to two-party systems, with simple majority rule (see Ordeshook, 1976: 304–306). 'Thus we witness a trade-off, with economics opting for theoretical and deductive rigour within the context of a narrowly but well defined set of issues while political science chooses descriptive accuracy within a broadly but poorly defined context' (ibid., p. 307). Ordeshook's statement is made with special reference to the spatial theory of elections.

In an early critique of this theory, Donald E. Stokes (1963/1966) discussed four critical assumptions, turning Anthony Downs' spatial model into a special case of a more complex prospective theory covering variable conditions. The first assumption, or 'axiom', is that of *unidimensionality*. This assumption is clearly not realistic, since political issues fall along several dimensions. This is not a serious limitation, since, as Stokes notices (ibid., p. 168), the spatial model may be easily extended to cover multiple dimensions. A second axiom is that of *fixed structure*. Unlike dimensions and positions in physical space, however, those in political space are subject to rapid change, as different issues come on the agenda. A third assumption is the axiom of *ordered dimensions*. But not all issues can be meaningfully assumed to be dimensional at all. Stokes makes the distinction between 'position issues' and 'valence issues' (ibid., p. 170). Only position issues are ordered along a dimension. Valence issues are issues that voters value either positively or negatively but do not position in space. Typical examples are competence and integrity, or incompetence and corruption, on the part of administrations. The spatial model of party competition does not apply to valence issues. The fourth axiom is called *common reference*. It is the assumption that all parties and all voters organize their subjective political space in the same way; that there is one intersubjective political space, common to all parties and voters. This is not the case. As Stokes points out, there is abundant evidence against each of these assumptions, or axioms. One way out is to turn them into the extremes of variables, which may be subjected to empirical investigation (ibid., pp. 176–179). As we shall see, part of Stokes' programme has been realized in the later development of the spatial theory of party competition. It has become multidimensional, and has incorporated agenda setting and the personality of candidates as elements in the theory, thus becoming less spatial and less economic.[6]

According to Peter C. Ordeshook (1976: 285), the above critique gave rise to 'a concerted effort to advance spatial theory along the lines suggested by Stokes and to render Downs's conceptualization more deductive and mathematically rigorous'. The latter development is the most conspicuous, but has turned out to be a somewhat mixed blessing. Every step in the direction of complexity and mathematical sophistication is also a step away from simplicity and lucidity. A further consequence of this is that the spatial theory of elections has become a concern mainly for a minority of political scientists, able to master the requisite mathematics, while remaining inaccessible to the rest. While unfortunate, this is certainly not an argument against the use of sophisticated mathematics, if only it increases our understanding of voting and party competition – and I have no doubt that it has. But there is still a feeling that the growth of knowledge lags somewhat behind the growth of technique. This feeling is widespread and well captured by the following statement by Kaare Strom (1990: 565):

> Since Downs (1957), rational choice theories have come to play an increasingly important role in the study of competitive political parties. Efforts to develop such models of political parties have been of tremendous benefit to political science. Theories based on simple assumptions of party and voter objectives have generated influential (though often controversial) results. But even though rational choice models of political parties have been both powerful and suggestive, they have failed to generate any single coherent theory of competitive party behavior or to produce robust results that apply under a variety of environmental conditions. There is little theory to help us choose between existing models, and where their assumptions fail, we are often left in the dark.

The feeling of being left in the dark is not confined to unbelievers. It is rather the case that we all walk in darkness and have not yet seen the great light. The overriding problem with spatial theory, as with the economic theory of politics, in general, is the difficulty of finding determinate outcomes, or equilibiria (Ordeshook, 1976: 292–298; Ordeshook and Shepsle, 1982; Austen-Smith, 1983).[7] In the absence of theoretical determinacy, it is also difficult to predict what will be the electoral outcome of rational individual choice. In spatial theory, as in game theory, the absence of solutions is also lack of empirical content and predictive power.[8] But it is not the only source of low empirical content. Another source is the lack of realism on the part of the basic assumptions. The recent history of spatial theory has been dominated by two major concerns: (1) how to solve the problem of indeterminacy and (2) how to incur more realism in spatial models. Both concerns are motivated by a desire to increase predictability of outcomes.

One reason why the spatial theory of mass elections has little predictive power is its dependence upon a totally unrealistic assumption of 'full' information. In reality candidates are badly informed about voters' policy preferences – what they know is based upon public opinion polls – and they have no chance of getting to know how people will vote and/or if they will vote. Candidates' choice of policy is a choice under uncertainty, as is the choice of voters. A massive body of evidence shows that most (American) voters are ignorant about politics; about candidates, parties, programmes, ideologies and issues (see pp. 140–142). Anthony Downs is aware of this evidence and assumes only a limited amount of information, on the part of voters, in his own theory of democracy.[9] But the problem remains: does not the spatial theory of voting imply more information than Downs is warranted to assume on the basis of existing evidence? If so, there is no reason to expect any convergence towards the centre of the ideological spectrum. Richard D. McKelvey and Peter C. Ordeshook (1990b) address this issue in a series of experiments, but do not arrive at a clear answer. They do find a weak tendency to convergence even with very limited knowledge, but warn against hasty inferences to real world events.

But tendencies usually make their way in the midst of countervailing forces, and the tendency to ideological convergence is no exception. There is always the risk that voters and members at the extreme will be disappointed. The result may be a new party. If ideology defeats vote-maximization, that is; and sometimes it does. As Dunleavy (1991: 143) points out, 'leaders in democratic parties often confront troublesome choices about maximizing their internal popularity with activists or their external appeal to voters'. (See also Robertson, 1976; Budge and Farlie, 1977.) For a modified spatial model, see Figure 3.3. It may be added, in this connection, that evidence suggests that voters at the extremes of the ideological spectrum are better informed about politics, more certain about how to vote and more likely to vote (Palfrey and Poole, 1987). Contrary to Downs' prediction, new parties may also occur at the centre of the ideological spectrum. This is the case in Great Britain, where we have recently witnessed the re-emergence of a Liberal party in between the Tory and Labour parties (see Heath, 1987).

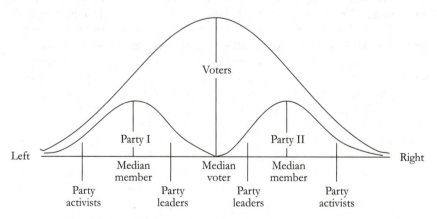

Figure 3.3 One-dimensional spatial politics in a two-party system

In case there should be a suspicion that I paint an overly negative picture of spatial theory, I would like to point out that leading representatives of this theory are also very much conscious of its problems and limitations. Ordeshook, for instance, concludes his review essay with the following statement:

> We have ... sought to outline how spatial theory might be modified to accommodate certain aspects of reality without abandoning its basic perspective. We find, nevertheless, that the theory possesses several major inadequacies as constituted at present. The first is its reliance on the concept of pure strategy equilibria for a definition of a solution to the election game. The second is its failure to consider election systems other than simple majority rule. Its third major inadequacy concerns the development of an adequate conceptualization of attitudes and preference and an appropriate statistical methodology. We agree, moreover, with those critics who argue that spatial analysis provides a poor *model* of election processes; but we disagree strongly with the assertion that it constitutes an inadequate *theory* of those processes.
>
> (Ordeshook, 1976: 309f.)

Ordeshook also comments on the limits and possibilities of game theory and rational choice in general. His tone is optimistic, since he believes 'that the rational choice paradigm, of which spatial analysis is a part, is sufficiently flexible to accommodate a great variety of alternative models of cognition and learning' (ibid., p. 310). The question, however, is how much it can accommodate 'without abandoning its basic perspective'. The tendency in the spatial theory of mass elections, I suggest, has been to introduce elements that are neither spatial nor economic.[10]

Enelow and Hinich (1984), for instance, introduce non-policy issues in their model of mass elections. Special importance is assigned to the personality of the candidate. It is assumed that voters prefer candidates with qualities such as integrity, ability, compassion, intelligence, etc. This is a perfectly reasonable assumption, the importance of which increases as a monotonic function of the mediatization of politics (see, e.g., Rosenberg *et al.*, 1986). It is only that the personal qualities of candidates have no location in policy space. Can they be fitted into an economic approach to politics? I believe the answer has to be: No! We may conceive of the personality of candidates as a matter of trust. This is in parallel to exchange on the market. Just as parties to market transactions must be able to trust one another, voters must be able to trust politicians. This is clearly in the rational self-interest of voters (cf. Popkin *et al.* 1976: 792–795, 799–805). The problem with an economic interpretation is that voters are supposed to value moral qualities, such as integrity and compassion, in candidates, whereas public choice tells us that they posses no such qualities. Either public choice is wrong, or the voters are wrong. But if voters are wrong to believe that candidates have moral qualities, then they are not as rational as the economic approach assumes that they are. It is, of course, possible to evade this dilemma by denying that the economic approach presupposes rational belief, but it is still not very convincing to operate with a model which assumes that the electorate is the victim of an illusion.

One of the most significant tendencies in recent spatial analysis has been institutionalism, especially in conjunction with agenda setting. This important development is found almost exclusively in the theory of committees, which I have decided not to discuss. One exception is William H. Riker, who brings the idea of agenda control to bear on the spatial analysis of mass elections. In his version, agenda control appears as one form of *heresthetic*, or the art of manipulating conditions of choice (Riker, 1986; 1990a: 47–54). Other forms of heresthetic are strategic voting and manipulation of dimensions, or redefinition of the situation. In addition to heresthetic, which influences outcomes by modifying the space, there is *rhetoric* which works upon voters' preferences.[11] Rhetoric, as a means of changing voters' preferences, lies definitely outside the scope of economic theory. It is a bit surprising, therefore, to read Riker's spirited defence of rational choice theory (Riker, 1990b). Neither heresthetic nor rhetoric is easily assimilated by a theory of rational choice. Heresthetic maybe,[12] but rhetoric hardly. Riker seems to be of another opinion:

> In order to understand rhetoric and persuasion in terms of the spatial model, it is necessary to have a spatial model in which acts of persuasion make sense. It is unfortunate that the spatial model as usually presented does not allow for voters' position to change and thus preclude persuasion.
>
> (Riker, 1990b: 56)

Unfortunate or not, it is a limitation of the spatial model, as of all economic models. A 'rational choice' theory enriched by heresthetic and rhetoric, therefore, is no longer an 'economic' theory, in the usual sense of this term (see Dunleavy, 1991: 98ff.; Keech, 1991: 607). While it is possible to explain why people use persuasion as a means to achieve their ends in terms of rational choice, it is not possible to understand persuasion itself – how it works – with this theory. A theory of persuasion, therefore, is necessarily auxiliary to economics as a theory of rational choice.

In the recent critique of spatial analysis, the assumption of fixed preferences has been a major target (Dunleavy, 1991: 90–110; Simmons, 1993: 35). Patrick Dunleavy, in particular, has argued that parties use *preference-shaping strategies* in addition to the *preference-accommodating strategy*, assumed by public choice theories. Two critics (Rabinowitz and Macdonald, 1989) of traditional spatial theory argue that it is seriously flawed as an empirical theory of voting, and suggest an alternative 'directional theory of issue voting' based upon the sociological idea of symbolic politics.

PERSUASION

Standard economic theory assumes certain things as given to analysis. These things include technology, institutions, preferences and, I would like to add, beliefs. My present concern is preferences and beliefs. Now this is, of course, a serious limitation to economic theory, since we wish to know how people come to acquire their preferences and beliefs and why they differ between individuals and cultures. Despite some attempts to explain preferences endogenously, it has been the concern of the other social sciences to explain the formation of preferences and beliefs. Now this is not exactly news. It is precisely what Gordon Tullock suggests in his article 'Economic Imperialism':

> Economists in general have been relatively little interested in the preferences that individuals have. They assume the preferences and then deduce what the outcome is but do not pay much attention to investigation of these preferences. Traditionally, an economist will tell you that this is a problem for the psychologist rather than the economist. In practice, however, it is not only the problem of the psychologist, it has to a very large extent been the problem of the sociologist and of the behavioralist political scientist. A great deal of the research of the sociologists, behavioralists, and political scientists concerns the type of person who is apt to be involved in some particular activity. This can be thought of as an effort to determine which people have certain sets of tastes and preferences.
>
> (Tullock, 1972: 323)

Tullock not only registers a traditional division of labour between the different social sciences, he goes on to argue that it is a proper and desirable division. '(M)y proposal for the future organization of social sciences is that they be divided into two grand domains, the sciences of choice and the sciences of preferences' (ibid., p. 324). I do not accept this division, at least not as stated by Tullock. As I have already indicated, preferences must be supplemented by beliefs. More importantly, norms cannot be reduced to 'preferences', as conceived by a theory of rational choice. What matter here, however, are preferences and beliefs.

But what is the point of arguing something that public choice theorists already know and admit? First, because I am not certain that all public choice theorists are aware of the implications of this limitation for public choice as a theory of politics. Second, because I do not believe that many social scientists, who are not economists, know that this is a limitation of economic theory. Third, because the assumption of fixed preferences has not been given as much attention as those of rationality and self-interest, neither by public choice theorists, nor by others.

One exception to the rule that economists assume fixed preferences is the dissenting voice of Albert Hirschman. While sometimes seen as a contributor to public choice (see, e.g., Mueller, 1979: 125), Hirschman is critical of its scientific imperialism (Hirschman, 1970: 19f.; 1981: 267ff., 298ff.) and his view of politics is fundamentally different. Public choice delimits the political domain to the provision of public goods. Others suggest the more inclusive category of collective action (Taylor, 1987: 20). As opposed to both these views, Hirschman derives his view of politics from his now famous distinction between *exit* and *voice*. As different ways of influencing the behaviour of an organization, exit belongs to the economic and voice to the political realm.

> The customer who, dissatisfied with the product of one firm, shifts to that of another, uses the market to defend his welfare or to improve his position; and he also sets in motion market forces which may induce recovery on the part of the firm that has declined in comparative performance. This is the sort of mechanism economics thrives on. It is neat – one either exits or one does not; it is impersonal – any face-to-face confrontation between customer and firm with its imponderable and unpredictable elements is avoided and success and failure of the organization are communicated to it by a set of statistics; and it is indirect – any recovery on the part of the declining firm comes by courtesy of the Invisible Hand, as an unintended by-product of the customer's decision to shift. In all these respects, voice is just the opposite of exit. It is a far more 'messy' concept because it can be graduated, all the way from faint grumbling to violent protest; it implies articulation of one's critical opinions rather than a private, 'secret' vote in the anonymity of a supermarket; and finally, it is direct and straightforward rather than roundabout. Voice is political action par excellence.
>
> (Hirschman, 1970: 15ff.)

I agree that voice is political action *par excellence*, but it is not the only type of political action. In the next section I will discuss the exercise of power, which is also political action, but something else. Nevertheless, Hirschman points to something important, and even though he does not address the issue of preferences at this point, the implication is clear: one, obvious, aim of raising one's voice is to change the preferences and beliefs of those in authority.

In a later work, *Shifting Involvements* (1982), Hirschman takes explicit issue with the economists' habit of working with fixed preferences (1982/1985: 5, 9ff.). His specific purpose, in this book, is to argue that there is a recurrent shift, or cycle, between the pursuit of private and public interest. Periods of withdrawal from public life and an exclusive concern with private happiness are followed by outbursts of collective action aimed at the transformation of society, or parts of it. The key to an understanding of preference change is disappointment, both with consumer goods and with political action. A serious deficit with the standard economic analysis of political activity, according to Hirschman (ibid. p. 85), is the failure to understand that such activities 'carry their own reward'. Participation in collective action is not in all circumstances a cost. In many cases people receive a benefit, not only from the results of such activity, but from the activity itself (see also Hirschman, 1981: 290–293 and 1985: 11–15). *Activism* might be a value, or 'good'. This is, no doubt, an important insight, but it is not a serious problem for rational choice theory. There is no obstacle to including benefits from participation in individuals' utility functions and many public choice theorists have done so (see Chapter 5).

Still later (1984: 89f.; 1985: 8–11), Hirschman makes the distinction between two kinds of preference change: (1) the usually unreflective change in tastes and (2) the reflective change in values. Behind this distinction is a theory of tastes and values as two types of preference related to each other as first-order preferences and second-order metapreferences. In addition to our preferences for consumer goods and services, we have metapreferences for our preferences. We reflect upon our first-order preferences and change them in accordance with the kind of person we want to be and with our values.[13]

The argument of this section is that public choice, by assuming preferences and beliefs as given to analysis, leaves out much of what is usually conceived to be essential to political life. I have already suggested that authority is important to political life. With Lindblom (1977: ch. 9), we may conceive of politics as 'The Struggle over Authority': how to get there and how to stay there. And for those who are not in positions of authority: how to control those who are. The way to achieve these things includes persuasion as an important part. The aim of persuasion, obviously, is to change people's preferences and beliefs. Much of political activity, therefore, lies outside the scope of public choice. But it definitely belongs to the traditional domain of sociology. In his *Sociologists, Economists and Democracy*, Brian Barry writes (1970/1978: 6), 'In place of rational maximisers with set goals, the sociological approach can allow for the development and change of motives, which themselves can be treated in a more complex way than simply as "goals".' 'Sociologists', for Barry, means Parsons, but we might broaden the concept and find that most of sociology's contribution to political science concerns the 'explanation' of preferences and beliefs.

Orthodox sociology explains behaviour in terms of values, norms and beliefs. To the extent that these are common and learned, they make up what is meant by the term 'culture'. But sociology (and social psychology) has also been much interested in how values, norms and beliefs are inculcated in new members of society. The process by which this takes place is called 'socialization'. Socialization is often thought of as completed at the entrance into adulthood, but clearly learning continues. It may be useful, therefore, to distinguish between 'primary' socialization, ending with adolescence, and 'secondary' socialization, ending with death. Applying this frame of reference to politics gives us the notion of 'political socialization' for the process by which individuals acquire their political values and beliefs and the term 'political culture' for the stock of shared political values, norms and beliefs in a society. The study of political socialization has been concentrated on two questions: (1) children's knowledge of and emotional attachment to political symbols and institutions, and (2) the early development of partisan attitudes and party identifications. The first question has to do with political system and the second with political regime. Children's attachment to their political institutions is turned into citizens' support. Its strength and stability is pivotal for the legitimacy of the political system. It was a common presumption that children develop their partisan attitudes and party identifications early in life and stick to them for the rest of their lives. Research in this area indicates that the stability of partisan attitudes and party identifications has been somewhat overrated, at least in the United States, but that it is still a highly significant fact of political life (Sears, 1975).

Among the most elusive concepts of political discourse is that of 'public opinion' (Bennet, 1980; Kinder and Sears, 1985). Though made up of the same stuff as political culture and partisan ideology, values and beliefs, it seems to occupy a place somewhere in between the two. It is more shifting and issue-specific than political culture and less divisive than partisan ideology. One reason for its contestability is probably its normative implications as part of liberal ideology. For critics of democracy, 'public opinion' is a derogatory label, designating uninformed popular prejudice. For believers in popular sovereignty, public opinion is, if not in fact at least potentially, the enlightened result of rational public debate. On both views, public opinion is the result of persuasion and outside the scope of an economic theory of politics.

Sociologists, on the other hand, have always taken an interest in the phenomenon called 'public opinion'. Among the first to do so was the French sociologist Gabriel Tarde, who made the distinction between a 'public' and a 'crowd'. While the latter is characterized by co-presence, the former may be physically dispersed and united only mentally. 'Opinion, as we define it, is a momentary, more or less logical cluster of judgements which, responding to current problems, is reproduced many times over in people of the same country, at the same time, in the same society' (Tarde [1898] 1969: 300). The historic precondition of a public and of public opinion was printing and the press. For Tarde, who was an elitist, public opinion was the opinion of the mass and, therefore, not to be relied upon.

Another early sociologist, who wrote about public opinion, was Ferdinand Toennies. For Toennies, who was an egalitarian, public opinion was in actual fact the opinion of an educated elite against the great mass of the people and, therefore, not democratic enough. Toennies also makes a distinction between 'popular sentiment' and 'public opinion'. In language borrowed from Adam Smith, he writes of public opinion as a spectator and judge:

Public opinion manifests its societal and political power by means of its approval and disapproval of political events, by demanding that the government take a certain position and abolish certain abuses, by insisting on reforms and legislative measures, in brief, by 'taking a stand' on certain questions of public policy, after the manner of a spectator or judge. Public opinion as power is thought of as a court of appeal, placed over and above popular sentiment and separated from it; public opinion may be dependent on popular sentiment, but is essentially an intellectual force.

(Toennies, [1923] 1971: 253f.)

Like Smith, Toennies is much concerned that public opinion might not be an *impartial* spectator and, also like Smith, he sees the main threat to impartial government in the power of business interest. For Toennies, this threat is the more serious as the press becomes part of business. As this happens, the press changes from being a medium, or forum, for the creation of public opinion, into an instrument for its manufacture in the interest of capital.

The year before Toennies' short piece on public opinion, the American political journalist Walter Lippman (1922) had published his well-known treatise on this subject. Influenced by Freud and by the sociological elite theorist Gustave Le Bon (see Chapter 6), Lippmann pointed to the fallibility and suggestibility of public opinion. With the help of symbols, leaders have an almost unlimited capacity to fabricate the consent they need from their following. The press, unfortunately, is no testifier of truth. Lippmann was led, by his analysis of public opinion, to take a rather disillusioned attitude to democracy. In the end, his hopes were pinned on the independent expert, who may provide the basis for a Socratic dialogue. But the people is no sovereign. It should interfere as little as possible in the affairs of government.

Among political scientists, the pioneer in this field was Harold Lasswell, who made political propaganda his main topic of investigation (Horwitz, 1961). Lasswell shared Lippman's view of the power and ubiquity of propaganda in modern society (Lasswell [1939] 1947: chs 2, 4). He defined it as 'the management of collective attitudes by the manipulation of significant symbols' (1927: 627). Lasswell was the first political theorist to draw serious attention to the use of symbols in politics (Lasswell, 1936/1958: ch. 2) and may, therefore, be considered the founder of the theory of symbolic politics (Merelman, 1981: 477–483, 496).

The possibility of managing collective attitudes by means of propaganda was soon to be demonstrated with fatal consequences by a number of emerging dictatorships, most clearly German Nazism.[14] Even so, Lasswell remained favourable to the use of political propaganda. The reason is that propaganda is not just a weapon in the hands of elites and dictators, but part of democracy (Lasswell [1942] 1947: ch. I:IV; [1943] 1947: ch. I:III).

When we reach the heyday of political sociology, opinions and attitudes become its major concerns. Whether this is due to their importance or to their susceptibility to investigation by survey methods, I don't know. Anyway, opinions and attitudes are legitimate topics of investigation and the early studies in this field started an avalanche of research, which today constitutes a vigorous branch of social science: mass communication, mass media and information.

I will not go into the huge field of mass communication and mass media. To do so would lead too far. There is one contribution, however, which it is hard not to mention: the early research, by Paul Lazarsfeld and his colleagues (Lazarsfeld *et al.*, 1944/1948: 40–51, 150–158; Berelson *et al.*, 1954/1956: chs 6 and 11; Katz and Lazarsfeld, 1955: 31ff., 309–320), on the effects of mass media and personal influence on the vote decision in political campaigns. Lazarsfeld *et al.* found that the effects of mass media on most citizens are indirect. Between the media and the atomized mass there are social interaction and social groups to which individuals belong, and in social groups there are informal 'opinion leaders'. These opinion leaders are more exposed to mass media than the average citizen and, therefore, better informed about candidates, programmes and issues. Information about politics is mediated twice: by mass media and by opinion leaders, before it reaches the majority of citizens. There is a 'two-step flow of communication'.[15]

Another finding of Lazarsfeld *et al.* was that the overall effect of mass media was less than expected by the theorists of mass society. People are not entirely atomized. They still belong to social groups and receive most of their opinions and beliefs from the other members of these groups. Even so, I take it that few would object to the following conclusion: *considering the role of mass media in modern society and, especially, in politics, a theory of mass media is an indispensable part of a theory of politics. Lacking a theory of mass media, therefore, is a serious lacuna in the economic theory of politics.* The model of the political market in Figure 3.4 is an illustration of this lacuna. An adequate model of the forces that shape policy must include the mass media as an autonomous influence.

In his important *The Structural Transformation of the Public Sphere* (1962/ 1989), Jürgen Habermas offers a historical-sociological critique of public opinion. As a social reality, public opinion, rightly understood, is wholly dependent upon the existence of a public sphere. Both phenomena belong to bourgeois society and are intimately connected with the rise of the press. As ideals, public opinion and the public sphere are children of the Enlightenment and of liberalism. The main thesis of Habermas' work is that bourgeois society has developed in a way that resulted in the destruction of the public sphere and the concomitant perversion of public opinion. In the absence of a public sphere, functioning as a breeding ground for true public opinion, it degenerates into mass opinion – an object of manipulation for those who control the mass media. The social psychological concept of 'public opinion' employed in behaviouralist political science and political sociology reflects this decay of public opinion.

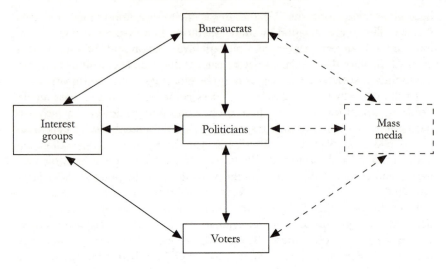

Figure 3.4 Mass media – a missing element in public choice

Like the economic theory of politics, Habermas maintains that party competition in liberal democracies has become increasingly like competition between firms on the market.

> Consequently the parties and their auxiliary organizations see themselves forced to influence voting decisions publicistically in a fashion that has its analogue in the way advertising pressure bears on buying decisions. There emerges the industry of political marketing. Party agitators and old style propagandists give way to advertising experts neutral in respect to party politics and employed to sell politics in an unpolitical way.
>
> (Habermas, 1962/1989: 216)

It is significant, however, that Habermas concentrates on advertising, the element of persuasion which is exogenous to economic theory. Habermas' conception of party competition as market competition does not derive from an economic theory of politics; it is part of a sociological theory of symbolic politics. According to Habermas, party competition becomes 'stylized into a show. Publicity loses its critical function in favor of a staged display; even arguments are transmuted into symbols to which again one cannot respond by arguing but only by identifying with them' (Habermas, 1962/1989: 206).

> Hence the presentation of the leader or the leader's team plays a central role; they too need to be packaged and displayed in a way that makes them marketable. The popularity index is a government's measure of how much it has the nonpublic opinion of the population under its

136

control or of how much publicity that can be translated into popularity its team of leaders must additionally obtain.

(ibid., p. 218)

Symbolic politics

The predominant sociological theory of mass elections is not altogether antithetical to spatial theory. In fact, these theories have much in common and differ only in a few, but crucial, respects. The similarity between the two theories is underscored by the fact that one man is counted as an important link in the development of both theories: the economist Joseph Schumpeter (cf. Pizzorno, 1985: 43f.; 1990: 297f.). For public choice theorists, Joseph Schumpeter is the first link in the development of the economic theory of democracy. For sociologists, he is but one link, however important, in the evolution of the sociological theory of democracy. Both views are correct, but in this section I am going to explore only the sociological version.

In his more realistic alternative to the classical theory of democracy, Schumpeter suggested that it consists in the competitive struggle for votes and, ultimately, for leadership, that is power. The role of the electorate is not to govern, as in the ideal of popular sovereignty, but to produce a government. Because of the importance he attaches to effective leadership, Schumpeter assigns to parliament a less prominent role than is usual in theories of democracy.

Schumpeter makes the analogy with competition in the economic sphere, and he does suggest that candidates and parties compete for office and power. This lends credibility to the public choice interpretation of Schumpeter's theory of democracy. But other elements of his theory points in another direction. First of all, Schumpeter's critique of the assumption of rationality in utilitarianism hits the spatial theory of mass elections too:

In particular, we still remain under the practical necessity of attributing to the will of the *individual* an independence and a rational quality that are altogether unrealistic. If we are to argue that the will of the citizen *per se* is a political factor entitled to respect, it must first exist. That is to say, it must be something more than an indeterminate bundle of vague impulses loosely playing about given slogans and mistaken impressions. Everyone would have to know definitely what he wants to stand for.

(Schumpeter, 1942/1954: 253)

Compare this view of the citizen with Ordeshook's (1976: 286) list of assumptions made about them in spatial theory:

(1) they employ a common set of criteria for evaluating election candidates;

(2) while their preferences may differ, the admissible range of alternative preferences on a criterion can be represented by a segment of the real line;

(3) citizens' preferences over this range are well defined.

Second, and more important, the main element in Schumpeter's market analogy is advertising. On this subject, he observes, economists have much to learn that they can't find in economic textbooks (Schumpeter, 1942/1954: 257, 263). The reason, as I have already pointed out, is that orthodox economics assumes fixed preferences. But Schumpeter does not. On the contrary, professional politicians compete, not with policies, but by means of persuasion.

> Human nature in politics being what it is, they are able to fashion and, within very wide limits, even to create the will of the people. What we are confronted with in the analysis of political processes is largely not a genuine but a manufactured will.
>
> (Schumpeter, 1942/1954: 263)

This is in contrast to Anthony Downs (1957: 47), who assumes 'that citizens' political tastes are fixed'. And yet public choice theorists are in the habit of refering to the 'Schumpeter–Downs' theory of democracy, as if it were one. For sociologists it is equally natural to see Schumpeter's theory as part of political sociology and especially as an elaboration of Max Weber's theory of democracy (Lipset, 1959/1963: 41; Held, 1987: ch. 5). Habermas, for instance, mentions 'the theory developed by Weber, extended by Schumpeter, and now unquestioned by modern political sociology' (Habermas, 1969/1971: 68) and also sees it as an example of 'democratic elite theories' (Habermas, 1973/1975: 37). There is much to support this view.

Schumpeter, himself, mentions Freud, Le Bon and Pareto as sources of inspiration (Schumpeter, 1942/1954: 256).[16] But why is there no mention of Max Weber, if Weber is indeed a main source of Schumpeter's theory of democracy? One possible reason is that Weber was German and, because of the war, everything German was unpopular in the United States at the time when Schumpeter published *Capitalism, Socialism and Democracy* (1942/1954). There is little doubt that Schumpeter knew Weber's theory of democracy[17] and there is no doubt at all that it exhibits striking similarities to his own theory (Parry, 1969: 145; Beetham, 1974/1985: 111).

Weber, we have seen (pp. 121–123), was worried that political power in modern society would fall into the hands of bureaucrats, who were without the calling and the capacity for leadership. In this situation, Weber saw a strong parliament as one possible countervailing power. Parliament could work as a training ground, from which political leaders might be recruited. A second countervailing power would be the mass of citizens supporting a 'plebiscitary' leader with demagogic skill and a party to back him/her up. Political leaders are likened to entrepreneurs, competing for the popular vote by means of demagogy. Democracy, for Weber, was not a matter of popular sovereignty, but a technique for the selection of political leaders. It is good to the extent that it allows the most capable leaders to assume power. It is bad to the extent that the emotional element will predominate in politics.[18]

In the latter half of this century, much political sociology has converged on a theory of politics as symbolic action. Such diverse figures as David O. Sears (see p. 85) and Alessandro Pizzorno (1985: 50–54; 1990: 307–312) pay allegiance to some version of this theory. Most closely associated with the idea of symbolic politics, however, is Murray Edelman, who gave this theory its name (1964, 1971).[19]

The programme of Edelman's first book, *The Symbolic Uses of Politics* (1964), was to reveal 'the mechanisms through which politics influences what they [people] want, what they fear, what they regard as possible, and even who they are' (ibid., p. 20). This programme is radically different from rational choice. Influencing what people want, is changing their first-order preferences. Influencing what is possible, is altering their perceived opportunity set. Influencing who they are, is changing their second-order, or metapreferences (see p. 132).

Edelman conceives of mass politics – as distinguished from interest group politics – as similar to a spectator sport, with strong elements of nonrational symbolic forms, such as myths and rites, used as means of political persuasion. Political action is instrumental and rational, no doubt, but it is also symbolic and expressive. The symbolic use of political language is evocative, rather than descriptive, or referential; it is intended to evoke emotions, rather than to inform about matters of fact. In addition to referential symbols, politics uses *condensation symbols* to 'evoke the emotions associated with the situation. They condense into one symbolic event, sign, or act of patriotic pride, anxieties, remembrances of past glories or humiliations, promises of future greatness' (Edelman, 1964: 6).

> The basic thesis is that mass publics respond to currently conspicuous political symbols: not to 'facts,' and not to moral codes embedded in the character or soul, but to the gestures and speeches that make up the drama of the state.
>
> (ibid., p. 172)

The mass public knows little about political issues and it doesn't really care. 'It ignores these things until political actions and speeches make them symbolically threatening or reassuring, and it then responds to the cues furnished by the actions and the speeches, not to direct knowledge of the facts' (Edelman, 1964: 172). Edelman's conclusion is similar to Schumpeter's, but different from that of Downs: 'It is therefore political actions that chiefly shape men's political wants and "knowledge," not the other way around' (ibid., p. 72).

The rationally ignorant voter

Public choice is a branch of rational choice, and a most vigorous branch at that. Its *most* vigorous branch, microeconomics, originally operated on the assumption of perfect information. In its later development, economics has relaxed this assumption in some contexts, which are characterized by risk or uncertainty. Rationality then becomes the maximization of *expected* utility. In his general model of rational choice, Jon Elster (1986a: 12ff.) now includes the assumption of rational belief, to supplement the assumption of rational action, or as part of it. The minimum requirement is that beliefs are internally consistent. In addition, rational action involves three optimizing operations: 'finding the best action, for given beliefs and desires; forming the best-grounded belief, for given evidence; and collecting the right amount of evidence, for given desires and prior beliefs' (Elster, 1991a: 117). Is political man rational, in this sense? I will consider the case of the voter.

Schumpeter depicts the voter as predominantly non-rational, irrational and irresponsible; acting from prejudice and impulse, and easily swayed by propaganda to follow the will of a charismatic leader (Schumpeter, 1942/1954: 256–264). As we have seen, Schumpeter borrowed this image of the citizen from sociological elite theorists.[20] Schumpeter's theory of democracy is advanced in explicit opposition to the 'classical doctrine' handed down to us from the Enlightenment. According to this theory, democracy is popular sovereignty and politicians are the representatives of the people.

This picture of the voter was largely corroborated in the behaviouralist revolution, when sociologists and political scientists began asking people questions about politics. To their dismay, they found that the typical voter is not the ideal citizen of classical democratic theory, but largely ignorant about matters political. A majority of voters have little knowledge about policy issues, lack a coherent ideology and are unable to distinguish between party programmes (Berelson *et al.*. 1954/1956: ch. 14; Campbell *et al.*, 1960: chs 8–10; Converse, 1964).

This image of the ignorant voter has not been unchallenged, however. The political scientist V.O. Key made a passionate attempt to rehabilitate the voter in *The Responsible Electorate* (1966). It seems to me, though, that he achieves this mainly by expecting less from the typical voter. 'From our analyses the voter emerges as a person who appraises the actions of government, who has policy preferences, and who relates his vote to those appraisals and preferences' (Key, 1966: 58f.). 'The only really effective weapon of popular control in a democratic regime is the capacity of the electorate to throw a party from power' (ibid., p. 76), or, in more colourful language, to 'throw the rascals out'. This is the view of democracy defended by Schumpeter (1942/1954: 269ff.) and Popper (1945/1966, vol. 1: 120ff., vol. 2: 127ff., 160ff.; 1962/1968: 344f., 350f.). It is a normative theory, aiming at realism, and it has the support of 'a positive theory of negative voting' (Fiorina and Shepsle, 1990), but it is a far cry from the classical theory of democracy.

Classical democratic theory presumed that the voter is rationally and responsibly oriented towards the future; that voting is *prospective*. Sociological voting studies demolished this presumption. Public choice agreed, but redefined ignorance as rational, from the point of view of the individual. V.O. Key (1966: 61f., 76) went further and argued that the electorate is largely responsible despite appearances to the contrary. Voters may not know a great deal about issues, ideologies and party programmes, but they know something about the performance of the incumbent government from their own experience (cf. Popkin *et al.*, 1976: 788). Voters' responsibility now lies in their *retrospective* appraisal of the past achievements of the party and/or candidate in power.[21]

The most thorough analysis of retrospective voting, to date, is by Morris P. Fiorina (1981). Without denying the existence of a prospective element in most voting, he argues that retrospective evaluation is fundamental for voters' choice of party or candidate. Like Key, Fiorina paints the electorate in rosy colours. It is rational and responsible enough to make politicians accountable for their actions.[22] The problem is with irresponsible politicians, a dissolving party system and, ultimately, with the political system generating this state of affairs (Fiorina, 1981: ch. 10). I find little to disagree with in Fiorina's model of retrospective voting. Voting appears as 'a function of future expectations, recent experiences and performance evaluations, and more distant experiences and judgements encapsulated in party identification' (ibid., pp. 155f.). This specification seems to exhaust the possible relevance of time. Admittedly, there is an asymmetry of information: we know something about the past, but nothing about the future, except what we can infer from past performance and from campaign promises. In this, chronological, sense, retrospection is necessarily prior to prospection. But this does not imply that people use only current, or even recent, experiences of economic conditions as a basis for their beliefs about the future. Recent research indicates that partisanship and beliefs about the competence of responsible politicians are important (see, e.g., Conover *et al.*, 1987: 565ff.; Lewis-Beck, 1988a; 1988b: ch. 8).

Despite occasional attempts to restore the voter's reputation, however, the less flattering picture dominates the scene (see, e.g., Ferejohn and Kuklinski, 1990). The American voter, at least, is ignorant about politics. What is the implication for rational choice?

Anthony Downs accepted the view of the citizen emerging from empirical research, but added the special twist that it is rational to be ignorant about politics. Considering the information costs involved in getting informed about politics, there is no reason to expect the average citizen ever to become the ideal citizen. According to Samuel Popkin (1991: 13), this is the central insight in Anthony Downs' *An Economic Theory of Democracy*. The rationality of the voter is low-information rationality.

A problem with theories introducing information costs, bargaining costs and transaction costs, not to speak of psychic costs, is that they are difficult to falsify (cf. Elster, 1979: 156). Since it is usually quite impossible to decide what is an optimal amount of information, the assumption of rationality easily becomes empty of content. We might add that Philip Converse (1964: 209ff.) found that many voters actually hold inconsistent beliefs about politics, thus apparently violating the minimum requirement for rationality, but Converse's results have been questioned (see, e.g. Rosenberg, 1988: 3ff.).

I will accept Downs' and Popkin's suggestion that voters are rationally ignorant about politics, but suggest an alternative interpretation of what happens in a political campaign and other forms of political communication.

Two years after the publication of Anthony Downs' *An Economic Theory of Democracy*, Talcott Parsons made his systems theoretic interpretation of voting in the American political system (Parsons, [1959] 1967). I will ignore his systems theory and concentrate on his analysis of the act of voting. Parsons' diagnosis of the vote situation is similar to that of Downs. Like Downs, he is aware that it is difficult to fit into a utilitarian frame. Since there are millions of voters, one vote is not likely to affect the outcome. Voting does not make sense in terms of self-interest. Also like Downs, Parsons suggests that voting is made in a situation of irredeemable uncertainty. Voters cannot possibly know enough about issues and candidates to make a rational decision (ibid., p. 239): 'voting is marginal and peripheral for the average citizen. He has many role-involvements in his sphere of private affairs and simply cannot be a sophisticated political expert (ibid., p. 248). Parsons' solution to this problem is different, however. Whereas Downs solved the problem of uncertainty with the help of ideology, as a way of cutting information costs, Parsons suggests that most voting is traditional and, therefore, nonrational:

> Since the intellectual problems involved in a rational solution are not practicably soluble, my thesis is that the mechanisms are typically nonrational. They involve stabilization of political attitudes *in terms of association with other members of the principal solidary groups in which the voter is involved*. In terms of party affiliation this may be called 'traditionalism'.
>
> (Parsons, [1959] 1967: 235)

It might be suggested that traditionalism is itself a rational solution to the problem of voting, but this does not make each traditional act of voting rational. 'The very conception of rationality implies a certain ordered responsiveness to changes and shifts in the external situation. There is hence an inherent connection between nonrationality and the relative absence of such flexible responsiveness' (ibid., p. 246).

According to Parsons, then, most voting is *traditional*, or habitual. But voting is also symbolic and *expressive*. People vote to express their allegiance to a certain party and their solidarity with other people voting for the same party. Voting is, in most cases, a traditonal and expressive act of solidarity with a group and of identification with a party. To the extent that this is so, political campaigns are without effects, they are *rituals* (ibid., p. 250).

Most theories of symbolic politics, emphasize the fickleness of the masses and their susceptibility to persuasion (see, e.g., Edelman, 1971: 3–7; 1975: 309ff.). Parsons differs from the mainstream by emphasizing stability. One reason for this is that Parsons' theory is based upon the results presented in *Voting*, the study by Berelson, Lazarsfeld and McPhee (1954/1956), which reported a high degree of stability in party preferences. Edelmans' judgement is based, instead, on the later studies by Campbell *et al.* (1960) and Converse (1964), which reported less stability in voting behaviour.

Parsons may have exaggerated the extent to which voting is traditional, or habitual, but he did recognize two alternatives to the traditionalist pattern. The first is the vacillating voter, with a low interest in politics and a social position inviting cross pressure. The second alternative is the extremist voter, responding to the emotionally charged messages of charismatic politicians. Of these, the vacillating voter will appear to be the more rational voter.

Symbolic versus rational politics

In this concluding section on persuasion, I will suggest three reasons why symbolic politics cannot be comprehended by a theory of rational choice. (1) Political language includes symbols, intended to arouse emotions rather than to convey information. (2) These emotions are often associated with collective identities and political ideals larger than self-interest. (3) There is no such thing as a neutral political language. Political descriptions of social reality involve persuasive definitions. Before political actors start acting strategically, they try to impose their definitions of the situation upon other actors.

Public choice conceives of communication as transmission of *information*.[23] What voters receive in political campaigns is information about *facts*. But this conception gives a seriously incomplete, and therefore distorted, understanding of the function of political language. Political messages are typically intended to persuade, not to inform receivers, and persuasion is not always information. Indeed, persuasion is often disinformation. It works by positive lying, or withholding of relevant information (cf. Bennett, 1988).

It is common to make a distinction between 'rational persuasion' and 'manipulative persuasion'. An overlapping, but not identical, distinction is between rational manipulation by logic and argument, and psychological manipulation by cause and effect.[24] Robert E. Goodin tries to show in his *Manipulatory Politics* (1980) that manipulation is more often rational and less often psychological than most people are inclined to believe. I have a feeling he overstates his case, but drawing the line between rational and psychological manipulation is not easy, and, for my purposes, less important. Both forms of manipulation are different from transmission of information and intended to prevent the formation of rational belief. Manipulation is a form of exercise of power acting contrary to the putative will of those subject to it (Goodin, 1980: 7–20).

Starting with Downs' rationally ignorant voter, Goodin suggests four ways to utilize this ignorance for manipulatory purposes: by lying, secrecy, propaganda (biased information) and information overload (too much information). For my purposes, however, some other ways of manipulation, also discussed by Goodin, are more important: laying linguistic traps, rhetorical trickery, the use of symbolic rewards.

The mark of symbolic politics is appeal to emotions. This emotional component of political messages has been entirely neglected by rational choice. This is not because emotions are incompatible with rationality. They are not. Emotions and rationality go a long way together, reason being slave to the passions. Emotions threaten rationality only in the case of affect, leading to impulsive action. When emotions burst out so suddenly and so strongly as to short-cut our cognitive activity; when there is no weighing of means and ends, no calculation of benefits and costs, then action can be deemed rational only at the cost of tautology. This is the reason Max Weber recognized the existence of affectual action besides instrumentally rational action (Weber, 1922/1978: 24f.).

My main argument is not, however, that emotions are incompatible with rationality. It is that they are often incompatible with self-interest. Emotions often attach to collective entities and to moral values and principles higher than self-interest. When symbolic politics appeals to emotions, it is usually to emotions attached to collective entities, such as class, race and church, nation, or to core values such as freedom, democracy, justice, etc (cf. Sniderman, Brody and Tetlock, 1991: chs 7–8).

An important observation is that emotions attach not only to reality, but to the symbols used to talk about, or to represent, reality. The philosopher Charles L. Stevenson distinguished between the *emotive* and *descriptive* meanings of signs and suggested that the two might drift apart: 'To whatever extent emotive meaning is *not* a function of descriptive meaning, but either persists without the latter or survives changes in it, let us say that it is "independent" '(Stevenson, 1944: 72). Ulf Himmelstrand has used the idea of independent emotive meaning to define 'symbol acts' as acts 'which have symbols as their exclusive objects, neglecting largely the objective or conceptual referent of the object' (Himmelstrand, 1960: 43). Symbol acts are expressive of attitudes, and verbal attitudes have what Himmelstrand calls 'independent affective loadings' (ibid., p. 47).

It is not difficult to find examples of symbol acts used for both destructive and constructive purposes. Saluting the flag may be a symbol act expressing a patriotic attitude. Nor is it difficult to find examples of the use of symbols to create collective identities. The history of nationalism is a sad spectacle of warmongers using national symbols to prepare people for war. A more constructive symbol act is demonstrating on the first of May as an expression of identification with the working class. James Johnson (1988: 232–237) mentions May Day as a tradition, with strong ritual and symbolic dimensions, invented to help create a working class by making workers aware of their common interest.

I will turn, instead, to emotions attached to moral values and principles. Political speeches are full of words like 'freedom', 'liberty', 'democracy', 'human rights', 'justice', 'equality', etc. These are the most highsounding words in political ideologies. Taking these words seriously, however, is incompatible with public choice, since they express values different from self-interest. Acting on values and principles is 'value-rational' action, in the sense of Max Weber (1922/1978: 24f.), action 'determined by a conscious belief in the value for its own sake of some ethical, aesthetic, religious, or other form of behaviour, independently of its prospect of success'. Ideologies, therefore, must be reinterpeted to mean something other than commitment to moral values if they are to be included in a theory of public choice.

The basic hypothesis of Anthony Downs 'states that political parties are interested in gaining office *per se*, not in promoting a better or ideal society' (Downs, 1957: 96). 'No *Weltanschauung* is accepted at face value, because it is seen as tainted with its espousers' desire to gain power' (ibid., pp. 96f.). In Downs' theory of democracy, then, the use of ideologies by politicians is a manifestation of sheer opportunism. Voters use ideologies differently. For them, the main problem is uncertainty about the consequences of their choice. Voters, therefore, use ideologies as a means of cutting their information costs. I do not deny that ideologies may function in both these ways, but it is only part of the truth, certainly not the whole truth. As many observers have pointed out, ideas cannot be used by opportunists if they are not genuinely felt and adhered to by others (see, e.g. Durkheim, 1983: 153). Pareto, for instance, makes this point with respect to religious ideas:

> For people whose thinking is governed by sentiment, the presence of hypocrites among believers in a given religion is an argument for depreciating its importance and often for condemning it. But for those who reason experimentally, the fact that a religion has hypocritical supporters is an indication of the faith's power, since men feign belief in something only if it is widely accepted by large numbers of their fellow men.
>
> (Pareto [1921] 1976: 319)

But ideologies are not made up of values alone. They consist of values *and* beliefs, and the two are usually inseparable, except as a matter of logic. I will return, therefore, to the assumption of rational belief and to the rational choice reduction of communication to information. This reduction presupposes that society is out there 'waiting' to be described; an object that we can decide to be more or less informed about. This commonsense realism is problematic in all theories, but more so in theories of society, and most of all in political theories. Language is rarely, if ever, used to describe neutral facts. It may be doubted, on epistemological grounds, whether there is such a thing as a neutral fact at all. Using a well-known term from the philosophy of science, facts are 'theory-laden' (Hanson, 1958/1965: 19).

It is a truism in anthropology and sociology that 'reality' or, at least, 'social reality' is, in some sense, a 'social construction', but also that we are prisoners of our language and our culture (cf. Goodin, 1980: ch. 3). According to Durkheim's sociological Kantianism, the categories of understanding – time, space, causality, number, class, substance, personality, etc. – are collective representations of social origin (1912/1965: 22–33, 165ff., 488–496; Durkheim and Mauss, 1903/1970). This may be going too far in sociologism, but there is a kernel of truth in it. Knowledge is a social phenomenon and society is, to a significant degree, constituted by our knowledge about it. The most ambitious attempt to turn this insight into systematic theory is the phenomenology of Alfred Schutz (1932/1972, 1962). In this theory, society is conceived of as a *lifeworld* of commonsense knowledge that we take for granted and act upon in our everyday life. The important point is that society is very much a cognitive order, constituted by our, largely tacit, knowledge of the social practices that keep it going (Giddens, 1984).

Phenomenology is often castigated for its concern with mental phenomena and, consequently, with a problematic of the human subject. Less objectionable, in the eyes of those who level this critique, is the linguistic version of the truism that society is a social construction. Most well known is the so-called Sapir–Whorf thesis, which says that 'reality', or at least 'social reality', is inconceivable except within some language:

> Human beings do not live in the objective world alone, nor alone in the world of social activity as ordinarily understood, but are very much at the mercy of the particular language which has become the medium of expression for their society. It is quite an illusion to imagine that one adjusts to reality essentially without the use of language and that language is merely an incidental means of solving specific problems of communication or reflection. The fact of the matter is that the 'real world' is to a large extent unconsciously built up on the language habits of the group. No two languages are ever sufficiently similar to be considered as representing the same social reality. The worlds in which different societies live are distinct worlds, not merely the same world with different labels attached.
>
> (Sapir [1929] 1949: 69)

The implication of this quite unassailable thesis is that beliefs are relative to the culture of which they are part; they are culture-bound. And this goes for rational beliefs too. No amount of information can bring knowledge that transcends the culture to which you belong, or to which you have access. This is not, of course, a fatal obstacle to rational choice, but it makes it appear in its right light, and it does constitute a problem when making cross-cultural and historical comparisons.

Problems begin when we confront the fact that there are conflicting beliefs within cultures. The sociological explanation of this fact is that beliefs are socially determined. In the words of Marx and Engels (1846/1976: 42): 'It is not consciousness that determines life, but life that determines consciousness.' 'Consciousness is, therefore, from the very beginning a social product, and remains so as long as men exist at all' (ibid., pp. 49f.). According to the Marxist theory of ideology, beliefs are manifestations of interests and especially of the interests of the ruling classes, which impose their beliefs on the rest of the population: 'The ideas of the ruling class are in every epoch the ruling ideas: i.e., the class which is the ruling material force of society is at the same time its ruling intellectual force' (ibid., p. 67). If this is true, we can speak of a 'dominant ideology', which helps the ruling class to attain 'hegemony', which is rule by consent rather than by force.

The Marxist theory of ideology was the main pillar of the sociology of knowledge (Mannheim, 1936). Another pillar was Vilfredo Pareto's theory of 'derivations' (Pareto, 1916/1980: chs 7–8), which is the Marxist theory of ideology, in other words. A third pillar was the idea of the 'definition of the situation', borrowed from symbolic interactionism.[25] The point of this notion is that people do not act upon objectively given situations, but upon situations as defined by themselves and/or others. Situations are socially constructed. This is also the message of Peter Berger and Thomas Luckmann (1966), who made the phenomenology of Alfred Schutz an important part of their sociology of knowledge.

I suggested above that facts are theory-laden and beliefs culture-bound. Political language, however, is not only theory-laden, it is *value-laden* as well, and beliefs are not only culture-bound, they are manifestations of interest. Political language thrives on selective information and 'persuasive definitions' (Stevenson, 1944: ch. 9). Political concepts, therefore, are, without exception, 'essentially contested concepts' (Gallie, 1956).

The notion of 'persuasive definition' was used by Charles L. Stevenson in the context of ethics, but is, of course, equally useful in the context of politics. Stevenson observed that definitions, in ethics, often have a function other than mere description. 'In point of fact, this is rarely the case; description is usually a secondary consideration. Ethical definitions involve a wedding of descriptive and emotive meaning, and accordingly have a frequent use in redirecting and intensifying attitudes' (Stevenson, 1944: 210). Persuasive definitions achieve this by utilizing the emotive meaning of words in attempts to alter their descriptive meaning. Thus, by describing a policy as 'just', politicians hope to make people accept it irrespective of its descriptive meaning of 'just', in this particular case. A precondition for persuasive definitions is that ethical terms are 'vague', or 'ambiguous'. Observers of politics will have no problem in finding examples of persuasive definitions. Politicians use them all the time.

The idea of 'essentially contested concepts' is closely associated with that of 'persuasive definition'. Essential contestability occurs because people try to persuade one another of the 'proper' meaning of words. W.B. Gallie makes no reference to Stevenson, but it is obvious that persuasive definition and essentially contested concepts are related phenomena. Like the former, the latter are possible because political terms are open to multiple interpretations. Both deal with appraisive terms and are exemplified by the same category of terms: freedom democracy, justice, power, etc. (Gallie, 1956: 168ff.; Connolly, 1973/1983). It might be added that persuasive definition is usually interested definition. As long as politics continues to involve conflicting values and interests, political concepts will remain essentially contested concepts – that is, for ever. Contested concepts are an essential part of politics and of the human condition.

The theory of symbolic politics is based on the sociology of knowledge. Beliefs are not based on 'information', or on information alone; they are part of people's attempts to make sense of reality. Language is used not only to describe an objective reality, but to create meaning and, according to Murray Edelman (1971: 31): 'Meaning is basically different from information and incompatible with it.' Social reality is constructed and politics is part of this construction. Politicians use language to proffer their own preferred definitions of social problems and their own solutions to them. Political language is used strategically to serve the objectives of politicians. 'The very concept of "fact" becomes irrelevant because every meaningful political object and person is an interpretation that reflects and perpetuates an ideology' (Edelman, 1988: 10).

Among the more common devices is to categorize other countries, or their regimes, as 'enemies' and 'threats' to national security, to describe social phenomena as 'problems' and to define certain situations as 'crises' (see Edelman, 1975, 1977, 1988). By using these words, politicians may, of course, give an accurate picture of the state of their country, but equally often the purpose is to justify certain policies, irrespective of the descriptive accuracy of their accounts. By inventing enemies, they motivate a strong national defence. By describing something as a problem they motivate whatever means are deemed necessary to solve it. By defining a situation as a crisis, finally, politicians usually want to justify extraordinary measures, which would not be accepted in a normal situation. That something other than information is involved in these categorizations and definitions is evident from the fact that people with different interests and different values rarely agree on them. What for some people appear as relations of free exchange, are by others conceived of as relations of power and exploitation. What some people see as legitimate claims to justice are by others dismissed as envy. When some people see unemployment and poverty as the result of a merciless economic system, others blame individuals for being lazy and, themselves, responsible for their situation.

Edelman contrasts symbolic politics with rational choice, which is 'one more symbol in the process of rationalization rather than the path to enlightenment' (Edelman, 1988: 4). Actually, Edelman's account of politics is not at all unlike that of public choice. Politicians are depicted as self-interested and manipulatory. Edelman also insists that 'language usage is strategic' (ibid., p. 108), a suggestion that fits nicely in a methodology of rational choice. A closer look, however, reveals a chasm between the two. Symbolic politics is similar to public choice in a respect, which makes both incompatible with rational choice. Manipulation changes people's preferences, or beliefs. This is against the assumptions of rational choice. The main reason why symbolic politics is incompatible with rational choice is that it makes the assumption of rational belief break down. If some people use symbolic politics strategically, and successfully, this implies that other people are manipulated either to change their preferences, or to entertain irrational beliefs.

POWER

According to a well-known, and once influential, characterization of the 'political system', its task is 'the authoritative allocation of values for a society'. Political science, consequently, is 'the study of the authoritative allocation of values for society' (Easton, 1953/1971: 129–141; 1965: 49f., 96f.). This definition is both too narrow and too broad. It is too narrow, because it excludes non-governmental political activity. In particular, it excludes much that has been the subject matter of political sociology; social movements, for instance. And maybe this is the intended objective: to achieve a clear division of labour between political science and political sociology. Easton's definition is too broad, because it turns every exercise of authority into politics and because it relies on a very broad definition of 'authority' (Ball, 1988). According to Easton (1953/1971: 132f.; 1965: 50), wherever there is obedience, there is authority. On this view, authority becomes indistinguishable from coercion and identical with power, as usually conceived.

An alternative route is followed by Talcott Parsons, who conceives of power as linked to, but not identical with, 'authority', as here understood. According to him, power is by definition legitimate. Unlike most other theorists, Parsons takes power to be a capacity of social systems, not of individuals – not even a relational property of individuals. In a manner not entirely clear to me, he suggests that power is a medium, analogous to money. 'Authority', as Parsons uses this term, is an institution; a complex of norms, or rights, surrounding the use of power (Parsons, 1958: 205; [1963] 1967: 319–321). '*Authority* is the politically crucial quality of a status in a social structure. *Power* I conceive, in contrast, to be a primary instrumentality of effective performance in that position' (Parsons, 1966: 79).

According to Parsons, power is the proper subject matter of political science. This is not the place to dig deeply into Parsons' complex theory of the social system. Suffice to say that he assigns to political science the task of analysing the polity, one of four subsystems of the total social system, or society. The others are the economy, the social and the cultural systems. The polity, or political system, is organized around the specific functional requisite of collective goal-attainment.

Easton tends to equate authority with power and Parsons to equate power with authority, as these phenomena are usually understood. This is not surprising. 'Power' and 'authority' are among the most contested concepts and phenomena in the social sciences. My purpose is neither to engage in conceptual analysis, nor to explore the real world of power and authority. I do take it for granted, though, that, however defined, 'power' and 'authority' refer to phenomena of some importance in politics (cf. Lively, 1976; Lindblom, 1977: 17–32, 119ff.). It is a matter of some consequence, therefore, that the economic theory of politics – at least to the extent that it is a theory of exchange – is unable to deal with these phenomena. This is the argument in this section.

Forms of power

Conceptions of power have been divided, by Steven Lukes (1978: 636) into two categories. There are the conceptions of power as a *collective capacity* (power$_1$) and there are the alternative conceptions of power as an *asymmetric relation* between individuals or groups (power$_2$). I am going to distinguish between three concepts of 'power'. In addition to power$_1$ and power$_2$, there is power$_3$, or the capacity of some actors to reward and/or punish other actors. Power$_2$ and $_3$ are species of power$_1$, and power$_3$ is a species of power$_2$.

The historical roots of power$_1$ are in the Roman concept of *potestas*. It has been defended, most consistently, by Hannah Arendt, who conceives of power as being necessarily collectivistic. '*Power* corresponds to the human ability not just to act but to act in concert. Power is never the property of an individual; it belongs to a group and remains in existence only so long as the group keeps together' (Arendt, 1969/1986: 64). 'Power', in Arendt's sense, means the consent and support of those governed, rather than the activity of those who govern. For Arendt, 'The fundamental phenomenon of power is not the instrumentalization of another's will, but the formation of a common will in a communication directed to reaching agreement.'[26] Similar, in certain respects, is Parsons' notion of 'power' as a

> generalized capacity to secure the performance of binding obligations by units in a system of collective organization when the obligations are legitimized with reference to their bearing on collective goals and where in case of recalcitrance there is a presumption of enforcement by nega-

tive situational sanctions – whatever the actual agency of that enforcement.

(Parsons [1963] 1967: 308)

Unlike Arendt, Parsons conceives of power as instrumental in the achievement of collective goals. 'Power in a collectivity is a means of effectively mobilizing obligations in the interest of collective goals' (Parsons, 1966: 85). But it rests on the consent and support of the governed. The use of force is a last resort and a limiting case. Also, unlike Arendt, Parsons uses 'power' to denote a property of a social system, not of actors. For Parsons, power is a medium of the political process, analogous to money in the economic process. Power is part of all collectivities. It is involved in collective goal-achievement, the political function, or aspect, of any collectivity. Most obviously, it is part of the political subsystem of society: the polity, or state apparatus.

Finally, Parsons conceives of power as a *non-zero-sum* collective property of social systems (Parsons, 1957: 139–143; [1963] 1967; 1966: 79–81, 103f.). An increase in power on the part of A is not necessarily a loss of power on the part of B. If A and B cooperate, the power of both may increase in terms of collective goal-achievement. In game-theoretic terms, this is merely a recognition of the existence of games of cooperation, or coordination, in addition to (zero-sum) games of conflict.[27]

A view, similar to the ideas of Arendt and Parsons in certain respects, but resolutely stripped of all systems thinking and assumptions of a harmony of interests, is advanced by Göran Ahrne in his *Social Organizations* (1994: 12–18; 116–125). A main theme in this book is that organizations are 'power containers' (cf. Giddens, 1985: 13) and that members of organizations get access to collective resources which significantly increase their power.[28] Relations within organizations take the form of authority and influence (Ahrne, 1994: 89–92). Relations between organizations take the form of conflict, competition, exchange or collaboration. For Ahrne (1994: 117), 'Power is relational.'

This brings me to power$_2$, best represented by Max Weber. On Weber's famous definition, ' "Power" (*Macht*) is the probability that one actor within a social relationship will be in a position to carry out his own will despite resistance, regardless of the basis on which this probability rests' (Weber, 1922/1978: 53). In the terminology of Habermas (1977/1986: 84f.), this concept of 'power' is not just 'instrumental', as Parsons', but 'strategic', since it directs attention to the competitive struggle for power between groups and individuals.

For Weber (1922/1978: 53), the above definition is too broad, at least for sociological purposes: 'All conceivable qualities of a person and all conceivable combinations of circumstances may put him in a position to impose his will in a given situation.' Weber, therefore, suggests the concept of 'domination', to replace that of 'power'. ' "Domination" (*Herrschaft*) is the probability that a command with a given specific content will be obeyed by a given group of persons.'

Weber also mentions discipline – habitual and automatic obedience – as a form of domination. Discipline is rarely mentioned in discussions of Weber's sociology of domination, even though it played an important part in his own analyses. Recently the theme of disciplinary power has been developed in great detail by Michel Foucault (1975/1977; [1976] 1980: 105–107). Weber would not, however, have endorsed Foucault's amorphous concept of 'power' as permeating all corners of society. This is exactly what Weber objects to in his argument for using the concept of 'domination' instead (1922/1978: 942f.). Of domination, there are two main types: economic power and authority, or in Weber's own words: 'domination by virtue of a constellation of interests (in particular: by virtue of a position of monopoly), and domination by virtue of authority, i.e., power to command and duty to obey' (1922/1978: 943).

The Weberian concept of 'power' is too narrow. First, because it does not recognize power as conceived by Arendt and Parsons. Second, because it implies a will, or intention, on the part of those who have power. I suggest that the *unintended* consequences of the actions of individuals and groups may also be manifestations of their power. 'Agency refers not to the intentions people have in doing things but to their capability of doing those things in the first place (which is why agency implies power . . .' (Giddens, 1984: 9).

I think there is room for both concepts of power. Following Giddens (1979: 88ff.; 1984: 14–16) and the critical realists (Isaac, 1987), I conceive of 'Power', in the generic sense (power$_1$), as a transformative capacity; a capacity to achieve something, to make a difference in the world.[29] Four points should be made. (1) Being a *transformative* capacity, power includes power over matter.[30] (2) Being a *capacity*, power does not have to be exercised. (3) 'Power', in this sense, is related to agency, but not to intention or will. (4) Power is based upon control over resources, of one kind or another, and these resources are usually a property of social structure rather than of individuals.

Giddens is actually indebted to Parsons for his generic concept of power and for the corollary view that social structures are both enabling and constraining (Giddens, 1984: 169–179).[31] Unlike Parsons, however, Giddens allows for the possibility that 'power', as a matter of definition, may be a property of individuals. I think this is a wise decision, even though personal power is unimportant for the purposes of social science. An interesting example is charisma, which is based on personal qualities, which become a matter for social science only because the charismatic person is able to gain a following, thus turning personal power into collective power.

In addition to the generic, or broad, concept, Giddens suggests an asymmetric concept of 'power' as 'domination' (power$_2$), borrowed from Weber (Giddens, 1979: 88–94; 1984: 29–33, 256–262; 1985: 7ff.). Giddens uses the concept of 'domination' to cover relations of autonomy and dependence between actors; individual or collective. Power, in the form of domination, is based on control over resources, which are of two types: *allocative* and *authoritative*. 'Allocative resources refer to capabilities – or, more accurately, to forms of transformative capacity – generating command over objects, goods, or material phenomena. Authoritative resources refer to types of transformative capacity generating command over persons or actors' (Giddens, 1984: 33). The distinction between allocative and authoritative resources corresponds to Weber's distinction between economic power and authority. Allocative resources are, of course, economic. Command over material objects is based on property rights. The main authoritative resource is the right to command, or to act, attached to a certain office, or position. It is of some importance to realize that both allocative and authoritative resources are based on social institutions in the form of rights.

An alternative classification of the main sources of power has been developed by Pierre Bourdieu. He distinguishes between three forms of capital:

> *economic capital*, which is immediately and directly convertible into money and may be institutionalized in the form of property rights; . . . *cultural capital*, which is convertible, on certain conditions, into economic capital and may be institutionalized in the form of educational qualifications; and . . . *social capital*, made up of social obligations ('connections'), which is convertible, in certain conditions, into economic capital and may be institutionalized in the form of a title of nobility.
>
> (Bourdieu, 1983/1986: 243)

There is no need to comment on economic capital. Cultural capital is less familiar. Its principal form is education, but it also includes such things as linguistic and cultural competence (*Bildung*). Cultural capital has something in common with 'human capital', as understood by economists, but is more general. Cultural capital is not confined to 'economic' uses, but is also (mainly?) used to confer status, or 'distinction', on its owners. Cultural capital is a form of 'symbolic capital' (Bourdieu, 1972/1977: 171–173; 1980/1990: 112–121). It is that form of symbolic capital which dominates in societies with a written language and the printing press. In addition to formal education, symbolic capital includes such things as honour, prestige, reputation and status, which were the most important sources of power in traditional society, but which are of some importance also in modern society. Social capital, finally, is the 'connections' we have, in the form of kin, friends and acquaintances; what are today referred to as 'social networks'. As a source of power, social capital was also more important in traditional society than in modern society, but it certainly plays a role in all societies. Today social capital seems to be more important in those parts of the world with least experience of bureaucratic administration and legal authority. Under Western eyes, power based on social capital appears as 'nepotism' and 'corruption'. Social capital is derived, or secondary, in the sense that it depends upon the primary resources of your connections. In this, it resembles the resources you command as a member of an organization – a phenomenon entirely neglected in Bourdieu's sociology.[32]

Bourdieu, then, assigns no independent place to authority in his theory of domination and this leads me to the third concept of 'power', or power$_3$. This concept arises in either of two ways: because you make a distinction between authority and power, or because you make no room at all for authority, as distinct from power.

Michael Taylor follows the first route. He mentions a number of ways of 'getting people to do things', including power and authority. Power works by affecting the incentives of people, so that it becomes rational for them to act in a certain way (Taylor, 1982: 11). A similar concept of 'power' has been suggested by Walter Korpi (1985). According to him, power is based on resources, which enable actors (individuals or collectives) to reward or punish other actors. Authority has no place at all in Korpi's analysis of power. Both Taylor and Korpi make an 'economic analysis of power', in the sense of Brian Barry (1976a), and both exemplify a third concept of 'power', or power$_3$.

There is no correct definition of 'power'. The choice between different concepts is a matter of convenience or, perhaps, of fertility. Considering the bewildering variety of concepts of power, I am inclined to believe that it is best to cast the net widely and, then, to distinguish between different *forms* of power.

Bertrand Russell (1938/1948: 35ff.) suggested three ways in which we might exert power, or 'influence', over an individual: 'A. By direct physical power over his body, e.g. when he is imprisoned or killed; B. By rewards and punishments as inducements, e.g. in giving or withholding employment; C. By influence on opinion, i.e. propaganda in the broadest sense.'

Russell's classification is useful, since it includes Steven Lukes' third face of power: the power to change other people's preferences by means of persuasion. If there is any truth in the characterization of the press as 'the fourth estate', we cannot neglect the power of the press in our conception of power. If the Marxist theories of ideology and hegemony are true, the third face of power deserves a place at the centre of an analysis of power in society.

Russell's classification is not exhaustive, however. In particular, I miss authority, or power based on authority, as a special form of power. Talcott Parsons' analysis of power makes it possible to remedy this defect. Parsons makes two distinctions: (1) the distinction between methods operating upon people's preferences and beliefs and methods operating upon their situation, and (2) the distinction between positive and negative sanctions. By combining these two distinctions, Parsons arrives at four ways in which an actor can produce a change in the behaviour of another actor (Parsons [1963] 1967: 310; see Figure 3.5):

Channel

	Intentional	Situational
Positive	Persuasion	Inducement
Negative	Activation of commitments	Coercion

Sanction

Figure 3.5 Ways of exerting power

I do not accept Parsons' analysis, but, like Brian Barry (1976a: 68), I believe that it is a useful start for an analysis of power. Most useful is the distinction between preferences and situation as channels for bringing about a change in the actions of individuals. Also important is the suggestion that we can do so by activating actors' commitments to rules. Following Barry (ibid., p. 68), I suggest that Parsons' table gives rise to three forms of power, not four.

Authority and *influence* (persuasion) operate upon the preferences and beliefs of people. Authority does so primarily by activating individuals' commitments to rules, while influence works on their preferences. Influence makes people change their minds. In a broad sense of the term, 'authority' includes influence, but for my present purposes, I see influence as distinct from authority. Coercion and inducement operate on people's opportunity sets. They give them an incentive to act in certain ways by means of threats, offers and their combination: throffers (see Barry, 1976a: 69ff. and Taylor, 1982: 11ff.). Coercion is negative. It consists in the ability to make credible and successful threats (Taylor, 1982: 14). Inducement, on the other hand, can be either positive or negative, and this is the case with most (all?) resources used as incentives. The distinction between coercion and inducement, therefore, is not well-founded. Like Barry, I suggest that we collapse coercion and inducement into one single form of power. I suggest that we call it 'power by sanction', or *sanctioning power*.[33]

In addition to the forms of power mentioned thus far, there is *physical force*, or violence (Barry, 1976a: 68). Force can be used in several ways. It can be used indirectly as a means of coercion in offers, threats and throffers, as implied in the felicitious phrase: 'I'll give you an offer you can't refuse'. Force can also be used directly to achieve intended effects. People can be moved, locked up and killed. But there is a third use of violence intended to teach victims a lesson, and by learning the lesson to comply with our wishes. This is

155

Mind	Situation	Body
Influence	Sanctioning	Physical
	power	force
Authority		

Figure 3.6 Forms of Power

the use of force to discipline people; to turn them into 'docile bodies' and willing subjects, as suggested by Foucault. Discipline has this much in common with influence. Both are intended to 'persuade' people to change their minds.

Different bases and forms of power are convertible into one another. Physical force, for instance, can be used to acquire economic resources and to coerce people to obey, by making threats credible (armed robbery exemplifies both). It can also be used to gain control over the means of persuasion, as when occupation troops, or a revolutionary army, takes control over the mass media. Physical force cannot be used to control people's minds, however, and it is not convertible into authority. There is rather a negative relation between these forms of power. Physical force is usually used as a substitute for authority. Coercion is subject to the same limitations as physical force. Influence is convertible to other forms of power, but in less obvious ways. It is to some degree convertible into economic resources (begging) and to authority: it is possible to conceive of one individual persuading another individual to obey a command. By the same token, it is possible to conceive of actors persuading other actors to use coercion or even violence, as in instigation of rebellion. The most current forms, or bases, of power, however, are authority and economic power. Authority is convertible into all other forms of power, if the rights on which it rests include these things. Political authority, for instance, may include the right to tax, to command an army, to use legal threats and to control mass media. Economic power, likewise, can be used, to buy means of violence and of persuasion. It can also be used to buy the right to command people's labour power and to coerce those who become dependent on your resources for their economic welfare.

Because of the convertibility of forms of power, most relations of domination rest on several forms of power. The power of capital over labour rests on economic resources, but money can buy authority, influence and physical violence, and economic resources can be used to coerce those who lack them. The much discussed domination of men over women is a combination of all forms of power. Since times immemorial, it is a form of traditional authority, which is now losing its hold over the minds of men and women alike. It is a

156

form of economic power, since men have much more economic resources, which they can use both to induce and to coerce women to comply with their wishes. The possibility of coercion is especially evident when women are dependent on their husbands, or other men, for their means of support. Because of subjection to traditional authority and lack of economic resources, women have inferior access to legal authority and to the means of persuasion. Violence, finally, is a last resort for men who cannot mobilize other forms of power and who cannot accept that domination has come to an end.

Authority

Authority had been a dominant theme in political philosophy long before it became a topic of social science. In political philosophy, the matter of authority is normative and concerns its possible justification. As such, it is related to the issue of political obligation (Green, 1988: ch. 8; Dunn, 1991). My interest is in authority as a social phenomenon, to be investigated by the social sciences, using mainly empirical methods. Some conceptual labour is also necessary in social science investigations, however, if only as a preparation for empirical research.

As we have already seen, it is common to make a distinction between power and authority. Originally, the Romans used the term 'power' (*potestas*), to designate collective power of the community and 'authority' (*auctoritas*) to refer to the asymmetric power of A over B (Lukes, 1978: 638f.; Ball 1988: 81f.).[34] The idea is that the community somehow authorizes some of its members to command other members in the common interest of the community. This distinction is obviously inadequate as a classification of forms of power, since it does not distinguish between authority and other ways in which A might exert power over B.

It has also been suggested that people comply with authority out of their own free will, but bow down to power only against their own will (see, e.g., De Jouvenal, 1957: 32; 1958: 161; Connolly, 1974/1983: 109, 113). This distinction is also inadequate as it stands, since it equates power with coercion, or the capacity to issue credible threats. But we certainly wish to call those people powerful, who get their way mainly by positive sanctions, or rewards. The suggestion that we obey authority by free will is better, but not entirely correct. Criminals rarely obey judges of their own free will, but the power exerted by judges is definitely what most people would call 'authority'.

One of the standing issues concerning the concept of 'authority' is whether it implies legitimacy, or not. The dominant view among social scientists has been to see authority as necessarily legitimate (Friedman, 1973/1990: 60). The prevailing opinion among philosophers seems to be that it is not (De George, 1985: 18; Green, 1988: 59–62). The reason for this difference is probably that social scientists treat legitimacy as a social fact, whereas philosophers treat it as a normative issue.[35] I follow the praxis of social scientists and conceive of 'authority' as 'legitimate power' – power is legitimate to the extent that people accept it as such – but concede to philosophers the point that authority is not, thereby, morally justified.

An important distinction is that between being *an* authority and being *in* authority (Peters, 1958/1967: 86ff.). Albert Einstein was an authority on physics and his cousin Alfred on music, especially Mozart. James Buchanan is an authority on economics. Being *an* authority, then, depends upon some special competence a person might have. This form of authority has been called 'epistemic authority' (De George, 1976; 1985: ch. 3). I find this term somewhat misleading, because too narrow. First, the term 'epistemic', today, makes us think of theoretical or discursive knowledge, whereas people may be authorities also in practical matters, if they possess some skill or master some art (*techne*). Second, because the term 'epistemic' seems, definitely, to exclude the *moral* authority of virtuous men and women.[36] It may be hard to come up with examples, but I suppose that Mahatma Gandhi and Mother Teresa qualify as candidates for being moral authorities. What characterizes *an* authority, then, is some personal attribute, which make us willing to follow his/her advice. An advice from an authority is *authoritative*. An authority is roughly equivalent to an expert, except that we may hesitate to talk about experts in the sphere of morality. An authority exerts power in the form of influence.

Some people wish to reserve the term 'authority' for this first type (e.g., Friedrich, 1959a: 128ff.; 1972: 47ff.; Taylor, 1982: 21–24). I find this usage hard to accept. It has been etymologically justified by Friedrich (see, however, Peters, 1958/1967: 85f.) and ideologically defended by Taylor, but it is completely at odds with common usage today. For most people, 'authority' means, above all, the right to command on the part of those *in* authority (see Benn, 1967: 215). While the authority of *an* authority rests on personal qualities, the authority of those *in* authority rests with their office, or position; what De George (1985: ch. 4) calls *executive authority*. It may be pointed out that both types of authority coincide if people are selected for offices because of their personal qualities, as in a technocracy or meritocracy.[37]

My concern here is with political authority, and for a theory of politics, executive authority is the more important (cf. Bayles, 1976). Executive authority may be divided into *performative* and *imperative* authority (De George, 1985: 63–68). Performative authority is simply the right to perform some action, while imperative authority is the right, on the part of someone in authority, to command other individuals subject to that authority. Another distinction of some importance is between *de jure* and *de facto* authority (Peters, 1958/1967: 84ff.; Benn, 1967: 215f.), both of which are distinct from authority as legitimate power. *De jure* authority which is not also *de facto*, is most probably illegitimate. *De facto* authority may be legitimate, but need not be. People may obey out of habit or self-interest.

Authority is in no way confined to the political sphere, however. It pervades every corner of society, especially organizations. In traditional society, elders used to have authority over younger people, and some of it remains to this day. Parents still have some authority over their own children. Authority is important also in the economic sphere. If relations between firms take the form of exchange, those within firms are, largely, in the form of authority. Even if there has been, recently, a tendency to flatten out organizations, most firms are still hierarchical structures of command and obedience. Authority within firms is based upon economic power. Employers buy the right to command their employees, and to organize their firms as authority structures, in much the same way as citizens, according to Hobbes, submit to the authority of the sovereign in exchange for order and security. In the contract beween capitalists and workers, the former buys the labour-power of the latter in exchange for a wage. This contract gives capitalists the right to order people about while at work. But the analysis could be taken one step further, because economic power depends, in its turn, upon property rights established in the constitution. We could, if we wish, talk about property rights as 'authority over resources'. All rights are grounded, ultimately, in the constitution, which might, therefore, seem to be rock-bottom. But the rights defined by a constitution lend authority only to the extent that it is legitimate, and not all constitutions are legitimate. Constitutions may be only *de jure* and defended, in the last analysis, by naked power.

The state, then, does not rule by authority alone. Max Weber defined the 'state' as a 'compulsory political organization' which 'successfully upholds the claim to the monopoly of the legitimate use of physical force in the enforcement of order' (Weber, 1922/1978: 54). To make legitimacy part of the definition of the state is unwise, since some states lack this asset, but to include physical force is certainly to the point. States rule by authority, or by force, as the case may be, but usually by both. The economic basis of the activity of the state is the right, or power, to tax. But this means that the state has vast economic resources, or economic power, in addition to authority and physical power. Much legislation aims at affecting the incentives of people and is, threrefore, a manifestation of coercion rather than authority. Ideally, state power is the rule of law, but since law is necessarily general, it does not dictate exactly what to do in each particular case. Because of this, officials are given discretionary powers which go beyond the authority of their office. This is a fact and a problem, which no critic of the state is likely to forget.

Authority has been much discussed by political scientists, of course, but also by sociologists. Robert Nisbet mentions authority as one of five 'unit ideas', which together constitute the sociological tradition (Nisbet, 1966/1970). Max Weber is the sociologist most often associated with this particular unit idea. For him, authority is legitimate power (see, however, Uphoff, 1989). People may obey a command for a number of reasons, but, in addition, there is normally a belief in its *legitimacy* (Weber, 1922/1978: 213). Weber goes on to distinguish three types of authority, or 'legitimate domination': *legal authority*, 'resting on a belief in the legality of enacted rules and the right of those elevated to authority under such rules to issue commands'; *traditional authority*, 'resting on an established belief in the sanctity of immemorial traditions and the legitimacy of those exercising authority under them'; *charismatic authority*, 'resting on devotion to the exceptional sanctity, heroism or exemplary character of an individual person, and of the normative patterns or order revealed or ordained by him' (Weber, 1922/1978: 215).

Weber's theory of authority has been much discussed and much criticized, but remains the major source of inspiration for social scientific treatments of this subject. Parsons complained that Weber neglected to analyse professional (epistemic) authority, something he associated with Weber's tendency to over-emphasize the coercive aspect (Parsons, 1947: 59f.). Habermas argues that the idea of legal authority is wanting, because legality does not guarantee legitimacy. Hence, the need for some additional grounding of positive law (Habermas, 1981/1984: 264–267). Anthony H. Birch (1993: 35–42) suggests that the main problem with Weber's analysis of authority is its limitation to the legitimacy of regimes. Authority also depends upon the legitimacy of economic systems (why not political systems?), political communities and policies. Economic systems and policies present no problems, but what is 'legitimacy of political communities'? It refers to situations when citizens reject their leaders, because of ethnic and cultural identities, as in colonies and some multiethnic political communities.

In his discussion of the legitimacy of economic systems, Birch draws on Offe's and Habermas' analysis of the legitimation crisis of the modern welfare state (see p. 52f.). This is, indeed, the most obvious example, but he could also have mentioned Seymour M. Lipset in this connection. Lipset noticed in 1959 that legitimacy was a neglected problem area and tried to turn it into a top priority in political sociology (Lipset, 1959/1965: 84, 108–114; see also 1959/1963: ch. 3; 1967: 440ff.). Lipset maintained that the stability of regimes and political systems alike depend upon their legitimacy and effectiveness, and the two are mutually reinforcing. Lipset's main interest was in the stability of democracy and he had much of interest to say about this important topic. Among other things, he claimed that the legitimacy of modern political systems depends upon their effectiveness, which depends upon constant economic development (Lipset, 1959/1963: 82). This is a truth, which has, unfortunately, been verified over the last thirty years.

In retrospect we might conclude that Lipset did not quite succeed in his attempt to instate legitimacy at the centre of political sociology. But legitimacy has certainly become one of its major concerns.

Public choice and power

The word 'power' is not part of the vocabulary of mainstream economics (see Bartlett, 1989: 4–8). The reason for this is obvious and well known. The neoclassical orthodoxy strips the market of all social relationships, including, of course, relations of power. Economic actors are price-takers, with no ability, alone, to influence prices, or to exert pressure on other actors. Prices are the unintended results of the buying and selling of many actors on the market.

But if mainstream economics lacks a theory of power, this must be the case also with public choice, which is mainstream economics applied to politics. This is, indeed, the case. Public choice, at least as a theory of exchange, is equally devoid of a theory of power. '"Power" is a concept frequently employed by political scientists and sociologists, and totally ignored by economists and practitioners of public choice' (Mueller, 1989: 248).

Lacking a theory of power is a calamity for any theory of politics, and, especially, for a theory with imperialist pretensions. Things get worse because of the fact that many applications of public choice are premised on the assumption that politicians and bureaucrats are *power seekers* (see Chapters 1–2). Is there a way out of this impasse?

In his book *The Politics of Bureaucracy* (1965), Gordon Tullock is perfectly clear about the decisive difference between politics and economics:

> *Generally speaking, 'politics' describes social situations in which the dominant or primary relations are those between superior and subordinate...* This general meaning can perhaps best be clarified by comparison and contrast with 'economics.' The latter, as a discipline, describes social situations in which persons deal with one another as freely contracting equals.
>
> (Tullock, 1965/1987: 11)

> Summarizing, we can say that economic theory is based on the assumption that the central behavioral relationship to be analysed is that among freely contracting individuals. This relationship is recognized to be an approximation to reality rather than an accurate description in all but a few limiting cases. Economic theory abstracts from the other aspects of the human relationship, and studies its own limited part of reality. There are important areas for which the economist's assumptions are clearly inapplicable, notably the governmental bureaucracy.
>
> (Ibid., pp. 13f.)

According to Tullock, then, there can be no economic theory of the state. And yet he advocates the economic approach to politics (Tullock, 1976: 1–6; Buchanan and Tullock, 1962/1965: ch. 3) and to all human behaviour (Tullock and McKenzie, 1975/1985: ch. 1). Public choice seems to be entangled in the most glaring contradictions. A possible solution to the puzzle about Tullock would be that he conceives of public choice somewhat differently from the economic theory of the market. While the latter assumes free exchange, the former is confined to making the assumption of self-interest (see Buchanan, 1986: 26).

But what of Buchanan, who identifies economics with exchange more than with self-interest? In his 'Foreword' to Tullock's book on bureaucracy, he suggests that it is 'economic' in approach only, but not in content. This is not an objection, however. Buchanan admits that the political relationship is different from the economic. Rather than looking upon it as a relation of authority, however, Buchanan sees the political relation as a form of slavery (1965/1987: 5). Buchanan is, thus, aware of the limits to an economic theory of politics at an early stage in his intellectual development (see [1963] 1979: 33ff). But this does not prevent him from propagating an economic theory of politics-as-exchange, while remaining silent (to my knowledge) upon the subject of the political relation of authority (which is surprising, indeed, for a follower of Hobbes). Until recently, that is. In the 1980s, Buchanan introduced the distinction between 'economics as catallaxy' and 'political science' or simply 'politics', the former being concerned with exchange and the latter with authority, or power. 'Interestingly enough, this dividing line between the two areas of social science inquiry is the same as that proposed by some political scientists and sociologists, for example, Talcott Parsons' (Buchanan, 1989a: 15; see also 1986: 21).[38]

Public choice is incapable of dealing with power only to the extent that it relies on the assumption that politics can be analysed as exchange between *free and equal* partners. *Rational choice*, on the other hand, is quite indispensable for the analysis of *sanctioning power* exercised in the exchange, or strategic interaction, of *unequal* partners (Baldwin, 1978; Dowding, 1991). I tend to believe, however, that rational choice is also insufficient for the analysis of sanctioning power. Rational choice typically takes resources, like preferences, as given. But we would like to know why people are unequal in the first place and how it is possible to maintain this unequal situation (cf. Münch, 1992: 140). To do this, we need to introduce social institutions and belief systems, which do not belong in a self-sufficient theory of rational choice.

The main stumbling-block to a rational choice theory of power, however, is not sanctioning power, but influence and authority. I have already argued that influence (persuasion) lies outside the scope of rational choice. The same goes for authority. Economics deals with relations of exchange, but authority means relations of command and obedience. It is possible to explain some relations of authority as the outcome of exchange, e.g. the contract between employers and employees, but certainly not all. The theory of the social contract is either *Gedankenexperiment*, or myth. But even if all authority relations could be explained in this way, this would still not establish the universality of rational choice. It would still be the case that relations of authority, *once they are instigated*, are not amenable to rational choice analysis.

The main reason why authority lies outside the scope of rational choice is that it is, by definition, *legitimate*. Relations of authority include activation of commitments, or normative beliefs, that a command issued by a person in authority ought to be obeyed. This is not a 'rational choice', as defined by the methodological approach with this name. An adherent of rational choice might reject this definition and maintain that authority is coercion, that ultimately obedience is always based on fear of sanctions. This is the Hobbesian theory of authority, which I will discuss and reject in Chapter 7. For the time being, I simply dismiss it as extremely unlikely. But once again: even if it were true that people in their daily lives of subordination to authority obey only because of fear, this would still not explain what happens *within* relations of authority. Figure 3.7, therefore, makes no sense in an economic theory of politics.

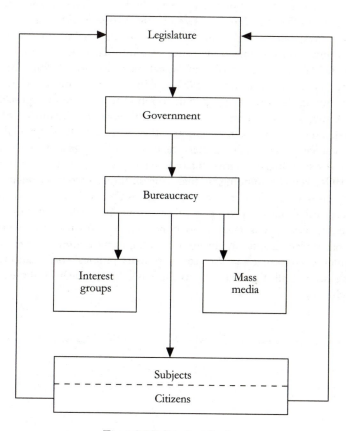

Figure 3.7 Political authority

We have, finally, arrived at a distinction of long standing in social thought. Herbert Spencer, for instance, divided societies into *militant* and *industrial* (1890: chs 17 and 18; [1891] 1969: 317ff.). The first type is characterized by compulsory, the second by voluntary, cooperation. The explicitly acknowledged source of Spencer's division is Sir Henry Maine's famous distinction between *status* and *contract* as two stages in the development of law (1861/1972: 100).

A distinction similar to, but not identical with, that between exchange and authority has been proposed by Friedrich von Hayek: the, nowadays, much celebrated distinction between a *cosmos*, or spontaneous order, and a *taxis*, or organization (see Hayek, 1978: 72–76; 1982, vol. 1, ch. 2). Hayek's distinction differs from the others by focusing upon the genesis of two types of order: the mark of a spontaneous order is that it has grown, as the unintended result of the actions of individuals, whereas an organization is consciously created and instituted by men.

Other relevant distinctions are those between *Markets and Hierarchies* (Williamson, 1975) and *Markt und Organisation* (Vanberg, 1982). Together with Viktor Vanberg, James Buchanan now makes a categorial distinction between 'the economy' and 'organizations', such as clubs, associations, unions, firms and states. 'The essence of organizational membership is subjection to the authority system' (in Buchanan, 1989b: 330). The recognition of the latter phenomenon leads Buchanan explicitly to repudiate economic imperialism.

I think this is a wise move. The most typical aspect of organizations is that they rest on authority. Organizations, therefore, largely defy analysis by rational choice. Joseph Schumpeter knew this and suggested that organizations are for sociologists to investigate (see Chapter 4, p. 171f.). Göran Ahrne (1990, 1994) keeps reminding us that 'organizations', broadly conceived, are the main component parts of society. If this is so, there is reason to be even more sceptical about the prospects of economic imperialism. For my present purposes, however, it is enough to point out that politics, to a very large extent, takes place inside organizations: states, parties, interest organizations, universities, even families, as the seat of primary political socialization. Much, but certainly not all, that happens in there is beyond reach by the economic approach.

4

INDIVIDUALISM

Having discussed self-interest and exchange, there remains individualism. Mainstream microeconomics is usually cited as the paradigm example of methodological individualism in social science. The economic theory of politics follows suit. Adherents of public choice profess their belief in methodological individualism (Buchanan, 1966: 25). It is a controversial issue whether methodological individualism implies ethical individualism, or not. Many adherents of methodological individualism deny that it does (see, e.g. Weber, 1922/1978: 18; Elster, 1982: 453; 1985a: 8). Schumpeter (1908: 90), who coined the term, made a distinction between 'political individualism' and 'methodological individualism'. I agree that you cannot deduce either one from the other – 'imply' is too strong a word – but I doubt that it is a mere accident that so many methodological individualists are also ethical and political individualists (Udehn, 1987: 77–83; Kingdom, 1992: 8–12). For many commentators, and not only adversaries, it is self-evident that methodological individualism is associated with ethical and political individualism internally, by bonds of meaning, rather than externally, or by accident (see, e.g. Brodbeck, 1954, 142; Sproule-Jones, 1984: 176). For my present purposes, however, this is of no importance. As a matter of fact, James Buchanan, like most people in the public choice camp, is an advocate of both methodological and ethical individualism. The matter becomes more complicated by the fact that Buchanan is a methodological in-dividualist in his normative theory of constitutional economics. Maybe this is the bridge that so often unites methodological and ethical individualism.

In this chapter, I am going to argue, first, that public choice is caught in a tension between individualism and institutionalism and, second, that James Buchanan's individualism is ethical rather than methodological. Ethical individualism is the one cardinal value of normative public choice, which is the subject of the second part of this chapter. The normative import of sociology is not equally explicit, but it tends to be more supportive of democracy and equality. In the final section of this chapter I suggest that some elements of public choice theory are best understood as part of

165

libertarianism, or the ideology of the New Right. Public choice is, first of all, a eulogy on the market and a theory of government failure.

METHODOLOGICAL INDIVIDUALISM

In an earlier work, I argued that there are many different versions of methodological individualism, but the following version, or something like it, seems to be most common: *Social phenomena must be explained in terms of individuals, their physical and psychic states, actions, interactions, social situation and physical environment* (Udehn, 1987: 40–43).

The individualist theory of society has a long history in Western thought. It can be traced to Greek Antiquity; to the doctrines of the Sophists and of Epicurus. It was part of the Renaissance and was at its strongest during the Enlightenment. Before the nineteenth century, individualism was equal to the theory of the social contract. In modern social science it has turned into *methodological* individualism and has been advocated by, among others, John Stuart Mill and the Austrian economist Carl Menger. First to use the term 'methodological individualism' was another Austrian economist, Joseph Schumpeter. According to him, methodological individualism means simply 'dass man bei der Beschreibung gewisser wirtschaftlicher Vorgänge von den Handeln der Individuen ausgehe' (the point of departure for descriptions of economic Phenomena is the actions of individuals) (Schumpeter, 1908: 90–91).

Among the most important advocates of methodological individualism, in this century, are Max Weber, Ludwig von Mises, Friedrich von Hayek, Karl Popper, J.W.N. Watkins and Joseph Agassi. The first three defended a subjectivist version of methodological individualism. This version might also be called 'Austrian methodological individualism', even if Max Weber was a German sociologist, not an Austrian economist. Weber was much inspired by Austrian economics and contributed to its further methodological development in the work of Ludwig von Mises and Friedrich von Hayek. Popper, Watkins and Agassi, on the other hand, advocated an objectivist version of methodological individualism, which might also be called 'Popperian methodological individualism', because Watkins and Agassi are pupils of Popper.

Austrian methodological individualism

Subjectivist methodological individualism found its first mature expression in the writings of Max Weber. According to him, it is primarily a principle of concept formation. In a much quoted letter to the economist Robert Liefmann, Weber writes:

> I do understand your battle against sociology. But let me tell you: If I now happen to be a sociologist according to my appointment papers, then I became one in order to put an end to the mischievous enterprise

which still operates with collective notions (*Kollektivbegriffe*). In other words, sociology, too, can only be practised by proceeding from the actions of one or more, few or many, individuals, that means, by employing a strictly 'individualist' method.

(Quoted in Roth, 1976: 306)

For Weber, methodological individualism is inseparably linked to the idea of an interpretive sociology, suggested as an alternative to organicism and functionalism. Its ultimate objective is the explanation of social phenomena in terms of the meaning people attach to their own behaviour, that is to their motives (Weber, 1922/1978: 4ff.).

Ludwig von Mises was much influenced by Weber, but was more of a Kantian and phenomenologist. For Mises, subjectivism is not only a matter of method, but of epistemology and ontology. 'Everything social must in some way be recognizable in the action of the individual. What would that mystical totality of the universalists be if it were not alive in every individual?' (Mises, 1933/1976: 43). In Mises, methodological individualism is turned, above all, against Marxism.

Society is a product of human action. Human action is directed by ideologies. Thus society and any concrete order of social affairs are the outcome of ideologies; ideologies are not as Marxism asserts, a product of a certain state of social affairs.

(Mises, 1949/1966: 145)

The most elaborate version of subjectivist methodological individualism can be found in the work of Friedrich von Hayek. In his case, it is part of an attack upon scientism: the slavish but misguided imitation of the natural sciences by social scientists.

In fact, most of the objects of social science or human action are not 'objective facts' in the narrow sense in which this term is used by the Sciences and contrasted to 'opinions', and they cannot at all be defined in physical terms. So far as human actions are concerned the things are what the acting people think they are.

(Hayek, 1955: 26–27)

A seeming consequence of this view would be that the social scientist must confine herself to the use of commonsense concepts. This is not an implication accepted by Hayek, however. Common sense is the starting point, but not the end of social science. The reason is that human actions have unintended consequences. The task of social science is to analyse social phenomena which are 'the unintended or undesigned results of the actions of many men' (Hayek, 1955: 25). Or rather, the social scientist constitutes these phenomena by constructing individualist models of them.

167

Popperian methodological individualism

Karl Popper is probably the most well-known advocate of methodological individualism, at least outside economics. He differs from his predecessors by defending an objectivist methodology also in the social sciences. What matters for the purposes of social science is not the meaning people attach to their actions, but the objective logic of the situation. Unfortunately, Popper's views on methodological individualism have not contributed to creating clarity as to its meaning and intent. The reason is that Popper builds his methodology out of two traditionally opposite elements: individualism and institutionalism.

Popper's first mention of methodological individualism is in *The Poverty of Historicism*,[1] where he warns against mistaking theoretical models for concrete things and declares that 'the task of social theory is to construct and to analyse our sociological models carefully in descriptive or nominalist terms, that is to say, *in terms of individuals*, of their attitudes, expectations, relations, etc. – a postulate which may be called "methodological individualism"' (Popper, 1957/1961: 136).

Popper takes great care to distinguish methodological individualism from psychologism, a doctrine which he rejects. The alternative to psychologism is a methodology based on situational logic and institutionalism. Situational logic is a generalization of the method used in economics and identical with what we now call 'rational choice'. What Popper means by 'institutionalism' is not equally clear, but examples of institutions are language and universities, two quite disparate phenomena. The task of institutionalism is to make sociology autonomous relative to psychology, but compatible with methodological individualism. This is where problems pile up.

> The human or personal factor will remain the irrational element in most, or all, institutional social theories. The opposite doctrine which teaches the reduction of social theories to psychology, in the same way as we try to reduce chemistry to physics, is, I believe, based on a misunderstanding. It arises from the false belief that this 'methodological psychologism' is a necessary corollary of methodological individualism – of the quite unassailable doctrine that we must try to understand all collective phenomena as due to the actions, interactions, aims, hopes and thoughts of individual men, and as due to traditions created and preserved by individual men.
>
> (Popper, 1957/1961: 157–158)

It is important to observe that Popper uses institutionalism to argue against the theory of the social contract, which he puts on a par with psychologism, because it explains social institutions in terms of human nature alone. Psychologism leads to the theory of the social contract by way of a regress into a state in which there are no social institutions; a state of nature, that is.[2]

It is a desperate position because this theory of a pre-social human nature which explains the foundation of society – a psychologistic version of the 'social contract' – is not only a historic myth, but also, as it were, a methodological myth. It can hardly be seriously discussed, for we have every reason to believe that man or rather his ancestor was social prior to being human (considering, for example, that language presupposes society).

(Popper, 1945/1966: 93)

Popper is not insensitive to the merits of psychologism, however, and the merit it has derives from its being a radical version of methodological individualism and, as such, opposed to methodological collectivism.

Psychologism is, I believe, correct only insofar as it insists upon what might be called 'methodological individualism' as opposed to 'methodological collectivism'; it rightly insists that the 'behaviour' and the 'actions' of collectives, such as states or social groups, must be reduced to the behaviour and to the actions of human individuals. But the belief that the choice of such an individualistic method implies the choice of a psychologistic method is mistaken (as will be shown below in this chapter) even though it may appear very convincing at first sight.

(Popper, 1945/1966, vol. 2: 91)

Despite his promise to do so, Popper never shows that methodological individualism differs from psychologism. The immediate impression that the former implies the latter, therefore, remains (Gellner, 1973: 15). Nor does Popper succeed in reconciling methodological individualism with institutionalism. What he has to adduce on this issue borders on contradiction. According to Popper, all social phenomena, social institutions included, must be explained in terms of individuals (Popper, 1945/1966, vol. 2: 98; 1962/1968: 125). This is the principle of methodological individualism. Against psychologism, however, Popper argues that the actions of individuals cannot be explained without reference to social institutions and to their manner of functioning (1945/1966, vol. 2: 90). One way to escape this seeming contradiction would be to argue that methodological individualism applies only to explanations of social phenomena, while psychologism applies to the explanation of the actions of individuals. I find this solution too farfetched to merit attention.

Another solution has been proposed by J.O. Wisdom. He agrees that Popper's methodological individualism looks reductionist and therefore incompatible with insitutionalism, but offers a way out of this dilemma. On Wisdom's interpretation, Popper holds that social wholes are 'partially' or 'distributively', but not 'globally' or 'collectively' reducible to the actions of individuals.

The 'reductionist' programme aims at dispensing with *all* institutional

169

wholes after the 'reduction' is carried out. Now, Popper is fully aware, I think, that this is impossible, for you can dispense with one or even more institutional wholes, but *only in an institutional setting* . . . [Popper's] view involves a partial reduction, in which any one institutional whole is 'reducible' though not all such wholes at once.

(Wisdom, 1970: 274)

As Wisdom later admits, this is 'a development from, though inconsistent with Popper's methodological individualism' (Wisdom, 1971: 143).

The tension between individualism and institutionalism in Popperian methodology led to its further development in two directions: J.W.N. Watkins followed the path of strict methodological individualism, while Joseph Agassi suggested a unity of opposites, called 'institutional individualism'. Watkins did much to clarify the true meaning and intent of methodological individualism, as originally conceived. Among his many statements I choose the following explication of methodological individualism:

This principle states that social processes and events should be explained by being deduced from (a) principles governing the behaviour of participating individuals and (b) descriptions of their situations.

(Watkins, 1953: 729; see also 1952: 187)

To this statement should be added the special clause that 'social situation' must refer to other individuals and material circumstances, but not to social entities of any kind. To admit of social entities as part of the situation is to smuggle in alien elements through the back door and to beg the whole issue of individualism versus social holism (cf. Lukes, 1973: 118–122).

Institutional individualism

In a suggestive article on 'methodological individualism' (1960), Joseph Agassi sets out 'to defend institutional individualism', which he considers 'to be Popper's great contribution to the philosophy of the social sciences' (Agassi, 1960: 244). According to Agassi, the controversy between holism and individualism has been based upon the implicit assumption that wholes, if they exist, have aims and interests of their own. Popper's great contribution is to have developed a *via media* between the traditional views by rejecting this assumption. Popper accepts the existence of social wholes, but denies that they have interests distinct from those of individual human beings. (Agassi, 1960: 277–278).

Thus . . . not the aims of institutions but rather their existence affects the individual's behaviour; the existing institutions constitute a part of the individual's circumstance which together with his aims determine his behaviour . . . While according to psychologistic individualism only material conditions may be considered as relevant circumstances, according to Popper the existence of institutions may be considered as relevant circumstances too.

(Agassi, 1960: 247)

This is a fair characterization of Popper's institutionalism, but it is wrong to believe that it originated with Popper. It is simply a restatement of traditional institutionalism in the social sciences. More original was Popper's combination of institutionalism with situational logic, or rational choice, which is what distinguishes the new institutionalism in economics from the old institutionalism.

Nevertheless, there is still a problem of reconciling institutionalism with individualism. Agassi eventually comes to realize this and confesses: 'Popper ... I now tend to agree with Gellner, is unclear about matters and so free for all. I do not mean to reaffirm the position I held in 1960, and I do not know whether today I will at all endorse methodological individualism' (Agassi, 1972: 326). In his article 'Institutional Individualism' (1975) Agassi did reaffirm his position, but without claiming that this position is methodological individualism.

I have argued that institutionalism is incompatible with original methodological individualism. This does not imply, of course, that institutional individualism is an impossible position. Quite the contrary, it is immeasurably superior to methodological individualism as a methodology for social science. I do not even mind calling it 'methodological individualism', as long as it is recognized that we have to do with two distinct methodological principles. Perhaps we could call them *strong* and *weak* methodological individualism, respectively.

The existence of social institutions has always been a problem for individualist theories of society. The most consistent version of individualism is the theory of the social contract. In this theory individuals are situated in a state of nature and institutions are wholly endogenous. This theory came under heavy attack in the nineteenth century by Romantic philosophers (and others) defending an organicist theory of society and the state. But it was also attacked by social scientists from all disciplines, defending institutionalism. It was at this time that Joseph Schumpeter intervened in the debate and coined the term 'methodological individualism'. Unlike most economists, however, Schumpeter was not a methodological individualist himself.

When Schumpeter invented the term 'methodological individualism', he opposed it to the 'social' approach used in sociology. He also believed that methodological individualism is inapplicable outside theoretical economics and, especially, in the theory of organization (1908: 91–95, 539–541).[3] Later, Schumpeter, more or less, equates sociology with institutional analysis. He points out the similarities between sociology and the institutional school in economics, and opposes this approach to the methodological individualism of marginalist economics (1954: 20f., 26f., 983–995, 864–877, 954). In his own work, Schumpeter was a methodological individualist only to the extent

171

that he practised theoretical economics. In his sociological works, he was not a methodological individualist.[4]

The opposition between individualism and institutionalism is particularly clear in economics, where 'the "institutional" view of economic activities' is contrasted with 'the individual or contractual aspect' (Knight, [1951] 1963: 18). The urge of neoclassical economics, and the purpose of its methodological individualism, is to endogenize all social institutions (see Boland, 1982: 30–32, 48ff.). Unlike the theory of the social contract, however, economics has never succeeded in eliminating social institutions. If contract theories give rise to an infinite regress taking us 'back' to a state of nature, the economic approach gives rise to a vicious circle of individuals and institutions, a chicken-and-egg problem about primacy (cf. Nozick, 1977: 353–361).

Public choice individualism

The tension between individualism and institutionalism recurs in public choice and is illustrated by the work of James Buchanan. From the beginning, Buchanan contrasts an 'individualistic' theory of the state with an 'organismic' theory. In the first, 'the state is represented as the sum of its individual members acting in a collective capacity' (1949: 496). 'The state has no ends other than those of its individual members and is not a separate decision-making unit. State decisions are, in the final analysis, the collective decisions of individuals' (Buchanan, 1949: 498). This view of (methodological) individualism, implying that only individuals decide and act, is the basic intuition behind Buchanan's methodological individualism in all his writings on this subject and turns it into an aspect of rational choice (Buchanan, 1989b: ch. 3; see also Sproule-Jones, 1984: 168f.). But Buchanan is also one of the most consistent advocates of institutionalism in modern economics. Supporting evidence for this suggestion is not necessary, since institutionalism pervades every corner of his work. Buchanan's methodological individualism, therefore, is identical with the institutional individualism of Popper and Agassi. 'First of all, methodological individualism does not imply or require that individual choice behavior is invariant over changes in the institutional setting' (Buchanan, 1989b: 38); 'there is no difficulty at all in analyzing individual choice behavior under differing institutional settings, and in predicting how these varying settings will influence the outcomes of the interaction process' (Buchanan, 1988: 105). This institutionalism is an important difference between public choice and mainstream microeconomics (Sproule-Jones, 1982: 794–797). Unlike Popper and Agassi, however, Buchanan is also a contractarian and this gives rise to a certain tension, or split, in his theory of politics-as-exchange.

Buchanan, the constitutional economist is, I suggest, engaged in two entirely different enterprises. Buchanan, the contractarian, assumes utility-maximizing individuals choosing between order and anarchy. In this analysis

172

rules are public goods, subject to complex exchange or agreement. But, then, there is also Buchanan the institutional political economist and follower of Smith, who compares different constitutions with respect to their effects. In this analysis, constitutions are not the objects of choice and exchange. They are given to analysis as rules assumed to be followed. Only then can they have effects. It is an entirely different matter that the ultimate purpose of this analysis is to guide people in the choice of constitution. Buchanan makes a distinction between choice within a constitution and choice of constitution. It is only in the first context that constitutions are treated as goods and subject to complex exchange. But Buchanan's comparative constitutional economics is not within that context. As a positive theory of the effects of different constitutions, it is entirely concerned with choices within constitutions. Only the normative relevance of this analysis lies within the context of choice *of* constitution. Buchanan's constitutional economics is not a theory of choice and complex exchange of constitutions. If economics is a theory of choice and exchange, therefore, Buchanan's constitutional economics is not an economic theory.

The argument, thus far, does not question the existence, or possibility, of an economic theory of rules, or institutions. I have not rejected the view that people create and obey rules for economic, selfish or altruistic, reasons. The point I wish to make is that once you start asking questions about the *effects* of rules, you assume that they are in fact followed, irrespective of the motive for adherence – they may be either economic or moral, or both, or neither. Thus, even if it were possible to explain the emergence and existence of rules in economic theory, a theory about the effects of rules already in existence is not an economic theory. Not if economics is about choice and exchange. To ask about the effects of rules, norms, institutions or social structure, in varying ways, is a common concern for anthropology, sociology, the old institutional economics and Marxism, but has not been a concern of neoclassical economics until recently.

What unites these 'non-economic' disciplines and theories is not only an interest in the working and effects of institutions, broadly conceived, but also a rejection of the economic theory of institutions, if for somewhat different reasons. Sociologists tend to emphasize the importance of social norms and habits of conduct. Marxists are closer to mainstream economists in assigning due weight to interest, but reject the contract, or exchange, part of the economic explanation as mere ideology. I suggest that rules are followed for different reasons: either economic or moral, or both, or neither. Many social norms, or codes, such as manners, or rules of etiquette, are neither instrumental, nor moral. They are followed out of ingrained habit, routine, or unthinking tradition. In the case of most rules, an economic explanation is highly problematic. They are a matter of principle, rather than of utility. What is more, their possible utility seems to depend upon the extent to which they are accepted as valid principles of action.

There is no contradiction between the two sides of Buchanan's work, however, since it is possible to see contractarianism and institutionalism as two complementary, rather than conflicting, perspectives. But if there is no conflict between contractarianism and institutionalism, or between two versions of methodological individualism, I suggest that there is a conflict between institutionalism and rational choice, if seen as universal approaches in social science (cf. Grafstein, 1991). Institutionalism, based on the conviction that institutions matter, implies that institutions have a power of their own. But if they do, we have an explanation of action in terms of rules, as distinguished from rational choice. Hence, rational choice is not a universal approach in social science.

NORMATIVE PUBLIC CHOICE

Public choice is not just a positive theory of politics. It is also, and perhaps above all (Wolfe, 1989b: 120 ff.), a normative theory of the ideal, or good, society, and what policies we should pursue to realize this ideal (Mueller, 1979: Part II; 1989: Part V). Before the rise of public choice, the task of normative economics was generally conceived as that of producing a social welfare function. There were always critical voices, especially the Austrians and other libertarian economists, but a strong alternative was lacking until public choice emerged on the scene. An important event in this development was Kenneth Arrow's demonstration of the problems involved in social choice.

I am not going to discuss welfare economics and I will only touch upon the theory of social choice. In this section, I will start by describing James Buchanan's development from an economist and theorist of positive public choice to a political philosopher preaching individualism as the basic value of normative public choice. But it is not simply individualism; it is what C.B. Macpherson (1962) has called 'possessive individualism', a kind of individualism which has the market as its presupposition and precondition. The Virginia School of public choice is the latest significant manifestation of an individualist social and political philosophy which originated with Hobbes and Locke. It is represented today most obviously by people belonging to the Austrian, Chicago and Virginia Schools of economics and by the philosopher Robert Nozick. As a political ideology it is called 'libertarianism' and, according to some, it is the manifestation of 'true individualism' and 'classical liberalism', as distinguished from the 'false individualism' of Rousseau and the intellectuals of the French revolution (Hayek, 1948).[5]

It is not a mere accident that many economists are possessive individualists and libertarians. The science of economics developed as a theory of the market and the free market still has a special place in economic theory. It is often pointed out that the market, as depicted in economic theory, has never existed. From a theoretical point of view, the market is an ideal type, in the sense of Max Weber, a simplified model of the real market. But as Max

Weber also pointed out – taking the economic theory of the market as his example – theoretical ideal types easily turn into normative ideal types (Weber [1917] 1949: 44).

But economists are not alone in turning theoretical models into normative ideals. Sociologists do so too, but they are probably a more heterogeneous bunch than are economists. The main sociological utopia, I suggest, is *community*. An alternative utopia for many sociologists is *civil society* (Wolfe, 1989b). Both concepts are polysemic and open to different interpretations and different utopias. For some, community means above all the family and other small and/or traditional groups. This is the interpretation made by conservative sociologists. In matters of policy, these sociologists join the libertarians in their onslaught on the state. Other sociologists dream of a *political* community, characterized by solidarity between its citizens. These sociologists are much more favourable to the state and tend to defend the welfare state against its critics. The political philosophy called 'communitarianism' is characterized by an ambiguity about the size and shape of the ideal community. It includes both conservative critics of the welfare state, and liberal and social democratic defenders of the welfare state as a political community of citizens. Believers in civil society are no less divided. There are conservative and libertarian sociologists celebrating civil society only because it is alternative to the state. There is also a Marxist tradition, conceiving of civil society as distinct from both market and state. The utopia of Marxism, communist society, bears traces of both community and civil society. Communist society is a community characterized by solidarity and equality, but it is not a political community, at least not in the form of a state. Communist society is a classless civil society free from exploitation. It is an association of free producers, without a state. Whether it is, or should, or could, be a market, or must be a centrally planned economy, is one of the most controversial issues in the history of Marxist thought (Udehn, 1981a).

Among economists, one of the few who have tried to find out what sociology is all about is Mancur Olson (1968, 1969). He observes, correctly, that sociology and economics suggest different solutions to the problem of order. For sociology, social order is based upon a common culture: common values, norms, attitudes and symbols, transmitted from one generation to the next through socialization. Of paramount importance, for social order, is the existence of institutions and organizations fulfilling the functions of socialization and social control. Economics, on the other hand, sees a spontaneous social order emerging as individuals enter into voluntary exchange with one another on the market. The precondition for this social order is that individuals have *different* values (tastes) and talents. Olson notes that Durkheim tried to capture something of this difference with his distinction between 'mechanic' and 'organic' solidarity; the first based upon a common morality, the second upon functional differentiation. It may be added that most theoretical sociologists have somehow been concerned with this difference. In contemporary sociology, the distinction is between 'social integration' and 'system integration' (Lockwood, 1964; Giddens, 1987: 28).

Olson goes on to argue that these two models of society are not only descriptive, but 'ideals' defended by sociologists and economists, respectively. He also agrees with the sociologists that there is a trade-off between the two types of social order, so that an increase in one of them is necessarily at the expense of the other. I assume that he also agrees that over the last two hundred years there has been a violent expansion of the market at the expense of community. Schumpeter has described it as a 'process of creative destruction' (Schumpeter, 1954: ch. 7). Marx and Engels' description of this process in *The Communist Manifesto* is worth quoting:

> The bourgeoisie, wherever it has got the upper hand, has put an end to all feudal, patriarchal, idyllic relations. It has pitilessly torn asunder the motley feudal ties that bound man to his 'natural superiors', and has left remaining no other nexus between man and man than naked self-interest, than callous 'cash payment'. It has drowned the most heavenly ecstasies of religious fervour, of chivalrous enthusiasm, of philistine sentimentalism, in the icy water of egotistical calculation. It has resolved personal worth into exchange value, and in place of the numberless indefeasible chartered freedoms, has set up that single, unconsionable freedom – Free Trade.
>
> (Marx and Engels, 1848/1967: 82)

Olson does not reveal his own preferences. A reading of his other works would make us believe that his sympathies are with the market. Be that as it may, when comparing the economic and sociological visions of society his conclusion is diplomatic: we need both. The problem is to find the optimal mix between them. The solution is as simple as it is elegant. The perfect combination would be one where people have different preferences for private goods, but common preferences for public goods. Now this is not the case and there are also widely differing opinions about which goods are, or should be, private or public. So, for all practical purposes, the problem remains.

Ethical individualism

Throughout his writings, Buchanan assumes the traditional separation of facts and norms (or values); the first stating what is, the second what ought to be (1962: 307–314; 1979a: 12; 1979b: 179; Brennan and Buchanan 1981: 195f.). Obviously, what is, or could be, has 'implications', or, better, relevance, for a discourse about what ought to be (Buchanan, 1978: 15–17; 1979a: 11–22; 1986: 22; Buchanan and Tullock, 1962/1965: 7, 24). Most public choice literature belongs clearly in the first realm. Buchanan is a bit more uncertain about the status of his own theory of constitutions. He seems to vacillate between a positive and a normative interpretation, with a drift, over time, towards the latter. In *The Calculus of Consent* (Buchanan and Tullock, 1962/1965), even though the stated purpose is normative (pp. 4, 24), the analysis is supposed to be *wertfrei* (value-free) (p. vii). Buchanan later suggests (1978: 9f.) that it was 'a mixture of a positive analysis of alternative decision rules and a normative defence of certain American political institutions that owe their origins to the Founding Fathers and to James Madison in particular'. He also informs us that later he has 'tried to move cautiously but clearly in the direction of normative understanding and evaluation, to move beyond the way rules work to a consideration of what rules work *best*' (ibid., p. 16). Even so, Buchanan saw his next important contribution to the theory of constitutions, *The Limits of Liberty* (1975), 'as a basically positive analysis, with ethical content squeezed to a minimum' (1979b: 176). In *The Reason of Rules* (1985), finally, discourse is explicitly normative. The overriding aim is to find normative criteria for the choice of constitution. Of course, this presupposes a comparative, positive analysis of how alternative sets of legal rules work (Brennan and Buchanan, 1985: xi, 134ff.). The distinction between positive and normative discourse now seems to be this: a positive analysis seeks facts, but has normative relevance. A normative analysis seeks the best society (in some respect), but leans upon positive analysis. It is a matter of ultimate purpose. In the last decade or so Buchanan has turned into a devoted advocate of a normative theory of constitutions along the lines of eighteenth-century political economy and closer to social philosophy (Buchanan, 1979b: 179; 1979a: 11–22; 1986: 260–274; Brennan and Buchanan, 1984: 382–394).

According to the most superficial view, discourse is normative to the extent that it uses words like 'ought', 'best', or 'good'. But, of course, things are a bit more complicated. Even in the absence of any explicitly stated evaluation, recommendation or prescription, all social theory is, irredeemably, more or less value-laden. In the case of public choice, it is 'more' rather than 'less'. The interesting question is why Buchanan originally believed that it is 'less'. One possible answer is: by taking (pre-Paretian) welfare economics as the paradigm of normative analysis. The purpose of this analysis is to arrive at a welfare function for society as a whole – an endeavour which, according to Myrdal (1929/1953: 54), involves a 'communistic fiction'. Buchanan is correct to argue that it is impossible to construct a social welfare function without the introduction of value-judgements. At least, if we are not allowed, on scientific grounds, to make interpersonal comparisons of utility. And, according to Buchanan (and the Austrians), we are not. Utility and cost are subjective phenomena, which are revealed only in the actions of individuals, but not amenable to objective measurement and quantification (see, e.g., Buchanan, 1969a, *passim*; 1979b: 81–91). This is the theoretical reason behind Buchanan's methodological individualism (Buchanan, 1962: 315–317; 1975a: 1f.; 1979a: 13f.; Buchanan and Tullock, 1962/1965: 3, 11–15; Brennan and

Buchanan, 1985: 19ff. See also Udehn, 1987). But, clearly, Buchanan is wrong to believe that the individualism of his contractarian approach is only methodological; an analytical method, but ethically neutral, or with normative content minimized. Buchanan's methodological individualism does not suggest a way to explain, or describe, any existing society, past or present. It depicts and justifies an imaginary society supposed to maximize individual freedom, or liberty. This society does not follow from *methodological* individualism alone. Buchanan eventually comes to realize this fact: 'A distinction must be drawn between the methodological individualism that builds on individual choice as the basic unit of analysis and a second presupposition that locates the ultimate sources of value exclusively in individuals' (Buchanan [1987] 1989b: 62). He realizes that his own constitutional economics relies on the second presuppostition.

Buchanan is also correct to argue that the social welfare functions suggested by economists reflect their own values. But he is wrong to assume that he can escape the dilemma by recommending constitutions instead. Constitutions are not ethically neutral, at least not if they define property rights, maybe the most controversial issue in history to this date. As we have seen, Buchanan eventually realizes that, like welfare economics, his own theory of constitutions is primarily normative. The difference is in the object of inquiry, not in their logical characteristics. Both theories are equally normative (see p. 181).

A second possible reason why Buchanan originally interpreted his theory of constitutions as positive is that it is based upon values that are common and uncontroversial in Western liberal society (Buchanan, 1979b: 152; 1986: 51f.). But, certainly, a theory is not less normative for promoting liberal values, even if those values happen to be commonly accepted in our Western society. It is, if anything, more ethnocentric. Weber has argued that all social theory is ethnocentric to some degree. We cannot escape our cultural heritage, but select problems because of their *cultural significance* (Weber, [1904] 1949: 74ff.). But Buchanan goes much further. He actively and wholeheartedly supports one single value – individual liberty – at the expense of other values, and defends a social organization, which, he believes, maximizes this value. But liberty is not the only value, not even in our Western society. There are also equality and social security. In the presumed trade-off between liberty and equality, Buchanan's preferences are all for the former.

The basic intuition behind Buchanan's analysis of politics-as-exchange is that politics ought to approximate the working of a perfectly competitive market. On the market, resource allocation is Pareto efficient, reflecting the tastes, or revealed preferences, of individuals. There is no special problem of distribution as distinct from allocation. The distribution of economic goods over individuals is a function of the allocation of resources to different uses.

In politics, things are different. As we have seen, there is little *simple* exchange between two parties. In politics, exchange is indirect, or *complex*

(Buchanan, 1975a: 43–48; 1986: 90; 1989a: 14f.; Brennan and Buchanan, 1985: 25). It takes the form of agreement, or consent. But if it is easy for two parties to exchange private goods to their mutual benefit on the market, it would seem impossible for millions of people to agree on the provision of public goods by the state or some other collective agency. Even in a democracy, policy does not reflect the preferences of all voters, but, at best, of a majority of them. As Kenneth Arrow (1951/1963) and Duncan Black (1958) have shown, no voting rule can transform the preferences of individuals into a consistent set of preferences for the community as a whole.

Arrow and Black are generally considered important forerunners of public choice – Black almost a member – and their results are incorporated as part of the doctrine. The reason is easy to see. The implication of Arrow's and Black's analyses seems to be that welfare economics is impossible. If we cannot derive a social welfare, or collective choice, function from the preferences of individuals, then it must reflect the preferences of the welfare economist himself – something the libertarian enemies of welfare economics had argued for a long time, but without formal proof. Arrow provided the proof. A further implication seems to be that the market is superior to politics as a mechanism for resource allocation cum distribution.

This was not Arrow's conclusion, however. The market mechanism fails equally to create a rational social choice (Arrow, 1951/1963). Why these diverging conclusions? The answer is that Arrow assumed that individuals have both *tastes* and *values*, the former pertaining to their direct consumption, the latter to their moral evaluation of different social states. On the market, there is not even the possibility to express preferences for social states, only tastes for consumption goods (Arrow, 1951/1963: 17–19). Buchanan (1954b) was among the first to react to Arrow's conclusions. While agreeing with the implications of Arrow's analysis for welfare economics, he criticized Arrow for suggesting the idea of rational social choice in the case of the market. The market is not a mechanism for social choice – it is a spontaneous order – and can, therefore, be, neither rational, nor irrational.

Buchanan's 'solution' is to pick up an idea of the Swedish (socialist) economist Knut Wicksell, who argued that the political analogue of economic (Pareto) efficiency is unanimous consent (see Buchanan, 1975a: 6–8, 149–151; 1986: 23; 1989b: 62f.; Buchanan and Tullock, 1962/1965: 8; Brennan and Buchanan, 1985: 135–137). The idea is simple and, in itself, unobjectionable: unanimous consent concerning public goods is the only obvious condition in which a change is impossible without making someone worse off. But of course it is no solution, since it does away with the problem. The problem of social choice occurs only because people have different preferences, making unanimity impossible. Buchanan's 'solution' consists in avoiding the problem by minimizing public choice to those issues, if any, where unanimous consent is possible.

In the case of most, if not all, public goods, however, unanimous consent

179

is impossible. We cannot expect entire populations completely to agree upon what public goods should be provided. Unanimous consent is utopian. If we demand unanimity, there is simply very little scope for public choice. But Buchanan does not go that far. As he observes, himself (1986: 90), 'such an inclusive decision rule would of course make political action almost impossible'. Exactly how far he wishes to go is difficult to tell. He certainly wishes to push decision rules in the *direction* of unanimity. And, of course, there is nothing sacred about simple majority. Also, we have to admit that unanimity is the ideal of democracy, however unattainable.

Confronted with the impossibility of everyone agreeing on the production of public goods and of accepting his/her share of private goods, Buchanan shifts attention from goods proper to the rules of the economic and political games, viz., the constitution.[6] If people do not agree upon the distribution of wealth, maybe they can be made to agree upon the rules governing its acquisition. If only the game is fair, people may accept the result. The precondition for accepting a particular distribution of wealth, or allocation of resources, is that individuals, when entering the game (the social contract), are uncertain about their future position in the social order. They do not know in advance whether they will eventually turn out to be winners or losers.[7] The picture is, of course, complicated by the introduction of time. A social contract may be binding for those who 'signed' it, but what is our obligation to a constitution enacted long before we were born? This complication seems to call for an intermittent renegotiation of the terms of the contract. But even so, Buchanan is willing to grant a certain primacy to the status quo, simply because, unlike other possible alternatives, it exists. '"We start from here," and not from somewhere else' (Buchanan, 1975a: 78). As to the present status quo, however, this primacy is not enough. Buchanan does not believe that we live in the best of worlds, or that the real is necessarily also the rational.[8] There is need for a constitutional revolution (Buchanan, 1975a: ch. 10; Brennan and Buchanan, 1985: ch. 9).

Buchanan's analysis, once again, is far removed from anything we observe in reality. No state and no constitution is, or was, the result of an actual social contract and unanimity is impossible in constitutional, as in other, matters. All constitutions are imposed; in most cases by a minority, nowadays more often by a majority. In some countries, the passing of a constitution even requires something more than a simple majority, but unanimity – never. Buchanan, of course, knows this. His intention is not to provide an historical account of what actually happened or, 'wie Es eigentlich gewesen war'. His purpose is to provide a 'conceptual', or 'logical', explanation of the origin of constitutions (Buchanan: 1962: 317–320; 1975a: 6, 54; Brennan and Buchanan, 1985: 19ff.). Buchanan even admits that the exchange paradigm is of less value in the study of politics than in the analysis of the market. But the difference is one of degree. In both cases, we have to do with idealizations. It is only that the exchange model is a bit more removed from reality in the case of politics than in the case of the market (see Buchanan, 1986: 21, 90; 1989a: 14ff.). Or so I interpret Buchanan. But he seems to be wavering. In *The Reason of Rules*, he writes, together with Geoffrey Brennan, that 'a requirement for unanimity may seem to be mere utopian romanticizing' (ibid., p. 27) and also that 'Critics might immediately suggest that unanimous agreement smacks of utopian absurdity' (ibid., pp. 136f.). Their defence is not in terms of descriptive realism, but in terms of normative relevance: 'there is no alternative criterion for the evaluation of proposals' (ibid., p. 137). Constitutional economics is a normative enterprise, like welfare economics, and is recognized as such (ibid., pp. 54–56, 65f.). The difference is that constitutional economics shifts 'the domain of normative inquiry from the set of imaginable *income distributions* to the set of feasible *institutional arrangements* from which income distributions will emerge' (ibid., p. 117). There is irony in this development. Public choice, we recall, started as a movement against welfare economics. The latter was accused of being normative and, above all, of lacking in realism. Public choice, on the contrary, was launched as uncompromising realism, depicting man as the selfish creature he really is. Today public choice itself appears no less 'idealistic', both descriptively and normatively.

I suggested above that Buchanan changed his focus from economic goods proper to the rules of the economic and political games. This is my view, not Buchanan's. According to him and most other economists, rules, including constitutions, are public goods on a par with parks, roads, the military, etc. I have some difficulty with this analysis. The differences seem more important than the similarities.

First of all, constitutions and other rules are not the kinds of thing that you can exchange on the market. This might not seem a serious problem, since in a way this is the case with all public goods. I still believe there are important differences, however. Ordinary public goods can in principle be owned and alienated. The problem here is practical. In the case of rules, on the other hand, it is inconceivable that they could ever be owned, bought or sold. Secondly, unlike ordinary economic goods, rules cannot be consumed, or even *used*. Rules are *obeyed* (or disobeyed), *followed* (or broken). According to a sociological or philosophical analysis that is, and Buchanan seems to agree: 'As Frank Knight emphasized, a human being is a rule-following animal. We live in accordance with a set of moral-ethical rules or norms for behavior, a set that we take, consciously or unconsciously, to be relatively absolute absolutes' (1989a: 43). This insight, unfortunately, has not left any trace in his economic theory of politics.

The economist might retort that economic analysis is in no way restricted to 'goods', or 'commodities', in a narrow sense. There is, for instance, the peculiar commodity of labour power, as analysed by Marx, and human capital, as analysed by Becker and others. There are also the various things called 'services'. The defining characteristic of an economic 'good' is that it confers utility upon individuals, anything that individuals value. It is difficult to deny

181

that rules may be 'goods' in this sense. A certain amount of order and security is a good thing, no doubt. Perhaps rules may be conceived of as some kind of goods of a higher order – as a form of capital (see Buchanan, 1975a: ch. 7).[9]

A first problem with this interpretation is that it is out of tune with Buchanan's suggestion that we restrict economic analysis to net *wealth* maximization (see Buchanan, 1979b: 66ff.). Rules are not part of wealth. But different rules may have different *effects* upon the wealth of nations and of individuals. May we not assume that individuals prefer those rules that favour themselves, in the first place, and their nation, in the second place? This is a possibility, but, if so, are the rules incorporated as arguments in individuals' utility functions? It does not seem so, because the whole purpose, or reason, of rules, according to Buchanan (1979a: 15f.; 1986: 31–33; 1989a: 36ff.; 1989b: 41ff.; Brennan and Buchanan, 1981: 441; 1985: 16–18), is to *constrain homo economicus*.[10] As we will see in the next section (pp. 189–195), the role of economic man is entirely different in Buchanan's constitutional economics and in orthodox economics.

> to model persons in *homo economicus* terms for this purpose of deriving constitutional structure is not the same thing at all as advancing predictions that persons will necessarily behave as *homo economicus*, even in some average or representative sense. The legitimate 'science of political economy' – of interaction among persons who behave in accordance with precepts of net wealth maximization – is not, and should not be conceived to be analogous to that 'science of economics' which is conceived to be exclusively concerned with the generation of refutable hypotheses.
>
> (Buchanan, 1986: 36)

Also, in Buchanan's 'conceptual explanation' of a constitution that is fair, individuals are absolutely uncertain about their future position. This means that utility-maximization is impossible. And, indeed, the *absence* of individual utility-maximization is the main precondition for unanimity in the choice of constitution. What, then, is economic about such explanation? Is it not the case that people, when deprived of the possibility of economic behaviour, choose according to their moral values? Buchanan does not deny this possibility, but his analysis takes another direction. Uncertainty has the further function of turning a fair constitution into the most rational alternative from a purely egoistic point of view. In the face of uncertainty, people will avoid the risk of becoming losers in an unequal society. Self-interest leads to a fair and equal society. This may be, if people start from nothing, or are forced to choose a constitution, but this does not turn the constitution itself into a public good. Nor is it apparent that anything even remotely resembling exchange takes place. In economics proper, exchange is based upon differences between individuals (see Buchanan, 1975a: 11; Buchanan and Tullock,

1962/1965: 4). People exchange because they have different tastes, abilities or property. In Buchanan's constitutional economics, the opposite is the case. Agreement is possible only if we remove all differences between individuals.[11]

Nevertheless, as I have already suggested, Buchanan does conceive of constitutions, and of rules generally, as public goods. In the state of nature there is Hobbesian *Warr* (War). Constitutions emerge as people agree to constrain their own behaviour in exchange for a similar constraint on the part of other individuals. But this order is not stable. There is still an incentive to defect. The next step, therefore, is the choice of a sovereign with the right to punish those who break the social contract.[12] In this contractarian perspective law, and order, the constitution and the state, or sovereign, are treated as public goods.

I suggest that the problem with an economic interpretation of rules is reflected in Buchanan's constitutional economics. If a constitution is a public good, like any other, then there is nothing sacred, or special, about it. It may be changed at any time, like any convention. But Buchanan feels that a constitution is, and must be, something more important and more permanent. He 'solves' the problem by making a distinction between short-term, or narrow, self-interest and long-term, enlightened, self-interest. While it is often in our narrow self-interest to deviate from legal rules, it is in our enlightened self-interest not to do so. But this is not a satisfactory solution. It is too much *ad hoc* and indeterminate. It allows us to have it both ways and so to make the economic theory of constitutions immune to critique.

There seems to be a schizophrenic split between Buchanan$_1$, the professional economist and Buchanan$_2$, the personal moralist. Buchanan$_1$ is the contractarian constitutional economist. Buchanan$_2$ goes as far as to argue for the need of a new civic religion (Brennan and Buchanan, 1985: 149f.). The problem is that it is self-defeating to argue for the need of a religion, or even of a secular morality, in terms of economic utility. The sacred is the exact opposite of the efficient, expedient or merely convenient, and even secularized morality is possible only as something distinct from the economic.[13] The morally good is categorically different from economic goods. The relation between them is that of inverse variation. To the extent that a law is seen as an economic good, it loses its moral force. Most legal rules, and constitutions in particular, are not just economic goods. They are moral goods as well. What is missing in any economic analysis of law is *The Moral Dimension* (Etzioni, 1988; Wolfe, 1989b).

As Buchanan frequently observes, a constitution has to be legitimate. Unanimity is, indeed, the ideal, but not because it is analogous to economic efficiency. Both the market and the rule of unanimity are legitimate to the extent that they correspond with individualism and democracy as cultural values of our Western civilization. In the case of the market, moral justification is relatively unimportant. It seems justified in terms of purely economic considerations. No viable alternative is at hand. In the case of the rule of unanimity, things are entirely different. Moral justification means everything. A broad consensus is important, because it corresponds with democracy as a moral value. A constitution that is passed in a democratic fashion may be accepted even by those who would prefer another constitution. But we should not expect, or demand, unanimity. And, here, Buchanan is too little outcome-oriented – which is unusual for an economist. Buchanan, the proceduralist, asks us to disregard the outcome, or end-state, if only the procedure is fair (see, however, Buchanan, 1984: 444). But this is wishful thinking. Most people do have moral beliefs about social states and quite a lot have strong moral convictions about distributive justice. What is more, lots of people judge the constitution by the outcome; the kind of society it gives rise to. Those who are egalitarians, for instance, will not give their consent to a constitution that gives rise to an elitist society, no matter how uncertain they are about their own fortune in this society. Failure to account for this fact is an obvious shortcoming of Buchanan's constitutional economics, in its positive and normative shapes alike.

Democracy

Democracy met with resistance from its very instigation. At first, critics of democracy were mainly conservatives (Roper, 1989). Eventually they were joined by libertarians.[14] In both cases, following Hirschman, we may refer to them as 'reactionaries'. In *The Rhetoric of Reaction* (1991), Hirschman distinguishes three theses advanced by reactionaries against democracy: (1) that democracy has perverse effects, (2) that democracy is futile and (3) that democracy is a threat to liberty. An acute observation is that reactionaries have recently tried a new tactic. Reactionary politics is presented as progressive, while defenders of democracy and equality are described as conservative. This rhetoric has been a marked feature of the political debate in Sweden for some ten years now.

Libertarians, then, have always taken a rather ambivalent attitude towards democracy. They accept it as a method, but not as a value; as a means, but not as an end (see, e.g. Hayek, 1960: ch. 7). Public choice has added to this ambivalence by voicing doubts also concerning democracy as a method. The only justification of democracy now seems to be that alternatives are lacking. A critic has described public choice as a theory of 'democracy-bashing' (Kelman, 1988); friends of public choice prefer to talk about its 'unromantic' view of democracy (Mitchell and Simmons, 1994). There are several reasons for this reluctant acceptance of democracy on the part of public choice theorists. David Beetham has usefully summarized the libertarian theory of democracy in four theorems:

> I shall call them, respectively, the *necessity theorem* (the market is a necessary condition for democracy); the *analogy theorem* (democracy is best

184

understood on the model or analogy of the market); the *superiority theo-rem* (the market is more democratic than the polity ever can be); the *disability theorem* (political democracy threatens or disables the operation of the free market). Each of these theorems highlights a different item in the neo-liberal litany of market virtues. The 'necessity theorem' de-fines the market as an essential locus of individual freedom. The 'analogy theorem' applauds the market's spontaneous mechanism of incentives and disincentives for reconciling the individual interest with the common good. The 'superiority theorem' emphasizes consumer sovereignty and the market's responsiveness to popular demand. The 'disability theorem' underlines the beneficial economic disciplines of the market, which we relax at our peril.

(Beetham, 1993: 188)

Beetham goes on to make an observation of utmost importance for an understanding of normative public choice: 'central to my concern will be a characteristic assumption which all four theorems betray, to the effect that the market constitutes the paradigmatic social institution, and offers the privi-leged vantage point, in relation to which all other social institutions must be understood and assessed' (ibid., p. 188). Thus, the market is not just the best mechanism for resource allocation, it is the best mechanism for political decision-making and for social interaction generally; the yardstick with which to measure the value of all social institutions. This is the result of using economic theory of the market – economics as catallactics – as a normative theory of politics.

I believe that there are three main reasons why public choice theorists are not particularly enthusiastic about the idea of democracy.

A first reason is that they tend to accept Tocqueville's celebrated diagnosis of the future of democracy in *Democracy in America* (1835–40). Democracy leads to a quest for equality and to a totalitarian mass society. For Tocqueville, this was a risk; for libertarians it is a historical necessity. The well-known story told by Hayek (1944/1962) and Talmon (1960), among others, is that democracy takes us on the road to serfdom. The intellectual roots of totalitar-ian democracy are to be found in Rousseau's theory of popular sovereignty, the trunk is Hegel's theory of the state and the most dangerous branch is Marx's idea of communist society. According to libertarianism, there is a necessary conflict between equality and liberty. Since liberty is primary, equal-ity must be sacrificed (Pennock, 1979: ch. 2).

A second, and related, reason is that the 'classical' theory of democracy is deemed unrealistic. Elite theorists had depicted the people as ignorant and capricious and, therefore, as unfit to be sovereign. Schumpeter solved this problem by redefining democracy as a method for the choice of sovereign. If the role of the people is reduced to casting a vote every third, or fourth, year, the risk of misgovernment is minimized. Schumpeter's solution does not calm James Buchanan, however. The democratic method may be a safeguard against the people, but not against self-seeking politicians and bureaucrats. The trouble with the democratic method is that it channels all interests in one direction, leading to government spending and budget deficit (see pp. 30–32).

A third reason is that democracy is deficient as a method of social choice. The works of Kenneth Arrow and Duncan Black showed that aggregating preferences is more problematic than anyone had suspected. Often it is impossible to arrive at a collective preference order. Some theorists see this problem as a fatal blow to the idea of 'populist democracy' (Riker, 1982: 238–271). Others are less worried about it. For James Buchanan, the problem of social choice is definitive proof that the market is superior to democracy as a method of resource allocation. Constitutional economics is an attempt to repair the defects of democracy. In his own words: '"democracy" assumes normative meaning only in a constitutional perspective' (Buchanan, 1986: 258f.). If individuals are the ultimate sources of value, 'the ultimate model of politics is *contractarian*. There simply is no alternative' (Buchanan, 1986: 240).

There are fewer libertarians among sociologists than among economists. Sociologists are more often liberals and socialists of various sorts,[15] and they are more likely to see democracy as an ultimate value. This is manifested in a concern with cultivating the value of democracy itself. Sociologists tend to regard a democratic culture as a precondition for a democratic political system (Almond and Verba, 1963; Pennock, 1979: ch. 6). Sociologists also tend to entertain a different conception of 'democracy'. They are more likely to pay allegiance to a liberal tradition, which celebrates freedom of mind and speech. The utopia of this tradition is a public sphere (see Habermas, 1962/1989) where public man (see Sennett, 1978) participates in the shaping of public opinion.[16]

David Miller's (1992) distinction between 'liberal' and 'deliberative' democracy captures the difference I have indicated. I don't find his terminology wholly adequate, though. What Miller calls 'liberal' democracy is better called 'libertarian', since 'deliberative' democracy is also very much part of the liberal tradition. Roland Pennock (1979: chs 2 and 5) has made a distinction between 'individualist' and 'collectivist' democracy, which overlaps that between liberal and deliberative democracy. Individualist democratic theory is represented, for Pennock, by public choice; collectivist democracy by Rousseau, Hegel, the British Hegelians and Marx. I find this distinction more to the point, but realize that the term 'collectivist' has a tendency to be associated with 'communism', which is unfortunate in a distinction between theories of democracy. What we have is a distinction between 'radical individualism' and theories of democracy as popular sovereignty.

Like Buchanan, sociologists have emphasized the importance of unanimity, or consensus, but they conceive of it in an entirely different way. Sociologists are not hampered by an assumption of fixed preferences. Reaching consensus, therefore, is not a matter of aggregating fixed preferences, but of shaping and changing people's values and beliefs, in order to reach agreement. Two ways of achieving consensus have been suggested by sociologists. The first is more authoritarian and justified only for propagating the value of democracy itself. Only the second is, itself, an expression of democracy and fit for the generation of a 'general will'.

The 'authoritarian' view emphasizes the importance of socialization, including education, as a condition of democracy. That education is the way to create citizens of democratic states is not an idea that sociologists were first to suggest, but they were quick to make it their own. One example is Emile Durkheim, who maintained that education is the means whereby all societies create the conditions for their own preservation (Durkheim, 1956: 71). Durkheim is not the best example, however, since he was theoretically interested in moral eduaction as a functional prerequisite of all societies, and practically interested mainly in its contribution to the creation of a French nation (Durkheim, 1925/1973). He occasionally addressed the intellectuals, however, with the exhortation to participate in public life as advisers and educators of the people ([1883, 1904] 1973: chs 2 and 5). A better example is Karl Mannheim, who saw education as groundwork for a democratic society. 'Democracy cannot exist unless all its institutions are thoroughly oriented to democratic ends' (Mannheim, 1951: 173). Mannheim is also a good example of the 'authoritarian' way of achieving consensus. He makes short work of a 'popular culture', which emerges in mass society. The people have to be enlightened before they become sovereign (ibid., ch. 10).

The second way of reaching agreement is through argument and debate between free and equal citizens in a public sphere. The obvious example, here, is the critical theory of Jürgen Habermas. The foundation of his theory of communicative action is a pragmatic theory of communicative competence. In order for communication, or mutual understanding, to be possible, certain conditions must be fulfilled. Habermas recognizes five validity claims immanently raised in communication: (1) truth of propositions and efficacy of teleological actions, (2) rightness of norms of action, (3) adequacy of standards of value, (4) truthfulness or sincerity of expression and (5) comprehensibility or well-formedness of symbolic constructs. To the extent that these validity claims are satisfied, we approach an ideal speech situation, which is also a precondition for an optimally functioning democracy.

Jürgen Habermas' theory of communicative action has been much discussed in recent political discourse and even influenced James Buchanan. Together with the German sociologist Viktor Vanberg, he now distinguishes two interpretations of the role of agreement in politics: 'the *social contract notion* and the *dialogue notion* of agreement' (Vanberg and Buchanan, 1989: 46). Buchanan's constitutional economics, of course, belongs in the first category, while Habermas' theory of communicative action equally obviously belongs in the second category. The main difference between them is that, while constitutional economics starts from given preferences and beliefs and seeks the preconditions for a compromise, the theory of communicative action assumes that it is possible to change people's preferences and beliefs so that they agree. 'Stated differently, *agreement* is viewed as a *discovery* process, a process by which persons not simply reach a compromise but "discover" what – in some objective sense – *is* fair or just' (ibid., p. 57).

I find Vanberg and Buchanan's article remarkable in several respects. First of all, it comes as a surprise to see an American libertarian take notice of a German critical theorist. More important, however, the article is yet another deviation, on the part of Buchanan, from public choice orthodoxy. The latter typically assumes that self-interest is all and rational argument nothing, or mere noise (see, however, Buchanan, 1954b: 120).

> Such interpretation disregards the relevance of the genuine *theoretical* component in all political and, *a fortiori,* in all constitutional preferences. And it ignores that *winning support for one's own visions and theories is an important part of the political process* [my italics]. The very fact that political discourse is carried out in terms of reasoning argument rather than simple declaration of interests, by itself imposes certain constraints on how one may seek support for one's own proposals.
>
> (Vanberg and Buchanan, 1989: pp. 60f.).

I have italicized part of the quote in order to make a point about public choice as a normative theory of politics. For some time now, Buchanan and his public choice fellows have been actively engaged in persuading the American people and the rest of the world that we need less democracy and more market. They have been quite successful, but their success cannot be explained by public choice theory itself. If politics is the aggregation of fixed preferences, there is no room for 'winning support for one's own visions and theories'. Public choice has been the most persuasive political message over the last twenty years or so, but has no way of explaining this fact, except to suggest that it is a manifestation of self-interest (cf. Weale, 1990: 524f.).

PUBLIC CHOICE AS IDEOLOGY

In the sociological classic *Ideology and Utopia* (1936), Karl Mannheim used the first term to denote a doctrine used to defend the status quo by hiding its true nature from view. The second term was used to refer to a reality-transcending ideal of social life – a vision of the good society. For Mannheim, the concepts of 'ideology' and 'utopia' are part of a view of history. Ideologies are in the interest of the ruling class if it is to preserve the prevailing social order, while utopias are in the interest of subordinated classes if they are to change it (Mannheim, 1936/1960: 36, 173ff.). Stripped of their dynamic and sociological connotations, Mannheim's concepts turn into the two dominating concepts of 'ideology' in contemporary social science: as a positive ideal to strive for and as a legitimizing falsification to debunk. Ideology$_1$ may be defined as a 'system of values and beliefs about the good society', an ideal to be realized. Ideology$_2$ may be defined as a 'misrepresentation of social reality, biased in a certain way to serve the interest of a social class, or social group'.

Public choice is an ideology in both these senses. In the former section, I discussed public choice as a normative theory, or ideology$_1$, based on the value of individualism and the belief that this value is maximized in by voluntary exchange – the market as utopia. In this section, I suggest that certain elements of public choice make it into an ideology also in the Marxist sense: a theory that misrepresents reality and introduces bias in order to justify a free market society.

The role of self-interest

The public choice view of human nature is in line with a long tradition of 'realism' in political theory represented, in varying degrees, by people like Machiavelli, Hobbes, Smith, Tocqueville, Marx, Weber, Pareto and Schumpeter. It is opposed to another tradition, based on the assumption that political man acts in the public interest. This assumption, implicit in most political theory, is not only wrong, but dangerous. It makes us unable both to understand political life and to guard against its dangers. If, on the other hand, we assume that political man pursues his own selfish ends, we are able to explain the growth of government and of bureaucracy and to defend ourselves against the new Leviathan.

The argument of Chapter 2 in this book was that the public choice assumption of self-interest is untenable. Political man is incomprehensible unless we recognize that he is also guided by altruism, morality and social norms. Interestingly, James Buchanan concedes this point, while defending the use of economic man for the purposes of an economic theory of politics. He not only admits, but insists, that the assumption of self-interest is descriptively false (Buchanan, 1972: 16ff.; 1979b: 70ff., 166; 1981: 384–386). Before many other economists, Buchanan argued for a multiple self. 'The elementary fact is, of course, that *homo economicus* does exist in the human psyche, along with many other men and that behaviour is a product of the continuing internal struggle between them' (Buchanan, 1979b: 207; see also pp. 224ff. and Buchanan and Tullock, 1962/1965: 20f.). Much like the sociologist Emile Durkheim (see Chapter 7), Buchanan argues that morality and social norms are necessary for social order (1979b: chs 12 and 13; 1986: ch. 11). Even the market depends, for its proper working, upon respect for certain rules that it is in the narrow self-interest of exchanging parties to break. Law and order is a public good (Buchanan, 1975a: 74–77, 107ff.; 1979b: 211; Brennan and Buchanan, 1985: 12–15). In this connection, Buchanan makes 'a distinction between "economic" and "noneconomic" behavior, between narrow self-interest and enlightened self-interest' (1979b: 70; see also 1986: 32ff., 88).

189

Together with Brennan, he expresses a hope that the decline of morality we have witnessed over the last two hundred years will come to an end and a new civic religion come into being (Brennan and Buchanan, 1985: 49f.). Unlike Durkheim, Buchanan and Brennan see no connection between the decline of morality, and the spread of market relations.

Buchanan's original argument for turning political man into economic man was a call for consistency. Man is one and the same and there is no reason to believe that he/she is different in politics than on the market. The presumption was, of course, that economic man is true man or, at least, much closer to human nature than political man. This argument is repeated as late as 1987 (Buchanan, 1989b: 63), but with little weight attached to it. As we have seen, Buchanan has changed his mind both about consistency and self-interest. A similar argument for methodological symmetry is now advanced in defence of using economic man for the purposes of comparative analysis of institutions. If we have two possible causes – men and institutions – and wish to isolate the effects of the latter, then we must keep the former constant. This is elementary experimental logic; John Stuart Mill's method of difference. There is a problem, however. Unlike many other variables, men and institutions do not exist apart. Institutions are not external to people. At least not to the people who man them. This follows from Buchanan's methodological individualism. But, according to Mill (1843/1950: 214–216), if we cannot isolate the effects of one variable (e.g. constitutions) upon that of another (e.g. social order), then we cannot use the method of difference. We have to rely, instead, on the method of concomitant variation. Now, empirical data pertaining to our problem suggest that political man acts also in various group interests and in the public interest. Hence, we cannot know what would be the effects of political institutions if political man were a rational egoist, except by thought experiment, or *Modell-Platonismus* (Albert, 1963). I do not deny the value of such experiments, but they do not replace real experiments. Also, in a case like this, when the purpose of comparison is *evaluation*, I see no point at all in assuming universal self-interest. If political man is observed usually to act against his/her self-interest, then any relevant evaluation of political institutions must be based upon this fact, not upon any contrafactual assumption of universal self-interest.

A third argument for methodological symmetry turns less upon experimental logic than upon the evaluation of the effects of different institutional arrangements. The basis of the argument is the hypothesis that the welfare losses of inefficiency are an increasing function of the distance from the efficiency ideal. If so, relatively more damage is done by a few egoists than what would be expected from an aggregation of 'average' behaviour. Thus we had better assume the worst and act upon a minimax strategy. I am unable to assess the validity of this argument, even though it looks plausible. The problem, of course, is how to test the hypothesis upon which it is based. There are serious, if not insurmountable, obstacles to measuring welfare losses, both in the private and the public sector, so how would we know? In the absence of such measures, any comparison of efficiency is bound to remain guesswork. More important, as I have argued above, the motivational assumptions used by public choice theorists to explain government failure do not presuppose self-interest. Both vote- and budget-maximization are compatible with the assumption that public officials try to serve the public interest. There is no need for the assumption of self-interest. This is even more obvious in a slightly different, extra-scientific, version of the above argument.

We should assume that politicians are self-interested, because it is dangerous not to assume the worst about those in power. Like Friedrich von Hayek before them, Brennan and Buchanan quote Lord Acton's famous dictum: 'All power corrupts, absolute power corrupts absolutely' (Hayek, 1944/1962: 100; 1960: 450; 1967: 145; Brennan and Buchanan, 1985: 64). Even if there were only a grain of truth in this saying, it would still be one of the most important truths about social life. The warning implied should remain constantly before our eyes. It is dangerous to invest people with too much power, especially if unchecked. But it has little to do with self-interest, or with economic man for that matter. To the extent that it is true, it is a sociological, rather than an economic, truth. Economics typically assumes that human nature is constant and that power is absent. But Lord Acton's dictum asserts that human nature changes as a result of power. Social position influences personality. This is a typical sociological argument.

Power, itself, is the problem, not petty self-interest. The most dangerous individuals are not the narrowly selfish ones who, according to Brennan and Buchanan (1985: 36), 'seek to maximize their own expected net wealth'. Potentially more dangerous are those committed to some impersonal cause, such as that of their race, religion, nation or class. Most dangerous are the fanatics, fundamentalists and madmen. The worst villains – Hitler, Mussolini, Stalin, Khomenei – defy economic analysis. What purely self-interested arguments enter a utility function that explains mass murder?

Max Weber and Karl Popper saw the problem more clearly. The really dangerous persons are those submitting to a cause much 'higher' than their own selfish interest; a cause for which they are prepared to sacrifice their lives and the lives of others. In the terminology of Weber, such persons are 'value-rational' and committed to an ethics of 'ultimate ends', as distinguished from an 'ethics of responsibility' (see, p. 312). According to Popper the root of the evil is utopianism, a type of political action which is rational, but unselfish (1962/1968: 358). Popper goes as far as to suggest that the real problem is that people are too good, but stupid, not that they are too bad. Most harm is created by people with the best intentions, but ignorant about the consequences of attempting to realize their ideals (1962/1968: 356ff.).

Buchanan eventually reaches a similar conclusion: 'The moral zealot in positions of political power may well be less desirable than the private self-seeker who is on the take more or less openly' (Buchanan, 1989b: 35).

A last argument: Throughout his writings, Buchanan upholds the thesis that morality is a scarce resource. In an often quoted article (see, e.g., Samuelson, 1970: 777; Phelps, 1975: 1; Kristol, 1981: 203), Dennis Robertson asked 'What does the Economist economize?' His answer was 'love', having in mind Christian love, that is altruism and morality.

> There exists in every human breast an inevitable state of tension be-
> tween aggressive and acquisitive instincts and the instincts of benevo-
> lence and self-sacrifice. It is for the preacher, lay or clerical, to inculcate
> the ultimate duty of subordinating the former to the latter. It is the
> humbler, and often the invidious, role of the economist to help, so far
> as he can, in reducing the preacher's task to manageable dimensions.
>   (Robertson, 1956: 148).

It may be added that Robertson, following Alfred Marshall, considers benevolence and self-sacrifice the higher, but aggression and acquisitiveness the stronger, forces of human nature. The implication is that the economist should assist in creating such institutions as prevent the lower instincts from being detrimental, if possible by channelling them in directions leading to the common good. The exemplar is, of course, the market where the individual, intending only his own gain, is, nevertheless, 'led by an invisible hand to promote an end which was no part of his intention' (Smith, 1776/1937: 423).[17]

But is 'love' a scarce resource? Margolis' model, discussed above, might seem to support this assumption. The idea of an allocation rule of 'fair share' (FS) suggested that 'The larger the share of my resources I have spent unselfishly, the more weight I give to my selfish interests in allocating marginal resources' (Margolis, 1982/1984: 36). For the purposes of static analysis, Margolis assumes that FS allocation is given once and for all. But he also considers the case of changing opportunities, making for a change in allocation between S-Smith and G-Smith (ibid., pp. 56f.). This is still in line with the assumption that love is a scarce resource. There is no assumption, however, that the weight attached to group-interest relative to self-interest is constant over time. Even though Margolis gives a biological argument for group-interest, there is nothing to suggest that the inside referee, U-Smith, is a constant of human nature. Quite the reverse, Margolis emphasizes the role of persuasion in changing preferences (ibid., pp. 13, 25). He also recognizes the reciprocal influence of individual preferences and culture, allowing for changes over long periods of time (ibid., p. 51).

Of course, love is not a scarce resource. We all know that those who have received much love have more to give. The founder of economics, Adam Smith, knew it: 'Kindness is the parent of kindness; and if to be beloved by our brethren be the great object of our ambition, the surest way of obtaining it is by our conduct to shew that we really love them' (Smith, 1759/1976:

369). The founder of sociology, Auguste Comte, also knew it, and based his hopes for a better society upon this fact. The problem, as Comte saw it, is to breed sympathy until it outgrows self-interest as the dominating motive force in society (Comte [1851–1854] 1975: 337ff., 407f.).

The argument for economizing on love is fundamentally flawed. The idea that we go about with a fixed amount of good deeds that can somehow ebb, like certain natural resources, is absurd. As Albert Hirschman has argued (1984: 93), morality is an *ability*, not a resource; and like all abilities, it may atrophy if we don't practise. Therefore, we should beware of demolishing those institutions that depend upon morality and civic duty for their proper functioning.

This leads to a reversal of Brennan and Buchanan's argument for assuming self-interest. Rather than minimizing our dependence upon morality, we should extend its scope. The market is the only place where self-interest meets with social approval or, at least, acceptance. We do not expect good deeds from businessmen, at least not in their ordinary business transactions. Brennan and Buchanan (1985: 60–63) suggest that there is a sort of Gresham's law in politics such that bad behaviour drives out good behaviour.[18] I don't wish to deny the existence of such a mechanism, but I certainly wish to argue that it is more effective on the market, at least if 'good behaviour' means benevolence. Because of competition, good deeds are virtually impossible on the market. Buchanan seems to argue that standards of morality are higher on the market than in politics (Buchanan, 1986: 89).[19] It is, of course, possible that there is more honesty in business than in politics, though I very much doubt it. But if there is, that is because trust is so very important for market exchange (McKean, 1975; Stigler, 1982: 22). Without honesty, people couldn't trust their business partners and the all-important institution of contract would cease to function and, ultimately, to exist. But honesty, however important, is far from all there is to morality. Business morality is a minimal morality. Therefore, if we wish more social morality, we should minimize market relations, relying instead upon institutions more conducive to good deeds.

I wish to advance a last argument why we should not assume universal self-interest, even for the purposes of an economic theory of politics. According to a well-known sociological, or social psychological, theory of the self, this somewhat elusive entity is, to a large extent, determined by the attitudes of others. We become what people tell us, or in other ways show us, that we are. This theory is usually associated with the name of Charles Horton Cooley, who talked about the 'looking-glass self' (1902/1964: 184). An important part of our selves is the way we imagine we appear in other people's minds. This theory of the 'social self' was developed into great sophistication by the American pragmatist George Herbert Mead (1934/1962: esp. ch. 3). According to him, the self arises in communication with others, by means of significant symbols. First, with 'significant others' (parents, teachers), later with the 'generalized other' (members of society in their various roles). Mead's self is a multiple self, consisting of an 'I' and a 'me'. The 'I' is the spontaneous element in human action, the 'me' the institutional element. The latter, which resembles Freud's Superego, exercises control over the former. As we have seen (p. 100), the theories of Cooley and Mead originate in the social psychology of Adam Smith.

My purpose in introducing this theory of the social self is not to repeat the argument that man is a social, or moral, animal, conforming to social norms. I accept this as an established fact. My purpose is rather to emphasize that this is something the individual becomes through socialization, primary and secondary. I wish to highlight the looking-glass self. My point is that people become more egoistic by being told that this is what they are. I don't wish to exaggerate the importance of economists as agents of socialization. But neither should we underestimate the impact of their teaching – and they teach us that we are selfish. By telling people, including politicians, that they are egoists, economists contribute to making them think of themselves, and to act, as such. If, by his very nature, man is a beast, who can blame him for acting as such? I certainly do not wish to go to the opposite extreme of suggesting that man is an angel – he/she is neither beast nor angel – but it might be a good idea to expect politicians to approximate this ideal and to disapprove strongly when they fail. I fear that the teaching of economists, especially public choice theorists, may have contributed to lowering the standards of morality in politics over the last decades – and this is certainly not what we need (cf. Ball, 1988: ch. 2).

Dennis Robertson suggested that it is for the preacher to teach morality. But if the economist is a preacher, teaching egoism? George Stigler (1982) admits that economists have increasingly assumed the role of preacher – equating preaching with policy recommendations – but denies that they have had much influence upon policy. According to Stigler, this is due mainly to their limited knowledge about the effects of different economic policies. He, therefore, impels his fellow economists to engage in more empirical research, aimed at providing a more secure base for policy proposals. But the economists' preaching is certainly not confined to recommending this or that economic policy. It is the conviction of many economists – perhaps a majority, including, most obviously, the members of the Austrian, Chicago and Virginia Schools of economics – that economics, like the other social sciences, teaches a morality (cf. Wolfe, 1989a: 222–226; 1989b: 7, 31ff.). Following F.H. Knight (1935), Stigler calls it the 'ethics of competition' (1982: chs 1–2). Self-interest is the central dogma of this economic ethic, preached with much confidence by economists, and especially those from Chicago and Virginia, during the last decades.

The main function of the assumption of self-interest seems to be ideological, in the sense that it favours market solutions (cf. Petracca, 1991: 181ff.; Scalia, 1991: 204, 208) – at least according to traditional economic analysis, which sees in the market the sole institution with the wonderful ability of turning private vice into public virtue. In politics, on the contrary, it leads to suboptimal waste and serfdom. *Ergo:* The best society is a free market society.

Government failure

In the previous section on normative public choice, we saw that its ultimate value is individualism or, more precisely, possessive individualism. The locus of possessive individualism is the market. But this is not its only advantage. The market has the unique quality of being *efficient,* by definition. Compared to the market, all other ways of coordinating human activity appear inefficient, also by definition. In particular, this is the case with the state.

The Virginia School of public choice was launched as a needed corrective to the theory of market failure, but has developed into a one-sided attack on government: the market is all good and government is all bad. A recent sympathetic review of public choice (Mitchell and Simmons, 1994), praised by the leading members of the movement, summarizes its message under two rubrics: 'In Dispraise of Politics' and 'In Praise of Private Property, Profits and Markets'. This is what it's all about. Public choice is, more than anything else, a theory of government failure (Buchanan, 1975a: 172; 1979a: 11; 1979b: 73–75, 209f., 271; 1986: 15). The argument is that government is too big, and public expenditure, in Western democracies, a gigantic waste of resources. Before criticizing this argument, I will briefly discuss some explanations of the growth of public expenditure.

Discussions of public expenditure usually start with a statement of 'Wagner's law'. At the end of the nineteenth century the German economist Adolph Wagner predicted that public expenditure would grow faster than, hence make up an increasing share of, the national economy. This 'law' was really no more than an empirical generalization. Its 'explanation, justification and cause is the pressure for social progress and the resulting changes in the relative spheres of private and public economy, especially compulsory public economy' (Wagner, 1883/1967: 8). More specifically, Wagner saw the task of the state as that of providing services, which are indispensable to economic life, but which will not be provided by private enterprises because of their public goods characteristics. Presumably Wagner believed that the need for such services would increase with industrialization. A second task of public finance is the promotion of social welfare.

> The redistribution of national income in favour of the lower classes is a conscious aim of modern social policy; the earlier practice of taxation in favour of the upper classes worked in the opposite direction but still represented regulatory interference with the distribution of national income, even though this was not always recognized.
>
> (Wagner [1883] 1967: 81)

The twentieth century did not see much in the way of a positive theory of public finance until Alan Peacock and John Wiseman wrote *The Growth of Public Expenditure in the United Kingdom* (1961). The immediate purpose of this study was to estimate and explain the increase in public spending in Great Britain from 1890 till 1955. During this period government spending, including transfers, increased ten times in real terms. The share of public spending in GNP increased from 9 per cent to 37 per cent. Why? Peacock and Wiseman considered a number of possible explanations, Wagner's law included. Their own contribution to an explanation was in terms of a 'displacement effect' and a related 'concentration process'. Peacock and Wiseman observed that public expenditure tended to rise dramatically in emergency situations, such as war, and to stay at the higher level after the crisis (cf. Wilensky, 1975: ch. 4). Assuming that there is such a thing as a 'tolerable tax burden', which sets limits to public expenditure, they argued that only an emergency can make people accept a substantial rise in their tax burden. Once they have got used to this new, higher level of taxes, however, they seem willing to tolerate the increased burden in the future. The 'concentration process' refers to the increasing importance of central government, relative to local government, associated with the growth of public expenditure (Peacock and Wiseman, 1961/1967: 24–30).

Thomas Borcherding has analysed public expenditure in the United States from 1870 to 1970. Before 1900 there was no increase in public expenditure relative to GNP. In this century, however, the public sector increased its share of GNP from 6.8 per cent in 1902 to 34.1 per cent in 1970 (Borcherding, 1977a: 26). Borcherding finds no support for a displacement effect in the United States (ibid., p. 38; cf., however, Cameron, 1985: 229–231), but tries to estimate the relative weight of a number of other factors contributing to the expansion of the public sector (Borcherding, 1977b, 1985). Dividing the contributory causes into 'economic', or 'a-institutional', and 'political', or 'institutional', he finds that the former – including relative prices of public services, increased affluence and a larger population – account for about half of the rise in public expenditure. The rest must be explained by politics, as conceived by public choice, which means the play of self-interest in representative democracy.

David Cameron (1978) compared public expenditure in 18 countries in order to assess the relative merit of five typical explanations of its dramatic growth after World War II. In 1980 most of the richest countries in the world had public sector spending of between 30 and 50 per cent of GDP. Two countries, Sweden and the Netherlands, used more than 60 per cent of GDP in the public economy (Cameron, 1985: 232).[20] The first explanation, mentioned by Cameron (1978: 1245), is the *economic*, which sees the expansion of the public sector as a function of economic growth (Wagner). The second explanation is *fiscal*, focusing on the 'fiscal illusion' (Buchanan). The third type of explanation is *political*. There are several varieties of this type, but public choice, to the extent that it sees public expenditure as the result of competitive bidding for popular support, obviously belongs here. A fourth type of explanation is *institutional*. It seeks the cause of public expenditure in the institutional structure of government; whether it is centralized or decentralized, for instance. The institutional type of explanation is not easily distinguished from the political. Public choice clearly belongs in both. There is, finally, a fifth explanation, called *international*, since it focuses on the place of the national economy in the international economy. Those, usually small, countries whose domestic economies are most open to the world market have developed the largest public economy. The reason, very briefly, would be that governments in these countries try to abate the, often disruptive, effects of exposure to external influence by state intervention. Surprisingly, perhaps, Cameron finds most support for the international explanation (ibid., p. 1253). The second most important factor turned out to be the political, but not exactly the public choice version. Cameron found a positive correlation between public expenditure and leftist (social democratic) government, indicating, of course, that interest is important (but not necessarily self-interest) and also that ideology matters to some extent (ibid., p. 1252; see also Cameron 1985: 233–240). By way of an ingenious combination of the international and political explanations, Cameron arrives at the following sequential explanation: a small, open, economy gives rise to high industrial concentration, but also to strong centralized unions, supporting social democratic governments, expanding the public economy (ibid., pp. 1256ff.; see also Alt and Chrystal, 1983: 216f.).

There are, thus, several alternative explanations for the growth of government, most of which have to do with the industrialization and democratization of the Western world.[21] Using broad categories, we may divide them into *economic* and *political*. I start with economic explanations (cf. Wilensky, 1975: ch. 2). It is generally agreed that government is necessary even for the market to work effectively. Hence, it seems reasonable to assume that if the market grows, government grows too. Even as a nightwatchman, the state would have to grow, because there is more to watch over. There is need for more law and more police. But that is not enough. Industry needs lots of things that the market does not provide, or that are better provided by government. I think of roads, railways, electricity and things like that, usually summarized as 'infrastructure', or 'social overhead capital'. But I think also of 'human capital' created through education. Industry needs educated people more than agriculture. But government is needed also to counteract, or mitigate, some of the negative effects of a free market: monopoly, external effects, business cycles.

Market failure may explain why governments grow, but why do they grow at a faster rate than national income, if, indeed, they do?[22] A common explanation is in terms of income elasticity. As people's real incomes grow, demand shifts from necessaries to 'luxuries', including government services, such as social welfare. The argument is usually strengthened by the observation that the production of government services is more labour intensive – whether for technical or motivational reasons – than industrial production. Public choice economists usually deny that market failure can account for the relative growth of government. So does Chicago economist Sam Peltzman (1980: 211–221), who argues that governments' increasing share of national income is due to political redistribution of income. Peltzman presents data showing a correlation between equality, ability (education) and growth of government. His interpretation seems to be that equality and ability are the independent variables in this nexus. Not overall equality, but pre-transfer equality within the group of beneficiaries and not all beneficiaries; only those with the ability to promote their self-interest (ibid., pp. 221–236).

Economic explanations, then, account for part of government growth. But not for all and not alone; if only because a *need* for government explains nothing at all in the absence of some agent(s) experiencing that need and ready to meet it. Thus, we are led to political explanations. They are of two sorts: *institutional* and *cultural*. In dealing, first, with institutional explanations, we tread on public choice ground. Democracy is the cause of government growth, but only in conjunction with self-interest (Fiorina and Noll, 1978). There is little doubt that democracy leads to increasing public expenditure, but self-interest is only part of the explanation for this development. Universal suffrage was probably a precondition for the rise of the modern welfare state, but this does not prove that self-interest is the sole motive of voters (see pp. 78–93). In accordance with the median voter theorem, public choice predicts that the middle classes will be winners, while both the rich *and* the poor will lose in the game of redistribution (Stigler, 1970; Meltzer and Richard, 1978, 1981; Borcherding, 1977b: 57f.; 1985: 370–372).[23] Evidence is mixed, but does not support the median voter theorem (Wilensky, 1975: ch. 5; Cameron, 1978: 1258f.; Page, 1983; Klein, 1985: 212f.). The poor usually gain from redistribution, but there are important differences between countries. There is much redistribution in the Scandinavian welfare states, but little in the United States and Switzerland. Other (OECD) countries fall somewhere in between these extremes (Korpi, 1983: ch. 9; 1994; Esping-Andersen, 1990; Castles and Mitchell, 1993). They certainly lose when right-wing governments put an end to redistribution (Moon and Dixon, 1985: 679; Walker, 1990; Castles, 1993a).

Another thesis of public choice is that bureaucrats influence the level of public spending twice: first in their capacity of budget-maximizing civil servants, second in their capacity of utility-maximizing voters. It has been observed that bureaucrats vote in larger numbers than the rest of the voting population. If they are consistently selfish, however, they should also consistently favour parties and candidates supporting an expanding public sector. This is not the case (see, pp. 83f.).

The franchise is not all there is to democratic politics. It is shaped in between elections and subject to the influence of a plurality of interests. Most important are interest groups and, of course, government itself, or government bureaucracy. The public choice theory of interest groups (see pp. 26–29) has no support in available evidence. There is nothing to indicate that strong interest organizations, engaged in rent-seeking, lead to social waste and to the decline of nations. (Pryor, 1984; Gray and Lowery, 1988; Wallace and Oates, 1988). If anything, the contrary seems to be true. Countries with strong interest organizations have a better record than other countries, at least if these organisations are part of some corporatist arrangement (see Schmitter, 1981; Castles, 1987).

The most influential public choice theory of bureaucracy is that of William Niskanen. In an article with the promising title 'Economic Models of Bureaucracy: Survey, Extensions and Evidence' (1977), William Orzechowski compares Niskanen's model with some other economic models. Unfortunately, for my purposes, budget-maximization is not the issue. Orzechowski's comparison focuses on the question of whether public bureaucracies produce efficiently or not. Cited evidence goes against Niskanen's assumption that they do, favouring instead the rival hypothesis that the public sector produces at a much higher cost than does the private sector. Maybe this calls for an explanation. In the public choice literature on public expenditure, we find two distinct types of inefficiency. There is first the thesis of social inefficiency, or social waste, implying that resources could be allocated in a better, Pareto-optimal, way. Second, there is the thesis that public enterprises produce inefficiently, or at too high costs, what Leibenstein (1976/1980) has called X-inefficiency. Both may be true, but Niskanen advances only the first.

In Niskanen's public choice theory of bureaucracy, the relation between a bureau and its political sponsor is modelled as a bilateral monopoly. There is a single buyer and a single seller. But because bureaux offer a total output that the sponsor cannot afford to reject, bureaucrats can act as discriminating monopolists. Also, since only bureaucrats know the production function, while politicians do not, the former can, and do, use their monopoly power to produce above social optimum.[24] Few have been willing to accept this picture of elected politicians as passive sponsors of bureaucratic expansion. Hettich (1975) is among the first to ask for a more accurate account of the demand mechanism (see also Margolis, 1975: 652ff.; Peacock, 1978: 120ff.). He points out that legislators are elected by citizens and must to some extent be responsive to their demands. A model which does not include voters remains seriously incomplete. Hettich is also sceptical about the power assigned to bureaucrats in their dealings with politicians. This is also the main complaint against Niskanen's model made by Breton and Wintrobe (1975: 198–204; 1979: 213–218). They argue that politicians have to control the bureaucracy if they wish to be re-elected. But since it is easier to control oversupply than to control inefficient production, the main problem with bureaucracy is X-inefficiency.

This was the conclusion reached by Orzechowski (see above). Robert E. Goodin (1982: 28), goes on to argue that 'there are mechanisms *available* to politicians for monitoring bureaucratic activities more effectively', than suggested by Niskanen. He also points out that the procedure assumed in Niskanen's model is a typical American institution. Goodin proposes a revised model based on the assumption that politicians and bureaucrats, alike, try to implement policies under conditions of oligopoly based upon trust. Another alternative is suggested by Gary J. Miller and Terry M. Moe (1983), who try to restore some power to politicians in their bargaining with bureaucracy. In particular, they assume that politicians know only too well their disadvantage in estimating the cost of production and, therefore, adopt some rule of thumb, such as revealing their intention to pay only a certain amount per unit of a public good or service. I don't know whether this assumption is based upon empirical observation, or not. The most effective refutation of Niskanen's assumption of passive politicians is provided by real world events at this very moment in world history. In several representative democracies, we see politicians cutting the budgets of bureaux and reducing the size of the public sector.

The further implication of this critique is that Niskanen's thesis of bureaucratic oversupply cannot be sustained (Hettich, 1985: 15f., 24; Goodin, 1982: 33; Miller and Moe, 1983: 298; Sörensen, 1987). At least not without further qualification. Common opinion suggests that whether bureaux produce too much or not – if, indeed, there is a way to decide what is 'too much' – depends upon the institutional setting. 'Niskanen's famous generalization, that bureaux will always oversupply their output, has been shown to be limited to the case of a bureau able to exercise perfect price discrimination in its relationship with its financial sponsor. The assumption of such a capability imputes an implausible degree of monopoly power to the bureau' (Conybeare, 1984: 497f.).

I believe that public choice is correct to suggest that public expenditure grows as a result of the play of interests.[25] I also agree that a decentralized government contributes to this multiplicity of voices. Demand is, indeed, excessive. Not necessarily each demand by itself, but in the aggregate. And not only because people are self-interested, but also because there is an infinity of needs to meet and things to change. There is no end to the tasks of those who wish to do good. This multiplicity of claims and requests creates a constant pressure, which is hard for any government to resist, and which pushes public expenditure constantly upwards until there comes a government sufficiently determined to cut expenses. But, once again, it is wrong to assume that interest is necessarily self-interest, as in the theory of rent-seeking. Self-interest is only one motive among others. There is also group-interest, which is irreducible to self-interest, and there is devotion to causes other than the pleasures of the self (see Chapter 2).

Institutional models tend to explain the growth of government as the unintended result of the actions of individuals and groups. Incrementalism, as developed by Lindblom (1958: 300ff.; 1959),[26] Braybrooke and Lindblom (1963: 62ff., 71ff., ch. 5) and Wildavsky (1964/1974: 216–219), is, perhaps, the most plausible model of such a process.[27] Alt and Chrystal (1983: ch. 10), suggest that politicians try to keep public expenditure at a constant share of national income, but that incremental changes add up to significant changes in the long run. A problem with incrementalism is that we seem to be witnessing an inevitable process beyond the control of human beings. The impression of inevitability has been strengthened by the observation that even right-wing governments, intent upon cutting expenses, have often ended up spending more (see, e.g., Myrdal, 1960: 9–13).

Government is largest in countries with a strong, organized, working class and long periods of leftist, especially social democratic, government. This is so, not simply because leftist parties represent voters gaining from redistribution. If this were the case, there would be no exceptions to class-voting. But there is. The welfare state is the result, not of interest alone, but of a commitment to the ideals of equality and social security. I suggest that we also have to invoke something larger than the ideologies and programmes of political parties; we have to make room for history and *political culture* (Wildavsky, 1985a; 1985b: 263–265; Castles, 1993a). It is the case, of course, that political culture is shaped in a field of forces, including political parties. But there are other forces, such as interest groups, social movements, religious creeds. The existence of a political culture helps to explain why governments are not 'free' to follow their programmes. Political culture lasts longer than governments. Political culture also helps to explain differences between countries, equally wealthy and with similar political systems (Wolfe, 1989a). In no other country is individualism as strong and concern about big government as great as in the United States (Feldman, 1983; Sniderman and Brody, 1977). This is so even though the United States has a small government compared to most countries in the West. Differences aside, however, there has been a broad consensus in all Western countries, including socialist and liberal ideologies, supporting the rise of the welfare state. This fact must be part of the explanation of an expanding public sector in all Western countries.

The contention of public choice – Anthony Downs (1960) excepted – is not just that the public economy is large, but that it is *too* large, much too large – at least twice as large as optimum size. This is not a scientific statement. It is not even an empirical statement. There is simply no scientific way to decide whether the public sector is too large or not (cf., e.g., Jackson, 1982: ch. 7). Niskanen's estimation that bureaux produce twice their optimal output is not accepted even within public choice quarters. According to Borcherding (1977b: 61), 'This is an exaggeration, no doubt'. Also, 'waste is directly related to a bureau's monopoly power' (ibid., p. 62). As we have seen, this is the really weak part of Niskanen's argument. Bureaucrats are not discriminating monopolists. Budgets are passed by politicians, elected by citizens. In the end, therefore, it is only voters who can decide whether the government spends too much. If the electorate accepts a certain level of public expenditure, then, by the only criterion available, it is not too high. If on the other hand, voters choose a party promising to cut public expenditure, then it is too high.

Public choice theorists are, of course, correct to emphasize the obscure relation between the costs and benefits of the public sector. This may easily lead to a level of public spending that deviates from the social optimum. But there is little, except public choice, to suggest that spending in democracies must necessarily be above optimum.[28] Buchanan invokes 'fiscal illusion' to explain why this is the case. People tend to underestimate the costs of public expenditure, especially if the costs are borne in the form of indirect taxes, deficits and inflation. It is not that I deny the presence of all sorts of illusions, including, perhaps, a fiscal illusion; I could think of some myself. I believe, for instance, that there is such a thing as a 'local illusion', making people overestimate the relative importance of their own contribution to the common good. Applied to bureaucracy, the local illusion would make each bureau, or department, overestimate the social utility of its own goods and services. I find it equally plausible, however, to assume a systematic tendency to underestimate the benefits of the public sector. Anthony Downs, for instance, argued (1960: 551–555) that we underestimate most government benefits because of their *remoteness*. In addition, people may become so accustomed to the goods and services provided by government that they fall victims to an illusion that they are free, like the air we breathe. Naturally, people do not want to pay taxes, but if they could be made to understand that there is, indeed, no such thing as a free lunch, they might be more willing to do so. The problem might be that people, or a majority of them, want the goods and services provided by government, but cherish the illusion that they can somehow have the benefits without the costs. One way to find out if people are really prepared to take the consequences of lower taxes is to see what happens to governments making drastic cuts in public expenditure.[29]

The growth of government and public expenditure in the last century is due to a multiplicity of causes, which are difficult to estimate in isolation. Alan Peacock, a major figure in this field, argues 'that the search for some all embracing theory of public expenditure is now generally recognised as a chimera' (1992: 54).

More interesting, for my argument, is the occurrence of some critical voices from within, or close to, public choice itself; voices suggesting, as I do, that the use of efficiency in the evaluation and comparison of government and market is ideological. According to this market ideology, the market is efficient and government inefficient by definition.

The first voice belongs to Gary Becker, who makes some cautious remarks concerning the issue of efficiency. He is critical of Mancur Olson and the theory of rent-seeking for seeing pressure groups only as dead weight. He suggests that competition between pressure groups may lead to an efficient allocation of subsidies; that public ownership may be an efficient way of subsidizing private enterprises and also that public enterprises, themselves, may appear to be less efficient than private enterprises only because subsidies are not included in their output (Becker, 1983: 386f.; 1985: 338, 344). These considerations 'illustrate some difficulties in evaluating the efficiency of the public sector, difficulties ignored by numerous casual evaluations' (Becker, 1983: 387).

Critical thoughts have also been voiced by Mancur Olson. In a recent article he argues apropos of government expenditure that 'such a huge, long-lasting and pervasive increase in the role of governments could not have occurred if there had not been a public demand for it'; 'Some of the complaints about big government come, of course, from those who have regularly espoused anti-government ideologies' (Olson, 1990: 215). Olson agrees that there is ineffectiveness in government provision of public goods, but the cause is neither self-interest, nor democratic institutions. Ineffectiveness is the result of irredeemable information problems. The recurrent promises by politicians to increase efficiency by privatization, therefore, are false. It cannot be done. The problem does not lie in the form of ownership, or in human motivation, but in the nature of public goods.

I conclude by quoting a political economist, who is close to public choice but does not share its ideological dead weight:

> In much of (American) Public choice a further conclusion has been reached: it is argued that markets are generally superior, and that politics is almost always inferior. However, this conclusion is based more on an ideological presupposition than on analysis, and it certainly does not follow from Political Economy.
>
> (Frey, 1992: 130)

For libertarians, government is always too big, irrespective of its size; and it is doomed to failure, no matter what its actual achievements. Already in the nineteenth century, libertarians complained about big government, despite its rather modest dimensions (see, e.g. Spencer, [1857–1891] 1969). Today, the critique of big government is strongest in those (OECD) countries with the smallest governments (Castles, 1993a).

At the turn of the century, Vilfredo Pareto advanced a theory of 'spoliation', which is, in all essentials, identical with the public choice theory of rent-seeking.

> Past history and contemporary observation shows us men at all times and in all places divided into groups, each of which generally procures economic goods for itself partly by producing them directly and partly by despoiling other groups, who despoil them in turn. These activities interact in a thousand of ways and their direct and indirect effects are extremely varied . . . With certain industrial groups, it is easy to see to

which side the balance tips; with others it is difficult to know whether on balance, they are gainers or losers by this system – one which, more-over, entails an enormous destruction of wealth of society in general.

(Pareto, [1902] 1976: 140f.)

For Pareto, as for contemporary public choice, this enormous destruction of wealth (at least in the modern world) hinges, ultimately, on the state and its regulations.

Despite the loss of efficiency supposed to be the inevitable result of big government and strong interest groups, however, there is no empirical sup-port for the public choice theory of government failure. There is not an inverse relation between size of government and economic growth (Agell, Ohlson and Lindh, 1995). If anything the relation is positive. The most 'developed' high-tax welfare states have done pretty well in the economic race between nations (Korpi, 1992), while many low-tax/small-government coun-tries are to be found at the bottom of the league for OECD countries (Castles, 1993a).

The absence of power

In Chapter 3, I criticized the view of politics as exchange. Politics is about power, not exchange. In this concluding section of Chapter 4, I will go further and suggest that not even the market is free from power. I will do it briefly and without an attempt to substantiate my claim in any detail.

Economic theory conceives of market exchange as free from power and other social relations (see pp. 160f.). This is fiction, not fact. But it is an abstraction which is perfectly legitimate, and wholly adequate, in a theoretical model. Libertarians go further, however, and argue that market exchange is *de facto* between free and equal partners. No actor on the market has power to coerce other actors. Coercion is a monopoly of the state (Hayek, 1960: 134ff.; 1982: ch. 15; Friedman, 1962/1982: ch. 1; Friedman and Friedman 1979/1990: ch. 1; Rothbard, 1970/1977; ch. 6; Buchanan, 1975: 18; Preston, 1984). This is ideology. As I have already suggested (p. 162), this is nothing that follows from the methodology of rational choice. It is a peculiarity of the (orthodox) economic theory of the market; a peculiarity that is, for obvi-ous reasons, particularly dear to libertarians.

The critique of this idyllic view of market exchange is well-known. Most famous, of course, is the critique by Marx, who used the economic theory of exchange as the paradigm of ideology$_1$; a theory which hides the true nature of a social phenomena in a way that protects the interest of the ruling class. According to Marx the relation between capitalists and workers is one of exploitation, not of free exchange (see Elster, 1985: ch. 4). Marx's attempt to prove his theory of exploitation was by way of a now discredited theory of value. Contemporary Marxists retain the theory of exploitation, but drop the attendant theory of value. The most influential theory of exploitation in modern Marxism is by John Roemer (1982; 1988).

Sociologists tend to agree with Marx that there is a relation of power between capitalists and workers; between those who own the means of production and those who do not. According to Weber, for instance,

> The formal right of the worker to enter into any contract whatsoever with any employer whatsoever does not in practice represent for the employment seeker even the slightest freedom in the determination of his own conditions of work and it does not guarantee him any influence on this process. It rather means, at least primarily that the more powerful party in the market, i.e., nomally the employer, has the possibility to set the terms to offer the job 'take it or leave it,' and, given the normally more pressing economic need of the worker, to impose his terms upon him. The result of contractual freedom, then, is in the first place the opening of the opportunity to use, by the clever utilization of property ownership in the market, these resources without legal restraints as a means for the acheivement of power over others.
>
> (Weber, 1922/1978: 729f.)

Also Durkheim and Parsons agree that there is an asymmetry of power between capitalists and workers, to the advantage of the former (Durkheim, 1893/1964: 216, 354ff; 1983: 212ff.). In a manner similar to contemporary Marxism, Parsons argued that Marx's theory of value is mainly of antiquarian interest, while his theory of exploitation is of permanent interest. Parsons agrees with Marx, that capitalists have bargaining power over workers and this is all that is necessary for a Marxian theory of exploitation (Parsons, 1937/1968: 109). Neither Durkheim, nor Parsons (see, however, pp. 154f.), did much to develop of theory of power and exchange though (their main interest was in harmony and consensus). The first ambitious attempt, by a sociologist, to do so was by Peter M. Blau in his *Exchange and Power in Social Life* (1964/1986).

If power is based on resources, as I have argued in Chapter 3, then, there can be no doubt that capital means power. Control over economic resources gives sanctioning power to the owner; power to manipulate the incentives of other people. The sanctioning power of one individual A over another individual B increases to the extent that B *depends* upon A for the satisfaction of his/her needs or desires (cf. Emerson, 1962; Blau, 1964/1986: 28f, 32).

In general, then, control over economic resources gives, to owners of capital, a considerable power over everything that money can buy, including people and, most importantly, politicians and the media. Public choice recognizes only one asymmetry of power; that between producer and consumer interests. But this is to forget about the power of money. Marxist and neo-corporatist theory is, no doubt, correct to point out that capitalists have the advantage, over other interests, of controlling huge amounts of money, which they can use to convince politicians and the public about the appropriateness of a certain policy. Even former pluralist Robert A. Dahl (1985; 1986) now admits that corporate capitalism exhibits economic power differentials, which are highly problematic, from a democratic point of view.

More specifically, capitalists have power over workers by means of their ownership of the means of production. Workers depend upon capitalists for earning a living (Blau, 1964/1986: 22). Libertarians, of course, deny that there is such a dependence involved in the exchange of labour power for a wage. There are lots of capitalists, and workers are free to choose between them. This is a simplified view, far removed from reality. For a serious attempt to disentangle the different ways in which employees depend upon employers, by a non-Marxist using neoclassical terminology, see Bartlett (1989: ch. 7).

The absence of power is a serious deficiency in the positive and normative versions of public choice alike. Considering the ubiquity and obviousness of power in social life, relations of exchange included, it is hard to avoid the conclusion that this conspicuous absence is 'ideological', in the special sense attached to this term by Marx, and by a majority of sociologists.

Part II

COLLECTIVE ACTION: A COMPARISON

5

THE ECONOMICS OF
COLLECTIVE ACTION

In Chapter 2, I started with a theory, or an assumption, and showed that it runs into serious trouble when confronted with available evidence. In this chapter, I proceed in the opposite direction: I start with a problem and discuss various attempts to solve it.

The subject of this chapter is the problem of collective action; if, indeed, there is such a problem. According to the economic approach, or some versions of it, there is. Collective action, like voting, is treated as something enigmatic; a practical dilemma and a theoretical paradox (Axelrod, 1970: ch. 3; Riker and Ordeshook, 1973: 57ff.; Margolis, 1982/1984: ch. 2; Olson, 1982: 17ff.; see, however, Hardin, 1982: 138ff.). Both involve a 'paradox of participation', in the sense that participation appears inexplicable in a narrowly economic perspective. In both cases, the apparent 'paradox' is a result of size and appears only in mass elections and large groups.

An important difference between the economic theory of voting and the economic theory of collective action is that, whereas the former assumes that self-interest explains voting, the latter implies that self-interest is not enough for collective action. Therefore, considering the amount and importance of collective action in the world, this theory does not lend unambiguous support to an economic theory of politics. Quite the contrary, the existence of collective action 'stands as an indication of the fundamental inadequacy of decision theory, a clear sign that its postulates are flawed' (Barnes, 1990: 274). After all, people do cooperate. The fact that people vote is the first serious anomaly of an economic theory of politics. The fact that they cooperate is the second (cf. Barnes, 1990: 286). Voting may, of course, be seen as an instance of collective action, or cooperation.

The problem of collective action is the subject of an enormous literature, and for a very good reason. It is a problem of fundamental importance for social life and, therefore, for social science. While originally raised in connection with interest-groups, the problem of collective action turns into the general problem of cooperation and, ultimately, into the problem of social order and of human existence.

The subject matter of this chapter is the *economic approach* to collective action. This does not imply that I will treat only those who are economists by profession. I will treat those – or some of them – who use, or discuss, an 'economic approach', a term which in this chapter is used in the broader sense of rational choice, rather than public choice. The reason for this extension is that I wish to sketch the internal development of the economic approach, and to show that this development leads in a direction away from the assumption of self-interest: from public choice to rational choice and beyond. There is a presumption that telling this story implies a critique of public choice. This is the case if the story is 'whiggish'; a story about progress, as, indeed, I believe it is.

THE PROBLEM OF COLLECTIVE ACTION

The classic in this field is, of course, Mancur Olson's *The Logic of Collective Action* (1965). In this work, Olson challenges conventional wisdom (including political science, sociology and Marxism), by arguing that 'unless the number of individuals in a group is quite small, or unless there is coercion or some other special device to make individuals act in their common interest, *rational, self-interested individuals will not act to achieve their common or group interest*' (ibid., p. 2). The reason is that interest groups trade in collective, or public, goods, which are characterized by non-excludability (ibid., p. 14). Public goods, if provided at all, have to be, or are best, supplied to all members of the group.[1] But if this is so, the most rational course of action, for a self-interested individual, is to take a free ride: to enjoy the benefits of the collective good without contributing to the cost. This is why labour unions often resort to coercive methods and taxes are compulsory (Olson, 1965/1971: chs 3–4).

Olson divides groups into small, intermediate and large (ibid., pp. 48–50). Free riding is not a problem if the group is small and 'privileged', which means that 'each of its members, or at least some one of them, has an incentive to see that the collective good is provided, even if he has to bear the full burden of providing it himself' (ibid., p. 50). This is the case when the value to any one individual (Vi) of a collective good is larger than the total cost of its production (C); when, therefore, the advantage (Ai) to this individual is a positive sum, or when $Ai = Vi - C > 0$. In small groups there are also a number of social incentives at work: friendship, social status, prestige, etc., which add to the benefit each individual receives from group membership (ibid., pp. 60–65). But, as the size of the group (Sg) increases, there is a decrease both in the relative importance of each individual's contribution to collective action and in each individual's share, or fraction (Fi), of the value of the collective good for the group as a whole (Vg). $Fi = Vi/Vg$. In the intermediate group no single member benefits enough to supply the collective good for the group. But an intermediate group is not large enough to let a free rider remain anonymous. Hence, there is the possibility of obtaining collective goods with some coordination and organization. Olson gives the example of oligopolistic interaction, which may take place when the number of firms on a particular market is, in his sense, 'intermediate'. In the large, or latent, group, however, free riding is easy and coordination difficult. Large groups, therefore, have to rely on selective incentives, such as journals or insurances, or on coercion, in order to secure support (ibid., p. 44). This conclusion leads Olson to advance the so-called 'by-product theory' of pressure groups (ibid., pp. 132ff.). If the provision of a public good is not enough to motivate people to join an organization, then they must also be organized for some other purpose. Lobbying for collective goods is a by-product of organizations that receive their strength from selective incentives. Olson's logic of collective action calls for a leader, or political entrepreneur, to explain the emergence and existence of interest groups (ibid., pp. 174ff.).

It should be pointed out, however, that Olson is more aware of the limits of self-interest and of his theory of collective action than many of his critics seem to have noticed. First, while assuming utilitarian rationality in his own analysis, he does not suggest that all action, or even all collective action, can be explained in this way. Olson's logic of collective action is intended to apply to special interest, or pressure groups, but not supposed to shed much light upon 'non-economic lobbies' with social, political, religious or philanthropic interests, or upon 'mass movements'. Collective action, on the part of these groups, is nonrational or irrational and, therefore, the subject matter of sociology (Olson, 1965/1971: 159–165). Second, and related, Olson acknowledges the existence of moral incentives, but excludes them from consideration on the ground that they are hard to verify. He criticizes the tendency to analyse all behaviour with economic models, but at the same time suggests how it can be done in the case of moral incentives. Interesting, for my purposes, is the following remark: 'The adherence to a moral code that demands the sacrifices needed to obtain a collective good therefore need *not* contradict any of the analysis in this study; indeed, this analysis shows the need for such a moral code or for some other selective incentive' (ibid., p. 61n.; see also p. 160n.).

Olson's theory of collective action is, in some respects, less restricted than those of many of his economic colleagues. First, even though the bulk of Olson's analysis relies on the assumption of self-interest, he claims that the assumption of rationality would be enough for his results to obtain, at least in the case of large groups. The reason is that in large groups even an altruistic contribution would not be perceptible (ibid., pp. 64, 159). Second, Olson's theory is not 'materialistic'. Many selective incentives are *social*: status, prestige, social pressure, etc. (ibid., pp. 60–65). Third, even while his *formal* analysis is atomistic and static, his *informal* analysis is interactionist and dynamic. Social control is effective only in a dynamic context. By pointing out the importance of social sanctions as selective incentives, Olson precipitates the results later obtained by the dynamic use of game theory. Fourth, Olson was well acquainted with institutional solutions to the collective action problem, such as leadership and formal organization, long before the new institutional-ism made an impact on the economic theory of collective action.

Olson's theory of collective action is sometimes discussed together with that of James Buchanan and both confirm the similarities (Olson, 1965/1971: 38, n. 58; Buchanan, 1965b: 13, n. 8). This fact should not obscure the dif-ferences between them. Buchanan defines public goods in terms of 'jointness of supply', or 'divisibility' (1968: ch. 4, 173ff.). He maintains that there are few pure public goods, such that they are equally available to all, and suggests that we should rather conceive of all goods as making up a spectrum of divisibility; from perfectly divisible private goods to pure, perfectly joint, public goods. Divisibility is not always and entirely a technical matter. To a large degree indivisibility is institutional. Jointness is created in the political process and other forms of cooperation.

The most obvious similarity between Olson and Buchanan is in the analy-sis of the effects of group size. Buchanan agrees that public goods provision becomes progressively more difficult as the number of parties to a contract increases. The reason is the increasing costs of reaching an agreement and of organizing for the provision of public goods (Buchanan, 1968: 83f.).[2] Bucha-nan also makes a distinction between small groups, in which strategic rational-ity and bargaining is possible, and large groups, in which rationality becomes a parametric play against nature. In this atomistic setting of independent players, free riding is the dominant strategy (1965b: 5ff.; 1968: 84ff.). A solu-tion to the public goods problem, therefore, has to be centralized and, to some degree, coercive. An important element of voluntariness may be re-tained by introducing a rule of unanimity. If a public good is provided only on condition that all, or nearly all, contribute to its provision, free riding becomes impossible, or extremely risky (1968: 92ff.). Under this rule, there-fore, people might be expected to contribute to the provision of public goods even in large groups.

Buchanan is probably the first to analyse the public goods problem as similar to a prisoner's dilemma (Buchanan, 1965b: 8). He suggests that it may be treated as a large-number, or N-person prisoners' dilemma as in Figure 5.1 (Buchanan, 1968: 87f.).

Because the provision of public goods usually involves cost-sharing and because most public goods are impure, the public goods problem is rarely a simple problem of provision. In addition to this problem, or as part of it, there is the problem of how to distribute costs and benefits among group members. Since costs and benefits are often independent and since contribu-tors and beneficiaries are sometimes different sets of people, this problem is two fold: how to distribute costs among contributors and how to distribute benefits among beneficiaries (ibid., pp. 178ff.).

Buchanan is most interested in public goods supplied by the state. In this case, the collective action problem is solved by coercive taxation. But the problem of reaching an optimal resource allocation remains and unanimity

212

Players N-I

		Contribute	Do not contribute
	Contributes	5,5	-5,0
Player I	Does not contribute	10,5	0,0

Figure 5.1 Buchanan on an N-person prisoners' dilemma (approximate payoffs when N is large)

is not feasible. One way to retain some efficiency, however, is to subject public goods provision to constitutional constraints unanimously agreed upon. Hence, Buchanan's new research programme for constitutional economics. A first contribution to this programme was made by Buchanan and Tullock in *The Calculus of Consent* (1962). The main part of this work was devoted to discussing the effects of different rules for decision-making. Buchanan returns to constitutional matters in *The Limits of Liberty* (1975). In this work constitutions, themselves, are analysed as public goods and the collective action problem turns into the problem of cooperation and social order.

Buchanan's approach to this problem is contractarian and, more specifically, Hobbesian. Like all theorists in the social contract tradition, Hobbes starts his analysis in the state of nature. More than others, however, he paints it black. In the state of nature there is a war of each against all, because every man is an enemy of every man. In this state there is no industry, no culture and 'no Society; and which is worst of all, continuall feare, and danger of violent death; And the life of man, solitary, poore, nasty, brutish, and short' (Hobbes, 1651/1968: 186). This being the case, reason suggests and the law of nature dictates that people should renounce their natural rights to other people's life and property and *'be contented with so much liberty against other men, as he would allow other men against himselfe'* (ibid., p. 190). These transfers of rights take the form of contracts, where people promise to fulfil whatever terms they have agreed upon. Unfortunately, men being what they are, they cannot be trusted to keep their promises. Contracts therefore will be void until there is created a coercive power, authorized to punish breaches of contract.

Covenants, without the Sword are but Words, and of no strength to

213

secure a man at all. Therefore notwithstanding the Lawes of Nature ...
if there be no Power erected, or not great enough for our security;
every man will and may lawfully rely on his own strength and art, for
caution against all other men.

(Hobbes, 1651/1968: 223)

Realizing this, people will eventually enter a social contract, where they
agree to subject themselves to a sovereign on the following terms: *'I
Authorise and give up my Right of Governing my selfe, to this Man, or to this
Assembly of men, on this condition, that thou give up thy Right to him, and Author-
ise all his Actions in like manner'* (ibid., p. 227). Thus is instituted the great
Leviathan which alone can guarantee peaceful cooperation and social order.

Buchanan's analysis of the constitutional contract is very close to that of
Hobbes. Like the latter, he denies the possibility of an anarchic solution to
the problem of cooperation. Like many others (e.g. Taylor, 1976: 101–114;
1987: 129–146), Buchanan conceives of cooperation in a state of anarchy as a
prisoners' dilemma, where free riding, or breaching of contracts, is the dominant strategy (Buchanan, 1975a: 27, 65). The state, therefore, is necessary, but
not in the form suggested by Hobbes. Buchanan does not endorse Hobbes'
absolutism. Leviathan may be necessary, but it is a necessary evil. Being wild,
it cannot be domesticated, and since it cannot be tamed, it must be fettered.
This is Buchanan's message in a nutshell.

Mancur Olson's main concern is interest groups, James Buchanan's is the
state. Neither of them is interested in social movements and Olson explicitly
relegates them to a place outside the scope of his theory. The lacuna created
by Olson's exclusion of mass movements from his analysis of collective
action has been filled by Breton and Breton (1969). They advance an economic theory of social movements, without the problem of collective action
but akin to the Schumpeter–Downs theory of party competition. Social movements are treated as analogous to firms and as operating on a market for
social change. The demand for social change is a function of people's welfare, relative to other people and to their expectations. Demand for social
change increases as economic growth decreases or fails to appear.[3] On the
supply-side, there are profit-seeking firms, but, above all, political entrepreneurs offering various ideologies for sale. Breton and Breton's theory of
social movements rests on some dubious assumptions, but self-interest is not
one of them, at least not explicitly.

More orthodox, in this respect, is Gordon Tullock's analysis of revolutions
(Tullock, 1971; cf. Popkin, 1979: 24). Tullock assumes that the payoff for
participating in revolutionary activity is decided by the public and private
goods the revolution might bring to an individual, multiplied by the likelihood
of its success. From this expected gain must be detracted the risk of penalty
imposed upon the revolutionary in case of failure and the risk of being killed
or injured in battle. Tullock finally adds an E term for the possible entertain-

214

ment value of participation. Now, Tullock's argument is that the public goods expected from a revolution cannot motivate people to participate, since they will enjoy these benefits even if they remain inactive and because their participation does not add significantly to the likelihood of victory. The incentives for participating in revolutions, therefore, are the private benefits and costs associated with the possible outcomes of such activity.[4]

Tullock observes the similarities between his own analysis of revolutions and Mancur Olson's analysis of pressure groups: 'Following Olson we are in essence espousing the byproduct theory of revolutions' (1971: 96). Like the latter, it is based on the assumption that self-interest is the dominating motive for participation in collective action (ibid., pp. 96f.).

As I have already mentioned, Olson denied that the logic of collective action applies to mass movements. It may come as a surprise, therefore, that he used it to refute Marx's theory of class action and of the proletarian revolution, which relies on the Mass Movement, with a capital M (cf. Gamson, 1975: 59). According to Olson (1965/1971: 105–110), Marx was wrong to assume that workers will act in their common interest. They will not, because no one individual makes a difference to the outcome and because the goals pursued are public goods; an open invitation to free riding. Olson's refutation of Marx's theory of revolution receives support from Allen Buchanan (1979), who argues that neither self-interest nor group-interest is sufficient motivation for revolution. The reasons he gives are those of Olson and Tullock. Particular emphasis is given to the point that not even non-selfish group-interest is enough for revolutionary collective action, since each contribution is negligible (ibid., p. 65). Buchanan considers some solutions to the collective action problem, but denies that they are compatible with the general tenor of Marx's social theory. Marx shared the rationalist and utilitarian premises of Olson, but came to a different conclusion. Since Olson is right, Marx must be wrong. It is not altogether clear to me whether Buchanan, himself, accepts these premises; nevertheless, his discussion of their implications is clarifying.

It will not do to write about the collective action problem and omit Garrett Hardin's famous article 'The Tragedy of the Commons' (1968). This article has generated a literature almost as voluminous as that following upon *The Logic of Collective Action*. The tragedy of the commons is the story about herdsmen and about the perverse effects of their free access to a common pasture. Since each herdsman seeks to maximize his own gain, he will add more animals to his own herd. But if all herdsmen act in this way, the pasture will soon be overgrazed and finally ruined. The reason for this is a certain asymmetry between benefits and costs. The benefit of adding more animals to a herd is private and accrues to the owner of the herd. The cost of overgrazing, however, is public and shared by all herdsmen alike. It has been objected that common pastures existed in Europe for many hundreds of years and also that a common pasture is not (technically) a public good, since it is divisible (Taylor, 1987: 3f., 26). This may be, but is, perhaps, not too important. I understand the tragedy of the commons as, essentially, a parable for the human condition: a rapidly increasing population incessantly engaged in draining limited natural resources and in polluting our one finite common: mother earth.

Garrett Hardin is a biologist and his concern is very different from, even opposite to, that of many economists. For him, economic growth is not a value, it is part of the tragedy. Even so, Hardin's view of the collective action problem and of a possible solution to it is identical with that of public choice economists. The trouble, as they see it, is that people are rational egoists and that appeals to their consciences, therefore, are in vain. The one remaining possibility is appeal to people's incentives. For Hardin, the only remedy is 'mutual coercion, mutually agreed upon by the majority of the people affected' (Hardin, 1968: 1247).

Olson's logic of collective action and Hardin's tragedy of the commons are examples of a larger class of social phenomena, in which the aggregate effect is an unintended, sometimes also an unanticipated, result of the actions of individuals. The paradigm of this class of phenomena is, of course, Adam Smith's invisible hand. In anthropolgy and sociology, such unintended consequences are sometimes referred to as 'latent functions'. Intended consequences are called 'manifest functions' (Merton, 1957: 60–82). Characteristic of functions, including the invisible hand of the market, is that they are collectively 'rational', or good. But there are also dysfunctions, where unintended consequences are 'irrational', or bad. Olson's logic of collective action (for large groups) and Hardin's tragedy of the commons exemplify the latter case. Both have the structure of an N-person prisoners' dilemma: for each person, defection dominates cooperation, irrespective of the choice of the rest. But if all defect, they will all be worse off than if they all cooperate. The problem of collective action, then, is the prospect of an outcome, the reverse of Adam Smith's invisible hand. It is the problem of how to avoid a situation where individual rationality leads to collective irrationality instead of to the common good (see Hardin, 1982: 1–2; Barry and Hardin, 1982: 23–26).

Thomas C. Schelling has given us a great many examples of such phenomena and suggested some typical ways to analyse them (Schelling, 1973, 1978). Some of the ideas and models launched by Schelling have become part of the common stock-in-trade in the analysis of collective action. One such idea is that of a 'critical mass', or 'critical point', at which some chain reaction gets started. Originally used in nuclear physics, the generalized term 'critical mass' refers to a certain proportion of elements that must be activated for an aggregate effect to take place. In social science, critical masses exist because 'people's behavior depends on how many are behaving a particular way, or how much they are behaving that way' (Schelling, 1978: 94).[5]

A second analytical tool, introduced by Schelling is a diagram, representing a multiple prisoners' dilemma (Figure 5.2). The Schelling diagram takes the form of two vertical axes for payoff and, in between, a horizontal axis for group size ($n + 1$). On the horizontal axis are drawn two curves, one representing the preferred choice (defection), the other representing the unpreferred choice (cooperation). The left end of the former curve is the zero point, indicating that as long as no one contributes, there is no payoff going to free riders. Of special importance is the point k, at which the latter (lower) curve intersects with the horizontal axis. At this point, benefits exceed

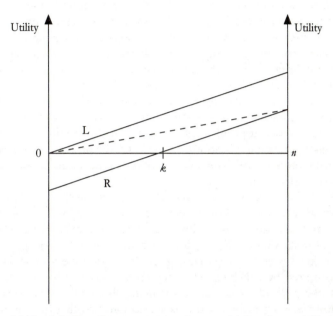

Figure 5.2 The Schelling diagram representing a multiple prisoners' dilemma.

costs, and there is the possibility that a coalition of cooperators might be willing to provide a public good, even if the rest defect. The dotted line represents the total (or average) benefit for different mixes of cooperators and defectors.

Figure 5.2 shows only one possible version of the multiple person prisoners' dilemma. It is the most simple version, with linear and equidistant payoff curves for cooperators and defectors. The highest point on the dotted curve gives the maximum payoff. In Figure 5.2 this point is reached with universal cooperation, but with other payoff functions maximum may well be reached when only some cooperate, while the rest take a free ride.

The Schelling diagram can be used to represent not only prisoners' dilemmas, but all sorts of interdependent binary choices (cf. Frohlich *et al.*, 1975). The prisoners' dilemma is only one of several types of situation in which individual rationality, or individual action, leads to collective irrationality, in the form of suboptimal outcomes (Schelling, 1978: 225). Schelling does not give the name 'collective action problem' to this class of problems, but it is certainly a candidate for a definition. A very wide definition it would be, since it includes not only problems of cooperation, but also the usually less severe problems of coordination. The problem of cooperation I define loosely as occurring because of an incentive to free ride. In the problem of coordination there is either one aggregate outcome preferred by all, if only they can coordinate their actions to reach it; or there are several outcomes 'equally' preferred. In the first case, the problem of coordination has the structure of an assurance game; in the latter case it becomes a matter of convention.[6] It may also be the case that there are several coordination equilibria, one being Pareto-superior to the rest; or several collectively equivalent equilibria with different implications for different individuals. In the latter case, we get a game called the 'battle of the sexes' (see below).

It should be added that problems of coordination are not always less serious than problems of cooperation. If there are multiple conventional equilibria they involve a problem of fairness, because multiple equilibria have multiple distributional implications. In this case, the problem of coordination turns into a problem of bargaining that might be more serious than the problem of cooperation (see p. 222).

Schelling's suggestions have turned out to be unusually fertile soil for the growth of ideas in the field of collective action. Among those who are most obviously indebted are Norman Frohlich, Mark Granovetter, Pamela Oliver, Gerald Marwell, Michael Taylor, Russell Hardin, Anthony de Jasay and, in particular, Jon Elster. Some psychologists, developing the idea of *social traps*, are also inspired by Schelling. The theoretical basis for this idea is not the logic but the psychology of action or, better, behaviour, since this basis is behaviourist learning theory. A trap is a situation such that the contingencies of reinforcement lead to perverse effects (Platt, 1973: 643; Cross and Guyer, 1980: 4, 11). There are several ways of classifying social traps. I will impose only some elementary distinctions. The first is that between *individual* and *collective* traps. I presume that this distinction is self-evident. It refers to the victim of the trap: is it the individual or the collective? A second, equally self-evident, distinction is between *immediate* and *delayed* traps. A third distinction is that between *traps* and *countertraps*, or fences. A trap is a situation in which a rewarding behaviour leads to negative consequences. A countertrap is a situation in which a punishing behaviour prevents the attainment of a good.

Some examples. Individual traps are typically delayed, as when the immediate gratification of smoking and eating ruin our health. Individual counter-traps occur when people refuse to test something new – it may be food, music, literature, or anything else – and are by their rigidity excluded from the pleasures that might ensue. But there are also immediate individual traps when the excitement of the moment makes people foolhardy: fast driving, gambling, etc.

My interest is, of course, in collective traps and countertraps, in which immediate rewards and punishments lead to immediate or delayed undesirable outcomes, maybe ruin, for the collective. The paradigmatic cases – Mancur Olson's logic of collective action and Garrett Hardin's tragedy of the commons – exemplify an immediate, or short-term, collective countertrap and a delayed, or long-term, social trap, respectively.[7] The logic of collective action applies also to delayed collective countertraps. Examples would be failure to invest in future public goods; in environment, infrastructure, public education, etc. Typical examples of immediate collective traps are crowding effects, as when all try to get home as quickly as possible from work, thereby creating a traffic jam, or when some rise from their seats in order to get a better view of some spectacle, forcing all to rise in order to see anything at all and less comfortably.[8]

Jon Elster has attempted to cover the ground of social traps with the help of rational choice. In that perspective, individual traps and countertraps appear as instances of the intrapersonal, intertemporal collective action problem (Elster, 1985b: 138; 1985c: 249ff.; 1989a: 19ff.). Failure to solve this problem is due to myopia and weakness of will; its solution depends upon the possibility of a more enlightened self-interest and upon pre-commitment. While this analogy is both interesting and fertile, it is not my business here. I turn, instead, to Elster's discussion of the original collective action problem.

According to Elster, there are several equally legitimate definitions of a 'collective action problem'. His first suggestion involves two: one strong and one weak:

> According to the strong definition, we have a collective action problem if two conditions are satisfied. First, each individual derives greater benefits under conditions of universal cooperation than he does under conditions of universal noncooperation. Second, each derives more benefits if he abstains from cooperation, regardless of what others do ... A weaker definition is provided by retaining the first condition that went into the strong definition while replacing the second by two others: cooperation is individually unstable and individually inaccessible. By individual instability I mean that each individual has an incentive to defect from a situation of universal cooperation, by individual inaccessibility that he has no incentive to take the first step away from a situation of universal noncooperation.
>
> (Elster, 1985b: 139f.)

The strong definition is simply an N-person prisoners' dilemma and need not detain us any more. The weak definition is more controversial. As

Brian Barry pointed out in his comment on Elster, there is no very good reason for retaining the first condition in the weak definition. Universal cooperation is much too strong a condition. There is a collective action problem, if some indefinite level of cooperation is Pareto superior to universal noncooperation (Barry, 1985a: 156). Elster is quick to accept Barry's point (Elster, 1985c: 239). The oddity is that he did not do this in the first place, since it follows from Schelling's discussion of the 'generic' collective action problem, with which Elster is very well acquainted and will eventually utilize in his own analysis of the technology of collective action (Elster, 1985c; 1989a: 27–34).

The other two conditions are clarified, by Elster, in terms of the games of assurance (also called the game of trust) and of chicken. A fourth game of some relevance for the collective action problem, is the battle of the sexes.[9]

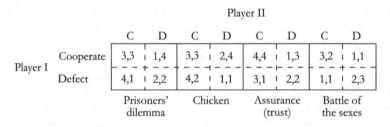

Figure 5.3 A Taxonomy of 2 × 2 games involving a collective action problem.

In the game of assurance, the cooperative solution is inaccessible because it takes two or, in the N-person game, N persons to reach a solution. This situation I have already dubbed 'the problem of coordination' (see p. 218). Elster calls it 'the problem of information', since it is assumed that, once people understand the situation, they will immediately cooperate. The 'game of assurance' was discussed and baptized by Amartya Sen (1967). In his version of the game, individuals prefer to cooperate and will do so if they are assured that others will do so too. But the payoff structure of this game can also be achieved by technical and institutional means. If a public good is *extremely* lumpy, it may be that it can only be produced if all contribute (cf. Elster, 1985b: 140). An institutional means to create an assurance game may be a decision rule to the effect that the public good will only be provided if there is an unanimous agreement to contribute (cf. Buchanan, 1968: 92ff.).

In the game of chicken, the cooperative solution is individually unstable, because each individual, even while preferring cooperation before universal noncooperation, prefers that someone else provides the collective good. Elster refers to this as the 'indeterminacy problem' and argues that it might be even more severe than the prisoners' dilemma (Elster, 1985b: 140). The relevance of the game of chicken for the analysis of collective action has been brought out most clearly by Michael Taylor and Hugh Ward (Taylor and Ward, 1982; Taylor, 1987: ch. 2; see also Jankowski, 1990). They question the ubiquity of the prisoners' dilemma as a paradigm for analysing collective action, maintaining that many collective action problems, including environmental ones, have the structure of a game of chicken. The characteristic feature of this game is that universal defection is the worst outcome. In the N-person version of this game it is assumed that a subgroup of cooperators is necessary and sufficient for the public good to be provided. This will be the case if the public good exhibits *some* lumpiness (step goods). Many versions of this game are possible (see Jankowski, 1990). To the extent that individuals make their choices conditional upon the choices of others, their decisions involve a risk. Assuming also that they are risk averse, they may choose to cooperate. If choices are sequential, the first may precommit themselves to a defecting strategy, forcing the rest to cooperate. As the remaining subgroup becomes small enough to make the cooperation of each necessary for the provision of a public good, the game transforms into a game of assurance. On balance, cooperation should be more likely when the problem of collective action is a game of chicken than in the case of a prisoners' dilemma (Taylor and Ward, 1982: 370; Taylor, 1987: xi, 58).

The battle of the sexes takes place when partners to a relationship want to do different things, but want to do it in the company of the other, rather than alone.[10] This game is characterized by the existence of multiple coordination equilibria unequally preferred by different players. Jean Hampton has argued that many collective action problems – including some of those interpreted by Taylor and Ward as games of chicken – have the structure of this game (Hampton, 1987: 246, 254n.). In the terminology of Olson, both chicken and the battle of the sexes are characterized by multiple 'privilege'; there are more than one individual and/or coalition willing to take upon themselves the provision of a public good. The difference is that the battle of the sexes has coordination equilibria, whereas the game of chicken has only Nash equilibria. In the former no one can be made better off by anyone acting otherwise; in the latter no one can be made better off by alone acting differently. Hampton argues that collective action problems turn into battles of the sexes in the case of pure step goods and criticizes Taylor and Ward for failing to appreciate this fact.

Elster and Taylor deny that the game of assurance presents a genuine collective action problem. This means that there are public goods, the provision of which does not involve a collective action problem. Taylor suggests that 'a collective action problem exists where rational individual action can lead to a strictly Pareto-inferior outcome, that is, an outcome which is strictly less preferred by every individual than at least one other outcome' (Taylor, 1987: 19). This definition is terminologically, but not intentionally, identical with that of Schelling (p. 218 above). For Taylor, it is a matter of definition that failure to achieve coordination spells lack of individual rationality. But the game of chicken also presents a problem in this respect. Because this game lacks a dominant strategy, it is not always clear what rationality prescribes (Taylor, 1987: 19). Perhaps the generic feature of collective action problems is the existence of an invitation to free ride. If so, there is a collective action problem whenever individual rationality dictates free riding. Since this is no less indeterminate in the case of chicken, as is Taylor's definition, we might opt for a psychological version: there is a collective action problem whenever there is a temptation, on the part of rational individuals, to free ride on the contributions of others. It may be an undesirable property of this definition that 'free riding' appears as a primitive term, but for my purposes it is an advantage with a definition that highlights the issue of self-interest.

If a collective action problem is defined by a temptation to free ride and if Hampton is correct to maintain that there is also a free rider problem in the battle of the sexes, then, of course, we have a collective action problem in this game too. It depends. Hampton suggests that there are free rider problems both in the *selection* of producers and in the actual *production* of a public good. The battle of the sexes occurs in the former. This may be, but most analysts of collective action prefer to see the problem of selection as a bargaining problem distinct from the collective action problem. According to James Buchanan (1968: 178ff.), Jon Elster (1985c: 247–249; 1989a: chs 2, 4; 1989b: ch. 14) and Elinor Ostrom (1990: 46–50), for instance, the collective action problem is often, perhaps usually, accompanied by problems of how to distribute the costs and benefits of public goods. These problems, which are typically solved by bargaining, may be even more severe than the pure collective action problem. The bargaining problem arises because there is rarely one cooperative 'solution' to a collective action problem. According to Elster (1985c: 247), there are two main sources of trouble: (1) the existence of multiple cooperative equilibria creates a *coordination problem* (cf. Hampton, 1987: 254–257). (2) The unequal distribution of costs and benefits creates a *fairness problem* (cf. Hardin, 1982: 90ff.). Important as it is, the problem of bargaining is not the subject of this chapter. It is a problem of social choice, rather than of collective action.

Philip Pettit has suggested a distinction between *free riding* and *foul dealing* in an N-person prisoners' dilemma. Unlike a free rider, a foul dealer makes suckers worse off than in the case of universal defection. 'The free rider seeks to benefit by the efforts of others, the foul dealer to benefit at their expense' (Pettit, 1986: 374). This is a defining characteristic of a two-person prisoners' dilemma and the reason why defection is the dominant strategy. In the two-person game, therefore, there could be no free riding, only foul dealing. In the N-person, case, however, there may be both free riding and foul dealing, as the case may be. It may be pointed out that free riding, while

222

tempting, is really not possible at all in a one-shot prisoners' dilemma. This is so, because all (rational self-interested) players will defect. For free riding to be possible, the game must be chicken or the battle of the sexes. In these cases, free riding, as distinguished from foul dealing, is most likely to occur. In the game of assurance, neither free riding nor foul dealing is possible on the part of rational players. This is because, in this game, all lose, while a foul dealer stands to gain by defecting. If someone were, nevertheless, to defect, in a game of assurance, he/she would be a saboteur, but not a foul dealer.

There may be no single definition capable of catching all real world collective action problems in one net. Maybe they are united, if at all, by family resemblance. In his latest treatment of the collective action problem, Jon Elster (1989a: 24–27), gives three definitions and suggests three ways in which even the weakest definition may be relaxed. In this chapter, the prisoners' dilemma will be used as a paradigmatic basis of an argument against the economic theory of collective action. Other types of collective action will be treated as deviations from this ideal type.

The collective action problem is something of an Achilles' heel for a positive economic theory of politics. As such, it has generated a vast body of literature devoted to solving it. Microeconomics relies on the assumption of rationality, and in most cases, including public choice, also on the assumption of self-interest. It is static and it is individualistic, or atomistic, in the sense that it precludes interaction of individuals. Finally, it is weak on institutional analysis and negligent of social structure. As I have already indicated, Olson makes some unorthodox openings, but does not go far enough to solve the problem of collective action. Attempts to do so have proceeded by relaxing one, or several, of the assumptions and limitations of the economic approach. In the case of Olson's theory, there are some additional assumptions, concerning the nature of collective goods and the effects of group size upon their provision, that have been disputed.

The only assumption that cannot be questioned, if economic theory is to remain a theory of rational choice, is the assumption of rationality. But it can be redefined, along with the situation to which it is applied. I intend the situation as conceived by presumptive participants, but there is also the 'objective' situation of other people acting in an institutional framework or social structure. My conviction is that the practical problem of collective action is solved because people are not entirely self-interested, at least not all of them. This implies that the theoretical problem of collective action cannot be solved without giving up the assumption of self-interest, without rejecting the core assumption of public choice. In the remainder of this chapter, I will first present some attempts to solve the collective action problem while retaining the assumption of self-interest, if only for methodological purposes. Secondly, I will discuss some other suggestions, going beyond self-interest, while remaining within the framework of rational choice – until it bursts, in the case of Elster. Thirdly, I will present some empirical research, supporting my sociological prejudice that cooperation is possible, mainly because people act from other motives than narrow self-interest.

GROUP SIZE

The first ambitious attempt to evade the discouraging implications of Olson's analysis was made by Norman Frohlich, Joe A. Oppenheimer and Oran R. Young in their *Political Leadership and Collective Goods* (1971). Their stated intention was to extend Olson's theory (p. xiii), but, in fact, it is more of a revision. Their basic idea is that collective goods are provided by political entrepreneurs seizing the opportunity to make a profit by providing collective goods to passive recipients. I suppose it is possible to say that political entrepreneurs turn large groups into intermediate ones. Or better, centralization makes it possible to achieve the same degree of coordination and control in a large group as in a decentralized intermediate group. There are three possible sources of revenue for the leader and his organization: donations, taxes and exchange of private goods (pp. 6ff., 18ff.). So far there is only an extension, no revision of Olson's analysis. But why should people contribute? I disregard taxes and private goods. Why should a single individual donate money to a political entrepreneur if her/his contribution makes no difference? This is the point where the analysis of Frohlich *et al.* differs significantly from that of Olson.

Olson used several arguments to show that members of large groups would not voluntarily contribute to the provision of collective goods, unless accompanied by some private good, used as a selective incentive. A first argument of Mancur Olson was that the benefit to each will be a declining fraction of group benefit, so that, in large groups, costs will certainly outweigh benefits. If this argument is correct, the above analysis of Frohlich *et al.* will be incorrect. Consequently, they reject Olson's first argument. While it is true that the benefit to each makes up a declining *fraction* of the total benefit from a public good as the group becomes larger, this does not imply that its absolute value to an individual declines too – and it is the absolute value that decides whether an individual will contribute to the provision of a public good, or not. The benefit an individual receives from a collective good decreases with group size only when there is a strong crowding effect, or diseconomies of scale, which is common, but not typical of collective goods (Frohlich and Oppenheimer, 1970: 107ff.; Frohlich *et al.*, 1971: 145–150).

A second argument follows directly from the first. If the benefit to each is a declining fraction of group benefit as the group becomes larger, then the less likely it is that the group will be privileged. This argument adds nothing new. A third argument of Olson was that organization costs increase with group size. This may be, but the important thing for the individual is per capita costs. As Frohlich *et al.* point out, cost-sharing arrangements may decisively alter the situation in which individuals decide whether to contribute or not. In large groups, mechanisms for cost-sharing may be furnished by political entrepreneurs. Pooling the resources of large numbers of contributors, they provide a demanded public good in exchange for a profit (Frohlich *et al.*, 1971: 22–25, 146f.; Frohlich and Oppenheimer, 1978: 49–55, 66ff.).

These three arguments are mentioned by Olson, himself, as 'three separate but cumulative factors that keep larger groups from furthering their own interests' (Olson, 1965/1971: 48). But there are others. A fourth argument, used by Olson, is that, in large groups, each contribution will be too small to make a noticeable difference to the outcome (ibid., 44f.). The rational thing to do, therefore, is not to contribute. This argument is based on the assumptions of atomism and paradigmatic rationality. Individuals do not take one another into account and no single contribution affects the pooled resources. Frohlich *et al.* replace this assumption by the alternative assumption that people act strategically on their estimation of other people's likely behaviour and the consequent probability that the collective good will, in fact, be provided. Since each individual is better off with the collective good, than without it, they will contribute if their expected utility exceeds their costs. The decision is taken in a situation of risk (Frohlich *et al.*, 1971: 20ff., ch. 5).[11]

Olson's most well-known argument is about free riding. Frohlich, Oppenheimer and Young claim to address this problem, but I think they evade it and offer an alternative analysis. If Olson is right, they are wrong, and I tend to believe that Olson is right, at least about the implications of narrow self-interest. If people's first inclination is to free ride when possible, and if they are not risk averse, they will do so as soon as they estimate the probability that the collective good will be provided anyway to more than 0.5 (cf. Buchanan, 1968: 88–91; Laver, 1980: 205). It is still possible, of course, that Frohlich, *et al.* are closer than Olson to the way most people actually think about collective goods.[12]

It is nowadays widely agreed that Olson's size arguments do not stand up to scrutiny (see, e.g., Chamberlain, 1974; Hardin, 1982: ch. 3; Taylor, 1976: 23–25; 1982: 39ff.; 1987: 7–11; Oliver and Marwell, 1988). Among the best discussions is that by Russell Hardin in his important *Collective Action* (1982). Hardin points out that Olson's analysis suffers from a conflation of two typologies: the distinction between privileged, hence manifest, and latent groups and the trichotomy of small, intermediate and large groups. Olson writes as if small groups were always privileged and large groups always latent, but there is really no necessary relation between the two dimensions. A small group may be latent and a large group privileged. The most dubious assumption made by Olson is that individuals' net benefit necessarily declines as the group becomes larger. Two circumstances could turn each group member's net benefit into a decreasing function of group size: (1) individual benefits decrease, (2) individual costs increase – or both. This may, but need not, be the case.

According to Olson, each individual receives a fraction *(Fi)* of the group gain *(Vg)*, such that $Fi = Vi/Vg$. This formula says nothing about the absolute value of the collective good to the individual *(Vi)*. But Olson's size argument obviously depends upon the assumption that individual benefit is a decreasing function of group size. Why else should he attach so much importance to fractions? Also, much that Olson says about the effects of group size simply does not make sense without this assumption. But the analytical truth that individual benefit is a fraction of group benefit does not imply the synthetic statement that individual benefit decreases with group size.

This point had already been made by Frohlich *et al.* It was repeated, with even more clarity and force, by John Chamberlain (1974) and is an important part of the recent argument of de Jasay (1989). According to Chamberlain, Olson's argument applies only to goods characterized by rivalness of consumption, goods that are 'exclusive', in the sense of Olson (1965/1971: 38). But for nonrival, or 'inclusive', public goods, 'the relationship between group size and the amount of the good actually provided is the opposite of that asserted by Olson' (Chamberlain, 1974: 712). This is so because in the absence of rivalness a decreasing fraction of total benefit does not imply a decreasing benefit to each individual. It could be, of course, that rivalness is the rule and nonrivalness an exception. There is no argument, by Olson or anyone else, to support such a contention.

De Jasay similarly argues that the conventional analyses of public goods assume constant returns to scale. Both marginal and average utility is $1/N$ of group benefit, where N is the number of beneficiaries. The usually unstated assumption behind this analysis is that public goods are perfectly divisible (de Jasay, 1989: 149–151), as if they were simply aggregates of private goods. But this assumption is most often false. Public goods are typically indivisible. Indeed, this is part of the very meaning of a 'public good'. De Jasay suggests that jointness is a special case of indivisibility (ibid., pp. 156ff.).[13]

According to Samuelson, jointness is a necessary condition and defining characteristic of collective goods (Samuelson, 1954: 387). A second, commonly accepted, defining characteristic is non-excludability. Mancur Olson chooses to emphasize the latter (Olson, 1965/1971: 14). But this choice is tendentious, since it supports his own argument. Non-excludability makes for free riding and works against the provision of public goods. Jointness works in the opposite direction. It tends to increase the probability that collective goods will be provided. 'Jointness' means that the utility one person derives from a good does not diminish as a result of its use by other people. A lighthouse is one commonly cited example. Legislation intended to give us clean air would be another. In the case of perfect jointness, therefore, individual benefit is independent of group size. Perfect jointness may be rare, but some degree of jointness characterizes all collective goods. Indeed, most collective goods sought by interest groups – laws and regulations, import quotas and tariffs, exemption from taxes, etc. are general and, therefore, perfectly joint, in a formal sense. Materially, varying degrees of rivalness occur as indirect effects of the implementation of governmental policy. The absence of jointness, however, means that a particular good is possible only as a private good.[14]

Many collective goods exhibit increasing returns to scale. This is especially so in all cases where the provision of the collective good depends on protest and revolt, or, more generally, on the active participation of the members of a social group or movement. Activities, such as riots, strikes, petitions, demonstrations, revolutions and wars often depend crucially upon numbers. The ability to exert pressure, not only in the form of force but also in the form of persuasion, is largely a function of group size. In the case of increasing returns to scale, individual benefit increases with group size.

Olson is rather brief about costs. He assumes that total costs will be a monotonically increasing function of the quantity produced of a collective good. He further assumes that fixed costs will usually be high, that marginal costs will eventually decline and finally rise again, so that the cost function will be U-shaped. The only costs explicitly discussed by Mancur Olson are organization costs, which are usually greater in large groups than in small groups, at least in the start-up of an organization. But these are largely overhead costs, which do not vary much with the size of the group. Once the organization is there, production of public goods often shows dramatically decreasing marginal costs. Always when this is the case, per capita costs decrease as a function of group size – but only when there is cost-sharing.

Olson mentions cost-sharing, but obviously does not believe that it can give rise to voluntary cooperation in large groups. For Olson, public goods will be provided only when $Ai = Vi - C > 0$. But if cost-sharing is feasible, $Ai = Vi - Ci$, where Ci is the cost to one individual (i) of providing some public good. Shared costs are necessarily lower for each individual than is the total cost of a public good. In the case of shared costs, since Ci is only a fraction of C, or total group cost, it is, of course, much more likely that Ai will take on a positive value. For Olson, however, cost-sharing is possible in large groups only by way of coercion, in which case Ci becomes a tax. This argument does not depend upon a pure size effect. It follows analytically from Olson's atomistic assumption of independent decision-making in large groups and causally from the hypothesis about free riding (cf. Frohlich and Oppenheimer, 1970).

The problem of crowding effects in the production of public goods is usually solved by organization. Large interest organizations usually divide into a small nucleus of active members that do the job and a large, passive troop

227

of supporters. In this way, the persuasiveness of number is combined with the effectiveness of organization and leadership to produce public goods at low cost to each member. The provision of a specific government may also be seen as a collective good with increasing returns to scale. As a collective good government is also characterized by an extreme 'lumpiness', since, in democratic countries, it can usually be produced only by a majority. In the case of government, lumpiness is institutional, but often it is technical. A bridge costs a lot, but once it is built it costs little to maintain and is extremely useful to lots of people. In the case of lumpy goods, cost-sharing is often the only possibility of obtaining a public good at all.

Interesting, in this connection, are the results of Oliver, Marwell and Teixeira's analysis (computer simulations) of the effects upon collective action of different production functions (see Figure 5.4). If the production function is decelerating, collective action is easy to get started, but will soon ebb away: in many cases too soon, because those most interested in a collective good will be first to contribute, while those less interested will free ride. This outcome is suboptimal, because it is determined by the marginal utility of those least interested in the collective good. The situation is very different in the case of accelerating production functions. Because of high initial costs, the collective action problem is more severe and collective action rare. But if collective action does take off – something that depends entirely upon the existence of

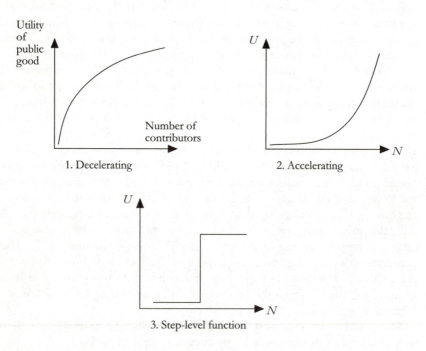

Utility of public good

Number of contributors

1. Decelerating

2. Accelerating

3. Step-level function

Figure 5.4 Three production functions for public goods

228

a critical mass – it will tend to snowball because of increasing marginal returns.

A special, but important, case is step functions, associated with step-level, or lumpy, goods (see Hardin, 1982: 55–61; Hampton, 1987: 248–250). In the extreme, a public good can only be provided if all group members contribute. In this case, free riding is impossible and the collective action problem turns into a game of assurance. At the other extreme, only one contribution is necessary for the public good to be provided. In this case, we may have a battle of the sexes, in which all members would be prepared to provide the good by themselves, but would prefer someone else to be the one to do it. In this case free riding is a real possibility. A public good can be provided if some number of individuals (K) cooperate, while the rest $(N - K)$ take a free ride. If K is large enough to yield a net benefit for this subgroup, as in the Schelling diagram (Figure 5.2, p. 217), then there is a possibility that the collective good might be provided. This case has been analysed by Michael Taylor and Hugh Ward as a game of chicken (pp. 220f).

Step functions may also be negative. Some public goods can only be provided by a small number of people, or by a single individual. Obvious examples are those that depend upon secrecy, or upon some special ability, talent or power for their supply. Spies and saboteurs often work alone and so do stars of all sorts. People with extraordinary powers, natural or institutional, may also be in the position of being the only ones capable of producing a certain public good. This is the step function for heroes: individuals who, alone, provide public goods of much value to lots of people.

Oliver, Marwell and Teixeira assume production functions to be always increasing, but marginal returns may also be negative. An additional contribution may give rise to a decrease in the total value of a collective good, or in the probability that it will be provided. Inspired by Oliver, Marwell and Teixeira, Jon Elster has analysed net, and average, benefits as functions of a number of contributors. Net benefits, of course, start decreasing long before gross benefits do, or when marginal costs exceed marginal returns. There are lots of collective action problems where average benefit decreases as the number of cooperators becomes too large. Average benefit may reach a maximum when only some cooperate, while the rest take a free ride. Jon Elster takes the example of everybody cleaning up after a party, even though the job could be more effectively done if some kept out of the way. Universal cooperation may even lead to an outcome that is worse than no cooperation at all. If everybody helps clean up litter after a garden party, the lawn may be ruined. Or, as the proverb says, 'too many cooks spoil the broth'. These examples are from ordinary life, but analogies from political activity are not hard to find (Elster, 1989a: 32–34, 189ff.; 1989b: 127–134).

The conclusion of this section would be that Olson's size argument is seriously deficient. There are many types of collective goods and Olson's argument applies only to some of them. One thing remains true, however: social control is more difficult in large groups. Therefore, if individuals are rational egoists, 'The size effect which ... should be taken most seriously is *the increased difficulty of conditional cooperation in larger groups*' (Taylor, 1987: 12).

TIME AND INTERACTION

Of much importance for the subsequent treatment of the collective action problem was Russell Hardin's interpretation of Mancur Olson's logic of collective action in large groups as identical with an N-person prisoners' dilemma (Hardin, 1971; 1982: chs 1–2; Barry and Hardin, 1982: 23–26). As we have seen, Hardin was not the first to make this interpretation. James Buchanan had done it before, but it was Hardin who introduced it among political scientists, with definite repercussions for the further analysis of collective action.

Of even greater consequence, however, was the analysis of the problem of collective action as an *iterated* prisoners' dilemma. The most famous example of this analysis is Robert Axelrod's computer tournament, reported in *The Evolution of Cooperation* (1984).[15] Axelrod invited a number of philosophers and social scientists to participate in the tournament, each using a strategy of his own choosing. The tournament consisted of an indefinite number of two-person prisoners' dilemma games, where all participants played against one another. To Axelrod's surprise, the strategy that emerged victorious was the simple 'tit-for-tat', suggested by the well-known game-theorist Anatol Rapoport. Tit-for-tat is the strategy of always cooperating in the first round and defecting only when the other player defects. What this result suggests is that, in the long run, it is rational even for the egoist to cooperate. The implication for social life – to the extent that it resembles an iterated two-person prisoners' dilemma – would be that cooperation, or social order, is possible even in the absence of government authority.

The result of Axelrod's computer tournament might seem to support an economic theory of collective action, or even of social order. But support is equivocal. It disappears if economics is a theory of rational *choice*.

> There is no need to assume that the players are rational. They need not be trying to maximize rewards. Their strategies may simply reflect standard operating procedures, rules of thumb, instincts, habits, or imitation ... The actions that players take are not necessarily even conscious choices. A person who sometimes returns a favor, and sometimes does not, may think about what strategy is being used. There is no need to assume deliberate choice at all.
>
> (Axelrod, 1984: 18)

Of all participants in the tournament, only one chose the winning strategy of tit-for-tat. If people in their daily lives often act upon this strategy, this is not because they are more 'rational' than the participants in the tournament, but because there is a *norm of reciprocity* (Axelrod, 1984: ch. 3). The prevalence of such a norm in society is not the result of rational choice, but of evolution (see also Axelrod, 1986).

Axelrod's theory of cooperation is 'economic', however, in the limited sense discussed here: it is based upon the assumption of self-interest. The question it seeks to answer is this: 'Under what conditions will cooperation emerge in a world of egoists without central authority?' (ibid., p. 3). His answer is that this is possible if there is a sufficiently large chance that people will meet again (ibid., p. 20). But then it should be observed that Axelrod is not talking about narrow self-interest. His analysis does not exclude a concern for others. 'The reason for assuming self-interest is that it allows an examination of the difficult case in which cooperation is not completely based upon a concern for others or upon the welfare of the group as a whole' (ibid., p. 6). Rather than assuming self-interest, Axelrod seems content not to exclude it. If this is the kind of 'self-interest' assumed in his theory, there is little reason to call it 'economic', rather than something else.

It does seem, however, that Axelrod's argument is that cooperation *could* occur even in a world of pure egoists. There are two conditions: 'that the cooperation be based on reciprocity and that the shadow of the future is important enough to make this reciprocity stable' (ibid., p. 173). The second condition is sometimes satisfied.[16] Under certain, not too unlikely, circumstances egoists are also likely to meet again. If they belong to the same social group, for instance, and the group is small (cf. Coleman, 1986). But can reciprocity ever become established in a world of pure egoists? As I understand Axelrod, a positive answer to this question hinges on the possibility that a small cluster of individuals hits upon the strategy of reciprocity by mere chance, learns that it is advantageous and defends it against invasion by other strategies. This, I submit, is unlikely to happen within either a rational choice or an evolutionary framework. In his 1986 article on the evolution of norms, Axelrod mentions three mechanisms that could sustain evolution: survival of the fittest, learning by trial and error, and imitation (Axelrod, 1986: 1097f.). Of these, Michael Macy has recommended a stochastic learning model as a less demanding framework for capturing the emergence of cooperation (Macy, 1989: 199ff.). I concur that something like this is needed and I welcome the attempt to rehabilitate the classical sociological theory of internalized norms in this way (Macy, 1990b: 246).

First to analyse the collective action problem as an iterated prisoners' dilemma, or a prisoners' dilemma *supergame*, was Michael Taylor in his *Anarchy and Cooperation* (1976).[17] According to him, it is a major shortcoming of Olson's formal analysis of collective action and of the theory of ordinary games alike that they are static. The simple insight that in real life people meet again, and often remember what happened last, is of paramount importance for an understanding of the logic of collective action. When people meet again they may make their actions conditional upon the prevoius actions of others. This feature of real life interaction may be captured by the prisoners' dilemma supergame. If people play the same game over and over again, they may choose a strategy that makes their choices in each round dependent upon the choices of others. Taylor's conclusion concerning the two-person supergame is similar to that of Axelrod. Cooperation is possible among rational egoists, if they use conditional cooperative strategies (tit-for-tat), if the number of two-person prisoners' dilemmas is indefinite and if the players do not discount the future too much, relative to their immediate payoffs (Taylor, 1976: 31–43, 86–89; 1987: ch. 3). Tit-for-tat is not the only possible conditional strategy, but it is the most salient one. If there are only two strategies: tit-for-tat (B) and consistent defection (D∞), then we have an assurance game with bilateral tit-for-tat (B,B) as the most preferred outcome for both players (Taylor, 1987: 67). Bilateral tit-for-tat is also a coordination equilibrium, since no player can be made better off by any player unilaterally switching to some other strategy (Taylor, 1987: 71–73; see also Hardin, 1982: 166).

Taylor is aware of the serious limitations of the two-person game and criticizes Axelrod for ignoring them. Above all, collective action, typically, does not consist of pairwise interaction. Also, people's cooperation is not dependent upon the cooperation of other players, one at a time, but upon enough others cooperating all the time. Collective action, therefore, is better captured by an N-person prisoners' dilemma supergame (Taylor, 1976: 43–61, 89–93; 1987: ch. 4). Taylor's analysis of this game, however, does not give rise to any very definite conclusions. Cooperation is possible, but only if a sufficient number of players are conditional cooperators.

As we have seen (p. 221f.), Taylor is also critical of the definition of the collective action problem as a prisoners' dilemma. Most importantly, there is also a collective action problem when preferences have the structure of a game of chicken (Taylor and Ward, 1982; Taylor, 1987: ch. 2). The significance of this fact is heightened by Taylor's argument that the N-person prisoners' dilemma supergame may develop into a game of chicken. This happens if it is rational for a subgroup of cooperators to provide a public good, but there are multiple equilibria. In this case all members would wish a subgroup to cooperate, but they would like it to be a subgroup not including themselves as members (Taylor, 1987: 92f.). In short, people prefer to free ride on the contribution of others. Even so, 'a subgroup of conditional Cooperators *might* emerge if enough players are sufficiently risk averse' (Taylor, 1987: 93) and if the public good is lumpy enough to make a subgroup of a certain size both necessary and sufficient for its provision.[18,19]

Jean Hampton has argued that some of the collective action problems identified by Taylor and Ward as games of chicken are really battles of the

232

sexes (Hampton, 1987: 254n.). She cites the following well-known passage from David Hume:

> Two neighbours may agree to drain a meadow, which they possess in common: because it is easy for them to know each other's mind; and each must perceive, that the immediate consequence of his failing in his part, is the abandoning of the whole project. But it is very difficult, and indeed impossible, that a thousand persons should agree in any such action; it being difficult for them to concert so complicated a design, and still more difficult for them to execute it; while each seeks a pretext to free himself of the trouble and expense, and would lay the whole burden on others.
>
> (Hume, 1738/1911, vol. 2: 239)

According to Hampton (1987: 251ff.), the situation described by Hume has the structure of a battle of the sexes. I have problems with this interpretation. In the first place, the two-person game is obviously a game of assurance, since unilateral defection leads to 'the abandonment of the whole project'. But this is unimportant, because Hampton is interested in the N-person case. She asks us to conceive of a thousand-person matrix, but uses a three-person matrix for purposes of illustration. The game-theoretic structure is assumed to be the same. What I do not understand is this: According to Hampton, a situation in which all cooperate is better for cooperators than a situation where only some do so (Hampton, 1987: 252), whereas a coordination equilibrium is characterized by the fact that 'no one would be better off if any one player . . . acted differently (ibid., p. 253). A situation where universal cooperation is better than being suckered is more like a game of chicken than a battle of the sexes.

Hampton takes no notice of the fact that Michael Taylor has also analysed the above passage from Hume (Taylor, 1976: 124–125; 1987: 159f.). His interpretation is entirely different. For Taylor, the important thing is Hume's size argument, which is identical with that of Mancur Olson. What Hume says about large groups, therefore, reflects an N-person prisoners' dilemma. The briefness of Hume's remark rules out anything like a valid interpretation, but I do find Taylor's suggestion more plausible. Hampton maintains that defection does not dominate in the situation depicted by Hume. But this applies to the case of two neighbours, not to a group of a thousand persons. In this case it is, according to Hume, impossible to reach agreement. Hence a rational individual should defect, no matter what others do. It should be added that Taylor agrees with Hampton's interpretation of Hume in the case of small groups, in which conventional solutions to coordination problems are supposed to be possible.

For Taylor and Ward, lumpiness played an important part in turning collective action problems into games of chicken. But for Hampton (1987: 248ff.), lumpiness creates battles of the sexes. I do not know which analysis is the more correct, but both games are common and important in real life.

I have given a brief account of the application of game theory to the problem of collective action. The obvious virtue of game theory is the clarity and precision it brings to the analysis of social phenomena. The main short-coming is excessive simplification. In the next section I will introduce some complexities that take us beyond game theory. Before I do, however, I will show that some of these complexities are also recognized by those who have made most fertile use of game theory in the analysis of collective action.

As we have seen, Michael Taylor used an N-person prisoners' dilemma in his analysis of collective action. But this game is inadequate as a representation of real life cooperation. The most important shortcoming, according to Taylor himself, is that it assumes a static environment. 'In some of the public goods problems of interest here, a more realistic description of reality would require a *changing* payoff matrix, possibly a changing set of available strategies, and even a changing set of players' (Taylor, 1987: 107). At this point, I suspect that we may have reached the limits of game theory. There is a theory of nested games, to be sure (see, e.g., Heckathorn, 1984; Tsebelis, 1990), and Taylor has shown how the games of chicken and of assurance may become nested within a prisoners' dilemma supergame, but complexity sets limits to the possible utility of this theory too. At this point we must opt for something less simple, less precise and less formal. Probably the only alternative is some kind of largely informal institutional analysis, as exemplified by the authors discussed in the next section.

This is the road trodden by Robert Axelrod after *The Evolution of Cooperation* (1984). While still using game theory in his formulation of the problem of collective action, he now turns to social norms and institutions for its solution (Axelrod, 1986; Axelrod and Keohane, 1985). Maybe this is a hint at the most fertile use of game theory in social science: as a heuristic tool more than as the source of explanatory models.

Russell Hardin, finally, goes beyond the theory of (noncooperative) iter-ated games in at least two important respects. First, in an iterated game it is possible not only to make cooperation conditional upon the cooperation of others, but to enter a contract by convention. This is true, but takes us beyond noncooperative game theory, which excludes this possibility by defini-tion. Second, the important thing for conditional cooperation is that people meet again, not that they play the same game over and over again. For this to happen, it suffices that people engage in overlapping activities. An individual defecting in one game may be punished in another. When a group of people engage in many overlapping activities, it is easy to punish free riders – the ultimate punishment being exclusion from the group (Hardin, 1982: ch. 11).

Hardin's transcendence of game theory points in the direction of a more institutional and more structural treatment of collective action. His analysis of contract and of overlapping activities, in fact, anticipates some of the weightiest arguments made by the new institutionalists.[20] On the other hand, most of these arguments are not at all new in the history of ideas. They are not even new in the short history of the economic theory of collective action. In fact, very little is added to Mancur Olson's informal analysis of collective action.

SOCIAL STRUCTURE

The superiority of the iterated, over the one-shot, prisoners' dilemma lies in the introduction of time and a rudiment of social interaction in the economic analysis of collective action. This is important, but more could be done to approximate real life. Game theory assumes that players are homogeneous in their preferences, if not in their strategies, but in reality they are not. Even though collective action presupposes a common interest, members of the collective also have diverging and more or less intense interests, and unequal resources to back them up. It is a serious lack of realism, therefore, to assume, as does the economic theory of collective action, that individuals are homogeneous and interchangeable (Elster, 1989a: 49, 152ff.). In this respect, use of the iterated prisoners' dilemma was a step back, relative to Mancur Olson's informal analysis, which allowed groups to be heterogeneous and, therefore, privileged, if some member(s) of the group want a collective good so much as to be willing to provide it for the whole group. Further steps in this direction have been taken by sociologists, borrowing the concepts of 'threshold' and 'critical mass' from Thomas Schelling and using them in their own *economic* approach to collective action.

Among sociologists, the notion of 'threshold' was first used to analyse collective action, or 'behavior', by Mark Granovetter (1978). It is a characteristic feature of social life that the actions of individuals depend, in different ways, upon the actions of other individuals.[21] This goes for collective action as well. The simplest form of interdependence is purely quantitative. People's binary decision whether or not to participate in collective action depends upon the number, or proportion, of others already participating. Since we know that people differ in their readiness to participate in collective action, we may define an individual's 'threshold' as the number, or proportion, of others who must take action before he/she does.

Granovetter's analysis is 'economic'. He assumes that people act so as to maximize their utility, and that this utility depends upon the actions of others. Unlike traditional economics, however, he also assumes that people take the actions of others into account when deciding whether to participate or not. Like Frohlich, Oppenheimer and Young, Granovetter assumes that people act strategically, but he differs from the former in making strategy depend upon knowledge of objective circumstances, rather than upon a subjective estimation of probabilities. In Granovetter's model people act on perfect information, not in a situation of risk. This is possible because his model is sequential; each person knows, at every instant, how many others have joined collective action. This is, in many cases of collective action, not a very realistic assumption. Granovetter's main example is participation in riots. Even in this case, information about the number and proportion of rioters is, of course, far from perfect. People know only what happens in their immediate surroundings. Information about more distant events often takes the form of rumours.

Nevertheless, some insights can be gained from Granovetter's analysis. One important insight is that collective action may be highly 'accidental', in the sense that small differences in the distribution of 'thresholds' in the population make a big difference to the aggregate outcome. Because of this, it is virtually impossible to infer the distribution of thresholds from the aggregate outcome. Granovetter illustrates with the following example: suppose we have a group with 100 members, where the distribution of thresholds takes the form of the following series: 0, 1, 2. . .99. In this group, the individual with threshold 0 will begin and the rest will follow, like the bricks in a game of dominoes. But if only one link in the chain had been missing, collective action would have failed to appear. The main burden of Granovetter's analysis is to demonstrate the possibility of domino, or bandwagon, effects in collective action.

The term 'critical mass' has been used by Pamela Oliver, Gerald Marwell and Ruy Teixeira (1985) to denote the well-known fact that much collective action depends crucially upon the money and labour of small groups of dedicated individuals, who provide collective goods for themselves and/or a much larger group of passive beneficiaries, or free riders. Oliver, Marwell and Teixeira discuss collective action as a function of two variables: (1) the heterogeneity of interests and resources and (2) the shape of the production function for various public goods.

A critical mass is simply a form of heterogeneity that makes collective action possible. As such, it has much in common with Mancur Olson's 'privileged group'. A novelty is that the former is made dependent not only upon interests but also upon resources. The critical mass typically consists of persons rich in resources: money, time and, above all, organizational skills. It is a well-known fact that the critical mass is often middle-class, while the passive mass of recipients equally often consists of less resourceful persons from the lower classes.

The introduction of heterogeneity into people's preferences and resources has opened some avenues for further research on the collective action problem. Among those who have taken this direction are Russell Hardin and Jon Elster. They both take the further step of assuming a qualitative, not just a quantitative, heterogeneity in preferences. I will return to this line of research in the section on mixed motivations (pp. 255–261).

There is an additional dimension in the analyses of Granovetter and Oliver *et al.* that I have not mentioned: the amount and structure of social ties and networks in the population. In a well-known article with this title, Granovetter argued for 'The Strength of Weak Ties' (1973). The idea is that strong ties

236

are possible only within small circles of friends, whereas ties that connect small groups with other groups usually are weak. The importance of weak ties lies in their possible function as channels for the diffusion of innovations and messages. As such, weak ties can also enhance the capacity of communities for collective action (1973: 1373–1376). In his article on thresholds of participation, Granovetter makes no mention of weak ties, but argues that strong ties of friendship may influence individuals' thresholds. They are lowered if our friends have already joined, and raised if our friends remain outside a collective endeavour (Granovetter, 1978).

The possible effects of social ties and networks on collective action was also investigated by Marwell, Oliver and Prahl (1988). Once again the method used was computer simulation. Results, therefore, should be treated with suspicion, even though there is little to arouse it. What came out of the computer confirms our prejudices. Marwell *et al.* mention, as an unanticipated result, that network centralization is conducive to collective action. Considering the importance usually attached to leadership and hierarchy in both sociological and economic theories of organization and collective action, I find it surprising that this result was unanticipated. The explanation Marwell *et al.* give of this result is in terms of *selectivity*. Network centralization, in combination with preference heterogeneity, makes it possible for organizers to pick out and concentrate their mobilizing efforts on individuals with a high propensity for collective action, thereby enhancing the overall probability of finding a critical mass triggering collective action (Marwell *et al.*, 1988: 503, 526–532).[22]

The reason social networks can sometimes solve the collective action problem, is that they make all-or-none contracts possible. People agree to contribute if all contribute (Marwell *et al.*, 1988: 509f.). Collective action, then, takes the form of a cooperative assurance game.[23] Commitment to the contract is binding and all that is needed for cooperation. In other cases, however, the temptation to break the contract is stronger and the game turns into the noncooperative game of prisoners' dilemma, necessitating the use of sanctions to achieve cooperation in the first place.

Appeal to social sanctions is one of the most prominent solutions to the problem of collective action. A problem with sanctions is that they are, themselves, collective goods subject to a collective action problem. The use of sanctions to solve the first collective action problem gives rise to a *second-order* collective action problem (Oliver, 1980).[24] This is especially so with negative sanctions, or punishments, because they are generally more costly to use. Using sanctions, then, complicates the picture, and forces the game theorist to analyse the collective action problem as a compounded, or nested, game (see Heckathorn, 1989). If effective sanctioning may be achieved by a subgroup, we get a game of chicken, because people would wish to stay outside that group (see Jankowski, 1990: 460f.).

Oliver suggests that use of sanctions may change the incentive structure in such a way as to make an initially 'irrational' collective action 'rational'. This is, of course, possible, especially with the use of positive sanctions. If, for instance, there is strong interest and resource heterogeneity in the group, those with much interest and resources may use side-payments to induce the rest to cooperate. In general, however, the necessity to use sanctions makes the problem of collective action more severe. This is because all sanctions are costly, therefore increasing the total cost of collective action. In the case of punishments, costs very soon become forbidding. Thus, even if the second-order collective action problem is usually less difficult than the first-order problem (Hardin, 1982: 172; Elster, 1989a: 41), the combined problem is usually more difficult, because more costly.

One deficiency in Oliver's analysis of the second-order collective action problem is the absence of a concept of 'opportunity cost'. Why should an individual accept punishment? Why not exit? The reason suggested by Hirschmann (1970) would be loyalty, but this is not an option in this case, because loyalty would make people cooperate in the first place. As a possible solution to the collective action problem, loyalty belongs to a sociological frame of reference. An economic alternative has been suggested by Michael Hechter. The use of punishment is an exercise of power. It is possible only when an individual is in some way *dependent* upon the group and, therefore, not 'free' to leave (Hechter, 1983b: 21–24, 50, 53). This is, of course, the case in many instances of collective action, but surely not in all.

Michael Hechter draws our attention to the monitoring costs involved in the use of sanctions (Hechter, 1984). Free riders must be detected in order that they can be punished. Hechter first divides monitoring costs into metering costs, sanctioning costs and allocation costs; the costs incurred by the problem of sanctioning the right people in the right way. Later, he recognizes two types of costs associated with social control: monitoring costs and sanctioning costs (Hechter, 1987: 150).

Hechter argues that the solutions to the collective action problem offered by Axelrod and Taylor are limited in scope. Informal control, in a state of anarchy, is possible only in small groups. In large groups, on the other hand, cooperation can be achieved only by the use of formal social control. The burden of this argument is, of course, to make collective action in large groups seem even more improbable. Hechter's way out of this predicament is to maintain that cooperation is possible in the case of *collective goods*, characterized by *excludability* (Hechter, 1987: 38). His main examples are rotating credit associations and insurance groups, in which people cooperate for their mutual benefit, without free riders.[25] It is a frequently repeated and confirmed thesis that trade unions often emerged out of such insurance groups, or mutual aid societies (see, e.g., Oberschall, 1973: ch. 4; Calhoun, 1982: ch. 6; 1983: 894ff.; 1988: 135, 145–154, 161–168). Hechter uses this historical fact to support his main thesis that large groups providing *public goods*, characterized by *non-excludability*, may emerge as a by-product of groups providing excludable collective goods (1987: ch. 6).

Fortunately, or perhaps unfortunately, there are institutional mechanisms available to economize on control costs in large groups. One such mechanism stands out as dominating the historical scene: hierarchic organization. All large groups tend towards hierarchy. The economic explanation of this fact is in terms of transaction costs (Williamson, 1975). In the case of collective action some organization and leadership is often necessary to achieve coordination, continuity and effectiveness. Control costs are part of transaction costs and they remain a part of all organizations. In private firms, as in most organizations, cooperation is to some extent secured by compensation in the form of wages. In the case of organizations providing public goods the possibility of free riding makes social control more of a necessity. A hierarchic structure of federated groups combines informal control in small groups with formal control from above (Hechter, 1987: 178–186). One special device is the use of group sanctions, from above, to increase the informal control in a group. Because group sanctions are collective goods, or bads, they create a new collective action problem in the group subjected to them (Heckathorn, 1988, 1990). A common control technique is to punish the whole group for some act committed by one of its members. If the punishment is severe, as it often is, this technique may be horridly effective.

Hechter's analysis of collective action is firmly rooted in the tradition of public choice. It is based upon a consistent use of the assumption of rational egoism and it exemplifies its development into a new institutionalism. In a similar vein, Bendor and Mookherjee (1987) argue that organizational structure is important for the maintenance of cooperation. According to them, two solutions to the collective action problem feature prominently in the literature: the centralized solution of Hobbes, Buchanan and Olson and the decentralized solution of Axelrod and Taylor. Both have their particular drawbacks. The decentralized solution is not feasible in large groups and the centralized solution makes free riding possible. A combination of them into a federal, or hierarchic, structure maintains the advantages, while avoiding the disadvantages, of both. In a federal organization, the decentralized units do the monitoring and the central unit the sanctioning of free riders.[26] Organization, then, is the solution to the maintenance of cooperation. But how is collective action possible in the first place? Bianco and Bates (1990) argue that the presence of a leader, controlling the reward structure of the remaining players, may suffice to resolve the collective action dilemma in the initial stage. The precondition is that the leader is motivated by strong enough incentives and has the capability of issuing credible and effective threats.

Elinor Ostrom's *Governing the Commons* (1990) is an attempt to apply institutionalism to real collective action problems. It is a study devoted to renewable common pool resources (CPR), such as fishing grounds, groundwater basins, grazing areas, irrigation canals, etc. (cf. Gardner *et al.*, 1990). Not surprisingly, she finds that people actually do solve collective action problems without help from outside. The conclusion, therefore, must be that the traditional approaches to collective action – Mancur Olson's 'logic of collective action', Garrett Hardin's 'tragedy of the commons' and Russell Hardin's prisoners' dilemma – are too pessimistic about the prospects of collective action. In particular, Ostrom stresses the 'capacity of individuals to restructure their own interdependent situation' (Ostrom, 1990: 46).[27] Game theory, while indispensable to the analysis of collective action, makes too many simplifying assumptions. As an equally indispensable complement, Ostrom advocates an institutional analysis of the variable conditions of collective action.

Among the things revealed by Ostrom's analysis, is the simple, but important, fact that people facing collective action problems do so under varying conditions, more or less conducive to their successful solution. The main message is that people can organize so as to restructure the situation they are in. Because of this, few things are absolutely given to analysis in the form of parameters. By turning constants into variables, we can expand the scope of analysis, thereby increasing its 'realism' and relevance. The inevitable loss of simplicity is a cost we have to bear (Ostrom, 1990: 23ff.). Ostrom's own contribution to an institutional analysis of collective action takes the form of a framework, compatible with a multiplicity of models. As a framework, it is intended to identify the relevant variables, rather than to specify a single, explanatory, model (ibid., ch. 6).

Moving beyond traditional economics and game theory, then, leads us to take a more sanguine look at collective action. Communication and organization facilitates collective action. But institutional analysis also makes us realize that, in certain respects, problems are worse than what is suggested by the traditional approach to collective action. First of all, a CPR problem, unlike a pure public goods problem, is not one, but two. In addition to the well-known provision problem, there is the equally serious appropriation problem. Because of the divisibility and private appropriation of common pool resources, appropriators must agree on the distribution of the produce of the resource (Ostrom, 1990: 30–33, 46–50; Gardner *et al.*, 1990: 340–346). Second, traditional approaches usually presume that collective action problems can be analysed at a single 'operational' level. Institutional analysis recognizes three levels. In addition to the operational level, there are two institutional levels: there is, first, the level of collective choice rules governing the operational level and, second, the constitutional level comprising rules for collective, or social, choice (ibid., 50–55). From a more practical point of view, a viable solution to a CPR problem must include solutions to the following problems: '(1) the problem of supplying a new set of institutions, (2) the problem of making credible commitments, and (3) the problem of mutual monitoring' (ibid., p. 42).

Despite her insistence on the importance of institutional analysis, Ostrom wishes to remain within rational choice, although the explanatory burden is shifted from individuals to institutions. The assumptions made about the individual are weak and empty. Individuals are assumed to be 'rational', in some unspecified sense, and to weigh the costs and benefits of alternative strategies. They are supposed to discount the future in varying degrees and to be guided by norms when evaluating alternative courses of action. The introduction of social norms might seem to imply a concession to the sociological approach. Ostrom denies that it does. The breaching of a norm incurs a psychic cost to be weighed against the benefit derived from acting in this way. This is the sort of reductionism I will criticize in the following section.

The new institutionalism has made us alert to some of the limitations of game theory. Michael Hechter, for instance, is critical of the solutions based on the N-person prisoners' dilemma supergame (Hechter, 1990a, 1990b). There are two problems: (1) N-person prisoners' dilemmas have multiple equilibria. (2) Solutions depend on the assumption that players have perfect information about the previous moves of other players. The problem with multiple equilibria is that they preclude a determinate solution. The problem with assuming perfect information is its lack of realism in large groups. The explicit address of Hechter's critique is Michael Taylor (Hechter, 1990b). As such, it is battering at an open door. Taylor is certainly aware of these problems and is careful not to make exaggerated claims concerning the viability of his analysis of the N-person prisoners' dilemma supergame.[28]

But institutional, or centralized, solutions to the collective action problem face their own insuperable difficulties. It had already been pointed out by Brian Barry (1970/1978: 37–40; see also Laver, 1980: 204–208) that political entrepreneurs cannot solve the collective action problem, because followers still face this problem. If leaders are invested with the capacity to provide selective incentives, we do not have a distinct solution, only a restatement of Mancur Olson's original view. Also, explanations in terms of political entrepreneurs fail to account for the emergence of organized interests. We may believe that political entrepreneurs join existing organizations for their own careers, but it is hard to believe that the early organizers of unions and other collective endeavours were motivated in this way. Jimmy Hoffa may have been so motivated, but hardly Joe Hill (Hardin, 1982: 35–37). The principal problem with any institutional solution to the collective action problem, at least if it rests on social control, is this: social control is itself a collective good subject to a collective action problem. The original, spontaneous collective action problem, therefore, must be solved prior to organization and social control (Taylor, 1987: 21ff., 30; 1990: 224ff.; Elster, 1989a: 17, 40ff.). If we remain within the economic frame, that is. If we transcend this framework and allow leaders and organizations to produce solidarity and ideology things become entirely different.

Hechter argues that game theory has contributed precious little to our understanding of collective action (Hechter, 1990b: 245, 248). I think that is a bit unfair, but counter with another provocation: there is not much that is novel in the new institutionalism either.

The recent analysis of the role of networks, organizations and leaders in collective action elaborates and improves upon themes already to be found in Mancur Olson's *The Logic of Collective Action*. Very little is definitely new and there is nothing to challenge his main conclusions. Networks, it is reasonable to assume, have the size of intermediate groups, in which collective action, according to Olson, is possible, if problematic. What Hechter has to say about the necessity of social control and its possibility in groups of different size merely confirms the previous conclusions of Olson. Hechter's theory of trade unions as a by-product of insurance groups seems to be a version of Olson's by-product theory of interest groups, even though Hechter himself denies it.

Hechter interprets Olson as maintaining that 'public-goods-seeking unions used insurance as a selective incentive to attract members; insurance groups are considered to be the by-product of trade unions' (Hechter, 1987: 121). According to Hechter, 'Olson's causal order should be reversed: it is far more likely that trade unions were the by-product of insurance groups than vice versa' (ibid., p. 123). But this is exactly what is implied by Olson's by-product theory of interest-groups:

> The lobbies of the large economic groups are the by-products of organizations that have the capacity to 'mobilize' the latent group with 'selective incentives'. The only organizations that have the 'selective incentives' available are those that (1) have the authority and capacity to be coercive, or (2) have a source of positive inducements that they can offer the individuals in a latent group.
>
> (Olson, 1965/1971: 133)

The reason selective incentives can perform this function is their excludability (ibid., p. 51). It is true that Olson does not say that insurance groups preceded trade unions in time. Nor does he suggest that insurances were the only selective incentives at work. Olson's main argument is that large trade unions, 'having the authority and capacity to be coercive', emerged out of small ones, relying on 'a source of positive inducement that they can offer the individuals in a latent group' (Olson, 1965/1971: 66ff.). Insurances are but one type of selective incentive. They were important in the early days of the railroad brotherhoods, but not in other trade unions (ibid., pp. 72f.). Nevertheless, the gist of Olson's argument is that some excludable selective incentive is necessary for the emergence of trade unions (ibid., chs 3 and 6). Therefore, unless we impute to Olson the highly controversial idea that an effect can precede its cause, we must intepret him, like Hardin (1982: 34), as maintaining 'that organization for selective benefit reasons preceded organizational pursuit of collective benefits'. Until we have some more substantial reason to believe that *all* labour unions, not to mention *all* interest groups, actually emerged out of insurance groups, I suggest we interpret Hechter's theory as a special case of Olson's by-product theory of pressure groups.

Bendor and Mookherjee's argument about the advantages of federation is stated clearly by Mancur Olson in *The Logic of Collective Action* (1965/1971: 62f.) and, before him, by many sociologists (see Chapter 4). Bianco and Bates' argument about leaders is a restatement of the analysis made by Frohlich, Oppenheimer and Young, and accepted by Olson in the appendix to the 1971 edition of *The Logic of Collective Action* (pp. 175ff.).

Elinor Ostrom, like Hechter, owes more to James Buchanan than to Mancur Olson, but this does not make much of a difference. In both cases, solutions to collective action problems depend on selective incentives – especially sanctions – which are the heart of the matter and my next topic.

SELECTIVE INCENTIVES

An early assessment of Olson's theory of collective action can be found in Brian Barry's *Sociologists, Economists and Democracy* (1970/1978). While, in the main, sympathetic, Barry nevertheless raises some objections. Most important, he is sceptical concerning the possibility of explaining actual collective action in terms of 'selective incentives' – unless, under this rubric, we include virtually everything which may motivate an individual to join an organization, in which case the allegedly economic explanation becomes empty (pp. 33–37).

> Obviously, the constant danger of 'economic' theories is that they can come to 'explain' everything merely by redescribing it. They then fail to be any use in predicting that one thing will happen rather than another. Thus if an organization maintains itself, we say 'It must have provided selective incentives'; and this is bound to be true since whatever motives people had for supporting it are called 'selective incentives'.
>
> (Barry, 1970/1978: 33)

I think Barry's admonitions concerning selective incentives should be taken seriously indeed. The reason is this: if we allow any kind of selective incentive *(Si)*, they will function as the notorious D term in the economic theory of voting: an unlimited reservoir, or potential, of *ad hoc* explanations that renders the economic theory of collective action immune to refutation.

$$Ai = Vi - C + Si > 0$$

What a free use, or interpretation, of Si achieves is a guarantee that Ai will turn into a positive sum and the economic theory of collective action thus confirmed (cf. Davis, 1992: 18f.). A good illustration of this risk is the introduction of an E term for 'entertainment value of participation' in the equation used by Gordon Tullock to express the payoff for participation in a revolution (see pp. 214f.). Tullock, himself, is not the worst sinner, even though it seems a bit *ad hoc* to shift from the heavy emphasis of decision-making costs in collective action in *The Calculus of Consent* to the use of E in his analysis of revolution. Considerably more objectionable is Morris Silver's reinterpretation of Tullock's E term as 'psychic income from participation in revolution'. As such, E includes 'the individual's sense of duty to class, country, democratic institutions, the law, race, humanity, the rulers, God, or a revolutionary brotherhood as well as his taste for conspiracy, violence, and adventure' (Silver, 1974: 64f.).

Edward N. Muller and Karl-Dieter Opp set out to remedy what they saw as deficiences in the models of Tullock and Silver, but ended up making things rather worse. They accept Olson's thesis that the material private benefits of collective action do not explain it. But they reject the by-product theory which says that private selective incentives will do the job. In particular, they reject the attempts by Tullock and by Silver to explain revolutionary action in terms of entertainment value and psychic income, respectively (Muller and Opp, 1986: 473, 485). Their own solution has two parts: first, they argue that collective goods benefits may be important, because people do not ask 'What's in it for me?', but 'What's in it for my group?' and because they overestimate the efficacy of their own contribution. Second, they add some 'soft' nonmaterial incentives, such as feelings of solidarity and psychic gratification from conformity to group norms (ibid., p. 474).

George Klosko argues that Mullers and Opp's model is not a strict rational choice model, since it violates the assumptions of narrow self-interest and of objective rationality, thereby destroying the simplicity, which is its main asset (Klosko, 1987). Muller and Opp reply that their model implies self-interest, but not egoism and subjective, but not objective, rationality (Muller and Opp, 1987). But that is exactly the problem. A concept of 'self-interest', which includes altruism, feelings of solidarity and conformity to norms (Opp, 1986: 90–92), is absolutely empty. A concept of 'subjective rationality' is not empty, and might indeed be necessary for many social scientific purposes, but it is, nevertheless, a problem, since it saves phenomena only by making rational choice much less useful, because less determinate.

Barry's complaints about selective incentives have been repeated and substantiated by a number of critics (see, especially, White, 1976: 268–276, but also Fireman and Gamson, 1979: 20; Chazel, 1990: 227–229), but has largely fallen on deaf ears. Or perhaps defenders of the assumption of rational egoism simply prefer parsimony to empirical content. Anyway, in the recent discussion about the economic theory of collective action, we can distinguish two main branches: one orthodox, the other revisionist. The former consists of those who try to retain the assumption of self-interest at all costs. Their main theoretical asset is the concept of 'selective incentive', rich in connotation, but including, above all, social sanctions of various sorts.[29] The latter consists of those who, like Barry, have become convinced that motives other than self-interest are involved in collective action and who resist the temptation of redefinition.[30] I will discuss the former in this section and the latter in the following section.

A second important critique of Mancur Olson's economic theory of collective action came from Bruce Fireman and William A. Gamson (1979). Their main arguments concern the use of selective incentives in the explanation of collective action in large groups (Fireman and Gamson, 1979: 12). First, if selective incentives are necessary, why bother with collective goods at all? And, since selective incentives are private goods, how come they are not provided by firms on the market? Since firms can produce these goods without the detour of collective goods, they must be able to produce them at a much lower cost. Isn't there something slightly absurd about a theory of interest groups, or collective goods, as by-products of organizations providing private goods, in the form of selective incentives, at an enormous competitive disadvantage? Also, if people join social movements mainly for the *social* selective incentives involved, why do they need a cause? Wouldn't a club be a better alternative? Do people need an excuse for sociability? This argument was hinted at by Frohlich, Oppenheimer and Young (1971: 18) and repeated by de Jasay (1989: 151n.). It is so devastating for Olson's account of collective action that my immediate reaction was to believe that it must be wrong. I haven't, as yet, been able to figure out what is wrong.

A second argument is directed at the interpretation of social control – the positive and negative sanctions sometimes used to promote collective action – as selective incentives. This interpretation creates a second-order collective action problem about sanctions: why would anyone wish to sanction other individuals out of self-interest? This problem occurs because sanctions are, themselves, collective goods contributing to social order (Fireman and Gamson, 1979: 19, 35; cf. Oliver, 1980). In addition to first-order norms against free riding, therefore, there are metanorms telling people to punish free riders (Axelrod, 1986: 1100ff.). 'If the second-order defection problem is solved through a metanorm sanctioning system, that gives rise to a third-order free riding problem and so forth' (Heckathorn, 1989: 80). Unlike Heckathorn, I maintain (Udehn 1993: 249) that the impending infinite regress can be stopped only by invoking solidarity and/or morality. 'Most obviously, perhaps, the problem of sanctioning nonconformers may be resolved by ethical motivations, as for example by a demand for fair play' (Hardin, 1982: 172).

Michael Hechter attempted to circumvent both these problems by suggesting that large groups providing public goods develop out of small groups providing only excludable goods, or 'selective incentives'. According to Hechter (1987: 121), 'There is no inherent reason why the members of an insurance group cannot convert their assets into a strike fund and reconstitute themselves as a trade union.' Hechter's argument hinges on the existence of formal control in the insurance group. With an effective control system, it is possible to make a switch in production from private to public goods.

This solution is as ingenious as it is simple. It rests on the cunning of history. And it does not lack support. Organizations often develop out of other organizations, and this seems to have been the case with many trade unions. But it is still a problematic story, especially when told about selfish people. First, even if some unions did in fact emerge in this way, it is quite impossible to believe that all did (see, e.g. Hardin, 1982: 34). E.P. Thompson (1963/1980: 459), for instance, suggests that, in England, friendly societies were often covers for trade union activity, in which case the 'causal' direction of by-productivity is reversed. It is, of course, even more impossible to believe that *all* collective action can be explained as the by-product of organizations providing jointly produced private goods. Second, why are there no private market substitutes for insurance groups? Samuel Popkin has stated this problem succinctly:

> But why then do the collective goods get produced? If the organizer is motivated to produce the collective goods whether or not they are required to generate the exchanges with individuals, but the others are motivated only by narrow self-interest, then someone should be able to produce the incentives more cheaply by not spending any of the profit on collective goods. If collective goods plus selective incentives cost more to produce than selective incentives alone, why do the goods ever get produced?
>
> (Popkin, 1988: 15)

Popkins' answer is that collective goods are more important than what is implied by the by-product theory of collective action. In particular, there are usually values other than economic benefits involved in social movements.

Third, would rational egoists ever agree to forgo insurance for the uncertain outcome of strikes? Fourth, how can trade unions keep their members after they have switched to public goods? One answer would be excludability in the form of the closed shop. (It has been tried and it exists, but it is far from universal.) The main answer, of course, is social control. But, then, we are back in the second-order collective action problem.

The futility of rational egoism

I am going to argue, in the rest of this section, that, despite appearances to the contary, social control, in the form of social sanctions, cannot be assimilated by an economic theory of collective action. The main reason for this is the second-order collective action problem. It is perfectly intelligible why rational egoists should seek rewards and avoid punishments, or the contrary, if they are masochists; but it is not at all clear why they should use them, unless they are sadists. Ultimately, social control rests upon internalized moral values and norms and the attempt to reduce them to rational egoism is doomed to failure. I will try to lend credibility to this argument by showing that the most sophisticated attempts to explain the emergence of cooperation in a population of rational egoists end up introducing alien elements in the form of social values and norms.

Robert Axelrod's evolutionary theory tells us how cooperation *could* have emerged, given some specified conditions. But did it emerge this way? This is an entirely different matter. I interpret Axelrod as maintaining that cooperation could emerge in a world of egoists, but can only be maintained by morality. This interpretation presupposes that the norm of reciprocity is a moral rule, rather than a mere convention. Axelrod does not discuss this matter explicitly, but it seems to me that he implies that the norm of reciprocity emerges as a convention and develops into a social norm or moral code. If this is a correct interpretation, Axelrod is in substantial agreement with Russell Hardin, who suggests that this is one typical pattern of development in the social evolution of cooperation (Hardin, 1990: 374–377). In any case, I submit that norms do not belong in the hard core of economics. If, as in Axelrod's theory, a norm of reciprocity is needed, for cooperation to be possible, this is a concession to the sociological perspective (cf. Bianco and Bates, 1990: 137; Dawes *et al.* 1990: 109; Macy, 1990a: 821).

The importance of social norms, for social life and, consequently, for social science explanations, is brought out more clearly in a couple of articles written after *The Evolution of Cooperation*. First, there is an emphasis on the fact that real games are played in the context of – indeed, are constituted by – people's beliefs, social institutions and social structure (Axelrod and Keohane, 1985). Second, there is the insight that sanctioning is costly and gives rise to a second-order collective action problem, since 'no one has an incentive to punish a defection' (Axelrod, 1986: 1100). One remedy would be the existence of a *metanorm*, telling people to punish those who do not punish defectors (ibid., p. 1101ff.). But this is no solution, unless the metanorm is internalized. For no one has an incentive to punish those who do not punish defectors. We are trapped in a third-order collective action problem and an infinite regress. Axelrod does not fall into that trap. He discusses a number of mechanisms to support norms. Internalization is one of them.

> The logic of the norms game suggests that lowering the temptation to defect might not be enough. After all, even if most people did not defect, if no one had an incentive to punish the remaining defectors, the norm could still collapse. This point suggests that we look for internalization, not only in the reduced incentive to defect, but also in an increased incentive to punish someone else who does defect.
>
> (Axelrod, 1986: 1104)

A more important problem concerns the relation between egoism and rationality or, rather, the lack of such a relation in the case of Axelrod. Most adherents of rational choice – including those discussed in this section – assume not only that man is an egoist, but that he is a *rational* egoist. Axelrod, as we have seen, drops the assumption of rationality. The issue I wish to raise, however, is this: is it meaningful to use the terms 'egoism' and 'altruism' to characterize actions which are not intentional; actions which are, in Axelrod's words: 'standard operating procedures, rules of thumb, habits, or imitation' and which involve no 'deliberate choice at all'? I am, of course, aware that biologists use the terms 'egoism' and 'altruism' to describe the behaviour of animals and even of genes, but I interpret this as an expression of anthropomorphism. As I see things, the terms 'egoism' and 'altruism' belong to an intentional and moral language game, and lose, or change, their meaning when used in other contexts.[31] It may be argued that a change in meaning does not affect the validity of Axelrod's argument, but it may change our interpretation of his theory. I suggest that Axelrod's evolutionary theory of cooperation has more in common with functionalist theory in anthropology and sociology than with an economic theory of rational choice.

Michael Taylor belongs to those who use the assumption of rational egoism for purposes of analysis only. Egoism and fixed preferences are part of the 'thin theory of rationality', which he defends (1988: 66). Here I am more interested in his deviation from this theory. A first departure is the analysis of altruism, positive and negative. Altruism is defined, by Taylor (1976: 69; 1987: 111), as regard for other persons' payoffs and utilities. Positive altruism is benevolence and negative altruism is malevolence. Against Mancur Olson, Taylor argues that altruism makes a real difference to collective action. As expected, positive altruism is shown to increase the likelihood of collective action. It does so, first of all, by increasing the ratio of benefits to costs, but also in more indirect ways. If, for instance, some individuals are altruists, they may form a critical mass, triggering collective action, or they may provide the collective good all by themselves.

In his *Community, Anarchy and Liberty* (1982), which is a companion volume to *The Possibility of Cooperation*, Taylor argues 'that in the absence of the state social order can be maintained *only* if relations between people are those characteristic of *community*' (ibid., p. 2; my italics). The core characteristics of a community are (1) that its members have beliefs and values in common, (2) that their relations are direct and many-sided and (3) that they practise reciprocity (ibid., pp. 25–33). This definition spells trouble. The concept of 'community' is a Trojan horse in a theory of rational choice. For most sociologists, to say that community is necessary for cooperation, is to say that rational egoism is *not* sufficient.

A first thing to notice is that community is an 'external' solution, whereas Taylor's game-theoretic solution is, of course, 'internal' (1987: 21–24). If there is an internal solution to the problem of collective action, why the need for an external solution? The only answer I can think of, is that the internal solution is not viable, but depends upon the external solution. This, by itself, does not imply the end to the thin theory of rationality, but it opens the door to motives other than self-interest.

According to Taylor, the third characteristic of community is reciprocity, consisting of 'a combination of what one might call short-term altruism and long-term self-interest' (ibid., p. 28). But the whole burden of the arguments of anthropologists and sociologists – including those discussed by Taylor – is that reciprocity is a norm; an obligation (see Chapter 7). Taylor is, of course, free to disagree, but unless he maintains that members of a community are actually and usually guided by considerations of long-term self-interest when helping each other – to my mind, an unnecessarily cynical assumption, making a mock of short-term altruism and his plea for community (1982: 53ff.) seem rather less attractive – he lands in functionalism, rather than rational choice. Eventually, Taylor agrees that reciprocity is a norm and a moral principle (Taylor, 1989: 139).

No less problematic is Taylor's first characteristic of community: that its members have beliefs and values in common. Unless committed to the view that people value only those things that further their self-interest, Taylor faces the problem that there might be a conflict between our values and our self-interest. If some of the values entertained by members of a community are moral values, as most sociologists would argue, this is certain to be the case. Most people have experienced such conflicts in their own consciences, and when doing the wrong thing, felt remorse. In another article, Taylor recognizes the existence of 'expressive rationality', or 'commitments to values, principles and ideals the individual cares about. It is clear that rationality in this sense would often require the individual to do things which the thin theory would deem non-rational' (Taylor, 1988a: 87f.).

What, finally, is Taylor's view of social norms? The typical rational choice approach is to reduce social norms, on a par with laws, to the positive and negative sanctions associated with them. Norms do not affect behaviour, directly, only through the incentive structures, or opportunity sets they create. This does not seem to be Taylor's view, however. According to him, 'a social norm is a prescription or standard with which most people actually comply' (Taylor, 1982: 49). He recognizes the role of socialization (1982: 66, 76–80) and observes that social norms may become internalized (1976: 7); in which case the individual prefers to conform without sanctions (1987: 29f.). It is not clear what are the implications of this view for his theory of collective action, but socialization is incompatible with fixed preferences.

One step in the direction of increasing clarity is taken in the recent article, 'Structure, Culture and Action in the Explanantion of Social Change' (1989), although it seems to me that he still conflates norms and values. Taylor now criticizes the reduction of norms to sanctions, arguing that they are ideals competing with self-interest as determinants of action (ibid., pp. 136f.). He also admits that, in *The Possibility of Cooperation*, he was not entirely clear about this (ibid., p. 158, n.37). Taylor still argues that the thin theory of rationality has an important place in the explanation of collective action, and even of the emergence of social norms, but it does not rule alone. There is a place also for explanations in terms of structure and culture, including, most importantly, values and normative beliefs (ibid., pp. 148–153). This is an important concession, coming from a defender of the thin theory of rationality.

Axelrod and Taylor are political scientists. In using an economic approach, they only follow the trend in political science since the beginning of the 1960s. If they find it necessary to introduce 'sociological' elements into their analysis, this is an indication that there are limits to economic analysis. It is otherwise with those sociologists, who in the 1980s – in some cases much earlier – turned to rational choice as a promising alternative to an 'exhausted' sociological approach (Lindenberg, 1985b: 246–248). To this group belong a number of American, German and Dutch sociologists with a particular interest in the emergence of social norms and institutions. My argument is that, despite serious efforts in this direction, they never succeeded in entirely eliminating the sociological element from their analysis. In the latest writings of members of this group there is not even the attempt to do so. The ambition now seems to be some kind of marriage between economics and sociology.[32] It will probably be a more stormy than happy marriage. Let's hope it will be a fertile one.

We have already met Michael Hechter and his contribution to a theory of collective action. Hechter's main concern, however, has been to develop a theory of group solidarity, based on the assumption of rational egoism. This might seem to be an impossible task, or an Indian rope trick, because 'solidarity' usually means the opposite of egoism. But Hechter means something else by this term. For him, 'solidarity' is a behavioural term. It means conformity to group norms. Group solidarity is a function of (a) the extensiveness of its corporate obligations and (b) the degree to which members comply with these obligations (Hechter, 1983b: 17; 1987: 18).

The term 'obligation' is no less of a problem. It simply has no place in an analysis based on the assumption of rational egoism. If we are under an obligation to do something, this means that we should do it even if it is not in our self-interest to do so. But let's not quarrel about words. It may be that Hechter also uses this term in an unusual sense. I don't think so. In his first contribution to a theory of group solidarity, he says: 'The existence of a moral element obliging members to act according to collective standards of conduct, or norms, is the distinguishing feature of any solidarity group' (Hechter, 1983b: 17). This is the orthodox sociological view which Hechter's theory is supposed to challenge, but there is no explicit redefinition of the concept of 'obligation'. In a typically individualist vein (see Udehn, 1987: 192–201), Hechter's theory shifts attention from the consequences to the genesis of moral obligations (Hechter, 1983b: 19), or prosocial behaviour (Hechter, 1987: ch. 4). This shift, however, does not do away with moral obligations – it assumes their existence. Now, Hechter's intention is not to enhance the importance of moral obligations, it is to argue for the necessity of formal control in the form of sanctions. But if his intention were to argue

250

that compliance to norms is a function solely of sanctions, then there would be no need – indeed it would only be confusing – to give such a central place to the concept of 'obligation'. Hechter's argument seems to be that social control is necessary for group solidarity and collective action in large groups, but not that it is sufficient. He certainly denies that internalization of moral obligations is sufficient, but this does not imply that it is unnecessary.[33]

There are some other elements in Hechter's analysis that square badly with the assumption of rational egoism. When explaining why people accept the extensive obligations that go along with membership of groups producing joint goods, he refers to 'immanent goods', or utility derived from participation: entertainment, enlightenment, love and friendship (Hechter, 1987: 42f., 171). These goods are important and people do derive selfish pleasure from them. But love and friendship are never entirely selfish. On the contrary, love and friendship involve altruism essentially. A merely instrumental attitude destroys these goods. Therefore, if love and friendship help to explain group solidarity in groups producing joint goods, we can infer the prevalence of altruism in these groups. Finally, we are informed that the insurance groups that preceded trade unions sought to admit only those of high moral character (Hechter, 1987: 118). If formal control is sufficient for group solidarity, this was an entirely unnecessary measure of precaution.

James Coleman was the pioneer and the most prominent figure of rational choice in sociology. We might even say 'public choice', because Coleman's early contribution to a theory of exchange was largely an importation of the programme of public choice into his own discipline (Coleman, 1964, 1966). Like public choice, Coleman sought and found his main inspiration in the writings of Thomas Hobbes and Adam Smith. What made the strongest impression on Coleman were their attempts to account for social order in terms of self-interest and exchange, but without recourse to mainstream sociology and the notion of 'social norms'. If there are social norms, the intellectual challenge is to explain their emergence and maintenance. This has been one of Coleman's main preoccupations ever since.

Another of Coleman's early interests was the theory of social choice, but he also recognized the problem of collective action (1966: 616). He even made a weighty critique of Robert Axelrod's evolutionary theory of cooperation long before it was published: a solution to the problem of collective action depends upon 'an implicit pact to make one's action contingent on that of all other's' [and this] 'requires a higher level of social organization than pairwise exchange' (Coleman, 1973: 105). Coleman repeats this critique, with explicit reference to Axelrod, thirteen years later, in an article on the emergence of social norms (Coleman, 1986: 66, 82). Two properties of an iterated prisoners' dilemma are especially restricting: (1) that players act simultaneously in each round of the game and (2) that sanctions are restricted to moves in the game. In real life, if people meet again they may use sanctions that are different from the actions they are sanctioning (Coleman, 1990a: 46).

In his 1986 and 1990 articles on the emergence of social norms, Coleman makes an economistic reduction of social norms to sanctions. 'Although I will use both the term "norm" and the term "sanction", I will mean by "norm" nothing more than the set of sanctions that act to direct the behavior in question' (Coleman, 1986: 56; 1990c: 250f). This definition has been justly criticized by Taylor (1989: 136f.) and Majeski (1990: 273ff.). I suppose, though, that it is a matter of convenience, not of principle. In another article, Coleman argues that a mature rational choice theory has to reckon with norms that are internalized (e.g. Coleman, 1987: 135f., 138, 148).

Coleman's theory construction culminates with his ambitious *magnum opus*, *Foundations of Social Theory* (1990b). This impressive work illustrates my argument very well. All serious attempts to explain cooperation in terms of rational egoism end by reintroducing the very elements originally excluded: altruism, solidarity, social norms.

Coleman starts with the assumption of self-interest and his explicit strategy is to use it as far as possible. But only for purposes of analysis and argument. 'Certainly norms do exists, persons do obey them (though not uniformly) and persons do often act in the interests of others or of a collectivity, "unselfishly" as we would say' (Coleman, 1990b: 31). My simple point is that Coleman's strategy is not very successful, as he admits himself:

> To begin with persons not endowed with altruism or unselfishness and lacking a shared normative system does not mean that in every part of the theory the persons who are actors are assumed to be without those added components of the self. To the contrary, most parts of the theory will assume that actors possess some of these components, although the assumptions are largely implicit. In general, the more universally held a norm or the more widespread a moral precept, the more likely I will be to overlook it, to take it always and everywhere as given, thus necessarily diminishing the scope of the theory. Some norms are not so widely shared and are therefore more readily recognized.
>
> (Coleman, 1990b: 32)

I have no objection, in principle, to this heuristic use of the assumption of rational egoism. I nevertheless see a problem with a theory that introduces non-selfish elements implicitly and leaves it to the reader to recognize them. This strategy is of no assistance if, like me, you are interested in the fertility and limits of the assumption of rational egoism.

As Coleman admits, himself, the major part of his theory contradicts the assumption of rational egoism. It uses concepts, such as 'rights', 'authority', 'trust' and 'social norms', which have no place in a public choice, or narrowly economic, analysis of social order. It may be pointed out that these concepts had no place in Coleman's earlier, more utilitarian, theory of exchange (1964, 1966; 1973: chs 2–4). Among the primitive concepts of this theory are 'actors', 'events', 'control of actors over events' and 'interest of actors in events' – nothing that is incompatible with the assumption of rational egoism.

Even though Coleman admits that there are limits to rational choice, and even more severe limits to public choice, I suggest that he often goes too far in assuming narrow self-interest on the part of actors. There is too much forced redefinition of familiar concepts, in order to make them fit into his own, utilitarian, framework. One example of this is Coleman's analysis of zealotry. It is a good illustration of the dangers pointed to by Barry and others at the beginning of this section. Free use of 'selective incentives' leads to loss of content.

According to Coleman, zealotry is or the opposite of free riding (Coleman, 1988; 1990b: 273–278). By a 'zealot', Coleman understands an individual who is willing to bear extreme costs seemingly out of proportion to the personal benefits involved. Examples would be people willing to risk their lives for some collectivity to which they belong: a country, class, religious community, party, etc. Coleman's explanation hinges on the existence of a network of social relations creating the possibility of almost costless selective incentives in the form of encouragement. There is no need to deny the potential power of encouragement in order to be suspicious of this explanation. It is a good illustration of what can be done with selective incentives: everything. That's the problem.

Another problem concerns the redefinition of 'zealot'. In Coleman's analysis, a zealot turns out to be as selfish as the rest of us. The benefits derived from encouragement exceed the, sometimes extreme, costs of zealotry. Coleman's explanation is plausible in the case of people with low self-esteem and an extreme need of encouragement and praise. Such people can be made to do almost anything for recognition by the group. But this is not what we normally understand by a 'zealot'. The common sense of this word is a person entirely devoted to a cause, without regard to self-interest. In the terminology of Max Weber, a zealot is an individual guided by an 'ethic of ultimate ends', rather than an 'ethic of responsibility' (Weber [1919] 1948: 120). Zeal is an example of value-rationality, not instrumental rationality (Weber, 1922/1978: 212f.). Therefore, a typical zealot is not a person being encouraged by others to do heroic deeds; it is a person who encourages and expects others to join her/him in acts of heroism.

Coleman's explanation of zealotry is an example of going too far in assuming rational egoism. But what is the exact status of his 'explanation'? Is it an exercise in heuristic model building, or does it aspire to truth? This is hard to know, because Coleman is clearly aware of a possible alternative explanation, and accepts this alternative in general (Coleman, 1990b: 292ff.). When discussing the possibility of norms becoming internalized, he points to the importance of socialization and argues that socialization and internalization are effective to the extent that individuals *identify* with the socializing agent. Also nation-states and other collective actors attempt to make members identify with the collective. Since Coleman acknowledges the importance of identification, would it not be better to explain zealotry in these, sociological, terms? Zealotry is possible because people sometimes identify very strongly with a group or a moral principle.

I am going to recapitulate and conclude the argument of this section. We have seen that the various attempts to explain collective action, or cooperation, in terms of self-interest have led to the introduction of social norms. Since social norms can have no place in the hard core of an economic research programme, if social norms are allowed at all, they must be endogenized. That is, social norms must be explained, but are not allowed to explain. The classic strategy of economic reductionism, accordingly, is to explain the *emergence* and *maintenance* of social norms in terms of rational egoism. This is the typical procedure in the social contract tradition. But it is a one-sided treatment of social norms. For if they emerge, they exist; and if they exist, they may be presumed to make some difference. There would be no point in creating rules nobody obeyed.

This leads to the next move of economic reductionism. Rules are obeyed, but only because of the sanctions attached to them. Indeed, rules, or norms, are sanctioning mechanisms. They work by altering the costs and benefits associated with different actions; what economists call the opportunity, or feasible, set. This move, however, leads to the second-order collective action problem, to metanorms, and, eventually, to an infinite regress, which can only be stopped by reinvoking the efficacy of social norms independently of sanctions.

There is another, equally important, argument. Complying with norms only because of the sanctions attached to them is sheer opportunism. According to this view, we are all like Molière's Tartuffe: opportunists, hypocrites, impostors. But this is absurd. Norms cannot be reduced to sanctioning mechanisms. Norms are not systems of threats and offers, punishments and rewards. We all know the difference between opportunists and honest people. The very possibility of identifying someone as an opportunist, or hypocrite, depends upon the existence of honest people. Paradoxically expressed, if all were equally opportunistic, there would be no 'opportunists', or there would be no word for them (see Smelser, 1962: 30). Coleman points out that people who have failed to internalize norms are called 'sociopaths' (Coleman, 1990b: 294). It might be added that these people were formerly called 'psychopaths', because they lack a conscience or superego. The diagnosis of pathology is possible only because normal adults are supposed to be equipped with a conscience of internalized norms.

Smelser's 'linguistic' argument has an 'ontological' counterpart (see Elster, 1989a: 128f.; 1989b: 118). The opportunistic interpretation of norms as means of rationalization and manipulation is self-defeating. Norms can have no instrumental value unless they have an independent power of their own –

they would be useless even for strategic purposes of manipulation – and whatever independent power norms may have derives from their internalization.

As a last resort, economic reductionists admit that social norms are internalized, but reduce people's consciences, or superegos, to internal sanctioning mechanisms (see Coleman, 1990: 293f.; Ostrom, 1990: 35, 205). Our consciences do indeed function this way. We feel guilt or shame when we violate internalized norms, and proud or self-righteous when we do our duty. But this is no proof of the universality of the economic approach, because the costs and benefits associated with internalized norms are derivative of moral consciousness. If people did not believe in right and wrong, they would feel neither guilt nor self-righteousness. Therefore, if economics is a theory of rational choice and sociology a theory about social norms, to treat moral consciousness as a sanctioning mechanism producing psychic costs and benefits makes economics parasitic upon sociology. Social norms return as exogenous variables in the economic theory of cooperation. The reductionist strategy of endogenization has failed. This is where we stand.[34]

Once it is admitted that social life is, to some extent, rule-governed, the economic theory of cooperation is doomed as a totalizing approach; doomed to partiality. The reason is that following a rule is utterly different from rational choice. 'When I obey a rule, I do not choose. I obey the rule *blindly*' (Wittgenstein, 1953/1974: 85). This is a statement about the nature of rules. It does not say that people actually do follow rules blindly. Of course, people always have the binary choice of obeying, or not obeying, a norm, even though individuals with strongly internalized norms: men and women of principle, may not feel that they have much of a choice. Thus, an economist might say of people obeying norms that they prefer to do so. But this tautology does not resurrect economic man, because a non-opportunistic obedience to norms is a 'preference' for sociological man.

MIXED MOTIVATIONS

There is an emerging insight among social scientists that not all collective action can be explained in terms of rational egoism. Even so, many social scientists prefer to keep this assumption for reasons of *parsimony*. This may be legitimate scientific practice, but it is not entirely without dangers. Like some religions, it may lead to otherworldliness; to a withdrawal from the complexity of the mundane world into a more simple world of pure abstraction. In this Platonic heaven of intellectual constructs, many social scientists feel at home, apparently satisfied with activities such as model-building and story-telling.

Others stick to economic man for *heuristic* purposes. Mancur Olson, for instance, acknowledges in his recent article on 'Dictatorship, Democracy and Development', that 'Since human nature is profoundly complex and individuals rarely act out of unmixed motives, the assumption of rational self-interest that I have been using to develop this theory is obviously much too simple to do justice to reality' (Olson, 1993: 574). His defence for nevertheless using this assumption is in terms of parsimony (ibid., p. 573). This is, of course, entirely unobjectionable, especially if coupled with a readiness to consider alternative models of man (cf. Willer, 1992).

Anthony de Jasay (1989: ch. 8) exemplifies the latter attitude. His use of the assumption of single-minded self-interest is only for the sake of argument. He wishes to show that voluntary cooperation is possible even in a world of egoists. De Jasay is in no doubt, however, that economic man is seriously inadequate as an all-purpose model of man in social science and also that real world cooperation is the result of other-regarding and moral considerations. *Homo economicus* appears as only one among several *dramatis personae*, to be found mainly on the market. In politics we have to reckon with more complex persons, guided by mixed motivations.

Other social scientists take the consequences of the apparent failure of economic theory to explain all collective action. They see their primary task as building models that fit the facts, simple or not. If so, models must be adjusted to what we know, or believe that we know, about the world. In our case, if we have reason to believe that motives other than self-interest explain collective action, we should introduce them in our models. This is, of course, what many social scientists have tried to do.

Terry M. Moe, for instance, would be an exemplary representative of this attitude. Pursuing the economic logic of collective action up to a point and for the sake of its simplicity, he is aware that it 'greatly idealizes the value structures of individuals, for we know that people respond to a complex assortment of incentives in virtually every area of social life'. These include 'altruism, belief in a cause or ideology, loyalty, beliefs about right and wrong, camaraderie, friendship, love, acceptance, security, status, prestige, power, religious beliefs, racial predjudice' (Moe, 1980: 113ff.). Moe is equally aware of the theoretical problems involved in doing justice to this variety of motivations, and of the measurement problems involved in their empirical specification, or operationalization. Nevertheless, he adopts the reasonable stance that, ultimately, it is an empirical, not a theoretical, matter what incentives motivate individuals to join interest organizations. I will return to empirical questions in the following section. In this section, I will mention some of the most influential theoretical models of mixed motivations in the context of collective action.

In his early critique of Mancur Olson, Brian Barry suggested that much collective action cannot be explained without invoking non-economic motives, such as altruism, duty or solidarity, most importantly in the form of class-consciousness (Barry, 1970/1978: 33–37). Earlier still, Amartya Sen had identified the problem of assurance, which may arise if we break the isolation of prisoners in the prisoners' dilemma. In the assurance game, defection is not the dominant strategy. Each player prefers to cooperate, if all others cooperate, and will do so if they are assured that all others will do so too (Sen, 1967: 114f.). The game of assurance has been used as a possible interpretation of the Marxist concept of 'class consciousness' (see p. 299).

To say that people might prefer to cooperate is not enough, however, as Amartya Sen was among the first economists to admit in his famous article 'Rational Fools'. We wish to know *why* people sometimes prefer to cooperate. Sen mentions two possible candidates: (1) sympathy and (2) commitment (Sen, 1979: 95ff.; 1985). Of these, commitment is most destructive for economic theory. Both replace self-interest, but commitment replaces economic 'rationality' too. This is so because 'commitment does involve, in a very real sense, counterpreferential choice' (1979: 96). Commitment replaces utility-maximization, because it does not imply that we prefer more to less.

Fireman and Gamson reached a similar conclusion as they tried to bring order to the possible motives for collective action. They do not deny the ubiquity of self-interest, but they emphatically deny that it is the sole motive for participation in social movements, which is their main concern.[35] In addition there is the possibility of solidarity among members of groups based on a common identity. This solidarity, in its turn, may be the basis of a particular *group-interest*, which is irreducible to any combination of self-interests (Fireman and Gamson, 1979: 21ff.). A third important motive is commitment to universal principles, such as justice and human rights (ibid., pp. 26f.). Thus, in addition to self-interest, 'Two different mechanisms operate, one acting through people's loyalty to a group with which they experience solidarity, and the other acting through people's responsibility to personal principles that are at stake in collective action' (ibid., p. 31).

Where Sen spoke of sympathy, Fireman and Gamson talk about solidarity growing out of a common identity. I do not know if they intend different things, but it might be useful to make a distinction. Sympathy seems to me more personal, while solidarity is more collective and, therefore, more indiscriminating. But, unlike commitment to principles, both sympathy and solidarity may be assimilated by a rational choice model acknowledging the existence of a group-interest in addition to self-interest.

The most well-known attempt to develop a new model of rational choice along these lines is by Howard Margolis. His basic idea, as we have seen (pp. 107–110), is to assign to the individual two separate interests, or selves: self-interest (S-Smith) and group-interest (G-Smith). The choices of S-Smith and G-Smith are mediated by an arbiter called U-Smith, allocating resources according to a rule of 'fair share' (Margolis, 1982/1984: 36ff.). One reason for advancing this alternative to public choice, was the inability of economic man to solve the problem of collective action.

The conventional economic model not only predicts (correctly) the existence of problems with free riders but also predicts (incorrectly) such severe problems that no society we know could function if its members actually behaved as the conventional model implies they will.

(Margolis, 1982/1984: 6)

Russell Hardin shares Margolis' doubts about Mancur Olson's economic theory of collective action. 'Under the logic of collective action, we should expect to see very little large-scale collective action motivated by narrow self-interest. . . Yet we know that many large-scale interests are organized' (Hardin, 1982: 101). This fact can only be explained by assuming 'extra-rational' (non-egoistic) motivations, such as morality, the desire for self-development through participation and ignorance of the relation between costs and benefits (ibid., pp. 102ff.). All these motivations may be interpreted in a way that make them consonant with Margolis' new model of rational choice.

Ignorance about the relation between costs and benefits is an endemic feature of most collective action. If conceived as a problem of informa-tion, it may be rationalized as costs of information in a redefinition of 'rationality' as satisficing. This is Margolis' solution to the problem of ignorance (Margolis, 1982/1984: 49–51). But it is not Hardin's solution. Hardin reckons with an ignorance that goes deeper and cannot be amended by information. He calls it 'misunderstanding' (Hardin, 1984: 112–117). What Hardin has in mind is the possibility that people system-atically overestimate the probability that their own contribution will make a difference to the provision of collective goods in large groups (see also Moe, 1980: 30–33). If this is the case, their actions are irrational and outside the scope of (objectivistic) rational choice. But it could still be self-interested action.

The desire for self-development through participation may also be con-ceived of as a manifestation of egoism. This is the case to the extent that participation is, itself, a good carrying its own reward (see, e.g., Buchanan and Tullock, 1962/1965: 347n; Hirschman, 1981: 290–293; 1982/1985: 85). For Margolis, participation is also a source of utility, but it derives from 'giving resources away for the benefit of others'; hence, 'participation altruism' (Margolis, 1982/1984: 21). It is not a matter of interdependent utility functions, however. Participation, itself, not the benefit others receive, is the source of utility in participation altruism. Utility derived from the benefit conferred on others is called 'goods altruism' (ibid., p. 21).

In my opinion, 'participation altruism' is a muddled concept. Goods altru-ism is clear enough, but participation for the benefit, but without concern, for others is not altruism. In the language of Elster, altruism is 'outcome-oriented', not 'process-oriented' (Elster, 1985b: 145ff.; 1989a: 37ff.). If partici-pation is entirely process-oriented, the benefit conferred on others is a by-product of selfish participation. But it is hard to believe that all participation in collective action is selfish. With Margolis (1982/1984: 24), I conclude that 'a pure participation model ... would not be satisfactory'. Participation is motivated mainly by outcome.

Returning to Hardin, we find that the emphasis is on self-development, rather than on participation. The suggestion is that people may wish to take part in the events of history and to shape the future as a means to 'self-realization'. Hardin admits that this motive, too, may be interpreted as narrowly selfish, but prefers, himself, to interpret it as a moral notion (Hardin, 1982/108–112). He does not, however, provide much of an argument for this interpretation.

Elster has argued, persuasively in my opinion, that participation is not enough for self-realization, or self-respect (Elster, 1989a: 45f.). It goes without saying that self-realization and self-respect cannot be achieved solely by participation, irrespective of the goals pursued. These 'goods' can only be attained by participating in movements devoted to goals conceived by the actor as worthy. Thus, self-realization depends necessarily upon the purpose of collective action. Elster advances this argument against Hirschman (1982/1985), but unjustly so. In my view, Hirschman's understanding of the benefits derived from participation gives additional strength to Elster's argument.

Hirschman makes a distinction between two types of preference change: (1) the usually unreflective change in tastes, or first-order preferences, and (2) the reflective change in values, or second-order metapreferences (Hirschman, 1982/1985: 66–76; 1984: 89f.; 1985: 8–11). While our tastes, or first-order preferences, concern goods and services, our values, or metapreferences, concern the kind of person we want to be, including what kind of utility function we want to have (Frank, 1987). Utilizing this idea, we might suggest, with Hirschman, that self-realization through participation is attained to the degree that it furthers goals consistent with people's metapreferences. If, for instance, political liberties and rights are among an individual's most strongly held values, he or she might attain self-realization and self-respect by working for Amnesty.

I return to Hardin and a third (his first) extra-rational motivation: 'morality'. As with self-realization, Hardin does not provide much of an explication of this notion. He mentions 'such moral or psychological motives as altruism, guilt, or a sense of injustice at having to suffer collective bads in order to profit others'. What moral motives have in common is that they differ from 'amoral' self-interest (Hardin, 1982: 167). But it is not clear that morality is extra-rational in the sense of being non-utilitarian, or non-consequentialist. Thus, it is not clear that 'morality' goes beyond Margolis' notion of 'group-interest', or is incompatible with his new model of rational choice (see Hardin, 1982: 99f.).

But there is a fourth extra-rational motivation: contractarianism (Hardin, 1982: ch. 6, 102). This motive may be entirely rational, or selfish, when circumstances permit effective sanctioning. In this case, Hardin speaks of a conventional norm of fairness (ibid., p. 161). But in many cases, cooperation is due to an ethical norm of fairness (ibid. pp. 216–219). What is morality and what is merely convention is in many cases difficult to tell. Convention and morality typically shade over into each other. Reference to ethical norms indicates a break, not only with self-interest, but with any utilitarian rationality. Yet I am not entirely certain that Hardin wishes to go that far in *Collective Action* (1982). In a recent article on 'The Social Evolution of Cooperation' (1990) he does, but he deems action motivated by interest to be much more common than action motivated by norms, at least in modern industrial society (Hardin, 1990: 366).

The final step is taken by Jon Elster, who eventually recognizes that it is necessary to go beyond not only self-interest but also utilitarianism and rational choice, in order to explain collective action. If economic man will not cooperate, or only conditionally, large-scale cooperation can only be explained by invoking sociological man. What Elster has to say about sociological man has, of course, been said by sociologists before, but not always with such acumen.[36] Sociologists, naturally, tend to take sociological man as given to analysis. Elster has reached his present position by a different route. He started as a defender of economic man and rational choice and has reached his hard-won conclusions by reflection, rather than by education. This fact, together with the unusual ability of this prolific writer, gives a special weight to his argument.[37]

It is Elster's contention that collective action can only be explained by assuming *mixed motivations* (1985b: 141ff.; 1986a: 16ff.; 1989a: 187ff.). Besides self-interest, there are altruism, morality and social norms. Altruism is a psychological motive directed at particular persons, whereas morality consists of general principles (Elster, 1985b: 148; 1989a: 47). Elster also makes a distinction between moral and social norms; the former being consequentialist, the latter nonconsequentialist (1985b: 145; 1986a: 8f.; 1989a: 100f.). What this means is that morality is concerned with the outcome of actions, while social norms tell us to act, or not to act, in certain ways, irrespective of the result. An alternative way of looking at this distinction would be to treat moral norms as a subclass of social norms, as those social norms that are justified in terms of the *Good*, whether it is freedom, justice, equality or some other moral value. In addition, there are other social norms, such as technical norms and mere conventions. The distinctions between altruism, morality and social norms are not sharp. Though different types of motivation, they shade off into each other. One reason for this is that they have a common basis in emotions (cf. Elster, 1989a: 99f.; 1989b: ch. 7).

Elster does not attach much importance to altruism in explaining collective action. The reason is that altruism is limited to a close circle of family and friends (1986d: 25). There remain two categories of non-selfish motivations: morality and social norms. Within these two categories, Elster (1989a: 187ff.; see also 1985b: 148ff. and 1986d: 8ff.) recognizes three specific types of special importance for collective action: Utilitarianism, everyday Kantianism and the norm of fairness. Utilitarianism is a morality oriented wholly to outcome. It motivates people to participate in collective action if it leads to increasing average benefit. Everyday Kantianism is a blend of morality and social norms, but more of the latter. It tells people to cooperate because it is their duty to do so, but only if universal cooperation is better for everybody than universal defection (Elster, 1989a: 192). The norm of fairness, finally, is conditional upon the cooperation of others. It is a norm against free riding.

Elster's idea is that these motivations interact and reinforce one another, so that the result is more than the sum of their isolated effects. They do so, in part, by being effective at different stages in the cumulative development of collective action. The explanation of collective action therefore requires a sequential model (Elster, 1989a: 204–206; 1989b: 132–134).[38] In the beginning only everyday Kantians cooperate, because they alone do so irrespective of success. Everyday Kantians, therefore, are necessary to trigger off collective action. If there are enough Kantians, the utilitarians might find it worthwhile to join, thereby creating the conditions necessary for the norm of fairness to come into play. The norm of fairness, by its very 'logic', functions as a multiplier leading to universal cooperation. This model lacks the simplicity and elegance of most economic models, but, according to Elster, something like this is the best we can hope for, in terms of simplicity, at least (1989a: 205). I agree.

THE EVIDENCE

As I pointed out at the beginning of this chapter, Mancur Olson's economic theory of collective action is apparently falsified by the very existence of society itself. What we see of collective action, cooperation and social order is not what we are led to expect by the economic logic of collective action. In the aftermath of Olson's pioneering work there have been many attempts to salvage pure logic by social mechanisms working to secure cooperation even among rational egoists. Even so, a majority of the most competent judges now seem to agree that motives other than self-interest are at work in social life and conducive to much of the cooperation we observe. This contention, I am now going to show, is supported by the main bulk of the empirical evidence pertaining to the matter.

While true, this is not an entirely uncontroversial statement. Douglas Heckathorn, for instance, suggests that the prediction of mutual defection in a prisoners' dilemma has considerable support in small group experiments (Heckathorn, 1984: 156). Michael Hechter maintains that experimental studies have 'produced a morass of inconsistent findings', but goes on to suggest that this is due to differences in experimental design. A careful design of a public goods situation – such as that created by Kim and Walker (1984) – however, permits free riding to emerge 'in full bloom' (Hechter, 1987: 27n.,

61). Writing from another perspective, Amitai Etzioni suggests that experimental evidence *against* the economic hypothesis of universal free riding is overwhelming (Etzioni, 1988: 59f.). There is no doubt that Etzioni is most in the right.

In order to appreciate this fact, it is necessary to realize what is implied by the economic theory of collective action. Earl R. Brubaker made the useful distinction between a 'strong' and a 'weak' version of the free rider hypothesis (Brubaker, 1975: 150). According to the strong version, a rational egoist will always free ride, in the absence of coercion or some other selective incentive. According to the weak version, public goods will be provided, but allocation will be suboptimal. The hypothesis derived from the economic theory of collective action, suggested by Olson, Buchanan and Garrett Hardin, is the strong version. The weak version is indeterminate and fully compatible with received wisdom in all branches of social science, with psychology and with common sense. No one in his right mind would deny the existence of free riding; it is part of our everyday experience, and frequently referred to in the social science literature, but in other terms (see Chapter 6). The issue, then, is the extent, not the existence, of free riding. The occurrence of free riding, therefore, is no evidence of the correctness of the economic theory of collective action, but voluntary cooperation is evidence against it. Brubaker, himself, cites some early experimental evidence showing 'beyond reasonable doubt that conditions exist under which free riding will not be the dominant response to a request for expressions of demand for a pure collective good' (Brubaker, 1975: 155). He believes that most people would be quite willing to contribute if they had some assurance that others would contribute too, so that their own scarce resources would not be wasted. One possible device would be a 'money back' guarantee if the public good is not provided (ibid., p. 151). Brubaker's hypothesis could be interpreted as suggesting that defection is motivated by a *fear* of losing one's scarce resources, rather than by *greed*.[39]

In a critical review by Pruitt and Kimmel (1977), the opinion of Michael Hechter seems, at first, to be vindicated. Their main critical point concerns the low external validity of experimental gaming (Pruitt and Kimmel, 1977: 367ff.). In addition, their own theoretical efforts – the so-called 'goal expectation theory' – go in the direction of assuming self-interested conditional cooperation and are, therefore, consistent with the theory of 'group solidarity' advanced by Hechter. The argument of Pruitt and Kimmel is not without ambiguity, however. Having criticized previous experimental gaming for lack of concern about external validity, they propose a theory that reproduces some of its most serious defects. The problem, they say, is that researchers are not interested in generalizing beyond the laboratory and do not know how to do it (Pruitt and Kimmel, 1977: 367f.). The solution is 'theory building in the context of concern about real-life applications. . . Hence we may be on soundest ground by building a theory about how individuals devise strategies and how groups develop social norms' (ibid, p. 370). But then they go on to suggest a theory that 'concerns the behavior of two people who are engaged in repeated interaction with one another and are trying to devise strategies for maximixing their own benefits' (ibid., p. 375). So much for real life and social norms. An interesting observation, though, is this: the lack of external validity implies a bias for 'cool calculation'. Experimental settings are typically such as to induce people to be more strategically rational than in real life.

> In such a setting, conventional social norms, attitudes, sentiments, and most social motives have relatively little impact on behavior because they seem irrelevant to the task at hand. Rather behavior is likely to be mainly a function of the nature of the surroundings, as interpreted in the context of the salient goals.
>
> (ibid., p. 375)

If so, there is reason to expect more cooperation in real life than in experimental games. This is probably not what Michael Hechter wished to suggest by complaining about the external validity of experimental games.

In a frequently cited survey of the psychological literature on 'social dilemmas' – a term used by many psychologists to denote a prisoners' dilemma – Robyn M. Dawes reviewed the results of experiments pertaining to the matter (Dawes, 1980). Evidence suggests that cooperation increases with communication, but decreases with group size. It is larger when choice is made public than when it is anonymous and larger when people expect others to cooperate. His conclusion – which follows from his review of proposed solutions to social dilemmas, but not obviously from the experimental results alone – was this:

> The hypothesis that follows from this survey and review is that there are two crucial factors that lead people to cooperate in a social dilemma situation. First, people must 'think about' and come to understand the nature of the dilemma, so that moral, normative, and altruistic concerns as well as external payoffs can influence behavior. Second, people must have some reason for believing that others will not defect, for while the difference in payoffs may always favor defection no matter what others do, the absolute payoff is higher if others cooperate than if they don't. The efficacy of both factors – and indeed the possibility of cooperative behavior at all in a dilemma situation – is based upon rejecting the principle of 'nonsatiety of economic greed' as an axiom of actual human behavior. And it is rejected.
>
> (Dawes, 1980: 170)

By Dawes that is, but not by psychologist Wolfgang Stroebe, or by Bruno S. Frey, who is a political economist closely associated with the theory of public choice (see Chapters 1 and 2). In their review of evidence about free riding, the model of selfish man in economics and psychology is an article of faith more than an hypothesis to be tested. Surprisingly, they find that strong evidence for free riding, and for the size effect, in psychological experimental games (Stroebe and Frey, 1982: 125), but much less so in economic and sociological simulations of market transactions (ibid., p. 127). 'However, since the total contribution to the public good of the groups observed was always greater than zero, no support was found for the strong free-rider hypothesis' (ibid., p. 131). Also, the size effect was not strong enough to support the extrapolation that it would ever become zero.

> Our review of the research on the free rider hypothesis, suggests that, at least in relatively small groups, free riding does not constitute a serious threat to social organization. Except in the case of experimental games researchers even appear to have had problems in demonstrating sizable free-riding effects.
>
> (ibid., p. 135)

Stroebe and Frey explain these results in terms of selective incentives. In particular, they invoke the sanctions attached to social norms and, especially, the feelings of guilt and loss of self-respect that are associated with violations of social norms and public morality (ibid., pp. 131, 134f.). As I have already argued, this analysis makes the economic model of man parasitic upon the sociological ditto, because feelings of guilt can only exist as by-products of internalized moral norms.

Another review, by Messick and Brewer, two of the most prominent figures in the field, confirms the importance of communication for the solution of social dilemmas, but they go further than Dawes by distinguishing four different ways in which communication has been shown to facilitate cooperation (Messick and Brewer, 1983: 22ff.): (1) By eliciting *information about the choices of others*, (2) by enhancing *trust in other group members*, (3) by activating *social values and responsibility* and by (4) creating a *group identity*. Much the same conclusion is reached in the review by Janusz Grzelak (1988: 296ff.), who adds that much cooperation seems to depend upon the individual's definitions of the situation – a classical sociological theme (see Chapter 6).

Making my own brief review of experimental evidence, I follow Dawes, and Messick and Brewer, in distinguishing two principal ways of solving social dilemmas: (1) changing the game until it is no longer a social dilemma (institutional solution); (2) relying on individuals' capacity for non-egoistic cooperation (motivational solution). Economic theory, resting on the assumption of rational egoism, has to rely on the first type of solution. Critics of this theory, including myself, maintain that motives other than self-interest must be invoked, in order to explain all collective action, cooperation and social order there is in the world. There is, of course, an interdependence between these solutions, such that certain motives come into play only in certain social situations and some social situations are created only by people with

264

mixed motives. A consequence of this is that it is sometimes difficult to tell which mechanism predominates in a particular instance of collective action.

Starting with institutional solutions, experimental evidence seems to confirm many of the hypotheses suggested in the first sections of this chapter. Social structures that facilitate interaction and social control invariably produce more cooperation. The problem with some of this evidence is that it does not discriminate between successful harnessing of self-interest and prosocial behaviour. There is, for instance, very strong evidence for conditional cooperation, both in iterated and in one-shot prisoners' dilemmas (see e.g. Pruitt and Kimmel, 1977: 375ff.; Kuhlman et al., 1986: 155; Liebrand, 1986: 125; Poppe, 1986: 147; Good, 1991: 231f.; Rabbie, 1991: 244–260). In iterated games, there is the possibility of punishing defectors, but there is ususally no possibility of knowing whether retaliation is motivated by enlightened self-interest or a norm of reciprocity. In one-shot games, retaliation is not possible, but cooperation is still conditional upon the cooperation of others. In this case too, we do not know whether cooperation is motivated by risk-averse self-interest, or by a norm of fairness. It is beyond doubt, however, that institutional modifications of incentives do have profound, often decisive, effects upon cooperation.

Samuelson, Wilke et al. conducted a number of experiments to test the hypotheses that inefficiency and inequity in the exploitation of a common resource would lead experimental subjects to hand over authority to a leader. Both hypotheses were confirmed. It was also found that leaders largely came up to expectations and behaved both prudently and fairly. The results were interpreted as lending support to the sociological hypothesis that leaders have two tasks: to promote collective goals and to be fair (Samuelson et al., 1986; Wilke et al. 1986a: 57–62).

Another attempt to test the effects of a changed incentive structure was made by Dawes et al. (1986). They transformed a prisoners' dilemma in two different ways, in order to discriminate between two motives for defection: fear and greed. If fear of being suckered is the dominant motive for defection, a money-back guarantee, if the public good is not provided, would suffice to ensure cooperation. The money-back guarantee transforms the prisoners' dilemma half-way into a game of chicken; being suckered yields the same payoff as mutual defection. If, on the other hand, greed is the dominant motive for defection, enforced contribution would be more effective. Enforced contribution changes the prisoners' dilemma half-way into a game of assurance; free riding does not pay.

Results were clearly in favour of enforced contribution, or fair share arrangements, as the more effective way of securing cooperation (0.81 versus 0.51). This result was replicated by Poppe (1986: 142), and counts as evidence against the hypothesis suggested by Brubaker. It should perhaps be pointed out that fear of being suckered is not identical with risk aversion, as proposed

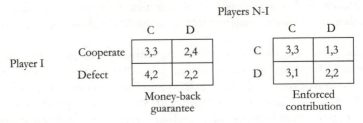

Figure 5.5 Payoff matrices for money-back guarantee and enforced contribution

by Frohlich *et al.* and by de Jasay. The risk involved in their explanations of cooperation is the risk of having to do without a public good, not the risk of losing a contribution to it. The indication that the latter is not an important motive for defection is rather indicative of the kind of conditional cooperation suggested by Frohlich and de Jasay.

Dawes *et al.* interpret their findings as providing a reason for the labour union policy of trying to exclude free riders. This may be, but we must not interpret their results as support for any hypothesis that greed is a dominant motive. Half of the experimental subjects contributed to the public good even in a prisoners' dilemma – a result which agrees with a large body of experimental social dilemmas, but not with a hypothesis about greed. This result cannot be explained by any institutional transformation of the incentive structure. It can only be explained in terms of other-than-selfish motives.

People do cooperate, even when rational egoism suggests free riding. But not all of them and not equally much. People differ in their propensity to cooperate in social dilemmas, and this propensity reflects their social values and orientations. In order to substantiate this hypothesis W.B.G. Liebrand (1986) classified people in four categories: (1) *altruism*, or the maximization of others benefit, (2) *cooperation*, or the maximization of joint benefit, (3) *individualism*, or the maximization of own benefit, and (4) *competition*, or the maximization of relative advantage. This classification was made prior to, and independent of, the experiment. The hypothesis was tested for three different games: prisoners' dilemma, chicken, and trust (assurance). A third independent variable was introduced: half of the experimental subjects were given 'positive feedback', or information that a majority of the other subjects had chosen a cooperative strategy; the other half received 'negative feedback', being told that a majority had already chosen a defecting strategy.

It was expected, of course, that people classified as altruists and cooperators would cooperate more in a social dilemma than those classified as individualists and competitors. It was further expected that defection would decrease in the game of chicken and decrease even more in the game of trust. It was finally expected that positive feedback would lead to increasing cooperation. All three hypotheses were corroborated (Liebrand, 1986: 123–125). Altruists and cooperators did cooperate more than individualists and competitors in all three games (0.79 versus 0. 60). Once again, about half of the experimental subjects cooperated in the prisoners' dilemma, two-thirds in the game of chicken and more than 90 per cent in the game of trust. The effect of feedback was different in the three games, but in the prisoners' dilemma, positive feedback resulted in significantly higher cooperation (0.72) than did negative feedback (0.42).

The effects of social values were also tested in a 'sequence dilemma' of the type made famous by Garrett Hardin in his 'tragedy of the commons' (Liebrand, 1986: 125–127). Seven individuals were allowed to take resources from a common pool subject to depletion, unless they showed restraint. The effect of social values was this: on average, altruists took $11.50, cooperators $13.48, individualists $15.08 and competitors $17.40.

The results reported by Liebrand were corroborated by Kuhlman et al. (1986), who also found that cooperativeness, individualism and competitiveness are stable personality traits of different individuals (ibid., p. 163). However, instead of interpreting these 'orientations' as manifestations of internalized social values, they go on to test the hypothesis that they are but different self-interested strategies based upon different expectations about the behaviour of others. Cooperators cooperate because they expect others to do the same and defectors defect because they expect others to do so. In the end, therefore, it all boils down to a matter of trust. This hypothesis implies a rejection of motivational solutions in favour of an institutional solution à la Axelrod and Taylor. Kuhlman et al. find their alternative interpretation supported (Kuhlman et al., 1986: 164–172). A problem with this hypothesis is that it does not explain the mass of experimental evidence that people also cooperate when defection, or free riding, is the dominant strategy. They suggest as a further implication of their hypothesis – an implication they also intend to test themselves – that cooperators are more sensitive to fear and competitors more sensitive to greed (Kuhlman et al., 1986: 172f.). As we have already seen, available evidence, so far, suggests that fear does not have a significant effect on cooperation at all.

Evidence against Kuhlman et al. can be found in the experiments reported by Orbell et al. (1984). The idea behind their experiment was that many social dilemmas involve, besides the two possibilities of cooperation and defection, the further option of exit from the group. The hypothesis they wished to test, was that cooperators exit more than defectors, since they gain more by choosing this option, relative to their previous choice to cooperate. I will not explain their rather complicated experimental design, merely report their findings. Contrary to their expectations, cooperators exited somewhat less than did defectors. Among the possible explanations for this result, Orbell et al. did consider the hypothesis suggested by Kuhlman et al., i.e. that cooperation depends upon the expectation that others will cooperate. Data did not support this hypothesis at all (Orbell et al., 1984: 156f.). Their own conjecture is that cooperators are motivated by a concern for the welfare of the group.

This suggestion is supported doubly: first by their decision to cooperate in the first place and second by their greater resistance to the temptation to exit. This consistency in cooperative behaviour strengthens the hypothesis that cooperativeness is a character trait of many individuals and reflects their internalized social values.

> The experimental result is significant, we believe, for emphasizing the importance of normative considerations as a factor behind the exit–stay decision as well as the cooperate–defect one and should be taken as showing the need for greater understanding of normative systems rather than as predicting general outcomes.
>
> (Orbell *et al.*, 1984: 160)

Strong evidence against the hypothesis of Kuhlman *et al.* has been provided by Dawes, Van de Kragt, *et al.* One of the most significant and consistent results of their experimentation over the years is that cooperation increases dramatically if people are allowed to communicate before being subjected to a social dilemma (Dawes, 1980: 185f.; Orbell *et al.* 1984: 154f.; Van de Kragt *et al.*, 1986: 189; see also Liebrand, 1986: 126). What, exactly, is achieved by communication? Dawes, Van de Kragt *et al.* have tried to answer this question in several series of experiments.

As a first step towards an answer, they tried to isolate the effect of prosocial persuasion from that of self-interested institutional rearrangement. This was achieved by comparing the separate and combined effects of two conditions: (1) eliminating the possibility of free riding by using a game of assurance, and (2) allowing group discussion. Both devices contributed equally much to cooperation by themselves, but only their joint presence produced Pareto optimality. In order to eliminate the possibility of punishment, contributions were anonymous and participants did not meet after the experiment. Having eliminated also the possibility that discussion facilitates self-interest by removing the fear of loss, Van de Kragt *et al.* assume, instead, that it triggers 'group-regarding motivations' (Van de Kragt *et al.*, 1986: 192). This assumption was tried in a new set of conditions removing the relation between contribution and self-interest altogether. Making the bonus of each depend on the contribution of others, only group regardingness could motivate players of the game. Also under these conditions, group discussion had a very strong effect on contributions: they increased about three times and were almost universal when bonus was made contingent upon the contribution of a designated set of five out of nine group members (van de Kragt *et al.*, 1986: 196).

In subsequent series of experiments, Dawes *et al.* have continued their attempt to find out, more exactly, why group discussion is so conducive to cooperation. They finally isolate group identity and, connected with it, solidarity as the most important factor. This conclusion is reached after consideration of four alternative solutions to social dilemmas: (1) Hobbes' centralized

Leviathan, (2) Axelrod's reciprocity, (3) Hardin's 'mutual coercion mutually agreed upon' and (4) a socially instilled conscience. I quote:

> We have . . . conducted a series of experiments over the past ten years, the results of which have led us, reluctantly at first, to conclude that the cooperation rate can be enhanced in the absence of egoistic incentives . . . Our experiments have led us to conclude that cooperation rates can be radically affected by one factor in particular, which is independent of the consequences for the choosing individual. That factor is group identity. Such identity – or solidarity – can be established and consequently enhance cooperation in the absence of any expectation of future reciprocity, current rewards or punishment, or even reputational consequences among other group members. Moreover, this identity operates independently of the dictates of conscience. In other words, our experiments indicate that group solidarity increases cooperation independently of the side payments – either external or internal – often associated with such identity.
>
> (Dawes, et al., 1990: 99; see also Dawes, 1991: 26ff.).

The evidence presented for this conclusion is three series of experiments. The first series is of the type described above (van de Kragt et al., 1986) and need not concern us here. The second series was intended to distinguish the effect of identity from that of conscience. It was assumed that group identity is characterized by particularism and conscience by universalism. If group identity is most important, contributions are high only when beneficiaries are group members. If, on the other hand, conscience is most important, contributions should not be affected if group members were replaced by strangers as beneficiaries. But it was. While discussion more than doubled cooperation when beneficiaries were group members, it did nothing to increase it when they were strangers. In a third series of experiments, the group identity hypothesis was tested against the effects of promising. It was found that promises were effective only if all group members made a promise to contribute. With less than universal promising, there was virtually no correlation at all between promise and contribution. This result does not establish the group identity hypothesis, but lends it additional support. The most likely, if not the only, interpretation is that universal promising is indicative of group identity.

Dawes, et al. (1990; see also Dawes, 1991) finally decide that social identity, or sociality, is a primordial fact about human beings and go on to criticize the evolutionary approach to cooperation advanced by Axelrod and others. This approach works only if we assume that sociality is historically prior to cooperation. 'Then it is clear that ease in forming group identity could be of individual benefit' (Dawes et al., 1990: 109). What is more:

> there have been no findings indicating that humans ever were not

social. It is fun and somewhat romantic to speculate about how isolates developed our most cherished characteristic, our ties to other humans. But once again, such speculations must be evaluated in terms of our knowledge of how humans behaved without such ties, and there is no evidence we ever did.

(ibid., p. 109)

The evidence mentioned thus far derives invariably from experiments with small groups in a laboratory. This is a problem, because Olson predicts failure of collective action only in large groups. It does not imply, however, that results from small groups are altogether invalidated as a test of Olson's theory. When there is no possibility of social control and the group is not privileged – as it is not in a prisoners' dilemma – self-interest dictates free riding also in small groups. Most experiments fulfil these conditions and count as evidence against the economic logic of collective action. There is also some evidence suggesting that cooperation does not necessarily cease as groups become larger (Bonacich et al., 1976; Liebrand, 1986: 128f.; Van de Kragt, et al., 1986: 191).

The strongest evidence of cooperation in large groups (80 members), comes from experiments made outside the laboratory by Gerald Marwell, Ruth E. Ames and Geraldine Afano. In these experiments we once again find unequivocal, and for the experimenters unexpected, evidence against the strong version of the free rider hypothesis. In a series of experiments they intended first to corroborate the hypothesis of free riding in a pure public choice situation and then to go on and change the situation in various ways in order to find out exactly what makes people contribute to the provision of public goods. Their hypothesis was refuted in the first experiment. On the average, people allocated almost half of their allotted resources to the provision of a public good, instead of free riding on the contributions of others (Marwell and Ames, 1979: 1349f.). Replications of the experiment with variations in resources, interests, group size, etc. confirmed the original results. Three variables had an effect on the outcome. When stakes were increased (by a factor of five), contributions to the provision of the public good sank to (on average) a third of people's resources (Marwell and Ames, 1980: 933–935). When the public good was changed from a divisible to an indivisible one, contributions increased to 80 per cent of the resources (Alfano and Marwell, 1981: 305ff.).

Most suggestive, perhaps, is the result obtained when subjects were divided into economics graduate students and other students. It was found that economics students free ride much more than others: only 20 per cent of their resources were allocated to the provision of public goods. Not only that; unlike other students, economics students did not attach any significance to the notion of 'fairness' (Marwell and Ames, 1981: 307–309). A clue to this fact may be the following circumstance: in order to make certain that their

270

experimental design captured the public goods problem, Marwell and Ames consulted five economists and one sociologist (all experts in the field). In addition to approving of the experimental set up, they were asked to predict the outcome (a) according to economic theory and (b) according to their own judgement. Five of them (the sixth did not answer) affirmed that economic theory predicts no contribution at all to the public good, while their own personal predictions were 20 per cent (average); the same as the economics students.

Experiments reported so far were conducted by psychologists, some sociologists, and at least one political scientist. Economists rarely engage in empirical research. The interesting thing is that, when they do, they seem to obtain results at odds with those of other social scientists and more corroborative of economic theory. Oliver Kim and Mark Walker, for instance, suggested that earlier refutations of the free rider hypothesis were due to mistakes in the experimental design that prevented an adequate test of the economic theory of public goods and the hypothesis about free riding. I will not comment on this verdict, except to point out that it is based upon a rather limited sample of previous experiments. I prefer to comment upon their own experiment, which, in the words of Michael Hechter, permits free riding to emerge in 'full bloom' (Hechter, 1987: 27n.). The first thing to notice is that 'full bloom' means *three* persons free riding out of *five*, which was the number of individuals participating in the experiment (Kim and Walker, 1984: 19). A second comment is that the design of Kim and Walker's experiment was such that I am surprised that anyone contributed. For me and, I suppose, for most people, contribution to a public good must make some sense, in terms of what the public good is good for. A game in which you are asked to invest some amount of money in order to receive a larger amount, on condition that other anonymous persons also invest, is simply too alienating to motivate people to contribute.

Isaac, McCue and Plott also report evidence that goes against the current. Contributions in a repeated game were far below optimum and only slightly above zero. Contributions in the first game were substantial (38 per cent of optimum) and confirm earlier evidence, but decrease dramatically with repetition. This result goes against Axelrod's tournament of iterated two-person prisoners' dilemmas, but support Taylor's analysis of an N-person prisoners' dilemma. Cooperation is indeed difficult and depends upon the existence of a sufficiently large number of conditional cooperators. In the experiment by Isaac *et al.*, this number was obviously insufficient. And it was not because experimental subjects were economics students. To test the result obtained by Marwell and Ames, they included one experiment (out of nine) with sociology students. The outcome was the same as with the economists (Isaac *et al.*, 1985: 69). I see no reason to doubt the validity of the results, even though the reliability obviously was not the best (see ibid., p. 58n.). Two points should be made, however. (1) Payoffs were such as to avoid lumpiness. Since many public goods are lumpy this limits the scope of the results. Also, since there is much to suggest that lumpiness is favourable to cooperation, results may be biased. (2) The experimental design was such as to prevent motives other than self-interest from coming into play. Only as an exception was communication allowed and this resulted in a small but stable increase in level of contribution (ibid., p. 67). The point is simply that if you create an economists' universe of isolated atoms, then there is of course no reason to expect people to cooperate. But social life is not like that. (3) In the experiments both by Kim and Walker and by Isaac *et al.*, contributions were above zero. This means that the strong free rider hypothesis was refuted in both cases.

There is a widespread scepticism concerning the external validity of experimental results, especially among those who do not find their theories and hypotheses confirmed (see, e.g., Klandermans, 1986a: 87; Hechter, 1987: 27n.; Taylor, 1987: xii). This scepticism is sound, up to a point. It is difficult to simulate real social dilemmas in the laboratory, especially since subjects know that they are participating in an experiment. But this does not mean that experimental evidence is of no value at all. Psychologists and sociologists doing experiments are, nowadays, well aware of the pitfalls involved, but nevertheless claim some validity for their findings (see, e.g., Messick and Brewer, 1983: 36–40; Dawes *et al.*, 1986: 1174f; cf. also Cross and Guyer, 1980: 7f.). In the words of D.A. Good (1991: 236): 'While they must be taken with caution, I believe it would be wrong totally to reject them.' This much must be granted and the concluding remark is something to reflect upon: 'Experimentalists have been criticized for the distance between the laboratory and the real world. It is tempting to suggest that the distance between that world and the theorists' *Gedankenexperiment* is even greater' (ibid., p. 236).

If experimental evidence is of limited value, the obvious thing to do is to step out of the laboratory into the real world. Going back to 1968, only three years after the publication of Olson's book, we saw a sudden increase in collective activity. It is an intriguing fact that Olson's book won such wide acclaim in a historical period which seemed to contradict its main thesis and also that this apparent falsification went largely unnoticed in the vast literature that followed in its wake (cf. Hirschmann, 1981: 211; 1982/1985: 78). The problem with such evidence is that we cannot isolate self-interest from other motives. The defender of the economic theory of collective action can always invoke selective incentives and the critic has to slip back to a mixture of theory, logic and common sense. Fortunately there are some attempts to test the economic theory of collective action outside the laboratory.

One attempt to use, more than to test, Olson's theory was made by Samuel L. Popkin in *The Rational Peasant* (1979; see also 1988). The main burden of Popkin's argument is that political economy is superior to 'moral economy' when it comes to explaining collective action among peasants in Vietnam.

Following Olson, Popkin assumes that they will not act to achieve their common good without selective incentives (Popkin, 1979: 24–27, ch. 6). Popkin is equally indebted to Frohlich *et al.*, however, and argues that political entrepreneurs will do the job of mobilizing peasants for action.

Popkin tries the competing approaches on the case of four peasant movements in pre-war Vietnam: Catholics, Cao Dai, Hoa Hao and the communists. He finds that evidence supports the political economy approach. I will not argue against Popkins' conclusion that political economy is superior to moral economy as an explanation of peasant collective action. I do wish to claim, however, that Popkins' case for political economy is not entirely convincing, because more than rational egoism seems to have been involved in the movements described. While arguing that Vietnamese peasants are acting from self-interest,[40] this does not seem to have been the case with the political entrepreneurs. When explaining why peasants followed their leaders, he repeatedly emphasizes their moral qualities, dedication to the task, egalitarianism and religious or political ethos (Popkin, 1979: 191–193, 198; 1988: 16f., 21, 25, 30). Other non-economic elements introduced by Popkin are the charismatic qualities, or 'personal magnetism', of Huynh Phu So, the leader of the millenarian Hoa Hao (Popkin, 1979: 203; 1988: 33) and the nationalism of the communists (Popkin, 1979: 217f.; 1988: 43–45). For the peasants, nationalism was part of a new Vietnamese identity, which presumedly had some effect on their willingness to act collectively (Popkin, 1979: 86, 243; 1988: 60). The *non-economic elements* introduced by Popkin are not just that (non-economic). As we will see in the next chapter, they are central elements in the sociology of collective action.

A direct attempt to test Olson's theory of collective action has been made by Edward N. Muller and Karl-Dieter Opp. As we have already seen (p. 244), they wish to stay within rational choice and even to retain the assumption of self-interest, but not of egoism. I disregard conceptual matters, but note that their empirical findings cast doubts upon the economic models of Olson, Tullock and Silver. Using survey data from New York and Hamburg, Muller and Opp sought to lay bare the motivation behind rebellious collective action. Results indicated that 'selective incentives', in the sense of Olson, are largely irrelevant, and that the hypotheses of Tullock and Silver about entertainment value and psychic income are equally wrong. Instead, they suggest the alternative hypothesis that people engage in rebellious collective action mainly for the collective goods involved. They do so because they act in the collective, not in their individual, interest and, therefore, use a collective, not an individual, concept of 'rationality' (Muller and Opp, 1986).

Karl-Dieter Opp goes further in his analysis of the Hamburg data, which concern participation in the anti-nuclear movement. Confronted with the fact that several independent variables intercorrelate, he hypothesizes the existence of an ideological syndrome of post-materialist values behind some of them (Opp, 1986: 103f.). His attempt to test this hypothesis gives supportive evidence in the case of legal, but not in the case of illegal, protest (Opp, 1990: 229f.).

Muller's and Opp's findings cast doubts upon the models of Tullock and Silver, but not on that of Olson, which was never intended to cover the case of rebellious collective action, or of social movements. More to the point are William Gamson's survey of 'challenging groups' and Terry M. Moe's data on the motives for joining interest groups.

Gamson is more interested in Olson's efficacy argument than in his argument from self-interest. From this point of view, it makes no difference whether we have to do with a mass movement, philanthropic society or a pressure group. What matters is size. Irrespective of purpose, a single contribution is inefficacious in large groups. Gamson's data on 53 challenging groups, with respect to success, indicate that both solidarity, or loyalty, and selective incentives are important. 'In short, groups may grow large without the use of selective incentives, but in their absence, they have difficulty converting size into success' (Gamson, 1975: 70). Moe's main interest is in the relative importance of economic selective incentives and political collective goods. His main finding is that the former play a major role in members' motives for joining interest groups.

Both Gamson and Moe interpret their findings as lending overall support to Olson's by-product theory of interest groups (Gamson, 1975: ch. 5; Moe, 1980: ch. 8).[41] This is, in both cases, a debatable interpretation. I fasten, instead, upon the doubts cast by their data upon Olson's by-product theory of interest groups. Gamson compares those challenging groups that rely solely on solidarity with those that rely on both solidarity and selective incentives. He finds that the use of selective incentives increases the likelihood of success between two and three times. But according to Olson, selective incentives mean everything, solidarity nothing. Moe finds that, besides economic selective incentives, individuals are motivated by political collective goods and by a responsibility for the organization. The latter motives, moreover, interact in the most active members of the organization. In the end, therefore, Moe concludes that Olson's argument does not provide an adequate explanation of the existence of interest groups (Moe, 1980: 217f.).

I suspect that both Gamson and Moe compare Olson's by-product theory with an alternative which is its contradiction: a theory which says that altruism, solidarity, duty, or whatever, means everything and self-interest nothing. From this point of view, Olson's theory receives considerable support and may even be superior. But, as I will show in the following chapter, no such alternative exists in the social scientific literature, so this is not the point at issue. The alternative to Olson's economic logic of collective action is some theory of mixed motivations, self-interest included. If this is the point of departure, there is no doubt that the data of both Gamson and Moe support the latter, not the former.

This is also the conclusion of the more large-scale attempt by David

Knoke to test Olson's by-product theory on a sample of interest groups. He begins by observing that 'The empirical literature on organizational incentives is a steady accumulation of findings that refute Olson's emphasis on selective goods as essential for collective action' (Knoke, 1990: 313). Knoke's sample focuses on three types of organization: professional societies, recreational clubs and women's associations. His test is premised on the assumption that there are three main types of incentive for participation in interest associations: utilitarian incentives, social incentives and normative incentives. It is hypothesized that different incentives are important for different individuals and in different types of organization. Expectations are largely met. Members of interest groups are a heterogeneous lot and the groups they constitute are equally diverse. Contrary to Olson's by-product theory, selective incentives were found to be least important in pressure groups. The dominant interest in these groups seem to be collective goods and the dominant motive normative: 'contributing one's share to the organization is the fair and equitable thing to do' (Knoke, 1990: 326). Another result concerns the strong effect of communication on members' commitment to organizational goals. Knoke interprets this finding as indication that economic theory is wrong to work with stable preferences. People do not enter interest groups ready-made and unchanging. Interest formation is a dynamic process and part of political struggle. In this process, individuals create and affirm both their personal and group identities (ibid., p. 327).

A considerable portion of *The Logic of Collective Action* is devoted to labour unions. Considering the importance of this special interest organization in Olson's theory and in social life, unions cannot be bypassed as a test case. Much has been written about the solidarity of the working class and of labour unions as a manifestation of this solidarity (see, e.g., Thompson, 1963/1980, 456–469, *passim;* Hanagan, 1980; Birnbaum, 1988: ch. 5; 1990; Gilbert, 1992). It has even been suggested that unions follow a 'logic of collective action' different from that of capitalists and deviating from the pattern suggested by Mancur Olson's theory of interest groups. While this theory suggests, and capitalists follow, an instrumental-monological pattern of collective action, labour unions rely on a dialogical pattern used to create a collective identity (Offe and Wiesenthal, 1980). Even so, I am not aware of more than a few attempts to test Olson's theory of interest groups on labour unions.[42] Terry M. Moe summarized the scattered data there was on the matter in 1980, but none of these data were designed to test Olson's economic logic of collective action: they were more concerned with the alternative thesis of working-class consciousness and solidarity. The investigations mentioned by Moe indicate that working-class solidarity is not as strong as it is assumed to be in some quarters (Moe, 1980: 168–180). A majority of union members seem to be motivated solely, or mainly, by economic self-interest, at least in the United States. Ideology and solidarity seem to be somewhat more important in Europe. There is, however, a presumption that ideology and solidarity were much stronger in the initial stages of union formation. The picture emerging is the traditional sociology of organizational dynamics: from social movement to bureaucratic organization, or in Weber's specific version, the routinization of charisma (see p. 311). One thing we learn from sociological investigations is the problematic character of survey data. What people answer in reply to the sociologists' questions is an unreliable guide to their subsequent actions. In the 1950s and 1960s, sociologists concluded with one voice that working-class consciousness and solidarity were phenomena of the past, only soon to find a significant increase in strikes and other militant activities. The relevance of this development for Olson's logic of collective action has been addressed by Bert Klandermans (1986a), who confirms the hypothesis that workers' willingness to strike is conditional and takes the form of an assurance game. Individual workers participate, if they feel assured that enough others will participate. 'So the crux of the matter is influencing people's beliefs about the behaviour of others' (Klandermans, 1986a: 108). Collective action is a dynamic process.

If there is reason *a priori* to expect more cooperation among workers than among capitalists, then, of course, the economic theory of collective action would be even more damaged by evidence that even the latter do cooperate. Such evidence has been presented by David Marsh (1976), for the case of the Confederation of British Industry (CBI). Interviews with members of this association indicate that selective incentives are relatively unimportant, while it is the collective good itself that matters. Marsh's results are modified by Moe (1980: 191–199), who reports some variety among types of business associations.

Attempts directly to test the economic theory of collective action are even more scarce in the case of common pool resources. I have mentioned the experiments by Samuelsson, Wilke *et al.* (p. 265), but it may be added that history shows that commons existed for hundreds of years without any tragedy (cf. Taylor, 1987: 26). A more systematic investigation can be found in Elinor Ostrom's *Governing the Commons.* The emphasis of Ostrom is on institutional solutions to the collective action problem, but she repeatedly suggests that the institutions created were not enough to remove the possibility and consequent temptation to free ride (Ostrom, 1990: 75, 86, 93). The fact that people cooperate even in the face of such temptation is explained by assuming the operation of social norms (ibid., pp. 88f., 93f.). I interpret Ostrom as maintaining, implicitly at least, that institutions solve collective action problems, not only by creating the possibility of agreement, monitoring and sanctioning, but also by helping to create mutual trust and community-like social relations (ibid., pp. 171f.; cf. Gardner *et al.*, 1990: 354).

There is no doubt, then, that empirical evidence refutes the strong free rider hypothesis and supports the alternative hypothesis of mixed motivations. Which version of the latter provides the best explanation of collective action is undecidable in the present state of our knowledge. Except for one thing, I tend to believe that Elster's sequential model is the most adequate so far. What is missing in Elster's model is a recognition of the importance of collective identity for collective action.[43] This phenomenon is at the centre of sociological theories of collective action.

6

THE SOCIOLOGY OF COLLECTIVE ACTION

GROUP THEORY

In *The Logic of Collective Action* (1965/1971: 1, 16ff., 57ff.), Mancur Olson raised a number of objections against the traditional theory of groups, advanced by social psychologists, sociologists and political scientists. Most importantly, Olson argued against the view, which he ascribed to the traditional theory, that groups always act to further their common interest and that they do so irrespective of the size of the group. This view assumes, explicitly or implicitly, that individuals in groups act out of self-interest or, at least, rationally.

It is easy to show that Olson is wrong. Take his view that the traditional theory of groups is based on the assumption of self-interest. Olson's main reference, on this particular point, is to the sociologist Robert MacIver (Olson, 1965/1971: 8, 15). But Olson has not understood what MacIver understands by the term 'common interest'. He interprets this term as linked to that of a 'public good', and there is some justification for such interpretation of the source that Olson uses (MacIver, 1932), but it is nevertheless wrong. Consulting MacIver's more extensive discussions of the concept of 'common interest', we arrive at an entirely different interpretation. MacIver makes a distinction between *like* interests and *common* interests, which, according to him, is of fundamental importance for sociological analysis, but subject to much confusion. Now, Olson does just that: he mistakes common interests for like interests. But, according to MacIver (1917: 101): 'The common interest is always a directly social interest', only 'the like interests are always egoistic'. What is more:

> *Common interests* [are] *as primordial as self-limited interests* . . . Man is at once egocentric and sociocentric. How can anyone say that either element dominates when they are so inextricably fused in all man is and does? He lives for himself and he lives for the causes that are dear to him . . . The manifestations of common interest are of special significance for the sociologist because they throw light on that essential solidarity

278

which makes men members of any community and which in the last resort holds society together.

(MacIver, 1937: 32)

MacIver here gives expression to a basic presumption of sociological thought. Solidarity is the cement of society, but it is also necessary for cooperation and collective action. Because of this, all associations try to cultivate the common interest, whether an *esprit de corps*, class spirit or nationalism. They do so in various ways, including the use of symbols to express their unity. But common interests also develop spontaneously: like interests breed common interests. In all groups, therefore, there is a mix of egocentric and sociocentric interests, even if the proportion of each varies widely between groups of different sorts and sizes. If there is an element of solidarity even in pure interest groups, there is, conversely, an element of egoism even in the most intimate relation. 'In all our relations with others it is difficult to evade the promptings of the intrusive self-interest' (MacIver, 1917: 101). Because of this intrusive self-interest, there is free riding and a collective action problem. But self-interest is not the only threat to collective action. Because individuals are members of several groups, their loyalties are divided and sometimes conflicting. If the collective action problem consists in achieving unity, free riding is, in many types of organization, a rather trivial problem.

The most difficult collective action problem is in the initial stage of mobilization for support. Contrary to Olson's belief, MacIver does not suggest that groups always act to further their common interest.

> The recognition of an interest which can be promoted by organization is not of itself sufficient to bring an association into being. There are inertias, prejudices, and problems of ways and means still to be overcome. Here is where the service of leadership is most manifest. Usually it is the initiative, enthusiasm, and energy of one or a small number which prepare the ground. The leaders, whether from sheer devotion to the cause or from the sense of incidental advantages to themselves in the form of place and power or prestige or economic gain – usually no doubt from a combination of these motives – accentuate the advantage of organization and seek to establish attitudes in the potential members favorable to its formation . . . The tasks of the leader in the nascent stage are to create or intensify the consciousness of the need for the new organization, or, in other words, the sense of the interest around which it is organized, to instill confidence in themselves and thus in the efficiency of the organization they propose, and to harness this heightened sense of need to the practical necessities of financial or other co-operation on the part of the members. In order to organize an interest, it must first be presented in a certain detachment from others, and then, *in its organized form*, it must be brought into harmony with the complex of interests of the members.
>
> (MacIver, 1937: 253)

Another theory, allegedly guilty of assuming that individuals will always pursue their common interest, is the so-called 'group theory' in political science (Olson, 1965/1971: 125f.). Even worse, this theory is inconsistent, since it couples this belief with the assumption that individuals are selfish. This assumption is presumably part of any concern with economic interest groups, which are, by definition, 'self-interested'. But since they are, they will not join an interest group. The notion of a voluntary interest group is a *contradictio in adjecto*. Olson is wrong again. The political theory of groups, including, most importantly, interest groups, does not rely on the assumption of self-interest.[1]

It is commonly agreed that Arthur F. Bentley and David B. Truman are the most important representatives of the group approach to politics (see, e.g., Weinstein, 1962; Greenstone, 1975). This seems to be Olson's opinion too. But what do they say? Starting with Bentley, there is simply no ground for the accusation of inconsistency, except Olson's own dogmatic belief that interest is necessarily selfish. Bentley, on the contrary, makes no assumption at all about the motives of individuals. He simply observes that there are groups engaged in political activities to further various ends. He calls these goal-directed activities 'interests' and the groups, whose activities they are, 'interest groups' (Bentley, 1908/1967: 211ff.). That is all there is to it. Bentley's concept of 'interest', then, may be criticized for being too empiricist, or behaviourist, but not for implying self-interest. The different interpretation has been suggested by Paul Wilkinson: 'Bentley claims that each group can be defined in terms of its "group interest". He conceives "interest" as the group members' normative commitment to a claim or claims made by the group upon another group' (Wilkinson, 1971: 48). Wilkinson's interpretation has more support (see Bentley, 1908/1967: 258ff.).

David B. Truman's *The Governmental Process* (1951) is commonly held to be the most important book on political group theory. One aim of this work is to remedy the deficiency of Bentley's empiricism by providing a theoretical concept of 'group'. It suffices to identify the sources of Truman's concept to realize that Olson is wrong in this case too. Digging in the literature of anthropology, sociology and social psychology, Truman arrives at an understanding of interest groups fundamentally different from that imputed to him by Olson. He, in fact, addresses the issue of self-interest explicitly, so there is no need to impute anything at all. Or is it because Truman voices serious doubts about the position adopted by Olson? Truman notes that interest groups are often held to be selfish and irresponsible (1951a: 33). But this is not a scientific statement: 'many such political interest groups are from almost any point of view highly altruistic'. Selfishness is part of the meaning of 'pressure group', which belongs to 'the language of political abuse'; an expression of disapproval, rather than a statement of fact (ibid., p. 38). As used by Truman , ' "interest group" refers to any group that, on the basis of one or more shared attitudes, makes certain claims upon other groups in the society for the establishment, maintenance, or enhancement of forms of that are implied by the shared attitudes' (ibid., p. 33). There is no presumption that these shared attitudes are selfish.

Thus, there is no inconsistency in the group theory of politics. But there is an inconsistency in Olson himself. In *The Logic of Collective Action*, he argues that the traditional – including the sociological – theory of groups is based on the assumption of self-interest. This seems to me more like the economic approach; and this is also how Olson, himself, defines 'economics' in a couple of articles written shortly after *The Logic of Collective Action* (see Olson, 1968, 98–102; 1969: 140–145). But it contradicts the characterization he now gives of the sociological approach. In these articles, Olson gives a fairly adequate depiction of sociology as concerned with values, norms, beliefs and attitudes, and their transmission from one generation to the next through socialization (Olson, 1968: 102ff.; 1969: 145ff.). But if this is so, why are these factors missing in Olson's account of the sociological theory of groups and of collective action? May it not be that a commitment to values and beliefs helps explain why people sometimes support organizations and social movements even when narrow self-interest suggests a free ride?

Mancur Olson is wrong also to suggest that the traditional theory makes no distinction between small and large groups. This is plainly wrong. But before I show that it is, I will focus briefly on a sociologist Olson excepts from the charge of neglecting the size of social groups, namely Georg Simmel (Olson, 1965/1971: 21). Simmel is the source of Olson's notion of an 'intermediate' group inserted between those that are 'privileged' and those that are 'latent' (ibid., p. 50).[2] He is also credited with the insight that 'smaller groups could act more decisively and use their resources more effectively than large groups' (ibid., p. 54). Contrary to Olson's argument, however, this is a sociological commonplace, not a sign of exceptional wisdom. But Olson is correct to point out that Simmel took a particular interest in the size of social groups.

More than other sociologists, Simmel made the social group his special concern. Simmel was also virtually alone, among sociologists, in focusing on group size, or the quantitative aspect of groups, *per se*. From the beginning, his analysis of groups was part of a theory of social differentiation and human individuation (Simmel, 1890). In early society, individuals belonged to one, small, group – a family or tribe – and they belonged to it with the whole of their personality. In the course of history both society and the individual became differentiated. In modern society there is a multiplicity of groups and each individual belongs to a plurality of them, but only with part of his/her personality.

The modern condition, then, is characterized by the fact that individuals have many interests and are affiliated to many groups. From this fact follows a first thesis about the effect of group size: *ceteris paribus*, the larger the group, the less interests members of the group have in common. A first corollary:

the larger the group, the more competing interests demand the attention of each member. A second corollary: the larger the group, the less of each member's energy is spent on the pursuit of the common interest. These are purely quantitative determinations, paying no attention to social structure. In real life, it may be that large numbers of people have much in common.

Nevertheless, size does increase the heterogeneity of the group, thereby aggravating the problem of collective action. Simmel is aware of the problem of free riding: 'Almost all sorts of human association, whatever be their specific content and character, have to work to secure the cooperation in social unity of parts that persist in following a certain egoistic impulse' (Simmel, 1898: 677). But egoism is not the main problem. Much more important is the inevitable unanimity of large groups, together with the division of loyalty and energy of their members. No individual can be an active participant in many groups. But because individuals are different, it may be that at least some individuals are prepared to take a more active part, while the rest remain passive. The activists may engage because of devotion to the cause, or because of the intrinsic rewards of participation and/or leadership. In the later development of a group, there is often the additional, egoistic, possibility of living *off*, rather than *for*, the group.

Heterogeneity, then, is the main problem with large groups. But heterogeneity is not a function of size alone. It is also a function of lack of interaction between members and the consequent lack of social control. Interaction is, of course, related to size, but the relation is not simple. Thus, groups with the same size may differ widely with respect to the amount of interaction going on between members. It is true, though, that small groups are definitely 'privileged' when it comes to developing that homogeneity, cohesion and social control which, according to Mancur Olson, is a precondition for voluntary pursuit of a common interest.

Large groups, in order to persist, have to compensate for their lack of homogeneity and informal social control. They do so primarily by the institution of an organization and by leadership (Simmel: 1898: 683ff.; [1908] 1950: 170ff.; [1908] 1971: 280f.; [1908] 1955: 88ff.). This is the view, not only of Simmel, but of most sociologists. It is also the view of Mancur Olson, but with an important difference: while the latter see only self-interest at work in this arrangement, sociologists see something else. According to Simmel ([1922] 1955: 133ff., 143, 177ff.), solidarity is also at work in larger groups. Important means by which a collective identity is maintained in large groups are the use of symbols expressing unity, such as flags, monuments and the like (1898: 675), and a code of honour attached to membership of the group (ibid., pp. 681f.; [1922] 1955: 163–166). Another important device is to divide a large group, or organization, into sub-units; in earlier times often with a exact number, such as 10 or 100, in each subgroup. The obvious advantage with this organizational structure is the stronger solidarity and ease of surveillance in the smaller group (Simmel, [1908] 1950: 110, 170–177).

An important theme, usually absent from the economic analysis of collective action, is conflict. For Simmel ([1908] 1955) society is not just a multiplicity of groups, but of groups in conflict. And this is important for an understanding of collective action. Groups, especially interest groups, often emerge and survive only because of conflict with other groups (ibid., ch. III). The simple reason for this is that interests are often conflicting, and conflict has the well-known effect of simultaneously increasing in-group cohesion and out-group hostility. Before a common enemy, even the most heterogeneous group may unite. Conflict has the further consequence of reinforcing the tendency towards centralization. This is so because conflict requires mobilization and no large group, not even the army, can be constantly mobilized, at least not at the high level necessitated by open conflict.

Another sociologist credited with a certain insight into the problem of size is George C. Homans. But praise is mixed with blame. Homans is wrong to assume that findings about small groups can be applied to large groups. 'The "privileged" group, and for that matter the "intermediate" group, are simply in a more advantageous position' (Olson 1965/1971: 57). To the extent that Olson's argument is about size, he is definitely wrong. One important argument in Homans' *The Human Group* (1951) is that the small group is in an advantageous position. But, of course, this does not imply that findings about small groups tell us nothing about large groups. 'We have been focusing on the small group, but much that we say can also be applied to larger social units' (Homans, 1951: 426). Homan's analysis of groups is in terms of a limited set of variables, including, most importantly, activity, interaction and sentiment. A main hypothesis is that the sentiments necessary for the survival of a group, its morale, are a function of the activity and interaction of its members. And, of course, interaction depends upon size (ibid., pp. 184, 446), as does social control: 'We have seen that in the small group, control over persons that threaten to depart from the norms of the group is often exceedingly effective but is not imposed from without' (ibid., p. 462). In the large group more depends upon leadership, at the same time as the distance between leaders and followers increases and makes morale and social control more difficult (ibid., pp. 103f., 184, 461ff.).

To the extent that Olson's argument against Homans is about size, then, it is wrong. If we are to believe some of Olson's critics (see, e.g., Frohlich and Oppenheimer, 1970), it would seem that Homans is the more correct: interaction, solidarity and social control are what make small groups superior in solving collective action problems, not size itself. But Olson argues also in terms of 'privileged', 'intermediate' and 'latent' groups, and, despite his confusing use of these terms, they do not properly refer to groups of different size. This goes especially for privileged groups, which, as Hardin and others have shown (see p. 224–230), are not necessarily small. 'A "privileged" group is a group such that each of its members, or at least some of them, has an incentive to see that the collective good is provided, even if he has to bear the full burden of providing it himself' (Olson, 1965/1971: 49f.). Privileged groups exemplify the game of chicken, or a straddle ranking, rather than a prisoners' dilemma. Because of this, we should expect them to be advantaged in overcoming the collective action problem. But they are not free from the problem. Also in privileged groups, there is a temptation to free ride on the contributions of others.

Homans had no access to the notion of a 'privileged' group. No one did before Olson. Maybe it takes an economist to see its importance, which relies heavily on the assumption of self-interest. For a sociologist, a privileged group would simply be one where at least one of its members is motivated enough to organize collective action. Not a very interesting statement. But Homans' *The Human Group* includes something else of interest for our understanding of collective action: an extensive analysis of the famous studies of the Western Electric Company's Hawthorne Works in Chicago, 1927–1932 (Homans, 1951, ch. III).[3] One of the most interesting findings of this research concerned the existence of a norm restricting output well below the capacity of the workers.[4] The method of payment was piece wages, determined for each worker on the basis of a mix of individual and group output. Piece wages are always a collective good, because the rate setting payment per piece is collective. But in this case jointness was enhanced by the element of group piece work. Restriction of output is a norm against free riding or, rather, foul dealing (see p. 220). It tells the workers in the group not to produce 'too much' or 'too little' but to do 'a fair day's work for a fair day's wage'. A worker who worked too fast, relative to the norm of output, was called 'rate-buster', or 'speed-king'. Workers turning out too little were called 'chiselers'. The penalties for failure to comply with the norm were 'merciless ridicule' and ostracism. A rate-buster is a foul dealer, because he shows management the possibility of producing well above the norm. This knowledge may result in various attempts to lower piece wages, so that workers will all end up working harder for equal pay. A chiseler is a foul dealer, because of his small contribution to group piece work.

The norm putting a restriction on output, then, is a solution to a collective action problem. Those who violate the norm are punished, but punishment is only a complement. The main support of the norm are the sentiments of friendliness and solidarity, expressed above all by actions of mutual help, that develops in a work group, and which makes workers restrict their output voluntarily.

> Friendship between wiremen is an example. While sentiments of self-interest affected or influenced the behavior of the men in the room, they did not solely determine that behavior. If these sentiments had been alone decisive, output would perhaps have been higher. That both self-interest *and* something else are satisfied by group life is the truth that is hardest for the hard-boiled – and half-baked – person to see. As

Mayo says, 'If a number of individuals work together to achieve a common purpose, a harmony of interests will develop among them to which individual self-interest will be subordinated.' This is a very different doctrine from the claim that individual self-interest is the solitary human motive.

(Homans, 1951: 96)

But if Olson is wrong about Homans, there is still the possibility that he is correct about the rest of sociologists, or at least about those who have contributed to the traditional theory of groups. Perhaps they fail to see any difference between small and large groups? I maintain that Olson is wrong again. Olson's charge is false with respect to the vast majority of sociologists, several of whom – e.g. Cooley, Durkheim, MacIver, Parsons – Olson mentions in his book. Sociologists typically make the distinction between community and association (see pp. 338ff.), which is not directly in terms of size, but which is definitely and importantly related to it. The distinction between community and association focuses on something that is even more important than size, but a function of it: interaction. Durkheim makes a similar distinction between 'mechanical' and 'organic' solidarity, and so does the American sociologist Charles Horton Cooley. In his terminology, we have 'primary' and, by implication, secondary groups; the former being characterized by 'intimate face-to-face association and cooperation', a common life and purpose, and a mutual identification as a *we* (Cooley, 1909/1962: 23). It is basic to the argument that the cohesiveness, or 'mechanical solidarity', of primary groups and communities is a function of their limited size and diminishes with the increasing size of the group. According to Cooley, the characteristic form of modern organization is the 'nucleated group'. It is a group.

composed of a large number of members who put very little of themselves into it, along with a few, or perhaps only one, who enlist the main part of their personality. This gives a happy union of breath and concentration, and if one will reflect upon the association to which he belongs he will find, I imagine, that nearly all are conducted in this way.

(Cooley, 1918/ 1966: 252)

Robert MacIver is no less clear on this point. He makes the distinction between the primary group and large-scale association (MacIver, 1937: ch. 12), and maintains that 'effective participation is possible only for quite limited numbers' (ibid., p. 238). 'Direct co-operation is as characteristic of the face-to-face group as specialization is of the large-scale association (ibid., p. 240). In the latter, the common interest is necessarily pursued by a special administrative mechanism, while the lay members take on a more passive role. An important organizational device for bridging the gap between leaders and led in large-scale association is the federative principle (MacIver, 1917: 284; 1937: 247ff.). Another principle is that of agency, implying that the officials, or representatives, of the organization are responsible before its members. Because of these important differences, large-scale associations cannot function as substitutes for primary groups (MacIver, 1937: 251).

The sociological approach, then, has no difficulty with Olson's thesis that larger groups are disadvantaged with respect to collective action. They are, because, other things being equal, larger groups have more difficulty developing a common interest, a strong group solidarity and collective identity, and also more difficulty with the coordination and social control of the activity of their members. These problems are solved by institutionalization. Most of the institutional solutions to collective action problems that you find in the economic approach, can already be found in the sociological theory of groups. The main difference remains: sociology never adopted the assumption of self-interest.[5] But since it is nowadays generally agreed that self-interest cannot explain all collective action, this is not a disadvantage.

Even though ultimately wrong, I believe that a stronger case can be made for the economic theory of collective action by incorporating part of the sociological and political theory of groups. The economic approach tends to separate the analysis of collective action from that of interest groups. The first is about egoistic individuals seeking their common interest. The second is about, already constituted, interest groups seeking rents. The sociological theory of groups, by contrast, assumes that much collective action is part of a competitive, or antagonistic, struggle between groups. If so, the analysis of collective action should not be separated from that of the conflict between interests.

Following the group approach to politics, if only for the sake of argument, we could conceive of politics as the result of a plurality of group interests. Most of the time, the system of group-interests is in a state of unstable equilibrium. Organized interest groups emerge in response to disruptive changes in the social system and, later, in response to other organized interests. The main function of economic interest groups is to protect members against negative consequences of social change and to defend the group against other groups, thereby maintaining the balance of the system (Truman, 1951a: ch. IV). I make no presumption that this 'equilibrium' is a democratic representation of interests in society. It is obvious, to me at least, that it is not. I am also unable to reconcile with the absence of the state in the group theory of politics and remain sceptical about the idea of a social system in *equilibrium*.

The hypothesis, suggested to me, is that people support large economic interest groups, not so much because of any particular benefit they expect to derive from their contribution, but because they are afraid of what would happen if the interest group were not there to look after their common interest. People do know that economic interest groups are important determinants of policy. We know that people are risk averse. Maybe they are more than willing to pay their membership fees simply to have an organization working to maintain the status quo; to defend their interest relative to other interests. Perhaps people are afraid that their relative position would weaken and their share of the pie diminish if they did not support their economic interest group(s).

This argument is analogous to that used by Ferejohn and Fiorina to explain voting (see pp. 88f). I suggest, however, that it possesses a much higher *prima facie* plausibility in the case of interest groups. The argument is also economic, since it rests on the assumption of self-interest. As such it does not solve the 'paradox' of collective action. This paradox cannot be solved, only dissolved. You have to change the premises. But if you do, the hypothesis suggested may give a hint of an explanation of the contribution of some people to some interest groups. Olson's main argument, his logic – as distinct from the rest of his analysis – suffers from excessive individualism. It takes no account of interaction, institutions, or the political system in which interest groups are implicated. Previous arguments against Olson have introduced interaction as a decisive element. My argument shifts the attention from individuals and their relations to groups and their relations to other groups. In this way, another game-like situation is created (cf. Johnson, 1988: 213ff.), in which the original collective action problem is mereologically implicated in a game played by group-interests. This situation may be captured by the payoff matrix shown in Figure 6.1.

The payoffs in the matrix in the upper-left cell make up the prisoners' dilemma of the original collective action problem. The payoffs in the larger matrix represent the group-benefits from organizing a group-interest in the face of other group-interests. According to public choice, this game is another prisoners' dilemma (Group-interest I rank outcomes in the following order: $Y > W > X > Z$). To organize for collective action is a dominant strategy. To free ride on the contributions of others is still the best strategy for the individual. It makes a difference, however, to be implicated in a game of group-interests where failure to organize is not just failure to provide a collective good, but leads to a disadvantaged position relative to other interests in the struggle for power and for scarce resources. It is reasonable to assume that people will be more risk-averse in the latter situation than in an ordinary collective action problem.

I have already indicated an important difference between economists, on the one hand, and sociologists and political scientists, on the other. The latter tend to be more favourably disposed towards interest groups. According to public choice, the group-interest game is a negative-sum game. A society without interest groups is better than a society with rent-seeking interest groups engaged in unproductive fighting for their share of the social product ($W > X$). According to the sociological and political theory of groups, it is the

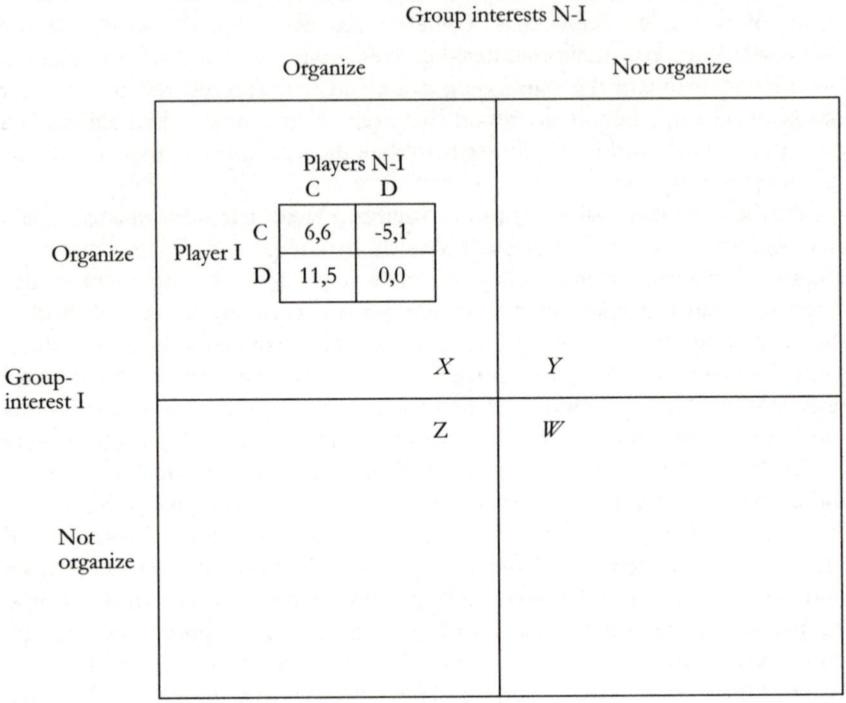

Group interests N-I

	Organize		Not organize

Players N-I

		C	D
Player I	C	6,6	-5,1
	D	11,5	0,0

Organize

Group-interest I

	X	Y
	Z	W

Not organize

Figure 6.1 The group-interest game.

other way round. A society with many groups, including interest groups, is better than a society without groups. The group-game is a positive-sum game $(X > W)$. More specifically, it is a game of deadlock (Group-interest I rank outcomes as follows: $Y > X > W > Z$). Several arguments support this view.[6] A first argument is that interest groups contribute to social integration by mediating between primary groups and the state.[7] A second argument is that interest groups contribute to representative liberal democracy (pluralism). A third argument is that interest groups contribute to civil peace and, therefore, to economic prosperity (corporatism).

The sociological concept of 'group' was originally a bit too inclusive. Groups were of all sizes and, usually, both latent and manifest. In the later development of sociological theory, 'groups' diminished in size until finally the term was reserved for small numbers of people interacting frequently with one another. As a consequence, groups became a concern mainly for social psychologists. Large, manifest, groups have become organizations, while latent groups are sometimes called 'collectives'. With this terminology, the problem of collective action becomes how to turn a collective into an organization, an interest group, a party, or a social movement.

288

COLLECTIVE BEHAVIOUR

Mainstream sociology did not possess a 'theory of collective action' until the assimilation of Marxism in the 1960s and 1970s. Instead, we find something called 'mass behaviour', or 'collective behaviour'. But this is entirely different, as we shall see. Before I turn to the sociological theory of collective action, I will touch briefly upon the subject of collective behaviour.

Virtually all early sociologists and psychologists were fascinated and preoccupied by a phenomenon they called 'mass behaviour'. And they were not alone. Writers and philosophers too took an interest in this subject, sometimes to a degree not far from obsession.[8] The sociological classic in this genre is Gustave Le Bon's *The Crowd* (1895/1960). According to him, in 1895 we were entering the 'era of crowds' – and this is not surprising, since, for Le Bon (ibid., Book III), not only every assembly of men and women, but every conceivable collective, is a crowd. The behaviour of crowds is typically irrational: it is not based on any calculation of benefits and costs, but largely is unconscious.[9] It is not self-interested: 'Personal interest is very rarely a powerful motive force with crowds, while it is almost the exclusive motive of conduct of the isolated individual' (ibid., p. 58). The crowd is not guided by social norms, but usually violates them. The revolutionary crowd always contains a crucial element 'recruited from the lowest dregs of the populace', 'a subversive social residue dominated by a criminal mentality' (Le Bon, [1912] 1979: 243). It is typically spontaneous and irresponsible and in the grip of some unscrupulous leader. 'A crowd is a flock that is incapable of ever doing without a master' (Le Bon, 1895/1960: 118). It is sometimes truly motivated by morality, but in most cases not at all, except, perhaps, as a rationalization. Above all, the crowd is in all respects, except power, inferior to the isolated individual.

Gabriel Tarde – another French sociologist and a friend of Le Bon – agreed with Le Bon in his estimation of the crowd, but made the useful division of masses into crowds and publics (Tarde [1901] 1969: ch. 16). While it is characteristic of crowds to exist in physical proximity, publics may be dispersed – and increasingly are in an age dominated by mass media. Le Bon's and Tarde's ideas were brought to America by Robert E. Park, but received their final, and most elaborated, form in the work of his pupil Herbert Blumer. In his hands, the theory of the crowd, or of mass behaviour, turned into a theory of 'collective behavior' (Blumer, 1946, 1957). Examples of collective behaviour are phenomena such as crowds, mobs, panics, festivals, carnivals, public opinion, propaganda, fashion, fads, revolts, rebellions, riots, revolutions, and social movements. 'Collective behaviour', in this sense, is really a heterogeneous category, but a common characteristic is an element of spontaneity and strong emotion: fear, hostility or joy. Blumer follows the early sociologists in conceiving of collective behaviour as essentially irrational. Its primary precondition is a state of social unrest. When this condition is satisfied, collective behaviour may occur as a result of three mechanisms, or stages: milling, collective excitement and social contagion. Blumer is not satisfied with Tarde's two types of masses. There are four forms of collective groupings: (1) the active crowd, (2) the expressive crowd, (3) the mass and (4) the public. I jump over these finer distinctions and turn to the real novelty: the addition of social movements as a development beyond elementary collective behaviour. Social movements are collective attempts to change the existing social order. As such, they involve a change in people's values. In addition to the three stages of elementary collective behaviour, Blumer recognizes five mechanisms, or stages of social movements: (1) agitation, (2) development of *esprit de corps*, (3) development of morale, (4) formation of ideology and (5) development of operating tactics. It is possible to see in this sequence of stages a development from emotion to cognition, or from irrational behaviour to rational action.

After Blumer, collective behaviour is no longer seen as typically irrational and disorderly.[10] Turner and Killian (1957/1972; Turner, 1964a, 1964b), for instance, argue that much collective behaviour displays a surprising degree of coordination and leads to the emergence of norms specific to the situation in which it takes place. Neil Smelser's *Theory of Collective Behavior* (1962) marks a major advance in the sociological understanding of the subject. In this work, increasing attention is paid to social movements. In the process, 'collective behaviour' is redefined as '*mobilization on the basis of a belief which redefines social action*' (Smelser, 1962: 8). After the redirection initiated by Turner, Killian and Smelser, social movements, public opinon and mass communication turned into subjects of their own, distinct from (elementary) collective behaviour.[11]

The early theories of the crowd and of collective behaviour have been subjected to devastating criticism on both empirical and ideological grounds. In its original form, the theory belongs definitely in the history of ideas, together with some other doubtful results of armchair theorizing. The amazing thing is that it dominated the scene for so long. Early critics, among sociologists, were Turner and Killian and Smelser; later also Berk (1974), who advocated a game-theoretic approach to collective behaviour.

Another early critic was the historian George Rudé (1964), who studied the politically active crowd in pre-industrial society 1730–1848.[12] Even though limited in its scope to the prototype of crowd behaviour, Rudé's investigation leads to a modified picture of the crowd. The pre-industrial crowd did not consist of a bunch of criminals, but of ordinary citizens from the lower classes. The crowd was violent, to be sure, but, with few exceptions, attacked property rather than people. It was not misled by unscrupulous leaders, but often acted on its own. Above all, the crowd was not particularly irrational.

> In short, the crowd was violent, impulsive easily stirred by rumor, and quick to panic; but it was not fickle, peculiarly irrational, or generally given to attacks on persons. The conventional picture of the crowd

290

painted by Le Bon and inherited by later writers is not lacking in shrewd and imaginative insight; but it ignores the facts of history and is, in consequence, overdrawn, tendentious, and misleading.

(Rudé, 1964: 257)

Of some relevance, in this connection, is that Rudé, like Le Bon, rejects the hypothesis of pocketbook motivation. Of course many riots, e.g. food riots, were motivated by immediate economic gain, but equally often the behaviour of the pre-industrial crowd is only comprehensible in terms of generalized beliefs about justice and the rights of man (ibid., ch. 14).

Rudé's view has been confirmed by later historical research, including that of E.P. Thompson (1971: 76ff., 107–115, 136) and Charles Tilly (1975b: 506ff.; 1978: 227; 1981a, 1981c; Shorter and Tilly, 1974: 336ff.; Tilly et al., 1975: 248ff., 280–300). Both deny that crowd behaviour is typically irrational, but they also deny that it is motivated solely by economic rationality. The following quotation, from Thompson, is interesting because it reverses the public choice argument against operating with different motivational assumptions:

> Too many of our growth historians are guilty of a crass economic reductionism, obliterating the complexities of motive, behaviour, and function, which, if they noted it in the work of their Marxist analogues, would make them protest. The weakness which these explanations share is an abbreviated view of economic man. What is perhaps an occasion for surprise is the schizoid intellectual climate, which permits this quantitative historiography to co-exist (in the same places and sometimes in the same minds) with a social anthropology which derives from Durkheim, Weber, or Malinowski. We know all about the delicate tissue of social norms and reciprocities which regulates life of Trobriand islanders, and the psychic energies involved in the cargo cults of Melanesia; but at some point this infinitely-complex social creature, Melanesian Man, becomes (in our histories) the eighteenth-century English collier who claps his hand spasmodically upon his stomach, and responds to elementary economic stimuli.

(Thompson, 1971: 78)

Thompson's argument is that the food riots in eighteenth-century England were motivated, not only by prospects of immediate economic gain, but by the 'moral economy' of pre-capitalist society. According to this paternalistic morality, producers of bread had an obligation to provide the local poor with their staple food, irrespective of the laws of the market. If farmers, millers and bakers failed to do their duty, the people had the right to seize grain, flour and bread by force and pay a price set by themselves.

A good critical discussion of the sociological theories of the crowd and of collective behaviour can be found in Clark McPhail (1991). One of his points is, exactly, that we should make a clear distinction between crowds and collective behaviour, simply because crowds, or gatherings, only occasionally engage in collective behaviour (ibid., ch. 5). Most behaviour in social gatherings is individual behaviour. An important failure of the early theory of collective behaviour was that it neglected to specify the phenomenon to be investigated; but under any specification, empirical evidence makes clear that the various types of violent behaviour conceived as typical are, in fact, rare. The thesis that the crowd is invariably irrational cannot be sustained. Collective behaviour is, at least in procedural terms, usually more rational than institutionalized behaviour. It is true that emotions are an important part of much collective behaviour, but emotion does not exclude cognition.

The sociological theories of the crowd and of mass society have also been attacked on ideological grounds, and justifiably so. In many cases, contributions to these theories reveal, above all, a reactionary combination of contempt for, and fear of, the people. Gustave Le Bon is a case in point. His writings are studded with the most unabashed manifestations of elitism and class prejudice. He was also a fierce critic, not only of socialism, but also of democracy, because it engenders equality and, in the end, socialism.[13]

As I have already pointed out, Le Bon was an important precursor of Joseph Schumpeter and, consequently, of public choice. At a general level, there is the curious asymmetry in simultaneously assuming a maximum of rational deliberation on the part of leaders and a minimum, or none at all, on the part of their followers, which is typical of the economic theory of democracy. But there is a much more specific continuity, as revealed by the following quotation, giving a summary statement of the argument in Buchanan and Wagner, *Democracy in Deficit* (1977):

> Should a member of an assembly propose a measure giving apparent satisfaction to democratic ideas, should he bring in a Bill, for instance, to assure old-age pensions to all workers, and to increase the wages of any class of state employees, the other Deputies, victims of suggestion in their dread of the electors, will not venture to seem to disregard the interests of the latter by rejecting the proposed measure, although well aware that they are imposing a fresh strain on the Budget and necessitating the creation of new taxes. It is impossible for them to hesitate to give their votes. The consequences of the increase of expenditure are remote and will not entail disagreeable consequences for them personally, while the consequences of a negative vote might clearly come to light when they next present themselves for re-election.
>
> (Le Bon, 1895/1960: 201)

There is one important difference, however. While inconsistent on this point, as on most points, Le Bon did not believe that people are motivated solely by self-interest, especially not as part of crowds. People are motivated by ideas, by dreams and hopes, and for these ideas they readily sacrifice their own interest:

> Let us remember ... that in spite of all appearances, it is not interest, powerful though it be in individuals, that leads the crowd. The crowd must have an ideal, a belief, and before it becomes impassioned by its ideal or belief, it must become impassioned by its apostles.
>
> (Le Bon [1898] 1979: 144)

Lest there should be any misunderstanding on this point, Le Bon's 'idealism' is not indicative of anything like a positive view of human nature. Le Bon is one of the most consistent misanthropes in the history of ideas. His insistence upon the importance of ideas as a motive force in history, comes to the fore mainly when he polemicizes with Marx, which is most of the time. The causally most efficacious ideal in the age of democracy is equality, but there is nothing to admire in the motives behind it:

> One of the chief results has been a general hatred of superiority. This hatred of whatever surpasses the average in social fortune or intelligence is today general in all classes, from the working class to the upper strata of the bourgeoisie. The results are envy, detraction, a love of attack, of scornful wit, of persecution, and a habit of attributing all actions to low motives, of refusal to believe in probity, disinterestedness and intelligence.
>
> (Le Bon, [1912] 1979: 254)

Despite all this justified critique, I believe that there is something important in the related ideas of mass behaviour and mass society that should not be dismissed out of hand (cf. Moscovici, 1985). First of all, the crowd, or mass, must have been a novel experience to many of those who, as a result of the industrial revolution, left their rural communities to lead a more anonymous life in the cities. This process was part of that great transformation of traditional into modern society, which was a major concern of all early sociologists. Second, the development of modern mass media has created new masses, in the form of publics, and new means of persuasion, unparalleled in the earlier history of society. Third, even if the most repugnant forms of mass behaviour are rare, their importance cannot be exaggerated. The theories of Le Bon and his followers may have been seriously deficient – Le Bon, himself, is a curious mixture of inconsistency, prejudice *and* insight – but they pointed to phenomena that show an uncanny tendency to reappear in modern society: the all too well-known horrors of Fascist, Nazi, communist and theocratic regimes.

One should not, however, see the above three points as steps in an argument. The once popular thesis – advanced most succinctly by William Kornhauser (1960) – that the social base of authoritarian mass movements is to be found among the most alienated, or isolated, elements of society, has been proved wrong. Supporters of extremist mass movements are usually well integrated in society, if not in the political system, but they often belong to declining social groups, representing the *ancien régime* in times of change (see, e.g., Gusfield, 1962; Obershall, 1973: 108–113; Birnbaum, 1988: 36–42).

'Collective behaviour', then – as conceptualized by sociologists and social psychologists until quite recently – is something utterly different from 'collective action'. It is characterized, not by the rational pursuit of some common good, but by the irrational behaviour of individuals when in a mass of people. Collective behaviour is the result of 'suggestion' and 'contagion', not of rational deliberation. The difference is clearly seen in one particular case of collective behaviour: the escape panic. What sociologists and social psychologists call 'collective behaviour' is, in this case, the failure to achieve 'collective action' in the sense of cooperation. An often cited example is the panic that breaks out in a public hall, say a theatre, in the case of a fire. When all rush to the exits, they will soon be blocked and people may be killed, both by the crowd and by the fire. The collective action problem involved has been conceived of as a prisoners' dilemma, where the optimal solution is how to achieve an orderly departure so that all, or at least some, might be saved (Brown, 1965: 738–743). The escape situation differs from an ordinary prisoners' dilemma in that the actions of each individual are consequential upon the actions of the others and also in that there is the possibility, if limited, of communication (see Coleman, 1990b: 203ff.). An important snag is uncertainty. Will cooperation save all, or only some? And if only some, which ones? This is an impossible problem of distribution and there is little time for bargaining. The cause of panic is, of course, that the stakes are terribly high. When it is a matter of life and death, cooperation might be expected to be difficult. 'Collective behaviour' may make 'collective action' impossible. But this is an empirical question and evidence suggests that panic is not at all a general response to life-threatening entrapment dilemmas (McPhail, 1991: 102).

In many cases, however, there is an interaction between collective behaviour and collective action (cf. Rule, 1989: 153ff.). Both hostile and expressive collective behaviour often accompany collective action, to which I now turn.

One of the most ambitious attempts to create a *Theory of Collective Behavior* was made by Neil J. Smelser in 1962. Written in the tradition of Parsonian 'grand theory', Smelser's book is, of course, much too complex even to try to recapitulate in a few sentences. The easiest way out is to cite his suggested explanation. Collective behaviour is the result of the following determinants, which together constitute the so-called 'value-added scheme': (1) structural conduciveness, (2) structural strain, (3) growth and spread of a generalized belief, (4) precipitating factors, (5) mobilization of participants for action and (6) the operation of social control (Smelser, 1962: 12–21). Without further explication, this enumeration, unfortunately, says very little. There are those who maintain that even with the further explication of Smelser, himself, the value-added scheme still does not say very much, at least not in the form of explanation. Nevertheless, Smelser claims that, together, these determinants make up the necessary and sufficient conditions for collective behaviour to take place. But that is not all. Being a value-added process, these conditions must appear in the sequential order suggested by the scheme. The main problem with Smelser's theory is that it is hard to imagine anything that would refute it (even though some have tried). For this reason, it is perhaps better to think of his scheme as a frame of analysis rather than as an explanation. Given the explanatory record of social science, I do not consider this a serious objection. And Smelser certainly deserves credit for analysing collective behaviour as a form of social action, involving values, norms, motives and resources (ibid., ch. 2).[14]

Another account of collective behaviour, written by a political scientist but falling squarely within the sociological tradition, is *Why Men Rebel* (1970), by Ted Robert Gurr. The subject matter of this book is collective violence, not collective action, generally; or even collective behaviour. Gurr's analysis is interesting in this connection, mainly because it relies on an important sociological idea signified by the term 'relative deprivation'. Put simply, the idea is that people assess their own situation, not in absolute terms, but relative to other people and, especially, to those belonging to their so-called 'reference group'; another sociological idea of some importance.[15] Obviously, the notion of 'relative deprivation' is best at home in a theory of social stratification as 'social status', still another relative notion. For the economist, it might be of some help to think of 'positional goods' (Hirsch). Status is a positional good and relative deprivation lack of it. Our reference group is the pond we choose as ours (Frank, 1985).

The big idea of Gurr is that collective violence is a function of 'relative deprivation', defined as 'actors' perception of the discrepancy between their value expectations and their value capabilities' (Gurr, 1970: 24). Relative deprivation may develop in any one of three ways: (1) because expectations rise, while capabilities remain constant, (2) because capabilities sink, while expectations remain constant, or (3) because expectations rise and capabilities sink at the same time (ibid., pp. 46–56). Gurr assigns special importance to the second pattern: 'Men are likely to be more intensely angered when they lose what they have than when they lose hope of attaining what they do not yet have' (ibid., p. 50). More specifically, this implies that one one should expect relatively more violence from groups that are on the decline. The third pattern coincides with James Davies' so-called 'J-curve' hypothesis, according to which 'Revolutions are most likely to occur when a prolonged period of objective economic and social development is followed by a short period of sharp reversal' (Davies, 1962: 6).

The psychological underpinning of Gurr's theory is the well-known frustration-aggression hypothesis, advanced by Miller and Dollard (1941: chs XIV–XV) to explain collective, or crowd, behaviour. Collective violence is a form of aggression caused by frustrated expectations. But frustration does not always lead to collective violence and only occasionally to political violence. A number of social conditions intervene in the process of turning relative deprivation into rebellion. There must be some normative and utilitarian justification and institutional support for rebellion, and a balance of power that makes it possible. As with Smelser, we are confronted with a model which is rather too complex to survey at a glance. I believe it is fair to say, though, that the main explanatory burden of Gurr's argument lies on relative deprivation.

What is the relevance of Smelser's and Gurr's analyses for the problem of collective action? There is no short answer to this question. Both conceive of collective behaviour as being, more or less, rational. In the case of aggressive behaviour, the element of utilitarian calculation of benefits and costs may, of course, sometimes be rather slight, but it is rarely altogether absent (Smelser, 1962: 1–12, 23ff.; Gurr, 1970: 210ff., 259f.). To the extent that collective behaviour is rational, there is the possibility of a collective action problem. But there is no paradox, or dilemma, in the sense of the economic theory of collective action. Neither Smelser (1962: ch. II, 270ff., 313ff.), nor Gurr (1970: 24–26, 68–71), assumes that self-interest is paramount, especially not Smelser. Collective behaviour is motivated by a belief in values and norms, many of which lack a clear connection to self-interest: democracy, equality, free enterprise, national autonomy, universal suffrage and many other things. To the extent that collective behaviour is governed by normative considerations, collective behaviour is not even utilitarian (cf. Gurr, 1970: ch. 6).

COLLECTIVE ACTION

The sociological theory of collective action starts with Karl Marx: 'The history of all hitherto existing society is the history of class struggles.' This is the opening sentence of Marx and Engels' *The Communist Manifesto* (1848/1967: 67) and it implies that collective action is, indeed, possible. How is it possible? Did Marx believe that a class of rational egoists will always act in their common interest? Mancur Olson, for one, believes that he did. And this was his big mistake.

> *For class-oriented action will not occur if the individuals that make up a class act rationally* . . . So the *rational* thing for a member of the bourgeoisie to do is to ignore his *class* interests and to spend his energies on his *personal* interests. Similarly, a worker who thought he would benefit from a 'proletarian' government would not find it rational to risk his life and resources to start a revolution against the bourgeois government . . . The crux of the matter, then, is that Marx's theory of social class is inconsistent insofar as it assumes the rational, selfish pursuit of individual interests.
>
> (Olson, 1965/1971: 105–108)

296

But did Marx assume that self-interest is the overriding motive? Olson is not absolutely certain. It may be that Marx admitted the existence of irrationality and of emotions. But evidence tends to suggest that 'Marx was offering a theory based on rational, utilitarian individual behavior' (ibid., p. 109).

Olson is not alone in interpreting Marx as a rationalist and utilitarian of sorts.[16] And maybe he was. The concept of 'interest' is of paramount importance for his class analysis, and material interest is a mighty force, according to historical materialism. But is it almighty? Reading Marx's concrete class analysis in *The Bourgeoisie and the Counter-Revolution* (Marx [1848] 1973a), *The Class Struggles in France: 1848 to 1850* (Marx [1850] 1973b) and *The Eighteenth Brumaire of Louis Bonaparte* (Marx [1852] 1973b) might certainly give this impression. Were it not for Marx's consistent use of a collectivist, instead of an individualist, methodology, these writings would appear as early contributions to public choice. Political man is depicted as an egoist engaged in what has later been called 'rent-seeking', or 'DUP activities'. The bureaucracy, in particular, is interested in an expansion of the public sector, while politicians try to buy the support of the masses. Since taxes are definitely not popular, the state finances its activity by borrowing from the financial aristocracy, thus creating an unhealthy state deficit (Marx, 1973b: 36ff., 186, 191, 243). Marx is also aware of the existence of a fiscal illusion. Like Buchanan, he recommends direct taxation on the following ground:

> Because indirect taxes conceal from an individual what he is paying to the state, whereas a direct tax is undisguised, unsophisticated, and not to be misunderstood by the meanest capacity. Direct taxation prompts therefore every individual to control the governing powers while direct taxation destroys all tendency to self-government.
>
> (Marx, *The Civil War in France* [1871] 1974: 92)

But here similarities end. Unlike public choice, Marx does not conceive of self-interest as a constant of human nature. The amount of egoism varies with social structure. It reaches unprecedented heights in bourgeois society and is strongest in the bourgeoisie itself. This theme, of unmistakable romantic origin, is most pronounced in Marx's early writings (see, e.g., *On the Jewish Question* [1843] 1974: 229–234; *Economic and Philosophical Manuscripts* [1844] 1974: 352, 373f.). It reaches its clearest expression in *The Manifesto of the Communist Party* (Marx and Engels [1948] 1967: 82): 'The bourgeoisie . . . has left remaining no other nexus between man and man than naked self-interest, than callous "cash payment"'. It has drowned feudal society 'in the icy water of egotistical relations'. The thesis of bourgeois, or capitalist, egoism became the received view of classical sociology. It recurs in Toennies' notion of 'society' (*Gesellschaft*), in Durkheim's concept of 'organic solidarity', in Weber's thesis of rationalization and in Simmel's *Philosophy of Money* (1900/1978: 437ff.).

The egoism of bourgeois society does not affect the working class to the same degree. Unlike the bourgeoisie, it is capable of acts of heroism and self-sacrifice. Marx, of course, has a tendency to exaggerate this difference, but he does not go as far as to deny that the bourgeoisie is incapable of collective action, or that the working class does not have a collective action problem. Both classes have a problem with competition between their own members.

The Marxist problem of collective action is often stated as that of turning a class-*in*-itself into a class-*for*-itself; a class organized for collective action (see, e.g., Calhoun, 1988: 134).[17] This distinction is equivalent to Olson's distinction between latent and manifest groups. A precondition for class formation is the development of class consciousness in the members of a class. Following Elster, we may define 'class consciousness as *the ability to overcome the free-rider problem in realizing class interests*' (Elster, 1985a: 347; cf. Shaw, 1984: 28). The issue then becomes whether class consciousness implicates something more than an awareness of a common interest on the part of a class of rational egoists. I believe that it does (cf. Barry, 1970/1978: 36; Elster, 1985a: 347; Shaw, 1984; Sabia, 1988).

> Large-scale industry concentrates in one place a crowd of people un-known to one another. Competition divides their interests. But the maintenance of wages, this common interest which they have against their boss, unites them in a common thought of resistance – *combination*. Thus combination always has a double aim, that of stopping competi-tion amomg the workers, so that they can carry on general competition with the capitalist. If the first aim of resistance was merely the mainten-ance of wages, combinations, at first isolated, constitute themselves into groups as the capitalists in their turn unite for the purpose of repres-sion, and in face of always united capital, the maintenance of the association becomes more necessary to them than that of wages. This is so true that English economists are amazed to see the workers sacrifice a good part of their wages in favour of associations, which, in the eyes of these economists, are established solely in favour of wages. In this struggle – a veritable civil war – all the elements necessary for a coming battle unite and develop. Once it has reached this point, association takes on a political character. Economic conditions had first trans-formed the mass of the people of the country into workers. The domina-tion of capital has created for this mass a common situation, common interests. This mass is already a class as against capital, but not yet for itself. In the struggle, of which we have pointed out only a few phases, this mass becomes united, and constitutes itself as a class for itself. The interests it defends become class interests. But the struggle of class against class is a political struggle.
>
> (Marx, 1847/1975: 159f.)

This is probably the best summary statement of Marx's theory of collective action (see also Marx and Engels 1848/1967: 88–94). The point of departure is the existence of a collective action problem in the form of competition between workers.[18] 'Trade unions originally sprang up from the *spontaneous* attempts of workmen at removing or at least checking that competition' (Marx, 'Instructions for Delegates to the Geneva Congress' [1867] 1974: 91). A first precondition for collective action, on the part of the working class, repeatedly emphasized by Marx, is exactly what frightened Le Bon and his elitist followers so much: the coming together of large masses of people in factories and in cities. The absence of this precondition also explains the presumed failure of peasants to organize for collective action (Marx [1952] 1973b: 238f.). A second preconditon for the development of class consciousness is the class struggle itself. Collective action, in the form of class struggle, is not only action *for* some collective good, but *against* a common enemy.

Class consciousness is mainly cognitive: it is consciousness, on the part of its members, of 'its position as a class', with a common interest.[19] But it is not only cognitive. Solidarity between members of a class, and especially between the members of the working class, is not only a fact, but a precondition for its emancipation: 'Citizens, let us remember the basic principle of the international: solidarity. We will only be able to attain the goal we have set ourselves if this life-giving principle acquires a secure foundation among the workers of all countries' (Marx, 1974: 325; see also pp. 81f.).

But if so, Olson and (Allan) Buchanan are wrong to suppose that Marxist 'class interest' is made up of nothing but self-interest. It has been suggested that workers, or most of them, do not play the prisoners' dilemma, but are engaged in the alternative game of *assurance* (Shaw, 1984, 21–28; Sabia, 1988; 64f.).[20] Workers prefer cooperation and contribute to the provision of collective goods, *if* a sufficient number of others do. In the terminology of Elster, the solidarity or altruism of workers is 'conditional' (Elster, 1979: 21; 1982; 468–470). They have a '*conditional preference for cooperation*' (1985a: 362). This suggestion has been advanced both as an interpretation of Marx and as an explanation of collective action on the part of the working class. I find it plausible in both cases.

Another well-known attempt to make sense of working-class collective action has been made by Claus Offe and Helmut Wiesenthal (1980). They make no claim that their attempt is in the Marxist tradition, but we are free to interpret it as such, even though their analysis is equally much in the tradition of mainstream sociology. The first step in their analysis is to argue that there is an asymmetry of power in the relation between workers and capitalists. In the second step it is suggested that, because of this power differential, there are more obstacles in the way of collective action in the case of the working class than in the case of capitalists. The conclusion is that workers have to rely on another strategy than do capitalists in order to achieve their aims.

Only to the extent that associations of the relatively powerless succeed in the formation of a collective identity, according to the standards of which the costs of organization are subjectively deflated, can they hope to change the original power relation ... No union can function for a day in the absence of some rudimentary notions held by the members that being a member is of value in itself, that the individual organization costs must not be calculated in a utilitarian manner but have to be accepted as necessary sacrifices, and that each member is legitimately required to practise solidarity and discipline, and other norms of a non-utilitarian kind.

(Offe and Wiesenthal, 1980: 78f.)

The notion of 'collective identity' could be interpreted as another explication of 'class consciousness', similar, if not identical, to Elster's 'conditional solidarity'. But obviously there is something wrong with such an interpretation. Elster is rather dismissive of Offe and Wiesenthal's analysis as a whole, and remains 'sceptical about the explanatory value of the concept of collective identity' (Elster, 1989a: 168). I, for my part, can see no convincing reason for being more sceptical about collective identity than about conditional solidarity. In fact, I am quite prepared to accept both. I will return to the concept of 'collective identity' later and argue – against Elster – that it is indispensable for the explanation of much collective action, including that of the working class in the early stages of its formation. As we have already seen, Marx assumed a difference between the bourgeoisie and the proletariat. Only members of the latter were capable of heroism and self-sacrifice. Elster himself has argued for a difference: 'By implication, I have suggested that capitalist collective action rests on selfish rationality in iterated games, whereas working-class collective action rests on externalities in the utility function' (Elster, 1985a: 363). He defends this departure from parsimony with reference to the extensive literature on working-class culture.[21] There really shouldn't be that much difficulty with the idea of a collective identity.

But if Marx did provide a theoretical solution to the collective action problem, why has the proletarian revolution failed to appear, or to appear as Marx predicted?[22] Marx expected the proletarian revolution to take place in England – the most advanced capitalist economy in his time – and then to spread to the rest of Europe and to the United States. The first communist revolution – proletarian or not – took place in Russia.[23] Marxists, ever since Marx, have tried to explain why his prophecy failed. A first explanation derives from Marx himself, and was nourished by Engels. Above the economic base rises a superstructure to protect it. Part of this superstructure is an ideology legitimizing the prevalent relations of production. Perhaps ideology is more potent than Marx expected. Perhaps ideology can prevent the development of a proletarian class consciousness. The seeds of this explanation can be found in a number of letters on historical materialism written by Engels after Marx's death. In one of them, Engels introduces the notion of a 'false consciousness', to denote the ideologically distorted consciousness of a class-in-itself. Important contributions to this type of explanation have been Antonio Gramsci's idea of 'hegemony' and Louis Althusser's theory of 'ideological state apparatuses'.

Another type of explanation derives from Robert Michels and his 'iron law of oligarchy'. Himself originally a socialist, Michels saw, to his great disappointment, how, eventually, the leaders of the labour movement developed interests of their own, distinct from those of the working class as a whole. The tragic consequence of this disappointment was that Michels turned into a supporter of Mussolini. The consequence for the Marxist theory of collective action was that social movements can be 'betrayed' by their leaders.

Lenin learned from Engels and anticipated Michels, but his lesson was different. The working class is unable to attain more than a false, 'trade union', consciousness. A true political class consciousness must be brought to the workers from without. Hence, the necessity of agitation and propaganda. Instead of concluding that a proletarian revolution is impossible, Lenin maintained that it has to be made, or led, by an intellectual elite of professional revolutionaries, on behalf of the proletariat (Lenin, *What Is to Be Done* [1902] 1963: 141ff., 197ff.). This is in direct opposition to Marx's view that 'the emancipation of the working classes must be conquered by the working classes themselves' (Marx, 1974: 82; see also 348ff., 375). But, of course, Lenin might be right. Perhaps a strong leadership is necessary to solve the collective action problem involved in a proletarian revolution. It is a further question whether leadership will lead to emancipation, or to oligarchy and a new class. Today, we have reason to believe that Leninist leadership is likely to lead to permanent oligarchy.[24]

In the further development of Western Marxism increasing doubts have been raised concerning the special position of the working class as a collective subject. Not only has it diminished in number and importance; it has become less revolutionary. What hope is still left for emancipation from exploitation and oppression must attach to new social groups and new social movements.

The simple answer to the above question – 'why has the revolution failed to appear?' – is that a revolution depends upon so much else than conditional solidarity. This is evident from Marx's own writings. His prediction of a breakdown or catastrophe, followed by revolution, is probably best seen as an expression of wishful thinking or, maybe, as an attempt at a self-fulfilling – it may turn out to be a self-defeating – prophecy, or both (cf. Elster, 1985a: 437ff.; 1988: 225). It is difficult to deny the utopian element, already pointed out by Bernstein (1899/1961: 204f., 209ff.). Perhaps it is closer to being a 'myth', in the sense of Sorel (1908/1961: 42ff., ch. 4),[25] or historical 'prophecy', as suggested by Weber ([1918] 1971: 205ff.) and Popper

(1945/1966, vol. 2: 135ff.; 1957/1961: 42ff.),[26] than a scientific prediction based upon an allegedly 'scientific socialism', as maintained by Engels (1878/1969, Part III; 1892/1970). Marx's scenario includes a development towards increasing exploitation and the final collapse of the capitalist mode of production, when, in the words of the *Manifesto*, 'The proletarians have nothing to lose but their chains.' This did not happen, or has not happened yet, and Marxists have advanced a number of arguments to explain why. I am not going to discuss the intricacies of Marxian economics. The most common explanation seems to have been that capitalism has survived thanks to imperialism and/or the state.

But possible answers could also be found at the level of strategic action. Marx seems to have underestimated the autonomy of the state and the strategic rationality of the capitalist class (Tilly 1978: ch. 4; Elster, 1988).[27] Both could be expected to do their best to prevent a revolutionary situation from ever arising. And this is what they have done in the capitalist countries of the West, together with the reformist labour movement. Also, Marx probably overestimated the extent to which solidarity may develop in a collectivity such as the working class, lacking the characteristics of community (see Chapter 7). Perhaps members of the labour movement simply acted rationally in choosing reform before revolution and capitalism before socialism? (see, e.g., Calhoun, 1982: 229–233; 1983: 901–911; 1988: 168–174; Przeworski, 1985: ch. 5; Wallerstein and Przeworski, 1988). There is no simple answer to these questions. Too much uncertainty surrounds decisions between alternative economic systems. It is a matter of *belief*, much more than of information. It seems reasonable to believe, however, that members of the working classes have acted rationally, given their beliefs and opportunities (see Offe and Wiesenthal, 1980: 103–109).

To conclude: even if Marx's prediction of a coming proletarian revolution is falsified, this does not imply that his analysis of collective action is all wrong. There are other forms of class struggle and we have seen lots of it in the last 150 years: much more than we should expect from Mancur Olson's theory of selective incentives. I concur with Sabia (1988: 50) that 'the charge of inconsistency is unfounded'. That, in fact, Marx identified a number of conditions under which collective action, if not revolution, is likely to occur.[28]

Except for indirect contributions, the sociological theory of collective action lay dormant until the revival of Marxism in the 1960s. Meanwhile, most forms of collective action were subsumed under the denigrating label 'collective behaviour', implying collectively induced irrationality. As I have already indicated, however, the theory of collective behaviour eventually turned into a theory of 'collective action', if by this term is understood behaviour that is governed by norms and/or is rational to some degree. This redefinition and reorientation is most clearly visible in the writings by Turner and Killian (1957/1972, Smelser (1963) and Turner (1964a, 1964b). In their works, collective behaviour becomes both less abnormal and less irrational. Participants in collective behaviour know what they are doing. They are invested not only with emotions and impulses, but with goals and reasons as well. Since much collective behaviour is not institutionalized, an important part of it is devoted to a definition, or redefinition, of the situation and to the creation and application of suitable norms (Turner, 1964a; 1964b; 1981: 19f.).

Smelser and Gurr are representatives of sociological orthodoxy in the 1960s. As such they were bound to be subjected to the attack of the impending radical challenge. A typical representative of this challenge is Charles Tilly, who is one of the most important contemporary sociologists preoccupied with a theory of collective action.[29]

RESOURCE MOBILIZATION

Tilly is highly critical of the theories of Smelser and Gurr and of the Durkheimian tradition to which they arguably belong (Tilly 1975b: 484–496; 1978: 18–24; 1981a: ch. 4; Shorter and Tilly, 1974: 6–11; Tilly et al., 1975: 4–6, 290–298). He seems suspicious of any attempt to find a universal explanation, suggesting instead a more historical approach, aimed at detecting different forms of collective action. Universal explanations are either truistically true, or false. Explanations in terms of structural strain or relative deprivation are false. Collective action is not more, but less, common among the most deprived groups in society.[30]

Without being, himself, an orthodox Marxist, Tilly's favourite among the sociological classics – at least when it comes to a theory of collective action – is clearly Karl Marx (Tilly, 1978: ch. 2; Tilly et al., 1975: ch. 6). Like many others, he is most impressed by Marx's analysis in *The Class Struggles in France: 1848 to 1850* and *The Eighteenth Brumaire of Louis Bonaparte*, where we find various classes and class fractions strategically contending for state power. Among the other sociological classics, Weber is also received favourably, because he recognized the importance of the state in capitalist society. Moving outside sociology, Tilly is also favourably disposed towards John Stuart Mill and the utilitarian tradition, to which Mancur Olson also belongs. Like Elster (1982: 463–478), Tilly draws attention to the potential utility of game theory in the analysis of class struggle (Tilly, 1978: 29–35, 1985: 742–745; 1990b: 212f.). 'That will be the general attitude of the analyses to follow: doggedly anti-Durkheimian, resolutely pro-Marxian, but sometimes indulgent to Weber and sometimes reliant on Mill' (Tilly, 1978: 48).

Tilly's conception of collective action is utilitarian: '*Collective action* consists of people's acting together in pursuit of common interests' (Tilly, 1978: 7). Alternatively, 'Collective action, for our purposes, consists of all occasions on which sets of people commit pooled resources, including their own efforts, to common ends' (Tilly, 1981b: 17). Thus, collective action is beset by the problem of free riding. The collective action problem is solved in practice by *organization* and, above all, *by the mobilization* of resources. A third precondition is *opportunity*, as determined by the specifics of the situation; most importantly, by the balance of power obtaining between groups at a particular moment. Tilly's view of collective action is summarized in his 'mobilization model' (Figure 6.2).

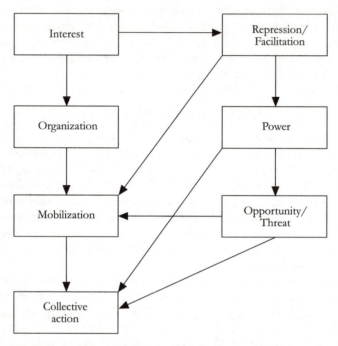

Figure 6.2 Charles Tilly's mobilization model (modified).
Source; adapted from Tilly (1978: 56).

In addition to organization, mobilization and opportunity, we find, on the right side of the model, repression and power as intermediate variables. Repression/facilitation is there to remind us that collective action depends upon the policy of the state; its repressiveness or permissiveness. The inclusion of 'power' needs no special justification, or explanation. Tilly's use of this contestable concept is, perhaps, another matter, but will not occupy me here.

I think it is true to Tilly's intention to conceive of this model as a framework for analysis, rather than as a theory, or an explanation. We have to do with a tentative working model used in, and based upon, Tilly's extensive empirical historical research on collective action. Thus, it is not intended to convey the *vérité* of collective action. It should, finally, be pointed out that Tilly's own research has been concentrated on certain important forms of collective action: revolutions, strikes and 'contentious gatherings'.

Tilly's analysis connects both with the sociological theory of groups, discussed in the previous section, and with the sociology of cooperation and social order, to be discussed in the next section. Like the former, Tilly sees collective action as implicated in conflict and part of struggles between contending groups. The economic theory of collective action is deficient, to the extent that it treats only singular collective actors seeking some collective good. This is the case with Olson's *Logic of Collective Action*, as with most economic treatments of the problem. Game theory is a useful tool for analysing strategic interaction, but breaks down before the complexity of social situations and the social relations they embody (Tilly, 1978: 24–37, 59–62, 74f., 84ff., 227ff.; 1990b: 214). All interaction is not strategic. Also, much collective action aims at changing the game, rather than seeking a certain payoff in a game that is pregiven to the actors. Besides, who are the actors and what are their interests? The economic approach to collective action, game theory included, has no answer to these questions. Finally, strategic collective action is usually surrounded by so much uncertainty, and often involves so much risk, as to defy any strict *logic* of collective action (Tilly, 1978: 99ff.).

But, once again, this critique of the economic approach may be turned into a defence. If we assume that people are risk-averse, as I suggested above (p. 287), then we may assume that groups engage in collective action simply to maintain their position in the prevailing status quo. This hypothesis is supported by Tilly (1978: 135): 'groups generally inflate the value of those things they already possess, when someone else is seeking to take them away'.

Among the results of Tilly's historical investigations may be mentioned the documentation of a development from *communal* to *associational* collective action (Tilly, 1973, 1975b: 505f.; 1978: 81–84; 1981a: 19–23; 1986a: 387–398; 1986b: 170–184; Shorter and Tilly, 1974: 15–20, ch. 3, 345–350). A change took place both in type of collective *and* of action. Until the beginning of the nineteenth century, the dominant type of collective actor was the community: the peasant village, the guild and the religious congregation. The most common types of contentious collective action were tax rebellions and food riots. From the middle of the nineteenth century, the dominant type of collective actor was the association: the party and the interest group. The most common types of contentious collective action, now, are the strike and the demonstration.

Tilly makes another, more analytic, categorization of forms of collective action, in terms of the claims made by contending groups. Claims may be *competitive, reactive,* or *proactive* (Tilly, 1975b: 506ff.; 1978: ch. 5; Tilly *et al.*, 1975: 48–55, 249–254). In competitive collective action, rival groups compete for goods, originally controlled by neither. In reactive collective action, a group defends its rights against a challenger, who engages in proactive collective action. The distinction between reactive and proactive collective action is most fertile in a dynamic context, where new groups rise to power while consigning others to oblivion. Thus, the collective action of communities was reactive, while associational collective action tends to be proactive, at least for a start.

The change from communal to associational collective action reflects the great transformation of the West produced by capitalism, with the kind assistance of the state, and resulting in the urbanization and proletarianization of large parts of the population. This transformation was the overriding concern of all classical sociologists, a concern which coloured their view of society and of social order in a way that I will indicate in the final chapter of this book.

The distinction between communal and associational collective action has generated a vast body of research, and not only by Tilly. Both George Rudé and E.P. Thompson observed a change in collective action, from a backward-looking, local type, defending the way of life in the old society, to a more forward-looking, political type, aimed at acquiring rights in the new society. The distinction between community and association goes back to the German sociologist Ferdinand Toennies, that between communal and associational collective action to Anthony Obershall. By combining this distinction with that between integrated and segmented collectivities, Obershall arrives at the classification shown in Figure 6.3 (Obershall, 1973: 120), which is also used by Tilly (1978: 82).

Links within collectives

		Communal	Weak	Associational
Ties to other collectivities	Integrated	A	B	C
	Segmented	D	E	F

Figure 6.3 A classification of collectivities.

I assume that the reader has a preliminary understanding of the distinction between community and association. I will treat it at some length in the next chapter. The distinction between integration and segmentation, concerns the degree to which collectivities are separated, or isolated, from one another. A society where people belong to superimposed groups, but with few ties and little interaction between the collectivities of superimposed groups, is highly segmented. A society with much overlap and mobility between groups, cross-cutting social cleavages, is highly integrated. Integration, in this case, means integration of groups in society, not integration of individuals in groups.

Obershall generates a number of hypotheses from his scheme (Obershall, 1973: 124ff.). By way of summary, they suggest that segmentation is highly conducive to mobilization for collective action. Social movements often mobilize by aligning pre-existing groups *en bloc* and by recruiting leaders from pre-existing organizations. In particular, the existence of communal groups, with strong ties of solidarity between their members, has proved to facilitate mobilization for collective action.

The importance of community and tradition for revolutionary mobilization has also been confirmed in the investigation of class struggle by Craig Calhoun (1982; 1983; 1988). He argues that reactionaries tend to be more radical than progressives. In particular, Calhoun claims that the strongest resistance to large-scale industrial capitalism came from artisans and small producers, rather than from the emerging proletariat. Only communities, such as existed before capitalism, create social ties strong enough to resist free riding. The modern proletariat is dependent on organization and leadership for collective action, but will not opt for radical upheaval.

Tilly and Obershall are often cited as representatives of the so-called 'resource mobilization approach' in the theory of collective action, or social movements (Orum, 1983: 327–330; Cohen, J.L., 1985: 674–690). Because of the obvious similarity of his analysis, Craig Calhoun may also be included in this group. This approach is often cited as being an example of rational choice. As we have seen, there is some justification for this view in the case of Tilly. He sees collective action as instrumental and strategically rational. He differs from traditional economics, however, in focusing on classes (and states), rather than on individuals, and in modelling these classes as involved in a contest for state power. But what about self-interest?

I interpret Tilly as arguing, like Marx, that class action is possible because of solidarity, but evidence for this interpretation is somewhat ambiguous. On the one hand, Tilly clearly ascribes to Marx the view that solidarity is important for collective action, and appears to accept this view himself: 'Karl Marx knew the importance of solidarity for collective action' (Tilly *et al.*, 1975: 271). 'The Marxian analysis ... generally traces collective action back to solidarity within groups and conflict of interest between groups, considers the solidarity and conflicts of interest to reinforce each other, and bases both of them on the organization of production' (Tilly, 1978: 14). On the other hand, solidarity has no explicit place in Tilly's model for the analysis of collective action. What he says about it, is included under the rubric 'mobilization' (Tilly, 1978: 69ff.), and he seems to be somewhat sceptical about the explanatory power of appeals to solidarity (Tilly, 1973: 214ff., 236f.). Tilly's objectivism and structuralism make him prefer explanations in terms of organization and social ties.

The case of Anthony Obershall is a bit different. He explicitly claims to erect his own sociological theory of mobilization on the foundation of Olson's economic theory of collective action (Obershall, 1973: 113–123). Much tells against this claim. First, sociology and economics are not easily joined together. Second, Obershall's own analysis is too sociological to be combined with Olson's theory of collective action. My impression is that he draws from the peripheral parts of Olson's theory, without touching the central part. In any case, Obershall obviously does not assume that mobilization for collective action succeeds because of an appeal to self-interest, except, perhaps, in the case of leaders, who are treated as political entrepreneurs. Sentiments of solidarity are considered vitally important (see, e.g., Obershall, 1973: 119, and *passim*), and so are cultural values and ideology (ibid., pp. 50, 65f., 178–184).

Eventually, Obershall arrives at a better understanding of the implications of his own theory (cf. Chazel, 1990: 223) The emphasis, now, is on group identity and solidarity (Obershall, 1978: 313): 'a mobilization theory based on the utilitarian rational-choice model leaves one somewhat unsatisfied, because strong passions, group consciousness, ideological appeal, and appeals to solidarity in group conflict are relegated to second place, if they are taken into account at all' (ibid., p. 307). He goes on to argue that solidarity also increases the scope of a rational choice theory of mobilization; first, because solidarity is, itself, a source of many benefits and costs for the individual and, second, because there is a positive relation between solidarity and social control in the form of rewards and punishments (Obershall, 1978: 308f.). This simple fact is the source of many attempts to reduce sociology to economics, but Obershall does not join the economistic movement.

Craig Calhoun is more extensive in his comments on Olson than is either Tilly or Obershall. He seems to accept Olson's theory of collective action as essentially correct and as providing a sufficient explanation for the lack of revolutionary zeal on the part of the working class (Calhoun, 1982, 1983, 1988). I disagree, because Olson's theory is about collective action, not just revolution, and the working class has engaged in much more collective action than we are warranted to expect from this theory. In particular, as many critics of Olson have pointed out, his theory cannot explain the emergence of large interest groups.

According to Calhoun, however, there is one solution to the collective action problem: community. But, if I understand Calhoun correctly, this solution is not inconsistent with Olson's theory. Community solves the problem by providing 'selective incentives' (Calhoun, 1982; 1983: 891, 900). There is reason to be sceptical about this interpretation. If we allow any kinds of selective incentive, they function as the notorious D term in the theory of voting: a reservoir for *ad hoc* explanations that would make Olson's theory of collective action immune to refutation, because empty of content (see pp. 273ff.). Mancur Olson is, to some extent, aware of this problem and excludes 'moral incentives' (Olson, 1965/1971: 61n.).

It is not altogether clear, too, whether Calhoun is prepared to follow Olson in this respect or not. Community solves the collective action problem by providing selective incentives; more specifically, social incentives such as friendship, social status, social esteem and social pressure. But, according to sociological orthodoxy, society is, to a large extent, a moral order and community is the type of social order where morality is strongest. Is Calhoun's concept of community economic or sociological? It seems to be both: 'A community may act as the source of selective inducements to participate in collective action – quite without depending on the individual's sense of belonging. It may produce collectively rational (useful) results which individual rationality would not have done' (Calhoun, 1980: 109). Also: 'To improve upon Marx's argument we need a sociological source for selective inducements to collective action. Olson suggests that we may find this in social pressure, within certain preexisting organizations. I concur . . .' (Calhoun, 1983: 891; see also 1982: 180, 234; 1988: 135). But Calhoun also recognizes the solidarity of traditional communities, without making it clear whether it is a selective inducement, or something additional to it (Calhoun, 1983: 900, 910). The ambiguity remains in the following passage:

> I suggest that the problems posed by Olson can be met in large part by my analysis of traditional communities. Not only does the sharing of tradition predispose individuals to similar analysis of their situations, but embeddedness in communal relations also produces an interdependence of interests among individuals.
>
> (ibid., p. 905; also quoted in 1988: 161)

One possibility is to interpret 'interdependence of interests' as interdepence of utility functions in the form of altruism, or solidarity. This interpretation is supported by the following quotation:

> it is inaccurate to see people in communities taking action solely as individuals (as much microeconomic theory and both psychologistic and economistic exchange theory do). Moreover, members of communities often desire that benefits should accrue to large social units with which they identify – kinship and descent groups, for example. If we fail to look at community, and instead look only at individuals, including individuals collectively described as action sets or social networks, a very significant part of social life must elude our analysis.
>
> (Calhoun, 1980: 127)

It is still possible to maintain that Calhoun remains within the 'logic', if not the economics, of collective action. Olson admitted the possibility of 'selfless', or 'unselfish', behaviour as long as it is rational from the point of view of the group (Olson, 1965/1971: 64). Oddly enough, Olson (ibid., p. 159) seems to argue that this possibility is most manifest in large groups. Calhoun, much more reasonably, argues the opposite: unselfish behaviour is much more common in small, primary, groups.

In Calhoun's latest writings on collective action, the theme of identity – both personal and collective – becomes much more prominent, and leads him definitely beyond economics and back to the centre of sociology. I will return to Calhoun, first, when discussing social movements and, a second time, when discussing the sociological idea of 'community'. It may be argued, though, that Calhoun was beyond economics all the time – maybe unawares – due to his conception of 'community' (Calhoun, 1980; 1982: 157ff.). Because of a certain 'structuralist' predisposition, Calhoun avoids a definition in terms of a feeling of 'belonging'. He defines community in terms of social relationships that are dense, multiplex and systematic. But the characteristic mark of communal bonds is that they involve obligations. Indeed: 'Moral obligations are essentially the stuff of community' (Calhoun, 1980: 112). It may be that Calhoun originally believed that moral obligations can be reduced to 'selective incentives', but that would be to conflate moral rules with the sanctions that go along with them – an all too common mistake, typically made by defenders of the economic approach.

SOCIAL MOVEMENTS

Mancur Olson's theory of collective action is not intended to apply to 'mass' movements (Olson, 1965/1971: 161f.). This information comes as a surprise, since Olson obviously believes that it applies to labour unions and that it falsifies Marx's theory of class action, which is all about the social movement, *par excellence:* the working-class movement. In the case of mass movements, Olson accepts the most dubious version of the theory of collective behaviour – the version depicting collective behaviour as irrational and many mass movements as being on the 'lunatic fringe' (Olson, 1965/1971: 162). Be that as it may, if social movements do not follow the logic of collective action, this is a serious limitation on the economic theory of collective action.

Sociology lacked a distinct theory of social movements until the middle of the twentieth century. This subject, like the subject of collective action more generally, was subsumed under the much discredited theory of collective behaviour. It is only 'natural', therefore, that Popper's *Poverty of Historicism* should culminate in a quest for an analysis of social movements (Popper, 1957/1961: 149).[31] A systematic treatment of social movements did not appear until the publication of Rudolf Heberle's *Social Movements* in 1951. On the other hand, Heberle's analysis is largely a synthesis of existing sociological knowledge, to the extent that it is relevant for an understanding of social movements; of Marx, of course, but also of Michels, Sorel, Mannheim and, especially, Weber. I discussed Marx in the previous section. Here I will complement the picture with some relevant issues, largely neglected by Marx but addressed by mainstream sociology. They are the issues of (1) leadership and (2) the 'role of ideas' in social movements.

The question of leadership, as we have seen, was tackled, in different ways, by Lenin and by Michels, who, besides being a socialist was also a sociologist, by profession. It is known that Lenin was acquainted with the work of Le Bon, and maybe he learned something about leadership from him.[32] Be that as it may, Lenin certainly exemplifies Le Bon's 'leader of crowds' (Le Bon, 1895/1960: 117–140) who, with his 'personal prestige' and 'magnetic fascination', is an obvious precursor of Weber's famous 'charismatic leader'.[33]

A charismatic leader is one who is obeyed because of exceptional personal qualities, ascribed to him by his followers. Typical examples are religious prophets, war heroes, demagogues and revolutionary leaders. Indeed, charisma is the most important revolutionary force in history – at least in pre-modern society. Charisma invariably means a break with tradition and other forms of routine. Charisma brings new values and beliefs in times of distress. But charisma is not limited to leaders of social movements. Parliamentary leaders too may be charismatic and, according to Weber, they should be.

It is constitutive of charisma to be indifferent towards economic and other worldly matters. The economic basis of the charismatic community is the voluntary gift; its principle of distribution communistic. In short, charisma is the negation of rational egoism. In Weber's terminology (see below), charisma is 'value rational', not 'instrumentally rational'.

But pure charisma cannot last for long. It can exist only *in statu nascendi*. Several factors conspire to make it a necessarily transient phenomenon. First of all, exceptional personal qualities are not easily transmitted to other persons. Second, 'idealism' is not stable, when invaded by competing material interests. Third, people cannot live permanently without routine. In addition to Michels' 'iron law of oligarchy', we may talk about Weber's 'iron law of the routinization of charisma'. For Weber, charisma and its routinization is a historical pattern of universal significance. If Weber is correct, there is a solution to the problem of initiating collective action. The solution is charismatic leadership. It has repeatedly been pointed out that Olson's by-product theory cannot explain the emergence of interest groups (see, e.g., Fireman and Gamson, 1979: 19; Turner, 1981: 14; Hardin, 1982: 34). Perhaps charisma is part of the explanation. There is little doubt that charismatic leaders have played an important role in the initial stages of many social movements.[34]

I turn to the role of ideas as motive forces in collective action. For Marx, the all-important form of collective action is class struggle, based upon common material interest. No independent role is assigned to ideas as motives for collective action. Also, Marx's historical *materialism* is opposed to any form of *idealism* that sees, in ideas, an important force in history. Ideas, at least in the form of ideology, belong in the 'superstructure'. But, on the other hand, ideology must be important too! Or else it could not fulfil the function assigned to it by historical materialism. Among orthodox Marxists, this fact is usually expressed by emphasizing that Marxism is a 'dialectical', as opposed to a 'mechanical', materialism. Anyway, sociology is usually interpreted as involving a denial of, or at least a corrective to, historical materialism. Mainstream sociology emphasizes the importance of ideas, of cultural values and beliefs, as motives for human action, including collective action (see, e.g., Alexander and Colomy, 1985).

311

The paradigmatic manifestation of sociologists' 'debate with the ghost of Marx' is Max Weber's famous thesis that the Protestant ethic contributed to the rise of capitalism (Weber, 1904–5/1930). Now, it should immediately be pointed out that Weber did not intend to put forward an alternative to historical materialism. His claim was limited to the much more modest thesis that Protestantism was, to some degree, conducive to the formation and spread of the capitalist spirit in the West (Weber, 1904–5/1930: 91, 183). Weber, in fact, often implies that material interests are more powerful, while insisting that ideas are important too. Thus, if Weber, especially in his sociology of religion, focused on 'the manner in which ideas become effective forces in history', this was not because he saw them as all-important. It was because they are important enough.

But ideas, as such, are unimportant. They become important only when internalized as motives in people's minds. Ideas turned into motives are called 'ideal interests'.

> Not ideas, but material and ideal interests, directly govern men's conduct. Yet very frequently the 'world images' that have been created by 'ideas' have, like switchmen, determined the tracks along which action has been pushed by the dynamic of interest.
> (Weber, 'The Social Psychology of World Religions' [1915] 1948: 280)

What made the Protestant ethic effective was not its propagation in books and sermons, even if that may have been a necessary precondition. What made the Protestant ethic really effective was its propagation in Protestant sects. In a vein similar to Olson's theory of selective incentives, Weber holds that ideas become effective as motives only if supported by group pressure and social approval. It is 'not the ethical *doctrine* of a religion, but that form of ethical conduct upon which *premiums* are placed that matters' (Weber, [1906] 1948: 321).

It is not absolutely clear from Weber's treatment, to what extent ideal interests are non-selfish. The example of the Protestant ethic indicates that ideal interests are not necessarily moral, or non-selfish. At other times, however, this seems to be the case. At the beginning of his treatment of the three types of legitimate domination, Weber makes a distinction between 'ideal (*Wertrationale*) motives' and 'material motives' (Weber, 1922/1978: 212f.), implying that ideal motives are, if not necessarily moral, at least non-selfish, because non-utilitarian. Value-rational (*Wertrationale*) action is defined as 'determined by a conscious belief in the value for its own sake of some ethical, aesthetic, religious, or other form of behavior, independent of its prospect of success' (Weber, 1922/1978: 24f.). But this is not what matters most. The important thing, here, is that the legacy of Weber – especially through the reception of his work by Talcott Parsons – has been a sociology that emphasizes the importance of ideas, of values and beliefs, as motives for action, including collective action. A corollary of this has been a rejection of

Marx's view that history is the history of class struggle. Other collectives than class – e.g. religious, ethnic and status groups, nations, tribes and sexes, some of them united primarily by common 'ideal interests' – may turn into collective subjects and become important forces in history.[35]

I have mentioned Weber's distinction between instrumentally rational and value rational action (contemporary rational choice theorists would not refer to the latter as 'rational'). Corresponding to this distinction is another, between two types of ethic: an 'ethic of ultimate ends', or 'principled conviction', and an 'ethic of responsibility' (Weber, [1919] 1948: 120; 1994: 359). The latter ethic is utilitarian, or outcome-oriented. The former is fundamentalist, in its disregard for consequences. The ideal politician, according to Weber, must be guided by both and possess the personal strength necessary to face the conflicts involved in such combination.

As an example of irresponsible value rationality, Weber mentions the syndicalist, promoting the general strike without a view to its consequences: 'You may demonstrate to a convinced syndicalist, believing in an ethic of ultimate ends, that his action will result in increasing the opportunities of reaction, in increasing the oppression of his class, and obstructing its ascent – and you will not make the slightest impression upon him' (Weber [1919] 1948: 120f.; cf. 1994: 360). This is certainly a correct interpretation of the attitude of the leading theoretician of syndicalism: George Sorel. I mention Sorel because he was deeply concerned with the collective action problem. Being a socialist, Sorel made this problem his own: 'I want to find out how the feelings by which the masses are moved form themselves into groups' (Sorel, 1908/1961: 58). This feeling is solidarity. Sorel was fully aware that self-interest is a bar to collective action, but, like most socialists, he believed, or hoped, that proletarian solidarity would be strong enough to solve the problem ([1899] 1976: 94–110). He also knew that solidarity is not a constant, but depends upon struggle and – this was Sorel's own contribution to a theory of collective action – motivating ideas, especially myths.

> Experience shows that the *framing of the future, in some indeterminate time*, may, when it is done in a certain way, be very effective, and have very few inconveniences; this happens when the anticipations of the future take the form of those myths, which enclose with them, all the strongest inclinations of a people, of a party or of a class, inclinations which recur to the mind with the insistence of instincts in all the circumstances of life; and which give an aspect of complete reality to the hopes of immediate action by which, more easily than by any other method, men can reform their desires, passions, and mental activity.
>
> (Sorel, 1908/1961: 124f.)

Examples of such myths are the early Christain beliefs in the return of Christ and in a coming catastrophe, Marx's prophecy of a revolution and the syndicalist idea of a general strike: 'the *myth* in which socialism is wholly comprised, i.e. a body of images capable of evoking instinctively all the sentiments which correspond to the different manifestations of the war undertaken by Socialism against modern society' (Sorel, 1908/1961: 127).

We may be tempted to conclude that Sorel's idea of a general strike itself turned out to be a myth, or fable. We may believe that Sorel's 'hypothesis' about the motivating power of myths has been refuted by historical development. But then it should, at least, be pointed out that Sorel did not intend to predict the occurrence of a general strike and the coming of socialism; he tried to bring it about, but failed. This failure may say something about the motivating power of myths and other ideas, but it does not prove that they are altogether impotent. Max Weber, who is justly admired for his sense of reality, took the threat of a general strike seriously indeed, at the time when it did appear as a threat to a 'class-conscious bourgeois'.[36]

Sorel was a bitter enemy of politicians and of intellectuals, especially academics and, among them, professional sociologists in particular. Politicians are described in the manner of public choice: as self-interested and unscrupulous manipulators, and in glaring contrast to the heroic and virtuous proletariat. Professional intellectuals are also self-interested, but, above all, cowards incapable of action. One seeming exception was Emile Durkheim, who receives some praise for having emphasized the importance of morality; a phenomenon sadly neglected by socialists, at least in the opinion of the moralist George Sorel ('The Socialist Future of the Syndicates' [1898] 1976: 90f.).

For Durkheim, morality is, indeed, an important phenomenon. It is also a collective phenomenon. Durkheim's central concept is that of 'collective consciousness' (*conscience collective*), being above all a collective *moral* consciousness. It might be expected, therefore, that Durkheim had something to say about collective action and about the role of ideas in collective action. And he had. But very little about contentious collective action and about social movements. Durkheim was interested in social order, not in contention and conflict.

I will return to Durkheim when discussing the sociological theory of social order. Here I will merely notice that Durkheim in his later writings highlighted the role of symbols for the integration of social groups. The concept of 'collective consciousness' is increasingly replaced by that of 'collective representations'. The most important source for Durkheim's later ideas is *The Elementary Forms of the Religious Life* (1912/1965). The general conclusion of this book 'is that religion is something eminently social. Religious representations are collective representations which express collective realities; the rites are a manner of acting which take rise in the midst of the assembled groups and which are destined to excite, maintain or recreate certain mental states in these groups' (Durkheim, 1912/1965: 22). The relevance of this conclusion for a theory of collective action would be that symbols, beliefs and symbolic actions, e.g. rites, may be means for the creation and maintenance of collective identity and solidarity in social groups and movements. Another thesis of Durkheim is that religions are idealizations of society (1912/1965: 469). This brings me to another topic, that of utopias; because there is a continuity between religious and utopian thought.[37]

Durkheim conceived of *The Elementary Forms of the Religious Life* as a contribution to a sociology of knowledge. A classic in this field is Karl Mannheim's *Ideology and Utopia* (1936), which is especially concerned with the role of ideas in social movements. Mannheim makes the distinction between ideologies, which are distortions of reality in the interest of particular social groups, and utopias which are ideals to be realized, if possible (Mannheim, 1936: 36). The main thesis advanced by Mannheim is that knowledge – at least knowledge about society – is, to some extent, a function of the social position of individuals and of their interests as members of social classes and other groups. Of special importance for social movements are utopias.

> Indeed, it may be stated further that it is a very essential feature of modern history that in the gradual organization for collective action social classes become effective in transforming historical reality only when their aspirations are embodied in utopias appropriate to the changing situation.
>
> (Mannheim, 1936: 187)

Utopias, then, belong to modern history. I will not, however, recapitulate Mannheim's account of the history of the utopian mentality.[38] I will quote, at length, instead, an interesting observation he makes about the transition from community-based to class-based collective action, which connects with the views of Tilly, Obershall and Calhoun, discussed in the previous section.

> Groups of pre-capitalistic origin, in which the communal element prevails, may be held together by traditions or by common sentiments alone. In such a group, theoretical reflection is of entirely secondary importance. On the other hand, in groups which are not welded together primarily by such organic bonds of community life, but which merely occupy similar positions in the social-economic system, rigorous theorizing is a prerequisite of cohesion. Viewed sociologically this extreme need for theory is the expression of a class society in which persons must be held together not by local proximity but by similar circumstances of life in an extensive social sphere. Sentimental ties are effective only within a limited spatial area, while a theoretical *Weltanschauung* has a unifying power over great distances. Hence a rationalized conception of history serves as a socially unifying factor for groups dispersed in space, and at the same time furnishes continuity to generations which continuously grow up into similar social conditions. In the formation of classes, a similar position in the social order and a unifying theory are of primary importance. Emotional ties which subse-

quently spring up are only a reflection of the already existing situation and are always more or less regulated by theory.

(Mannheim, 1936: 116f.)

Mannheim's sociology of knowledge is based upon the presumption that knowledge is situationally determined. The main source of inspiration for this view is the famous thesis of Marxist materialism: 'It is not consciousness that determines life, but life that determines consciousness' (Marx and Engels, 1846/1976: 42), together with the theories of ideology and of 'false consciousness'. But Mannheim couples these Marxist insights with the symbolic interactionist notion of a 'definition of the situation' (Mannheim, 1936: 19).[39] What this notion helps to bring home is the simple fact that people act upon the situation, not as 'it really is', but as they believe it is. This is not an epistemological statement, implying relativism. Neither Mannheim, nor I, wishes to maintain that it is never possible to arrive at an objectively correct description of a situation. Nor do I wish to deny that the objective situation sets limits to the number of possible, or plausible, definitions. *But*, for sociological purposes, it is of fundamental importance to recognize that reality is socially constructed;[40] that people, belonging to different cultures and groups, *do* have rival definitions of many situations (I assume that it is possible to speak of definitions without also speaking of situations, in the plural).

Philosophers have argued that there are 'essentially contestable concepts'. But concepts are used to interpret situations. If so, there are also essentially contestable definitions of situations, and for the same reason. Many concepts and definitions of situations are part of ideologies and linked to interests. Conflict is inescapable, unless we believe, with Marx, in the possibility of a classless society. What is 'free exchange' to some, is 'exploitation' to others. Of special importance for collective action, are definitions of situations as *unjust* (Turner and Killian, 1972: 259–268), or as *crisis*. Is there an environmental crises? Is there an economic crisis? (cf. Chapter 3, p. 147).

I believe that the notion of 'definition of the situation' based upon the insight that social reality is, to a large extent, a construction, is of great potential importance to the theory of rational choice and, especially, to game theory. I intend the descriptive part of definitions, even though I know that this part is rarely free from normative considerations. For rational choice, people's 'knowledge' of situations is a matter of information, if it is not characterized by uncertainty. Because information is costly, rationality is usually imperfect, or bounded. But many rival definitions of situations are resistant to any amount of information. People may be in fundamental disagreement about what situation they are in and what *kind of game* they are playing. What are the implications for rational choice? Elster has suggested that 'the theory of rational choice must be supplemented by a theory of rational belief' (Elster, 1986b: 1). Considering the nature of cultural beliefs in general, and ideological beliefs in particular, this demand makes the application of

316

rational choice highly problematic in most political situations (cf. Axelrod and Keohane, 1985: 230f., 234, 247).

I have recapitulated part of the theoretical background to the sociological theory of social movements. As I have already mentioned, the first systematic effort to create such a theory was made by Rudolf Heberle in 1951. As a pioneering attempt, Heberle's achievement is impressive. His first task, naturally, was to give some kind of preliminary definition of a 'social movement' and to distinguish this phenomenon from other social phenomena. The main defining characteristic of a social movement is, not surprisingly, that its aim is *change*. This is not controversial. The 'essence of a social movement is change' (Cameron, 1966: 8; see also Banks, 1972: 7ff., chs 3–4). More controversial is Heberle's suggestion that a social movement 'aims to bring about fundamental changes in the social order, especially in the basic institutions of property and labor relationships' (Heberle, 1951: 6). This seems to exclude reform movements aiming at minor changes in the social order and religious and moral crusades directed at individuals. A less demanding definition was proposed by David Cameron (1966: 7): 'A social movement occurs when a fairly large number of people band together in order to alter or supplant some portion of the existing culture or social order.' Probably an adequate definition should also allow the possibility of conservative social movements resisting change (Turner and Killian, 1957: 383f.; Cameron, 1966: 22f.). It may be argued, though, that change is primary, because resisting change makes sense only if there is an expectation of change. A social movement, then, is an indefinite number of people, more or less organized, who act with the express purpose of achieving (or resisting) a change in (1) the social order, or some part of it; and/or (2) in the beliefs, values or preferences of individual human beings.[41]

A second defining trait is more interesting for my purposes:

> A sense of group identity and solidarity is required, for only when the acting individuals have become aware of the fact that they have sentiments and goals in common – when they think of themselves as being united with each other in action through these sentiments and for these goals – do we acknowledge the existence of a social movement.
>
> (Heberle, 1951: 7; see also 128ff.)

This means that the collective action problem is solved by definition. A collective of individuals without the necessary identity and solidarity does not count as a social movement.[42] Even so, there are, of course, varying degrees of group consciousness in existing social movements (Heberle, 1968: 439).

Most sociologists would probably prefer to treat the question of identity and solidarity as an entirely empirical matter and not as part of the definition of a 'social movement'. Another, related characteristic, also pointed out by Heberle, has seemed more essential. Social movements are constituted by certain normative ideas, to which their members are committed and which

317

may be called their 'ideologies' (Heberle, 1951: 12f., 23ff.; 1968: 440). According to Wilkinson (1971: 27), an 'ideology', in this sense, is treated as a defining characteristic of social movements by virtually all leading scholars in the field (see, e.g., Turner and Killian, 1957: ch. 15; Smelser, 1962, chs 9–10; Killian, 1964: 430, 434–439; Gusfield, 1968: 445). As we shall soon see, this proposition was falsified only a few years after it was written. The theory of 'new social movements' ignores ideology.

A third defining characteristic of social movements (the second in Wilkinson's own enumeration), is 'a minimal degree of organization' (Wilkinson, 1971: 27). This raises the question of the peculiar composition and distinction of social movements. Social movements are usually distinguished from interest groups and political parties, although both of these may be parts of, or in other ways related to, the former. Social movements are wider and/or less integrated than organizations, but usually contain an organizational nucleus. Their composition typically comprises leaders, followers or rank-and-file members and sympathizers. Considering the fact that social movements often try to achieve their aims by influencing public opinion, the third category is far from unimportant. Nor is a fourth, external, category: the opponents of a social movement. Leaders are often divided into types, such as agitators, prophets, ideologues, statesmen, etc. Among the more useful classifications is that into charismatic, administrative and intellectual leaders (Killian, 1964: 441).

The paradigmatic example of a social movement is the working-class movement. And this is no accident, because this is how the term 'social movement' was originally used by Lorenz von Stein in his *Geschichte der Sozialen Bewegung Frankreichs von 1789 bis auf unsere Tage* (1850). The social movement was the labour movement. In the later development of the concept of a 'social movement' a generalization has taken place, so that that the set of social movements now includes all class movements, as well as those based upon sex, age, race, ethnicity, nationality, religion and lifestyle: moral crusades and new social movements such as the peace movement and the ecological movement.

NEW SOCIAL MOVEMENTS

The sociological theory of social movements fared no better than the main branch of sociological orthodoxy. By the end of the 1960s there was the radical challenge and in the 1970s a theoretical shift (Morris and Herring, 1986: 178–182). In the case of social movements, as in the case of collective action generally, the main challenge was the 'resource mobilization approach'. I have discussed some of the leading representatives of this approach (Tilly and Obershall) in the previous section, and do not intend to engage in unnecessary repetition. A short complementary addition concerning the special application of this approach to social movements may be justified, however.

The 'resource mobilization approach' was first clearly articulated by John D. McCarthy and Mayer N. Zald and launched as an alternative to the

318

'classical' sociological approach to social movements (McCarthy and Zald, 1973: 1f.). Instead of a social psychological concern with motives and a traditional sociological concern with ideology and values, McCarthy and Zald focused on 'structure', meaning, in their case, resources, organization and its environment. Their aim was not to replace the classical approach, but to instigate a focus of attention better adapted to the needs of social movements. Discontent is more or less constant, and can be treated as given to analysis; the point is to turn it into action (McCarthy and Zald, 1977: 1213, 1215).

Besides the pragmatic reason for a change in focus is another: there has been a change in the structure of social movements themselves, resulting from changes in society at large. Most important is the growth of a middle class willing to allocate some of its income, and of students willing to allocate some of their time, to social movements. Another important change is the invention and use of new mass media facilitating the spread of messages. Earlier, the strength of a social movement depended, to a large extent, upon participation and mass mobilization of those directly concerned. The social movements emerging in the 1960s exhibit a somewhat different pattern. They depend primarily upon the active participation of a small number of increasingly professional political activists drawing resources from various funds (McCarthy and Zald, 1973: 3–17).

McCarthy and Zald make extensive use of economic models in their analysis. The most distinct element in their approach derives not from Olson, but from Downs' theory of party competition and Breton and Breton's economic theory of social movements. Like the latter, McCarthy and Zald see the totality of social movements as a sector (SMS), comprising a number of social movement industries (SMI), within which a number of social movement organizations (SMO), headed by political entrepreneurs, compete for the support of individuals and funds with a preference for change, and choosing between alternative ways of allocating their support (McCarthy and Zald, 1977). I suspect that more dark than light is cast upon the subject by this market analogy.

McCarthy and Zald have a more ambiguous relation to Mancur Olson's theory of collective action. On the one hand, they accept his thesis that the costs of participation may be too high in large groups, so that people prefer to free ride on the activity of others (McCarthy and Zald, 1973: 7, 22n.; 1977: 1216). On the other hand, they suggest that social movements are less dependent on self-interest, because they can rely, instead, upon support from funds and from adherents that are not beneficiaries. But, as McCarthy and Zald admit (1977: 225f.), these so-called 'conscience adherents' are definitely not self-interested. They now maintain that Olson's logic applies to altruistic, as much as to egoistic, behaviour (ibid., p. 1222). This is correct to the extent that the argument depends upon the insignificance of each contribution, but it is also true that Olson did assume self-interest in his application of this logic, as did McCarthy and Zald in their first article. Like Olson, they

319

associate 'free riding' with self-interest, even though it is possible to conceive of free riding also in the case of altruism. McCarthy and Zald's analysis ends with a curious division of people into egoistic beneficiaries, moved only by selective incentives, and other adherents, with a conscience (McCarthy and Zald, 1977: 1227f., 1231). I find this division rather suspect, even though I agree that a good conscience is a luxury some people cannot afford.

In the early contributions to the resource mobilization approach, allegiance was usually paid to Mancur Olson's logic of collective action. My guess would be that this fact had more to do with a repudiation of the sociological tradition than with any merits of the former. Anyway, it did not take long before traditional sociological themes re-entered the discussion. In the previous section, we saw this happen in the cases of Obershall and Calhoun. It happened with the theory of social movements too. In an important article, two of the leading representatives of the resource mobilization approach, Bruce Fireman and William A. Gamson, made a joint attack on the utilitarian logic. The article implies a resurrection of the sociological tradition and precipitates some arguments later to gain wide currency. It also bridges the gap between the interest-oriented and the identity-oriented approaches to social movements.

Fireman and Gamson also offer an interesting rebuttal of the utilitaristic reduction of solidarity and/or morality to selective incentives. Most important is their argument against interpreting social control – the positive and negative sanctions sometimes used to promote collective action – as selective incentives. This interpretation creates a second-order collective action problem about sanctions: why should anyone wish to sanction other individuals out of self-interest? This problem occurs because sanctions are, themselves, collective goods contributing to social order (Fireman and Gamson, 1979: 19, 35). The impending infinite regress can be stopped only by invoking solidarity and/or morality (see Chapter 5, p. 245).

The resource mobilization approach met with surprisingly little resistance from more orthodox quarters. Ralph Turner did meet the challenge, but in a rather conciliatory manner, making room for both. This reaction was made easier by McCarthy and Zald's claim to advance a partial theory. Not surprisingly, Turner's main complaint concerns the flirtation with economic theory. He points out that in most instances of collective action the conditions for self-interested rationality are very far from being satisfied. Goals are not clearly stated, the situation is not defined and consequences are uncertain. In such a situation strong rationality is out of the question and weak rationality indeterminate. Because of this, much collective action is symbolic, or *expressive* (Turner, 1981: 9–13).[43] This view is in fundamental agreement with an approach that emphasizes collective identity, rather than collective interest, in the explanation of collective action. Thus, Turner agrees with Fireman and Gamson that individual selves are made up of social identities to a degree that makes it difficult clearly to separate self-interest from group-interest

320

(1981: 14). This view derives from the symbolic interactionist tradition in social psychology, to which Turner, himself, and the theory of collective behaviour, belongs. But 'Klapp's . . . interpretation of social movements as "collective search for identity" builds on this tradition, though few collective behaviorists would emphasize this process so disproportionately' (1981: 6). It is to this identity-oriented interpretation that I will now turn.

The resource mobilization approach was inspired by the experience of the rise of a number of new social movements in the United States, in the 1960s and 1970s: the civil rights movement, the anti-war movement, the student movement, the women's movement, etc. In fact, most of those contributing to the emergence of a new approach to social movements had direct experience of work in these movements (Morris and Herring, 1984b: 182–184).

Turning to Europe, the new social movements gave rise, not only to a new approach, but to a new concept (Melucci, 1980; Habermas, 1981; Eder, 1982; Cohen, 1983). The word 'new' in the concept of 'new social movements' indicates that we have to do, not only with new specimens of a kind, but with a new kind. Examples of new social movements would be the women's movement, the environmental movement, the anti-nuclear movement, the peace movement, the youth movement and various minority movements.

What, then, is new in the new social movements? There is no unanimous answer to this question, but the following characteristics are commonly agreed upon (cf. Offe, 1985b: 825ff.; Dalton *et al.*, 1990: 10–16): (1) New social movements are not engaged in struggles over distribution. They do not pursue 'material' interests at all, but 'postmaterial' values (Inglehart, 1990: 52f.), such as individual autonomy and participatory democracy, personal and collective identity, a healthy social and physical environment and the survival of mankind. (2) New social movements do not organize in the same way as old ones. They avoid hierarchy and leadership and favour more informal and 'democratic' forms of organization. To a large extent, new social movements are their own ends. They are innovations in forms of life, or 'lifestyles', rather than instruments for further ends. The immediate aims of new social movements are not 'political' in a narrow sense of this term, but 'cultural'. They operate not within the state apparatus, but in 'civil society', where they try to open up a new 'public space' for the expression of shared values and beliefs (cf. Melucci, 1985). (3) The new social movements have no clear class base, but a majority of their supporters are recruited from the new and expanding middle class, or 'petit bourgeoisie' (Eder, 1985; Olotsson 1988).

The idea of 'new social movements' is part of a novel approach centring around the notion of 'identity'. The situation in the sociological analysis of social movements now is that we have two competing, but possibly complementary, approaches (cf. Scott, 1990: 109): the 'resource mobilization' approach dominating the scene in the United States and the 'identity-oriented', or 'new social movement', approach dominating Western Europe (Cohen, 1985; Klandermans, 1986b). The origin of the identity-oriented approach is usually traced to the works of two distinguished sociologists: Alain Touraine and Jürgen Habermas (Cohen, 1982: 26ff.; Eder, 1982: 10ff.; Melucci, 1984a: 821; 1985: 791). Its most energetic defender, however, is Alessandro Pizzorno. Since it is sometimes presented as a novel approach, I wish to stress its deep roots in the sociological tradition, as indicated by the quotation from Turner above.

For Touraine, the occurrence of new social movements is linked to that of 'post-industrial', or 'programmed', society; a society where accumulation, or economic growth, does not depend primarily upon the exploitation of workers, but on the use of knowledge (Touraine, 1969/1971). In post-industrial society, the central conflict is no longer that between labour and capital, but the struggle against the dominating technocracy. The class opposing technocracy does not yet exist, but is in a formative stage of identification.

Very much like Tilly and the conflict tradition in sociology, Touraine sees social movements as parts of social conflict, or class struggle. This struggle is political, but does not necessarily involve the state. Social movements belong in civil society, but occasionally take part in historical struggles aiming at the replacement of one social system by another. In these cases, the state becomes the focus of contention (Touraine, 1978/1981: chs 5–6).

Touraine differs from the resource mobilization approach, however, in denying that social movements are engaged in conflicts of *interest*. While always present, interest is never the sole motive for participation in social movements (Touraine, 1978/1981: 63; 1985: 753, 762f., 769). This view, as we have seen, conforms to that of Mancur Olson (see p. 211). Touraine does not agree with Olson, however, that the non-rational motive is irrational. The characteristic mark of social movements, unlike interest groups, is their normative, or cultural orientation (Touraine, 1978/1981: 57ff., 80; 1985: 760ff.). Social movements are engaged in struggles over 'historicity'. The stakes in these struggles are cultural patterns and values. According to Touraine, the main threat to social movements is the egotism of utilitarian consumer society. And this is not just because self-interest leads to free riding. New social movements fight a society where utilitarianism is the dominant cultural pattern and the new 'opium of the people'. 'The utilitarian tradition is the main limit and obstacle to social movements today as religion was in more traditional cultures' (Touraine, 1985: 779).

Touraine's role in the development of the identity-oriented approach to social movements stems from his analysis of social movements in terms of the three principles of identity, opposition and totality. A social movement is the combination of three elements: 'the defense of the unity of the action – what we shall call a principle of identity, I; the struggle against a social adversary – the principle of opposition, O; the reference to the whole of society – the principle of totality, T' (Touraine, 1969/1971: 132; see also 1978/1981: 80ff.). But what, more precisely, does 'identity' mean? Touraine observes that the theme of identity has become increasingly popular in the social sciences, but also that it is an ambiguous notion (Touraine, 1984/1988: 75–82). Well, Touraine ought to know what it means, since he is one of those who contributed to making it such a popular notion. I recognize three distinct senses of the term 'identity', as used by Touraine (1974). There is (1) 'social identity', or an individual's social role; his/her assigned place in society. There is (2) 'personal identity', or an individual's self, as something distinct from his/her social roles. Both (1) and (2) play a part in Touraine's explanation of the rise of social movements. Some social movements defend traditional social roles against changes that threaten to make them obsolete. Other social movements, such as the 'new social movements', are more concerned to defend some personal autonomy and integrity against impending 'social forces'. But it is the third sense of 'identity' which is most important. Touraine uses the term 'social identity' in a second sense, in which it is constitutive of social movements. This is (3) 'social identity' as the result of common experiences and common struggles. I prefer to call this third form of identity 'collective identity'.

Habermas, like Touraine, first met with a new type of social movement in the shape of the student movement of 1968. For Habermas (1969/1971: 24–34), this movement signified a bourgeois (youth) revolt against bourgeois society; against competition, status-seeking and possessive individualism. A characteristic feature of this protest was its independence of, and contempt for, any instrumental criterion of success. Movement, protest, activity, participation turned into a lifestyle, a counterculture, an end in itself (cf. Hirschman, 1982/1985: ch. 4).

In his later writings, Habermas occasionally returns to the topic of new social movements, which are now analysed with the help of his celebrated distinction between *system* and *lifeworld* (Habermas, 1981; 1981/1987: 391–396). New social movements protest against the colonization of the lifeworld by the state and the economy. They protest against the roles assigned to individuals by these systems; the roles of citizen and client of the state, and of employee and consumer in the economy. New social movements are defensive attempts to restore a threatened lifeworld; threatened lifestyles and, more fundamentally, personal and collective identities. In this respect, the new social movements resemble the romantic reaction to early industrial society. An exception is the women's movement, which is more on the offensive and more continuous with traditional social movements, such as the labour movement. The main objectives of the women's movement have been freedom from male oppression, the dissolution of patriarchy, and the realization of equality of rights and opportunities.

The idea of 'new social movements' has met with some healthy scepticism from Alan Scott. I find his doubts about the qualitative novelty of the new social movements largely justified, as is his critique of the tendency to neglect important differences between them (Scott, 1990: ch. 4, 152–156; cf. also Brand, 1990). Scott's argument, however, is not incompatible with the view that the new social movements are 'new' in some less demanding sense (see, e.g., Kuechler and Dalton, 1990: 282; Opp, 1990). One reason why their novelty has been exaggerated may be the initial concentration on the student movement, and its turning into a paradigm. Scott seems more inclined to assume that it is a consequence of holistic reasoning. Maybe? Anyway, I share Scott's doubts about Alain Touraine's belief that the new social movements will eventually coalesce into *the* social movement engaged in the struggle over historicity (Scott, 1990: 60–69). Touraine may be critical of Hegelian teleology, but this belief smacks of Hegelian essentialism. What else would make us believe that social movements must follow some pattern known *a priori*?

Scott's objections do not concern the identity-oriented approach, which he seems to endorse without reservations (Scott, 1990: ch. 5); only it is recognized that identity is not something peculiar to new social movements, but a characteristic of all social movements. Scott raises the issue of identity in a direct encounter with Mancur Olson and the economic theory of collective action. He does so without any reference to Alessandro Pizzorno; surprisingly, since Pizzorno is probably the most well-known advocate of an identity-oriented approach as a complement to the more established interest-oriented approach.

Pizzorno's first move is to problematize the concept of 'interest'. Interests are not the sort of primordial and fixed entities that economic theory assumes they are. Interests arise and change in the flux of events. Collective interests, in particular, do not arise from a mere juxtaposition of individual interests. A precondition for the existence of collective interests is the formation of collective identities.

> There is a category of action which may be observed in social conflicts, that can be understood only if it is asked of them not what gains and what losses they will produce for the actors, but whether they will produce solidarity or not. These are the actions connoting a process of formation of a collective identity. Here expressive conduct will replace instrumental conduct. Direct participation will be felt to be necessary since representation is excluded and trust is not yet grounded. And the Olsonian law that participation for the acquisition of collective goods is uneconomical is suspended.
>
> (Pizzorno, 1978: 293)

For Pizzorno, then, identification always precedes interest (cf. Johnston, 1991: 101–105). The reason identity is so important in the case of the new social movements is simply that they are new. They are still in the process of identification (Pizzorno, 1981: 278–282). The relation between identity and interest, then, is temporal. But it is also structural. Pizzorno distinguishes three levels of political action: (1) the social basis of interest, (2) the active members of parties and social movements and (3) the leaders, or professional

324

politicians. Olson's logic of collective action operates at levels (1) and (3), while collective identity and solidarity is necessary at level (2).[44]

Against the economic theory of collective action, sociologists maintain that collective action is usually surrounded by so much uncertainty as to make strong rationality quite impossible (see, e.g., Turner, 1981, 1991). Pizzorno shares this view and argues that it correctly describes the situation of most political activity. Collective identity can be understood as a way of coping with uncertainty and defending long-term interests in an ever-changing environment (Pizzorno, 1985: 50–64; 1990: 307–324). Similar considerations have led Patrick Dunleavy to suggest an economic approach to group identity. His proposal is a well-known move in the repertoire of economic imperialism, used, this time, to save the public choice theory of interest groups. Group identity is a rational guide to self-interest in a state of imperfect information (Dunleavy, 1988: 32ff.). Group identity becomes analogous to ideology in Downs' theory of voting. This is not the view of collective identity defended by Pizzorno and the sociological approach. In sociology, collective identity spells solidarity (Pizzorno, 1985: 50–64; 1990: 307–324).

'Identity' is an important notion in philosophy. As such, it invites endless disputes. The situation is not much better in social science, but at least you feel permitted to proceed without getting to the bottom of the problem. Identity has to do with the unity and persistence of entities. This is true of social entities as well.

In sociology, three identities dominate: (1) personal or ego identity, (2) social or role identity and (3) collective or group identity.[45]

Most prominent in traditional sociology is the idea of social identity. Before anything else, *homo sociologicus* is man as bearer and/or performer of social roles. This identity, however, has been least important in the sociological theory of social movements.

Personal identity is the self as an entity distinct, or possibly distinct, from the various roles an individual plays. It is an article of faith in sociological theory that personal identity is, to a large extent, a 'social' identity, in the sense of being a social product. The personal self is a 'social self' because it is the end product of socialization and of the attitudes of others. Self is indissolubly linked to self-image and self-image is a mirror image, the mirror being other people.[46]

The degree to which an individual's personal identity is autonomous relative to his/her social roles is called 'role distance'. A second article of faith of sociological theory is that role distance and personal autonomy has increased as a result of historical development. In the beginning, personal identity was weak, or non-existent. Individuals were their social and collective identities. But historical development (in the West) led to increasing differentiation *and* individuation, and to personal identities of increasing autonomy. The ultimate expression of this development is existentialism, or the idea that we are free to choose our personal identities.

Existentialism has a counterpart in rational choice and the idea of 'metapreferences': the idea that we are free to choose our own preferences, or utility function (Hirschmann, 1982/1985: 66ff.; 1984: 89f.; 1985: 8ff.; Frank, 1987). This is going too far in the eyes of many sociologists. So, for instance, Pierre Bourdieu has criticized both existentialism and rational choice for excessive voluntarism (Bourdieu, 1972/1977: 72ff.; 1980/1990: 42ff.). His by now famous concept of *habitus* is used to argue that our choices, or preferences, are also socially predetermined.[47]

In any case, sociologists have argued that personal identity is at stake in new social movements and plays a role in the explanation of most collective action. The argument, as we have seen, is that at least some of the new social movements may be explained as rejections of the personal identities created by modern society and as attempts to create new personal and collective identities. In the case of the ecological movement something more is at stake: it is a matter of survival, or biological identity. This introduces the problematic dimension of time. What becomes of rationality and self-interest in the long run?

Rational choice theorists have tackled this problem only recently. The traditional assumption in economics was that individuals discount the utility of future consumption. And this is probably a perfectly justified assumption in the case of ordinary consumption goods. But when it comes to more important things, such as occupation, a place to live, health and a good environment, more prudent behaviour might be possible. But prudence means solving the potential conflict between short-term and long-term interest. Increasing attention is paid to the fact that our short-term interest in smoking cigarettes, having another drink, driving cars and consuming as much as possible is detrimental to our long-term interest in health and a good environment. One way to analyse this problem is to see it as analogous to the collective action problem (cf. pp. 218f.). In the case of a good environment, it is, of course, a collective action problem in the original sense, since it involves a collective good. But it is also a temporal problem involving several generations. My present interest, however, is in private goods. Divide a person into a plurality of successive selves and you get an intertemporal, intrapersonal 'collective action' problem. The equivalent of self-interested free riding is myopia and weakness of will. The way for an individual to solve this intertemporal collective action problem is precommitment (Elster, 1979b, part II; Schelling, 1984; Ainslie, 1986).

The introduction of time in rational choice has made not only interest, but also personal identity, problematic. Precommitment may be seen as a kind of metapreference for a certain personal identity. It may also be seen as a private norm (cf. Ainslie; 1986: 145f.; Elster, 1989a: 102–104). In this case, it bursts the frame of economics and rational choice.

More relevant for the explanation of collective action is the possibility of people identifying with some purpose other than personal welfare. It is a fact no economist can deny that individuals sometimes take great risks for a cause higher than themselves. Such bravery might not be very common, but it does exist.[48] This is the point of departure for Craig Calhoun's explanation of the protests in Beijing in Spring 1989 (Calhoun, 1991b). Himself a witness to these events, Calhoun became convinced that they cannot be explained in terms of interest. A satisfactory explanation must include reference to the personal and collective identities of the protesting students. Included in their personal identities, was a defence of certain values, such as freedom, national pride and personal integrity, associated with the traditional Chinese notion of 'honour'.[49]

Calhoun rejects the possibility of analysing personal identity in terms of interest (Calhoun, 1991b: 66f.). Thus, it was not a matter of the students having a preference for a certain personal identity. The identification of the students with certain values was not instrumental. It was 'value-rational', in the sense of Max Weber: a commitment to a value for its own sake, without regard to outcome. But commitment does not exclude consequentialism. It excludes only self-interest. People may also be committed to the cause of a group (see Sen, 1979: 95–109). According to Calhoun, this was the case with the students in Beijing. They identified not only with impersonal values, but also with their class and with their nation (Calhoun, 1991b: 55ff., 69f.). And, indeed, this is inevitable, since values are always cultural values and, as such, the property of some collective.

'Collective identity', finally, refers to the unity and persistence of a collective. Such unity, however, cannot exist without a collective consciousness, or we-feeling – a sense of belonging on the part of the members of the collective, which is the basis of solidarity. It is mainly to this collective consciousness sociologists refer, when invoking collective identity in the explanation of collective action. Economists admit that altruism is possible in the family, but tend to deny that it is possible in larger groups or collectives.[50] Sociologists, on the other hand, tend to believe that a we-feeling, or collective identity, may develop in much larger groups – including classes, races, ethnic groups, nations, sexes and churches – and sometimes does. We have already met with this belief in the case of the sociological theory of the group, in Marx's theory of class and, now, in the sociological theory of social movements. We will meet it again, more fundamentally, in the sociological notion of 'community' (cf. Jenks, 1990: 54).

The idea of collective identity is incompatible with public choice, but not with rational choice. The reason is that rational choice, unlike public choice, does not presuppose self-interest, as evidenced, for instance, by Howard Margolis' new model of rational choice (1981, 1982/1984). Even so, some advocates of rational choice express doubts concerning the explanatory power of the concept of 'collective identity' (see, e.g., Elster, 1989a: 168 and Przeworski, 1990: 72). Przeworski, who seems willing to accept that identity, or 'preference', formation is a social process, nevertheless accuses adherents

327

of the identity-oriented approach of mistakenly believing that this invalidates the rational choice approach. This is, of course, not the case, since once preferences are formed people act upon them and rational choice is fully applicable (ibid., p. 70). This must be granted, but Przeworski is wrong to assume that defenders of the identity-oriented approach deny this. Not at all and quite the contrary. As we have seen, this is exactly Pizzorno's view: identity formation precedes, but does not replace, interest. Later, Pizzorno suggests that the distinction between identity and interest is analytic. 'The two components coexist in the same person and are complementary' (Pizzorno, 1985: 63; see also 1990: 323). The claim is not that rational choice, or the interest-oriented approach, is invalid, but that it is incomplete. It does not capture the whole truth about collective action. This is perfectly clear also in Eyerman's and Jamison's (1991) cognitive approach to social movements. Collective identities are shaped in the search for new knowledge and new values, but neither knowledge nor values are independent of interests.

So far I have discussed only theories, approaches and beliefs, but is there any evidence? It would be possible to invoke the whole history of religious wars and crusades, wars between tribes and nations, wars of national liberation and ethnic separation, class struggles, etc., and argue that this history is overwhelming evidence of the existence and significance of collective identity, since self-interested individuals would not risk their lives for the possible benefits of these instances of collective action; but, presumably, this will not impress adherents of an economic approach to politics. An economic interpretation is always possible. Still, I insist that it is not credible. I, for one, cannot see how it is possible to understand what is happening in the former Soviet Union and Yugoslavia today, for instance, without recourse to the idea of collective identity. Not that I deny that self-interest is an important ingredient in these conflicts, as in most conflicts, but more important, still, is group-interest, and before we can even identify these group-interests, we must understand the complex of religious, national, ethnic and class identities involved in the articulation of these interests.

7

COOPERATION AND SOCIAL ORDER

We saw in Chapter 5 that the problem of collective action generalized into the problem of cooperation and, ultimately, of social order. This was possible because the problem of collective action is that of the provision of collective goods and social order may be conceived of as a collective good of sorts.

A considerable advance was made, in the economic theory of collective action, with the introduction of 'history', in the form of iterated prisoners' dilemmas. A 'solution' was found to the collective action problem as soon as it was possible for people to meet again. Robert Axelrod found that a strategy of tit-for-tat, or reciprocity, would lead to the evolutionary emergence of cooperation. His results were confirmed by Michael Taylor, who went on to argue that reciprocity is a characteristic mark of communities. Hence, cooperation is possible in the absence of a centralized authority, or state, only if social order takes the form of community.

Axelrod and Taylor take an economic approach to 'reciprocity' and 'community', at least as a start (as I have argued on pp. 247–250, they both came to accept the sociological view of reciprocity as a social norm). But both concepts have a long history in anthropology and sociology, where they signify something entirely different from, even opposed to, any economic interpretation. I will end this book with a presentation of the anthropological/sociological ideas of 'reciprocity' and 'community', since I believe that this is the best way to clarify the difference between the economic and sociological approaches to cooperation and social order.

RECIPROCITY

Reciprocity, in the writings of Axelrod and Taylor, is negative reciprocity, or punishment for defection. But reciprocity may also be positive, as in the case of reward for cooperation. In any economic theory, however, reciprocity must act upon the incentives at work in the rational choice of individuals. Reciprocity is the result of individuals' long-term interest in cooperation. While it pays to defect in the short run, it pays to cooperate in the long run.

In his *Community, Anarchy and Liberty* (1982), Michael Taylor makes exten-

329

sive use of anthropological literature to substantiate his own ideas on reciprocity and community. It does not emerge, from his references to anthropological work, however, that virtually all of the anthropologists mentioned took a radically different view of the matter. In fact, most of them are critical of the use of the economic approach in the study of the economies of non-market societies. One reason for this is exactly that the pervasive phenomenon of reciprocity defies standard economic analysis.

Taylor's references on the subject of reciprocity are to Marcel Mauss and Marshall Sahlins. But both Mauss and Sahlins, like the majority of anthropologists, see in the phenomenon of reciprocity a limit to economic analysis. The reason is that reciprocity is not at all a matter of free exchange, or of rational choice, but of obligation.

Among the first anthropologists to call attention to the pervasive role of reciprocity in 'savage society' was Bronislaw Malinowski. This is unfortunate for me, since Malinowski may be interpreted as lending support to an economic interpretation of reciprocity (see, e.g. Davis, 1973). The case is complex, because of an inconsistency in his work, but there is no doubt that Malinowski eventually came to maintain that the 'savage' was about as selfish as a modern businessman. He never argued, however, that either is entirely selfish. In his *Argonauts of the Western Pacific* (1922) Malinowski describes and analyses the famous *Kula*: a sort of indirect exchange of ceremonial gifts between (members of) tribes on the Trobriand Islands. Associated with this ceremonial gift exchange are ordinary trade and other activities. The important point to notice, for me, however, is '*that the whole tribal life is permeated by a constant give and take*. That every ceremony, every legal and customary act is done to the accompaniment of material gift and counter gift; that wealth, given and taken, is one of the main instruments of social organization, of power of the chief, of the bonds of kinship, and of relationship in law' (Malinowski, 1922/1961: 167). Economic life on the Trobriands, thus, does not take the form of free exchange, but is subject to strict rules of privilege and duty, associated with social status, especially kinship. Malinowski, then, is one of the main sources of the idea that, in primitive society, economic activity is not differentiated from other social phenomena, but part of 'Total social phenomena' (Mauss), or 'embedded' in social relationships (Polanyi).

Another notion which must be exploded, once and for ever, is that of the Primitive Economic Man of some current text books. This fanciful, dummy creature, who has been very tenacious of existence in popular and semipopular economic literature, and whose shadow haunts even the minds of competent anthropologists, blighting their outlook with a preconceived idea, is an imaginary, primitive man, or savage, prompted in all his actions by a rationalistic conception of self-interest, and achieving his aims directly and with a minimum of effort. Even *one* well established instance should show how preposterous is this assumption that man, and especially man on a low level of culture, should be actuated by pure economic motives of enlightened self-interest. The primitive Trobriander furnishes us with such an instance, contradicting this fallacious theory.

(Malinowski, 1922/1961: 60)

This statement seems clear enough, but is based upon a narrow view of self-interest as limited to a craving for economic, or material, gain. Against this view, Malinowski holds that primitive man is motivated, above all, by prestige. Wealth is important, but only because of the social prestige and power it confers on its possessor, and most prestigious is to give it away (Malinowski, 1922/1961: 62, 166ff.). Thus, primitive economic man is not a wealth maximizer. But he/she might still be a utility-maximizer in some more inclusive sense. And, of course, the lust for power and prestige is not disinterested. This is something that Malinowski came to realize in his *Crime and Custom in Savage Society* (1926). In this book, Malinowski attempts to explode the prevalent conception of primitive man as ruled entirely by custom and of primitive society as perfectly cohesive. Against this myth, Malinowski now argues that primitive man is more or less like modern man: individualistic, opportunistic and hypocritical; ruled by ambition, pride and self-interest (Malinowski, 1926: 27, 36, 48, 67, 73f., 80, 115f.). If primitive man fulfils his/her obligations, this is because it pays to do so. First, because gifts are given and returned in a way that balances in the long run (ibid., p. 26). Second, because of the sanctions attached to defection (ibid., p. 52f.). Instead of the noble savage, Malinowski gives us a picture of primitive man as governed by enlightened self-interest. But only partly (ibid., p. 30). Malinowski's aim is to demolish one exaggeration, not to replace it with another (ibid., pp. 55f., 58).

The fact is that no society can work in an efficient manner unless laws are obeyed 'willingly' and 'spontaneously'. The threat of coercion and the fear of punishment do not touch the average man, whether 'savage' or 'civilized', while, on the other hand, they are indispensable with regard to certain turbulent or criminal elements in either society. Again, there is a number of laws, taboos and obligations in every human culture which weigh heavily on every citizen, demand great self-sacrifice, and are obeyed for moral, sentimental or matter-of-fact reasons, but without any 'spontaneity' . . . that it is not enforced by any wholesale motive like fear of punishment, or a general submission to all tradition, but by very complex psychological and social inducements – all this is a state of affairs which modern anthropology has so far completely overlooked

(Malinowski, 1926: 13–15; see also pp. 20, 53)

Malinowski was the pioneer in the anthropological study of gifts and of gift exchange,[1] but the classic in this field is Marcel Mauss' *The Gift* (1925). A

331

basic theme of this book is that *homo oeconomicus*, the calculating machine, is the creation of modern market society. At times it would seem that Mauss, like the early Malinowski, had a rather restricted view of economic man as bent only upon material gain. Thus, he does not deny that men and women in early civilizations had interests, but they differed from those that predominate in our culture. Mauss even admits that a classic example of seeming generosity, such as the Potlach (a ceremonial gift common among the Indians living on the North West coast), is not free from self-interest (Mauss, 1925/1969: 72f.). 'The form usually taken is that of a gift generously offered; but the accompanying behaviour is formal pretence and social deception, while the transaction itself is based on obligation and self-interest' (ibid., p. 1).[2] The dominant theme of Mauss' work, however, is that reciprocal gift-giving is very different from free exchange for mutual adavantage. Being the nephew and disciple of Emile Durkheim, Marcel Mauss attempts to show that the essence of *Kula* exchange, Potlach, and other gifts, is the *obligation* to give (ibid., pp. 37–41).[3]

One of the most important critics of economic theory, among anthropologists, is Karl Polanyi, the head of the substantivist camp in economic anthropology. Like Mauss, Polanyi maintains that economic man is the offspring of market society, but unknown to people in non-market societies. It may be argued that Polanyi's critique also rests on a restricted conception of 'economic man' as a maximizer of net wealth. This seems to be the view of Michael Hechter (1983a: 164–168), who also seems to suggest that Polanyi's view of human motivation is compatible with a less restricted theory of rational choice. If this is Hechter's view, he is wrong.[4] Rational choice can assimilate some of the motives mentioned by Polanyi, but not all of them.

Polanyi accuses economists of working with an altogether inadequate theory of human motivation.

> Honor and pride, civic obligation and moral duty, even self-respect and common decency, were now deemed irrelevant to production, and were significantly summed up in the world 'ideal'. Hence man was believed to consist of two components, one more akin to hunger and gain, the other to honor and power. The one was 'material,' the other 'ideal'; the one 'economic,' the other 'non-economic'; the one 'rational,' the other 'non-rational.'
>
> (Polanyi [1947]1971: 69f.)

> On closer investigation, [man is] still found to be acting on remarkably 'mixed' motives, not excluding those of duty toward himself and others – and maybe, secretly, even enjoying work for its own sake.
>
> (Polanyi, 1971: 69)

Suggesting that we should include things like honour and pride in people's 'utility functions' is compatible with Gary Becker's more inclusive concept of 'utility-maximization' (1976: 5; Stigler and Becker, 1977). Mention of self-respect anticipates Thomas Schelling's idea of metapreferences, and the possibility of enjoying work for its own sake antedates an argument to this effect by Albert Hirschman. All these motives may be included in a rational choice model, but not civic obligation and moral duty.

Polanyi's most well-known thesis is that economic activity, in non-market societies, is embedded in social relations of religion, kinship and political authority (Polanyi [1957] 1971: chs 6–7; see also 1944/1957: ch. 4 and 1966: xv–xxvi). Only in modern market economies is the economic system a relatively autonomous sphere of human activity. In all other systems, economic activity is subordinated to the rights and obligations of social status. This fact has important implications for economic analysis. There are two meanings of the term 'economic' (Polanyi [1957] 1971: 139ff.). According to the traditional, *substantive* concept, 'economics' refers to the way people satisfy their (material) needs. In the modern *formal* conception, 'economics' means economizing on scarce resources. An undesirable consequence of the formal concept is that only modern market societies can be said to have an economy. The reason is that only in modern market economies is 'economic' activity identical with economizing. Only in market society are prices determined by market exchange, which alone makes economizing possible, or better, the predominant mode of economic activity (see also Sahlins 1972/1988: 277–314).

I will not discuss the historical accuracy of Polanyi's theses about the singularity of market society and the absence of economizing in non-market societies. Some commentators have suggested that the difference between societies may not be that great; that embeddedness in premarket societies was less deep than claimed by the substantivists, and, in particular, that exchange in market society is also embedded in social relations, if less institutionalized (Granovetter, 1985: 483ff.; 1993; Macneil, 1986: 577ff., 591–593; Davis, 1992: 7f.). This is an important corrective, but does not affect the issue of reciprocity. The important point, for my purposes, is Polanyi's insistence that market exchange is only one form of economic transaction and only one way of integrating economic activity. Other forms of economic integration are reciprocity and redistribution.

Empirically, we find the main patterns to be reciprocity, redistribution, and exchange. Reciprocity denotes movements between correlative points of symmetrical groupings; redistribution designates appropriational movements toward a center and out of it again; exchange refers here to vice versa movements taking place as between 'hands' under a market system. Reciprocity, then, assumes for a background symmetrically arranged groupings; redistribution is dependent upon the presence of some measure of centricity in the group; exchange in order to produce integration requires a system of price-making markets.

(Polanyi [1957] 1971: 149)

All these forms of integration can coexist in one society and typically do. But, according to Polanyi, reciprocity dominated in primitive society and redistribution in archaic society, while exchange dominates only in modern Western society.[5]

Taylor's main reference on reciprocity is to Marshall Sahlins, who builds upon the works of Malinowski, Mauss and Polanyi, and belongs to the substantivist school in economic anthropology (Sahlins, 1969). A virtue of Sahlins' analysis is its comprehensiveness; it is based upon an extensive survey of the anthropological literature on the different forms of reciprocity in a large variety of cultures. One result of this survey is a refutation of the

> popular tendency to view reciprocity as balance, as unconditional one-for-one exchange. Considered as a material transfer, reciprocity is often not that at all. Indeed, it is precisely through scrutiny of departures from balanced exchange that one glimpses the interplay between reciprocity, social relations, and material circumstances.
>
> (Sahlins, 1965: 144; 1972/1988: 190)

> The casual received view of reciprocity supposes some fairly direct one-for-one exchange, balanced reciprocity, or a near proximation of balance. It may not be inappropriate, then, to footnote this discussion with a respectful demur: that in the main run of primitive societies, taking into account directly utilitarian as well as instrumental transactions, balanced reciprocity is not the prevalent form of exchange.
>
> (Sahlins, 1965: 178; 1972/1988: 223)

In Sahlins' scheme of reciprocity, three concepts cover the extremes and the mid-point of a continuum, stretching from (1) *generalized reciprocity*, the solidary extreme, over (2) *balanced reciprocity*, the mid-point of direct exchange, to (3) *negative reciprocity*, the unsociable extreme (Sahlins, 1965: 147–149; 1968: 82f.; 1988: 193–195). The fertility of this scheme is displayed in its correlation with certain structural dimensions of tribal society: kinship distance, kinship rank, wealth and type of good or valuable. Not surprisingly, generalized reciprocity is strongest among kinsmen and expected, above all, from those high in rank. Outside kin groups, generalized reciprocity is expected, above all, from the wealthy. A special weight is attached to food, which is generally expected to be shared with those in need.

The most important basis of reciprocity, in tribal society, is kinship. Generalized reciprocity is strongest in the household and strong also in the lineage, less strong in the village, transforms into balanced reciprocity in the tribe and turns negative in dealings with other tribes.

Generalized reciprocity may expand and replace balanced reciprocity at the village and tribal levels. This development is typically associated with the rise of a big man, or chief, whose responsibility it becomes to administer generalized reciprocity by a pooling and reallocation of resources. 'Big-men and chiefs are compelled to relieve shortages among the people – just like the ordinary kinsmen but even more so, for the tribal leader is a paragon among kinsmen and his concern for community welfare is a kind of centralization of kinship morality' (Sahlins, 1968: 78). Generalized reciprocity thus develops into redistribution (Sahlins, 1965: 141–143; 160–164; 1968: 86–95; 1972/1988: 188–190, 206–210). There is a presumption, common among anthropologists, that the transition from reciprocity to redistribution in tribal economy, since it implies the existence of a centre, has something to do with the emergence of political authority and, eventually, the state (Mauss, 1925/1969: 73; Polanyi, 1944/1957: 48–53; 1966: ch. 3; 1971: 153ff., 306ff.; Sahlins, 1968: 94; Service, 1975: 72–80). If this is so, the welfare state can be seen as a modern version of the original state.

Balanced reciprocity may also expand and replace negative reciprocity as a pattern of intertribe relations. According to Sahlins, gift exchange is the main vehicle of pacification of relations between tribes. In an interpretation of Mauss' essay on the gift, Sahlins suggests that we might read this work as a treatise on political philosophy, offering an alternative to Hobbes. 'The primitive analogue of social contract is not the State, but the gift. The gift is the primitive way of achieving the peace that in civil society is secured by the state' (Sahlins 1972/1988: 169). The gift is a way to come to terms with members of other tribes and even to become friends with them, thus creating the conditions necessary for the development of ordinary trade and other activities.

For all its fertility as an instrument of analysis, there is something odd about Sahlins' scheme of reciprocity (cf. Service, 1966: 15f.). 'Generalized reciprocity' means altruism, sharing and generosity. This sounds more like benevolence. True, Sahlins mentions a diffuse obligation to reciprocate in some way, but it seems to me that the ideal type of reciprocity is balanced reciprocity.

'Negative reciprocity' is also problematic, since it means the absence of reciprocity, or the one-sided attempt to get something for nothing (cf. Davis, 1992: 24). This sounds more like the extreme of unequal exchange, or exploitation (cf. Gouldner 1960: 165–167). It may also be mentioned that Sahlins misinterprets Alvin Gouldner, who is the source of this term. According to Gouldner, 'negative reciprocity' means reciprocal malevolence; the reciprocal infliction of harm, as in revenge, retaliation, vendetta and other feuds (ibid., p. 172).

Alvin Gouldner sees in the norm of reciprocity a cultural universal, on a par with the more well-known incest taboo. In its most general, it prescribes: '(1) people should help those who have helped them, and (2) people should not injure those who have helped them' (Gouldner 1960: 171). The norm of reciprocity does not necessarily imply equivalence of value, or *quid pro quo*, but this is the ideal and it is important to distinguish reciprocity from complementarity of rights and duties (Gouldner 1960: 167–169, 172f.). It might be argued that Sahlins' generalized reciprocity obscures this distinction, as well as the distinction between the general norm of reciprocity and the general *norm of beneficence* (Gouldner, 1975: ch. 9). At least, Gouldner's examples of beneficence are identical with the examples Sahlins gives of generalized reciprocity. The norm of beneficence 'requires men to give others such help as they *need*'.[6]

> As we view it here, the norm of beneficence is a diffuse one encompassing a number of somewhat more concrete normative orientations such as 'altruism', 'charity', or 'hospitality'. In short, the norm calls on men to give something for nothing.
>
> (Gouldner 1975: 266)

An important idea, for my purposes, is Gouldner's suggestion that the norms of reciprocity and beneficence might work as 'starting mechanisms' for regular interaction. Malinowski had criticized utilitarian economics for ignoring 'the deep tendency to create social ties through exchange of gifts' (Malinowski, 1922/1961: 175). Mauss and Sahlins analysed the gift as a way to make peace and become friends with members of other tribes. This is what Gouldner means by a 'starting mechanism'.

The existence of such starting mechanisms is compatible with Robert Axelrod's analysis of the emergence of cooperation, except for the basic assumption of self-interest. I would even suggest that it provides a much-needed complement to that analysis, because it suggests a way that cooperation might start.[7] The gift, as analysed by Malinowski, Mauss and Sahlins, is the equivalent of cooperating in the first round of an iterated prisoners' dilemma. The important difference is this: while Axelrod's analysis relies upon the possibility that self-interested individuals might hit upon the strategy of reciprocity by mere chance, Gouldner suggests that it is a matter of good will.

It has been argued, by a number of critics, that the economic theory of collective action cannot explain how it gets started. This argument was advanced by Gouldner in his 1960 article on reciprocity. 'From the standpoint of a purely economic or utilitarian model, there are certain difficulties in accounting for the manner in which social interaction begins' (Gouldner 1960: 177). The analysis of the norm of reciprocity as a starting mechanism was intended to solve this problem:

> The norm of reciprocity may serve as a starting mechanism in such circumstances by preventing or enabling the parties to break out of this impasse. When internalized in both parties, the norm *obliges* the one who has first received a benefit to repay it at some time; it provides some realistic grounds for confidence, in the one who first parts with his valuables, that he will be repaid. Consequently, there may be less

hesitancy in being the first and a greater facility with which the exchange and the social relation can get underway.

(Gouldner 1960: 177)

In his later article on the norm of beneficence, Gouldner suggests, more plausibly, that it is the norm of beneficence that triggers an interaction subsequently based on reciprocity (Gouldner, 1975: 275–277). This latter suggestion is supported by two considerations.

First, the gift, when used as a starting mechanism, is not intended as the first move in a prisoners' dilemma. It is intended to break the isolation of the 'prisoners'. It is not even intended as part of a purely instrumental exchange. It is intended to create a relationship of mutual trust that may become the basis of other forms of interaction, including ordinary trade. The gift is ceremonial. It is a symbolic act of generosity, a gesture carrying the message that the donor wishes to create a social relationship.

Second, bestowing gifts upon individuals from other tribes is a generalization, or extension, of the morality governing tribal relations to relations with other tribes (Sahlins, 1972/1988: 196–204, 219ff., 279f., 302; see also Service, 1966: 17–20). In the *Kula*, individuals from different tribes create lifelong relations of friendship with their exchange-partners (Malinowski, 1922/1961: 85, 91, 275–281). This seems to be the typical pattern of intertribal interaction. But it also happens that trading partners become so close as to conceive of each other as kin, or quasi-kin; referred to as 'kin' and treated as such (Sahlins, 1965: 155–158, 176; 1972/1988: 201–204, 221, 281, 285, 302).

COMMUNITY

A precondition for reciprocity is that people meet again. This condition is satisfied most fully in the type of social structure called 'community'. Michael Taylor has, therefore, suggested that cooperation is possible in this type of social structure. Indeed, (1) reciprocity is one, of three, defining characteristics of community. The other two characteristics are (2) common values and beliefs, and (3) direct and many-sided relations.

In the light of the argument in the previous section, I would like to suggest that community is characterized by the norm of beneficence even more than by the norm of reciprocity. Concerning common values and beliefs, I wish to remind the reader of my argument in Chapter 5 (pp. 248–250) to the effect that Taylor eventually adopted views incompatible with an economic theory of collective action. This happens when you accept that some values and beliefs are moral and that the norm of reciprocity is a virtue, not just a strategy.[8] For an economic theory of cooperation, the important thing about community is that relations are direct and many-sided. This makes it possible to use the strategy of tit-for-tit, as in a prisoners' dilemma and, more important, using tit-for-tat, as in social control by means of selective incentives (see also Hechter, 1987: ch. 8). Taylor's definition of community, however, omits one characteristic of central importance to the sociological concept of 'community': a sense of belonging to, and of identification with, the group, that turns it into a community.[9]

Taylor maintains the exact opposite of the sociological theory of community. According to him, members of a community are poor and, therefore, more self-interested than people living in industrial society, who can afford the luxury of altruism, self-expression and commitment to values (1988a: 92). This, however, is in contradiction to Taylor's critique of the liberal theory of the state, which rests on the explicit assumption that the destruction of community involves a decay of altruism (1982: 53–59; 1987: 168–175). Taylor's critique of the liberal theory of the state, at first, looks very much like traditional anthropology and sociology: the transition from community (primitive, traditional society) to (modern, industrial) society involves a loss of common beliefs and values and of the efficacy of norms, but an increase of instrumentally rational action. It turns out to be the opposite. When Taylor laments the destruction of community, this is not because, in the terminology of Durkheim, it leads to 'anomie', but because it removes the conditions of rational collective action. Surprisingly – to a sociologist, at least – Taylor actually maintains that instrumentally rational action is more prevalent in communities than in modern societies. As a consequence, a thin theory of rationality is more applicable to the former than to the latter (1988a: 90–93). This view is diametrically opposed to that of Max Weber, who saw the development of the West as a process of rationalization: a gradual replacement of traditional action by instrumentally rational action. A corollary of Weber's rationalization thesis is the increasing applicability of the ideal type of instrumentally rational action in modern society (Weber, 1908/1975: 33). I have raised some objections to Weber's conclusions concerning methodology elsewhere (Udehn, 1981b), but I still find his analysis far more convincing than that of Taylor. It may be that some conditions for rational action are better satisfied in a community than in modern, complex and atomistic society. But this does not imply that the conditions for rational action, in general, are better. A careful analysis of this matter must take into account the development of culture and of social institutions. For Weber, the rationalization of the Western world had much to do with religion; with the disenchantment of the world and with institutional factors, such as the introduction of book-keeping and, more generally, with the rise of markets, the modern state and other bureaucracies.

The classic treatise on 'community' is Ferdinand Toennies' *Community and Association* (1955; *Gemeinschaft und Gesellschaft*, 1887).[10] Toennies does not give us a nutshell definition of this term, but its meaning emerges clearly from a reading of the book. The most general sense seems to be a state, and feeling, of 'belonging together' (Toennies, 1887/1955: 26f.), resulting from living together, working together, or sharing a common faith, fate or situation. The

338

three pillars of community are kinship (*Gemeinschaft* of blood), neighbour-hood (*Gemeinschaft* of place) and friendship (*Gemeinschaft* of spirit, or mind); its prototype the family (ibid., pp. 48ff., 223). From this nucleus, community widens in concentric circles to include the household, the village, the town and the commonwealth, as forms of living together; the place of work, the guild, the cooperative and the occupational group as forms of working to-gether. The most obvious example of a community of mind is the religious congregation, order, sect or church.

The typical relations of association (*Gesellschaft*) are exchange and contract; its prototype the market and its primary manifestation capitalism. But to *Gesellschaft* belong, also, all sorts of consciously created and contractually instituted organizations, including interest groups and the state.[11]

Community and association, as forms of social life, are based upon two distinct forms of human will. The psychic basis of community is 'natural will' (*Wesenwille*), the basis of association is 'rational will' (*Kürwille*). The latter concept is easier to grasp, because more clearcut. Rational will is the will of economic man. It is calculated self-interest. The concept of 'natural will' is more complex. As a help for economists, we might point out that it includes, most importantly, the phenomenon of interdependent utility functions. As such, natural will has both a positive and a negative side: it is benevolence, but also malevolence, especially towards those outside one's own community. Inclusion is always also exclusion. Without much argument, however, Toen-nies, like some other sociologists, chooses to concentrate exclusively on the positive side of community and natural will.[12] With this limitation, natural will becomes, in the most generalized form, reciprocal affirmation.

The germinal form of natural will is love, as exemplified, most perfectly, by the relation between mother and child. In less intimate relations, natural will transforms into sympathy and solidarity, and, eventually, into a morality of obligation, or duty. While rational will emanates from *consciousness* and is ex-pressed in self-criticism, natural will spells *conscience* and is accompanied by remorse or shame. Rational will is a manifestation of the intellect, of reason; natural will feeds on feelings, sentiments, emotions. This does not at all mean that natural will is irrational, or that it excludes intellect, or reason. Nor does it mean that rational will is totally free from emotions. It is more like this: in natural will, intellect is subordinated to sentiments and obligations, which give it direction. In rational will, emotions and morality are suppressed by a calculat-ing spirit and an attitude of emotional and moral indifference.

Natural will and rational will give rise to, and depend upon, two different types of social institution. The former is associated with concord, custom and religion; the latter with convention, positive law and public opinion. They are also accompanied by two different concepts of justice: to natural will corresponds *distributive justice*, to rational will *commutative justice*.

The distinction between 'community' and 'association' is ideal typical (Toennies, 1887/1955: 141f., 171–173).[13] Reality is always a mix between them. There is no real community without an element of calculated self-interest and no association without, at least, a rudimentary sense of belonging and solidarity. The ideal typical character of the concept of 'community' does not imply, however, that its realization is merely a utopian fantasy. An important part of Toennies' argument is that communities – if only as approximations of the ideal type – have existed as empirical forms of culture, indeed have dominated the short history of man.[14] Association, on a large scale, is a relatively late phenomenon. It is the thesis of Toennies – as of most sociologists – that development, at least since the rise of capitalism, has involved a constant increase of the element of association at the expense of community.

We may observe that Toennies classifies interest groups and the state as associations. This might seem to lend support to Olson's view of interest groups and to Hobbes' theory of the state. If I understand Toennies correctly – which in this particular case is difficult – he is also aware of the free rider problem (Toennies, 1887/1955: 248–250). Concerning special interest groups, however, it might be added that Toennies seems to have 'associations of capital for the purpose of usury, trade and production' (1887/1955: 225) in mind. By the 'state', Toennies intends the modern nation-state, not any form of political commonwealth.

If we turn from interest groups and states to various types of collectives, the picture becomes less clear. By a 'collective', Toennies understands 'a number of individuals united by some biological, psychic or social characteristic' (Toennies, [1925] 1971: 135), such as sex, race, nation, ethnicity, religion, estate or class. In *Community and Association*, Toennies classifies nations and classes as associations, belonging to *Gesellschaft*. In his later writings, these collectives acquire a community-like character:

> these collectives are more likely to be formed in combination with deep-seated feelings, such as love for one's kind, for one's native country, for one's language and customs, pride in one's ancestors, in possessions, especially in landed property and wealth. But it may also be combined with sentiments which spring from the lack of such privileges and goods, and these again may develop feelings of solidarity and comradeship, perhaps focused and expressed in a common love and admiration of the leader of a party, a common faith, and a common hope.
>
> (Toennies, [1931] 1971: 147; see also [1931] 1955: 5–6)

A second important source for a sociological understanding of *Community* (1917), is Robert MacIver's book with this title. In my opinion, however, MacIver's original treatment is improved upon in *The Elements of Social Science* (1921) and much improved in his *Society* (1937). For MacIver, although he emphasizes that community is a question of degree (1917: 23), there seems to be no absolute limit to the size of community. Cities and nations are examples of communities as much as are tribes and villages (1921: ch. 2). What happens, as the small communities of traditional society are progressively destroyed, in the course of social development, is not that the phenomenon of community disappears, but that people attach to larger communities instead and, especially, to nations. 'In the world of our present-day civilization the nation is the largest effective community. By this we mean that the nation is the largest group which is permeated by the consciousness of comprehensive solidarity' (MacIver, 1937: 154). Lest there should be any misunderstanding, I should perhaps point out that MacIver is no supporter of this development. 'In the modern world, as a limit to the range of community, nationalism is disastrous' (MacIver, 1937: 159).

For MacIver, as for Toennies, community has a 'distinctively territorial character. It implies a common soil as well as a common living' (MacIver, 1937: 147). But community is, above all, a sentiment, and this is the reason it can transcend life in the village or the circle of friends. For MacIver, community sentiment takes the form of identification:

There is the sense of communion itself, of collective participation in an indivisible unity, the feeling that makes men identify with others so that when they say 'we' there is no sort of distinction and when they say 'ours' there is no thought of division. This 'we-sentiment,' or the 'we-interest,' ... is found wherever men have a common interest, but it takes profound character where the interest is the commonweal itself. It is the sentiment which swells most strongly when the commonweal is threatened, so that men are ready to sacrifice all their private interests in order to save it. Yet even here, even in the white heat of such devotion, we should be cautious in using the ethical judgement which distinguishes between self-interest and altruism. It is rather that the interest of the individual is identified with or merged in the larger interest of the group, so that he feels indissolubly bound up with it, so that in his thought the community is 'bone of his bone and flesh of his flesh'.

(MacIver, 1937: 151)

The sad side of nationalism, as of other expressions of community sentiment, is the fear, suspicion and aggression it breeds towards strangers and other communities. On the positive side, we might cite the solidarity it creates, a solidarity which makes a community take care also of its less fortunate members. Sometimes, this solidarity embraces the nation – in rare cases it extends to all human beings and even to animals and plants – and results in the attempt to alleviate the lot of the poor and needy, and to attain some measure of distributive justice. Needless to say, there are limits to the solidarity of larger communities, such as nations. Social cleavages, based on class, race and religion, create antagonistic interests and competing loyalties (MacIver, 1937: 160–165). Most important in modern society is the economic cleavage between classes. While different from communities and disruptive of community sentiment, classes foster an identity of their own; a class sentiment

341

or what Marxists use to call 'class-consciousness' (MacIver, 1937: 173–177).

The sociological concept of 'community' has two parts: one *structural*, the other *cultural* (cf. Cohen, 1985/1989: 11ff., 70). The structural part connotes direct and intimate social relations, as in living and/or working together.[15] The cultural part of community is the experience of belonging to, and identifying with, this social structure. Community as social structure is primary in the sense that living and/or working together creates a sense of belonging. A conception of 'community' that comprises both parts has been suggested by Talcott Parsons, who emphasizes its territorial reference as a place of residence and/or work, but adds that a community is a normative order of legitimate authority and a communicative complex with a common language and a common culture (Parsons, 1959).[16]

A strong emphasis on the structural part of the definition has led to the thesis about a loss, or eclipse, of community. As traditional society is replaced by modern society, communities are replaced by associations. This thesis is sometimes accompanied by nostalgia for traditional (medieval) society and by an idealization of community life. But not always. There is a tendency automatically to classify sociologists writing about community as conservative. This is misleading. While sociologists have argued that community, as a closed social structure with definite boundaries, is on the decline in world history, they have not implied that communities will vanish altogether. Also, community is not a matter of all or nothing; there is also an element of community in distinctly modern social structures. Third, there is the presumption that people can develop a collective identity with collectivities much larger than structural communities.

The latter suggestion has been elaborated by Robert Nisbet in *The Quest for Community* (1953). It is a thesis of this work that people do have a strongly felt need for the intimate social relations that are characteristic of communities. Without them – and this is an axiom of the sociological tradition – individuals are lost in this world. Cut off the social bond and individuals become alienated and experience a 'loss of meaning' (Nisbet, 1953/1990: chs 1 and 3; cf. Habermas, 1981/1987: 140–148). A longing for community, therefore, far from being a characteristic mark of sociologists, is a feeling that is widespread in society and, at times, reaches climactic heights. The argument of Nisbet's book – which I reject – is that the destruction of community is the work of the state, whose representatives cunningly exploit the loneliness and insecurity of individuals for their own expansionist and totalitarian purposes (Nisbet, 1953/1990: 89ff.).

I do accept the presupposition of Nisbet's argument, however. People do have a need for material, emotional and intellectual security. In traditional society this security was provided by communities. I also accept the further argument that the destruction of communities creates a vacuum, somehow to be filled, and may result in a transfer of collective identity to some larger collectivity, such as church, class, race, ethnic group, region, gender or nation-state. Allegiances are shifting and often competing, but class and nation-state have probably been the most consequential in the last hundred years, or two, at least in the West. I have discussed class in the section on 'Collective action' and mentioned some other collectives in the section on 'New social movements' in Chapter 6. I will add a few remarks on nationalism as an ideology and as a feeling of collective identity with the nation-state.

Nationality and nationalism have not received much scholarly attention in the last hundred years, at least not in the West. This is in sharp contrast to the hundred years before, when intellectuals were the most important progenitors of nationalism (Weber, 1922/1978: 926; Smith, 1991: 91–98, 119–123). There are several reasons for the relative lack of interest in nationality and nationalism as social phenomena. One reason is that the role of nationalism in war and in racism has turned it into something demonic, not to be evoked. This is in contrast to another opinion, which sees nationalism as a secondary and passing phenomenon on the wane. This was the view of Marx at a time when nationalism was definitely increasing in strength.

> National differences, and antagonisms between peoples, are daily more and more vanishing, owing to the development of the bourgeoisie, to freedom of commerce, to the world market, to uniformity in the mode of production and in conditions of life corresponding thereto.
>
> (Marx and Engels, 1848/1967: 102)

According to Marx and Engels, of course, capital is primary relative to nation and the proletariat is a force stronger than nationalism – 'working men have no country'.

Max Weber combines the above reasons into the view that nationalism is normally rather weak, but can occasionally and suddenly flare up and give rise to outbursts of national sentiment and action. According to Weber, nationalism is strongly emotional and, therefore, quite irrational (Weber, 1922/1978: 924f.). This is one reason for the problematic nature of 'nationality' and 'nationalism' as concepts in social science.

A third reason why social scientists, until recently, have paid little attention to nationalism and nationality is the difficulty of coming to terms with these phenomena. Max Weber, who was himself a nationalist, at least in his youth, despaired of finding a referent, both for 'nationality' and for 'ethnic group', sometimes used to define 'nation' (Weber, 1922/1978: 387–398).

> If the concept of 'nation' can in any way be defined unambiguously, it certainly cannot be stated in terms of empirical qualities common to those who count as members of the nation. In the sense of those using the term at a given time, the concept undoubtedly means, above all, that *it is proper* to expect from certain groups a specific sentiment of solidarity in the face of other groups.
>
> (Weber, 1922/1978: 922)

343

A similar conclusion was reached by Robert MacIver, who suggested that 'No quality or interest, however common, can be the basis of nationality unless it is regarded as common by those who possess it, and any quality or interest whatever, if so regarded, can be the basis of nationality' (MacIver [1915] 1970: 94). Also:

> it is of the very essence of nationality that it rests on the consciousness of difference no less than on likeness. For each nationality is determined by contrast with others, and nationality regards itself not only as distinct from others, but nearly always as possessing some *exclusive* common qualities, being thereby separated from others as well as united within itself.
>
> (ibid., p. 95)

A fourth reason for the relative scarcity of works on nationalism and national identity is probably that contemporary social scientists, in the West, make up a free-floating cosmopolitan intelligentsia, with a poorly developed national identity and a limited capacity for empathic understanding of other people's national sentiment. In the last ten years, however, the situation has changed markedly, probably because of a new wave of nationalism in various parts of the world. We now have a number of good works on nationalism and nationality. Even so, surprisingly little has been added to the few, but acute, observations made by Weber and MacIver at the beginning of this century.

One thing that emerges from recent research on nationalism, is that, contrary to a common belief, the state begets the nation, rather than the other way around. Nations are not awakened, but created. They are produced by means of nationalism, 'a political principle, which holds that the political and the national unit should be congruent' (Gellner, 1983: 1ff., 39ff.; see also Hobsbawm, 1990: 9f.). Nationalism is an ideology used to create nations and to legitimize the nation-state as a political community (Nisbet, 1953/1990: 145–148). It produces that modicum of solidarity, cohesion and patriotism, or national identity, for short, which is necessary for reasons of state (Balibar, 1991; Smith, 1991: ch. 4).

Another thing that emerges from recent research is that the nation-state is a typically modern phenomenon (Anderson, 1983/1991: 11f.; Hobsbawm, 1990: ch. 1). There is no agreement about the exact cause of nationalism and of the rise of the nation-state, except that it is complex. Most observers argue that it has something to do with the development of capitalism, or industrial society. Benedict Anderson emphasizes the development of 'print capitalism' and of a vernacular print language as a necessary condition for the development of nationalism. The popular press and literature contributed to develop a national culture and a national consciousness (Anderson, 1983/1991: 36ff.). Ernest Gellner provides a functional explanation of nationalism in terms of the need, in industrial society, for a homogeneous and educated population, capable of running this type of society (Gellner, 1983: ch. 3; 1987: ch. 2). I believe that Gellner's structural explanation can be provided with the requisite micro-foundations to give us one important clue to the age of nationalism. Most obviously, we would like to know who has a stake in the creation of a national 'high culture'. For Weber (1922/1978: 926), it 'goes without saying that, just as those who wield power in the polity invoke the idea of the *state*, the intellectuals ... are specifically predestined to propagate the *"national"* idea'. Anthony D. Smith (1991: 120f.) mentions professionals as a category with a special interest in the rise of the nation-state.

Thus, interest is part of the explanation of nationalism. But only part. 'There is, one must repeat, no need to assume any conscious long-term calculation of interest on anyone's part. The nationalist intellectuals were full of warm and generous ardour on behalf of the co-nationals' (Gellner, 1983: 61). Indeed, what nationalism requires of the citizens of the state is exactly that they should sacrifice their self-interest for the sake of the nation (Poole, 1991: 92–94, 97). So what is the nation? As we have already seen, Weber and MacIver despaired of finding a precise answer to this question, and so do contemporary writers. Neither a common homeland, descent or polity, nor a shared language, ethnicity or religion, suffices as a basis of nationality – but they all facilitate the creation of national identity. They do so in a double capacity of reality and myth. The existence of real common features certainly makes nationalism more potent. But the lack of common features does not block the road to national identity. If the citizens of a state lack a homeland, a common ancestry and a common history, these can be invented in the form of myths about a common destiny and reinforced by national symbols (see Smith, 1991: ch. 2; Poole, 1991: 95ff.).

Related to the question of national identity is Benedict Anderson's influential idea of nations as 'imagined communities'. Since all 'real', or structural, communities are characterized by co-presence, nations must be symbolically constructed (cf. Cohen, 1985/1989). 'In fact, all communities larger than primordial villages of face-to-face contact (and perhaps even these) are imagined' (Anderson, 1983/1991: 6). There is nothing new in the idea of imagined social entities. But Anderson succeeds in extracting some new substance out of it, and of giving it a striking name. The 'materialist' reader will, of course, be sceptical about the power of ideas, in general, and imagined communities, in particular.[17] But I concur, with Anderson, that imagined communities do exist and sometimes have effects that are clearly anomalous to an economic theory of collective action. Such a theory cannot 'explain the *attachment* that peoples feel for the inventions of their imaginations', and certainly not 'why people are ready to die for these inventions' (Anderson, 1983/1991: 141; see also Calhoun, 1991a: 106–114).

345

Before my discussion of nationalism, I agreed with Nisbet that the political community may assume the role of substitute for communities proper. Nisbet is not alone in suggesting this possibility. Several writers have pointed out that the nation-state is often idealized as a family writ large (Balibar, 1991: 98ff.; Poole, 1991, 100ff., 109; Smith, 1991: 78f., 91, 161–163). But there is a more homologous substitute for lost communities: the utopian community.

Rosabeth Moss Kanter (1972, 1973) studied utopian, or intentional, communities in the United States with special regard to their survival value.[18] She recognized three types of community: the religious, the political and the psychological. The earliest utopian communities were religious. Political communities developed in the wake of the industrial revolution and represent the response to the destruction of traditional communities. They include the utopian experiments of the followers of Robert Owen, Charles Fourier and Etienne Cabet. The psychological type, finally, emerged in the 1960s, as part of the rebellion of youth.

Kanter's aim was to find out what makes communities successful, as measured by their longevity. She assumed that viability depends upon the commitment of members and hypothesized that communities will survive to the extent that they make successful use of commitment mechanisms. Borrowing from Talcott Parsons' action theory, Kanter further assumed that individuals orient themselves to communities instrumentally (the *cognitive* mode), affectively (the *cathectic* mode) and morally (the *evaluative* mode) (Kanter, 1972: 68). Identifying a number of specific commitment mechanisms exemplifying these modes of orientation, she went on to investigate the relation between use of commitment mechanisms and longevity in nineteenth-century communes. For most mechanisms, she found a strong positive correlation with success (Kanter, 1972: ch. 4).

Michael Hechter (1987: ch. 8) uses Kanter's study in his economic theory of group solidarity, but suggests a different interpretation of her results. Hechter's interpretation is, I believe, an example of that kind of redescription and economic reductionism, at all costs, that I criticized in Chapter 4 (pp. 243–255). He maintains (Hechter, 1987: 164) that Kanter's analysis is '(mostly implicit) normativist', when, in fact, it is explicitly based on Talcott Parsons' theory of the social system. This is about as explicit as you can get about the 'normativism' of your analysis. Hechter does not seem to appreciate the fact that concepts, such as 'authority' and 'obligation', for most sociologists, include a normativist element as part of their connotation. He also seems to believe that a normativist (sociological) position rules out a concern with instrumental rationality in the form of free riding. As I have tried to demonstrate throughout this chapter, this is a misconception of the sociological approach. An additional proof of this is the fact that Parsons' and Kanter's theory of group solidarity includes instrumental action as one of three modes of orientation of an individual to a collective. Before Hechter made his own insightful analysis (Hechter, 1987: 161–167) of the role of opportunity, or exit, costs in people's decision whether to stay in a group, or to leave it, Kanter made a similar analysis of this matter (Kanter, 1972: 70–72).

Making use of Talcott Parsons' theory of social action, Kanter's analysis of nineteenth-century communes stands squarely in the sociological tradition. So does her analysis of more recent counterculture communes as 'value-based' social movements in the sense of Neil Smelser (Kanter, 1973).

SOCIAL ORDER

The central problem for social science is to explain social order. How do people manage to live together? One can discern two ways of answering this question. The first view is normative and communal: people learn from their culture customs that provide an internal compass guiding them to act in ways that minimize conflict and ensure comity. The second view is rationalistic and individualistic: order is created by explicit and implicit agreement entered into by self-seeking individuals to avert the worst consequences of their predatory instincts. In the first view, order is natural and prior to any social contract or government institution; in the second, it is contrived and dependent on agreements and sanctions. Rules are obeyed in the first case because they have moral force, in the second because they convey personal advantage. In the first view, compliance is automatic and general; in the second, it is strategic and uncertain.

(Wilson, 1993: 1)

This quotation is from James Q. Wilson's presidential address to the American Political Association, 1992. I am not sure that the problem of social order is *the* central problem for social science. It is certainly one of its perennial problems and, like most such problems, likely never to be solved. What we find in the history of social thought is a vacillation between these two answers alternating in the position of being the dominant view. In modern social science, sociology is the main expression of the first view of the matter, while economics represents the second view. Wilson goes on to observe that the sociological, or

normative view has been under heavy attack for several decades for at least three reasons: it seems to imply a complacent functionalism; it appears to minimize or deny the value of conflict; and it lacks the theoretical power found in the assumption that people always seek their own interest. I believe that one can grant, up to a point, all of these objections and still be left dissatisfied with the alternative, namely, that social order is contrived, based on calculation, and dependent on individual assent.

(ibid., p. 1)

347

I agree with Wilson. I am not in a position, however, to be able to offer anything better than the traditional sociological critique of the economic answer to the problem and of putting the orthodox sociological answer in its stead.[19]

Jon Elster (1989a: 1ff.; 1989b: 101) recognizes two problems of order.[20] The first is Hobbes' problem of why there is not a *war* of each against all, or why there is *cooperation*. The second problem of order could be associated with Hume. It is the problem of why there is order rather than *chaos*, or why there is *coordination*, or at least, predictability. Social science has been more concerned with Hobbes' than with Hume's problem of order. Recently, however, both rational choice and sociology have shifted their focus of attention from the former to the latter.

There are, at least, three versions of the economic, or rational choice, theory of social order (cf. Taylor, 1982: 53ff.). According to the first version, social order is possible in a market society, where rational egoists exchange for their mutual benefit, but without the state. This position may be called 'anarcho-capitalism'. It is possible to interpret John Locke as a proponent of this view. Even if he defended a minimal state, Locke argued that cooperation and exchange are possible in the state of nature.[21] The second version maintains that social order is possible in a market society, but only if there is a state that guarantees property and contract. This is the theory of order, commonly ascribed to Thomas Hobbes. A third theory says that social order is possible among rational egoists if they live in communities. This version is launched by Michael Taylor (1982).[22]

Of these three versions, anarcho-capitalism is the most radical and least important. The most influential version is the Hobbesian theory of the social contract. The 'communitarian' solution to the problem of order is a recent addition to economic theory. It is borrowed from anthropology and sociology, but transformed in the process. In anthropological and sociological theories, communities are characterized by solidarity and a common morality. According to economic theory, communities, like the state, maintain order by sanctioning defection.

Sociology developed very much as a critique of the rationalist theory of society; of the theory of the social contract, of economic theory and of utilitarian philosophy. Virtually all sociologists agree that social order is to some degree a normative order; that society is not possible without, at least, a modicum of morality (Wolfe, 1989: 19–23). This view of society is most explicit in the works of Emile Durkheim and Talcott Parsons, but is clearly expressed by other major sociologists as well. George Simmel, for instance, denies that the existence of a criminal code is enough for social order. 'The minimum of ethical, peaceful behavior without which civil society could not exist thus goes beyond the categories guaranteed by the criminal code' (Simmel [1908] 1955: 65). Pareto, who became famous as an economist, turned to sociology because he saw clearly the limits of economic theory.

According to him, there are many motive forces besides self-interest. Benevolence, for instance, is mentioned as a sentiment, 'without which society probably could not exist' (Pareto [1902] 1976: 138). One class of motives, or 'residues', has to do with 'group-persistence', or the 'persistence of aggregates'. As the name indicates, they are vital for social order: 'The sentiments we have called persistence of aggregates . . . are the cement of all human societies' (Pareto [1921] 1976). 'Looking a little deeper, one may say that society is grounded in group-persistences' (Pareto, 1916/1980: 360).[23]

The thesis that society is to some extent a normative order is implicit even in the theories of Marx and Weber. In Marx, it appears in the idea that *ideology* is necessary for the maintenance of relations of production involving exploitation. Normative order is fully recognized in Antonio Gramsci's concept of *hegemony* (Gramsci, 1971: 333),[24] which has much in common with Max Weber's concept of legitimate power, or authority. In Weber, then, normativity assumes the shape of *legitimacy*. A social order is legitimate if those subject to it believe that it is binding, or obligatory; that it is their duty to obey its maxims of behaviour, even when these conflict with self-interest (Weber, 1922/1978: 31–33). In a bureaucracy, which is the specifically modern form of legitimate domination, reasons for actions are of two sorts: 'subsumption under norms, or a weighing of ends and means' (Weber, 1922/1978: 979). According to Weber, a social order of domination based on self-interested calculation of advantage, or fear of consequences, is necessarily unstable. Not even affectual and ideal motives of solidarity are sufficient. 'In addition there is normally a further element, the belief in legitimacy' (Weber, 1922/1978: 213).

One important element in the sociological critique of the theory of the social contract was the idea of 'community', which I explored in the previous section. My short presentation of the ideas of Toennies and MacIver made it patently clear that the sociological approach to community is different from the economic one. While social control is an important part of community life, its basis is solidarity, not self-interest. A main target of Axelrod's, Taylor's, de Jasay's and Ostrom's analyses is Hobbes' and Buchanan's theory of the state. Against this theory, it is argued that cooperation is also possible in a stateless, 'anarchic', society. But this has been evident to anthropologists and sociologists since the instigation of these disciplines. The name – or one name – of this possibility is 'community'.

In every society, save during the throes of revolution, there is a firmament of order. The acceptance of its terms is an expression of the sentiments that bind men everywhere in social union. They obey the law not merely because they recognize the legitimacy of its source, nor mainly because they are convinced of the rationality of its content. They obey not merely because they consider it their obligation to the state. And they certainly do not obey solely because they fear the sanctions attached to the law, 'The fear of consequences' on which Thomas Hobbes laid such stress. Neither the fear of punishment nor the fear of the larger consequences of law-breaking to society can explain the common observance of the law. All the motivations we have here mentioned are involved but they do not operate in their simplicity as single and sufficient determinents of men's behavior.

(MacIver, 1947/1965: 58)

According to MacIver, then, law-abidingness is a matter of mixed motivations. If we are to believe MacIver, however, people obey the law primarily because that is what they have been taught to do:

Men obey because they are social beings – or, if you prefer it, because they are socialized beings, trained and indoctrinated in the ways of their society. All the motivations that are evoked and active in their social circle conspire to make them, on the whole, law-abiding. We cannot then answer the question why men obey the law by adducing merely *political* considerations. Law-abidingness is the pragmatic condition of and response to the whole firmament of social order.

(MacIver, 1947/1965: 58)

Hobbes' individualist theory of the state is often contrasted to the 'organic' theory of Hegel and his followers, as if these were the only alternatives (see, e.g., Buchanan, 1949: 496–498). The writings of Toennies and MacIver attest to the possibility and historical actuality of such an alternative. Both are critical of Hobbes and the theory of the social contract.[25] But they are equally critical of Hegel and the organic theory of the state.[26]

Toennies and MacIver agree with Hobbes that the modern nation-state is an association instituted to further a common interest, but they both lean towards Marx's view that it is the particular interest of the bourgeoisie, more than the general interest of the community as a whole, that is promoted (Toennies, 1887/1955: 250–253; [1905] 1971: 125–127; MacIver, 1926/1964: 46–50; 1947/1965: 23–29). Toennies consistently expressed a very high opinion of Hobbes, whom he calls a 'genius' and 'great thinker'. In the Preface to the second edition of *Gemeinschaft und Gesellschaft* (1912), we find the following passage:

I admire the energy and consistency of the Hobbesian construction of the state. However, when I traced the powerful influence of Hobbesian concepts in England and elsewhere, down to the nineteenth century, I was astounded by the decline of this rationalistic and individualistic philosophy of law, which in the eighteenth century had been accepted as the pinnacle of wisdom.

(Toennies, 1971: 31)

In fact, Toennies' own theory of association (*Gesellschaft*), derives to a large

350

extent from Hobbes' theory of the state (see Toennies, 1896: 214ff.). In the end, however, Hobbes' analysis is lop-sided.

> Why is this? Because the final piece is missing, that is, the clear and complete distinction of a commonwealth, not just from any society or from sociability at large but as much from the 'great and lasting societies,' from alliances, from all forms of social life, which are possible also in the state of nature, and actually occur in it, and which as such belong to the state of nature. Again we must ask, Why?
>
> (Toennies, [1923] 1971: 52f.)

What is missing from Hobbes' analysis is, of course, an account of community. The reason it is missing, is Hobbes' rejection of Aristotle's notion of man as a *zoon politikon*; his individualism. Instead of dismissing Hobbes as a bad historian and an equally bad sociologist, however, Toennies emphasizes the ideal typical character, and prophetic quality, of Hobbes' theory of the social contract. The individualist theory of society is an ideal type that is increasingly realized in modern society.

MacIver is, on the whole, less appreciative of Hobbes than is Toennies. While praising his consistency, he considers Hobbes' theory – as all other theories of the social contract, except Rousseau's – fundamentally flawed.

> The old doctrine spoke of a *social* contract or covenant, and would have escaped the fallacies of which it is accused if it had only distinguished community from State and recognised that while all associations, the State included, rest on covenant, community itself is prior to and the necessary precondition of all covenant. A social will to establish society (or community) is a contradiction. A social will to establish and maintain the State is a great reality. It is visible in the obedience men pay to political laws determined by a majority alone; it is visible in the continuous transformation of the State, in accordance with changes in the social will. Community is co-evil with life, associations are merely its products.
>
> (MacIver, 1917: 128f.)

The fault with Hobbes' theory of the state is that it sees no other alternative than state absolutism and a war of each against all (MacIver, 1926/1964: 238–246). The fault with the theory of the social contract is that it posits an a-social man, who, for all that we know, never inhabited the earth and who would not be able to create either society or state. The autonomous and rational individual presupposed by the theory of the social contract is, in fact, *social* man, the result of a long historical development (MacIver, 1937: 38–42).

The theory of the social contract, then, is a myth. But not just a historical myth of the origin of society. If we accept Toennies' interpretation, Hobbes should be freed from this charge. Nor is it just a methodological myth, as suggested by Popper (1945/1966, vol. 2: 93). According to MacIver, the

351

theory of the social contract is, above all, a myth of legitimation, serving as a justification of the modern nation-state (MacIver, 1947/1965: Part I). It is but one in a series of myths of authority. While the modern state is about 500 years old, government, in the sense of political authority, is much older and in the sense of authority, pure and simple, about as old as man. In its germinal form, as an attribute of parenthood and old age, authority needed no special justification. But as political authority developed into a special function, a chief or king, increasingly detached from the community, it had to be legitimized by some myth. By far the most common myth of political authority before the modern nation-state, was religion. Chiefs and kings were either of divine origin, or ruled on special commission by God. By the end of the Middle Ages, this myth began to lose its force. The theory of the social contract is simply the myth most appropriate for the modern nation-state. It is a myth of sovereignty, but there are diverging opinions on who should be the sovereign: king or people. Hobbes' *Leviathan* is the ultimate defence of absolutism. As MacIver observes, 'The most complete exposition of a social myth often comes when the myth itself is waning. It was so with the *Leviathan*' (MacIver, 1947/1965: 55).

But there is the opposite myth of the state as an indivisible whole, or organism, propagated most consistently, perhaps, by G. W. F. Hegel and his followers. Despite their opposite metaphysical presuppositions, however, Hobbes and Hegel seem to have something highly objectionable in common. They both seem ready, if for different reasons, to invest the state with unlimited powers over its subjects, or citizens. In Hobbes, it took the form of absolutism; in Hegel, it takes the form of totalitarianism. 'The state is the actuality of the ethical Idea' (Hegel, 1821/1967: 155). As such it has 'supreme right over the individual, whose supreme duty it is to be a member of the state' (ibid., p. 156). This is not the place for a lengthy exposition of Hegel's doctrine of the state. By way of extreme simplification, and utilizing a terminology that is by now familiar, I suggest that Hegel wished to turn the state from an 'association' into a 'community'. While actual states are associations, the idea, purpose and destiny of the state is to become a community.

Toennies' main charge against Hegel is an echo of Marx's (see [1843] 1975: 105, 109, 113, 196). Hegel stands accused of a 'glorification of the state', in general, and of the conservative Prussian state, in particular (Toennies, [1912] 1971: 27). For MacIver (1937: 283ff.; 1947/1965: 270ff., 303ff.), as for Popper (1945/1966, 1957/1961), both writing in the shadow of Nazism and World War II, Hegel appears as the most important representative of a disastrous doctrine that paved the way for Fascism and Nazism. Much earlier, however, MacIver had criticized Hegel for his organicism and for his identification of community and state or, rather, the absorption of the former by the latter (MacIver, 1911; 1917: 28–38; 1921/1929: 149ff.; 1926/1964: 447ff.; 1937: 42–45; 1947/1965: 144–155).

I am not going to discuss the fairness of MacIver's and Popper's reading of Hegel. I merely note that there are other readings.[27] On one point, however, I wish to question MacIver's interpretation. I find it hard to accept MacIver's view that Hegel simply identified state and community (or society), when, as Toennies correctly observes ([1925] 1971: 62), Hegel is often, if mistakenly, credited with the discovery of society, or 'civil society', as distinct from the state. As Toennies points out, the term 'civil society' was used, in this sense, much earlier and definitely by Adam Ferguson (*Essay on the History of Civil Society*, 1767). But it is, nevertheless, indisputable that Hegel was important as a propagator of the idea of 'civil society', and of sociology, or so I wish to argue (cf. Wolfe, 1989: 15 ff.).

I believe that Hegel was a more important progenitor of sociology than either Comte or Spencer, which is not to say that the latter two were unimportant. Hegel is the disputed, but undeniable, intellectual father of Marx. By some, he is also seen to figure prominently behind Comte (see, e.g., Toennies, 1912/1971: 29; Hayek, 1955, Part III). Most important, Hegel was the single most important thinker to create the soil of nineteenth-century German thought, which was the most important breeding ground for sociology. Other important forces were the Romanticism of Johan Gottfried von Herder and the Historical School of jurisprudence, headed by Frederick Charles von Savigny. The first generation of American sociologists went to Germany to study and so did Talcott Parsons. English and French sociologists did not. But there is an important exception: Emile Durkheim. Nor should we forget that neo-Hegelianism was a strong intellectual force in the United States and in the United Kingdom around the turn of the century, or at the time when sociology became an academic discipline.

Of paramount importance for sociology was the Hegelian critique of the theory of the social contract and of the abstract (isolated) individual it assumes. If anything ever united sociologists, it used to be this – before the recent encroachment of economic imperialism. The state, according to Hegel, is not a contract of rational egoists, but the crowning achievement of ethical life in society. We may disagree, but it should be observed that, for Hegel, ethical life has three dialectical moments: family, civil society and state, or thesis, antithesis, synthesis. Ethical life has its origin in the family. Civil society, which for Hegel is equivalent to the economic system, is a disintegrating sphere, where men pursue their own private interests. In the state, finally, men are once again united in the pursuit of their common interest. The point of Hegel's dialectical argument is, of course, that the state should be a true community of men rather than a liberal nightwatchman. The point I wish to make, however, is that, in addition to the state, there are two parts: family and civil society. In Hegel's division of ethical life, or society, it is the family, not civil society, which is the prototype of community, later to become a special, but not the only, concern for sociologists. In their attempts to establish a province of their own, sociologists have highlighted a domain that lies 'outside' both state and market, but which is of the utmost importance for society, because it comprises those types of social relations that are necessary for solidarity or social integration. Two sociologists, in particular, have contributed to making social integration a major sociological concern: Emile Durkheim and Talcott Parsons.[28]

Among the classical sociologists, Durkheim distinguishes himself by launching sociology primarily as a theory of social order. It is a main theme of his work that society is a normative, or moral, order, and possible only as such. From this point of view, the economic theory of society is seriously defective. Society is not possible among rational egoists. Durkheim is a consistent critic of economic theory and of the theory of the social contract.

Durkheim attributes to economists the position I have called 'anarcho-capitalism': the belief that market exchange is possible among rational egoists without any moral authority (Durkheim, 1887/1993: 59ff.; 1983: 10ff.). His main target of critique, however, is the sociologist Herbert Spencer, who shared the economists' worldview and depicted the industrial type of society as a system of market exchange between free and equal partners.

> Social solidarity would then be nothing else than the spontaneous accord of individual interests, an accord of which contracts are the natural expression. The typical social relation would be the economic, stripped of all regulation and resulting from the entirely free initiative of the partners. In short, society would be solely the stage where individuals exchanged the products of their labour, without any action properly social coming to regulate this exchange.
>
> (Durkheim, 1893/1964: 203)

This is not an entirely accurate rendering of Spencer's position, but it is a succinct statement of the most radical version of the economic theory of social order. Durkheim's argument against this theory is that exchange is not possible except within a legal and moral framework of rights and duties. 'For everything in the contract is not contractual.' The contractual element consists of free exchange. 'But wherever a contract exists, it is submitted to regulation which is the work of society and not that of individuals, and which becomes ever more voluminous' (Durkheim, 1893/1964: 211). It would be more accurate to speak of 'exchange', where Durkheim says 'contract', and to say that exchange is not possible without contract, where contract is a social institution regulating exchange (cf. Parsons and Smelser, 1956: 104–114). At least, this is the gist of Durkheim's argument. If the division of labour produces solidarity, this is 'not because it makes each individual an *exchangist*, as the economists say; it is because it creates among men an entire system of rights and duties which link them together in a durable way' (Durkheim, 1893/1964: 406). In support of this argument, Durkheim traces the history of the institutions of property and contract, which are not primordial, but emerged as part of the development of society and which are the preconditions for exchange (Durkheim, 1983: chs 11–18).

This argument strikes at the heart of a consistent anarcho-capitalist position, but it is not sufficient to defuse Spencer's theory, which relies on a theory of natural rights (Spencer [1884] 1969: 161–183). The most well-known adherent of a theory of natural rights, or natural law, is not Herbert Spencer, however, but John Locke. According to Locke, individuals in the state of nature respect one another's natural rights to life and property. The state of nature, or liberty, is not a 'state of licence'.

> The *State of Nature* has a Law of Nature to govern it, which obliges every one: And Reason which is that Law, teaches all Mankind, who will but consult it, that being all equal and independent, no one ought to harm another in his Life, Health, Liberty, or Possessions.
>
> (Locke, 1690/1965: 311)

For Durkheim, this is no way out. There are no natural rights. Whatever rights individuals have, emanate from society. Rights are something individuals have acquired in the course of historical development. In the beginning there was force and no rights at all. In the early stages of development of society, there was a lot of force and few rights. In modern society it is the other way around: there are many rights and little force. The theory of natural law, which assigns to the state the role of protecting individuals' natural rights, fails to realize that, historically, the state has been a source of many of those rights (Durkheim, 1983: 52ff.).

Durkheim agrees with Hobbes, against Locke, in his image of the state of nature, at least if this state is conceived of as the absence, not only of a state, but of society. The possibility of spontaneous cooperation in the state of nature hinges on a belief in a predominant harmony of interests. But this belief is mistaken. 'For where interest is the only ruling force each individual finds himself in a state of war with every other since nothing comes to mollify the egos, and any truce in this eternal antagonism would not be of long duration' (Durkheim, 1893/1964: 203f.).

Durkheim does not accept Hobbes' solution to the problem of order, however. 'If contracts were observed only by force or through fear of force, contractual solidarity would be very precarious. A wholly external order would badly cover disturbances too general to be indefinitely controlled' (Durkheim, 1893/1964: 382). The clearest statement to this effect is, probably, in Durkheim's early treatise of the German positive, or scientific, theory of morals (*La science positive de la morale en Allemagne*, 1887). The following statement is, actually, an account of the views of the German jurist Rudolf Jhering, but there is little doubt that it is also an expression of Durkheim's own view:

> If the whole legal order rested on fear, society would be nothing but a prison where people only move where they see the whip raised above them. For society to be possible there must be some unselfish feelings

in us. These tendencies of which the two principle types are love (*die Liebe*) and the sense of duty (*das Pflichtgefühl*), surpass the domain of pure morality (*die Sittlichkeit*) without which the law could not endure.

(Durkheim, 1887/1993: 86)

The theory of the social contract is false, not only as a matter of historical fact, but on every reasonable interpretation.

Thus, the conception of a social contract is today difficult to defend, for it has no relation to the facts. The observer does not meet it along his road, so to speak. Not only are there no societies which have such an origin, but there is none whose structure presents the least trace of a contractual organization. It is neither a fact acquired through history nor a tendency which grows out of historical development. Hence to rejuvenate this doctrine and accredit it, it would be necessary to qualify as a contract the adhesion which each individual, as adult, gave to the society when he was born, solely by reason of which he continues to live. But then we would have to term contractual every action of man which is not determined by constraint. In this light, there is no society, neither present nor past, which is not or has not been contractual, for there is none which could exist solely through pressure.

(Durkheim, 1893/1964: 202)

At the most basic level, Durkheim criticizes the individualist theory of society for radically misconceiving the nature of man and society: 'man is man only because he lives in society. Take away from man all that has a social origin and nothing is left but an animal on a par with other animals' (Durkheim, 1983: 60) Since man is a social animal, it is simply wrong to conceive of *asocial*, but rational, individuals agreeing to form a society. For Durkheim, this is to put the cart before the horse. The truth of the matter is the opposite of that suggested by the individualist theory of society. The autonomous and rational individual postulated in the state of nature is, actually, the result of a long historical development.

According to Durkheim, society is a spontaneous order, not a conscious and rational creation. On this point, Durkheim agrees with Herbert Spencer and with those economists who suggest that the market is a spontanenous order (Durkheim, 1893/1964: 386).[29] He does not agree, however, that it is the spontaneous order *par excellence* and *par préférence*, and, as we have seen, he emphatically denies that it is self-regulating.

Durkheim's arguments, so far, have been directed at anarcho-capitalism and at the theory of the social contract. It is still possible to argue, however, that it is unfair to Herbert Spencer. While characterizing industrial society as a system of voluntary cooperation, Spencer also maintains that it is not possible among rational egoists. It is possible only because 'in addition to their selfish interests, men have sympathetic interests, which, acting individually and cooperatively, work out results less remarkable than those which the selfish interests work out' (Spencer [1871] 1969: 301).

Durkheim is aware that Spencer recognizes the existence of altruism, but argues that he does not attach due importance to non-selfish motives – he certainly considers self-interest the stronger motive (see, e.g. Spencer [1881] 1969: 174). I am not certain that Durkheim is fair to Spencer, but it is a point that could be made against many economists, who grant the existence of altruism and morality and who see it is an asset, but who seem to believe that we could do without it.

> Thus, altruism is not destined to become, as Spencer desires a sort of agreeable ornament to social life, but it will forever be its fundamental basis. How can we ever really dispense with it? Men cannot live together without acknowledging, and, consequently, making mutual sacrifices, without tying themselves with strong, durable bonds. Every society is a moral society.
>
> (Durkheim, 1893/1964: 228)

According to Durkheim, then, social order is impossible among rational egoists. Cooperation, even in the form of exchange for mutual advantage, presupposes morality. Law has its origin in customs and customs are based on two equally primordial motives, or sentiments: self-interest and altruism.[30]

After Durkheim, it was, above all, Talcott Parsons who contributed to turning sociology into a theory of social order. In his first major work, *The Structure of Social Action* (1937), Parsons intended to lay the foundation for sociology as a social science beside economics and political science. It was a synthetic attempt, based upon interpretations of the theories of the economist Alfred Marshall, the economist and sociologist Vilfredo Pareto and the sociologists Emile Durkheim and Max Weber. Before embarking upon his main task, however, Parsons gives a short account of the utilitarian system, which dominated social thought before the rise of the social sciences and the first social science to emerge from philosophy: classical economics. He suggests that it was characterized by four features: atomism, rationality, empiricism and randomness of ends (Parsons, 1937/1968: 60).[31]

In his historical sketch of the development of the utilitarian system, Parsons starts with Hobbes, who posed the famous problem of order, which besets every theory based on utilitarian premises. According to Parsons (1937/1968: 93), 'Hobbes saw the problem with a clarity which has never been surpassed, and his statement of it remains valid today. It is so fundamental that a genuine solution of it has never been attained on a strictly utilitarian basis'.

Hobbes' problem of order is, of course, the theoretical problem of explaining why, if human beings are rational egoists, there is not a war of each against all. Hobbes' own solution, the social contract, is dismissed by Parsons as obviously untenable:

> This solution really involves stretching, at a critical point, the conception of rationality beyond its scope in the rest of the theory, to a point where the actors come to realize the situation as a whole instead of pursuing their own ends in terms of their immediate situation, and then take the action necessary to eliminate force and fraud, and, purchasing security at the sacrifice of the advantages to be gained by their future employment.
>
> (Parsons, 1937/1968: 93)

What Parsons objects to is Hobbes' use of the familiar device of enlightened self-interest, which make individuals refrain from acting upon their immediate self-interest for the long-term benefits of cooperation.

Unlike Hobbes, John Locke did not see the problem of order, or security, as very serious, even within a utiliarian framework. According to Parsons (1937/1968: 95ff.), Locke evaded the problem of order in two ways: first, by introducing the idea of a divine natural law, which individuals know by the force of their own reason. Second, by introducing the metaphysical assumption of 'identity of interests'. I prefer the expression 'harmony of interests'.

The idea of natural law, or natural rights, is untenable from a scientific point of view and without foundation in the utilitarian system. The assumption of a harmony of interests is untenable on empirical grounds. I am not certain, however, that Locke is committed to making such an assumption. When explaining why people prefer life in political society before life in the state of nature, Locke describes the latter state as 'very unsecure, very unsafe' and 'however free, is full of fears and continual dangers' (Locke, 1690/1965: 395). Parsons is more correct to point out that the assumption of a harmony of interests is an integral part of economic theory as a theory of exchange. He is also correct to maintain that there is no acceptable, only desperate, solutions to Hobbes' problem of order within the utilitarian system.

In his conclusion to *The Structure of Social Action*, Parsons suggests a division of labour between the social sciences which coincides, without being identical, with the three versions of the rational choice theory of social order. The classification is analytical and does not refer to concrete objects of investigation. Economics is the most abstract of the social sciences and, because of this, the theoretically most simple. Economics abstracts from all social relationships, including power relations. Its explanations are in terms of exchange between rational and atomized individuals, with given wants on a market. Political science is based on the insight of Hobbes, that social life involves conflict of interest and a struggle for power among individuals, as a means to other ends (and also as an end in itself). Political science is the study of power. Sociology, finally, is based on the insight, expressed most clearly by Emile Durkheim, that social order is based, neither on voluntary exchange, nor on fear of consequences, but on the existence of a moral community. Sociology is the science of social, or 'common-value integration' (Parsons, 1937/1968: 768).

Around 1950, Parsons switched from action theory to system theory. From then on, the division of labour between the social sciences is conceived in terms of different subsystems of the total social system. The division is still analytical. The total social system consists of four subsystems: economy, polity, society and culture; each system answering one of four functional imperatives: adaptation, goal-attainment, integration and pattern-maintenance, all of them necessary for the survival of the system.[32] This is not the place to penetrate Parsons' intricate theory of the social system. I merely note what is, perhaps, self-evident: economics is about the economy and political science about the polity. Sociology is about society and culture, or about social integration and pattern-maintenance (Parsons, 1951/1970: 545–555; Parsons and Smelser, 1956: 5–8, 295–309).

'Economic theory is, in a technical theoretical sense, by far the most developed and sophisticated branch of the behaviour sciences.' (Parsons and Smelser, 1956: 308). But this is not a justification of economic imperialism. To admit that economics is superior, in certain respects, to the other social sciences 'is not to say that other social systems should be treated as if they were economies; clearly they are not' (Parsons and Smelser). While it is true that the other social sciences would benefit from using the economic approach to human behaviour, it is also the case that sociological theory is relevant for the explanation of the working of the economic subsystem, which is, of course, what Parsons and Smelser attempt to demonstrate in their *Economy and Society*.

In the 1960s strong doubts were raised concerning the fertility of orthodox sociology. It was criticized for being too 'grand' (Mills, 1959/1970: ch. 2), for utilizing an 'oversocialized conception of man' (Wrong, 1961), for being conservative (Gouldner, 1971) and for being functionalist (Giddens, 1977: ch. 2). A majority of sociologists came to reject the idea of sociology as a theory of order, and the further idea of social order as a normative or moral order (see, e.g., Giddens, 1977: ch. 6). Another strain of sociological thought, originating in the sociology of knowledge, in symbolic interactionism, phenomenology and ethnomethodology, has focused attention on society as a *cognitive order* (see, e.g., Knorr-Cetina and Cicourel, 1981). In a word borrowed from Giddens, human beings are 'knowledgeable'.

This was no doubt an important correction to the predominantly moral view of social order, but it neglects the extent to which the orthodox consensus was itself 'cognitive'. Durkheim, for instance, was a pioneer in the sociology of knowledge. His work on 'primitive classification' and his idea of 'collective representations' are important contributions to a theory of society as a cognitive order. Also, cognitive order does not, by itself, exclude moral order. It is true that social order depends upon individuals being competent members of society, knowing its practices, or rules, but some of these rules are moral rules. Normative, or moral, order, therefore, presupposes cognitive order.

I conjecture that part of the discontent with orthodox sociology was due to its emphasis on society as a normative, or moral, order. The rise of exchange theory and rational choice theory within sociology is one manifestation of this discontent (Sciulli, 1992: 161ff.). Recent sociological theories, other than rational choice, prefer to conceive of society as made up of rules, or social practices (Bourdieu, 1972/1977, 1980/1990; Giddens, 1984). I do not believe that the difference between orthodox sociology and this new sociology really is that great, but I will not argue this point here. Implicit in these novel theories is that there are different types of rules. In addition to moral rules, there are conventions (customs, manners, traditions) and technical rules. An important, but neglected, type of rule is linguistic rules or, more generally, rules of signification. Like other disciplines, sociology has witnessed a 'linguistic turn'.

This shift, in sociology, from a theory of moral order to a theory of cognitive order, corresponds to a shift in rational choice from the problem of cooperation to the problem of coordination. To solve coordination problems, we do not need moral rules, we need only conventions. An indication of this shift, is a change of interest from the work of Thomas Hobbes to that of David Hume. A problem with games of coordination is that they have multiple equilibria. Rational choice, therefore, ends in indeterminacy. There is no way to tell which equilibrium will actually be reached (see pp. 218–222).

In an interesting article, John Ferejohn (1991) has suggested that both rational choice and interpretive sociology are incomplete, but complementary, approaches. His argument starts from the so-called 'folk theorem', which suggests that rationality is, in many situations, indeterminate with respect to a number of equally possible outcomes. Rational choice is, therefore, unable to predict the selection of one, particular, outcome, without some auxiliary hypothesis. Thomas Schelling (1960: 57, 68–70) introduced the idea of a 'focal point' as a possible 'solution' to coordination games. A focal point is an outcome that stands out as the most salient, or most 'natural', among a number of equilibria.

> It is here that an interpretivist approach offers a valuable and unique contribution. There is something in the meanings shared by members of that time and place, in their identities and self-understandings that make some equilibrium outcomes not just plausible but more natural, and even more inevitable than others ... Intersubjective understandings happen to play the part of the auxiliary hypothesis, or 'focal point,'

permitting agents to coordinate their strategic behavior in complex social interactions.

(Ferejohn, 1991: 298f.)

By 'interpretive meanings', Ferejohn understands the 'intersubjective meanings embedded in institutions and practices' (Ferejohn, 1991: 283). I find Ferejohn's analysis full of insight and his synthesis basically sound. It might be added, though, that not all institutions and practices are solutions to games of coordination. There are also norms of cooperation and of partiality (Ullmann-Margalit, 1977), and norms regulating externalities (Coleman, 1987: 138ff.; 1990b: 249ff.) and a host of other social institutions and practices as well. It might, finally, be pointed out that many rational choice theorists will not let the matter rest with a compromise, but use rational choice to explain the emergence of norms, or institutions. The works of Ullman-Margalit and Coleman exemplify this strategy.

Another strategy, used by many economists, is to supplement, or replace, rational choice by a theory of evolution based on a mechanism of selection. Prominent examples of this strategy are Andrew Schotter's *The Economic Theory of Social Institutions* (1981) and Robert Sugden's *The Economics of Rights, Cooperation and Welfare* (1986). This is still an expanding field which has led to a renaissance of Austrian economics, the theories of Carl Menger and Friedrich von Hayek in particular. In my opinion, this evolutionary institutionalism brings economics closer to sociology. I will not, however, develop this argument here.

361

CONCLUSION

In the latter half of this century, the theory of politics has been enriched by the economic approach to this topic. There is no doubt that the use of economic models has meant a revitalization of the theory of politics. Knowledge thrives on theoretical competition – a suggestion which may itself be interpreted as a theorem derived from economic theory (cf. Ghiselin, 1987). The economic approach has brought a new perspective to bear on the subject, and our understanding of it has increased thereby; both by the positive contributions of economic theory itself and by the changes incurred on other theories. In the end, the main contribution of public choice may very well turn out to be that it roused the other approaches from their dogmatic slumbers.

Among the positive contributions, I tend to believe that the general approach has been more important than the particular content. Rational choice is a useful methodology, not only in economics, but in all social sciences, even though I am convinced that it is less useful in the other (non-economic) social sciences (Udehn, 1992). In particular, I believe that formal models, such as game theory, spatial theory and the theory of social choice, have helped to clarify matters only vaguely comprehended before. Formal models have brought precision to the discussion of problems that are absolutely central to political theory, e.g. voting and collective action. Game theory, in particular, is an important heuristic device. It helps to lay bare the structure of interdependence between actors in many situations; what Karl Popper has called 'the logic of the situation'. Because of this, game theory is indispensable for identifying theoretical problems and for generating hypotheses.

There is a glaring discrepancy, however, between the sophistication of *theoretical* public choice and the barrenness of *empirical* public choice. The reassurance and confidence with which the message of public choice is still trumpeted over the world of social science and politics – by some of its adherents at least – is out of all proportion to the rather meagre achievements of public choice in terms of prediction and explanation. The objective of this book, therefore, has not been to praise the economic theory of politics – we have seen enough of that – but to warn against its over-utilization. This book has been about the failures and limitations of public choice.

There is, on the part of many proponents of the economic approach, a naive belief in the universality of economic theory – a phenomenon called 'economic imperialism'. This tendency is, in my opinion, not a panacea to truth, but a detriment to social science. Being a sociologist, my main concern has been to defend the sociological approach to politics. It has been my objective in this book to demonstrate the limited applicability of the economic approach to politics and to argue that the sociological approach is an indispensable supplement.

Amartya Sen has argued, in a famous article (Sen, 1979), that economic man has too little structure. This is a justified complaint. The assumptions of rationality and self-interest have failed when confronted with available evidence. On these assumptions, it is impossible to explain why people vote (see Chapter 2) and why they engage in collective action (see Chapter 5). The assumption of rational egoism has to be replaced by an assumption of *mixed motivations* (see pp. 255–261). This is not to say we should never use the simplifying assumptions of economic theory. For heuristic purposes, there are definitive advantages of simplicity, but for explanatory purposes, simplicity is not enough. We have to assume mixed motivations, as does sociological theory. In addition to self-interest, sociological theory recognizes collective identity and social norms as potent sources of human action.

But it is not only economic man who lacks structure. Even more conspicuous is the lack of social structure in economic theory. Traditional economic theory is individualistic, or atomistic. Individuals are not parties to social relations and they do not take each other's actions into account. The only interaction allowed by traditional economics is impersonal exchange between free and equal individuals on the market. On this assumption, much of social and political life, naturally, becomes incomprehensible, or falls outside the province of economic theory. People do belong to groups and it is only because of this that they are 'human' beings with a language and culture. People also belong to organizations, characterized by relations of command and obedience. People, finally, enter relations which are not at all free and equal, but include the power to coerce.

To the extent that public choice tries to mimic the economic theory of the market, it is subject to the same limitations, and these limitations hit the former much harder. To ignore social relations is a dubitable simplification in a theory of the market, but it borders on absurdity in a theory of politics. This is not to deny that there is exchange also in politics.

Game theory is a more adequate tool when dealing with the subject of politics. Strategic interaction is certainly more common than exchange. But game theory too is of limited use. It now seems as if most 'real life' games either lack equilibria or have multible equilibria. When this is the case, game theory can neither predict nor explain the actions of individuals. Perhaps they follow some rule, as sociologists believe that they do most of the time. Another serious limitation of the theory of non-cooperative games is that people are not assumed to communicate. People do communicate and, presumably, something comes out of it. Empirical evidence suggests strongly that communication helps people solve the collective action problem and to cooperate. One effect of communication, especially if it is frequent, is that people may develop collective identities and feelings of solidarity. This is probably the explanation of most collective action.

There is also a cooperative game theory, which is not handicapped by assuming mute individuals. I have not at all discussed cooperative game theory in this book, but it is indispensable for analysing bargaining and, as such, an important part of a theory of politics. Cooperative game theory is also limited, however, by the assumption of stable preferences made by all economic theories. People do change their preferences. Communication is used to persuade people to do so. Persuasion may be instrumental, or strategic; used to achieve some objective. In that case, persuasion is rational action at least on the part of the sender of the message. The receiver of the persuasive message, however, typically breaks the rules of rational choice by changing preferences. Many public choice theories exhibit an asymmetry of assumptions. Some actors are assumed to be strategically rational, others mere objects of manipulation. There is, however, a form of communication, for which we might reserve the name 'communicative action', which is not strategic at all, but aims at mutual understanding.

Public choice has introduced some social structure in economic theory in the form of institutions. This is an important step in the direction of increasing realism. It is also a step in the direction of convergence with sociology and traditional political science. Both these disciplines have been institutionalist all the time. The difference is that public choice always starts with the individual making a choice. Institutions are in the background, affecting the individual's opportunity set. It is a moot point, whether institutionalism is compatible with methodological individualism, or not. By investing social institutions with the bulk of explanatory power, public choice breaks with original methodological individualism, which insisted that social phenomena should be explained in terms of individuals and nothing else. Even more problematic is the relation between institutionalism and rational choice. Institutions are rules and the existence of institutions presupposes that rules are followed, but rule-following is not rational choice. Institutionalist rational choice, therefore, is incoherent. There are, of course, a number of ways in which public choice tries to evade this problem. I have tried in this book to show that these attempts are in vain. There is no getting away from the fact that people do follow rules for reasons not reducible to rational choice.

Sociology is not hampered by the limiting assumptions of the economic approach . For most sociologists this is seen as an advantage over economics. For most economists, it is what is wrong with sociology. I believe both positions are wrong. There is no either–or. The simplicity and elegance of economic models is a result of economics' simplifying assumptions. The lack of simplicity and elegance on the part of sociological theory is a result of not making these simplifying assumptions. But because there is a trade-off between simplicity and realism, there are advantages *and* disadvantages with both.

Unlike economics, sociology is premised on the assumption that the human individual is essentially a social being. Individuals belong to groups, organizations and collectives. The social nature of the human individual is closely associated with the use of language. Human beings communicate by means of language and other symbols. Because of this simple truism sociology is able to address some issues which escape the attention of economists and to explain some facts which are anomalous to economic theory. Sociology can at least provide some sort of explanation for the obvious facts that people cooperate and that they change their preferences.

NOTES

INTRODUCTION

1 The territorial metaphor should not be taken seriously. Disciplinary borders are unimportant. What is important, is how to understand and how to explain politics, hence my concern with *approaches* to politics. Nor do I wish to allege that economics and sociology are somehow superior to political science. I agree with Ordeshook (1992), that political scientists have contributed greatly to the development of rational choice, as they have also contributed to sociology. What eventually emerged as the economic and sociological approaches, from an undifferentiated social, or political, philosophy, was a historical accident and, as such, largely arbitrary (cf. Olson, 1990: 213).

2 Another way to achieve a more integrated analysis would be to attempt a more interdisciplinary venture. If political actors and institutions must be considered for an understanding of macroeconomic phenomena, isn't it reasonable to assume that other disciplines have something to contribute by way of variables exogenous to economic theory? This was the assumption behind a project (IDEA = Interdisciplinary Dimensions of Economic Analysis), led by the sociologist Ulf Himmelstrand, in which I took part. The most tangible result of this project was the anthology *Interfaces in Economic and Social Analysis* (Himmelstrand, 1992a). My contribution to this anthology is the origin of the present study.

3 The story I tell about political science is all about the state and development of this discipline in the United States. This narrow focus is justified by the fact that 'political science, for better or worse, has been, more than the other social sciences, an American creation and export' (Gunnell, 1988: 34). While there are now several centres of political science, the rest of the world has until now been a periphery, relative to the United States (Anckar and Berndtson, 1988a). For a less ethnocentric view see, e.g., Easton *et al.*, (1991).

4 For an excellent introductory account of the sociological approach to politics, referred to as 'the behavioral persuasion', see Eulau (1963).

5 Thus, Truman (1951a) maintained that group theory is part of behavioralism and Almond (1960: 4) that functionalism is so too.

6 I think especially of the Colombia studies of the Bureau of Applied Social Research (BASR): Paul F. Lazarsfeld, Bernard Berelson and Hazel Gaudet, *The People's Choice* (1944) and Bernard Berelson, Paul F. Lazarsfeld and William N. McPhee, *Voting. A Study of Opinion Formation in a Presidential Campaign* (1954). The sociological approach of these studies was replaced by a more social psychological approach in the studies by Michigan's Survey Research

Center (SRC): Angus Campbell, Gerald Gurin and Warren E. Miller, *The Voter Decides* (1954), Angus Campbell, Philip E. Converse, Warren E. Miller and Donald E. Stokes *The American Voter* (1960) and *Elections and the Political Order* (1966). For an overview, see W. Berns (1962), who prefers the social psychological approach of the Michigan group, J. S. Dryzek (1992), who defends the sociological approach of the Columbia group against the 'counter-revolutionary' attack from Michigan and Miller (1994), for an insider view of the matter.

7 According to Emile Durkheim (1895/1964: lvi), 'Sociology can ... be defined as the science of institutions, of their genesis and of their functioning'. Talcott Parsons, likewise, suggests that sociology, as the theory of social systems, is 'centered on the phenomena of the institutionalization of patterns of value-orientation in roles' (Parsons, 1951/1970: vii).

8 Gabriel A. Almond (1990: 23f., 48ff.) argues that public choice theorists, by using the paraphernalia of hard science; mathematics and advanced statistics, have succeeded in capturing the highest positions in the status hierarchy of political scientists, relegating the rest to a prescientific status.

9 Mitchell was first an advocate of the sociological approach to politics and wrote a book on Talcott Parsons (Mitchell, 1967), but was eventually convinced that the economic approach is superior to political sociology.

10 The most determinist faction of political sociology was that of Lazarsfeld and his colleagues, not the structural-functionalists. According to the former, 'a person thinks, politically, as he is, socially. Social characteristics determine political preference' (Lazarsfeld *et al.*, 1944/1948: 27). But not even this kind of determinism implies a denial of state, or governmental, autonomy. The heavy emphasis of the Columbia group on the strength of the group and of personal influence would rather make for autonomous political institutions. In retrospect, Lazarsfeld explains the lack of attention to top decision-makers, with the difficulty, for social scientists, of getting access to the political institutions of the state (Lazarsfeld, 1964: 177).

11 Giovanni Sartori (1969: 66–69) has argued both that there is a division of labour between political sociology and political science *and* that the former is reductionist. This is inconsistent if by 'reduction' is meant what it usually means: a complete explanation of the topic of one theory by another theory. If political sociology and political science have different topics, or treat different aspects of the same topic, no reduction is possible.

12 The term 'theory' has a special connotation in political science, as exemplified by the controversy over 'political theory' (Almond, 1966; Gunnell, 1983, 1988). In a first, somewhat unusual, sense, 'political theory' denotes the history of political ideas. In another, more usual, sense it denotes theory as part of political science. I use the term 'political theory' in the latter sense, but recognize that its roots are in the history of political ideas. By 'political philosophy', I understand a predominantly normative enterprise, as opposed to 'political science', which is mainly concerned with the description and explanation of political phenomena. I am, of course, aware that no normative theory can afford to disregard facts and no positive theory succeed in eliminating values.

13 When the sociologist John H. Goldthorpe (1984b: 1–3) refers to the 'new political economy', he has in mind an economic theory informed by political science and sociology, an interdisciplinary theory that is. See also Wyn Grant (1985a: 12), who uses the term 'political economy' to reflect an effort 'to bring the insights of political science and sociology to bear on the analysis of economic problems' and 'to develop a genuine political economy, i.e. one that does not use economic theories to explain political outcomes, but combines the insights

of a number of social science disciplines in the exploration of common concerns'.

14 The notion of 'hard core' was introduced by the Popperian philosopher of science Imre Lakatos. The hard core is that part of a scientific research programme which is beyond dispute and, therefore, not tested within the research programme (Lakatos, 1970: 133).

15 For a recent explication, not of the economic approach, but of 'the economic theory of rational action', see Monroe (1991: 4). This theory assumes that (1) actors pursue goals, (2) reflecting their self-interest; (3) choices are conscious (4) and made by individuals; (5) preferences are consistent and stable, and (6) maximize expected utility; (7) individuals possess 'extensive information' about alternatives.

16 For a comprehensive critical assessment of the economic approach to politics, see Laver (1981), and especially the various contributions to Monroe (1991) and especially, Green and Shapiro (1994). Critical appraisals focusing on particular aspects of the economic approach include Toye (1976), Granqvist (1987), Mansbridge (1990), Lewin (1991), Lindberg (1992) and Udehn (1992).

17 This is a procedure I have learned from my friend and colleague Thomas Coniavitis (1984).

18 Barry, as we have seen, argues that the economic approach to politics is vastly superior to the sociological approach. I don't think this is fair. If they are interested in different things they are not comparable. Barry (1970/1978: 180) seems to admit this: 'We cannot come to any simple conclusion about the relative merits of our two approaches, because they are so little of the time competing in the same league.'

19 According to Mitchell (1988: 117): '"Public Choice" was chosen as a title to supplant that of *Papers on Non-Market Decision Making* and as a name of the Society for the Study of Public Choice at its annual meeting in 1967. James S. Coleman and the present author may claim authorship of the term which won by a small plurality over "social choice," the "new political economy," and the "economics of politics".'

20 See, however, Tullock (1987), Wintrobe (1990) and Olson (1993), for discussions of aspects of dictatorships, from a public choice perspective.

1 TWO APPROACHES TO POLITICS

1 For a more comprehensive introduction to the economic theory of economics, or public choice, see especially Mueller (1976, 1979, 1989), but also Abrams (1980), McLean (1987), Mitchell (1988) van den Broeck (1988), Peacock (1992), and Mitchell and Simmons (1994). For an annotated bibliography, see Lovrich and Neiman (1984). Anthologies on public choice include Buchanan and Tollison (1972, 1984), Buchanan *et al.* (1978) and Rae and Eismeier (1979). On political economy, see Frey (1978a), Frohlich and Oppenheimer (1978), Alt and Chrystal (1983) and Alt and Shepsle, eds (1990). Stigler, (1988) is a useful anthology of Chicago studies in political economy.

2 A similar theory of democracy, as essentially an institutional mechanism, a method for selecting a government, was advanced by Karl Popper, but without any mention of Schumpeter's work (see Popper, 1945/1966, vol. 1.: 124ff.; vol. 2: 151; 1962/1968: 344f., 350f.). There is no mention of Schumpeter's work in Friedrich A. Hayek's *The Road to Serfdom* (1944) either. In *The Constitution of Liberty* (1960: 443), Hayek quotes, with approval the following statement by Schumpeter (1942/1954: 242): 'Democracy is a political *method*, that is to

say, a certain type of institutional arrangement for arriving at political-legislative and administrative decisions and hence incapable of being an end in itself, irrespective of what decisions it will produce under given historical conditions.'

3 A good discussion can be found in Riker and Ordeshook (1973: chs 11–12). The spatial theory of voting is not uncontested, however. For a critique, directed mainly at the assumption of dimensional space in which voters occupy a definite position, see Rabinowitz and Macdonald (1989).

4 An early attempt in this direction can be found in Gordon Tullock (1967b: ch. 4).

5 For the analysis of log-rolling, Buchanan and Tullock (1962/1965: 120–124) model politics as a series of games, a sequence of decisions over time. Their analysis bears an interesting resemblance to the game theoretic analysis of reciprocity in collective action (see Chapter 5). For a discussion of vote trading, see Brams (1975: ch. 4).

6 For a further discussion of coalition games, see Riker and Ordeshook (1973: ch. 7) and Brams (1975: ch. 6).

7 A book with a similar title is Alan Peacock's *The Economic Analysis of Government and Related Themes* (1979). The similarity is probably not accidental, since Peacock expresses his admiration for Breton's work, but since Peacock's work is less systematic (a collection of previously published articles, together with a new introduction) and less explicit about basic assumptions, it does not call for special attention (at least not in this chapter). As an economic analysis of politics, Peacock's work depends more on the assumption of exchange than on the assumption of self-interest.

8 A summary of this book can be found in Breton (1978).

9 In the discussion following Breton (1978), he suggests that one can apply his analysis to the political business cycle (Buchanan *et al.*, 1978: 65).

10 Another contribution to the theory of political business cycles was Lindbeck (1976). My reason for neglecting Lindbeck's article is not that I find it unimportant – I believe that it is superior to those of Nordhaus and MaCrae – but that I hesitate to include him in the public choice camp. Lindbeck agrees with public choice in the quest for 'endogenous politicians', but is less anti-Keynes. He is also less willing to accept *homo economicus* wholesale. Politicians are both benevolent and selfish, but more selfish as they approach election day. Another reason for neglecting Lindbeck's contribution is the similarity of his model to that of Bruno S. Frey.

11 Frey has written extensively on politico-economic models and cycles. An early contribution is Frey (1974). The best source is probably Frey (1978a: chs 10–11), but see also (1978b). On 'politometrics', see Frey (1979). For easy reading, see his textbook Frey (1983).

12 There is, in addition, the press as an important political power, but public choice has nothing at all to say about it. Probably that is because the mass media have no place in a theory which assumes stable preferences (see pp. 130–149).

13 For a generalization and modification of Stigler's theory of regulation, see Peltzman (1976). In Peltzman's model, regulation is not necessarily inefficient and consumers do have a say. The differential advantage, or relative power, of producers and consumers is dependent, among other things, upon business cycles and upon elasticity of demand.

14 For an introduction to the theory of rent-seeking see, e.g., Tollison (1982) and Mueller (1989: ch. 13). The most important articles on the subject are assembled in Buchanan, Tollison and Tullock (1980). Another important collection

of articles, most of them written by people outside the public choice camp, is Colander (1984).

15 In the United Kingdom, Samuel Brittan diagnosed the politico-economic system with the help of both Virginia public choice and Mancur Olson. He found that the disease was a combination of excessive expectations on the part of voters and the pursuit of group-interest in the market (Brittan, 1975: 9ff.; 1977, 247ff.).

16 Without explicitly saying so, I have already dealt with theories of public finance. The theory of political business cycles may be conceived as belonging to this field and the theories of Niskanen and Breton definitely so. But it is Buchanan who has done most in this field. Before he became a constitutionalist economist and political philosopher, his main speciality was public finance.

17 See also Buchanan and Wagner (1978).

18 In the United States, monetary policy is in the hands of the central bank, the Federal Reserve Board, which is outside governmental control. According to Buchanan and Wagner (1977: 116–119), however, this is only formally so. In reality, monetary policy is a complement to fiscal policy in the financing of public expenditure. Politicians have the power to put pressure on the monetary authorities and the latter, being personal utility-maximizers, like the rest of us, are unable to resist this pressure.

19 James T. Bennett and Thomas J. Di Lorenzo (1984) argue that constitutional rules against budget deficits are of little or no help, since political entrepreneurs answer by creating off-budget enterprises.

20 See also Downs (1957: 28), Stigler (1982: 136ff.), Mueller (1989: 1f.) and Crain and Tollison (1990: 3).

21 In a similar vein, Assar Lindbeck (1976) calls for an economic analysis with 'endogenous politicians'. It should be pointed out, however, that Lindbeck is more macro-oriented and less willing to accept *homo economicus* wholesale. Politicians are both selfish and benevolent, but increasingly selfish as they approach election day. Cf. also Gwartney and Wagner (1988a: 7).

22 The most glaring lacuna in this introductory treatment of political sociology is the omission of social movements, by many considered the special province of political sociology. I compensate for this omission in Chapter 6 on 'The Sociology of Collective Action'. For an introduction to political sociology, see Orum (1978/1983), Rush (1992) and Bottomore (1979/1993). A good introduction to classical political sociology is Zeitlin (1968).

23 See, however, Parsons (1957: 142), where he criticizes socialists for romanticizing a 'mystical "popular will" or " public interest". . .'.

24 Seymor Martin Lipset's *Political Man* (1959), is probably the work that best represents the typical concerns of traditional political sociology.

25 See Enelow and Hinich (1984: 2–6) for a similar characterization of the difference between the economic (spatial) and sociological (social-psychological) approaches to politics (voting).

26 See, e.g., Dalton *et al.* (1984); Crewe and Denver (1985); Dalton (1988), Denver (1989; ch. 3 on Great Britain).

27 There are recent data indicating that class voting (Erikson, 1989) and party identification (Miller, 1991) have become as important as ever in Reagan's and Bush's United States. These findings support the guess that the 1960s and 1970s might turn out to be, in some respects, a parenthesis rather than a permanent change.

28 For an account of the recent development of political sociology, see King (1986) and Riley (1988).

29 Good discussions of elite theory can be found in Bottomore (1966) and Parry (1969). For a recent presentation, focusing on Mosca, see Albertoni (1985).

30 To these might be added the French sociologist Gustave Le Bon and the Spanish philosopher José Ortega y Gasset, who developed the complementary theory of mass society. I will return to Gustave le Bon in Chapter 6. Ortega y Gasset won undeserved renown for his boring lamentations over the loss of authority, distinction and traditional values in modern societies, in *The Revolt of the Masses* (1930/1957). He differs from the elite theorists in his concern with a cultural, rather than a political, elite. Of some interest, in this connection, is the French syndicalist, and later Fascist, George Sorel, whose ideas influenced Pareto.

31 The first German edition of *Political Parties* appeared in 1911. The English translation is from the Italian edition of 1915.

32 Pareto elaborated on his elite theory in most of his writings, from *Cour d'economie politique* (1896), to *Tranformazione della Democrazia* (1921). A useful selection, including his most important contributions to elite theory, is assembled in *Vilfredo Pareto. Sociological Writings* (1976). Pareto's fullest treatment of the subject is in his *Trattato di Sociologia General* (1916), translated as *The Mind and Society* (1936). I have used a translation of an abridged version of this work, approved by the author himself (1920), with the title *Compendium of General Sociology* (1916/1980). See also *The Rise and Fall of the Elites* (1901/1968), which is a translation of an essay Pareto wrote in 1901.

33 Robert Michels was a socialist who became disillusioned with socialism and democracy by observing the oligarchic tendencies in the German Social Democratic Party and eventually set his hope on a charismatic leader, such as Mussolini. Pareto has been described, by Ferrarotti (1985), as a disenchanted and pessimistic conservative. Gustave le Bon and Ortega y Gasset took a somewhat different stance. They despised the masses and feared socialism more than Mosca and Pareto, but they also believed that the masses would actually insert themselves in power. For Le Bon and Ortega y Gasset, popular sovereignty was not a myth; it was on its way to becoming reality.

34 For another pluralist reaction, see Talcott Parsons' review of Mills' *The Power Elite* (Parsons, 1957). Among the critical points are that Mills exaggerates the power of business and underrates the importance of parties and parliament, and that his depiction of the United States as a mass society fails to appreciate the role of professional organizations and other associations.

35 P. Digeser (1992) argues that there is a fourth face of power revealed by Michel Foucault, involving the creation, or production, of human subjects. I do not see the qualitative leap from the third to the 'fourth' face of power. Shaping peoples' wants, in the way described by Lukes (1974: 23) *is* shaping people. This is not, however, to belittle the contribution of Foucault to our understanding of power. He has done a lot to focus our attention on the third face of power; the various forms it takes, its close relation to knowledge and its ubiquity in modern society (see, e.g. Foucault, 1980).

36 Even so, J.C. Isaac has argued that Lukes' concept of power is not Marxist, or realist, enough. 'In short, Lukes seems unable to articulate the structural nature of social power which, he rightly notes, is so important' (Isaac, 1987: 15). According to Isaac, social power, the power of one agent over another agent, is parasitic upon each agent's power, or capacity, to act. Social power, then, becomes *'the capacities to act possessed by social agents in virtue of the enduring relations in which they participate'* (ibid., p. 22). Among sociologists, Anthony Giddens (1984) 14–16, 246–252; 1985: 7–17) has most explicitly adopted the realist conception of 'power' and also incorporated Foucault's complex power-

knowledge-surveillance in his own analysis of modernity. See Ball (1988: 91–105), for a short survey of the recent discussion of 'power'.

37 Often cited surveys are Jessop (1977) and (1982).

38 The main source for Habermas is C. Offe, *Strukturprobleme des kapitalistischen Staates* (1972). Offe's ideas on the matter of crisis management are available in English in a number of translated articles some of them assembled in Offe (1984).

39 Much of the literature on corporatism is in the form of anthologies: Schmitter and Lehmbruch (1979), Berger (1981), Lehmbruch and Schmitter (1982), Goldthorpe (1984c), Cawson (1985) and Grant (1985b). In addition there is Cawson (1986), by one of the leading theorists on corporatism. A good guide to the subject is Williamson (1989). An early review from a Marxist perspective is Panitch (1980). For a critical review, see Wilson (1983), Cox (1988a, 1988b) and O'Sullivan (1988).

40 Many commentators complain that different authors mean different things by the term 'corporatism' (Panitch, 1980: 159; Cox, 1988a: 35ff.; 1988b: 295ff.; O'Sullivan, 1988: 7). I agree that this is a problem, but it is not a very serious problem. Above all it is not a problem that is unique to 'corporatism'. I would say that this is the plight of most terms in social science.

41 Cawson's definition and discussion of 'corporatism' has been criticized by Cox (1988a, 1988b) in a voice that is too loud for the weight of the argument. In particular, Cox does not seem to be altogether clear about the nature of *ideal types*. See Cawson (1988) for a reply to Cox's criticism.

42 Cawson (1985: 10–21; 1986: chs 5 and 6) has also made a distinction between macro-, meso- and micro-corporatism, which I bypass altogether.

43 A typical representative of this view is the sociologist Emile Durkheim. See the well-known preface to the second edition (1902) of his *Division of Labor in Society* (1893/1967) and *Professional Ethics and Civil Morals* (1983, passim).

44 On the importance of the parties' respective definitions of the situation for corporatism to occur, see Nedelmann and Meier (1979: 107–117).

2 SELF-INTEREST IN POLITICS

1 Cf. Riker (1984: 15): 'This more or less general motivation is, so I believe, what makes generalization about politics possible. Most participants have the same goal, namely, to win on whatever is the point at issue. Assuming they think seriously about how to achieve their goals, they may be expected to behave in similar ways.' This may be true, but whether it is true or not is independent of any assumption of self-interest.

2 William H. Riker (1990b: 178) considers the median voter theorem to be 'certainly the greatest step forward in political theory in this century'. I wouldn't be so sure, but I accept it as one important contribution to a science of politics. Riker goes on to cite this contribution as proof of the 'salutary impact' of rational choice theory on political science (ibid., p. 180). I accept this too, but repeat that the median voter theorem is strictly independent of any assumption of self-interest for its validity.

3 We may note that Black speaks about nations being 'selfish'. He also assumes that there is such a thing as a national interest (Black, 1958: 142, 154). I suppose that Buchanan, together with most public choice theorists, would brand this mode of expression as a flagrant violation of the principle of methodological individualism. Of course, nations have no selves, and no interests.

4 The distinction between economics as a pure logic of choice and as a positive, predictive, theory is stated most clearly in Buchanan (1969b).

5 For a more realistic, sociological, account of economic policy, inspired in varying degrees by Marxism, see e.g., Alt and Chrystal (1983), Korpi (1983), the various articles in Lindberg and Maier (1985), Borooah (1988) and most important for my present purposes, Hibbs (1987a, 1987b) and Hibbs and Dennis (1988). I do not wish to suggest that all these authors share a common perspective, but they have at least this much in common: they all believe that power, institutions and social groups with conflicting interests are important determinants of economic policy.

6 See, especially, the various contributions to Eulau and Lewis-Beck (1985), but also Hibbs, (1985a: ch. 5; 1985b: ch. 6) and Alesina, Londregan and Rosenthal (1993: 22). See, however, Leithner (1993) for evidence from Australia, Canada and New Zealand, suggesting that economic voting may not be ubiquitous.

7 See Hibbs (1987b: ch. 11, first published in 1977 and 1987a: ch. 7; Yantek, 1988: 198–208, on the cases of Reagan and Thatcher) on unemployment and inflation, and Alt (1985) on unemployment only. Alt's data suggest that the difference is most pronounced at the beginning of terms. This observation is supported by Alesina (1988: 34) and Alesina and Rosenthal (1989: 374f.).

8 The studies by Kau and Rubin and Kalt and Zupan have been criticized by Jackson and Kingdon (1992) for being poor in method: the proxies used to measure ideology are inadequate and too close to their supposed effects. Hence, the risk of tautology. Jackson and Kingdon do not, however, 'question the truth of the observation that ideology matters in legislative decisions and in policy outcomes. Indeed, we are convinced that it does, and we believe this literature has had the salutary effect of reminding scholars of the importance of ideology' (Jackson and Kingdon, 1992: 816).

9 See Whiteley, Seyd, Richardson and Bissell (1993), for a study of party activists in the British Conservative party, which suggests that the economic theory of political participation is incomplete. The most important missing element is party identification: 'expressive motives ... grounded in a sense of affection and loyalty for the party' (Whiteley *et al.* 1993: 87).

10 For a summary of the critique against Niskanen, see Smith (1988: 166–176) and Lewin (1991, ch. 4).

11 In the same year appeared an article by Sears and Lau (1983), arguing that there is a methodological artifact operating in the opposite direction. Because, in many survey interviews, questions concerning personal economic situation and political attitudes follow close upon each other, respondents tend to answer in an apparently more self-interested way than would otherwise be the case. They do so either by personalizing political attitudes or by politicizing their personal economic situation. Sears and Lau support their argument with experimental evidence. Lewis-Beck (1985) tested their hypothesis with data from national election surveys, but could not find anything to support the hypothesis of pocketbook voting as a methodological artifact.

12 Shanto Iyengar (1989) argues that attribution of causal and treatment responsibility for specific issues, such as racial inequality, poverty, crime, terrorism, etc., is of major importance for citizens' political preferences, and for their consequent evaluation of politicians and policies.

13 Concerning the issue of busing, evidence against self-interest has been criticized by Green and Cowden (1992) as unreliable, because based on opinions. Turning from opinions to protests, they find strong support for the efficacy of self-interest.

14 In *The American Voter* (1960), Campbell *et al.* seem to be somewhat more impressed

by the power of self-interest. They now argue that an individual's ideology is largely determined by self-interest (pp. 203–209). Does this interpretation of ideology reflect a reading of Anthony Downs' *An Economic Theory of Democracy*?

15 To vote because of duty is not, of course, 'irrational' in a broader sense of this term. There is an argument by Quattrone and Tversky (1986; 1988: 732–734), however, to the effect that voting may be to some extent irrational. Drawing upon well-known phenomena occurring in other contexts, and upon experiments by themselves, they suggest that voting may be based upon mistaking diagnosis for cause. People may delude themselves into believing that their own voting for a particular candidate is diagnostic of many people doing the same thing. Hence they vote. Quattrone and Tversky do not propose this argument as an alternative to earlier explanations. In addition to benefits deriving from the prospect of casting the decisive ballot, there are additional benefits including 'fulfilling one's duty as citizen, participating in a common social ritual and signalling to others that voting is essential for the survival of democracy. To these rational causal consequences of voting, we suggest adding a less rational diagnostic aspect' (ibid., p. 49). Jon Elster (1989a: 195ff.) goes further and suggests that this type of 'magical thinking' underlies 'everyday Kantianism'.

16 See, e.g., the articles by Strom, Stephens, Mayer and Good, Beck and Tullock in *American Political Science Review*, 69, 1975.

17 A rather desperate attempt to save public choice can be found in Mueller (1989: ch. 18). Mueller is forced to admit that voting cannot be explained without the 'ethical voter hypothesis'. But, for some reason – which I am at a loss to understand, except as an expression of an economist's disciplinary prejudice against sociology – the ethical voter hypothesis does not provide an explanation, only 'an ex post rationalization of the act' (ibid., p. 362; cf. Margolis, 1982/1984: 12). In this situation, Mueller's last resort is this: the existence of 'ethical preferences' is best explained by behaviourist learning theory, in the selfish terms of 'reward' and 'punishment'. This argument is easily rebutted. (1) Behaviourism is not the best theory of moral development. (2) Even if it were, it would not eliminate ethical preferences. To argue thus, is to commit the genetic fallacy. (3) In order to establish 'the postulate that man is innately a selfish animal' (ibid., p. 363), Mueller's last resort must be biology rather than psychology. But biology tells us that there is altruism among animals. Is the gene 'selfish'? Opinion among biologists is divided. A remarkable aspect of Mueller's argument is that he is willing to sell out the assumption of rational *choice* in order to retain that of self-interest (ibid., pp. 363f.). This is so because behaviourism entails the denial of rational choice. In order to save the assumption of utility-maximization, Mueller's escape is Alchian's 'as if maximization', selection by competition. But this does not work. There are no mechanisms of selection, analogous to the market, at work in politics and there certainly is none in the case of voting. Why should selection favour ethical voting? Mueller vaguely refers to 'society's collective interest' (ibid., p. 364), but this is to create a new problem, not to solve an old one. In the end, Mueller tells us the story of how parents and teachers tell their children and pupils generally to cooperate and to vote because this is their duty as citizens. Appearances should not delude anyone into believing that this is a sociological story. It is only an *as if* sociological story, told by an economist. For a similar attempt to rationalize voting, see the sociologist James S. Coleman (1990b: 289ff.).

18 For a historical account of the idea of self-interest see, e.g., Hirschman (1977), Vaughan (1982), Myers (1983) and Lux (1990: chs 6, 8 and 9).

19 In the recent literature on Adam Smith, Werhane (1991) is most emphatic in rejecting the mistaken interpretation of Adam Smith as an advocate of one-

dimensional economic man and of *laissez-faire*. For a balanced and very readable full-length portrait of Smith, see Muller (1993). For a more libertarian, but also very reliable interpretation, see West (1990). Good introductions are West (1976) and Raphael (1985).

20 I think it is possible to recognize a somewhat less confident defence of economic man in some of Stigler's more recent articles (see Stigler [1981] 1982: chs 1–3).

21 As Brennan and Buchanan (1985: 53) pointed out, Smith does not even claim that market transactions are wholly self-interested: 'we can agree with Adam Smith that the consumer does not depend for his supper's meat on the benevolence of the butcher, without in the least ruling out the existence of such benevolence. The butcher may or may not be benevolent toward his customers. The crucial point is that such benevolence *need* not be present, and hence whether or not it is present is essentially irrelevant.'

22 For a comprehensive argument that the origin of sociology is in the Scottish Enlightenment, see Eriksson (1988), unfortunately available only in Swedish.

23 For a good statement of Smith's social psychology of moral sentiment, see Campbell (1971).

24 James Buchanan (1986: 32) lumps together Hobbes, Mandeville, Hume and Smith as thinkers with a similar view of the relation between self-interest and collective interest. This is misleading. Not only Smith, but also Hume, was a strong critic of the 'economic reductionism' of Hobbes and Mandeville (see Holmes, 1990).

25 Another threat was that division of labour will lead to such simple and uniform tasks as to make the lower ranks of the population ignorant and apathetic (Smith, 1759/1976: 734ff.; see also Harpham, 1984: 770–773).

26 James Buchanan mentions Wicksteed's idea of 'non-tuism' often in his writings (see, e.g., Buchanan, 1969a: 79; Buchanan and Tullock, 1962/1965: 18; Brennan and Buchanan, 1981: 383; 1985: 36), but it does not lead him to drop economic man.

27 Amartya Sen (1985: 347) distinguishes between 'self-centered welfare', 'self-welfare goal' and 'self-goal choice'. The first is narrow self-interest, the second admits of interdependent utility functions and the third is 'guided by the pursuit of one's own goal (and in particular, it is not restrained by the recognition of other people's pursuit of their goals)'. Wicksteed's non-tuism is closest to 'self-goal choice', but requires the qualification that one's own goals are not restrained by the recognition of the goals of parties to market exchange. The difference becomes significant when we turn from traditional economics to game theory. On non-tuism, see also Lux (1990: 156ff.) and Collard (1991: 18).

28 This is not the only inconsistency to be found in the writings of Stigler. In the midst of his argumentation for assuming universal utility-maximization, not excepting the behaviour of economists, Stigler (1982: 60, 77, 83) explains the delayed adoption of this assumption by economists, in terms of *cultural values and ideas*. To me, this seems like a sociological explanation of the delayed triumph of the economic approach. As a plea for economic imperialism, it is self-defeating.

29 This is the title of Max Weber's famous speech in Munich University in 1918, translated and reprinted in Weber (1948, 1994).

30 Also Tullock (1984a) now believes that people act, to some extent, in the public interest. While weak, the public interest is, nevertheless, decisive in explaining why people support government provision of public goods, such as military defence and police protection.

31 See, however, Brennan and Buchanan (1985: 145), where it is argued that 'The professional economist must look at the governmental-political process as

driven by the same forces that drive the market process, even when analysis incorporates the recognition that self-interested behavior is not nearly so amenable to simple modeling in political as in market choice.'

32 The best source is the article 'The Motivation of Economic Activities' (1970) in Parsons (1954), but see also Parsons (1949).

33 Parsons uses the same tripartition to analyse individuals' commitment to collectivities. In this he comes close to David Hume, who divides factions into those of interest, affection and principle (Hume 1741–42/1963: 58).

3 POLITICS AS EXCHANGE

1 The sociologist James C. Coleman (1964: 170ff.; 1966: 621ff.; 1972: 145ff.; 1973: 60, 75ff.) has developed a theory of social exchange that seems to be a generalization of the phenomenon of log-rolling.

2 For an overview of different ways of conceiving the relation between politicians and bureaucrats, see Peters (1987).

3 George J. Stigler (1972: 98–100), has argued that even minority votes influence policy, so that there is, nevertheless, a 'basic similarity between political and economic competition'. This is surprising. The usual libertarian message is that the market is vastly superior to government with respect to pluralism, diversity, alternatives.

4 The spatial theory of committees is perhaps an equally valuable contribution – according to Riker (see p. 372, note 2 to Chapter 2), Duncan Black's median voter theorem is 'certainly the greatest step forward in political theory in this century' – but, unlike mass elections, committee voting will probably never be a central concern of political science.

5 The assumption of an ideological continuum stretching from left to right, or from liberal to conservative, was criticized from within the rational choice camp by Popkin et al. (1976: 796–799).

6 In a recent critique of the spatial model of party competition, Rabinowitz and Macdonald (1989) maintain that it has failed to overcome the weaknesses pointed out by Stokes and especially the problem created by the axiom of ordered dimensions. Their own solution to this problem is a 'directional theory of issue voting' based upon a theory of symbolic politics. See also Dunleavy, (1991: 90–98) for a recent critique of the assumptions of spatial theory, especially the assumptions of single-peakedness and proximity (that voters always choose to support the party that is nearest to them).

7 In the spatial theory of committees the problem is, of course, that of cycling majorities. The main strategy used to come to terms with this indeterminacy has been institutionalism. Special attention has been called to institutions that permit some candidate(s) to set the agenda; to decide which alternatives to choose between and in what order (Enelow and Hinich, 1984: ch. 8; Rosenthal, 1990).

8 Summarizing their survey of experimental research on spatial models, McKelvey and Ordeshook (1990a: 140) conclude 'that the large body of theoretical research into spatial models of committees and elections is not without sound empirical content'. This may be, but a lack of empirical content would be disastrous for a positive theory of politics. When it comes to the spatial theory of mass elections, it seems to be widely agreed that it has low empirical content and predictive power (see, e.g., Johnson, 1991: 115–117).

9 According to Gordon Tullock (1990: 208), 'Political scientists have realized since Downs (1957) that if voters do not pursue politics as a hobby, they are usually very badly informed about it.' But this is not something that Downs

discovered; it is something that he assumed on the basis of massive evidence from from sociological studies (see Downs, 1957: 298; cf. Fiorina, 1981: 3; McKelvey and Ordeshook, 1990b; Popkin, 1991: 12–15). Downs' contribution was to suggest that costs of information make it rational for voters to be ignorant about politics (see, Popkin *et al.*, 1976: 786ff.; Frohlich *et al.*, 1978: 180f; Fiorina, 1990: 332; Popkin, 1991: 13–15). Tullock (1967b: ch. 7) accepts Downs' analysis, but seems to be, himself, ignorant about the research on which it is based: 'Not enough research has been done on the amount of effort put into political study by the common man, but it is reasonably certain that the figure would be small' (ibid., p. 101). While Tullock may be justified in maintaining that not *enough* research has been done, it is also true that *much* research had already been done by 1967.

10 Ordeshook (1976: 295f.) mentions party identification on the part of voters, and ideological commitment and dependence on party and financial contributors on the part of candidates, as sources of spatial constraint. He points out, though, that these elements are *ad hoc* relative to spatial theory. Cf. Dunleavy (1991: 131–136) on the rigidities created by these spatial constraints. Austen-Smith (1983: 454) mentions 'appeal to nonspatial features such as candidate personality or family background', constituting 'an ad hoc extension to the basic spatial framework'.

11 See also Riker's presidential address to the American Political Science Association (1984), where he analyses the use of heresthetic and rhetoric in the decision on the Constitutional Convention of 1787. A further purpose of this analysis is to argue for a more dynamic model of decision-making and also that rational choice escapes the defects of both determinism and indeterminism.

12 Jon Elster (1986b: 12ff.) incorporates belief in his model of a rational choice explanation. So there seems to be some room for people's definition of the situation. But a theory of rational choice presupposes a theory of rational belief (ibid., p. 1). This is a problem for Riker's heresthetic. Manipulation by means of a redefinition of the situation indicates rationality on the part of the manipulators, but hardly rational belief on the part of the manipulated.

13 Cf. Amartay Sen (1979: 102ff.). Hirschman's analysis also connects with the idea of lexigraphic preferences, as used by Blegvad and Collins (1992) and Himmelstrand (1992b).

14 An early attempt to understand the rise to power of Adolf Hitler and his Nazis was made by Serge Chakotin in *The Rape of the Masses. The Psychology of Totalitarian Political Propaganda* (1939/1971). The analysis is burdened by too much reliance on a defunct psychology of reflexes and instincts, but also contains valuable observations on the use of symbolism in propaganda (ibid., pp. 98ff.).

15 The 'theories' of opinion leaders and of a two-step flow of information have turned out to be lasting contributions to political theory. See e.g., Popkins (1991: 12f., 47–49) and Zaller (1992).

16 It has been argued, by Parry (1969: 144), that Mosca's reconciliation with democracy in his second, extended, edition of *The Ruling Class* (1939), points in the direction of a pluralist democracy, as depicted by Schumpeter and others.

17 Schumpeter was personally acquainted with Weber and intellectually indebted to him in many respects (see Swedberg, 1991: 92f.).

18 The main source for Weber's theory of democracy is 'Parliament and Government in Germany in a Reconstructed Germany' (1918), published as Appendix II to *Economy and Society* (1922/1978: 1381–1469) and with a slightly different title in Weber, *Political Writings* (1994: 130–271). Other sources are 'Suffrage and

Democracy in Germany' (Weber [1917] 1994: 80–129) and his famous speech 'Politics as a Vocation' ([1919] 1948: 77–128), published as 'The Profession and Vocation of Politics' in *Political Writings* (1994: 309–369). For a trustworthy account of Weber's theory of democracy, see the excellent book by David Beetham, *Max Weber and the Theory of Modern Politics* (1974/1985: ch. 4).

19 I have already mentioned Harold Lasswell as a founding father of the theory of symbolic politics. Another precursor, mentioned by Edelman (1964: 10–12), is Ulf Himmelstrand (1960), who launched the idea of 'symbol acts'. The main intellectual heir of Edelman is W. Lance Bennett (1980, 1988).

20 It is difficult not to see in Schumpeter's view of human nature in politics an expression of deep pessimism, following upon political events in Europe before the publication of his book in 1943. But this does not necessarily detract from the realism of the picture.

21 The notion of 'retrospective voting' is often linked to that of 'economic voting' – as in the hypothesis that voters punish incumbent administrations for a bad economic record, at least in presidential elections (Fiorina, 1978; Kiewiet and Rivers, 1984; Erikson, 1989). As we have seen, this hypothesis was part of the theory of political business cycles and supported by evidence about the aggregate behaviour of voters (Kramer, 1971). Kramer's evidence has been criticized by Stigler (1973), who suggests that economic conditions *do not* influence and *should not* influence the vote. If voters are rational – and Stigler assumes that they are – they know that short-term economic changes are due to many other things than government performance. As we saw in Chapter 2, aggregate evidence clearly support the hypothesis of economic voting.

22 Cf. Chappell and Keech (1985), for a model that assumes an even higher level of sophistication on the part of the electorate.

23 See, e.g. Ferejohn and Kuklinski (eds) *Information and Democratic Processes* (1990), which contains many contributions representing rational choice.

24 Both distinctions have something to do with the ancient distinction between (Socratic) dialectics and (Sophistic) rhetoric, used by both Plato and Aristotle.

25 The notion of the 'definition of the situation' goes back to the American sociologist W.I. Thomas, famous for his so-called 'theorem': 'if men define situations as real, they are real in their consequences' (See Chapter 6, note 39).

26 See Habermas (1977/1986), which also includes a critique of Arendt's concept of 'power' and an illuminating comparison of the views of power of Arendt, Parsons and Weber.

27 See Giddens ([1968] 1977: ch. 10) for a critique of Parsons' concept of 'power'. Parsons does not deny conflict between sectional interests, but, according to Giddens, he entirely neglects it, as he does the relational concept of power involving A's power over B. As has been pointed out, again and again, by his numerous critics, Parsons' view of society recognizes only consensus and harmony of interests. This is the main defect of his sociology.

28 For individuals with limited resources of their own, number and organization may be the only way to gain power. Marx knew this when he urged workers to unite and organize a party (see ch. 6., pp. 298ff.).

29 For a critique of this general definition of power, see Connolly (1974/1983: 107f.) and Lukes (1986a: 5ff.), both of whom seem to doubt that it is a good idea to fit all forms of power into one picture. See also Dowding (1991: 1).

30 Cf. Russell (1938/1948: 35): 'there is power over human beings and there is power over dead matter or non-human forms of life. I shall be concerned mainly with power over human beings, but it will be necessary to remember that the chief cause of change in the modern world is the increased power over matter that we owe to science.'

31 Michael Mann (1986: 6) is another sociologist who draws on Parsons' analysis of power. He makes the distinction between 'collective' (non-zero-sum) and 'distributive' (zero-sum) aspects of power.

32 A difference between organizational resources and social capital is that the former multiplies as a function of organization, whereas the latter is aggregative. Organizations are not just power containers, they are power multipliers. The power of an organization is more than the sum of the power of its individual members.

33 Parents offering their children sweets, toys or money, in exchange for their compliance, use their economic power to induce them in a certain direction. If parents threaten to withdraw their children's weekly pocket-money, and the threat is credible, they use economic power as coercion. Threatening to lock them up in their room, if they don't behave, is also coercion, if the threat is credible, which such threats rarely are. Commanding children to do their homework, while hoping that they will sense a duty to obey, is to rely on authority. If parents try to make them switch from sweets to fruit, by telling them that sweets are bad for their teeth and fruit good for their health, they try persuasion.

34 A somewhat different account is given by Carl J. Friedrich (1967: 127f.). In his version, *auctoritas* was conferred upon a law when the old men of the senate uttered: 'yes, the law also pleases us; we are in agreement'. In this way, a law 'acquired authority because the decision of *will* on the part of the popular assembly had been enlarged by a decision of "reason," as the old men reflected upon the wisdom of the legislation in terms of tradition and religion'.

35 According to Green (1988: 5), 'A state is legitimate only if, all things considered, its rule is morally justified. (It is absurd to say, as some political scientists do, that the state is legitimate if it is believed to be legitimate by its citizens; for what are we to suppose they believe in believing *that*?)'. A social scientist might retort that, for one thing, citizens might believe different things in different cultures and in different historical epochs and all these different beliefs might lend legitimacy to the state, so perhaps the fact that they do entertain this belief is more important than the content of the belief, at least for the purposes of social science.

36 According to Durkheim ([1906] 1974: 54ff.; 1925/1961: 88ff.), moral authority ultimately resides with the collective, with society.

37 For a critique of authority based on technical knowledge, or 'epistemocratic authority', see Ball (1988: 115–120).

38 It is an irony that Parsons conceived of his own theory of politics as a theory of exchange on a par with economics (see, e.g., Parsons [1963] 1967: 345).

4 INDIVIDUALISM

1 *The Poverty of Historicism* was first published as articles in *Economica* (1944), on the initiative of the editor, Friedrich von Hayek.

2 Popper's argument against psychologism and the theory of the social contract is not his own. It is a standard argument against the individualist view of society, stated very clearly by, among others, Émile Durkheim in *The Rules of Sociological Method* (1895/1964: 102ff.).

3 Schumpeter, in fact, believed that methodological individualism is limited in its application to a narrow range of phenomena. 'Wir wollen gewisse wirtschaftliche Vorgänge beschreiben und auch dass innerhalb ganz enger Grenzen. Die tieferen Gründe derselben mögen interessant sein, aber sie berühren unsere

Resultate nicht. Sie gehören zu dem Gebiete der Soziologie und daher kann unsere Auffassung auch nicht durch den Nachweis unmöglich gemacht werden, dass man die Vorgänge in einer Volkswirtschaft tatsächlich nicht als rein individuelle erklären könne' (Schumpeter, 1908: 94).

4 Schumpeter ([1927] 1951: 135) mentions Gustav Schmoller, Emile Durkheim and Othmar Spann as the main sources of inspiration for his own theory of class. This is enough to exclude the possibility that Schumpeter's theory of class is individualistic. See also Schroeter (1985: 163). When Elster (1983: 113) says that 'Schumpeter practised the doctrine of methodological individualism', this is true, but not the whole truth. He also practised methodological collectivism.

5 Emile Durkheim ([1890, 1898] 1973, chs 3–4) made much the same distinction between two forms of individualism, but argued that the tradition emanating from Kant and Rousseau is 'true' individualism, because it, alone, realizes that the individual depends for her/his autonomy and individuality upon society.

6 Of vital importance for an understanding of Buchanan's constitutional economics, is his distinction between decision-making within a framework of rules and decisions about the rules themselves (1975a: x; 1989: 57f.; Brennan and Buchanan, 1985: 5–7). A more complete analysis reveals at least three levels: (1) decisions within a legal framework, (2) decisions about laws and regulations, but within a constitution, and (3) decisions about the constitution, which are necessarily also about the constitution, or we end in an infinite regress (cf. Buchanan and Tullock, 1962/1965: 6, 15). The legal framework, then, is a two-layered structure (cf. Buchanan, 1984: 440ff.). The constitution has a special status, since it comprises laws about legislation. The implication for public choice is this: while private market transactions take place within the constitution *and* other laws and regulations, decisions about public goods by the state are regulated only by the constitution (cf. Buchanan, 1975a: 35ff.).

7 Buchanan's approach has a certain similarity to that of John Rawls in *A Theory of Justice*. Buchanan accepts Rawls' analysis of justice as *fairness* and sees in his own (and Tullock's) use of uncertainty about future position in constitutional choice an analogue to Rawls' 'veil of ignorance' (Buchanan, 1975a: 70f., 175–177, 181 n.4; 1979b: 196 n.5; 1986: 126ff., 168, 243ff.; 1989a: 27f., 65f.).

8 Unlike his more conservative fellow libertarian Friedrich von Hayek, Buchanan does not believe in the 'wisdom' of cultural evolution. See Buchanan (1975a: x, ch. 10; 1986, ch. 8; Brennan and Buchanan, 1985: 9f.).

9 On the idea of norms as social capital, see also Coleman (1987b; 1990b: ch. 12) and Putnam (1993: 167ff.), who also includes social networks in social capital.

10 See, however, Buchanan (1989a: 37f.), where he denies the existence of a one-dimensional preference ordering over all goods. Our choice of rules is dictated by our (meta)preferences for constraints. Cf. the analysis of lexigraphic preferences by Blegvad and Collins (1992), and by Himmelstrand (1992b).

11 This is not entirely correct. In *The Limits of Liberty* (1975a: pp. 54f.) Buchanan makes room for inequality in tastes and capacities (there is no property) in the pre-constitutional state. But this is only to make the analysis more realistic. Inequality is still a hindrance to, not a precondition for, the emergence of a constitutional contract.

12 For a critique of this second step in Hobbes' (and Buchanan's) analysis, see Michael Taylor (1987: ch. 6).

13 See Nisbet (1966/1970: ch. 6). The sacred character of morality was emphasized, most strongly, by the sociologist Emile Durkheim [1914] 1973: ch. 10; 1906/1974: 48ff.; 1925/1973: 10). It may be pointed out, a propos Buchanan,

that Durkheim (1898/1973: ch. 4) saw individualism as the 'religion' of our time. We treat the human personality as a sacred object and engage in a 'cult of the individual'.

14 Libertarians are those liberals who see economic, or market, freedom as the 'essence' or basis, of a free society. They see the need for a state as a 'nightwatchman', but wish to minimize its activity, as indeed all political activity to providing a minimal number of public goods.

15 Important exceptions to this rule are the elitist political sociologists mentioned in Chapter 1 (pp. 42–46) and in Chapter 6 (pp. 289ff.).

16 Marxism is a special case, which does not fit my description of sociology. Marxists are suspicious of common values, because they are considered part of dominant ideologies helping ruling classes to maintain hegemony. Unlike public choice, Marxism does not see heterogeneous preferences as much of a problem. The problem is private property and class conflict. But once classes are abolished, heterogeneous preferences mysteriously cease to be a problem.

17 It may also be noted that Robertson, while talking about self-interest, uses examples that are not individuals. Among his examples are unions failing to show wage-restraint and nation-states not contributing to international cooperation. This is group-interest, not self-interest. Because of this confusion, Robertson's article is a poor source of support for Buchanan's argument.

18 A similar argument can be found in Friedrich von Hayek's *The Road to Serfdom* (1944/1971), Chapter 10, with the title: 'Why the Worst Get on Top'.

19 See, however, Brennan and Buchanan (1981: 387ff.), where they seem to admit that political man is a better or, at least, less egoistic man than is economic man. For a history of the defence of commerce, relative to politics, see Hirschman (1977).

20 'Public expenditure' is, of course, a highly problematic concept, making comparison extremely difficult. There is, for instance, the problem of whether to count public enterprises as part of the public sector. There is also the problem of transfers, which are not, strictly speaking, expenditure. More generally, public expenditure is not coextensive with public activity. Governments may legislate about off-budget activity that makes no difference to total costs but makes a big difference in nominal public expenditure. For a good discussion see Klein (1985: 199–205).

21 See, e.g., Lindberg (1992: 147–149). For an overview of the different explanations of the growth of public expenditure, see Tarschys (1975), Alt and Chrystal (1983: ch. 8) and Wildavsky (1985b).

22 In a well-known article by Morris Beck (1976), it is argued that, in real terms, government output decreased, as a share of GDP, in most industrial countries between 1950 and 1970. This result was obtained by using a deflator for price changes. The explanation for this surprising result would be in terms of increasing salaries for civil servants and a higher labour-intensity in the public sector. If Beck is correct, the critics of public sector growth should focus on productive, rather than allocative, inefficiency.

23 Peltzman (1980: 235, 267f.) equally assumes that the poor will lose, mainly because they lack the ability (education) to look after their own interests. For a good discussion of the role of redistribution in the expansion of the public sector from a perspective close to public choice, see Lindbeck (1985). While assuming that narrow self-interest is the most important motive behind redistribution, Lindbeck also assigns a role to 'welfare altruism and ideology', and to 'attitudes towards consequential externalities' (ibid., p. 311). By the latter expression is meant a wish to remove poverty because it is ugly and

possibly dangerous. This motive is self-interest on the part of benefactors rather than beneficiaries.

24 Niskanen defines optimum as production that maximizes net benefits (1971: 47; 1973: 29). This is what a profit-maximizing monopolist would do, but it is not a Pareto-efficient level for the economy as a whole (see de Bruin, 1987: 53–59).

25 This assertion should not be interpreted as allegiance to a pluralist, as distinguished from an elitist, or a corporatist view of the distribution of power in society. The latter views are closer to the truth.

26 The title of Lindblom's 1959 article is 'The Science of "Muddling Through"'. When writing the passage about incrementalism, I came upon the following passage in Robert Musil's novel *The Man without Qualities*, ([1932] 1979: 70) 'Digression number two: the law of world history, it now occurred to him, was nothing but the fundamental principle of government in old Kakania, namely that of "muddling through".'

27 Incrementalism is, of course, closely akin to Karl Popper's method of 'piecemeal engineering' (Popper, 1957/1961: 64–70). The main difference is that the 'incrementalism' is intended to be descriptive of politics in Western democracies or, at least, the United States, while the idea of piecemeal social engineering is, first of all, normative.

28 Arguments to the contrary exist (Chappell and Keech, 1990; Williams, 1990), but are equally difficult to sustain.

29 There are other arguments, in terms of productive efficiency, to show that the public sector is too large relative to the private sector. There is, for instance, the general argument that the public sector drains the private sector of resources and in the end threatens to crowd it out. There is the dynamic argument about a trade-off between equality and efficiency. Increasing equality decreases the incentive to work. It also leads to a decrease in private capital accumulation and a consequent retardation of economic growth. An argument more closely associated with public choice is that public enterprises produce less efficiently than private enterprises (Spann, 1977; Mueller, 1989: 261–266). This is an old observation (see, e.g., Wagner, 1883/1958: 3) which has come to attain the status of folk wisdom (see, e.g., Parkinson, 1958).

5 THE ECONOMICS OF COLLECTIVE ACTION

1 The original definition of a collective, or public, good is that of Paul A. Samuelson. For Samuelson, the important feature of a collective, or public, good, is 'jointness of demand' (1954: 389): 'each individual's consumption of such a good leads to no subtraction from any other individual's consumption of that good' (ibid., p. 387; see also Samuelson 1955: 350).

2 This point was really made by Buchanan and Tullock before Olson. In the *Calculus of Consent* (1962/1965: chs 6–8), they analysed collective action as a function of group size, arguing that decision-making costs increase with size. But since the external costs are imposed by other individuals in the absence of the public good, the combined cost curve will be U-shaped, with costs first decreasing and then increasing as a function of group size.

3 This part of the theory is closely akin to certain sociological theories of revolution, such as James Davies' theory of the J-curve and Ted R. Gurr's theory of relative deprivation (see Chapter 6).

4 The equation Tullock uses to determine the payoff for participating in the revolution, on the revolutionary side, is this:

$$Pr = Pg(Lv + Li) + Ri(Lv + Li) - Pi[1 - (Lv + Li)] - Lw \times Ir + E,$$

where Pr is 'total payoff to subject if he joins action'; Pg is 'public good generated by successful revolution'; Lv is 'likelihood of revolutionary victory assuming subject is neutral'; Li is 'change in the probability of revolutionary success resulting from individual participation in the revolution'; Ri is 'private reward to individual for his participation in revolution if revolution succeds'; Pi is 'private penalty imposed on individual for participation in revolution if revolt fails', Lw is 'Likelihood of injury through participation in revolution'; Ir is Injury suffered in action and E is 'entertainment value of participation' (Tullock, 1971: 89–91). Because of the insignificance of Li and the fact that an individual will enjoy Pg even if he/she remains inactive, an individual's gain from participation reduces to this:

$$Gr \approx Ri \times Lv - Pi(1 - Lv) - Lw \times Ir + E,$$

where Gr stands for 'opportunity cost (benefit) to individual from participation rather than remaining neutral'.

5 Schelling subsumes two different, but related, ideas under the rubric of 'critical mass'. The first and most proper use of the term is to denote that proportion of individuals that must act, for a collective action to take place. The second use is that of a 'critical point', or threshold, designating the proportion of others that must act before a single individual decides to join. A 'critical mass' is a property of the collective; a 'threshold' is a property of an individual. Both notions have been used in the analysis of collective action. The idea of a threshold for participation has been utilized by Mark Granovetter and that of critical mass, by Pamela Oliver *et al.*

6 It is an obvious advantage if all drivers use one side of the road, in each direction. It does not matter very much which side it is. This is largely a matter of convention. But it does matter to some extent, because many drivers occasionally visit foreign countries by car. The optimal global solution, therefore, is that all drivers on earth use the same convention. In Sweden, there was until 1967 left hand traffic, when the government decided to switch to right hand traffic. The reason was, of course, that most other countries have right hand traffic. With increasing traffic over borders it was expected that a switch to the most common convention would lead to a decrease in the number of accidents. This example is an illustration of one situation mentioned by Schelling: when there are two self-enforcing equilibria, but one of them is slightly better than the other. Even though all, or most, would prefer the collectively better solution, they may be trapped in the less attractive situation until a central authority enforces a shift. The shift cannot be achieved without coordination.

7 Cross and Guyer (1980: 133) point out that Hardin goes too far in assuming that the commons will be overgrazed. At some point in the successive destruction of the pasture it will be not only collectively but individually irrational to add another animal to the herd. The cost of an additional animal will exceed marginal benefit before the pasture is ruined. In its long-term consequences, the tragedy of the commons is a game of chicken, rather than a prisoners' dilemma (cf. Taylor and Ward, 1982).

8 Another typology of collective action problems has been proposed by Russell Hardin (1982: ch. 4). One dimension in his typology is 'internal provision versus external provision of the good or bad' (ibid., p. 51). 'Internal provision' means that a public good is provided by the group members themselves; 'external provision' that it is provided by some external agency: by the state, for instance, or by some charity organization.

9   These games were identified and described by Anatol Rapoport and Melvin Guyer in their taxonomy of 2 x 2 games . The game of assurance, or trust, however, is not identified by name, but mentioned as a no-conflict game with an absolutely stable equilibrium (Rapoport and Guyer, 1966: 206).

10 The name of this game derives from the following example provided by Luce and Raiffa (1957/1985: 91): a man and a woman each have two choices for an evening's entertainment Each can either go to a prize fight or to a ballet. Following the usual cultural stereotype, the man much prefers the fight and the woman the ballet. However, both prefer the company of the other to going out alone.

11 Another argument stems from assuming imperfect information about benefits and costs. Terry M. Moe suggests (1980: 30–34), as a possibility, that individuals systematically overestimate the efficacy of their own contribution to achieving the goals of interest groups. If so, they may well participate even in large groups, while being subjectively rational. Moe's data supports this assumption (ibid., pp. 205–207, 214).

12 An extended and improved presentation of this argument can be found in Frohlich and Oppenheimer (1978: 55–63). They now recognize clearly that neither cost-sharing nor expected utility-maximization solves the collective action problem.

13 This distinction between indivisibility and jointness was made before by Alfano and Marwell (1981: 301).

14 Michael Taylor (1987: 11) makes a distinction between imperfect jointness, or crowding, and rivalness. If there is crowding, the amount of a collective good available to each individual decreases with increasing group size. If there is rivalness, it is the individual's benefit that decreases. Crowding is objective and rivalness subjective.

15 See also Axelrod (1981) and Axelrod and Dion (1988), where further research on the evolution of cooperation is discussed.

16 See, however, Bendor (1987), who shows that there might be a problem if we consider the possibility of 'noise', in the form of error and other unintended consequences, affecting the determinism of tit-for-tat. To the extent that this is the case, individuals face a situation of uncertainty, and if they are risk-averse might choose some other strategy less conducive to cooperation.

17 See also *The Possibility of Cooperation* (1987), which is a revised edition of *Anarchy and Cooperation* and 'Cooperation and Rationality: Notes on the Collective Action Problem and Its Solution' (1990), which is based upon parts of *The Possibility of Cooperation*.

18 An analysis similar to that of Taylor and Ward can be found in Anthony de Jasay's *Social Contract, Free Ride* (1989). Like the former, he denies that the public goods problem is typically a prisoners' dilemma: 'Not subscribe' is not necessarily a dominant strategy. Important for de Jasay's argument is the claim that many public goods are lumpy (step-level goods). There are often no returns at all until contributions reach a level at which the marginal contribution becomes pivotal. In this situation, the risk that not enough others will contribute, will lead most people to do so (ibid., pp. 169–172).

19 Richard Jankowski agrees with Taylor and Ward that chicken games may develop out of N-person prisoners' dilemmas (1990: 450–458), but adds two other classes of chicken games: those arising in cases of positive externalities and those associated with punishment of defectors (ibid., pp. 458–461). As an example of the former, he mentions vaccination. For most diseases, all are protected if the majority are vaccinated. If so, we might prefer to belong to the minority that

free rides on the vaccination of others. Punishment of defectors gives rise to a game of chicken, especially if we have reason to be afraid of retaliation.

20 On the importance of overlapping activities, or closure of social interaction, for the possibility of sanctioning defectors, see Coleman (1986; 1990a: 41–52; 1990b: 266ff., 318–320). On the use of exclusion as a punishment for defection, see Hechter (1984: 175; 1987: 36–39, 161–167). The effectiveness of this sanction is, of course, a function of the dependence of the individual on the group as a source of personal welfare.

21 According to Max Weber's famous, but untenable, definition; 'Action is "social" insofar as its subjective meaning takes account of the behaviour of others and is thereby oriented in its course' (Weber (1922/1978: 4).

22 The idea of 'critical mass' has also been used by Michael C. Macy (1990), in a computer simulation based on learning theory instead of rational choice. His contention is that a critical mass of cooperators may arise as the result of a stochastic learning process involving sanctioning of defectors. Sanctioning may be pragmatic or normative. If it is normative, it goes beyond self-interest. Macy's model has certain similarities with Axelrod's evolutionary model, but does not rely on selection. Adaptation through learning is a shorter way to develop a critical mass of cooperators.

23 An all-or-none contract differs from an assurance game in the sense of Amartya Sen, and a convention in the sense of Russell Hardin, since it depends for its viability upon an enforcement mechanism.

24 The second-order collective action problem was recognized by Parsons (1966: 74f.): 'In cases of continuing noncompliance, insistence inevitably includes the threat of imposing negative sanctions as a consequence of noncompliance. *Then their implementation becomes a commitment of the threatener.* As will be made clear later, this in no way implies that fear of negative sanctions is the principal motive for honoring collective commitments' (my italics).

25 Cf. Spencer ([1871] 1969: 302) for a similar account of the origin of Insurance societies.

26 Bendor and Mookherje are wrong to attribute to Olson a centralist position. Olson saw the importance of 'social incentives' in small groups and also the possibility of a federalist solution to the collective action problem in large groups (Olson, 1965/1971: 62f.). In fact, Olson argued that large interest groups, such as contemporary labour unions, are only possible by a fusion of small, local, unions (ibid., 66ff.). But the federal solution to the collective action problem is older than Olson: it is an established part of the sociological theory of groups (see Chapter 6).

27 The insight that human beings typically transform the game situations they are in was a key element in Buckley, Burns and Meeker (1974: 278f., 289ff.).

28 In a recent article (Taylor and Singleton, 1993), Taylor discusses institutional solutions to the collective action problem, with special reference to Heckathorn and Ostrom.

29 It should be pointed out that some in the orthodox camp use the assumption of self-interest as a heuristic device, rather than as an all-powerful explanation of collective action. This is unobjectionable if combined with a readiness to consider alternative explanations.

30 Mancur Olson himself is aware of the problematic trade-off between parsimony and empirical content and, therefore, excludes 'moral incentives' (Olson, 1965/1971: 61n.).

31 Genetically, it is probably the other way around. According to Georg Simmel ([1908] 1950: 260) 'The original content of morality is of an altruistic-social nature. The idea is not that morality has its own life independent of this

content and merely absorbs it. Rather, the devotion of the "I" to the "thou" (in the singular or plural) is the very idea, the definition of the moral. Philosophical doctrines represent, by comparison, a much later phase.'

32 See Hechter, Opp and Wippler (1990), Lindenberg (1990) and, especially, Hechter (1992, 1994) for a critical discussion of the role of values in rational choice analysis.

33 In an article written together with Debra Friedman and Satoshi Kanazawa, Hechter writes: 'No state has sufficient resources to maintain order solely via policing; this is why Weber invoked the famous concept of *legitimacy*' (Hechter *et al.*, 1992: 79). I take this statement as an indication that moral obligation is necessary for group solidarity, despite the authors' belief that the concept of 'legitimacy' belongs in the rational choice tradition.

34 For a somewhat exaggerated, but very effective, critique of the equally exaggerated claims of economic reductionists, see Davis (1992: 17–22).

35 It may be pointed out that Gamson is responsible for one of the most comprehensive empirical investigations there is on voluntary interest groups (Gamson, 1975).

36 I think especially of Elster's effective rebuttal of the various forms of economic reductionism (1989a: 125–151; 1989b: ch. 12; 1989c: 544–550; 1991: 116–126). For a suggestive treatment of the collective action problem by two sociologists and a mathematician, see Buckley, Burns and Meeker (1974). See also Burns (1994).

37 By the same token I am, of course, obliged to attach special importance to the views of James Coleman and other rational choice sociologists, who have abandoned sociological man for economic man. If I am not mistaken, however, the tendency in rational choice sociology is definitely away from economic man (cf. note 32).

38 Sequential models have been used before, by Granovetter and Oliver, Marwell and Texeira, for instance (see pp. 235f. above). All such models depend upon the assumption of some kind of heterogeneity: in resources and/or intensity of preferences for a collective good. The important novelty in Elster's model is the assumption of heterogeneity, not only in the strength, but in the *kind*, of motives for engaging in collective action.

39 The distinction between fear and greed was made by Coombs (1973) in his parametrization of the prisoners' dilemma game. Greed is defined by the positive inducement for each player to defect. Fear is the risk that the other player will defect if I cooperate.

40 Popkin uses the assumption of self-interest only for methodological purposes and then with the following qualification: 'Many persons equate rationality and self-interest – with self-interest defined as "interest only in one's own welfare." I most emphatically deny that persons are self-interested in this narrow sense. It is clearly the case that, at different times, peasants care about themselves, their families, their friends, and their villages. However, I do assume that a peasant is primarily concerned with the welfare and security of self and family. Whatever his broad values and objectives, when the peasant takes into account the likelihood of receiving the preferred outcomes *on the basis of individual actions*, he usually will act in a self-interested manner' (Popkin, 1979: 31).

41 Data are also interpreted as casting doubt upon traditional pluralist theory. I am not convinced about the relevance of his data for pluralist theory. As Moe observes himself (Moe, 1980: 160), the latter simply has very little to say about individuals' motives for joining interest groups. Because of this, I find it unjust to compare pluralist theory to Olson's theory entirely on terms dictated by the latter. If economic selective incentives are important for members of interest

groups, this adds to our understanding, but it does not necessarily contradict pluralist theory, which treats interest groups as given to analysis.

42 There are more empirical studies confirming the importance of social norms in wage bargaining, with equally negative implications for an economic theory of interest groups.

43 Elster is 'sceptical about the explanatory value of the concept of collective identity' (Elster, 1989a: 168). Considering the experiments of Dawes, *et al.*, he should perhaps give the matter a second thought.

6 THE SOCIOLOGY OF COLLECTIVE ACTION

1 There seems to be some justification for Olson's critique in the case of Robert A. Dahl, a third representative of the group approach. In his famous *Who Governs* (1961b: ch. 19), Dahl appears to assume that both *homo civicus* and *homo politicus* are largely self-interested. But not entirely so. The list of resources used in political activity 'might also include solidarity: the capacity of a member of society to evoke support from others who identify him as like themselves because of similarities in occupation social standing, religion, ethnic origin, or racial stock'.

2 There is reason to believe that Olson's theory of large interest-groups as 'by-products' also derives from Simmel: 'Formally speaking, competition rests on the principle of individualism. Yet as soon as it occurs within a group, its relation to the social principle of the subordination of every individual interest under the uniform group interest is not at once clear. To be sure, the single competitor pursues his own purpose; he uses his energies for asserting his own interests. The competitive struggle is carried on by means of objective accomplishments, usually yielding a result which is somehow valuable to a third party. The purely social interest makes this result into an ultimate goal, while for the competitors themselves it is only a by-product' (Simmel, [1908] 1955: 72).

3 The results of these studies are reported in E. Mayo, *Human Problems of Industrial Civilization* (1933), T. N. Whitehead, *The Industrial Worker* (1938), F. J. Roethlisberger and W. J. Dickson, *Management and the Worker* (1939) and G. C. Homans, *Fatigue of Workers* (1941).

4 This norm, which is well known to all workers, was also known to sociologists well before the Hawthorne studies. Max Weber, for instance, observes in his little-known empirical study of industrial workers, that 'the so-called "runners" are usually compelled, directly or indirectly, by the solidarity of their fellow-workers, "to put the brake on", i.e. remain within the limits of average effort which will permit the others to "keep up", and which eliminates the danger, always in the workers' minds, of increases in earnings due to particularly high output possibly causing the employer to reduce the piece-rate' (Weber, 1908/1971: 133). Alain Touraine (1978/1981: 70) interprets collective slow-down as an indication of class consciousness. In his view, recognition of this phenomenon marks the birth of industrial sociology.

5 One important exception to mainstream sociological group theory is Robert Michels' classic: *Political Parties. A Sociological Study of the Oligarchic Tendencies of Modern Democracy* (1915/1962). In this work is advanced the famous 'iron law of oligarchy', which maintains that, not only political parties, but all large-scale organizations develop into oligarchies. Part of the argument is technical-organizational. This part is fully in line with mainstream sociology. But there is a second part of the argument relying on the assumption of the egoism of leaders. This part is more in line with public choice and, in fact, belongs to its

intellectual heritage. Robert Michels was a forerunner of Joseph Schumpeter, who was an important precursor of public choice.

6 The sociological view of this matter receives some support from Robert D. Putnam's recent study of civic traditions in modern Italy (Putnam, 1993).

7 This argument has been advanced most clearly and explicitly by Hegel, Tocqueville, Durkheim and Parsons. The difference between the economic and sociological theories of social groups and organizations is clearly illustrated by comparing Mancur Olson's *The Rise and Decline of Nations* (1982) and George Caspar Homans' *The Human Group* (1951: ch. XVIII).

8 On the importance of the mass, or crowd, in the writings of Edgar Allan Poe, Victor Hugo and Charles Baudelaire, see Benjamin (1973: 48ff.). The most important 'law' of mass psychology is implied in Thomas Hardy's *Far From The Madding Crowd* (1874). Robert Musil's *The Man without Qualities* (1932/1979, vol. 2, ch. 120) includes an episode of a political demonstration, that reveals thorough familiarity with the social psychology of crowds. Elias Canetti, finally, tells us in his autobiography vol. 2, *Torch in My Ear* (1990), how certain events in Vienna made him devote his life to reflection on mass behaviour. The result of these reflections was his *Power and Mass* (1962). Was it the same events – hunger riots – that inspired Musil and Canetti, which made the young Karl Popper turn away from Marxism (see Popper, 1976: 32ff.).

9 Le Bon's theory of mass behaviour is the point of departure for Freud's speculations on this subject in *Group Psychology and the Analysis of the Ego* (1921/1959).

10 For a good summary of the theory of collective behaviour from the 1950s, see Marx and Wood (1975).

11 See, e.g., Faris (ed.), *Handbook of Modern Sociology* (1964), where collective behaviour and social movements are treated in separate chapters, by Ralph H. Turner and Lewis M. Killian respectively. See also Rosenberg and Turner (eds), *Social Psychology* (1981), where John F. Lofland treats 'Collective Behavior: The Elementary Forms', Louis A. Zurcher and David A. Snow discuss 'Collective Behavior: Social Movements' and Gladys Engel Lang and Kurt Lang write about 'Mass Communications and Public Opinion: Strategies for Research'. Smelser does not make a distinction between collective behaviour and social movements. He recognizes five types of collective behaviour: the panic, the craze, the hostile outburst, the norm-oriented movement and the value-oriented movement (Smelser, 1962: 83ff.). While it seems reasonable to see the first three as examples of collective behaviour and the last two as examples of reformist and revolutionary social movements respectively, Smelser, himself, does not admit any such discontinuity.

12 Rudé was not alone in investigating the social composition of the revolutionary crowd in the 1950s. Studies by Albert Soubol and Kare Tonnesson reached a similar conclusion. See Tilly (1964: 111–121) for a summary of these findings.

13 See *The Crowd*, Book III, ch. IV, and, especially, *Gustave Le Bon. The Man and His Works* (Liberty Press, 1979), comprising generous selections from Le Bon's major writings, including *The Psychology of Socialism* (1898), *Opinions and Beliefs* (1911) and *The Psychology of Revolutions* (1912).

14 For a critique of Smelser, see Marx and Wood (1975: 406–413).

15 The term 'relative deprivation' was first used by Samuel Stouffer and his associates in *The American Soldier* (1949) – a classic of *empirical* sociology. It received its first theoretical elaboration by Robert K. Merton in the second edition of his *Social Theory and Social Structure* (1957) – a classic in *theoretical* sociology – where it is tied to the concept of 'reference group', originally introduced by Muzafer Sherif in *An Outline of Social Psychology* (1948).

16 Olson (1965/1971: 105, n. 22), cites C. Wright Mills and Talcott Parsons in support of this interpretation. Parsons' argument to this effect is first stated in *The Structure of Social Action* (1937/1968: 110).

17 As Jon Elster has pointed out (1985a: 346), Marx (probably) did not use the expression 'class-in-itself' (*Klasse an sich*) himself.

18 Johnson (1988) and Przeworski (1990: 79f.) have argued, correctly I believe, that the workers' strategic situation is not captured by Olson's logic of collective action. The problem is not the provision of a public good that they lack, but that they are in a situation of ruinous competition. Putting an end to this competition is a collective good, but the defector is not a free rider, he is a 'foul dealer', in the sense of Philip Pettit (1986).

19 For an extreme cognitivist, or epistemic, and objectivist interpretation of class consciousness, see G. Lukacs, *History and Class Consciousness* (1922/1971). For him, 'class consciousness consists in fact of the appropriate and rational reactions "imputed" (*zugerechnet*) to a particular typical position in the process of production' (p. 51). Thus, one should not mistake '*the actual, psychological state of consciousness of proletarians for the class consciousness of the proletariat*' (p. 74). Lukacs' analysis of class consciousness is embedded in a kind of Hegelian historicism, which assigns to the proletariat a special historical mission as the subject-object of history. The proletariat is in a unique position of epistemic privilege, which permits it to adopt a totalizing point of view and to put an end to the antithesis of subject and object, and to reification.

20 The game, or problem, of assurance was identified by Amartay Sen (1967: 114f.) and distinguished from the isolation paradox in the prisoners' dilemma. In the assurance game defection is not a dominant strategy. Each player prefers to cooperate, if all others cooperate, and all will do so if they are assured that the others will do so too. In the case of such assurance, a Pareto-optimal solution of universal cooperation will be achieved.

21 One notable contribution to this literature is *Arbeiderkollektivet* by Elster's fellow-countryman Sverre Lysgaard (1961/1981). The leitmotif of this book is that there is, indeed, such a thing as a workers' collectivity, united by a collective identity: a capacity to feel and act as a 'we' against 'others'. In particular, collective identity makes it possible for the workers' collectivity to mobilize for (defensive) collective action against management. Lysgaard and his colleagues investigated this collective identity at the level of the shop floor, but presume that it reaches to the working class as a whole (ch. 8). Lysgaard's analysis of the workers' collectivity is corroborated by Korpi (1978: 150–154), who also confirm the thesis of a declining class consciousness, as indicated by an eroding union solidarity on the part of young Swedish metal workers (ibid., pp. 172–182). Michael Mann (1973: 13), conceives of 'class *identity* – the definition of oneself as working-class, as playing a distinctive role in common with other workers in the productive process' – as one element of class consciousness, arising in 'dialectical interaction' with the second element of 'class *opposition* – the perception that the capitalist and his agents constitute an enduring opponent to oneself'. A third element, derived from Lukacs, is the grasp of society as a *totality*, defined by the above opposition. The fourth, and final, element is the conception of an *alternative* society.

22 For a critical discussion of Marx's theory of collective action, see Calhoun (1982: ch. 8; 1983, 1988).

23 As we know today, peasants have turned out to be more revolutionary than proletarians, as witnessed by the revolutions in France, Russia and China (see Skocpol, 1979 and Calhoun, 1982: 236–240).

24 A possible clue to this development are the views expressed by Lenin in *The State and the Revolution* ([1917] 1963, vol. 2) and in subsequent works (see, e.g., *The Proletarian Revolution and the Renegade Kautsky* [1918] and *Left-Wing Communism – An Infantile Disorder* [1920]; both in Lenin, 1963, vol. 3). A main theme is the necessity, maintained by Marx, of smashing the bourgeois state apparatus and replacing it with the dictatorship of the proletariat. A second, related, theme is the necessity of centralization, both in economics and in politics. 'Bourgeois democracy' must be replaced by 'proletarian democracy', characterized by what has come to be known as 'democratic centralism'. The most prominent theme, however – at least in *The State and the Revolution* – is Marx's idea of 'the withering away of the state'. The repetitiveness with which this slogan is cited makes it look like an incantation. As we all know, it did not work. The state did not wither away and the Russian revolution ended as far from a collective good.

25 'There is no process by which the future can be predicted scientifically, nor even one which enables us to discuss whether one hypothesis about it is better than another; it has been proved by too many memorable examples that the greatest men have committed prodigious errors in thus desiring to make predictions about even the least distant future' (Sorel, 1908/1961: 124). Hopefully, this is common knowledge today. At the time Sorel wrote, it was not. But if a scientific prediction of the future of society is impossible, Marx's prediction of a socialist revolution must be something else. According to Sorel, it may be interpreted as a myth: 'Marx wishes us to understand that the whole preparation of the proletariat depends solely on the organization of a stubborn, increasing, and passionate resistence to the present order of things' (ibid., p. 135).

26 For all their difference in political outlook, there are some striking similarities between Sorel and Popper. They are both fierce critics of theories of historical inevitability and of utopianism, and they both see historical historicism as a theory guilty of both (Sorel, *Critical Essays in Marxism* [1902] and *Materials for a Theory of the Proletariat* [1919–21], see also Sorel, 1976; 1908/1969). They both suggest that social scientists fail to see the difference between scientific prediction in celestial mechanics and prediction of historical development. But whereas Popper cites no example at all of social scientists committing this mistake (Popper, 1957/1961: 36ff.), Sorel mentions Fourier (*Critical Essays. . .* [1902] 1976: 133; see also *Materials. . .* [1919–21] 1976: 232ff.). Both suggest that the only patterns ascertainable in history are trends, not laws (Popper, 1957/1961: 105ff.). Sorel does not use the term 'trend', but talks about the 'grouping of certain facts' ([1902] 1976: 124). Popper's refutation of historicism in the preface to *The Poverty of Historicism* (1957/1961) can already be found in Sorel. Popper's argument is that it is impossible to predict the future course of human history, because historical development depends upon the growth of scientific knowledge, which of course, we cannot predict. In *Critical Essays. . .* ([1902] 1976: 168), Sorel says that 'There is no procedure for deducing a technique from a past technique, therefore, no precision [sic] is possible.' The context clearly indicates that it should be 'prediction', not 'precision'. Finally, Popper's 'methodological nominalism' and his critique of 'methodological essentialism' are also anticipated by Sorel: 'For the ancients, science was concerned with *concepts*, that is to say, with kinds of things . . . But modern science is concerned with laws, that is with relations' (Sorel, *The Utility of Pragmatism* [1921] 1976: 258).

27 As Theda Skocpol (1979) has argued, the success of revolutions hinges more on the weakness of the state than on the strength of the revolutionary movement.

28 See, however, Calhoun (1982: 227–235; 1988: 154–175), who agrees that Marx was not inconsistent, but who, nevertheless, concurs with Olson that working-class collective action rests on selective incentives provided by formal organization.

29 For a short presentation of Tilly's theory of collective action, see Hunt (1984). For an attempt to develop sociological orthodoxy in a way that makes it less vulnerable to the radical critique, see Alexander and Colomy (1985). Their strategy is 'ecumenical' and consists in the effort to achieve a synthesis between symbolic interactionism (Turner and Killian) and a neofunctionalism which is capable of accommodating the idea of a conflict of interests (Eisenstadt). I find their synthesis rather attractive and also believe that it is representative of the state of the art of sociology at the present moment.

30 I have a feeling that Tilly is a bit unfair to Smelser and Gurr – possibly also to Durkheim (see Birnbaum, 1988: 16) – since none of them said that strain, or deprivation, is a sufficient condition for collective behaviour. For a more positive evaluation of Durkheim's sociology in relation to a theory of collective action, see Robert J. Holton (1978). But, then, Holton emphasizes another aspect of Durkheim's work – the importance of rituals and symbols for the collective sentiments of the crowd.

31 *The Poverty of Historicism* was originally published as articles in *Economica* in 1944–45.

32 In her 'Introduction' to *Gustave Le Bon. The Man and his Work*, Alice Widener maintains (1979: 13) that Lenin, together with Mussolini, Theodore Roosevelt and Sigmund Freud, was strongly influenced by Le Bon. She also claims (ibid., p. 41) that after the October revolution in 1917, Le Bon's *Psychological Laws of the Evolution of Peoples* could be found on Lenin's work table, 'with passages heavily marked and underlined. Later, the "little book" was studied by Benito Mussolini and Adolf Hitler.'

33 It may be observed that one of Le Bon's greatest admirers, the American president Theodore Roosevelt, is mentioned by Weber (1922/1978: 1130, 1132), as a typical example of a modern charismatic plebiscitary leader and demagogue.

34 Weber's 'theory' of charisma and its routinization has become incorporated as a disputed part of mainstream sociology. As we have already seen, something like it is part of the sociological theory of the group. It is also part of the sociological theories of organization and of social movements (see, e.g., Parsons, 1951/1970: 525, n. 15). For a critical assessment of the application of Weber's theory to social movements, see Zald and Ash (1966), Banks (1972: ch. 3) and Marx and Wood (1975: 396–398).

35 It may be pointed out that Weber (1895/1980) referred to himself as a 'class-conscious bourgeois' and a nationalist. In his own hierarchy of values, the national interest of Germany stood above his interest as a member of the bourgeoisie. Against Marx, he held that the masses in times of national crisis, would likewise subordinate their class interest to that of their nation. A main theme of Weber's political writings, and a personal problem for himself, was the fact that Germany lacked a politically mature class for the recruitment of political leaders.

36 See Weber, ([1906] 1994: 63); see also 'Socialism' ([1918] 1994: 296–299) and 'Parliament and Government in Germany under a New Political Order' ([1918] 1994: 192), also in Weber (1922/1978: 1428).

37 Cf. Pareto's view of socialism and other ideologies as secular religions (Pareto, 1901/1968: 42ff.; 1916/1980: 185–205, 235ff.; [1921] 1976: 313f.).

38 The first form of the utopian mentality, according to Mannheim, was the orgiastic chiliasm of the Anabaptists. For a brief discussion of chiliasm, or millenarianism, as social movements, see Wilkinson (1971: 70–75).

39 The origin of this notion is the American sociologist W.I. Thomas ('Situational

Analysis: The Behavior Pattern and the Situation' [1927] 1966: 154–167), most famous as the source of the so-called Thomas' theorem: 'If men define situations as real, they are real in their consequences' (Thomas, 1928: 572).

40 I have mentioned two important sources for this idea: Marxism and symbolic interactionism. A third source is Durkheim and his sociological Kantianism. A fourth important source is the phenomenology of Afred Schutz. A fifth source would be sociology of knowledge itself (Scheler, Mannheim). All these traditions are ably synthesized in Peter L. Berger and Thomas Luckmann's *The Social Construction of Reality* (1966). For an interesting application of the sociology of knowledge and of social contructivism to social movements, see Eyerman and Janison, *Social Movements. A Cognitive Approach* (1991).

41 It may be noticed that this definition turns social movements into a phenomenon entirely out of the reach of ordinary economic theory. Standard economic theory takes both the social order (institutions) and individuals' preferences as given, or exogenous, to analysis.

42 Heberle pays some attention to the motives people may have for joining a social movement. Following Weber, he distinguishes between a value-rational concern for some moral good, an emotional attachment to a charismatic leader, a traditional committment to social movements that one's parents and relatives belong to, and a purposive-rational motivation of personal advantage (Heberle, 1951: 95–99). Self-interest, then, is only one out of four possible motivations. But it is a quantitatively important one: 'A few are drawn into political action by a lust for power, or by a personal sense of civic duty, or perhaps by a tradition in their family or social set. But the broad masses are likely to be activated only if their immediate personal interests are affected by some measure of the government' (Heberle, 1951: 93).

43 A more comprehensive critique of the use of rational choice models in theories of collective behaviour and in social psychology can be found in Turner (1991).

44 In a later article, Pizzorno (1985: 46ff.) also excepts the professional politician from utilitarianism.

45 For a good discussion of these identities, see Habermas (1976/1979: ch. 2, 106–116; 1981/1987: 43–62, 96–111).

46 The main source of the sociological theory of personal identity is the American pragmatist philosopher and social scientist George Herbert Mead (1934/1962).

47 Does this view cast any light upon the difference between economics and sociology, as stated by Duesenberry: 'Economics is all about how people make choices; Sociology is all about how they don't have any choices to make' (quoted in Granovetter, 1985: 484).

48 Another conspicuous example of everyday heroism is the rescuing of Jews in Nazi Europe, as analysed by Monroe, Barton and Klingeman (1991). Like Calhoun, they reject every form of rational choice explanation of this phenomenon and opt for an explanation in terms of identity. The typical reason given by the rescuers, themselves was that they had no choice but to help.

49 Honour might not be very important in modern society, but in traditional society its role is difficult to overestimate. A well-known phenomenon is the norm of reciprocity obliging members of hostile clans to go on killing each other indefinitely and for no other purpose than the honour of the clan. For an analysis of honour in Kabyle society, see Bourdieu (1966).

50 One notable exception is Albert Hirschmann, who is clearly influenced by the sociological approach, including the identity-oriented approach, in his analysis of collective action (1982/1985, 1984, 1985).

392

7 COOPERATION AND SOCIAL ORDER

1 Malinowski made a classification, including seven forms of gifts, distributed along a continuum from 'pure gifts' to 'trade pure and simple' (Malinowski, 1922/1962: 176–191).

2 Referring to this statement, Jack Hirschleifer (1985: 57f.), claims that Mauss' analysis of the gift supports the model of economic man. This is, of course, very far from the truth.

3 Cyril Belshaw (1965: 48) maintains that 'despite the force of social imperatives, Mauss has overstressed them at the expense of entrepreneurial and choice elements'.

4 Hechter's argument is based upon a long quotation from Polanyi's *The Great Transformation* (1944/1957: 46f.), which admittedly supports his point, as do other statements in this book (see, e.g., p. 153), but other (later) works by Polanyi point in another direction.

5 In *Dahomey and the Slave Trade* (1966), which is Polanyi's most important attempt to apply his concepts to a historical society, he mentions four patterns of the economy: redistribution, reciprocity, exchange and *householding*. The latter is the typical mode of production of peasant society.

6 This focus upon needs 'explains' the primacy of food in generalized reciprocity. Food is our primary need.

7 See, however, Ziegler (1990) for a game-theoretic invisible-hand explanation of *Kula* exchange as a solution to the problem of order.

8 See Lawrence C. Becker (1986: 146ff.) for an analysis of reciprocity as a fundamental virtue.

9 Short surveys of the concept of 'community', before sociology, can be found in Friedrich (1959a) and Catlin (1959). On community as the most fundamental unit idea in the sociological tradition, see Nisbet (1966/1970: ch. 3). For a recent discussion of the meaning of 'community' as a key idea in anthropology and sociology, see Cohen (1985/1989).

10 The dichotomy of *Gemeinschaft–Gesellschaft* is basic to Toennies' sociology and recurs in most of his later writings. See, e.g., the articles, 'The Nature of Sociology' (1907), a 'Prelude to Sociology' (1925), 'The Concept of Gemeinschaft' (1925) and 'The Divisions of Sociology' (1926), all reprinted in F. Toennies, *On Sociology: Pure, Applied and Empirical* (1971). See also the article 'Gemeinschaft und Gesellschaft' (1931), reprinted as an introduction to *Community and Association* (1887/1955). See, finally, Toennies' second important contribution to sociological theory, *Einführung in die Soziologie* (1931/1981), *passim*, but especially *Erstes Buch*, p. 4.

11 It may be pointed out that Toennies was not only influenced by, but personally acquainted with the German economist Adolph Wagner, the author of Wagner's law, which was mentioned in Chapter 4 (p. 195). At one occasion, Toennies ([1932] 1971: 6) refers to Wagner as 'my learned protector'. Toennies' French contemporary Emile Durkheim was also indebted to Adolf Wagner and the other 'Academic Socialists': by their critique of the Manchester School of political economy, their programme for social welfare and by Wagner's law of public expenditure (Durkheim, 1887/1993: 58–77; 1983: 53f.).

12 Karl Marx would seem to be an obvious exception, but antagonism between classes is not antagonism between communities. A better example is Georg Simmel (1898: 45–50; 1908/1950), who made conflict between groups an important theme of his sociology and who also emphasized the integrating effects of

conflict. Another exception is Norbert Elias, who in *The Civilizing Process* (1939/1982) similarly emphasized the violence of a social life based upon community.

13 Cf. Weber (1922/1978: 40–43) on communal and associative relationships. Weber relates this distinction to his well-known classification of social actions (ibid., pp. 24f.) in the following way: communal relationships consist of affectual and traditional actions, associative relations of instrumentally rational and value-rational actions. Toennies disagrees with this understanding of community. According to him (Toennies, 1931/1981: 6) association is the result of instrumentally rational action (rational will), while community rests on affectual, traditional and value-rational action (natural will) together. I guess that this difference reflects a more basic difference in their respective views of morality. Toennies tends to see the basis of morality in emotions, Weber in reason.

14 Since there has been, recently, much interest in the phenomenon of 'the common', as tragedy and as historical reality, it might be pointed out that, for Toennies (1887/1955: 67–70), the common is a typical manifestation of community. For Toennies, its disappearance, whether tragedy or not, had nothing to do with self-interested overgrazing. It was the result of the legislation of the modern state and ultimately of the victory of capitalism over feudalism. Cf. Simmel (1908/1971: 278): 'The evolving centralist states struck down community holdings, the common pasture land. Part of this, as a public commodity, was absorbed into the property of the state and was attached to the administrative organism of the polity. The rest, to the degree that this did not occur, was distributed among enfranchised persons as private property.'

15 For a structural definition of 'community', see Calhoun (1980). In his latest writings Calhoun seems to have moved away from a purely structuralist to a more culturalist position with regard to community and collective action (Calhoun, 1991a, 1991b).

16 It may be pointed out (Martindale, 1964: 65) that Parsons' famous pattern-variables was an attempt to replace the *Gemeinschaft–Gesellschaft* dichotomy with something better (Parsons and Shils, 1951/1962: 49). Thus we may conceive of them as ideal typical descriptions of *Gemeinschaft* and *Gesellschaft* (cf. Martindale, 1964). In a community, role-definitions are characterized by affectivity, collectivity-orientation, particularism, ascription and diffuseness. In a 'society', or an association, role-definitions are characterized by affective neutrality, self-orientation, universalism, achievement and specificity (on pattern-variables, see Parsons, 1951/1970: 58–67, 101–112; Parsons and Shils, 1951/1962: 48f., 76ff.).

17 Paul James (1992) has suggested the less subjective term 'abstract community', to denote communities integrated in other ways than by face-to-face interaction, but without implying that they are, therefore, imagined.

18 The notion of an 'utopian', or 'intentional', community is a contradiction in terms, if we follow Toennies' distinction between community and association. Being intentionally and rationally instituted, an intentional community is an association, rather than a community. Hence, the contradiction 'associational communities'.

19 Wilson's argument is that there is an inborn ability to prosocial behaviour in human beings, detectable even in newborn children. This is in line with the view of orthodox sociology, which has always insisted that altruism is as much a part of human nature as is egoism.

20 Parsons (1937/1968: 91) makes a similar (identical?) distinction between a

'normative order' and a 'factual order', only that Parsons suggests that chaos is the opposite of normative order, while randomness, or chance, is the opposite of factual order.

21 It may be denied that Locke's theory is economic as defined here. Locke does not postulate rational egoists. Interaction in the state of nature is subjected to natural law. A modern defender of 'anarcho-capitalism' is Murray Rothbard (1970).

22 A similar classification of theories of social order can be found in Pizzorno (1991: 232f.). Instead of community, Pizzorno mentions a 'value integration view'. He also adds a fourth theory of social order, inspired by the work of Michel Foucault. It is referred to as 'disciplining'.

23 For a recent sociological critique of the individualist theory of social order, see Pizzorno (1991).

24 Antonio Gramsci's *Prison Notebooks* were written in prison between 1929 and 1935. They were first published in Italy between 1948 and 1951.

25 It may be pointed out that Toennies was one of the leading authorities on Hobbes of his time. Not only did he write a book about Hobbes' life and teaching (*Hobbes Leben und Lehre*, 1896), he is also the editor of two of Hobbes' works: the early *Elements of Law. Natural and Political* (1640) and the late *Behemoth or the Long Parliament* (1668), being a treatise on contemporary history (1640–1660). Toennies testifies to the importance of Hobbes to his own work in an article of 1932. It begins: 'I wish to characterize briefly my relation to sociology. I had been early engaged in philosophical studies, and approximately since 1877 these were centred on Thomas Hobbes, especially on his writings about the philosophy of law and government' (Toennies, 1971: 3). In the Preface to the second edition of *Gemeinshaft und Gesellschaft* (1912), we read: 'For I had taken my departure from Hobbes, to whose biography and philosophy I had devoted diligent studies in the years 1877 to 1882' (Toennies, 1971: 31).

26 MacIver is one of the most consistent critics of the organic theory of the state in the history of social science. See, e.g., MacIver (1911; 1926/1964: 447ff.; 1947/1965: 303ff.).

27 See, e.g., Plant (1972/1983), who interprets Hegel as an early spokesman of the welfare state and Taylor (1979) who sees in Hegel a source of inspiration for a communitarian ideology.

28 I should perhaps point out that I do not agree with this delimitation of sociology. My concern here is merely to sketch a sociological theory of order, which I believe is essentially correct.

29 Durkheim's position is, in many respects, close to that of Friedrich von Hayek in our own day. Like the latter, Durkheim makes a distinction between society as a spontanous order and the state as an organization (Durkheim, 1983: 79f.). Interesting, in particular, is Durkheim's argument about the limited and local knowledge of each member of society. This argument has turned into a cornerstone of Austrian economics (Durkheim, 1887/1993: 72f.).

30 A clue to Durkheim's theory of the development of law and morality is, once again, his early work on the German theory of morality, especially the part which deals with Wilhelm Wundt, who was a major influence on Durkheim's sociology (Durkheim, 1887/1993: part III).

31 By 'randomness of ends', Parsons means that utilitarianism does not take upon itself to explain the ends of individuals. In economics, this is manifested by the familiar fact that wants, or preferences, are exogenous and taken as given to analysis (Parsons, 1937/1968: 344).

32 Actually Parsons changes terminology over the years. The only constant elements are economy and polity. 'Society' is also called 'the integrative system', 'societal community' and the 'social sub-system'. 'Culture' is also called the 'pattern-maintenance system' and 'the cultural sub-system'.

BIBLIOGRAPHY

Abrams, R. (1980), *Foundations of Political Analysis. An Introduction to the Theory of Collective Action*, New York: Columbia University Press.

Agassi, J. (1960), 'Methodological Individualism', *British Journal of Sociology*, 11, 244–270.

Agassi, J. (1972), 'Listening in the Lull', *Philosophy of the Social Sciences*, 2, 319–332.

Agassi, J. (1975), 'Institutional Individualism', *British Journal of Sociology*, 26, 144–155.

Agell, J., Lindh, T. and Ohlson, H. (1995), 'Growth and the Public Sector: A Critical Review Essay', Uppsala University: Department of Economics, *Working Paper 1995:9*.

Ahrne, G. (1990), *Agency and Organization. Towards an Organizational Theory of Society*, London: Sage Publications.

Ahrne, G. (1994), *Social Organizations. Interaction Inside, Outside and Between Organizations*, London: Sage Publications.

Ainslie, G. (1986), 'Beyond Microeconomics. Conflict among Interests in a Multiple Self as a Determinant of Value', in Elster (1986d).

Ainsworth, S. and Sened, I. (1993), 'The Role of Lobbyists: Entrepreneurs with Two Audiences', *American Journal of Political Science*, 37, 835–866.

Albert, H. (1963), 'Modell-Platonismus: Der neoklassische Stil des ökonomischen Denkens in kritischer Beleuchtung' in H. Albert, *Marktsoziologie und Entscheidungslogik*, Neuwied am Rhein: Hermann Luchterhand.

Albertoni, E.A. (1985), 'Ruling Class, Elites and Leadership Interpreted by Mosca, Pareto, Ostrogorskij and Michels', *History of Sociology*, 6–7, 131–150.

Aldrich, J.H. (1993), 'Rational Choice and Turnout', *American Journal of Political Science*, 37, 246–278.

Alesina, A. (1988), 'Macroeconomics and Politics', in *Macroeconomic Annual*, Cambridge, Mass.: MIT Press.

Alesina, A. and Rosenthal, H. (1989) 'Partisan Cycles in Congressional Elections and the Macroeconomy', *American Political Science Review*, 83, 373–398.

Alesina, A., Londregan, J. and Rosenthal, H. (1993), 'A Model of the Political Economy of the United States', *American Political Science Review*, 87, 12–33.

Alexander, J.C. and Colomy, P. (1985), 'Social Differentiation and Collective Behavior', *Sociological Theory*, 3, 11–23, reprinted in J.C. Alexander, *Action and Its Environments. Toward a New Synthesis*, New York: Columbia University Press, 1988.

Alfano, G. and Marwell, G. (1981), 'Experiments on the Provision of Public Goods III: Non-divisibility and Free Riding in "Real" Groups', *Social Psychology Quarterly*, 43, 300–309.

Alford, R.R. (1967), 'Class Voting in the Anglo-American Political Systems', in Lipset and Rokkan (1967).

Almond, G.A. (1956), 'Comparative Political Systems', *Journal of Politics*, 18, 391–409.

Almond, G.A. (1960), 'Introduction: A Functional Approach to Comparative Politics', in Almond and Coleman, (1960).

Almond, G.A. (1966), 'Political Theory and Political Science', *American Political Science Review*, 60, 869–879.

Almond, G.A. (1983), 'Corporatism, Pluralism, and Professional Memory', *World Politics*, 35, 245–260.

Almond, G.A. (1988), 'The Return to the State', *American Political Science Review*, 82, 853–874, reprinted in Almond (1990).

Almond, G.A. (1990), *A Discipline Divided. Schools and Sects in Political Science*, London: Sage Publications.

Almond, G.A. (1991), 'Rational Choice Theory and the Social Sciences', in Monroe (1991). Also reprinted in Almond (1990).

Almond, G.A. and Coleman, J.S. (eds) (1960), *The Politics of the Developing Areas*, Princeton, N.J.: Princeton University Press.

Almond, G.A. and Powell, G.B. (1966), *Comparative Politics: A Developmental Approach*, Boston: Little, Brown.

Almond, G.A. and Verba, S. (1963), *The Civic Culture. Political Attitudes and Democracy in Five Nations*, Princeton, NJ: Princeton University Press.

Alt, J. (1985), 'Political Parties, World Demand and Unemployment', *American Political Science Review*, 79, 1016–1040.

Alt, J.E. and Chrystal, K.A. (1983), *Political Economics*, Brighton, Sussex: Wheatsheaf Books.

Alt, J.E. and Shepsle, K.E., (eds) (1990), *Perspectives on Positive Political Economy*, Cambridge: Cambridge University Press.

Alvarez, R.M., Garrett, G. and Lange, P. (1991), 'Government Partisanship, Labor Organization and Macroeconomic Performance', *American Political Science Review*, 85, 539–556.

Anckar, D. and Berndtson, E. (1988a), 'Introduction: Centers and Peripheries, Styles and Strategies', in Anckar and Berndtson (1988b).

Anckar, D. and Berndtson, E., (eds) (1988b), *Political Science Between the Past and the Present*, Helsingfors: Finnish Political Science Association.

Anderson, B. (1983/1991), *Imagined Communities*, London: Verso.

Arendt, H. (1969/1986), 'Communicative Power', in Lukes (1986).

Aristotle, (1962), *The Politics*, Harmondsworth: Penguin.

Arrow, K.J. (1951/1963), *Social Choice and Individual Values*, New Haven: Yale University Press.

Arrow, K.J. (1972), 'Gifts and Exchanges', *Philosophy and Public Affairs*, 1, 343–362, reprinted in Phelps (1975).

Arrow, K.J. (1986), 'Rationality of Self and Others in an Economic System', in Hogarth and Reder (1986).

Austen-Smith, D. (1983), 'The Spatial Theory of Electoral Competition: Instability, Institutions, and Information', *Environment and Planning*, 1, 439–459.

Austen-Smith, D. (1993), 'Information and Influence: Lobbying for Agendas and Votes', *American Journal of Political Science*, 37, 799–833.

Axelrod, R. (1970), *Conflict of Interest. A Theory of Divergent Goals with Applications to Politics*, Chicago: Markham.

Axelrod, R. (1981), 'The Emergence of Cooperation among Egoists', *American Political Science Review*, 75, 306–318.

Axelrod, R. (1984), *The Evolution of Cooperation*, New York: Basic Books.

Axelrod, R. (1986), 'An Evolutionary Approach to Norms', *American Political Science Review*, 80, 1095–1111.

Axelrod, R. and Dion, D. (1988), 'The Future Evolution of Cooperation', *Science*, 242, 1385–1390.

Axelrod, R. and Keohane, R.O. (1985), 'Achieving Cooperation under Anarchy: Strategies and Institutions', *World Politics*, 38, 226–254.

Bachrach, P. and Baratz, M.S. (1962), 'Two Faces of Power', *American Political Science Review*, 56, 947–952.

Bachrach, P. and Baratz, M.S. (1963), 'Decisions and Nondecisions: An Analytical Framework', *American Political Science Review*, 57, 641–651.

Badie, B. and Birnbaum, P. (1979/1983) *The Sociology of the State*, Chicago: University of Chicago Press.

Baine Harris, R., (ed.) (1976), *Authority: A Philosophical Analysis* Alabama: University of Alabama Press.

Balbus, I. (1975), 'Politics as Sport: An Interpretation of the Political Ascendancy of the Sports Metaphor in America', in Lindberg, *et al.*, (1975).

Baldwin, D.A. (1978), 'Power and Social Exchange', *The American Political Science Review*, 72, 1229–1242.

Balibar, E. (1991), 'The Nation Form: History and Ideology', in E. Balibar and I Wallerstein, *Race, Nation, Class. Ambiguous Identities*, London: Verso.

Ball, T. (1988), *Transforming Political Discourse. Political Theory and Critical Conceptual History*, Oxford: Basil Blackwell.

Banks, J.A. (1972), *The Sociology of Social Movements*, London: Macmillan.

Barnes, B. (1990), 'Macro-economics and Infant Behaviour: A Sociological Treatment of the Free-rider Problem', *Sociological Review*, 28: 272–292.

Barry, B. (1970/1978), *Sociologists, Economists and Democracy*, Chicago: University of Chicago Press.

Barry, B. (1976a), 'Power: an Economic Analysis', in Barry (1976b).

Barry, B. (ed.) (1976b), *Power and Political Theory. Some European Perspectives*, Chichester: John Wiley.

Barry, B. (1982), 'Methodology versus Ideology: The "Economic" Approach Revisited', in Ostrom (1982).

Barry, B. (1985a), 'Comment on Elster', *Ethics*, 96, 156–158.

Barry, B. (1985b), 'Does Democracy Cause Inflation? Political Ideas of Some Economists', in Lindberg and Maier (1985).

Barry, B. and Hardin, R. (eds) (1982), *Rational Man and Irrational Society?* Beverly Hills: Sage Publications.

Bartlett, R. (1989), *Economics and Power*, Cambridge: Cambridge University Press.

Bayles, M.D. (1976), 'The Function and Limits of Political Authority', in Baine Harris (1976).

Beck, M, (1976), 'The Expanding Public Sector: Some Contrary Evidence', *National Tax Journal*, 29, 15–21.

Beck, N. (1987), 'Elections and the Fed: Is There a Political Monetary Cycle?', *American Journal of Political Science*, 31, 194–216.

Becker, G.S. (1976), *The Economic Approach to Human Behavior*, Chicago: University of Chicago Press.

Becker, G.S. (1983), 'A Theory of Competition among Pressure Groups for Political Influence', *The Quarterly Journal of Economics*, 48, 371–400.

Becker, G.S. (1985), 'Public Policies, Pressure Groups, and Dead Weight Costs', *Journal of Public Economics*, 28, 329–347.

Becker, G.S. (1990), 'Interview', in Swedberg (1990).

Becker, L.C. (1986), *Reciprocity*, London: Routledge and Kegan Paul.

Beetham, D. (1974/1985), *Max Weber and the Theory of Modern Politics*, Cambridge: Polity Press.

Beetham, D. (1993), 'Four Theorems about the Market and Democracy', *European Journal of Political Research*, 23, 187–201.

Belshaw, C.S. (1965), *Traditional Exchange and Modern Markets*, Englewood Cliffs, N.J.:Prentice-Hall.

Bendor, J. (1987), 'In Good Times and Bad: Reciprocity in an Uncertain World', *American Journal of Political Science*, 31, 531–558.

Bendor, J. and Mookherjee, D. (1987), 'Institutional Structure and the Logic of On-going Collective Action', *American Political Science Review*, 81, 129–154.

Benjamin, W. (1973), *Charles Baudelaire. A Lyric Poet in the Era of High Capitalism*, London: Verso.

Benn S. (1967), 'Authority', in *The Encyclopedia of Philosophy*, vol. 1, P. Edwards (ed.), New York: Macmillan and the Free Press.

Bennett J.T. and DiLorenzo, T.J. (1984), 'Political Entrepreneurship and Reform of the Rent-Seeking Society', in Colander (1984).

Bennett, W.L. (1980), *Public Opinion in American Politics*, New York: Harcourt Brace Jovanovich, Inc.

Bennett, W.L. (1988), *News: The Politics of Illusion*, New York: Longman.

Bentley, A. (1908/1967), *The Process of Government*, Cambridge, Mass.: Belknap Press of Harvard University Press.

Berelson, B.R., Lazarsfeld, P.F. and McPhee, W.N. (1954/1956), *Voting: A Study of Opinion Formation in a Presidential Campaign*, Chicago: University of Chicago Press.

Berger, P.L. and Luckmann, T. (1966), *The Social Construction of Reality*, Harmondsworth: Penguin.

Berger, S. (ed.) (1981), *Organizing Interests in Western Europe. Pluralism, Corporatism, and the Transformation of Politics*, Cambridge: Cambridge University Press.

Berk, R.A. (1974), *Collective Behavior*, Dubuque, Iowa: Wm. C. Brown.

Berlin, I. (1969), *Four Essays on Liberty*, Oxford: Oxford University Press.

Berns, W. (1962), 'Voting Studies', in Storing (1962).

Bernstein, E. (1899/1961), *Evolutionary Socialism*, New York: Schocken Books.

Bhagwati, J.N., Brecher, R.A. and Srinivasan, T.N. (1984), 'DUP Activities and Economic Theory', in Colander (1984).

Bianco, W.T. and Bates, R.H. (1990), 'Cooperation by Design: Leadership, Structure and Collective Dilemmas', *American Political Science Review*, 84, 133–147.

Birch, A.H. (1993), *The Concepts and Theories of Modern Democracy*, London: Routledge.

Birnbaum, P. (1982), 'The State versus Corporatism', *Politics and Society*, 11, 477–501.

Birnbaum, P. (1988), *States and Collective Action: The European Experience*, Cambridge: Cambridge University Press.

Birnbaum, P. and Leca J. (eds) (1990), *Individualism. Theories and Methods*, Oxford: Clarendon Press.

Black, D. (1958/1971), *The Theory of Committees and Elections*, Cambridge: Cambridge University Press.

Blais, A. and Dion, S. (1990), 'Are Bureaucrats Budget Maximizers? The Niskanen Model and its Critics', *Polity*, 22, 655–674.

Blau, M. *Exchange and Power in Social Life*, New Brunswick: Transaction Books.

Blegvad, B.M. and Collins, P. (1992), 'Law as an Exogenous Factor in Economic Analysis', in Himmelstrand (1992).

Blaug, M. (1980), *The Methodology of Economics*, Cambridge: Cambridge University Press.

Blumer, H. (1946), 'Collective Behavior', in A. McClung Lee (ed.) *New Principles of Sociology*, New York: Barnes and Noble.

Blumer, H. (1957), 'Collective Behavior', in J.B. Gittler (ed.) *Review of Sociology. Analysis of a Decade*, New York: John Wiley and Sons.

Boland, L.A. (1982), *The Foundations of Economic Method*, London: George Allen and Unwin.

Bonacich, P., Shure, G.H., Kahan, J.P. and Meeker, R.J. (1976), 'Cooperation and Group Size in the N-Person Prisoners' Dilemma', *Journal of Conflict Resolution*, 20, 687–705.

Borcherding, T. (1977a), 'One Hundred Years of Public Spending', in Borcherding (ed.) (1977c).

Borcherding, T. (1977b), 'The Sources of Growth of Public Expenditures in the United States, 1902–1970', in Borcherding (1977c).

Borcherding, T. (ed.) (1977c), *Budgets and Bureaucrats: The Sources of Government Growth*, Durham, NC: Duke University Press.

Borcherding, T. (1985), 'The Causes of Government Expenditure Growth: A Survey of the US Evidence', *Journal of Public Economics*, 28, 359–382.

Borooah, V.K. (1988), 'Public Choice Theory and Macroeconomic Policy', in van den Broeck (1988).

Bottomore, T.B. (1966), *Elites and Society*, Harmondsworth: Penguin.

Bottomore, T. (1979/1993), *Political Sociology*, London: Pluto Press.

Bourdieu, P. (1966), 'The Sentiment of Honour in Kabyle Society', in J.G. Peristiany (ed.) *Honour and Shame. The Values of Mediterranean Society*, Chicago: University of Chicago Press.

Bourdieu, P. (1972/1977), *Outline of a Theory of Practice*, Cambridge: Cambridge University Press.

Bourdieu, P. (1979/1986), *Distinction. A Social Critique of the Judgement of Taste*, London: Routledge and Kegan Paul.

Bourdieu, P. (1980/1990), *The Logic of Practice*, Stanford, California: Stanford University Press.

Bourdieu, P. (1983/1986), 'The Forms of Capital', in J.G. Richardson (ed.) (1986) *Handbook of Theory and Research for the Sociology of Education*, New York: Greenwood Press.

Bourdieu, P. and Coleman, J.S. (eds) (1991), *Social Theory for a Changing Society*, Boulder Colorado: Westview Press.

Boyne, G.A. (1987), 'Bureaucratic Power and Public Policies: a Test of the Rational Staff Maximization Hypothesis', *Political Studies*, 35, 79–104.

Brams, S.J. (1975), *Game Theory and Politics*, New York: The Free Press.

Brand, K.-W. (1990), 'Cyclical Aspects of New Social Movements: Waves of Cultural Criticism and Mobilization Cycles of Middle-class Radicalism', in Dalton and Kuechler (1990).

Braybrooke, D. and Lindblom, C. (1963), *A Strategy of Decision. Policy Evaluation as a Social Process*, New York: The Free Press.

Brennan G. and Buchanan, J.M. (1980), *The Power to Tax. Analytical Foundations of a Fiscal Constitution*, Cambridge: Cambridge University Press.

Brennan, G. and Buchanan, J.M. (1981), 'The Normative Purpose of Economic "Science": Rediscovery of an Eighteenth-Century Method', in Buchanan and Tollison (1984).

Brennan, G. and Buchanan, J.M. (1983), 'Predictive Power and the Choice Among Regimes', in Buchanan (1989b).

Brennan, G. and Buchanan, J.M. (1984), 'Voter Choice. Evaluating Political Alternatives', *American Behavioral Scientist*, 28, 185–201.

Brennan, G. and Buchanan, J.M. (1985), *The Reason of Rules. Constitutional Political Economy*, Cambridge: Cambridge University Press.

Brennan, G. and Lomasky, L. (1985), 'The Impartial Spectator Goes to Washington', *Economics and Philosophy*, 1, 189–211.

Brennan, G. and Lomasky, L.E. (1987), 'The Logic of Electoral Preference. Response to Saraydar and Hudelson', *Economics and Philosophy*, 3, 131–138.

Brenner, R. (1980), 'Economics – An Imperialist Science?', *Journal of Legal Studies*, 9, 179–188.

Breton, A. (1974), *The Economic Theory of Representative Government*, London: Macmillan.

Breton, A. (1978), 'Economics of Representative Democracy', in Buchanan, *et al.* (1978).

Breton, A. and Breton, R. (1969), 'An Economic Theory of Social Movements', *American Economic Review. Papers and Proceedings of the American Economic Association*, 59, 198–205.

Breton, A. and Wintrobe, R. (1975), 'The Equilibrium Size of a Budget-maximizing Bureau: A Note on Niskanen's Theory of Bureaucracy', *Journal of Political Economy*, 83, 195–207.

Breton, A. and Wintrobe, R. (1979), 'Bureaucracy and State Intervention: Parkinson's Law?', *Canadian Public Administration*, 22, 208–226.

Breton, A. and Wintrobe, R. (1982), *The Logic of Bureaucratic Conduct. An Economic Analysis of Competition, Exchange, and Efficiency in Private and Public Organizations*, Cambridge: Cambridge University Press.

Brittan, S. (1975), 'The Economic Contradictions of Democracy', *British Journal of Political Science*, 5, 129–159.

Brittan, S. (1977), *The Economic Consequences of Democracy*, London: Temple Smith.

Brodbeck, M. (1954), 'On the Philosophy of the Social Sciences', *Philosophy of Science*, 21, 140–156.

Brown, R. (1965), *Social Psychology*, New York: The Free Press.

Brubaker, E.R. (1975), 'Free Ride, Free Revelation, or Golden Rule?', *Journal of Law and Economics*, 18, 147–161.

Buchanan, A. (1979), 'Revolutionary Motivation and Rationality', *Philosophy and Public Affairs*, 9, 59–82.

Buchanan, J.M. (1949) 'The Pure Theory of Government Finance. A Suggested Approach', *Journal of Political Economy*, 57, 496–505.

Buchanan, J.M. (1954a), 'Individual Choice in Voting and the Market', *The Journal of Political Economy*, 62, 334–343.

Buchanan, J.M. (1954b), 'Social Choice, Democracy and Free Markets', *The Journal of Political Economy*, 62, 114–123.

Buchanan, J.M. (1958), *Public Principles of Public Debt*, Homewood, Illinois: Richard D. Irwin.

Buchanan, J.M. (1962), 'Marginal Notes on Reading Political Philosophy', in Buchanan and Tullock (1962/1965).

Buchanan, J.M. (1965a), 'An Economic Theory of Clubs', *Economica*, 32, 1–14.

Buchanan, J.M. (1965b), 'Ethical Rules, Expected Values, and Large Numbers', *Ethics*, 76, 1–13.

Buchanan, J.M. (1966), 'An Individualistic Theory of Political Process', in Easton (1966).

Buchanan, J.M. (1967), *Public Finance in Democratic Process*, Chapel Hill: University of North Carolina Press.

Buchanan, J.M. (1968), *The Demand and Supply of Public Goods*, Chicago: Rand McNally.

Buchanan, J.M. (1969a), *Cost and Choice. An Inquiry in Economic Theory*, Chicago: University of Chicago Press.

Buchanan, J.M. (1969b), 'Is Economics the Science of Choice?', in E. Streissler (ed.), *Roads to Freedom. Essays in Honour of Friedrich A. von Hayek*, London: Routledge and Kegan Paul.

Buchanan, J.M. (1972), 'Toward Analysis of Closed Behavioral Systems', in Buchanan and Tollison (1972).

Buchanan, J.M. (1973), 'The Coase Theorem and the Theory of the State', in Buchanan and Tollison (1984).

Buchanan, J.M. (1975a), *The Limits of Liberty. Between Anarchy and Leviathan*, Chicago: University of Chicago Press.

Buchanan, J.M. (1975b), 'The Political Economy of the Welfare State', in Buchanan and Tollison (1984).

Buchanan, J.M. (1975c), 'The Samaritan's Dilemma', in Phelps (1975).

Buchanan, J.M. (1977), 'Why Does Government Grow?', in Borcherding, (1977c).

Buchanan, J.M. (1978), 'From Private Preferences to Public Philosophy: The Development of Public Choice', in Buchanan *et al.* (1978).

Buchanan, J.M. (1979a), 'Politics without Romance: A Sketch of a Positive Public Choice Theory and its Normative Implications', in Buchanan and Tollison (1984).

Buchanan, J.M. (1979b), *What Should Economists Do?* Indianapolis: Liberty Press.

Buchanan, J.M. (1980a), 'Reform in the Rent-Seeking Society', in Buchanan *et al.* (1980).

Buchanan, J.M. (1980b), 'Rent-Seeking and Profit Seeking', in Buchanan *et al.* (1980).

Buchanan, J.M. (1984), 'Constitutional Restrictions on the Power of Government', in Buchanan and Tollison (1984).

Buchanan, J.M. (1986), *Liberty, Market and State*, Brighton: Wheatsheaf Books.

Buchanan, J.M. (1988), 'The Constitution of Economic Policy', in Gwartney and Wagner (1988b).

Buchanan, J.M. (1989a), *Essays on the Political Economy*, Honolulu: University of Hawaii Press.

Buchanan, J.M. (1989b), *Explorations into Constitutional Economics*, College Station: Texas A&M University Press.

Buchanan, J.M. and Tollison, R.D. (eds) (1972), *Theory of Public Choice. Political Applications of Economics*, Ann Arbor: University of Michigan Press.

Buchanan, J.M. and Tollison, R.D. (eds) (1984), *The Theory of Public Choice – II*, Ann Arbor: University of Michigan Press.

Buchanan, J.M. and Tullock, G. (1962/1965), *The Calculus of Consent. Logical Foundations of Constitutional Democracy*, Ann Arbor: University of Michigan Press.

Buchanan, J.M. and Vanberg, V. (1989), 'Organization Theory and Fiscal Economics: Society, State and Public Debt', in Buchanan (1989b).

Buchanan, J.M. and Wagner, R. (1977), *Democracy in Deficit. The Political Legacy of Lord Keynes*, New York: Academic Press.

Buchanan, J.M. and Wagner, R. (eds) (1978), *Fiscal Responsibility in Constitutional Democracy*, Leiden: Martinus Nijhoff Social Sciences Division.

Buchanan, J.M., et al. (1978), *The Economics of Politics*, London: Institute of Economic Affairs.

Buchanan, J.M., Tollison, R.D. and Tullock, G. (eds) (1980), *Toward a Theory of the Rent-Seeking Society*, College Station: Texas A&M University Press.

Buckley, W., Burns, T. and Meeker, L.D. (1974), 'Structural Resolutions of Collective Action Problems', *Behavioral Science*, 19, 277–297.

Budge, I. and Farlie, D. (1976), *Voting and Party Competition: A Theoretical Critique and Synthesis Applied to Surveys From Ten Democracies*, London: John Wiley and Sons.

Budge, I. and Laver, M.J. (1986), 'Office-Seeking and Policy-Pursuit in Coalition Theory', *Legislative Studies Quarterly*, 11, 485–506.

Budge, I. and Laver, M.J. (1992a), 'Coalition Theory, Government Policy and Party Policy', in Laver and Budge, eds (1992).

Budge, I. and Laver, M.J. (1992b), 'The Relationship Between Party and Coalition Policy in Europe: An Empirical Synthesis', in Laver and Budge, eds (1992).

Budge, I. and Laver, M. (1993), 'The Policy Basis of Government Coalitions: A Comparative Investigation', *British Journal of Political Science*, 23, 499–519.

Budge, I., Crewe, I and Farlie (eds) (1976), *Party Identification and Beyond. Representations of Voting and Party Competition*, New York: John Wiley and Sons.

Bull, M.J. (1992), 'The Corporatist Ideal-Type and Political Exchange', *Political Studies*, 40, 255–272.

Burns, T.R. (1994), 'Two Conceptions of Human Agency: Rational Choice Theory and the Social Theory of Action', in P. Sztompka, ed., *Agency and Structure: Reorienting Social Theory*, Amsterdam: Gordon and Breach.

Calhoun, C.J. (1980), 'Community: Toward a Variable Conceptualization for Comparative Research', *Social History*, 5, 105–129.

Calhoun, C.J. (1982), *The Question of Class Struggle*, Chicago: Chicago University Press.

Calhoun, C.J. (1983), 'The Radicalism of Tradition: Community Strength or Venerable Disguise and Borrowed Language?', *American Journal of Sociology*, 88, 886–914.

Calhoun, C.J. (1988), 'The Radicalism of Tradition and the Question of Class Struggle', in Taylor (1988b).

Calhoun, C.J. (1991a), 'Indirect Relationships and Imagined Communities: Large-Scale Social Integration and the Transformation of Everyday Life', in Bourdieu and Coleman (1991).

Calhoun, C.J. (1991b), 'The Problem of Identity in Collective Action', in J. Huber (ed.), *Macro-Micro Linkages in Sociology*, London: Sage Publications.

Cameron, D.R. (1978), 'The Expansion of the Public Economy', *American Political Science Review*, 72, 1243–1261.

Cameron, D.R. (1985), 'Does Government Cause Inflation?', in Lindberg and Maier (1985).

Cameron, W.B. (1966), *Modern Social Movements. A Sociological Outline*, New York: Random House.

Cammack, P. (1989), 'Review Article: Bringing the State Back In', *British Journal of Political Science*, 19, 261–290.

Campbell, A. and Converse, P.E. (eds) (1972), *The Human Meaning of Social Change*, New York: Russell Sage Foundation.

Campbell, A., Gurin, G. and Miller W.E. (1954), *The Voter Decides*, Evanston/White Plains: Row, Peterson.

Campbell, A., Converse, P.E., Miller W.E. and Stokes, D.E. (1960), *The American Voter*, New York: John Wiley and Sons.

Campbell, A., Converse, P.E., Miller, W.E. and Stokes, D.E. (1966), *Elections and the Political Order*, New York: John Wiley and Sons.

Campbell, T.D. (1971), *Adam Smith's Science of Morals*, London: Allen and Unwin.

Castles, F.G. (1987), 'Neocorporatism and the "Happiness Index", or What the Trade Unions Get for their Cooperation', *European Journal of Political Research*, 15, 381–393.

Castles, F.G. (1993a), 'Changing Course in Economic Policy: The English-Speaking Nations in the 1980s', in Castles, ed. (1993b).

Castles, F.G., ed. (1993b), *Families of Nations: Patterns of Public Policy in Western Democracies*, Aldershot: Dartmouth.

Castles, F.G. and Mitchell, D. (1993), 'Worlds of Welfare and Families of Nations', in Castles (1993b).

Catlin, G.E.G. (1959), 'The Meaning of Community', in Friedrich (1959b).

Cawson, A. (1978), 'Pluralism, Corporatism and the Role of the State', *Government and Opposition*, 13, 178–198.

Cawson, A. (1985a), 'Varieties of Corporatism: The Importance of the Meso-Level of Interest Intermediation', in Cawson (1985b).

Cawson, A., (ed.) (1985b), *Organized Interests and the State*, London: Sage.

Cawson, A. (1986), *Corporatism and Political Theory*, Oxford: Basil Blackwell.

Cawson, A. (1988), 'In Defence of the New Testament: A Reply to Andrew Cox, "The Old and New Testaments of Corporatism"', *Political Studies*, 26, 309–315.

Cawson, A. and Saunders, P. (1983), 'Corporatism, Competitive Politics and Class Struggle', in King (1983).

Chakotin, S. (1939/1971), *The Rape of the Masses. The Psychology of Totalitarian Political Propaganda*, New York: Haskell House.

Chamberlain, J. (1974), 'Provision of Collective Goods as a Function of Group Size', *American Political Science Review*, 68, 707–716.

Chappell, H.W. and Keech, W.R. (1985), 'A New View of Political Accountability', *American Political Science Review*, 79, 10–27.

Chappell, H.W. and Keech, W.R. (1990), 'Citizen Information, Rationality, and the Politics of Macroeconomic Policy', in Ferejohn and Kuklinski (1990).

Charlesworth, J.C. (ed.) (1967), *Contemporary Political Analysis*, New York: The Free Press.

Chazel, F. (1990), 'Individualism, Mobilization and Collective Action', in Birnbaum and Leca (1990).

Coase, R.H. (1976), 'Adam Smith's View of Man', *Journal of Law and Economics*, 19, 529–546.

Cohen, A.P. (1985/1989), *The Symbolic Construction of Community*, London: Routledge.

Cohen, E.S. (1989), 'Justice and Political Economy in Commercial Society: Adam Smith's "Science of a Legislator"', *Journal of Politics*, 51, 50–72.

Cohen, J.L. (1982), 'Between Crisis Management and Social Movements: The Place of Institutional Reform', *Telos*, 52, 21–40.

Cohen J.L. (1983) 'Rethinking Social Movements', *Berkeley Journal of Sociology*, 28, 97–113.

Cohen J.L. (1985), 'Strategy or Identity: New Theoretical Paradigms and Contemporary Social Movements', *Social Research*, 52, 663–716.

Colander, D.C. (ed.) (1984), *Neoclassical Political Economy. The Analysis of Rent-Seeking and DUP Activities*, Cambridge, Mass: Ballinger.

Coleman, J. (1964), 'Collective Decisions', *Sociological Inquiry*, 34, 166–181.

Coleman, J. (1966), 'Foundations for a Theory of Collective Decisions', *American Journal of Sociology*, 71, 615–627.

Coleman, J. (1972), 'Systems of Social Exchange', *Journal of Mathematical Sociology*, 2, 145–163.

Coleman, J.S. (1973), *The Mathematics of Collective Action*, London: Heinemann Educational Books.

Coleman, J.S. (1986), 'Social Structure and the Emergence of Norms among Rational Actors', in A. Diekmann and P. Mitter (eds), *Paradoxical Effects of Social Behavior. Essays in Honor of Anatol Rapoport*, Heidelberg: Physica Verlag.

Coleman, J.S. (1987), 'Norms as Social Capital', in Radnitzky and Bernholz (1987).

Coleman, J.S. (1988), 'Free Riders and Zealots: The Role of Social Networks', *Sociological Theory*, 6, 52–57.

Coleman, J.S. (1990a), 'The Emergence of Norms', in Hechter *et al.* (1990).

Coleman, J.S. (1990b), *Foundations of Social Theory*, Cambridge, Mass: Belknap Press of Harvard University Press.

Coleman, J.S. (1990c), 'Norm-Generating Structures', in Cook and Levi (1990).

Coleman, J.S. and Fararo, T.J. (eds) (1992), *Rational Choice Theory. Advocacy and Critique*, Newbury Park: Sage Publications.

Collard, D. (1991), 'Love Is Not Enough', in Meeks (1991)

Comte, A. (1974), *The Crisis of Industrial Civilization. The Early Essays of Auguste Comte.* London: Heinemann.

Comte, A. (1975), *Auguste Comte and Positivism. The Essential Writings*, New York: Harper and Row.

Coniavitis, T. (1984), *Metodologisk Pluralism. Till Kritiken av den Existerande Sociologin*, Uppsala: Almqvist and Wicksell International.

Connolly, W.E. (1973/1983), *The Terms of Political Discourse*, Oxford: Martin Robertson.

Conover, P.J. (1984), 'The Influence of Group Identifications on Political Perception and Evaluation', *Journal of Politics*, 46, 760–785.

Conover, P.J. (1985), 'The Impact of Group Economic Interests on Political Evaluations', *American Politics Quarterly*, 13, 139–166.

Conover, P.J. (1988a), 'Feminists and the Gender Gap', *Journal of Politics*, 50, 985–1010.

Conover, P.J. (1988b), 'The Role of Social Groups in Political Thinking', *British Journal of Political Science*, 51–76.

Conover, P.J. and Feldman, S. (1986), 'Emotional Reactions to the Economy: I'm Mad as Hell and I'm Not Going to Take It Anymore', *American Journal of Political Science*, 30, 50–78.

Conover, P.J., Feldman, S. and Knight, K. (1986), 'Judging Inflation and Unemployment: The Origins of Retrospective Evaluations', *Journal of Politics*, 48, 565–588.

Conover, P.J., Feldman, S. and Knight K. (1987), 'The Personal and Political Underpinnings of Economic Forecasts', *American Journal of Political Science*, 31, 559–583.

Converse, P.E. (1964), 'The Nature of Belief Systems in Mass Publics', in D. Apter (ed.), *Ideology and Discontent*, New York: The Free Press.

Converse, P.E. (1966), 'The Concept of a Normal Vote', in Campbell *et al.* (1966).

Converse, P.E. (1972), 'Change in the American Electorate', in Campbell and Converse (1972).

Converse, P.E. (1976), *The Dynamics of Party Support. Cohort-Analyzing Party Identification*, London: Sage Publications.

Conybeare, J.A.C. (1984), 'Bureaucracy, Monopoly, and Competition: A Critical Analysis of the Budget-Maximizing Model', *American Journal of Political Science*, 28, 479–502.

Cook, K.S. and Levi, M. (eds) (1990), *The Limits of Rationality*, Chicago: University of Chicago Press.

Cooley, C.H. (1902/1964), *Human Nature and the Social Order*, New York: Schocken Books.

Cooley, C.H. (1909/1962), *Social Organization*, New York: Schocken Books.

Cooley, C.H. (1918/1966), *Social Process*, Carbondale/Edwardsville: Southern Illinois University Press.

Coombs, C.H. (1973), 'A Reparameterization of the Prisoner's Dilemma Game', *Behavioral Science*, 18, 424–428.

Coughlin, R.M. (ed.) (1991), *Morality, Rationality and Efficiency. New Perspectives on Socio-Economics*, Armonk, NY: M.E. Sharpe.

Cox, A. (1988a), 'Neo-Corporatism Versus the Corporate State', in Cox and O'Sullivan (1988).

Cox, A. (1988b), 'The Old and New Testaments of Corporatism: Is it a Political Form or a Method of Policy-Making?', *Political Studies*, 36, 294–308.

Cox A. and O'Sullivan, N. (1988), *The Corporate State. Corporatism and the State Tradition in Western Europe*, Aldershot: Edward Elgar.

Crain, W.M. and Tollison, R.D. (1990a), 'Empirical Public Choice', in Crain and Tollison, eds (1990).

Crain, W.M. and Tollison, R.D. (eds) (1990b), *Predicting Politics. Essays in Empirical Public Choice*, Ann Arbor: The University of Michigan Press.

Crewe, I. and Denver, D. (eds) (1985), *Electoral Change in Western Democracies. Patterns and Sources of Electoral Volatility*, London: Croom Helm.

Cross, J.G. and Guyer, M.J. (1980), *Social Traps*, Ann Arbor: University of Michigan Press.

Crouch, C. (1985), 'Corporatism in Industrial Relations: A Formal Model', in Grant (1985).

Crouch, C. and Pizzorno, A. (eds) (1978), *The Resurgence of Class Conflict in Western Europe since 1968, Volume 2: Comparative Analyses*, London: Macmillan.

Crozier, C. (1991), 'The Relational Boundaries of Rationality', in Monroe (1991).

Curry, R.L. and Wade, L.L. (1968), *A Theory of Political Exchange. Economic Reasoning in Political Analysis*, Englewood Cliffs, N.J.: Prentice-Hall.

Dahl, R.A. (1958), 'A Critique of the Ruling Elite Model', *American Political Science Review*, 52, 463–469.

Dahl, R.A. (1961a), 'The Behavioral Approach in Political Science: Epitaph for a Monument to a Successful Protest', *American Political Science Review*, 55, 763–772, reprinted in Eulau (1969b).

Dahl R.A. (1961b), *Who Governs? Democracy and Power in an American City*, New Haven: Yale University Press.

Dalton, R.J. (1988), *Citizen Politics in Western Democracies. Opinion and Political Parties in the United States, Great Britain, West Germany and France*, Chatham, N.J.: Chatham House Publishers.

Dalton, R.J., Flanagan, S.C. and Beck, P.A. (eds) (1984), *Electoral Change in Advanced Industrial Societies: Realignment or Dealignment?*, Princeton, N.J.: Princeton University Press.

Dalton, R.J., Kuechler, M. and Bürklin, W. (1990) 'The Challenge of New Movements', in Dalton and Kuechler (1990).

Dalton, R.J. and Kuechler, M. (eds) (1990), *Challenging the Political Order: New Social and Political Movements in Western Democracies*, Cambridge: Polity Press.

Davies, J.C. (1962), 'Toward a Theory of Revolutions', *American Sociological Review*, 27, 5–19.

Davis, J. (1973), 'Forms and Norms: The Economy of Social Relations', *Man*, 8, 159–176.

Davis, J. (1992), *Exchange*, Buckingham: Open University Press.

Dawes, R.M. (1980), 'Social Dilemmas', *Annual Review of Psychology*, 31, 169–193.

Dawes, R.M. (1991), 'Social Dilemmas, Economic Self-Interest, and Evolutionary Theory', in Coughlin (1991).

Dawes, R.M., Orbell, J.M., Simmons, R.T. and Van de Kragt, A.J.C. (1986), 'Organizing Groups for Collective Action', *American Political Science Review*, 80, 1171–1185.

Dawes, R.M., van de Kragt, A.J.C. and Orbell, J.M. (1990), 'Cooperation for the Benefit of Us – Not Me, or My Conscience', in Mansbridge (1990).

De Alessi, L. (1987), 'Nature and Methodological Foundations of Some Recent Extensions of Economic Theory', in Radnitzky and Bernholz (1987).

De Bruin, G.P. (1987), 'Economic Theory of Bureaucracy and Public Goods Allocation', in Lane (1987).

De George, R.T. (1976) 'The Nature and Function of Epistemic Authority', in Baine Harris (1976).

De George, R.T. (1985), *The Nature and Limits of Authority*, Lawrence: University Press of Kansas.

De Jasay, A. (1989), *Social Contract, Free Ride. A Study of the Public Goods Problem*, Oxford: Clarendon Press.

De Jouvenal, B. (1957), *Sovereignty. An Inquiry into the Political Good*, Chicago: University of Chicago Press.

De Jouvenal, B. (1958), 'Authority: The Efficient Imperative', in Friedrich (1958).

Denver, D. (1989), *Elections and Voting Behaviour in Britain*, London: Philip Allan.

Derthick, M. and Quirk P.J. (1985), *The Politics of Deregulation*, Washington, DC : Brookings Institution.

Deutsch, K.W. (1963/1966), *The Nerves of Government*, New York: The Free Press.

Deutsch, K.W. (1970), *Politics and Government. How People Decide Their Fate*, Boston: Houghton Mifflin.

Digeser, P. (1992), 'The Fourth Face of Power', *The Journal of Politics*, 54, 977–1007.

Dowding, K.M. (1991), *Rational Choice and Political Power*, Aldershot: Edward Elgar.

Downs, A. (1957), *An Economic Theory of Democracy*, New York: Harper and Brothers.

Downs, A. (1960), 'Why the Government Budget is Too Small in a Democracy', *World Politics*, 12, 541–663.

Downs, A. (1962), 'The Public Interest: Its Meaning in a Democracy', *Social Research*, 27, 1–36.

Downs, A. (1967), *Inside Bureaucracy*, Boston: Little, Brown.

Downs, A. (1991), 'Social Values and Democracy', in Monroe (1991).

Dryzek, J.S. (1992), 'Opinion Research and the Counter-Revolution in American Political Science', *Political Studies*, 40, 679–694.

Dunleavy, P. (1985), 'Bureaucrats, Budgets and the Growth of the State: Reconstructing an Instrumental Model', *British Journal of Political Science*, 15, 299–328.

Dunleavy, P. (1988), 'Group Identities and Individual Influence: Reconstructing the Theory of Group Interest', *British Journal of Political Science*, 18, 21–49.

Dunleavy, P. (1991), *Democracy, Bureaucracy and Public Choice*, London: Harvester Wheatsheaf.

Dunn, J. (1991), 'Political Obligation', in Held (1991).

Durkheim, E. (1887/1993), *Ethics and the Sociology of Morals*, Buffalo: Prometheus Books.

Durkheim, E. (1893/1964), *The Division of Labor in Society*, New York: The Free Press.

Durkheim, E. (1895/1964), *The Rules of Sociological Method*, New York: The Free Press.

Durkheim, E. (1912/1965), *The Elementary Forms of the Religious Life*, New York: The Free Press.

Durkheim, E. (1925/1973), *Moral Education. A Study in the Theory and Application of the Sociology of Education*, New York: The Free Press.

Durkheim, E. (1956), *Education and Sociology*, New York: The Free Press.

Durkheim, E. (1973), *On Morality and Society*, Chicago: University of Chicago Press.

Durkheim, E. (1974), *Sociology and Philosophy*, New York: The Free Press.

Durkheim, E. (1983), *Professional Ethics and Civic Morals*, New York: Greenwood Press.

Durkheim, E. (1986), *Durkheim on Politics and the State*, Cambridge: Polity Press.

Durkheim, E. and Mauss, M. (1903/1970), *Primitive Classification*, London: Routledge and Kegan Paul.

Easton, D. (1953/1971), *The Political System. An Inquiry into the State of Political Science*, New York: Alfred Knopf.

Easton, D. (1957), 'An Approach to the Analysis of Political Systems', *World Politics*, 9, 383–400.

Easton, D. (1965), *A Framework for Political Analysis*, Englewood Cliffs, N.J.: Prentice-Hall.

Easton, D. (ed.) (1966), *Varieties of Political Theory*, Englewood Cliffs, N.J.: Prentice-Hall.

Easton, D. (1967), 'The Current Meaning of "Behavioralism"', in Charlesworth (1967).

Easton, D. (1969), 'The New Revolution in Political Science', *American Political Science Review*, 63, 1051–1061, reprinted as 'Epilogue A' to Easton (1953/1971)

Easton, D. (1991), 'Political Science in the United States: Past and Present', in Easton *et al.* (1991).

Easton, D., Gunnell, J.G. and Graziano, L. (eds) (1991), *The Development of Political Science: A Comparative Survey*, London: Routledge.

Edelman, M. (1964), *The Symbolic Uses of Politics*, Urbana: University of Illinois Press.

Edelman, M. (1971), *Politics as Symbolic Action. Mass Arousal and Quiescence*, Chicago: Markham.

Edelman, M. (1975), 'Symbolism in Politics', in Lindberg *et al.* (1975)

Edelman, M. (1977), *Political Language. Words that Succeed and Policies that Fail*, New York: Academic Press.

Edelman, M (1988), *Constructing the Political Spectacle*, Chicago: University of Chicago Press.

Eder, K. (1982), 'A New Social Movement', *Telos*, 52, 5–20.

Eder, K. (1985), 'The "New Social Movements": Moral Crusades, Political Pressure Groups, or Social Movements', *Social Research*, 52, 869–890.

Elias, N. (1939/1982), *The Civilizing Process, Volume II: Power and Civility*, Oxford: Basil Blackwell.

Elster, J. (1979), *Ulysses and the Sirens. Studies in Rationality and Irrationality*, Cambridge: Cambridge University Press.

Elster, J. (1982), 'Marxism, Functionalism and Game Theory: The Case for Methodological Individualism', *Theory and Society*, 11, 453–482.

Elster, J. (1983), *Explaining Technical Change*, Cambridge: Cambridge University Press.

Elster, J. (1985a), *Making Sense of Marx*, Cambridge: Cambridge University Press.

Elster, J. (1985b), 'Rationality, Morality, and Collective Action', *Ethics*, 96, 136–155.

Elster, J. (1985c), 'Weakness of Will and the Free Rider Problem', *Economics and Philosophy*, 1, 231–265.

Elster, J. (1986a), 'Introduction' to Elster (1986d).

Elster, J. (1986b), 'Introduction' to Elster (1986e).

Elster, J. (1986c), 'The Market and the Forum: Three Varieties of Political Theory', in Elster and Hylland (1986).

Elster, J. (ed.) (1986d), *The Multiple Self*, Cambridge University Press.

Elster, J. (ed.) (1986e), *Rational Choice*, Oxford: Basil Blackwell.

Elster, J. (1986/1989), 'Self-Realization in Work and Politics: The Marxist Conception of the Good Life', in J. Elster and K.O. Moene, eds, *Alternatives to Capitalism*, Cambridge: Cambridge University Press.

Elster, J. (1988), 'Marx, Revolution and Rational Choice', in Taylor, ed. (1988b).

Elster, J. (1989a), *The Cement of Society. A Study of Social Order*, Cambridge: Cambridge University Press.

Elster, J. (1989b), *Nuts and Bolts for the Social Sciences*, Cambridge: Cambridge University Press.

Elster, J. (1989c), 'Rationality and Social Norms', in J.E. Fenstad, I.T. Frolov and R. Hilpinen, (eds), *Logic, Methodology and Philosophy of Science VIII*, Amsterdam: North-Holland.

Elster, J. (1991a), 'The Possibility of Rational Politics', in Held (1991).

Elster, J. (1991b), 'Rationality and Social Norms', *Archives Européennes de Sociologie*, 32, 109–129.

Elster, J. and Hylland, A. (eds) (1986), *Foundations of Social Choice Theory*, Cambridge: Cambridge University Press.

Emerson, R.M. (1962) 'Power-dependence Relations', *American Journal of Sociology*, 27, 31–41.

Enelow, J.M. and Hinich, M.J. (1984), *The Spatial Theory of Voting. An Introduction*, Cambridge: Cambridge University Press.

Enelow, J.M. and Hinich, M.J. (eds) (1990), *Advances in the Spatial Theory of Voting*, Cambridge: Cambridge University Press.

Engels, F. (1878/1969), *Anti-Dühring*, Moscow: Progress Publishers.

Engels, F. (1884/1891/1972), *The Origin of the Family, Private Property and the State*, London: Lawrence and Wishart.

Engels, F. (1888/1976), *Ludwig Feuerbach and the End of Classical German Philosophy*, Peking: Foreign Language Press.

Engels, F. (1892/1970), *Socialism: Utopian and Scientific*, Moscow: Progress Publishers.

Erikson, R.S. (1989), 'Economic Conditions and the Presidential Vote', *American Political Science Review*, 83, 567–573.

Erikson, R.S. (1990), 'Economic Conditions and the Congressional Vote: A Review of the Macrolevel Evidence', *American Journal of Political Science*, 34, 373–399.

Erikson, R.S., Lancaster, T.D. and Romero, D.W. (1989), 'Group Components of the Presidential Vote, 1952–1984', *Journal of Politics*, 51, 337–345.

Eriksson, B. (1988), *Samhällsvetenskapens Uppkomst*, Uppsala: Hallgren and Fallgren.

Eriksson, B. (1993), 'The First Formulation of Sociology. A Discursive Innovation of the 18th Century', *Archives Européennes de Sociologie*, 34, 251–276.

Esping-Andersen, G. (1990), *The Three Worlds of Welfare Capitalism*, Cambridge: Polity Press.

Etzioni, A. (1988), *The Moral Dimension. Toward a New Economics*, New York: The Free Press.

Etzioni, A. (1989), 'Toward a Deontological Social Science', *Philosophy of the Social Sciences*, 19, 145–156.

Eulau, H. (1963), *The Behavioral Persuasion in Politics*, New York: Random House.

Eulau, H. (1967), 'Segments of Political Science Most Susceptible to Behavioristic Treatment', in Charlesworth (1967).

Eulau, H. (1968), 'The Behavioral Movement in Political Science: A Personal Document', *Social Research*, 35, 1–29.

Eulau, H. (1969a), 'Tradition and Innovation: On the Tension between Ancient and Modern Ways in the Study of Politics', in Eulau (1969b).

Eulau, H. (ed.) (1969b), *Behavioralism in Political Science*, New York: Atherton Press.

Eulau, H. and Lewis-Beck, M.S. (1985), *Economic Conditions and Electoral Outcomes: The United States and Western Europe*, New York: Agathon Press.

Evans, P., Rueschemeyer, D. and Skocpol, T. (eds) (1985), *Bringing the State Back In*, Cambridge: Cambridge University Press.

Eyerman, R. and Jamison, A. (1991), *Social Movements. A Cognitive Approach*, Cambridge: Polity Press.

Feiwel, G.R. (1974), 'Reflection on Kalecki's Theory of Political Business Cycles', *Kyklos*, 27, 21–48.

Feldman, S. (1982), 'Economic Self-Interest and Political Behavior', *American Journal of Political Science*, 26, 446–466.

Feldman, S. (1983), 'Economic Individualism and American Public Opinion', *American Politics Quarterly*, 11, 3–29.

Feldman, S. (1984), 'Economic Self-Interest and the Vote: Evidence and Meaning', *Political Behavior*, 6, 229–251.

Feldman, S. (1988), 'Structure and Consistency in Public Opinion', *American Journal of Political Science*, 32, 416–440.

Ferejohn, J. (1991), 'Rationality and Interpretation', in Monroe (1991).

Ferejohn, J.A. and Fiorina, M.P. (1974), 'The Paradox of Not Voting: A Decision Theoretic Analysis', *American Political Science Review*, 68, 525–536.

Ferejohn, J.A. and Fiorina, M.P. (1975), 'Closeness Counts Only in Horseshoes and Dancing', *American Political Science Review*, 69, 920–925.

Ferejohn, J.A. and Kuklinski, J.H. (eds) (1990), *Information and Democratic Processes*, Urbana: University of Illinois Press.

Ferrarotti, F. (1985), 'Vilfredo Pareto: The Disenchanted World of Conservative Pessimism', *History of Sociology*, 6–7, 49–64.

Festinger, L. (1957), *A Theory of Cognitive Dissonance*, Stanford, California: Stanford University Press.

Fiorina, M.P. (1978), 'Economic Retrospective Voting in American National Elections: A Micro-Analysis', *American Journal of Political Science*, 22, 426–443.

Fiorina, M. P. (1981), *Retrospective Voting in American National Elections*, New Haven: Yale University Press.

Fiorina, M.P. (1990), 'Information and Rationality in Elections', in Ferejohn and Kuklinski (1990).

Fiorina, M.P. and Noll, R.G. (1978), 'Voters, Bureaucrats and Legislators. A Rational Choice perspective on the Growth of Bureaucracy', *Journal of Public Economics*, 9, 239–254.

Fiorina, M.P. and Shepsle, K.A. (1990), 'A Positive Theory of Negative Voting', in Ferejohn and Kuklinski (1990).

Fireman, B. and Gamson, W.A. (1979), 'Utilitarian Logic in the Resource Mobilization Perspective', in M.N. Zald and J.D. McCarthy (eds), *The Dynamics of Social Movements*, Cambridge, Mass: Winthrop Publishers.

Flanigan, W. and Fogelman, E. (1967), 'Functional Analysis', in Charlesworth (1967).

Foucault, M. (1975/1977), *Discipline and Punish. The Birth of the Prison*, Harmondsworth: Penguin.

Foucault, M. (1980), *Power/Knowledge. Selected Interviews and Other Writings 1972–1977*, Brighton: Harvester Press.

Frank, R.H. (1985) *Choosing the Right Pond: Human Behaviour and the Quest for Status*, New York: Oxford University Press.

Frank, R.H. (1987), 'If *Homo Economicus* Could Choose his Own Utility Function, Would He Want One With a Conscience?', *American Economic Review*, 77, 593–604.

Freud, S. (1921/1959), *Group Psychology and the Analysis of the Ego*, New York: W.W. Norton.

Frey, B.S. (1974), 'The Politico-Economic System: A Simulation Model', *Kyklos*, 27, 227–254.

Frey, B.S. (1978a), *Modern Political Economy*, Oxford: Martin Robertson.

Frey, B.S. (1978b), 'Politico-Economic Models and Cycles', *Journal of Public Economics*, 9, 203–220.

Frey, B.S. (1978c), 'The Political Business Cycle: Theory and Evidence', in Buchanan *et al.* (1978).

Frey, B.S. (1978d), 'A Politico-Economic Model of the United Kingdom', *The Economic Journal*, 88, 243–253.

Frey, B.S. (1979), 'Politicometrics of Government Behavior in a Democracy', *Scandinavian Journal of Economics*, 81: 308–322.

Frey, B.S. (1983) *Democratic Economic Policy. A Theoretical Introduction*, Oxford: Martin Robertson.

Frey, B.S. (1992), 'Comment', in Peacock (1992).

Frey, B.S. and Schneider, F. (1982), 'Politico-Economic Models in Competition with Alternative Models: Which Predict Better?', *European Journal of Political Research*, 10, 241–254.

Friedman, M. (1953), *Essays in Positive Economics*, Chicago: University of Chicago Press.

Friedman, M. (1962/1982), *Capitalism and Freedom*, Chicago: The University of Chicago Press.

Friedman, M. and Friedman, R. (1979/1990), *Free to Choose*, London: Pan Books.

Friedman, R.B. (1973/1990), 'On the Concept of Authority in Political Philosophy', in Raz (1990).

Friedrich, C.J. (ed.) (1958), *Authority*, Nomos I, Cambridge Mass.; Harvard University Press.

Friedrich, C.J. (1959a), 'The Concept of Community in the History of Political and Legal Philosophy', in Friedrich (1959b).

Friedrich, C.J. (ed.) (1959b), *Community*, Nomos II, New York: Liberal Arts Press.

Friedrich, C.J. (1967), *An Introduction to Political Theory*, New York: Harper and Row.

Friedrich, C.J. (1972), *Tradition and Authority*, London: Pall Mall Press.

Frohlich, N. and Oppenheimer, J.A. (1970), 'I Get By With a Little Help From My Friends', *World Politics*, 23, 105–120.

Frohlich, N. and Oppenheimer, J.A. (1978), *Modern Political Economy*, Englewood Cliffs, N.J.: Prentice-Hall.

Frohlich, N., Oppenheimer, J.A. and Young, O.R. (1971), *Political Leadership and Collective Goods*, Princeton, N.J: Princeton University Press.

Frohlich, N., Hunt, T., Oppenheimer, J. and Wagner, R.H. (1975), 'Individual Contributions for Collective Goods. Alternative Models', *Journal of Conflict Resolution*, 19, 310–329.

Frohlich, N., Oppenheimer, J.A., Smith, J. and Young, O.R. (1978), 'A Test of Downsian Voter Rationality: 1964 Presidential Voting', *American Political Science Review*, 72, 178–197.

Gallie, W.B. (1956), 'Essentially Contested Concepts', *Proceedings of the Aristotelian Society*, New Series, 56, 167–198.

Gamson, W.A. (1975), *The Strategy of Social Protest*, Homewood, Illinois: Dorsey Press.

Gardner, R., Ostrom, E. and Walker, J.M. (1990), 'The Nature of Common-Pool Resource Problems', *Rationality and Society*, 2, 335–358.

Gellner, E. (1973), *Cause and Meaning in the Social Sciences*, London: Routledge and Kegan Paul.

Gellner, E. (1983), *Nations and Nationalism*, Oxford: Basil Blackwell.

Gellner, E. (1987), *Culture, Identity, and Politics*, Cambridge: Cambridge University Press.

Ghiselin, M.T. (1987), 'The Economics of Scientific Discovery', in Radnitzky and Bernholz (1987).

Giddens, A. (1977), *Studies in Social and Political Theory*, London: Hutchinson.

Giddens, A. (1979), *Central Problems in Social Theory. Action, Structure and Contradiction in Social Analysis*, London: Macmillan.

Giddens, A. (1984), *The Constitution of Society*, Cambridge: Polity Press.

Giddens, A. (1985), *The Nation-State and Violence. Volume Two of A Contemporary Critique of Historical Materialism*, Cambridge: Polity Press.

Gilbert, D. (1992), *Class, Community and Collective Action. Social Change in Two British Coalfields*, 1850–1926, Oxford Clarendon Press.

Goldthorpe, J.H. (1984a), 'The End of Convergence: Corporatist and Dualist Tendencies in Modern Western Societies', in Goldthorpe (1984c).

Goldthorpe, J.H. (1984b), 'Introduction' to Goldthorpe (1984c).

Goldthorpe, J.H. (ed.) (1984c), *Order and Conflict in Contemporary Capitalism. Studies in the Political Economy of Western European Nations*, Oxford: Clarendon Press.

Good, D.A. (1991), 'Cooperation in a Microcosm: Lessons from Laboratory Games', in Hinde and Groebel (1991).

Goodin, R.E. (1980), *Manipulatory Politics*, New Haven: Yale University Press.

Goodin, R.E. (1982), 'Rational Politicians and Rational Bureaucrats in Washington and Whitehall', *Public Administration*, 60, 23–41.

Gouldner, A. (1960), 'The Norm of Reciprocity: A Preliminary Statement', *American Sociological Review*, 25, 161–178, reprinted in Gouldner (1975).

Gouldner, A. (1971), *The Coming Crisis of Western Sociology*, London: Heinemann.
Gouldner, A. (1975), *For Sociology. Renewal and Critique in Sociology Today*, Harmondsworth: Penguin.
Grafstein, R. (1991), 'Rational Choice: Theory and Institutions', in Monroe (1991).
Gramsci, A. (1971) *Prison Notebooks*, New York: International Publishers.
Granovetter, M. (1973), 'The Strength of Weak Ties', *American Journal of Sociology*, 78, 1360–1380.
Granovetter, M. (1978), 'Threshold Models of Collective Behavior', *American Journal of Sociology*, 83, 1420–1443.
Granovetter, M. (1985), 'Economic Action and Social Structure: The Problem of Embeddedness', *American Journal of Sociology*, 91, 481–510.
Granovetter, M. (1993), 'The Nature of Economic Relationships', in Swedberg (1993).
Granqvist, R. (1987), *Privata och kollektiva Val. En kritisk analys av public choice-skolan*, Lund: Arkiv förlag.
Grant, W. (1985a), 'Introduction' to Grant (1985b).
Grant, W. (ed.) (1985b), *The Political Economy of Corporatism*, London: Macmillan.
Gray, V. and Lowery, D. (1988), 'Interest Group Politics and Economic Growth in the United States', *American Political Science Review*, 82, 109–131.
Green, D.P. and Cowden, J.A. (1992), 'Who Protests: Self-Interest and White Opposition to Busing', *Journal of Politics*, 54, 471–495.
Green, L. (1988), *The Authority of the State*, Oxford: Clarendon Press.
Greenstein, F.I. and Polsby, N.W. (1975), *Handbook of Political Science*, 6 vols, Reading, Mass.: Addison-Wesley.
Greenstone, J.D. (1975), 'Group Theories', in Greenstein and Polsby, eds, (1975, *Volume 2: Micropolitical Theory*).
Greer, S. (1969), 'Sociology and Political Science', in Lipset (1969b).
Grier, K.B. (1987), 'Presidential Elections and Federal Reserve Policy: An Empirical Test', *Southern Economic Journal*, 54, 475–486.
Grier, K.B. (1989), 'On the Existence of a Political Monetary Cycle', *American Journal of Political Science*, 33, 376–389.
Gruber, J.E. (1987), *Controlling Bureaucracies. Dilemmas in Democratic Governance*, Berkeley: University of California Press.
Grzelak, J. (1988), 'Conflict and Cooperation', in M. Hewstone, W. Stroebe, J-P Codol and G.M. Stephenson (eds), *Introduction to Social Psychology*, Oxford: Basil Blackwell.
Gunnell, J.G. (1983), 'Political Theory: The Evolution of a Sub-Field', in A.W. Finifter (ed.), *Political Science: The State of a Discipline*, Washington: American Political Science Association.
Gunnell, J.G. (1988), 'American Political Science, Liberalism, and the Invention of Political Theory', in Anckar and Berndtson (1988b).
Gurr, T.R. (1970), *Why Men Rebel*, Princeton, N.J.: Princeton University Press.
Gusfield, J.R. (1962), 'Mass Society and Extremist Politics', *American Sociological Review*, 27, 19–30.
Gusfield, J.R. (1968), 'The Study of Social Movements', in *The Encyclopedia of the Social Sciences*, 14, 445–452, New York: Macmillan.
Gwartney, J.D. and Wagner, R.E. (1988a), 'Public Choice and the Conduct of Constitutional Economics', in Gwartney and Wagner (1988b).
Gwartney, J.D. and Wagner, R.E. (eds) (1988b), *Public Choice and Constitutional Economics*, Greenwich, Connecticut: JAI Press.
Habermas, J. (1962/1989), *The Structural Transformation of the Public Sphere*, Cambridge: Polity Press.

413

Habermas, J. (1969/1971), *Toward a Rational Society. Student Protest, Science and Politics*, London. Heinemann.

Habermas, J. (1973/1975), *Legitimation Crisis*, Boston: Beacon Press.

Habermas, J. (1976/1979), *Communication and the Evolution of Society*, Boston: Beacon Press.

Habermas, J. (1977/1986), 'Hannah Arendt's Communications Concept of Power', in Lukes (1986).

Habermas, J. (1981), 'New Social Movements', *Telos*, 49, 33–37.

Habermas, J. (1981/1984), *The Theory of Communicative Action*, Vol. 1: *Reason and the Rationalization of Society*, Boston: Beacon Press.

Habermas, J. (1981/1987), *The Theory of Communicative Action*, Vol. 2: *Lifeworld and System: A Critique of Functionalist Reason*, Boston: Beacon Press.

Hahn, F. (1991), 'Benevolence', in Meeks (1991).

Hammond, T.H. and Knott, J.H. (1988), 'The Deregulatory Snowball: Explaining Deregulation in the Financial Industry', *Journal of Politics*, 50, 3–30.

Hampton, J. (1987), 'Free-Rider Problems in the Production of Collective Goods', *Economics and Philosophy*, 3, 245–273.

Hanagan, M.P. (1980), *The Logic of Solidarity. Artisans and Industrial Workers in Three French Towns*, Urbana: University of Illinois Press.

Hanson, N.R. (1958/1965), *Patterns of Discovery*, Cambridge: Cambridge University Press.

Hardin, G. (1968), 'The Tragedy of the Commons', *Science*, 162, 1243–1248.

Hardin, R. (1971), 'Collective Action as an Agreeable n-prisoners' dilemma', *Behavioral Science*, 16, 472–481.

Hardin, R. (1982), *Collective Action*, Baltimore: Johns Hopkins University Press.

Hardin, R. (1990), 'The Social Evolution of Cooperation', in Cook and Levi (1990).

Harpham, E.J. (1984), 'Liberalism, Civic Humanism, and the Case of Adam Smith', *American Political Science Review*, 78, 764–774.

Hartley, K. (1992), 'Exogenous Factors in Neo-Classical Microeconomics', in Himmelstrand (1992a).

Hayek, F.A. von (1944/1962), *The Road to Serfdom*, London: Routledge and Kegan Paul.

Hayek, F.A. von (1948), *Individualism and Economic Order*, Chicago: Henry Regnery.

Hayek, F.A., von (1955), *The Counter-Revolution of Science. Studies on the Abuse of Reason*, New York: The Free Press of Glencoe.

Hayek, F.A. von (1960), *The Constitution of Liberty*, Chicago: Henry Regnery.

Hayek, F.A. von (1967), *Studies in Philosophy, Politics and Economics*, New York: Simon and Schuster.

Hayek, F.A. von (1972), *Individualism and Economic Order*, Chicago: Henry Regnery.

Hayek, F.A. von (1978), *New Studies in Philosophy, Politics, Economics and the History of Ideas*, London: Routledge and Kegan Paul.

Hayek, F.A. von (1982), *Law, Legislation and Liberty*, London: Routledge and Kegan Paul.

Heath, A.F. (1987), 'The Economic Theory of Democracy: The Rise of the Liberals in Britain', in Radnitzky and Bernholz (1987).

Heberle, R. (1951), *Social Movements. An Introduction to Political Sociology*, New York: Appleton-Century-Crofts.

Heberle, R. (1968), 'Types and Functions of Social Movements', in *Encyclopedia of the Social Sciences*, 14, 438–444, New York: Macmillan.

Hechter, M. (1983a), 'Karl Polanyi's Social Theory: A Critique', in Hechter (1983c).

Hechter, M. (1983b), 'A Theory of Group Solidarity', in Hechter, (1983c).

Hechter, M. (ed), (1983c), *The Microfoundations of Macrosociology*, Philadelphia: Temple University Press.

Hechter, M. (1984), 'When Actors Comply: Monitoring Costs and the Production of Social Order', *Acta Sociologica*, 27, 161–183.

Hechter, M. (1987), *Principles of Group Solidarity*, Berkeley: University of California Press.

Hechter, M. (1990a), 'Comment: On the Inadequacy of Game Theory for the Solution of Real-World Collective Action Problems', in Cook and Levi (1990).

Hechter, M. (1990b), 'The Emergence of Cooperative Social Institutions', in Hechter *et al.* (1990).

Hechter, M. (1992), 'Should Values Be Written Out of the Social Scientist's Lexicon?', *Sociological Theory*, 10, 214–230.

Hechter, M. (1994), 'The Role of Values in Rational Choice Theory', *Rationality and Society*, 6, 318–333.

Hechter, M., Opp, K.-D. and Wippler, R. (eds) (1990), *Social Institutions. Their Emergence, Maintenance and Effects*, Berlin: Walter de Gruyter.

Hechter, M., Friedman, D. and Kanazawa, S. (1992), 'The Attainment of Global Order in Heterogenous Societies', in Coleman and Fararo, (1992).

Heckathorn, D.D. (1984), 'A Formal Theory of Social Exchange: Process and Outcome', *Current Perspectives in Social Theory*, 5, 145–180.

Heckathorn, D.D. (1988), 'Collective Sanctions and the Creation of Prisoners' Dilemma Norms', *American Journal of Sociology*, 94, 535–562.

Heckathorn, D.D. (1989), 'Collective Action and the Second-Order Free-Rider Problem', *Rationality and Society*, 1, 78–100.

Heckathorn, D.D. (1990), 'Collective Sanctions and Compliance Norms: A Formal Theory of Group-Mediated Social Control', *American Sociological Review*, 55, 366–384.

Hedström, P. (1986), 'From Political Sociology to Political Economy', in Himmelstrand (1986).

Hee-Soh, B. (1986), 'Political Business Cycles in Industrialized Democratic Countries', *Kyklos*, 39, 31–46.

Hegel, G.W.F. (1821/1967), *The Philosophy of Right*, Oxford: Oxford University Press.

Held, D. (1987), *Models of Democracy*, Cambridge: Polity Press.

Held, D. (ed.) (1991), *Political Theory Today*, Cambridge: Polity Press.

Hesse, M. (1980), *Revolutions and Reconstructions in the Philosophy of Science*, Brighton: Harvester Press.

Hettich, W. (1975), 'Bureaucrats and Public Goods', *Public Choice*, 15, 15–25.

Hibbs, D.A. (1987a), *The American Political Economy. Macroeconomics and Electoral Politics*, Cambridge Mass.: Harvard University Press.

Hibbs, D.A. (1987b), *The Political Economy of Industrial Democracies*, Cambridge Mass.: Harvard University Press.

Hibbs D.A. and Dennis, C. (1988), 'Income Distribution in the United States', *American Political Science Review*, 82, 467–490.

Himmelstrand, U. (1960), *Social Pressures, Attitudes and Democratic Processes*, Stockholm: Almqvist and Wicksell.

Himmelstrand U. (ed.) (1986), *Sociology. From Crisis to Science? Volume 1: The Sociology of Structure and Action,* London: Sage.

Himmelstrand, U. (ed.) (1992a), *Interfaces in Economic and Social Analysis*, London: Routledge.

Himmelstrand, U. (1992b), 'Towards a Lexicographic Preference-Actor-Structure Theory', in Himmelstrand (1992a).

Himmelstrand, U., Ahrne, G., Lundberg, L. and Lundberg, L. (1981), *Beyond Welfare Capitalism. Issues, Actors and Forces in Societal Change*, London: Heinemann.

Hinde, R.A. and Groebel, J. (eds) (1991), *Cooperation and Prosocial Behaviour*, Cambridge: Cambridge University Press.

Hirschleifer, J. (1985), 'The Expanding Domain of Economics', *American Economic Review*, 75, 53–68.

Hirschman, A.O. (1970), *Exit, Voice and Loyalty. Responses to Decline in Firms, Organizations and States*, Cambridge, Mass: Harvard University Press.

Hirschman, A.O. (1977), *The Passions and the Interests. Political Arguments for Capitalism before its Triumph*, New Jersey: Princeton University Press.

Hirschman, A.O. (1981), *Essays in Trespassing. Economics to Politics and Beyond*, Cambridge: Cambridge University Press.

Hirschman, A.O. (1982/1985), *Shifting Involvements. Private Interest and Public Action*, Oxford: Basil Blackwell.

Hirschman, A.O. (1984), 'Against Parsimony: Three Easy Ways of Complicating Some Categories of Economic Discourse', *American Economic Review*, 74, 89–96.

Hirschman, A.O. (1985), 'Against Parsimony: Three Easy Ways of Complicating Some Categories of Economic Discourse', *Economics and Philosophy*, 1, 7–21. Revised version of Hirschman (1984).

Hirschman, A.O. (1991), *The Rhetoric of Reaction. Perversity, Futility, Jeopardy*, Cambridge, Mass.: Belknap Press of Harvard University Press.

Hobbes, T. (1651/1968), *Leviathan*, Harmondsworth: Penguin.

Hobsbawm, E.J. (1990), *Nations and Nationalism since 1780. Programme, Myth, Reality*, Cambridge: Cambridge University Press.

Hollander, S. (1976), 'Adam Smith and the Self-Interest Axiom', *Journal of Law and Economics*, 19, 133–152.

Holmberg, S. and Gilljam, M. (1987), *Väljare och Val i Sverige*, Stockholm: Bonniers.

Holmes, S. (1990), 'The Secret History of Self-Interest', in Mansbridge (1990).

Holt, R.T. (1967), 'A Proposed Structural-Functional Framework', in Charlesworth (1967).

Holton, R.J. (1978), 'The Crowd in History: Some Problems of Theory and Method', *Social History*, 3, 219–233.

Homans, G.C. (1951), *The Human Group*, London: Routledge and Kegan Paul.

Hood, C. (1992), 'Looking after Number One? Politicians' Rewards and the Economics of Politics', *Political Studies*, 40, 207–226.

Hood, C., Huby, M. and Dunshire, A. (1984), 'Bureaucrats and Budgeting Benefits: How do British Central Governments Measure Up?', *Journal of Public Policy*, 4, 163–179.

Horwitz, R. (1961) 'Scientific Propaganda: Harold Lasswell', in Storing (1961).

Hudelson, R. (1987), 'A Note on the Empirical Adequacy of the Expressive Theory of Voting Behavior', *Economics and Philosophy*, 3, 127–130.

Hume, D. (1738/1911), *A Treatise of Human Nature*, 2 vols, London: J.M. Dent & Sons Ltd.

Hume, D. (1741–42/1963), *Essays. Moral, Political and Literary*, Oxford: Oxford University Press.

Hunt, L. (1984), 'Charles Tilly's Collective Action', in T. Skocpol (ed.), *Vision and Method in Historical Sociology*, Cambridge: Cambridge University Press.

Inglehart, R. (1971), 'The Silent Revolution in Europe: Intergenerational Change in Post-Industrial Society', *American Political Science Review*, 65, 991–1017.

Inglehart, R. (1977), *The Silent Revolution. Changing Values and Political Styles among Western Publics*, Princeton N.J.: Princeton University Press.

Inglehart, R. (1990), 'Values, Ideology and Cognitive Mobilization in New Social Movements', in Dalton and Kuechler, eds (1990).

Isaac, J.C. (1987), 'Beyond the Three Faces of Power: A Realist Critique', *Polity*, 20, 4–31.

Isaac, R.M., McCue, K.F. and Plott, C.R. (1985), 'Public Goods Provision in an Experimental Environment', *Journal of Public Economics*, 26, 51–74.

Iyengar, S. (1989), 'How Citizens Think about National Issues: A Matter of Responsibility', *American Journal of Political Science*, 33, 878–900.

Jackson, P.M. (1982), *The Political Economy of Bureaucracy*, Oxford: Philip Allan.

Jackson, J.E. and Kingdon, J.W. (1992), 'Ideology, Interest Group Scores, and Legislative Votes', *American Journal of Political Science*, 36, 805–823.

James, P. (1992), 'Forms of Abstract "Community". From Tribe and Kingdom to Nation and State', *Philosophy of the Social Sciences*, 22, 313–336.

Jankowski, R. (1990), 'Punishment in Iterated chicken and Prisoners' Dilemma Games', *Rationality and Society*, 2, 449–470.

Jessop, B. (1977), 'Recent Theories of the Capitalist State', *Cambridge Journal of Economics*, 1, 353–373.

Jessop, B. (1979), 'Corporatism, Parliamentarism, and Social Democracy', in Schmitter and Lehmbruch (1979).

Jessop, B. (1982), *The Capitalist State*, Oxford: Martin Robertson.

Johnson, J.D. (1988), 'Symbolic Action and the Limits of Strategic Rationality: On the Logic of Working-Class Collective Action', *Political Power and Social Theory*, 7, 211–248.

Johnson, J.D. (1991), 'Rational Choice and Reconstructive Theory', in Monroe (1991).

Johnston, D. (1991), 'Human Agency and Rational Action', in Monroe (1991).

Kalecki, M. (1943), 'Political Aspects of Full Employment', *Political Quarterly*, October–December, 322–331.

Kalt, J.P. and Zupan, M.A. (1984), 'Capture and Ideology in the Economic Theory of Politics', *American Economic Review*, 74, 279–300.

Kanter, R.M. (1972), *Commitment and Community. Communes and Utopias in Sociological Perspective*, Cambridge, Mass.: Harvard University Press.

Kanter, R.M. (1973), 'Utopian Communities', *Sociological Inquiry*, 43, 263–290.

Kaplan, M.A. (1968), 'Systems Theory and Political Science', *Social Research*, 35, 30–47.

Katz, E. and Lazarsfeld, P.F. (1955), *Personal Influence. The Part Played by People in the Flow of Mass Communication*, Glencoe, Illinois: The Free Press.

Kau, J.B. and Rubin, P.H. (1979), 'Self-Interest, and Logrolling in Congressional Voting', *Journal of Law and Economics*, 22, 365–384.

Keech, W.R. (1991), 'Politics, Economics, and Politics Again', *Journal of Politics*, 53, 597–611.

Kelman, S. (1988), 'On Democracy-Bashing: A Sceptical Look at the Theoretical and "Empirical" Practice of the Public Choice Movement', *Virginia Law Review*, 74, 199–273.

Kelman, S. (1990), 'Congress and Public Spirit: A Commentary', in Mansbridge (1990).

Key, V.O. (1966), *The Responsible Electorate*, Cambridge, Mass: Belknap Press of Harvard University Press.

Khalil, E.L. (1990), 'Beyond Self-Interest and Altruism. A Reconstruction of Adam Smith's Theory of Human Conduct', *Economics and Philosophy*, 6, 255–273.

Kiewiet, D.R. (1983), *Macroeconomics and Micropolitics. The Electoral Effects of Economic Issues*, Chicago: University of Chicago Press.

Kiewiet, D.R. and Rivers, D. (1984), 'A Retrospective on Retrospective Voting', *Political Behavior*, 6, 369–393.

Killian, L.M. (1964), 'Social Movements', in R.E.L. Faris (ed.), *Handbook of Modern Sociology*, Chicago: Rand McNally.

417

Kim, O. and Walker, M. (1984), 'The Free Rider Hypothesis: Experimental Evidence', *Public Choice*, 43, 3–24.

Kinder, D.R. and Kiewiet, D.R. (1979), 'Economic Discontent and Political Behavior: The Role of Personal Grievances and Collective Economic Judgements in Congressional Voting', *American Journal of Political Science*, 23, 495–527.

Kinder, D.R. and Kiewiet, D.R. (1981), 'Sociotropic Voting: The American Case', *British Journal of Political Science*, 11, 129–161.

Kinder, D.R. and Sears, D.O. (1985), 'Public Opinion and Political Action', in G. Lindsay and E. Aronson, eds, *Handbook of Social Psychology*, Vol. 2, New York: Random House.

Kinder, D.R., Adams, G.S. and Gronke, P.W. (1989), 'Economics and Politics in the 1984 American Presidential Election', *American Journal of Political Science*, 33, 491–515.

King, R. (ed.), (1983), *Capital and Politics*, London: Routledge and Kegan Paul.

King, R. (1986), *The State in Modern Society. New Directions in Political Sociology*, Chatham, N.J.: Chatham House.

Kingdom, J. (1992), *No Such Thing as Society? Individualism and Community*, Buckingham: Open University Press.

Klandermans, B. (1986a), 'Individual Behaviour in Real Life Social Dilemmas: A Theory and Some Research Results', in Wilke *et al.*, (1986b).

Klandermans, B. (1986b), 'New Social Movements and Resource Mobilization: The European and the American Approach', *International Journal of Mass Emergencies and Disasters*, 4, 13–37.

Klapp, O.E. (1969), *Collective Search for Identity*, New York: Holt, Rinehart and Winston.

Klein, R. (1985), 'Public Expenditure in an Inflationary World', in Lindberg and Maier (1985).

Klosko, G. (1987), 'Rebellious Collective Action Revisited', *American Political Science Review*, 81, 557–561.

Knight, F.H. (1935), *The Ethics of Competition and Other Essays*, London: Allen and Unwin.

Knight, F.H. (1963), *On the History and Method of Economics*, Chicago: Chicago University Press.

Knoke, D. (1990), 'Incentives in Collective Action Organizations', *American Sociological Review*, 53, 311–329.

Knorr-Cetina, K. and Cicourel, A.V. (eds) (1981), *Advances in Social Theory and Methodology. Toward an Integration of Micro-and Macro-Sociologies*, London: Routledge and Kegan Paul.

Koford, K.J. and Colander, D.C. (1984), 'Taming the Rent-Seeker', in Colander (1984).

Kogan, M. (1973), 'An Over-simplified Model', Comment on Niskanen in Niskanen (1973).

Kornhauser, W. (1960), *The Politics of Mass Society*, London: Routledge and Kegan Paul.

Korpi, W. (1978), *The Working Class in Welfare Capitalism. Work, Unions and Politics in Sweden*, London: Routledge and Kegan Paul.

Korpi, W. (1983), *The Democratic Class Struggle*, London: Routledge and Kegan Paul.

Korpi, W. (1985), 'Power Resources Approach vs. Action and Conflict: On Causal and Intentional Explanations in the Study of Power', *Sociological Theory*, 3, 31–45.

Korpi, W. (1991), 'Political and Economic Explanations for Unemployment: A Cross-National and Long-Term Analysis', *British Journal of Politcal Science*, 21, 315–348.

Korpi, W. (1992), *Halkar Sverige efter? Sveriges ekonomiska tillväxt 1820–1990 i jämförande belysning*. Stockholm: Carlsson.

Korpi, W. (1994), 'Old Age Pensions and Poverty', in P. Guidicini and G. Pieretti, eds, *Urban Poverty and Human Dignity*, Milano: FrancoAngeli.

Kramer, G.H. (1971), 'Short-Term Fluctuations in US Voting Behavior, 1896–1964', *American Political Science Review*, 65, 131–143.

Kramer, G.H. (1983), 'The Ecological Fallacy Revisited: Aggregate versus Individual-level Findings on Economics and Elections, and Sociotropic Voting', *American Political Science Review*, 92–107.

Kramer, R.M. and Brewer, M.B. (1986), 'Social Group Identity and the Emergence of Cooperation in Resource Conservation Dilemmas', in Wilke, *et al.* (1986b).

Krasner, S.D. (1984), 'Approaches to the State. Alternative Conceptions and Historical Dynamics', *Comparative Politics*, 16, 223–246.

Kristol, I. (1981), 'Rationalism in Economics', in D. Bell and I. Kristol (eds), *The Crisis in Economic Theory*, New York: Basic Books.

Krueger, A.O. (1974/1980), 'The Political Economy of the Rent-Seeking Society', *American Economic Review*, 64, 291–303, reprinted in Buchanan *et al.* (1980).

Kuechler, M. and Dalton, R.J. (1990), 'New Social Movements and the Political Order: Inducing Change for Long-term Stability', in Dalton and Kuechler (1990).

Kuhlman, D.M., Camac, C.R. and Cunha, D.A. (1986), 'Individual Differences in Social Orientation', in Wilke, *et al.* (1986b).

Kuhn, T.S. (1962/1970), *The Structure of Scientific Revolutions*, Chicago: University of Chicago Press.

Laidler, D. (1981), *Introduction to Microeconomics*, Oxford: Philip Allan.

Lakatos, I. (1970), 'Falsification and the Methodology of Scientific Research Programmes', in I. Lakatos and Musgrave (eds), *Criticism and the Growth of Knowledge*, Cambridge: Cambridge University Press.

Landau, M. (1968), 'On the Uses of Functional Analysis in American Political Science', *Social Research*, 35, 48–75.

Lane, J.-E. (ed.) (1985), *State and Market: The Politics of the Public and the Private*, London: Sage Publications.

Lane, J.-E. (ed.) (1987), *Bureaucracy and Public Choice*, London: Sage Publications.

Lane, J.-E. and Ersson, S.O. (1991), *Politics and Society in Western Europe*, 2nd edn, London: Sage Publications.

Lane, R.E. (1981), 'Markets and Politics: The Human Product', *British Journal of Political Science*, 11, 1–16.

Lasswell, H.D. (1927) 'The Theory of Political Propaganda', *American Political Science Review*, 21, 627–631.

Lasswell, H.D. (1936/1958) *Politics: Who Gets What, When, How*, New York: World Publishing.

Lasswell, H.D. (1947) *The Analysis of Political Behaviour. An Empirical Approach*, London: Kegan Paul, Trench, Trubner.

Lavau, G. (1990), 'Is the Voter an Individualist?', in Birnbaum and Leca (1990).

Laver, M. (1980), 'Political Solutions to the Collective Action Problem', *Political Studies*, 28, 195–209.

Laver, M. (1981), *The Politics of Private Desire*, Harmondworth: Penguin.

Laver, M.J. and Budge, I., eds (1992), *Party Policy and Government Coalitions*, London: Macmillan.

Laver, M. and Shepsle, K.A. (1990), 'Government Coalitions and Intraparty Politics', *British Journal of Political Science*, 20, 489–507.

Lazarsfeld, P.F. (1964), 'Political Behavior and Public Opinion', in B. Berelson (ed.), *The Behavioral Sciences Today*, New York: Harper and Row.

Lazarsfeld, P.F., Berelson, B. and Gaudet, H. (1944/1948), *The People's Choice*, New York: Columbia University Press.

Le Bon, G. (1895/1960), *The Crowd. A Study of the Popular Mind*, New York: Viking Press.

Le Bon, G. (1979), *Gustave Le Bon. The Man and His Works,* A. Widener, ed., Indianapolis: Liberty Press.

Lehmbruch, G. (1979a), 'Consociational Democracy, Class Conflict and the New Corporatism', in Schmitter and Lehmbruch (1979).

Lehmbruch, G. (1979b), 'Liberal Corporatism and Party Government', in Schmitter and Lehmbruch (1979).

Lehmbruch, G. (1979c), 'Concluding Remarks: Problems for Future Research on Corporatist Intermediation and Policy-Making', in Schmitter and Lehmbruch (1979).

Lehmbruch, G. (1984), 'Concertation and the Structure of Corporatist Networks', in Goldthorpe (1984c).

Lehmbruch, G. and Schmitter, P.C. (1982), *Patterns of Corporist Policy Making,* London: Sage.

Leithner, C. (1993), 'Economic Conditions and the Vote: A Contingent rather than Categorial Influence', *British Journal of Political Science,* 23, 339–372.

Lenin, V.I. (1963), *Selected Works,* Moscow: Progress Publishers.

Lewin, L. (1991), *Self-Interest and Public Interest in Western Politics,* Oxford: Oxford University Press.

Lewis-Beck, M.S. (1985), 'Pocket-Book Voting in US National Election Studies: Fact or Artifact', *American Journal of Political Science,* 29, 348–356.

Lewis-Beck, M.S. (1986), 'Comparative Economic Voting: Britain, France, Germany, Italy', *American Journal of Political Science,* 30, 315–346.

Lewis-Beck, M.S. (1988a), 'Economics and the American Voter: Past, Present, Future', *Political Behavior,* 10, 5–21.

Lewis-Beck, M.S. (1988b), *Economics and Elections. The Major Western Democracies,* Ann Arbor: University of Michigan Press.

Liebrand, W.B.G. (1986), 'The Ubiquity of Social Values in Social Dilemmas', in Wilke *et al.* (1986b).

Lindbeck, A. (1976), 'Stabilization Policy in Open Economies with Endogenous Politicians', *American Economic Review. Papers and Proceedings,* 66, 1–19.

Lindbeck, A. (1985), 'Redistribution Policy and the Expansion of the Public Sector', *Journal of Public Economics,* 28, 309–328.

Lindberg, L.N. (1992), 'Political Science and the Study of the Economy', in Himmelstrand (1992).

Lindberg, L.N. and Maier, C.S. (eds) (1985), *The Politics of Inflation and Economic Stagnation. Theoretical Approaches and International Case Studies.* Washington, DC: The Brookings Institution.

Lindberg, L.N., Alford, R., Crouch, C. and Offe, C. (eds) (1975), *Stress and Contradiction in Modern Capitalism,* Lexington, Mass.: Lexington Books.

Lindblom, C. E. (1958), 'Policy Analysis', *American Economic Review,* 48, 298–312.

Lindblom, C. E. (1959), 'The Science of "Muddling Through"', *Public Administration Review,* 19, 78–88.

Lindblom, C.E. (1977), *Politics and Markets. The World's Political-Economic Systems,* New York: Basic Books.

Lindenberg, S. (1985a), 'An Assessment of the New Political Economy', *Sociological Theory,* 3, 99–114.

Lindenberg, S. (1985b), 'Rational Choice and Sociological Theory: New Pressures on Economics as a Social Science', *Zeitschrift für die gesamte Staatswissenschaft,* 14, 244–55.

Lippmann, W. (1922/1946), *Public Opinion,* New York: Penguin.

Lipset, S.M. (1959/1963), *Political Man,* London: Mercury Books.

Lipset, S.M. (1959/1965), 'Political Sociology', in R. Merton, L. Broom and L.S. Cottrell, Jr. (eds), *Sociology Today, Volume 1: Problems and Prospects,* New York: Harper and Row.

Lipset, S.M. (1963/1967), *The First New Nation: The United States in Historical and Comparative Perspective*, New York: Doubleday.

Lipset, S.M. (1967), 'Political Sociology', in N.J. Smelser (ed.), *Sociology: An Introduction*, New York: John Wiley and Sons.

Lipset, S.M. (1969a), 'Politics and the Social Sciences: Introduction', in Lipset (1969b).

Lipset, S.M. (ed.) (1969b), *Politics and the Social Sciences*, New York: Oxford University Press.

Lipset, S.M. and Rokkan, S. (eds) (1967), *Party Systems and Voter Alignments: Cross-National Perspectives*, New York: The Free Press.

Lively, J. (1976), 'The Limits of Exchange Theory', in Barry (1976b).

Locke, J. (1690/1965), *Two Treatises of Government*, New York: New American Library.

Lockwood, D. (1964), 'Social Integration and System Integration', in G.K. Zollschan and W. Hirsch (eds), *Explorations in Social Change*, Boston: Houghton Mifflin.

Lofland, J.F. (1981), 'Collective Behavior: The Elementary Forms', in M. Rosenberg and R.H. Turner (eds), *Social Psychology. Sociological Perspectives*, New York: Basic Books.

Lovrich, N.P. and Neiman, M. (1984), *Public Choice Theory in Public Administration. An Annotated Bibliography*, New York: Garland.

Lowi, T.J. (1988), 'The Return to the State: Critique', *American Political Science Review*, 82, 885–891.

Luce, R.D. and Raiffa, H. (1957/1985), *Games and Decisions. Introduction and Critical Survey*, New York: Dover Publications.

Lukacs, (1922/1971), *History and Class Consciousness*, London: Merlin Press.

Lukes, S. (1973), *Individualism*, New York: Harper and Row.

Lukes, S. (1974), *Power. A Radical View*, London: Macmillan.

Lukes, S. (1978), 'Power and Authority', in T. Bottomore and R. Nisbet (eds), *A History of Sociological Analysis*, London: Heinemann.

Lukes, S. (1986a) 'Introduction' to Lukes (1986b).

Lukes, S. (ed.) (1986b), *Power*, Oxford: Basil Blackwell.

Lux, K. (1990), *Adam Smith's Mistake. How a Moral Philosopher Invented Economics and Ended Morality*, Boston: Shambhala.

Lysgaard, S. (1961/1981), *Arbeiderkollektivet*, Oslo: Universitetsforlaget.

McCallum, B.T. (1977), 'The Political Business Cycle: An Empirical Test', *Southern Economic Journal*, 44, 504–515.

McCarthy, J.D. and Zald, M.N. (1973), *The Trend of Social Movements in America: Professionalization and Resource Mobilization*, Morristown, N.J.: General Learning Press.

McCarthy, J.D. and Zald, M.N. (1977), 'Resource Mobilization and Social Movements: A Partial Theory', *American Journal of Sociology*, 82, 1212–1241.

McClennen, E.F. (1975), 'Comment' on Buchanan in Phelps (1975).

Macfie, A.L. (1967), *The Individual in Society*, London: Allen and Unwin.

MacIver, R.M. (1911), 'Society and State', *The Philosophical Review*, 20, 30–45.

MacIver, R.M. (1917), *Community. A Sociological Study*, London: Macmillan.

MacIver, R. M. (1921/1929), *The Elements of Social Science*, London: Methuen.

MacIver, R.M. (1926/1964), *The Modern State*, London: Oxford University Press.

MacIver, R.M. (1932), 'Interests', in *Encyclopedia of the Social Sciences*, 7, New York: Macmillan.

MacIver, R.M. (1937), *Society. A Textbook of Sociology*, New York: Farrar and Rinehart.

MacIver, R.M. (1947/1965), *The Web of Government*, New York: The Free Press.

MacIver, R.M. (1970), *On Community, Society and Power*, Chicago: University of Chicago Press.

McKean, R.N. (1975), 'Economics of Trust, Altruism and Corporate Responsibility', in Phelps (1975).

McKelvey, R.D. and Ordeshook, P.C. (1990a), 'A Decade of Experimental Research on Spatial Models of Elections and Committees', in Enelow and Hinich (1990).

McKelvey, R.D. and Ordeshook, P.C. (1990b), 'Information and Elections: Retrospective Voting and Rational Expectations', in Ferejohn and Kuklinski (1990).

McKenzie, R.B. (1979), 'The Non-Rational Domain and the Limits of Economic Analysis', *Southern Economic Journal*, 46, 145–157.

MacKenzie, W.J.M. (1967), *Politics and Social Science*, Harmondsworth: Penguin.

MacKenzie, W.J.M. (1970), 'Political Science', Ch. 2 in *Main Trends of Research in the Social and Human Sciences. Part One: Social Sciences*, Paris: Unesco.

McLean, I. (1987), *Public Choice. An Introduction*, Oxford: Basil Blackwell.

Macneil, I.R. (1986), 'Exchange Revisited: Individual Utility and Social Solidarity', *Ethics*, 96, 567–593.

McPhail, C. (1991), *The Myth of the Madding Crowd*, New York: Aldine de Gruyter.

Macpherson, C.B. (1962), *The Theory of Possessive Individualism. Hobbes to Locke*, Oxford: Oxford University Press.

MacRae, C.D. (1977), 'A Political Model of the Business Cycle', *Journal of Political Economy*, 85, 239–263.

Macy, M.C. (1990), 'Learning Theory and the Logic of Critical Mass', *American Sociological Review*, 55, 809–826.

Macy, M.W. (1989), 'Walking out of Social Traps. A Stochastic Learning Model for the Prisoner's Dilemma', *Rationality and Society*, 1, 197–219.

Macy, M.W. (1991a), 'Chains of Cooperation: Threshold Effects in Collective Action', *American Sociological Review*, 56, 730–747.

Macy, M.W. (1991b), 'Learning to Cooperate: Stochastic and Tacit Collusion in Social Exchange', *American Journal of Sociology*, 97, 808–843.

Maier, C.S. (1981), 'Fictitious Bonds of Wealth and Law: On the Theory and Practice of Interest Representation', in Berger (1981).

Maier, C.S. (1984), 'Preconditions for Corporatism', in Goldthorpe (1984).

Maine, H. (1861/1972), *Ancient Law*, London: J.M. Dent and Sons.

Majeski, S.J. (1990), 'Comment on Coleman: An Alternative Approach to the Generation and Maintenance of Norms', in Cook and Levi (1990).

Malinowski, B. (1922/1961), *Argonauts of the Western Pacific*, New York: E.P. Dutton.

Malinowski, B. (1926), *Crime and Custom in Savage Society*, London: Routledge and Kegan Paul.

Mann, M. (1973), *Consciousness and Action among the Western Working Class*, London: Macmillan.

Mann, M. (1986), *The Sources of Social Power. Volume 1: A History of Power from the Beginning to AD 1760*, Cambridge: Cambridge University Press.

Mannheim, K. (1936/1960), *Ideology and Utopia. An Introduction to the Sociology of Knowledge*, London: Routledge and Kegan Paul.

Mannheim, K. (1951), *Freedom, Power and Democratic Planning*, London: Routledge and Kegan Paul.

Mansbridge, J.J. (ed.) (1990), *Beyond Self-Interest*, Chicago: University of Chicago Press.

March, J.G. and Olsen J.P. (1984), 'The New Institutionalism: Organizational Factors in Political Life', *American Political Science Review*, 77, 281–297.

March, J.G. and Olsen J.P. (1989), *Rediscovering Institutions. The Organizational Basis of Politics*, New York: The Free Press.

Marcus, G.B. (1988), 'The Impact of Personal and National Economic Conditions on the Presidential Vote: A Pooled Cross-Sectional Analysis', *American Journal of Political Science*, 32, 137–154.

Margolis, H. (1981), 'A New Model of Rational Choice', *Ethics*, 91, 265–279.

Margolis, H. (1982/1984), *Selfishness, Altruism, and Rationality. A Theory of Social Choice*, Chicago: University of Chicago Press.

Margolis, H. (1990), 'Dual Utilities and Rational Choice', in Mansbridge (1990).

Margolis, H. (1991), 'Incomplete Coercion: How Social Preferences Mix with Private', in Monroe (1991).

Margolis, J. (1975), 'Comment', on Niskanen (1975), *Journal of Law and Economics*, 18, 645–659.

Marsh, D. (1976), 'On Joining Interest Groups: An Empirical Consideration of the Work of Mancur Olson Jr.', *British Journal of Political Science*, 6, 257–271.

Martindale, D. (1964), 'The Formation and Destruction of Communities', in G.K. Zollschan and W. Hirsch (eds), *Explorations in Social Change*, Boston: Houghton Mifflin.

Marwell, G. and Ames, R.E. (1979), 'Experiments on the Provision of Public Goods. I. Resources, Interest, Group Size, and the Free-Rider Problem', *American Journal of Sociology*, 84, 1335–1360.

Marwell, G. and Ames, R.E. (1980), 'Experiments on the Provision of Public Goods. II. Provision Points, Stakes, Experience, and the Free-Rider Problem', *American Journal of Sociology*, 85, 926–937.

Marwell, G. and Ames, R.E. (1981), 'Economists Free Ride, Does Anyone Else? Experiments on the Provision of Public Goods, IV', *Journal of Public Economics*, 15, 295–310.

Marwell, G., Oliver, P.E. and Prahl, R. (1988), 'Social Networks and Collective Action: A Theory of the Critical Mass. III', *American Journal of Sociology*, 94, 502–534.

Marx, G.T. and Wood, J.L. (1975), 'Strands of Theory and Research in Collective Behavior', *Annual Review of Sociology*, 1, 363–428.

Marx, K. (1847/1975), *The Poverty of Philosophy*, Moscow: Progress Publishers.

Marx, K. (1859/1970), *A Contribution to the Critique of Political Economy*, Moscow: Progress Publishers.

Marx, K. (1973a), *Political Writings, Volume I: The Revolutions of 1848*, Harmondsworth: Penguin.

Marx, K. (1973b), *Political Writings, Volume 2: Surveys from Exile*, Harmondsworth: Penguin.

Marx, K. (1974), *Political Writings, Volume 3: The First International and After*, Harmondsworth: Penguin.

Marx, K. (1975), *Early Writings*, Harmondsworth: Penguin.

Marx, K. and Engels, F. (1846/1976), *The German Ideology*, Moscow: Progress Publishers.

Marx, K. and Engels, F. (1848/1967), *The Communist Manifesto*, Harmondsworth: Penguin.

Marx, K. and Engels, F. (1975), *Selected Correspondence*, Moscow: Progress Publishers.

Mauss, M. (1929/1960), *The Gift. Forms of Exchange in Archaic Societies*, London: Routledge and Kegan Paul.

Mead, G.H. (1934/1962), *Mind, Self and Society from the Standpoint of a Social Behaviorist*, Chicago: University of Chicago Press.

Meehl, P. E. (1977), 'The Selfish Voter Paradox and the Thrown-Away Vote Argument', *American Political Science Review*, 71, 11–30.

Meeks, J.G.T. (ed.) (1991), *Thoughtful Economic Man*, Cambridge: Cambridge University Press.

Meltzer, A.H. and Richard, S.F. (1978), 'Why Government Grows (and Grows) in a Democracy', *The Public Interest*, 52, 11–118.

Meltzer, A.H. and Richard, S.F. (1981), 'A Rational Theory of the Size of Government', *Journal of Political Economy*, 89, 914–927.

Melucci, A. (1984a), 'The New Social Movements: A Theoretical Approach', *Social Science Information*, 19, 199–226.

Melucci, A. (1984b), 'An End to Social Movements?', *Social Science Information*, 23, 819–835.

Melucci, A. (1985), 'The Symbolic Challenge of Contemporary Movements', *Social Research*, 52, 789–816.

Merelman, R.M. (1981) 'Harold D. Laswell's Political World: Weak Tea for Hard Times', *British Journal of Political Science*, 11, 471–497.

Merton, R.K. (1957), *Social Theory and Social Structure*, revised and enlarged edn, New York: The Free Press.

Messick, D.M. and Brewer, M.B. (1983), 'Solving Social Dilemmas. A Review', *Review of Personality and Social Psychology*, 4, 11–44.

Michels, R. (1915/1962), *Political Parties. A Sociological Study of the Oligarchic Tendencies of Modern Democracies*, New York: The Free Press.

Mill, J.S. (1843/1950), *Philosophy of Scientific Method*, New York: Haffner.

Miller, D. (1992), 'Deliberative Democracy and Social Choice', *Political Studies*, 40, Special Issue, 54–67.

Miller, G.J. and Moe, T.M. (1983), 'Bureaucrats, Legislators, and the Size of Government', *American Political Science Review*, 77, 297–322.

Miller, N.E. and Dollard, J. (1941) *Social Learning and Imitation*, New Haven: Yale University Press.

Miller, W.E. (1990), 'Party Identification, Realignment, and Party Voting: Back to Basics', *American Political Science Review*, 85, 557–568.

Miller, W.E. (1994), 'An Organizational History of the Intellectual Origins of the American National Election Studies', *European Journal of Political Research*, 25, 247–265.

Mills C.W. (1956/1959), *The Power Elite*, New York: Oxford University Press.

Mills, C.W. (1959/1970), *The Sociological Imagination*, Harmondsworth: Penguin.

Mises, L. von (1933/1976), *Epistemological Problems of Economics*, New York: New York University Press.

Mises, L. von (1949/1966), *Human Action*, Chicago: Contemporary Books.

Mitchell, W.C. (1967), *Sociological Analysis and Politics. The Theories of Talcott Parsons*, Englewood Cliffs, N.J.: Prentice-Hall.

Mitchell, W.C. (1968), 'The New Political Economy', *Social Research*, 35, 76–110.

Mitchell, W.C. (1969), 'The Shape of Political Theory to Come: From Sociology to Political Economy', in Lipset (1969b).

Mitchell, W.C. (1988), 'Virginia, Rochester, and Bloomington: Twenty-five Years of Public Choice and Political Science', *Public Choice*, 56, 101–119.

Mitchell, W.C. and Munger, M.C. (1991), 'Economic Models of Interest Groups: An Introductory Survey', *American Journal of Political Science*, 35, 512–546.

Mitchell, W.I. and Simmons, R.T. (1994), *Beyond Politics. Markets, Welfare, and the Failure of Bureaucracy*, Boulder Colorado: Westview Press.

Moe, T.M. (1980), *The Organization of Interests*, Chicago: University of Chicago Press.

Monroe, K.R. (ed.) (1991) *The Economic Approach to Politics. A Critical Reassessment of the Theory of Rational Action*, New York: HarperCollins.

Monroe, K.R., Barton, M.C. and Klingemann, U. (1991), 'Altruism and the Theory of Rational Action: An Analysis of Rescuers of Jews in Nazi Europe', in Monroe (1991).

Moon, B.E. and Dixon, W.J. (1985), 'Politics, the State and Basic Human Needs: A Cross-National Study', *American Journal of Political Science*, 29, 661–694.

Morris, A. and Herring, C. (1986), 'Theory and Research in Social Movements: A Critical Review', *Annual Review of Political Science*, 2, 137–198.

Mosca, G. (1896/1923/1939), *The Ruling Class*, New York: McGraw-Hill.

Moscovici, S. (1985), *The Age of the Crowd. A Historical Treatise on Mass Psychology*, Cambridge: Cambridge University Press.

Mueller, E. (1963), 'Public Attitudes toward Fiscal Programs', *Quarterly Journal of Economics*, 77, 210–235.

Mueller, D.C. (1976), 'Public Choice: A Survey', in Buchanan and Tollison (1984).

Mueller, D.C. (1979), *Public Choice*. Cambridge: Cambridge University Press.

Mueller, D.C. (1989), *Public Choice II*, Cambridge: Cambridge University Press.

Muller, E.N. and Opp, K.-D. (1986), 'Rational Choice and Rebellious Collective Action', *American Political Science Review*, 80, 471–487.

Muller, E.N. and Opp K.-D. (1987), 'Rebellious Collective Action Revisited', *American Political Science Review*, 81, 557–564.

Muller, J.Z. (1993), *Adam Smith in His Time and Ours. Designing the Decent Society*, New York: The Free Press.

Münch, R. (1992), 'Rational Choice Theory: A Critical Assessment of Its Explanatory Power', in Coleman and Fararo (1992).

Musgrave, R.A. and Peacock, A.T. (eds) (1967), *Classics in the Theory of Public Finance*, London: Macmillan; New York: St Martin's Press.

Myers, M.L. (1983), *The Soul of Modern Economic Man. Ideas of Self-Interest. Thomas Hobbes to Adam Smith*, Chicago: University of Chicago Press.

Myrdal, G. (1929/1953), *The Political Element in the Development of Economic Theory*, London: Routledge and Kegan Paul.

Myrdal, G. (1960), *Beyond the Welfare State*, New Haven: Yale University Press.

Nedelman, B. and Meier, K.G. (1979), 'Theories of Contemporary Corporatism: Static or Dynamic?', in Schmitter and Lehmbruch (1979).

Nie, N.H., Verba, S. and Petrocik, J.R. (1976), *The Changing American Voter*, Cambridge, Mass.: Harvard University Press.

Nisbet, R.A. (1953/1990), *The Quest for Community. A Study in the Ethics of Freedom and Order*, San Francisco: ICS Press.

Nisbet, R.A. (1966/1970), *The Sociological Tradition*, London: Heinemann.

Niskanen, W.A. (1971), *Bureaucracy and Representative Government*, Chicago: Aldine–Atherton.

Niskanen, W.A. (1973), *Bureaucracy: Servant or Master?* London: Institute of Economic Affairs.

Niskanen, W.A. (1975), 'Bureaucrats and Politicians', *Journal of Law and Economics*, 18, 617–643.

Niskanen, W.A. (1978), Competition among Government Bureaus', in Buchanan, *et al.* (1978).

Noll, R.G. (1985a), 'Government Regulatory Behavior: A Multidisciplinary Survey and Synthesis', in Noll (1985b).

Noll, R.G. (1985b), *Regulatory Policy and the Social Sciences*, Berkeley: University of California Press.

Nordhaus, W.D. (1975), 'The Political Business Cycle', *Review of Economic Studies*, 42, 169–190.

Nordlinger, E.A. (1987), 'Taking the State Seriously', in M. Weiner & S.P. Huntington (eds), *Understanding Political Development*, New York: HarperCollins.

Nordlinger, E.A. (1988), 'The Return to the State: Critique', *American Political Science Review*, 82, 875–885.

Nozick, R. (1977), 'On Austrian Methodology', *Synthese*, 36, 353–392.

Obershall, A. (1973), *Social Conflict and Social Movements*, Englewood Cliffs, N.J.: Prentice-Hall.

Obershall, A. (1978), 'Theories of Social Conflict', *Annual Review of Sociology*, 4, 291–315.

Offe, C. (1981), 'The Attribution of Public Status to Interest Groups: Observations on the West German Case', in Berger (1981), reprinted in Offe (1985a).

Offe, C. (1984), *Contradictions of the Welfare State*, London: Hutchinson.

Offe, C. (1985a), *Disorganized Capitalism*, Cambridge: Polity Press.

Offe, C. (1985b), 'New Social Movements: Challenging the Boundaries of Institutional Politics', *Social Research*, 52, 817–868.

Offe, C. and Wiesenthal, H. (1980), 'Two Logics of Collective Action: Theoretical Notes on Social Class and Organizational Form', in M. Zeitlin (ed.), *Political Power and Social Theory*, Greenwich, Connecticut: JAI Press, reprinted in Offe (1985a).

Oliver, P.E. (1980), 'Rewards and Punishments as Selective Incentives for Collective Action', *American Journal of Sociology*, 85, 1356–1375.

Oliver, P.E. and Marwell, G. (1988), 'The Paradox of Group Size in Collective Action: A Theory of the Critical Mass. II', *American Sociological Review*, 53, 1–8.

Oliver, P.E., Marwell, G. and Teixeira, R. (1985), 'A Theory of the Critical Mass. I. Interdependence, Group Heterogeneity, and the Production of Collective Action', *American Journal of Sociology*, 91, 522–556.

Olofsson, G. (1988), 'After the Working-class Movement? An essay on What's "New" and What's "Social" in the New Social Movements', *Acta Sociologica*, 31, 15–34.

Olson, M. (1965/1971), *The Logic of Collective Action. Public Goods and the Theory of Groups*, Cambridge, Mass: Harvard University Press.

Olson, M. (1968), 'Economics, Sociology and the Best of All Possible Worlds', *Public Interest*, 12, 96–118.

Olson, M. (1969), 'The Relationship between Economics and the Other Social Sciences: The Province of a "Social Report"', in Lipset (1969b).

Olson, M. (1982), *The Rise and Decline of Nations. Economic Growth, Stagflation, and Social Rigidities*, New Haven: Yale University Press.

Olson, M. (1990), 'Toward a Unified View of Economics and the Other Social Sciences', in Alt and Shepsle (1990).

Olson, M. (1993) 'Dictatorship, Democracy, and Development', *American Political Science Review*, 87, 567–576.

Opp, K.-D. (1986), 'Soft Incentives and Collective Action: Participation in the Anti-Nuclear Movement', *British Journal of Political Science*, 16, 87–112.

Opp, K.-D. (1990), 'Postmaterialism, Collective Action, and Political Protest', *American Journal of Political Science*, 34, 212–235.

Orbell, J.M., Schwartz-Shea, P. and Simmons, R.T. (1984), 'Do Cooperators Exit More Readily than Defectors?', *American Political Science Review*, 78, 147–162.

Ordeshook, P.C. (1976), 'The Spatial Theory of Elections: A Review and Critique', in Budge *et al.*, (1976).

Ordeshook, P.C. (1990), 'The Emerging Discipline of Political Economy', in Alt and Shepsle (1990).

Ordeshook, P.C. (1992), 'The Reintegration of Political Science and Economics', in Radnitzky (1992).

Ordeshook, P.C. and Shepsle, K.A. eds (1982), *Political Equilibrium*, Boston: Kluwer-Nijhoff Publishing.

Orren, G.R. (1988), 'Beyond Self-Interest', in Reich (1988).

Ortega y Gasset, J. (1930/1957), *The Revolt of the Masses*, New York: W.W. Norton.

Orum, A.M. (1978/1983), *Introduction to Political Sociology*, (2nd edn), Englewood Cliffs, N.J.: Prentice-Hall.

Orzechowki, W. (1977), 'Economic Models of Bureaucracy: Survey, Extensions, and Evidence', in Borcherding (1977c).

Ostrom, E. (ed.) (1982), *Strategies of Political Inquiry*, London: Sage Publications.

Ostrom, E. (1990), *Governing the Commons. The Evolution of Institutions for Collective Action*, Cambridge: Cambridge University Press.

O'Sullivan, N. (1988), 'The Political Theory of Neo-Corporatism', in Cox and O'Sullivan (1988).

Page, B.I. (1983), *Who Gets What from the Government*, Berkeley: University of California Press.

Page, E.C. (1985), *Political Authority and Bureaucratic Control*, Brighton: Harvester Wheatsheaf.

Pahl, R.E. and Winkler, J.T. (1974), 'The Coming Corporatism', *New Society*, 10 Oct., 72–76.

Paldam, M. (1979), 'Is There an Election Cycle? A Comparative Study of National Accounts', *Scandinavian Journal of Economics*, 323–342.

Paldam, M. (1981), 'An Essay on the Rationality of Economic Policy', *Public Choice*, 37, 287–305.

Palfrey, T.R. and Poole, K.T. (1987), 'The Relationship between Information, Ideology, and Voting Behavior', *American Journal of Political Science*, 31, 511–530.

Panitch, L. (1979), 'The Development of Corporatism in Liberal Democracies', in Schmitter and Lehmbruch (1979).

Panitch, L. (1980), 'Recent Theorizations of Corporatism: Reflections on a Growth Industry', *British Journal of Sociology*, 31, 159–187.

Pareto, V. (1901/1968), *The Rise and Fall of the Elites. An Application of Theoretical Sociology*, Totowa, N.J.: Bedminster Press.

Pareto, V. (1916/1980), *Compendium of General Sociology*, Minneapolis: University of Minnesota Press.

Pareto, V. (1976), *Vilfredo Pareto. Sociological Writings*, Oxford: Basil Blackwell.

Parkinson, C.N. (1958), *Parkinson's Law or the Pursuit of Progress*, London: John Murray.

Parry, G. (1969), *Political Elites*, New York: Frederick A. Praeger.

Parsons, T. (1937/1968), *The Structure of Social Action (Volume I: Marshall, Pareto Durkheim; Volume II: Weber)*, New York: The Free Press.

Parsons, T. (1947), 'Introduction' to M. Weber, *Social and Economic Organization*, New York: The Free Press.

Parsons, T. (1949), 'The Rise and Decline of Economic Man', *The Journal of General Education*, 4, 47–53.

Parsons, T. (1951/1970), *The Social System*, London: Routledge and Kegan Paul.

Parsons, T. (1954), *Essays in Sociological Theories*, New York: The Free Press.

Parsons, T. (1957), 'The Distribution of Power in American Society', *World Politics*, 10, 123–143.

Parsons, T. (1958), 'Authority, Legitimation, and Political Action', in Friedrich (1958).

Parsons, T. (1959), 'The Principal Structures of Community: A Sociological View', in Friedrich (1959b).

Parsons, T. (1963), 'Power and the Social System', in Lukes (1986b).

Parsons, T. (1966), 'The Political Aspect of Social Structure and Process', in Easton (1966).

Parsons, T. (1967), *Sociological Theory and Modern Society*, New York: The Free Press of Glencoe.

Parsons, T. and Shils, E.A. (1951/1962), 'Values, Motives, and Systems of Action', in T. Parsons and E.A. Shils (eds), *Toward a General Theory of Action*, New York: Harper and Row.

Parsons, T. and Smelser, N.J. (1956), *Economy and Society. A Study in the Integration of Economic and Social Theory*, New York: The Free Press.

Peacock, A. (1978), 'The Economics of Bureaucracy: An Inside View', in Buchanan *et al.* (1978).

Peacock, A. (1979), *The Economic Analysis of Government and Related Themes*, Oxford: Martin Robertson.

Peacock, A. (1992), *Public Choice Analysis in Historical Perspective*, Cambridge: Cambridge University Press.

Peacock, A. and Wiseman, J. (1961/1967), *The Growth of Public Expenditure in the United Kingdom, 1890–1955*, London: Allen and Unwin.

Peltzman, S. (1976), 'Toward a More General Theory of Regulation', *Journal of Law and Economics*, 19, 211–240, reprinted in Stigler, ed. (1988).

Peltzman, S. (1980), 'The Growth of Government', The *Journal of Law and Economics*, 23, 209–287. Reprinted in Stigler (1988).

Pennock, J.R. (1979), *Democratic Political Theory*, Princeton N.J.: Princeton University Press.

Peters, B.G. (1987), 'Politicians and Bureaucrats in the Politics of Policy-making', in Lane (1987).

Peters, R.S. (1958/1967), 'Authority', in A. Quinton (ed.), *Political Philosophy*, Oxford: Oxford University Press.

Petracca, M.P. (1991), 'The Rational Actor Approach to Politics', in Monroe (1991).

Pettit, P. (1986), 'Free Riding and Foul Dealing', *Journal of Philosophy*, 83, 361–379.

Phelps, E.S. (ed.) (1975), *Altruism, Morality and Economic Theory*, New York: Russell Sage.

Pizzorno, A. (1978), 'Political Exchange and Collective Identity in Industrial Conflict', in Crouch and Pizzorno (1978).

Pizzorno, A. (1981), 'Interests and Parties in Pluralism', in Berger (1981).

Pizzorno, A. (1985), 'On the Rationality of Democratic Choice', *Telos*, 63, 41–69.

Pizzorno, A. (1990), 'On Rationality and Democratic Choice', in Birnbaum and Leca (1990).

Pizzorno, A. (1991), 'On the Individualistic Theory of Social Order', in Bourdieu and Coleman (1991).

Plant, R. (1972/1983), *Hegel. An Introduction*, Oxford: Basil Blackwell.

Platt, J. (1973), 'Social Traps', *American Psychologist*, August 1973, 641–651.

Polanyi, K. (1944/1957), *The Great Transformation. The Political and Economic Origins of Our Time*. Boston: Beacon Press.

Polanyi, K. (1966), *Dahomey and the Slave Trade. An Analysis of an Archaic Economy*, Seattle: University of Washington Press.

Polanyi, K. (1971), *Primitive, Archaic and Modern Economies*, Boston: Beacon Press.

Poole, R. (1991), *Morality and Modernity*, London: Routledge.

Popkin, S.L. (1979), *The Rational Peasant*, Berkeley: University of California Press.

Popkin, S.L. (1988), 'Political Entrepreneurs in Vietnam', in Taylor (1988b).

Popkin, S.L. (1991), *The Reasoning Voter*, Chicago: University of Chicago Press.

Popkin, S., Gorman, J.W., Phillips, C. and Smith, J.A. (1976), 'Comment: What Have You Done for Me Lately? Toward an Investment Theory of Voting', *American Political Science Review*, 70, 779–805.

Poppe, M. (1986), 'Effects of Change in a Common Good and Choice Behaviour in a Social Dilemma', in Wilke *et al.* (1986b).

Popper, K.R. (1945/1966), *The Open Society and Its Enemies, Volume II: The High Tide of Prophecy: Hegel, Marx and the Aftermath*, London: Routledge and Kegan Paul.

Popper, K. R. (1957/1961), *The Poverty of Historicism*, London: Routledge and Kegan Paul.

Popper, K.R. (1962/1968), *Conjectures and Refutations. The Growth of Scientific Knowledge*, New York: Harper and Row.

Popper, K.R. (1976), *Unended Quest. An Intellectual Biography*, Glasgow: Fontana/Collins.

Poulantzas, N. (1968/1978), *Political Power and Social Classes*, London: Verso.-

Preston, L.M. (1984), 'Freedom, Markets, and Voluntary Exchange', *The American Political Science Review*, 78, 959–970.

Pruitt, D.G. and Kimmel, M.J. (1977), 'Twenty Years of Experimental Gaming: Critique, Synthesis, and Suggestions for the Future', *Annual Review of Psychology*, 28, 363–392.

Pryor, F.L. (1984), 'Rent-Seeking and the Growth and Fluctuations of Nations. Empirical Tests of Some Recent Hypotheses', in Colander (1984).

Przeworski, A. (1985), *Capitalism and Social Democracy*, Cambridge: Cambridge University Press.

Przeworski, A. (1990), 'Marxism and Rational Choice', in Birnbaum and Leca (1990).

Przeworski, A. and Wallerstein, M. (1982), 'The Structure of Class Conflict in Democratic Capitalist Societies', *American Political Science Review*, 76, 215–238.

Przeworski, A. and Wallerstein, M. (1988), 'Structural Dependence of the State on Capital', *American Political Science Review*, 82, 11–29.

Putnam, R.D. (1993), *Making Democracy Work. Civic Traditions in Modern Italy*, Princeton, N.J.: Princeton University Press.

Quattrone, G.A. and Tversky, A. (1986), 'Self-Deception and the Voter's Illusion', in Elster (1986a).

Quattrone, G.A. and Tversky, A. (1988), 'Contrasting Rational and Psychological Analyses of Political Choice', *American Political Science Review*, 82, 719–736.

Quirk, P.J. (1988), 'In Defense of the Politics of Ideas', *Journal of Politics*, 50, 31–41.

Quirk, P.J. (1990), 'Deregulation and the Politics of Ideas in Congress', in Mansbridge (1990).

Rabbie, J.M. (1991) 'Determinants of Instrumental Intra-Group Cooperation', in Hinde and Groebel (1991).

Rabinowitz, G and Macdonald, S.E. (1989), 'A Directional Theory of Issue Voting', *American Political Science Review*, 83, 93–121.

Radnitzky, G. (ed.) (1992), *Universal Economics. Assessing the Achievements of the Economic Approach*, New York: Paragon House.

Radnitzky, G. and Bernholz, P. (eds) (1987), *Economic Imperialism. The Economic Method Applied outside the Field of Economics*, New York: Paragon House.

Rae, D. and Eismeier, T.J. (1979), *Public Choice and Public Policy*, London: Sage Publications.

Raphael, D.D. (1985), *Adam Smith*, Oxford: Oxford University Press.

Rapoport, A. and Guyer, M. (1966), 'A Taxonomy of 2 × 2 Games', *General Systems*, 11, 203–214.

Rawls, J. (1972), *Theory of Justice*, Oxford: Oxford University Press.

Raz, J. (ed.) (1990), *Authority*, Oxford: Basil Blackwell.

Reich, R.B. (ed.) (1988), *The Power of Public Ideas*, Cambridge, Mass.: Ballinger.

Reisman, D. (1990), *The Political Economy of James Buchanan*, London: Macmillan.

Rhodebeck, L.A. (1993), 'The Politics of Greed? Political Preferences among the Elderly', *Journal of Politics*, 55, 342–364.

Riker, W.H. (1962), *The Theory of Political Coalitions*, New Haven: Yale University Press.

Riker, W.H. (1982a), 'Implications From the Disequilibrium of Majority Rule for the Study of Institutions', in Ordershook and Shepsle (1982).

Riker, W.H. (1982b), *Liberalism Against Populism. A Confrontation Between the Theory of*

Democracy and the Theory of Social Choice, Prospect Heights, Illinois: Waveland Press, Inc.

Riker, W.H. (1984), 'The Heresthetics of Constitution-Making: The Presidency in 1787, with Comments on Determinism and Rational Choice', *American Political Science Review*, 78, 1–16.

Riker, W.H. (1985), 'Comment' on M.P. Fiorina, 'Group Concentration and the Delegation of Legislative Authority', in Noll (1985).

Riker, W. (1986), *The Art of Political Manipulation*, New Haven: Yale University Press.

Riker, W.H. (1988), 'The Place of Political Science in Public Choice', *Public Choice*, 57, 247–257.

Riker, W.H. (1990a), 'Heresthetic and Rhetoric in the Spatial Model', in Enelow and Hinich (1990).

Riker, W.H. (1990b), 'Political Science and Rational Choice', in Alt and Shepsle (1990).

Riker, W.H. and Ordeshook, P.C. (1968), 'A Theory of the Calculus of Voting', *American Political Science Review*, 62, 25–42.

Riker, W.H. and Ordeshook, P.C. (1973), *An Introduction to Positive Political Theory*, Englewood Cliffs, N.J.: Prentice-Hall.

Riley, M. (1988), *Power, Politics and Voting Behaviour. An Introduction to the Sociology of Politics*, London: Harvester Wheatsheaf.

Robbins, L. (1935/1972), *An Essay on the Nature and Significance of Economic Science*, London: Macmillan.

Robbins, L. (1978), 'Discussion', in Buchanan *et al.* (1978), 64–69.

Robertson, D. (1976), *A Theory of Party Competition*, London: John Wiley & Sons.

Robertson, D.H. (1956), *Economic Commentaries*, London: Staples Press.

Roper, J. (1989), *Democracy and Its Critics. Anglo-American Democratic Thought in the Nineteenth Century*, London: Unwin Hyman.

Rosenberg, S.W. (1988), *Reason, Ideology and Politics*, Cambridge: Polity Press.

Rosenberg, S.W., Bohan, L., McCafferty, P. and Harris, K. (1986), 'The Image and the Vote: The Effect of Candidate Presentation on Voter Preference', *American Journal of Political Science*, 30, 108–127.

Rosenthal, H. (1990), 'The Setter Model', in Enelow and Hinich (1990).

Roth, G. (1976), 'History and Sociology in the Work of Max Weber', *British Journal of Sociology*, 27, 306–318.

Rothbard, M. (1970/1977), *Power and Market. Government and the Economy*, Kansas City: Sheed Andrews and McMeel.

Rudé, G. (1964), *The Crowd in History: A study of Popular Disturbance in England and France 1730–1848*, New York: John Wiley and Sons, Inc.

Rule, J.B. (1989), 'Rationality and Non-Rationality in Militant Collective Action', *Sociological Theory*, 7, 145–160.

Rush, M. (1992), *Politics and Society. An Introduction to Political Sociology*, New York: Prentice-Hall.

Russell, B. (1938/1948), *Power. A New Analysis*, London: Allen and Unwin.

Sabia, D.R. (1988), 'Rationality, Collective Action, and Karl Marx', *American Journal of Political Science*, 32: 50–71.

Sahlins, M.D. (1965), 'On the Sociology of Primitive Exchange', in M. Banton (ed.), *The Relevance of Models for Social Anthropology*, London: Tavistock Publications. Also in Sahlins (1972/1988).

Sahlins, M.D. (1968), *Tribesmen*, Englewood Cliffs, N.J.: Prentice-Hall.

Sahlins, M.D. (1969), 'Economic Anthropology and Anthropological Economics', *Social Science Information*, 8, 13–33.

Sahlins, M.D. (1972/1988), *Stone Age Economics*, London: Routledge and KeganPaul.

Samuelson, C.D., Messick, D.M., Wilke, H.A.M. and Rutte, C.G. (1986), 'Individual Restraint and Structural Change as Solutions to Social Dilemmas', in Wilke *et al.* (1986b).

Samuelson, P.A. (1954), 'The Pure Theory of Public Expenditure', *Review of Economics and Statistics*, 36, 387–389.

Samuelson, P.A. (1955), 'Diagrammatic Exposition of a Theory of Public Expenditure', *Review of Economics and Statistics*, 37, 350–356.

Samuelson, P.A. (1963), 'Problems of Methodology: Discussion', *American Economic Reveiw*, 53, 231–236.

Samuelson, P. (1970), *Economics*, 8th edn, New York: McGraw-Hill.

Sandler, T. (1992), *Collective Action. Theory and Applications*, London: Harvester Wheatsheaf.

Sapir, E. (1949), *Culture, Language and Personality*, Berkeley: University of California Press.

Saraydar, E. (1987), 'Preferences and Voting Behavior. Smith's Impartial Spectator Revisited', *Economics and Philosophy*, 3, 121–126.

Sartori, G. (1969), 'From the Sociology of Politics to Political Sociology', in Lipset (1969b).

Scalia, L.J. (1991), 'Self-Interest and Democratic Theory', in Monroe (1991).

Schelling, T.C. (1960), *The Strategy of Conflict*, Oxford: Oxford University Press.

Schelling, T.C. (1971), 'On the Ecology of Micromotives', *Public Interest*, 25, 61–98.

Schelling, T.C. (1973), 'Hockey Helmets, Concealed Weapens, and Daylight Saving. A Study of Binary Choices with Externalities', *Journal of Conflict Resolution*, 17, 381–428.

Schelling, T.C. (1978), *Micromotives and Macrobehavior*, New York: W.W. Norton.

Schelling, T.C. (1984), 'Self-Command in Practice, in Policy, and in a Theory of Rational Choice', *American Economic Association. Papers and Proceedings*, 74, 1–11.

Schlozman, K.L. and Verba, S. (1979), *Injury to Insult: Unemployment, Class, and Political Response*, Cambridge Mass.: Harvard University Press.

Schmitter, P.C. (1979a), 'Modes of Interest Intermediation and Models of Societal Change', in Schmitter and Lehmbruch (1979).

Schmitter, P.C. (1979b), 'Still the Century of Corporatism?', in Schmitter and Lembruch (1979). Originally published in *Review of Politics* (1974).

Schmitter, P.C. (1981), 'Interest Intermediation and Regime Governability in Contemporary Western Europe and North America', in Berger (1981).

Schmitter, P.C. (1985), 'Neo-Corporatism and the State', in Grant (1985).

Schmitter, P.C. and Lehmbruch, G. (eds) (1979), *Trends toward Corporatist Intermediation*, London: Sage Publications.

Schotter, A. (1981), *The Economic Theory of Social Institutions*, Cambridge: Cambridge University Press.

Schroeter, G. (1985), 'Ideal Types: Beacons or Blinders?, *History of Sociology*, 6, 161–166.

Schumpeter, J. (1908), *Das Wesen und Hauptinhalt der theoretischen Nationalökonomie*, Leipzig: Duncker und Humblot.

Schumpeter, J.A. (1942/1954), *Capitalism, Socialism and Democracy*, London: Unwin University Books.

Schumpeter, J. (1951), *Imperialism and Social Classes*, New York: Augustus M. Kelley.

Schumpeter, J. (1954), *History of Economic Analysis*, London: Allen and Unwin.

Schutz, A. (1932/1972), *The Phenomenology of the Social World*, London: Heinemann.

Schutz, A. (1962), *The Problem of Social Reality. Collected Papers 1*, The Hague: Martinus Nijhoff.

Sciulli, D. (1992), 'Weaknesses in Rational Choice Theory's Contribution to Comparative Research', in Coleman and Fararo (1992).

Scott, A. (1990), *Ideology and the New Social Movements*, London: Unwin.

Sears, D.O. (1975), 'Political Socialization', in Greenstein and Polsby, (1975).

Sears, D.O. and Funk, C.L. (1990), 'Self-Interest in Americans' Political Opinions', in Mansbridge (1990).

Sears, D.O. and Lau, R.R. (1983), 'Inducing Apparently Self-Interested Political Preferences', *American Journal of Political Science*, 27, 223–253.

Sears, D.O. Hensler, C.P. and Speer, L.K. (1979), 'Whites' Opposition to "Busing": Self-Interest or Symbolic Politics?', *American Political Science Review*, 73, 369–384.

Sears, D.O., Lau, R.R., Tyler, T.R. and Allen, H.M. (1980), 'Self-Interest vs. Symbolic Politics in Policy Attitudes and Presidential Voting', *American Political Science Review*, 74, 670–684.

Sen, A.K. (1967), 'Isolation, assurance and the Social Rate of Discount', *Quarterly Journal of Economics*, 81, 112–124.

Sen, A.K. (1979), 'Rational Fools: A Critique of the Behavioural Foundations of Economic Theory', in F. Hahn and M. Hollis (eds), *Philosophy and Economic Theory*, Oxford: Oxford University Press.

Sen, A.K. (1985), 'Goals, Commitment, and Identity', *Journal of Law, Economics, and Organization*, 1, 341–355.

Sen, A.K. (1987), *On Ethics and Economics*, Oxford: Basil Blackwell.

Sennett, R. (1978), *The Fall of Public Man*, New York: Vintage Books.

Service, E.R. (1966), *The Hunters*, Englewood Cliffs, N.J.: Prentice-Hall.

Service, E.R. (1975), *Origins of the State and Civilization. The Process of Cultural Evolution*, New York: W.W. Norton .

Shaw, W.H. (1984), 'Marxism, Revolution and Rationality', in T. Ball and J. Farr (eds), *After Marx*, Cambridge: Cambridge University Press.

Shorter, W. and Tilly, C. (1974), *Strikes in France 1830–1968*, London: Cambridge University Press.

Silver, M. (1974), 'Political Revolution and Repression: An Economic Approach', *Public Choice*, 17, 63–71.

Simmel, G. (1890/1989), 'Über Soziale Differenzierung', in G. Simmel, *Gesamtausgabe Band 2*, Frankfurt am Main: Suhrkamp.

Simmel, G. (1898), 'The Persistence of Social Groups', *American Journal of Sociology*, 3, 662–698, 829–836, and 4, 35–50.

Simmel, G. (1900/1978), *The Philosophy of Money*, London: Routledge and Kegan Paul.

Simmel, G. (1950), *The Sociology of Georg Simmel*, New York: The Free Press.

Simmel, G. (1955), *Conflict* and *The Web of Group-Affiliation*, New York: The Free Press.

Simmel, G. (1971), *On Individuality and Social Forms*, Chicago: University of Chicago Press.

Simmons, J.R. (1992), 'Economic Theory of Democracy Revisited and Revised', *New Political Science*, 1, 29–49.

Skocpol, T. (1979), *States and Social Revolutions*, Cambridge: Cambridge University Press.

Skocpol, T. (1982), 'Bringing the State Back In', *Items*, 36, 1–7.

Skocpol, T. (1985), 'Bringing the State Back In: Strategies of Analysis in Current Research', in Evans *et al.* (1985).

Smelser, N.J. (1962), *Theory of Collective Behavior*, New York: The Free Press.

Smith, A. (1759/1976), *The Theory of Moral Sentiments*, Indianapolis: Liberty Classics.

Smith, A. (1776/1937), *The Wealth of Nations*, New York: The Modern Library.

Smith, A.D. (1991), *National Identity*, Harmondsworth: Penguin.

Smith, B.C. (1988), *Bureaucracy and Political Power*, Brighton: Wheatsheaf Books; New York: St Martin's Press.

Sniderman, P.M. and Brody, R.A. (1977), 'Coping: The Ethics of Self-Reliance', *American Journal of Political Science*, 21, 501–521.

Sniderman, P.M., Brody, R.A. and Tetlock, P.E. (1991), *Reasoning and Choice. Explorations in Political Psychology*. Cambridge. Cambridge University Press.

Sorel, G. (1908/1961), *Reflections on Violence*, London: Collier Macmillan.

Sorel, G. (1908/1969), *The Illusions of Progress*, Berkeley: University of California Press.

Sorel, G. (1976), *From George Sorel. Essays in Socialism and Philosophy*, New York: Oxford University Press.

Sörensen, R. (1987), 'Bureaucratic Decision-making and the Growth of Public Expenditure', in Lane (1987).

Spann, R.M. (1977), 'Public versus Private Provision of Governmental Services', in Borcherding (1977c).

Spencer, H. (1890), *Principles of Sociology*, Vol 2, New York: Appleton.

Spencer, H. (1969), *The Man versus the State*, Harmondsworth: Penguin.

Sproule-Jones, M. (1982) 'Public Choice Theory and Natural Resources: Methodological Explication and Critique', *American Political Science Review*, 76, 790–804.

Sproule-Jones, M. (1984), 'Methodological Individualism. Challenge and Response', *American Behavioral Scientist*, 28, 167–183.

Stevenson, C.L. (1944), *Ethics and Language*, New Haven: Yale University Press.

Stigler, G.J. (1970), 'Director's Law of Public Income Redistribution', *Journal of Law and Economics*, 13, 1–10, reprinted in Stigler (1988).

Stigler, G.J. (1972), 'Economic Competition and Political Competition', *Public Choice*, 12, 91–106.

Stigler, G.J. (1973), 'General Economic Conditions and National Elections', *American Economic Review*, 63, 160–167.

Stigler, G.J. (1975), *The Citizen and the State. Essays on Regulation*, Chicago: University of Chicago Press.

Stigler, G.J. (1982), *The Economist as Preacher*, Oxford: Basil Blackwell.

Stigler, G.J. (1984), 'Economics – The Imperial Science?', *Scandinavian Journal of Economics*, 86.

Stigler, G.J. (ed.) (1988), *Chicago Studies in Political Economy*, Chicago: University of Chicago Press.

Stigler, G.J. and Becker, G. S. (1977), 'De Gustibus Non Est Disputandum', *American Economic Review*, 67, 76–90.

Stokes, D.E. (1963/1966), 'Spatial Models of Party Competition', *American Political Science Review*, 57, 368–377, reprinted in Campbell *et al.* (1966).

Storing, H.J. (ed.) (1961), *Essays on the Scientific Study of Politics*, New York: Holt, Rinehart and Winston.

Stroebe, W. and Frey, B.S. (1982), 'Self-interest and Collective Action: The Economics and Psychology of Public Goods', *British Journal of Social Psychology*, 21, 121–137.

Strom, K. (1990), 'A Behavioral Theory of Competitive Political Parties', *American Journal of Political Science*, 34, 565–598.

Sugden, R. (1986), *The Economics of Rights, Co-operation and Welfare*, Oxford: Basil Blackwell.

Svallfors, S. (1991), 'The Politics of Welfare Policy in Sweden: Structural Determinants and Attitudinal Cleavages', *British Journal of Sociology*, 42, 609–634.

Swedberg, R. (ed.) (1990), *Economics and Sociology*, Princeton, N.J.: Princeton University Press.

Swedberg, R. (1991), *Joseph A. Schumpeter. His Life and Work*, Cambridge: Polity Press.

Swedberg, R. (ed.) (1993), *Explorations in Economic Sociology*, New York: Russell Sage Foundation.

Talmon, J.L. (1960), *The Origins of Totalitarian Democracy*, New York: Frederick A. Praeger.

Taschys, D. (1975), 'The Growth of Public Expenditures: Nine Modes of Explanation', *Scandinavian Political Studies*, 10, 9–31.

Tarde, G. (1969), *On Communication and Social Influence*, Chicago: University of Chicago Press.

Taylor, C. (1979), *Hegel and Modern Society*, Cambridge: Cambridge University Press.

Taylor, I. (ed.) (1990), *The Social Effects of Free Market Policies. An International Text*, New York: St Martin's Press.

Taylor, M. (1976), *Anarchy and Cooperation*, Chichester: John Wiley.

Taylor, M. (1982), *Community, Anarchy and Liberty*, Cambridge: Cambridge University Press.

Taylor, M. (1987), *The Possibility of Cooperation*, Cambridge: Cambridge University Press.

Taylor, M. (1988a), 'Rationality and Revolutionary Collective Action', in Taylor (1988b).

Taylor, M. (ed.) (1988b), *Rationality and Revolution*, Cambridge: Cambridge University Press.

Taylor, M. (1989), 'Structure, Culture and Action in the Explanation of Social Change', *Politics and Society*, 17, 115–162.

Taylor, M. and Singleton, S. (1993), 'The Communal Resource: Transaction Costs and the Solution of Collective Action Problems', *Politics & Society*, 21, 195–214.

Taylor, M. (1990), 'Cooperation and Rationality: Notes on the Collective Action Problem and Its Solution', in Cook and Levi (1990).

Taylor, M. and Ward, H. (1982), 'Chickens, Whales, and Lumpy Goods: Alternative Models of Public Goods Provision', *Political Studies*, 30, 350–370.

Therborn, G. (1991), 'Cultural Belonging, Structural Location and Human Action. Explanation in Sociology and in Social Science', *Acta Sociologica*, 34, 177–191.

Thomas, W.I. (1928), *The Child in America*, New York: Alfred A. Knopf.

Thomas, W.I. (1966), *On Social Organization and Social Personality*, Chicago: The University of Chicago Press.

Thompson, E.P. (1963/1980), *The Making of the English Working Class*, Harmondsworth: Penguin.

Thompson, E.P. (1971), 'The Moral Economy of the English Crowd in the Nineteenth Century', *Past and Present*, 50, 76–136.

Tilly, C. (1964), 'Reflections on the Revolutions of Paris: An Essay on Recent Historical Writing', *Social Problems*, 12, 99–121.

Tilly, C, (1973), 'Do Communities Act?', *Sociological Inquiry*, 53, 209–240.

Tilly, C. (1975a), 'Reflections on the History of European State-Making', in C. Tilly (ed.), *The Formation of National States in Western Europe*, Princeton, N.J.: Princeton University Press.

Tilly, C. (1975b), 'Revolutions and Collective Action', in Greenstein and Polsby, (1975), Vol. 3: *Macropolitical Theory*.

Tilly, C. (1978), *From Mobilization to Revolution*, Reading, Mass.: Addison-Wesley.

Tilly, C. (1981a), 'Introduction', to Tilly and Tilly (1981).

Tilly, C. (1981b), *As Sociology Meets History*, New York: Academic Press.

Tilly, C. (1981c), 'The Web of Contention in Eighteenth-Century Cities', in Tilly and Tilly (1981).

Tilly, C. (1985), 'Models and Realities of Popular Collective Action', *Social Research*, 52, 717–747.

Tilly, C. (1986a), *The Contentious French*, Cambridge, Mass.: Belknap Press of Harvard University Press.

Tilly, C. (1986b), 'European Violence and Collective Action since 1700', *Social Research*, 53, 159–184.

434

Tilly, C. (1990a), *Coercion, Capital and European States, AD 990–1990*, Oxford: Basil Blackwell.

Tilly, C. (1990b), 'Individual Mobilization and Collective Action', in Birnbaum and Leca (1990).

Tilly, C. and Tilly, L. (eds) (1981), *Class Conflict and Class Action*, London: Sage Publications.

Tilly, C., Tilly, L. and Tilly, R. (1975), *The Rebellious Century*, Cambridge, Mass.: Harvard University Press.

Titmuss, R.M. (1970), *The Gift Relationship. From Human Blood to Social Policy*, London: Allen and Unwin.

Tocqueville, A. de (1835–40/1961), *Democracy in America*, 2 vols, New York: Schocken Books.

Toennies, F. (1887/1955), *Community and Association*, London: Routledge and Kegan Paul.

Toennies, F. (1896), *Hobbes. Leben und Lehre*, Stuttgart: Friedrich Frommans.

Toennies, F. (1931/1981), *Einführung in die Soziologie*, Stuttgart: Ferdinand Enke.

Toennies, F. (1971), *On Sociology: Pure, Applied and Empirical*, Chicago: University of Chicago Press.

Tollison, R.D. (1982), 'Rent Seeking: A Survey', *Kyklos*, 35, 575–602.

Touraine, A. (1969/1971), *The Post-Industrial Society*, London: Wildwood House.

Touraine, A. (1974), *Pour la Sociologie*, Paris: Editions du Seuil.

Touraine, A. (1978/1981), *The Voice and the Eye. An Analysis of Social Movements*, Cambridge: Cambridge University Press.

Touraine, A. (1984/1988), *Return of the Actor. Social Theory in Postindustrial Society*, Minneapolis: University of Minnesota Press.

Touraine, A. (1985), 'An Introduction to the Study of Social Movements', *Social Research*, 52, 749–788.

Toye, J. (1976), 'Economic Theories of Politics and Public Finance', *British Journal of Political Science*, 6, 433–447.

Truman, D. (1951a), *The Governmental Process*, New York: Alfred A. Knopf.

Truman, D. (1951b), 'The Implications of Political Behavior Research', *Items*, 5, 37–39.

Truman, D. (1955), 'The Impact on Political Science of the Revolution in the Behavioral Sciences', Brookings Lectures, *Research Frontiers in Politics and Government*, 202–231, also reprinted in Eulau (1969b).

Truman, D. (1965), 'Disillusion and Regeneration: The Quest for a Discipline', *American Political Science Review*, 59, 865–873.

Tsebelis, G. (1990), *Nested Games. Rational Choice in Comparative Politics*, Berkeley: University of California Press.

Tufte, E.R. (1978), *Political Control of the Economy*, Princeton, N.J.: Princeton University Press.

Tullock, G. (1965/1987), *The Politics of Bureaucracy*, New York: University Press of America.

Tullock, G. (1967a), 'The General Irrelevance of the General Impossibility Theorem', *Quarterly Journal of Economics*, 81, 256–70, reprinted in Tullock (1967b).

Tullock, G. (1967b), *Toward a Mathematics of Politics*, Ann Arbor: University of Michigan Press.

Tullock, G. (1967c), 'The Welfare Costs of Tariffs, Monopolies and Theft', *Western Economic Journal*, 5, 224–232, reprinted in Buchanan *et al.* (1980).

Tullock, G. (1971), 'The Paradox of Revolution', *Public Choice*, 11, 89–99.

Tullock, G. (1972), 'Economic Imperialism', in Buchanan and Tollison (1972).

Tullock, G. (1976), *The Vote Motive*, London: Institute of Economic Affairs.

Tullock, G. (1980), 'Rent Seeking as a Negative-Sum Game', in Buchanan *et al.* (1980).
Tullock, G. (1984a), 'A (Partial) Rehabilitation of the Public Interest Theory', *Public Choice*, 42, 89–99.
Tullock, G. (1984b), 'How To Do Well While Doing Good', in Colander (1984).
Tullock, G. (1987) 'Autocracy', in Radnitzky and Bernholz (1987).
Tullock, G. (1990), 'The Costs of Special Privilege', in Alt and Shepsle (1990).
Tullock, G. and McKenzie, R.B. (1975/1985), *The New World of Economics. Explorations into the Human Experience*, Homewood, Illinois: Richard D. Irwin.
Turner, R.H. (1964a), 'Collective Behavior', in R.E.L. Faris (ed.), *Handbook of Modern Sociology*, Chicago: Rand McNally.
Turner, R.H. (1964b), 'Collective Behavior and Conflict. New Theoretical Frameworks', *Sociological Quarterly*, 5, 122–132.
Turner, R.H. (1981), 'Collective Behavior and Resource Mobilization as Approaches to Social Movements: Issues and Continuities', *Research in Social Movements, Conflict and Change*, 4, 1–24.
Turner, R.H. (1991), 'The Use and Misuse of Rational Models in Collective Behavior and Social Psychology', *Archives Européenes de Sociologie*.
Turner, R.H. and Killian, L.M. (1957), *Collective Behavior*, Englewood Cliffs, N.J.: Prentice-Hall.
Turner, R.H. and Killian, L.M. (1972) *Collective Behavior*, 2nd edn, Englewood Cliffs, N.J.: Prentice-Hall.
Udehn, L. (1981a), 'Central Planning: Postscript to a Debate', in U. Himmelstrand (ed.), *Spontaneity and Planning in Social Development*, London: Sage Publications.
Udehn, L. (1981b), 'The Conflict between Methodology and Rationalization Thesis in the Work of Max Weber', *Acta Sociologica*, 24, 131–147.
Udehn, L. (1986), 'Economics, Exogenous Factors and Interdisciplinary Research', *Social Science Information*, 25, 259–276.
Udehn, L. (1987), *Methodological Individualism – A Critical Appraisal*, Uppsala: Diss.
Udehn, L. (1992), 'The Limits of Economic Imperialism', in Himmelstrand (1992a).
Udehn, L. (1993), 'Twenty-five Years with *The Logic of Collective Action*', *Acta Sociologica*, 36, 239–261.
Ullmann-Margalit, E. (1977), *The Emergence of Norms*, Oxford: Clarendon Press.
Uphoff, N. (1989), 'Distinguishing Power, Authority and Legitimacy: Taking Max Weber at his Word by Using Resource-Exchange Analysis', *Polity*, 22, 295–322.
Vanberg, V. (1982), *Markt und Organization*, Tübingen: J.C.B. Mohr.
Vanberg, V. and Buchanan, J.M. (1989), 'Interests and Theories in Constitutional Choice', *Journal of Theoretical Politics*, 1, 49–62.
Van de Kragt, A..C., Dawes, R.M. and Orbell, J.M. (1986), 'Doing Well and Doing Good as Ways of Resolving Social Dilemmas', in Wilke *et al.* (1986b).
Van den Broeck, J. (ed.) (1988), *Public Choice*, Dortrecht: Kluwer Academic Publishers.
Van Winden, F.A.A.M. (1988), 'The Economic Theory of Political Decision Making: A Survey and Perspective', in Van den Broeck (1988)
Vaughan, F. (1982), *The Tradition of Political Hedonism. From Hobbes to J.S. Mill*, New York: Fordham University Press.
Wagner, A. (1883/1967), 'Three Extracts on Public Finance', in Musgrave and Peacock (1967).
Wagner, R.W. (1977), 'Economic Manipulation for Political Profit: Macroeconomic Consequences and Constitutional Implications', *Kyklos*, 30, 395–410.
Walker, A. (1990), 'The Strategy of Inequality: Poverty and Income Distribution in Britain, 1979–89', in Taylor, ed. (1990).
Wallerstein, M. and Przeworski, A. (1988), 'Workers' Welfare and the Socialization of Capital', in Taylor (1988).

436

Wallis, J.J. and Oates, W.E. (1988), Does Economic Sclerosis Set in with Age? An Empirical Study of the Olson Hypothesis', *Kyklos*, 41, 397–417.

Watkins, J.W.N. (1952), 'The Principle of Methodological Individualism', *British Journal for the Philosophy of Science*, 3, 186–189.

Watkins, J.W.N. (1953), 'Ideal Types and Historical Explanation', in H. Feigl and M. Brodbeck (eds), *Readings in the Philosophy of Science*, New York: Appleton-Century-Crofts.

Weale, A. (1990), Can *Homo Economicus* Have a Political Theory?', *Political Studies*, 38, 517–525.

Weatherford, M.S. (1983), 'Economic Voting and the "Symbolic Politics" Argument: A Reinterpretation and Synthesis', *American Political Science Review*, 77, 158–174.

Weber, M. (1895/1980), 'The National State and Economic Policy' (Freiburg Address), *Economy and Society*, 9, 429–449. Also in Weber (1994).

Weber, M. (1904–5/1930), *The Protestant Ethic and the Spirit of Capitalism*, London: Unwin Books.

Weber, M. (1908/1971), 'A Research Strategy for the Study of Occupational Careers and Mobility Patterns', in J.E.T. Eldridge, (ed.), *Max Weber: The Interpretation of Social Reality*, London: Nelson.

Weber, M. (1908/1975), 'Marginal Utility Theory and the Fundamental Law of Psychophysics', *Social Science Quarterly*, 56, 21–36.

Weber, M. (1918/1971), 'Socialism', in J.E.T. Eldridge (ed.), *Max Weber: The Interpretation of Social Reality*, London: Nelson; also in Weber (1994).

Weber, M. (1922/1978), *Economy and Society*, Berkeley: University of California Press.

Weber, M. (1948), *From Max Weber: Essays in Sociology*, London: Routledge and Kegan Paul.

Weber, M. (1949), *The Methodology of the Social Sciences*, New York: The Free Press.

Weber, M. (1978), *Weber. Selections in Translation*, Cambridge: Cambridge University Press.

Weber, M. (1994), *Political Writings*, Cambridge: Cambridge University Press.

Weinstein, L. (1962), 'The Group Approach: Arthur Bentley', in Storing (1961).

Werhane, P.H. (1991), *Adam Smith and His Legacy for Modern Capitalism*, Oxford: Oxford University Press.

West, E.G. (1976), *Adam Smith. The Man and His Works*, Indianapolis: Liberty Classics.

West, E.G. (1990), *Adam Smith and Modern Economics. From Market Behaviour to Public Choice*, Aldershot: Edward Elgar.

White, L. G. (1976), 'Rational Theories of Participation. An Exercise in Definitions', *Journal of Conflict Resolution*, 20, 255–278.

Whitehead, J.W. (1991), 'The Forgotten Limits: Reason and Regulation in Economic Theory', in Monroe (1991).

Whiteley, P.F. Seyd, P., Richardson, J. and Bissell, P. (1993), 'Explaining Party Activism: The Case of the British Conservative Party', *British Journal of Political Science*, 24, 79–94.

Wicksteed, P.H. (1910), *The Common Sense of Political Economy*, London: Macmillan.

Widener, A. (1979), 'Introduction' to *Gustave Le Bon. The Man and his Work*, Indianapolis: Liberty Press.

Wildavsky, A. (1964/1974), *The Politics of the Budgetary Process*, Boston: Little, Brown.

Wildavsky, A. (1985a), 'A Cultural Theory of Expenditure Growth and (Un)Balanced Budgets', *Journal of Public Economics*, 28, 349–357.

Wildavsky, A. (1985b), 'The Logic of Public Sector Growth', in Lane (1985).

Wildavsky, A. (1987), 'Choosing Preferences by Constructing Institutions: A Cultural Theory of Preference Formation', *American Political Science Review*, 81, 3–21.

Wilensky, H.L. (1975), *The Welfare State and Equality. Structural and Ideological Roots of Public Expenditure*, Berkeley: University of California Press.

Wilke, H.A.M., Rutte, C.G., Wit, A.P., Messick, D.M and Samuelson, C.D. (1986a), 'Leadership in Social Dilemmas: Efficiency and Equity', in Wilke *et al.* (1986b).

Wilke, H.A.M., Messick, D.M. and Rutte, C.G. (eds) (1986b), *Experimental Social Dilemmas*, Frankfurt am Main: Peter Lang.

Wilkinson, P. (1971), *Social Movement*, London: Macmillan.

Willer, D. (1992), 'The Principle of Rational Choice and the Problem of a Satisfactory Theory', in J.S. Coleman and T.J. Fararo (1992).

Williams, J.T. (1990), 'The Political Manipulation of Macroeconomic Policy', *American Political Science Review*, 84, 767–795.

Williamson, O.E. (1975), *Markets and Hierarchies: Analysis and Antitrust Implications*, New York: Free Press.

Williamson, P.J. (1989), *Corporatism in Perspective. An Introductory Guide to Corporatist Theory*, London: Sage Publications Ltd.

Wilson, F.L. (1983), 'Interest Groups and Politics in Western Europe. The Neo-Corporatist Approach', *Comparative Politics*, 16, 105–123.

Wilson, J.Q. (1993), 'The Moral Sense', *American Political Science Review*, 87, 1–11.

Wilson, J.Q. and Banfield, E.C. (1964), 'Public-Regardingness as a Value Premise in Voting Behavior', *The American Political Science Review*, 58, 876–887.

Winkler, J.T. (1976), 'Corporatism', *Archives Européennes de Sociologie*, 17, 100–136.

Wintrobe, R. (1990) 'The Tinpot and the Totalitarian: An Economic Theory of Dictatorship', *American Political Science Review*, 84, 849–872.

Wisdom, J.O. (1970), 'Situational Individualism and the Emergent Group-Properties', in R. Borger and F Cioffa (eds) *Explanation in the Behavioural Sciences*, Cambridge: Cambridge University Press.

Wisdom, J.O. (1971), 'Science versus the Scientific Revolution', *The Philosophy of the Social Sciences*, 1, 123–144.

Wittgenstein, L. (1953/1974), *Philosophical Investigations*, Oxford: Basil Blackwell.

Wolfe, A. (1989a), 'Market, State, and Society as Codes of Moral Obligation', *Acta Sociologica*, 32, 221–236.

Wolfe, A. (1989b), *Whose Keeper? Social Science and Moral Obligation*, Berkeley: University of California Press.

Wright, E.O. and Cho, D. (1992), 'State Employment, Class Location, and Ideological Orientation: A Comparative Analysis of the United States and Sweden', *Politics and Society*, 20, 167–196.

Wright, J.R. (1989), 'PAC Contribution, Lobbying, and Representation', *Journal of Politics*, 51, 713–729.

Wrong, D. (1961), 'The Oversocialized Conception of Man in Modern Sociology', *American Sociological Review*, 26, 183–193.

Yantek, T. (1988), 'Polity and Economy under Extreme Economic Conditions: A Comparartive Study of the Reagan and Thatcher Experiences', *American Journal of Political Science*, 32, 196–216.

Zald, M.N. and Ash R. (1966), 'Social Movement Organizations: Growth, Decay and Change', *Social Forces*, 44. 327–340.

Zald, M.N. and McCarthy, J.D. (1979), *The Dynamics of Social Movements*, Cambridge, Mass.: Winthrop Publishers, Inc.

Zeitlin, I.M. (1968), *Ideology and the Development of Sociological Theory*, Englewood Cliffs, N.J.: Prentice-Hall, Inc.

Ziegler, R. (1990), 'The Kula: Social Order, Barter and Ceremonial Exchange', in Hechter, Opp and Wippler (1990).

INDEX

action: class 307–8, 315–16; classified 114;
communicative 187–8, 364; cultural
belonging 7, 37; rational 313, 338, 368
(n15); structural location 7, 37; *see also*
collective action
Adams, G. S. 81
advertising 136–7, 138
Afano, Geraldine 270
Agassi, Joseph 170–1
agenda setting 47, 129
Ahrne, Göran 151, 164
Aldrich, John A. 89
Alford, Robert A. 39–40
Almond, Gabriel A. 55, 58, 115
Alt, James 68, 201
Althusser, Louis 301
altruism: bureaucrats 78; love 192;
motivations 260–1; participation 108–9,
258–9; positive/negative 248; rationality
107; self-interest 17; social order 357
Ames, Ruth E. 270–1
anarcho-capitalism 348, 354, 356
Anderson, Benedict 344, 345
anthropology 7–8, 330–1, 332
approach, and theory 6
Arendt, Hannah 150
Aristotle 112
Arrow, Kenneth 17, 174, 179
association: collective action 305, 306, 337–8;
and community 285–6, 339–40, 350–1;
mass society 43; relations 339; social
order 350–1
assurance game 220, 221–2, 233, 237, 256–7,
389 (n20)
authority 157–60; community 157; exchange
164; incentives 154; influence 155–7;
legitimacy 157–8, 159–60, 162–3, 349;
myths 352; organization 164; political 132,

149, 158–9, 163; power 149, 154, 155–60;
public choice 93–4; state 159
Axelrod, Robert 63, 230–1, 234, 247–8,
336

Bachrach, Peter 47
Banfield, Edward C. 79
Baratz, Morton S. 47
Barry, Brian 3, 65, 111, 132, 220, 241, 243,
256–7
Becker, Gary 7, 27, 118, 202, 332–3
Beetham, David 184–5
behaviouralism 1–2, 47, 132
beliefs 130, 145–7, 312–13, 316–17
benevolence 97, 111, 192, 337, 349
Bentley, Arthur F. 2, 280
Black, Duncan 19, 62, 179
Blau, Peter M. 205
Blumer, Herbert 289–90
Borcherding, T. 196, 201
Bourdieu, Pierre 153, 326
bourgeoisie 50–1, 297–8, 300
bravery 327
Brennan, Geoffrey 90–2, 181
Breton, Albert 21, 25–6, 61–2, 214
Brewer, M. B. 264
bribery 118; *see also* corruption
Buchanan, A. 215, 299
Buchanan, James 9–10; *Calculus of Consent*
19–20, 64–5, 177, 213; collective action
212–13; conflict of interest 64;
constitutions 172–4, 177–8, 180–1,
182–3, 214; *Demand and Supply of Public
Goods, The* 30; *Democracy in Deficit* 30–1;
economics 34; exchange 34, 117–19, 161–
2; *homo economicus* 105; institutionalism
172–4; *Limits of Liberty* 177, 213; market
186; methodological individualism 172,